"A rich and detailed study Cistercians, from his childh Hexham, through his formative years at the Scottish court, to his conversion and entry into the Yorkshire Cistercian abbey of Rievaulx, and his subsequent monastic career as monk, novice-master, and abbot. This is far more than a narrative: Burton demonstrates how Aelred's life before and after he became a monk, and his engagement with the world outside the cloister, were permeated by the importance of friendship and love, and by his search for harmony, reconciliation, and unity, through friendship, with God."

—Janet Burton
    Professor of Medieval History
    University of Wales Trinity Saint David (Lampeter)

"In this beautiful and sensitive study, Pierre-André Burton gives readers a holistic examination of Aelred of Rievaulx's personal biography and writings, arguing that the holistic approach is the key to understanding both Aelred the man and the rich theology, anthropology, and spirituality Aelred offers to readers. Using his profound familiarity with the entirety of Aelred's written *oeuvre*—spiritual treatises, historical writings, sermons—as well as other medieval Cistercian writings, Burton produces a richly woven narrative whose separate threads provide striking insights in their own right and a unified image in their sum. This unique study, translated here into elegant English by Christopher Coski, is much more than the sum of its parts, which is precisely what it shows was the case with Aelred's individual actions and writings as well."

—Elizabeth Freeman
    Senior Lecturer in Medieval European History
    University of Tasmania

"Aelred was the son of a married priest at a time when that institution was fast disappearing. Aelred's intellectual development at the count of the Scottish king, his conversion to monastic life in the new and flourishing Cistercian order, and his role as teacher, as monk, and as abbot have given rise to the intense scholarship displayed in this work. Burton builds his profound insight into Aelred's spirituality on the framework supplied by his study of the stages in Aelred's life. This work is both historically profound and theologically insightful. Burton's work is a masterful study of a spiritual giant."

—John R. Sommerfeldt
Professor Emeritus
University of Dallas

CISTERCIAN STUDIES SERIES: NUMBER TWO HUNDRED SEVENTY-SIX

Aelred of Rievaulx (1110–1167)

An Existential and Spiritual Biography

Pierre-André Burton, OCSO

Translated by Christopher Coski

α

Cistercian Publications
www.cistercianpublications.org

LITURGICAL PRESS
Collegeville, Minnesota
www.litpress.org

A Cistercian Publications title published by Liturgical Press

Cistercian Publications
Editorial Offices
161 Grosvenor Street
Athens, Ohio 45701
www.cistercianpublications.org

This book is translated from Pierre-André Burton, OCSO, *Aelred of Rievaulx (1110–1167): De l'homme éclaté à l'être unifié. Essai de Biographie Existentielle et Spirituelle* (Paris: © Les Éditions du Cerf, 2010), with permission from Les Éditions du Cerf.

Scripture texts in this work come from the Biblia Sacra Vulgata.

1   2   3   4   5   6   7   8   9

Library of Congress Cataloging-in-Publication Data

Names: Burton, Pierre-André, author. | Coski, Christopher, translator.
Title: Aelred of Rievaulx (1110-1167) : an existential and spiritual biography / Pierre-André Burton ; translated by Christopher Coski.
Other titles: De l'homme éclaté à l'être unifié. English.
Description: Athens, Ohio : Cistercian Publications ; Collegeville, Minnesota : Liturgical Press [2020] | Series: Cistercian studies series ; number two hundred seventy-six | "This book is translated from Pierre-André Burton, OCSO, De l'homme éclaté à l'être unifié. Essai de Biographie Existentielle et Spirituelle (Paris: Les Éditions du Cerf, 2010), with permission from Les Éditions du Cerf." | Includes bibliographical references and indexes. | Summary: "Burton considers the influence of both English and church history on Aelred's personality and purpose as Christian, abbot, and writer. He emphasizes the place of the crucified Christ at the center of Aelred's life while calling spiritual friendship the "hermeneutic key" to his teaching"-- Provided by publisher.
Identifiers: LCCN 2020027628 (print) | LCCN 2020027629 (ebook) | ISBN 9780879072766 (paperback) | ISBN 9780879077082 (epub) | ISBN 9780879077082 (mobi) | ISBN 9780879077082 (pdf)
Subjects: LCSH: Aelred, of Rievaulx, Saint, 1110-1167. | Cistercians—England—Biography. | Christian saints—England—Biography. | Abbots—England—Biography. | England—Church history—1066-1485.
Classification: LCC BR754.A325 B8713 2020 (print) | LCC BR754.A325 (ebook) | DDC 271/.1202 [B]—dc23
LC record available at https://lccn.loc.gov/2020027628
LC ebook record available at https://lccn.loc.gov/2020027629

In memory of Father Charles Dumont,
deceased on Christmas Eve 2009.
We learned of his passing into our Father's kingdom
as we completed this biography.
It owes so much to him, and he would have so loved to read it.

Pierre-André Burton

Therefore will he give them up even till the time wherein she that travaileth shall bring forth: and the remnant of his brethren shall be converted to the children of Israel. And he shall stand, and feed in the strength of the Lord, in the height of the name of the Lord his God: and they shall be converted, for now shall he be magnified even to the ends of the earth. And this man shall be our peace. (Mic 5:3-5)

L'homme, par son action morale, ne réalise et ne retrouve l'unité qu'en unifiant le monde dans un sens qui l'unifie lui-même. (Man, by his moral action, realizes and recovers wholeness only by unifying the world in a way that unifies himself.) (Éric Weil, *Philosophie morale* [Paris: Vrin, 1981], 33)

Contents

Abbreviations

Series and Journals

CCCM	Corpus Christianorum, Continuatio Mediaevalis
CF	Cistercian Fathers series, Cistercian Publications
Cîteaux	*Cîteaux: Commentarii cistercienses*
Coll	*Collectanea Cisterciensia*
Cons	Constitutions of the Order of the Cistercians of the Strict Observance
CS	Cistercian Studies series, Cistercian Publications
CSQ	*Cistercian Studies Quarterly*
PL	Patrologia Latina. Ed. J.-P. Migne
RAM	*Revue d'Ascétique et de Mystique*
RB	*RB 1980: The Rule of St. Benedict.* Ed. and trans. Timothy Fry. Collegeville, MN: Liturgical Press, 1981.
RBen	*Revue Bénédictine*
SBOp	Sancti Bernardi Opera. Ed. Jean Leclercq, Henri Roche, and C. H. Talbot. Rome: Editiones Cistercienses, 1957–1977.

Aelred's Works

Anima	*De Anima; Dialogue on the Soul*
Bello	*Relatio de Bello Standardii; The Battle of the Standard*
Epil	Epilogue, *De quodam miraculum mirabili; A Certain Wonderful Miracle*

Gen angl	*Genealogia Regum Anglorum; Genealogy of the Kings of the English*
Iesu	*De Iesu puero duodenni; On Jesus at the Age of Twelve*
Inst incl	*De institutione inclusarum; The Formation of Recluses*
Lam D	*Lamentatio Davidis, regis Scotorum; Lament for David, King of the Scots*
Mira	*De quodam miraculum mirabili; A Certain Wonderful Miracle*
Oner	*Homiliae de Oneribus Propheticis Isaiae; Homilies on the Prophetic Burdens of Isaiah*
Orat	*Oratio Pastoralis; The Pastoral Prayer*
Pref B	Prefatory letter to Bernard in *De Speculum caritatis* (CF 17:73–75)
Pref H	Prefatory letter to King Henry in *Genealogy of the Kings of the English*
Spec car	*De Speculum caritatis; Mirror of Charity*
Spir	*De spiritali amicitia; On Spiritual Friendship*
Hexham	*De sanctis ecclesiae Hagulstadensis: The Saints of the Church of Hexham and their Miracles*
Vita E	*Vita Sancti Edwardi, Regis et Confessoris; The Life of Saint Edward, King and Confessor*
Vita N	*Vita Sancti Niniani; The Life of Saint Ninian*

Bernard's Works

Apo	*Apologia ad Guillelmum*
Pref Ep	Prefatory letter to Aelred's *Speculum caritatis*, CF 17:69–72

Walter Daniel's Works

Lament	Walter Daniel, *Lament for Aelred*
Letter	Walter Daniel, *Letter to Maurice*
VA	Walter Daniel, *Vita Ailredi / Vita Aelredi*

Translator's Note and Acknowledgments

Wherever possible, I replaced non-English quotations in Burton's work with quotations from English-language versions of the same texts. Chapter and paragraph numbers in Aelred's works come from the English versions, even when they differ from those in the Latin editions. Where English versions of quotations did not already exist, I have translated them into English. In all cases, unless otherwise noted, Latin annotations, biblical references, and emphasis in quotations are Burton's, not those of the quotations' original authors or editors. The Latin annotations are drawn from Burton's source texts, such as PL, CCCM, and SBOp. All biblical verses cited in English are taken from the English Vulgate, except where Aelred himself quotes the Bible.

I wish to express my deepest gratitude to several individuals whose generous contributions were vital in completing this work: first, to Lewis White, who allowed the use of excerpts from his (at the time) in-progress translation of Aelred's *Homilies on the Prophetic Burdens of Isaiah*; second to my colleagues and friends, Molly Morrison and Neil Bernstein, who assisted in translating quotations from Italian and Latin, respectively; and finally to Emily Stuckey, who compiled the indices. I could not have completed this project without their help. Above all, I'd like to thank Marsha Dutton, who offered me the opportunity to translate this work in the first place and who worked tirelessly to polish the final product.

General Introduction

1066–1167
From a Battlefield to the Chapter House of Rievaulx, or One Century of English History

> On January 12, 1167, at the age of 57, Aelred was laid to rest in Christ's peace, loved by God and man. He lived thirty-three years of monastic life, including twenty years of abbacy at the Cistercian monastery of Rievaulx. Blessed be his memory forever!

Such could have been the obituary drafted by Walter Daniel, personal secretary and posthumous biographer of the abbot of Rievaulx, to announce the death of the man he tended through many long years of illness, whom we, in turn, memorialize by retracing his life.

Aelred was born in 1110 in Hexham, a small Northumberland town on the banks of the Tyne near Hadrian's Wall, that miniature rampart whose construction the Romans began in 122 to mark the frontier between the Empire and the barbarian populations of what would one day become Scotland. In 1114, when Aelred was four years old, a painful event occurred that would profoundly trouble his early family life. The bishops of the diocese of York—first Thomas, and subsequently his successor Thurstan—applied canonical norms laid down by the Gregorian Reforms and decided to replace married clergy with monks or priests who had taken vows of celibacy. Aelred's father, Eilaf, was hit hard by this decision as he, following in

1

his forebears' footsteps, exercised a parochial appointment as guardian of the sacred relics kept in the church of Hexham, a future Augustinian priory. At this time or shortly thereafter—the exact date is unknown—Aelred was sent to be educated in the cathedral school at Durham, a highly reputable religious and intellectual center where the memory of the Venerable Bede was cherished.

In 1124, Aelred's father benefited from the accession of King David to the Scottish throne to gain entrance for his eldest son into the royal court. Aelred was to spend ten years there, years rich and fruitful in every regard. However, in 1134, to the surprise of many and after at least two years of intense spiritual struggle, Aelred decided to renounce what promised to be a brilliant career and instead entered a recently founded monastery, Rievaulx. Rievaulx belonged to an entirely new religious order, the Cistercians, then in rapid growth thanks to the prodigious influence of Saint Bernard of Clairvaux and his monastic doctrine of humanistic spiritualism and Christocentric theological anthropology, founded on the search for union with God through the affective power generated by, and through, charity.

Thirteen years later, in 1147, after a brief period of pastoral responsibility related to the founding of Rievaulx's daughter house of Revesby in 1144, Aelred was elected head of his own monastery and became the abbot of Rievaulx, a position he would hold for twenty years.

Another span of twenty years passed between Aelred's entry into the monastery and what could be considered his entry into politics. Starting in 1153–1154, when the Anarchy ended and Henry Plantagenet was recognized as Stephen of Blois' legitimate successor, Aelred became one of the most visible English ecclesiastical figures of his time. This consequence occurred primarily because of Aelred's treatises on national history, by which he became directly involved in the social and political affairs of the kingdom, directing their course as far as his abilities and rank allowed.

After more than ten years of painful illness that forced Aelred to relax his Cistercian austerity, he died in the night of January 12, 1167, roughly one hundred years after the downfall of the previously unbroken Anglo-Saxon dynasty. That dynasty had ended with the last legitimate Anglo-Saxon king, Edward the Confessor, who had died on January 5, 1066, with no direct heir. The subsequent Norman invasion was led by William the Conqueror with the blessing of Pope Alexander II. William's victory at Hastings on October 14, 1066, had made the end of the Anglo-Saxon dynasty definitive.

Aelred, the third abbot of Rievaulx, was buried on January 14, 1167, in the monastery's chapter house, beside his predecessor, the venerable William, Saint Bernard's former secretary, whom Bernard had sent to be Rievaulx's founder and first abbot.

From 1066 to 1167, between the Norman conquest and Aelred's death, a century of English history unfolded. Some may find it strange to frame Aelred's life between these two chronological reference points. The second is certainly justified: it marks the ending of the terrestrial pilgrimage of him who has been called the Doctor of Spiritual Friendship. As for the first reference point, which places the start of Aelred's life forty-four years before his birth, we have ample opportunity to demonstrate the date's pertinence. The national psychological trauma suffered by England in 1066 affected all aspects of the country's history deeply and for a very long time, even well after Aelred's death one century later. We will see, however, that many aspects of his life—the political responsibilities he took on, the self-awareness he acquired, the role he felt called to play in society, and even the "theology of history" that he gradually formulated—were in large part determined by the far-reaching consequences of the new dynasty's establishment on the English throne, a dynasty at first exclusively Franco-Norman and then, through gradual assimilation, Anglo-Norman. We will also see how, as abbot of a cenobitic monastery, Aelred sought to transpose the ecclesiastical model that had served as a foundation for the edification of his own monastic community to the context of his country's political life. Or, to put it another way, using a symbolism borrowed from Saint Augustine and omnipresent in Aelred's own thought, he attempted to transform the worldly City of Man, remodeling it in the image of the City of God.

Aelred in fact had but a single desire. It was constant throughout the diverse stages of his existence, and its trace is noticeable in the manner in which he assumed the multiple responsibilities assigned to him over time, even before he entered Rievaulx. In short, Aelred's great aspiration was to anticipate the *Heavenly Jerusalem* (the "Vision of Peace") in the *Babylon of this world* (the "City of Confusion"). To this end, he unceasingly strove to bring down the walls of hatred and rivalry, which—much like Hadrian's wall, whose vestiges lingered in Hexham and on whose ruins he may well have played with his childhood friends—divided the people of his time and caused much of the disaster and devastation he witnessed through the greater part of his life, especially before 1153–1154.

Henry Plantagenet's designation as Stephen of Blois' legitimate heir, after almost twenty years of civil war, changed the atmosphere and opened up to Aelred avenues of action he could never otherwise have hoped for. His manner and station permitted him henceforth to contribute to peace-building in his country by establishing himself as both the counselor of princes and the edifier of a national consciousness federated of all the hope and good will of a people bled white by long, painful years of civil war.

On this subject we attempt to answer at least two principal and related questions. First is the question of how Aelred came to take such an active part in the social and political life of his time. Some might argue that engagement in the affairs of his era contradicted his identity as a monk who, by his own sense of vocation, had chosen to withdraw into the silence of the cloister and devote himself as wholly as possible to an ascetic life of solitude and prayer. The second question regards the manner in which, and the theological and spiritual basis on which, Aelred so firmly engaged himself in the building of a society ultimately to be established on solid principles of peace and justice.

Two theses, then, need to be demonstrated. The first is that Aelred's social and political engagement as abbot of Rievaulx, as well as the manner in which he conceived of his pastoral responsibility toward the community confided to his care, found their source not only in his abbacy's inherent obligations but, even more important, were rooted in the depths of his personal and foundational life experiences. We will emphasize how, because of the singular circumstances of his personal narrative and its historical context, Aelred found himself thrust between the primary lines of fracture in his era's civil and religious society. We will emphasize how as he was particularly sensitized to the schisms forming in their wake he spared no effort in every personal, interpersonal, communal, ecclesiastical, social, or political context to navigate toward unity, harmony, conciliation, and reconciliation. Among the divisional lines we will take into account, the following ones derive from the chronological reference points highlighted earlier.

First, consider 1114: the fracture was simultaneously social, familial, and emotional. The decision on the part of Bishop Thomas and his successor Thurstan to replace married with unmarried clergy suddenly cast Aelred's family into an uncertain future and a relatively precarious socio-economic situation. Eilaf, Aelred's father and Hexham's priest, suddenly risked finding himself homeless and without an income with which to provide for his family. The shock was brutal. Whether it was then or slightly later that Aelred was sent to Durham is unclear. Either way, the social fracture was soon compounded by Aelred's sooner-than-planned departure from his early childhood environment. Furthermore, the brutality and suddenness with which these events succeeded each other would certainly have shaken the young child and thrown off his internal compass. Given the profound traces this departure appears to have left in his heart, there is every reason to think that this separation was deeply painful to Aelred, and that it resulted in a new fracture, emotional this time, whose exact depth we cannot measure.

In that same year we also see a socio-religious fracture. Although Aelred was too young at the time to understand the full importance of all the issues involved, he later discovered that the same episcopal decision that had upset the equilibrium of his family life was going to force two antagonistic ecclesiastical models to violently collide. The first, Celtic and Saxon, soon destined to disappear, raised no particular objection to the existence of married clergy. The second, newer and imported from the continent, met savage resistance. This model aimed to impose the canonical norms of a church reformed according to the Roman Gregorian model, so called after Gregory VII, the eleventh-century pope who was the principal artisan of a reform initiated years earlier by Pope Leo IX.

A second important date in the chronology is 1124. This time, the fracture was primarily socio-cultural. First, Aelred quit the predominantly and essentially religious environment in which he had spent the first fourteen years of his life in order to enter a universe that was socially very different, even if piety was certainly not absent from it. This new social milieu was the Scottish court. Additionally, Aelred's entry into the Scottish court marked a second, equally important split of a cultural and intellectual nature. In leaving Durham to enter into the service of King David, Aelred had to acquire the use of a third language. In addition to his native English and the Latin he had mastered while studying at Hexham and Durham, Aelred now had to learn French, held in esteem by the king of the Scots, who himself had learned it in the royal English court where he was in part educated.

But more than simply marking the passage from one language or one culture to another, this date above all effected a radical change in Aelred's mindset. At that time, Durham was an intellectual center of high repute, focused on theological study and scholarly historical research reminiscent of the Venerable Bede's work. Aelred never forgot the time of his study at Durham. Indeed, he appears to have retained throughout his life a pronounced and permanent penchant for the study of history in general and of his country in particular. At the same time, he obtained a particularly valuable intellectual advantage from his arrival at the Scottish court, with its cultural openness to Europe, and his acquaintance with King David, who like his mother, Saint Margaret, wished to Christianize his country and modernize its outdated institutions. From all of this he obtained a broader worldview, one that focused not nostalgically on the past, whatever its prestige, but instead encompassed the future and its promises.

A third vital moment in the chronology occurs in 1134–1135. Rievaulx was a monastery belonging to the comparatively new Cistercian Order, a community of French origin and the only order at the time with an openly transnational character. By choosing to enter Rievaulx, Aelred left behind what Aelred Squire has rightly called the "Hexham-Durham-York triangle."[1] Until that time, Aelred had lived most of his life in that triangle. His departure thus consummated a rupture with, but not a rejection of, the Anglo-Saxon environment of his birth and his native Celtic religious culture. This choice ratified and brought to an end the journey he had begun ten years earlier on entering the Scottish court. Paradoxically, at the very moment that he made this choice, opening himself to a form of universality transcending national and cultural differences, he became the saddened and powerless eyewitness to a twenty-year civil war, which did not end until 1153–1154.

Thus Aelred found himself confronted with two new fractures in 1134, both institutional in nature. The first of these affected vowed religious life, at the time in full transition and moving toward a renewed and more radically evangelical expression in its institutional forms. Bernard himself brought

1. Aelred Squire, "Historical Factors in the Formation of Aelred of Rievaulx," *Coll* 22 (1960): 262–82.

Aelred into this high-stakes debate. The second institutional fracture affected the feudal structures of medieval civil and political society. The interplay of political alliances and allegiances, as well as that of private interests, led many who had formerly considered themselves kin or friends to engage in a pitiless and merciless war to the devastation of the civil population, innocent victims of princely rivalries.

Finally, a last major reference point is 1153–1154, which saw the accession of Henry II to the English throne. This was a year of hope and the beginning of a new era that would be marked by a possible reconciliation among the peoples and cultures that made up post-conquest England. Sensing the promise and hope of a national sacred union, Aelred would have felt no further risk of fracture if he had not seen the gathering of threatening clouds and heard the first thunderous rumblings of a coming storm—one that would take shape in the open conflict that from 1163 on opposed King Henry II and Thomas Becket, his former chancellor become archbishop of Canterbury. Aelred would know neither of the conflict's fatal conclusion in Becket's assassination on December 29, 1170, nor of its tragic consummation in the nearly irreparable rupture this murder would create between medieval society's "Two Swords," between ecclesiastical hierarchy and political authority, between the church and the state. This ignorance is no doubt for the better, for had he lived to see it, he would have been faced with the collapse of his ardent socio-political dream of an ecclesiastical-political collaboration.

Later we examine each of these fractures, as they all, taken either individually or together according to the close connections between them, represented for Aelred either a challenge that he had to confront personally or a social debate in which he was sure to engage. From the outset, however—and this is the second thesis we set forth—it is notable that the manner in which Aelred deals with these personal challenges and fuels reflection on these social debates was remarkably constant throughout his life. Naturally sustained by what Aelred Squire calls a fundamentally "conciliatory temper,"[2] the future abbot of Rievaulx did not see these fractures as lines of demarcation for erecting divisive walls, but rather as providential opportunities offered to build a new society, unified and harmonious, prefiguring the City of God.

However, Aelred proceeded speculatively, aided by the progressive elaboration of a spiritual doctrine based on the transposition to a wider scope of something he considered a fundamental and primary human experience: friendship. We will show that the doctrine of spiritual friendship furnishes the common and binding thread of Aelred's existence and thought. It is a thread seen in his existence even from his earliest childhood and adolescence, continuing through his years of abbatial responsibility, and extending into his final public and political engagements. Similarly, the thread runs through his thought, beginning with a humanism of friendship, based on a Ciceronian model. It then passes through the construction of a brotherly monastic community constituting an ecclesiastical model based on the exemplar offered by the early community of the apostles. Eventually the thread passes through the construction of a civil society founded on social justice and the close collaboration between political and religious powers, representing a feudal societal model informed by Aelred's moderate interpretation of the "Two Swords Theory." Finally the thread evolves into a cosmic theology of universal friendship, based on a theological model that is both trinitarian in its communication of idioms and Christocentric in its focus on Christ as head of the church and the cornerstone in whom all things are recapitulated.

The foregoing should suffice to make clear that our approach to Aelred's life is multidimensional—inextricably anthropological and ethical, existential and spiritual, historical and doctrinal. We follow the course of Aelred's life and

2. Squire, "Historical Factors," 265.

discover the full breadth and depth of the man Aelred was throughout his existence. We highlight the obstacles that blocked his way and the challenges he had to overcome in his lifetime. Examining these obstacles and challenges, we take into account the historical circumstances—familial and cultural, social and political, or religious and ecclesiastical—external to his life proper, and show how he was shaped by the world around him. We also show how, by his personal choices, he shaped himself and contributed to shaping the world and the various environments in which he himself evolved. We will thus be in a position to verify how tightly entwined were Aelred's existence and doctrine. Or, to put it another way, we will see how in his itinerary from man, to monk, to abbot, to moral conscience of his society, the progressive unification of his whole being (body, soul, heart, and mind) and the gradual elaboration of his doctrinal synthesis (monastic anthropology and ethics, spiritual theology, and mystic life) cooperated. The latter was framed and constructed through the experiences of the former, and the former was firmly seated and supported on the foundation of the latter.

Our biography begins with an introductory section, a single chapter explaining our methods. In chapter 1 we draw up a brief survey of the existing historical literature surrounding the figure of Aelred. We consider its origins (namely Walter Daniel's *Life of Aelred*), the first attempts at "dehagiographization" to which historians such as Maurice Powicke devoted themselves at the start of the twentieth century, and finally contemporary studies by Charles Dumont, Aelred Squire, Anselm Hoste, Gaetano Raciti, Marsha Dutton, Brian McGuire, Elizabeth Freeman, and John Sommerfeldt, to cite only the best known. Following this, we outline our own methodology, as well as the specific focus we hope to give the present inquiry. The reader who is eager to begin the narrative of Aelred's life immediately can skip this first part if he so wishes.

Subsequently our narrative proper is broken into four principal stages, each corresponding to the four periods just outlined.

Part II addresses Aelred as a man, concentrating on his pre-monastic period from 1110 to 1134, and is divided into three chapters. Chapter 2 is devoted to the cultural and political context of Aelred's life, chapter 3 to the human and intellectual development he underwent before entering Rievaulx, and chapter 4 to his conversion in 1134.

Part III presents Aelred as a monk, emphasizing the initial period of his monastic instruction during the years 1134 to 1143, and consists of two chapters. Chapter 5 focuses on the early years of his monastic life at Rievaulx until 1141. Chapter 6 examines the composition of *The Mirror of Charity* (1142–1143) and the corresponding role Aelred took on in his community as instructor in the ways of monastic life.

Part IV deals with Aelred as abbot and pastor, concentrating on Aelred's "Time of Great Pastoral Responsibility" during the years 1143 to 1153. This part focuses on Aelred's monastic ministry, first practiced at Revesby (1143–1147) and then at Rievaulx (1147–1153). This part also consists of two chapters. Chapter 7 is primarily event-based, examining the external circumstances leading Aelred to take on these two charges. Inversely, chapter 8 is almost exclusively doctrine-based, studying Aelred's role as "Master Architect Building a Community."

Finally, part V accounts for the last fourteen years of Aelred's life, or "The Time of Spiritual Maturity," from 1153 until Aelred's death in 1167. Chapter 9 examines Aelred's political engagements in England's social and civil life. Analyzing his seven historical treatises, we demonstrate Aelred's claim to the title "moral conscience of his time." We see in those writings the progressive development of a theology of history that is the subject of chapter 10, in which we bring out what can be considered Aelred's cosmic mysticism of history.

This four-stage narrative is followed by chapter 11, a general conclusion, in which we synthesize certain fundamental points that our research has brought to light.

To close this introduction, we would like to express one hope, one wish, and several thanks.

It is our hope to do honor to the project outlined in the present introduction.

It is our wish that—in addition to discovering Aelred's endearing but vigorous spiritual physiognomy—the reader will find as much pleasure in reading this biography as we had in writing it. Our labors will be all the more worthwhile if they can awaken in the reader the fervent desire to learn more for himself.

Finally we offer our thanks. These are first addressed to Father Charles Dumont, who instilled our earliest desire to study the Fathers of Cîteaux, and who taught us to appreciate two of its most illustrious representatives: Aelred of Rievaulx, to whom the present biography is devoted, and his master, Saint Bernard. For some twenty-five years they have been faithful companions in our journey. We also wish to thank Father Paul Christophe of Les Éditions du Cerf. His obstinate persistence in requesting this biography finally succeeded— and not without difficulty, as he will certainly attest—in overcoming our own obstinate resistance to undertaking such a task. Our thanks are addressed finally to all those who, during the nearly two years required to complete this book, supported our efforts with their constant encouragement.

Part 1
Methodology

Chapter One

Historiography, Methods, and Perspectives

In this chapter, we offer a brief summary sketch of historical methodology and research relating to Aelred's life and works. This rapid survey delineates the principal stages of Aelred's rediscovery from the beginning of the twentieth century to the present. We thus contextualize from a historical, methodological, and doctrinal standpoint the unique perspectives of the present biography.

Many worthy works before this study have already traced a biographical portrait of Aelred, who, after serving as *dispensator* of the Scottish King David I, became abbot of the English Cistercian monastery at Rievaulx (founded in 1132 by Bernard of Clairvaux) and helped make the monastery famous. In this chapter, we comment on historians and scholars whose work has preceded our own and without which we could never have imagined its undertaking. Such a commentary permits us to pay the immense debt we owe to them, and simultaneously to outline, in context, the methodology and perspective adopted in our work. This survey consists of three parts. We begin with a presentation of Walter Daniel's *Life of Aelred*, a source text composed by a privileged eyewitness to Aelred's life. We then briefly present various nineteenth- and twentieth-century efforts to "dehagiographize" Aelred's life. Finally, we sketch our own process, clarifying the goals and principles guiding our research. This leads to our contention that Aelred's conception of spiritual friendship can be considered the hermeneutical key *par excellence* that unlocks access simultaneously to his spiritual doctrine, his personality, his life, and his multiple human engagements.

A Pioneering Testament: Walter Daniel's *Life of Aelred*

The premier historian to examine Aelred's life, both chronologically and through his eyewitness account, is Aelred's contemporary, Walter Daniel. Walter entered Rievaulx at the age of twenty-five, probably around 1150. He was Aelred's secretary and, during Aelred's final illness, an exceedingly (perhaps even excessively) devoted caregiver. The clearly expressed purpose of his *Life*, composed shortly after Aelred's death on January 12, 1167, was to defend Aelred's unjustly trampled-upon memory. Two chapters bear witness to this goal and report certain accusations brought against Aelred. The first of these concerns was the suspicion raised by detractors during Aelred's lifetime that personal ambition alone led to his abbacy (VA 26). The second is more insidious. It concerns not only the quality of Aelred's monastic life, but also the nature of his abbatial ministry. Some critics tried to frame him as a self-indulgent monk of loose discipline. They called him a "glutton and a wine-bibber"[1] and, perhaps even more gravely, accused him of excessive tolerance toward the moral weaknesses of others during his abbacy, describing him as "a friend of publicans" (VA 26, 27, 29, etc.).

Oriented as it is toward the defense and illustration of Aelred's monastic piety, the *Life* fails to avoid the pitfalls of ancient and medieval hagiography: an inflation of the facts, a rhetorical exaggeration, and above all a taste for the fantastic. Nonetheless, as biased as it may seem today, we mine this vital

---

1. VA 26, 27 (Walter Daniel, *The Life of Aelred of Rievaulx*, trans. F. M. Powicke, CF 57 [Kalamazoo, MI: Cistercian Publications, 1994], 115).

source of information, as have so many of our predecessors, appreciating its pertinence as a faithful reflection of what we know of Aelred through his own writings.

It should not be forgotten—however concerned Walter may have been with establishing the historical truth of the Aelred's life, or with reestablishing it wherever it seemed to him to be trod upon—that the *Life* was above all written as an act of filial piety.[2] Composing it was a way of honoring and defending the memory of the man he had viewed as a father from the time that Aelred, as Walter recalls, "begot me to the Life of Saint Benedict" (VA 1). In other words, we should not expect from this disciple's homage to his master the same rigor or historical reliability that we demand from a historian educated in proper methods of historical criticism. Walter's purpose, in fact, is rather to offer his reader a mirror in which truth can be seen—not simply historical truth but, more important, spiritual and ethical truth. In the final analysis, Walter offers his readers a model of monastic and abbatial life that deserves to be both contemplated and imitated (VA 1).

Between the life Aelred lived (or history proper) and the inevitably interpreted life written on paper (the *Life* as a hagiographical work), Walter places a railway switch to change the reader's trajectory. By means of this switch, he shunts readers off the track of the external appearances of Aelred's life and its purely historical eventfulness and sets them rolling down a track leading to the hidden mystery of Aelred's being and his spiritual physiognomy, which defies, at least in part, any objective and scientifically verifiable observation.

Such intent and perspective allow us to explain with a certain degree of plausibility an apparently curious aspect of the *Life's* literary composition. A rapid reading of the work shows that in composing his narrative, Walter mostly followed the

2. On this point, see the introduction to the French translation of Walter Daniel, *La Vie d'Aelred*, trans. Pierre-André Burton (Oka, Canada: Abbaye Notre-Dame-du-Lac, 2004), 18.

chronological order of Aelred's life. He divides it into four distinct and neatly identified periods: from Aelred's youth at the Scottish court until his conversion in 1134, his initial monastic instruction and his first responsibilities at Rievaulx from 1134 to 1143, his abbacy at Revesby from 1143 to 1147, and finally his abbacy at Rievaulx from 1147 to 1167. But after this initial chronological approach to the text, a detailed analysis brings to light a flagrant disproportion. While Walter devotes a little less than half of the *Life* (twenty-seven chapters out of sixty) to the thirty-seven-year stretch of the first three periods in Aelred's life, he reserves more than half (the last thirty-three chapters) to Aelred's twenty years of abbacy at Rievaulx.

At first glance this disproportion may not seem inordinate. Aelred's abbacy at Rievaulx is no doubt the most important period of his lifetime, as it coincides with the time of his human and spiritual maturity and the apogee of his influence. On the other hand, the disproportion becomes obvious as soon as one notes that twenty of the *Life's* last thirty-three chapters (chapters 40–60, exactly one-third of the narrative) are exclusively devoted to the four final years of Aelred's life, from 1163 to 1167. It is even more surprising to find that of these twenty chapters, the last thirteen take into consideration only the last year, and even more specifically only the final week, of Aelred's life. Obviously, then, Walter's narrative provides an extremely focused look at an essentially old and sickly Aelred.

We might be saddened by this hagiographic choice, which obscured broad segments of Aelred's life. Among these we might cite everything related to Aelred's temporal administration of his monastery, his role in Rievaulx's four daughter houses, over which he exercised canonical paternity, and his engagement in the social, political, and ecclesiastical affairs of his time.[3] There are simply too many aspects of Aelred's life that to our modern eyes are insufficiently explored in the *Life*.

---

3. For a map of England showing the location of Rievaulx's daughter houses, see Peter Fergusson and Stuart Harrison, *Rievaulx Abbey: Community, Architecture, and Memory* (New Haven: Yale University Press, 1999), 43.

It would, however, be unbecoming and unfair to hold all this against Walter. On numerous occasions in the course of his narrative, he explains the intentions that guided him and influenced his authorial choices. The passage that most clearly shows this purpose is found at the beginning of chapter 40. In this chapter, which opens the long section of the *Life* devoted to Aelred's four final years, Walter stresses his deliberate choice to narrow his work's scope and focus solely on the spiritual dimension of his abbot's life. His wish, he adds, is to show that Aelred never ceased to devote himself body and soul to the spiritual edification of his entire being, thanks to a rigorous religious asceticism (VA 40, 41) and a growing intensity in his life of prayer and intimacy with Christ (VA 42, 48), despite an increasingly pitiable state of health: "God willing, I shall briefly describe how in those four years, like a second Noah, he compacted the ark of his life within the breadth of a single cubit and, keeping the fabric of the pure temple, his body, in good repair, renewed and perfected it, and polished all the stones of the spotless sanctuary, his breast, and made them all square, and with the plummet of exact living built them into a house of perfection" (VA 40).

We shall not linger too long on this text, which has already been the object of detailed study. Here we simply note that Walter anchored his proposed project in the metaphor of Aelred as a "new Noah." This image is completed by two others converging with the first to furnish a narrative thread that stretches throughout the *Life*, and especially its final part. The first of these two images is introduced in chapter 41 and parallels the conflation of Aelred and Noah. Walter underlines the ascetic hue of this comparison by affirming that Aelred subjected his life to "a second circumcision" (VA 41), mercilessly cutting out from his life all superfluity and limiting himself to strict necessities, as befitted an adherence to the Cistercian reform and the ideal of Saint Bernard.

The second image is that of Aelred as a "new Moses" (see VA 43, 47, and 58). Contiguous to the first comparison, it demonstrates the way the asceticism to which Aelred unceasingly gave himself up over the years progressively led to a complete transformation of his being and literally transfigured his countenance, which was irradiated by and radiating with divine light. From this set of images emerges the idea that Walter wished above all to alleviate the suspicions that weighed upon Aelred's character during his lifetime and after his death, and to leave the dual portrait of a monk who was not only a veritable ascetic (a "new Noah") but also an authentic mystic (a "new Moses").

One can hypothesize that it is at least in part because of the twofold image of Aelred Walter wished to leave that he largely neglected exposition of Aelred's public stature and his role in the social, political, and ecclesiastical life of his time. But we should not overstate this point. That Walter insufficiently stressed the public dimension of Aelred's life does not mean that he ignored it entirely, as is most eloquently evidenced by the frequency with which he describes Aelred as *peacemaker*.[4] However unfamiliar one might be with the mindset of the medieval West, so overflowing with biblical thought and culture, the attentive reader of the *Life* cannot help but remark, by way of a subtle allusion to Hebrew etymology, that this simple qualification of Aelred as peacemaker allows Walter implicitly to present Aelred as a new Solomon. At a single stroke, the allusion suggests at least two other complementary ideas. First, in the manner of Solomon, Aelred becomes the model political administrator, exercising in the management of temporal wealth and authority the same prudence and wisdom as this biblical king. Second, in line with the etymology of the name *Solomon* ("king of peace"), Aelred is shown to be an ardent promoter of peace in his society.

"New Noah," "new Moses," "new Solomon": such are the three main aspects of Aelred's character Walter underscores in the course of his narrative. However, of these three roles—ascetic, mystic, and peacemaker—only the last seems, in our view,

---

4. E.g., Walter, VA 125.

to lack real substance. Preoccupied with Aelred's posthumous defense by presenting Aelred's monastic life as exemplary, Walter seems to have intentionally avoided framing Aelred in the context of his socio-cultural environment and relationships. Walter had little desire to expound Aelred's political engagements, even though these were well documented by Aelred's own historical works and other texts. From this dual limitation resulting from authorial intent, it follows that the *Life* is unable to shine a light on Aelred's full historical impact, an impact that led his contemporaries to say "almost the equal of Bernard is our Aelred [*Bernardo prope, par Aelredus noster*]."[5]

In fact, it was not until the late nineteenth and early twentieth centuries that this shortcoming in the presentation of Aelred's rich personality was overcome. In particular the unearthing of various archival and library collections, putting a number of medieval primary sources from Aelred's era into the hands of historians, allowed scholars to give a more substantive historical foundation to Aelred's life. It is to this renewal of Aelredian studies in the nineteenth and twentieth centuries that we now turn our attention.

The Renewal of Historical Research and Aelredian Studies

A Pioneer: F. M. Powicke

Among the historians who contributed to the renewal of Aelredian studies, the greatest pioneer is no doubt twentieth-century scholar Ferdinand Maurice Powicke. We are especially indebted to him for two publications that marked a turning point in Aelredian historiography. These works offer the first true historical research on Aelred and largely paved the way for all subsequent studies.

---

5. D. B. Tissier, citing Nicholas of Rievaulx, *Ac imprimis, Notitia altera*; PL 195:208. Pierre-André Burton, "An Illiterate, or a True Master of Spiritual Teaching?" in *A Companion to Aelred of Rievaulx (1110–1167)*, ed. Marsha L. Dutton (Leiden: Brill, 2017), 218.

The first of Powicke's publications is a long study appearing in 1922, still considered authoritative.[6] In *Ailred of Rievaulx and his Biographer Walter Daniel*, Powicke published the fruit of his research on the personality of Walter. Among other things, Powicke revealed the recent discovery of a fourteenth-century manuscript (today preserved at Jesus College, Cambridge, QB 7) containing the original unabridged text of the *Life of Aelred*, which until that time was known only through condensed versions from the sixteenth and seventeenth centuries. The second of these two publications, appearing in 1950, is a critical edition of the *Life*, accompanied by its English translation and preceded by a substantial introduction.[7]

Powicke's merit is not limited to this work. Not content with simply exhuming the *Life* from the archives, Powicke made every effort to appreciate its historical value by comparing Walter's testament to various other medieval sources. Such comparison permitted him better to illuminate the vast network of human relationships through which Aelred moved throughout his life. Powicke thus removed Aelred from the outlines in which Walter had drawn him, as an aging and ailing abbot, confined to his cell in the infirmary. Thanks to Powicke's efforts, other historians were now free to pursue the "dehagiographization" of Aelred's life.

Among the authors who have pursued and extended Powicke's inaugural work, a handful are of particular importance. We can group these scholars in twos and threes by reason of their approaches, which, if not identical, are at least similar. First are Aelred Squire and Father Charles Dumont, who employ a doctrinal and literary approach. Then more recently there are Marsha Dutton and Elizabeth Freeman, along with Brian Patrick McGuire, who employ socio-historical and psycho-historical approaches respectively.

6. Maurice Powicke, *Ailred of Rievaulx and his Biographer Walter Daniel* (London: University Press-Longmans, Green and Co., 1922). This study was the springboard for the 1950 publication.

7. Walter Daniel, *The Life of Ailred of Rievaulx*, trans. F. M. Powicke (Oxford: Clarendon, 1950, 1978).

The Literary and Doctrinal Approach of Aelred Squire and Charles Dumont

To our knowledge, Aelred Squire is the first to have proposed a complete and detailed biography of Aelred of Rievaulx. Modestly titled *Aelred of Rievaulx: A Study*, this work appeared in English in 1969 and has unfortunately never been translated into another language. It built on the substantial and fertile historical information brought to light by Powicke, who attempted to articulate that information with an attentive reading of the doctrinal content of Aelred's works.

Little more than twenty years later, in 1990, Dumont published a study as an introduction to the English translation of Aelred's *Mirror of Charity* that was less amply developed but equally compelling.[8] Through a literary and doctrinal perspective similar to Squire's, Dumont managed to inscribe Aelred's life and works within the spiritual and theological context of the Cistercian reform as a "school of charity." He paid particular attention to the doctrine of charity and the place of friendship in Aelred's human and spiritual journey.

The Sociohistorical Approach of Marsha Dutton and Elizabeth Freeman

Dutton's more sociological approach shines a new light on two particular aspects of Aelred's life. The first is the socio-religious and socio-historical context of Aelred's conversion and Cistercian vocation; the second is Aelred's historical writing and its concrete implications in twelfth-century English political history.

---

8. Charles Dumont, "Aelred of Rievaulx, His Life and Works," in *Aelred of Rievaulx, The Mirror of Charity*, trans. Elizabeth Connor, CF 17 (Kalamazoo, MI: Cistercian Publications, 1990), 11–67. The text was subsequently republished in French as Charles Dumont, "Aelred de Rievaulx: Introduction à sa vie et à ses écrits," in *Une éducation du cœur: la spiritualité affective de saint Bernard de Clairvaux et de saint Aelred de Rievaulx* (Oka, Canada: Abbaye Notre-Dame-Du Lac, 1997), 193–236.

In the first instance, Dutton measures with precision the impact of the Gregorian Reform on Aelred's choice to join the monastery of Rievaulx. By means of the restrictive norms the reform laid down regarding accession to the priesthood, Aelred was effectively constrained by a sort of historical and contextual necessity to make that choice. Similarly Dutton revisits, in order better to assess its validity, the accusation cast against Aelred during his own lifetime that his Cistercian vocation was stained by the vice of secret ambition.[9]

The second area of research explored by Dutton,[10] to which Elizabeth Freeman has recently added significant contributions,[11]

9. Concerning this dual inquiry, see Marsha L. Dutton, "The Conversion and Vocation of Aelred of Rievaulx: A Historical Hypothesis," in *England in the Twelfth Century*, ed. Daniel Williams (London: Boydell, 1990), 31–49. A Spanish translation of this article is also available: Marsha L. Dutton, "Conversión y vocación de San Elredo de Rievaulx," *Cistercium: Revista monástica* 45 (1993): 307–30.

10. In this area, several articles and studies are worth noting. Apart from Dutton's substantial introduction to the life of Aelred in the republishing of the English translation of the *Life of Aelred* (VA), the following titles are of note: "Aelred historien: deux nouveaux portraits dans un manuscrit de Dublin," Coll 55 (1993): 208–30 (with a subsequent English translation: "Aelred, Historian: Two Portraits in Plantagenet Myth," CSQ 28 [1993]: 112–43). More recently there appeared "A Historian's Historian: The Place of Bede in Aelred's Contributions to the New History of his Age," in *Truth as Gift: Studies in Cistercian History in Honor of John R. Sommerfeldt*, ed. Marsha L. Dutton, et al., CF 204 (Kalamazoo, MI: Cistercian Publications, 2004), 407–48; "*Sancto Dunstano Cooperante*: Collaboration between King and Ecclesiastical Advisor in Aelred of Rievaulx's *Genealogy of the Kings of the English*," in *Religious and Laity in Northern Europe 1000–1400: Interaction, Negotiation, and Power*, ed. Emilia Jamroziak and Janet Burton (Turnhout: Brepols, 2007), 183–95. It should also be noted that we owe to Dutton the complete collection of Aelred's historical works translated into English in two volumes: Marsha L. Dutton, ed., *Aelred of Rievaulx: The Historical Works*, trans. Jane Patricia Freeland, CF 56 (Kalamazoo, MI: Cistercian Publications, 2005); and *Aelred of Rievaulx: The Lives of the Northern Saints*, trans. Jane Patricia Freeland, CF 71 (Kalamazoo, MI: Cistercian Publications, 2006).

11. Of particular note is Freeman's doctoral thesis on Cistercian historiography, the first part of which is entirely devoted to Aelred's contribution. See

concerns Aelred's historical works. A deep study of these demonstrates that by playing a leading role in events, Aelred became an eminent actor in the history of his time. This thesis is developed along two distinct but connected axes. First, as historiographer and historian, Aelred was, so to speak, a creator of history. This is to say that his historical writings, as acts of semiotic interpretation and articulation of historical events, helped to shape the collective representation of those events for both his own era and posterity.[12] Such an affirmation is particularly pertinent to the royal myth that Aelred helped weave around the figure of Henry II in order to firmly establish the political legitimacy of the new Anglo-Norman monarchy.

It is precisely because Aelred was a creator of history in the sense we have just described that he was also an eminent actor in that history. As a historian, he hoped to accomplish more than simply to outline past events. He also aimed to have an impact on history by making himself the counselor of kings. In other words, the study of Aelred's historical works is of particular value in shedding light on the distinctly political role that he voluntarily, albeit indirectly, assumed.

The Psychohistorical Approach of Brian Patrick McGuire

Finally, we must say a word about Brian Patrick McGuire's provocatively titled 1994 biographical essay *Brother and Lover: Aelred of Rievaulx.*[13] Although writing from a completely different perspective, McGuire shares with Dutton the same desire to inscribe Aelred's vocation within a larger historical context in order to account for the multiple facets of his rich and engaging personality. Two items in particular retain

---

Elizabeth Freeman, *Narratives of a New Order: Cistercian Historical Writing in England, 1150–1220* (Turnhout: Brepols, 2002).

12. In particular, the study of the manuscript tradition of Aelred's historical works reveals that these texts enjoyed a lengthy posterity.

13. Brian Patrick McGuire, *Brother and Lover: Aelred of Rievaulx* (New York: Crossroad Press, 1994).

McGuiire's attention. On the one hand, McGuire assesses, as Dutton does, the influence of the Gregorian Reform on Aelred's choice to become a monk at Rievaulx and the part Aelred's psychoaffective orientation must have played in making this choice. It is not the place here to reexamine in detail the elaborate argument McGuire lays out.

It suffices to underscore two points. First, by situating his research as an extension of John Boswell's work on the history of tolerance and homosexuality in the heart of western Christianity,[14] McGuire aims to reveal a homosexual psychoaffective framework underlying Aelred's personality, and, on the basis of this supposed psychological structure, he examines in more precise focus the second of the two reproaches formulated against Aelred by certain contemporaries, according to which the abbot was "a glutton and a wine-bibber and a friend of publicans" (VA 26). Furthermore, McGuire's proposed interpretation would show that Aelred was indeed an abbot far too "tolerant" of the "weaknesses" of his brothers (VA 27, 29, 30) and that by the example of his own life Aelred would have encouraged them to integrate their homosexual tendencies into their monastic vocation.

It goes without saying that the publication of this book, preceded by others of a similar nature,[15] provoked a wave of reaction all the more critical for McGuire's having contributed, without ever proposing it explicitly, to the widespread diffusion

14. See John Boswell, *Christianity, Social Tolerance, and Homosexuality: Gay People in Western Europe from the Beginning of the Christian Era to the Fourteenth Century* (Chicago: Chicago University Press, 1980).

15. For reference, here is a partial list of McGuire's other works, in chronological order: Brian Patrick McGuire, "Monastic Friendship and Toleration in Twelfth-Century Cistercian Life," in *Monks, Hermits and the Ascetic Tradition*, ed. W. J. Sheils (Oxford: Blackwell, 1985), 147–60; "Aelred of Rievaulx and the Limits of Friendship," in *Friendship and Community: The Monastic Experience (350–1250)*, CS 95 (Kalamazoo, MI: Cistercian Publications, 1988), 296–338; and "Sexual Awareness and Identity in Aelred of Rievaulx (1110–1167)," ABR 45 (1995): 184–226.

of an image of Aelred as a homosexual—an image contested by many. Quite rightly, some will regret such a consequence, but no less legitimately, others will rejoice in the fact that the polemic raised by the publication of this book had at least two beneficial effects. The book incited numerous researchers and historians again to take up the question and examine it from angles as diverse as cultural history, spirituality, moral theology, and the literary study of autobiographical Aelredian texts. Just as important, this debate, now fortunately calmed, breathed new life into Aelredian studies in general.

The Aim of the Present Work

Before concluding this broad overview of Aelredian historiography, it remains to outline our main goals in undertaking a new biography of Aelred. It is up to readers to judge the degree of our success at the end of the journey. We begin by indicating how we have attempted to frame the study.

Confronted with the richness and diversity of the current approaches to Aelred's life and personality just outlined, we should specify the motivation that sparked this work and became its guiding principle. No doubt this principle itself constitutes the limit of our study, but it also furnishes—at least so we hope—its unique character. We do not pretend to present original facts surrounding Aelred's life, nor to contribute any new or previously unpublished texts to the existing Aelredian canon. In that respect, we are merely dwarves standing on the shoulders of the giants who preceded us. To a large extent we are but the beneficiaries of their labors. At most, we hope to present the reader the fruit of our twenty-year immersion in Aelred's and other scholars' works and, through that immersive experience, to help the reader better understand the man Aelred was.

Consequently our intention is to portray Aelred's human, spiritual, and monastic physiognomy by focusing on the innermost recesses of his heart. Our conviction is that this intimate anchor point will permit us to acquire the most unified vision possible of the varied facets of Aelred's existence and his diverse connections to the broader social, political, and ecclesiastical life of his era.

A First Principle: Unifying One's Life Through Christ

Our work has been consistently guided by two principles. The first relates to the monastic framework in which Aelred inscribed his existence. If there is one desire that naturally fills the heart of every monk, it is the quest to unify his life. For anyone wishing to better know the monk that Aelred was, there is no more fruitful path than to examine Aelred's efforts to realize this goal over the course of his lifetime. The historian who examines Aelred's life from this perspective has a great advantage, as this point recurs throughout Aelred's writings. Similarly, its frequent recurrence leads the historian to conclude that attaining this internal unification constituted the major challenge of Aelred's existence.

The dual image of the "spiritual ark of the heart" and the "single cubit" that dominates Aelred's two master works, *The Mirror of Charity* and *Spiritual Friendship*, reveals Aelred's driving desire to unify (*componere*) his entire spiritual and affective life by building it around Christ and by making it converge (*constringere in, traducere ad, revocare ad*) fully toward him, the form (*forma*), the exemplar, and the sole measure of all things. This image is so central and illuminating that Walter could find nothing better, using the image to speak of the manner in which Aelred "compacted the ark of his life within the breadth of a single cubit" (VA 40).

A Second Principle: The Cosmic and Divine Order of Charity in the World

The second principle is less existential and more epistemological than the first. It is founded on what John R. Sommerfeldt has rightly called the "cosmological roots" (but also anthropological) of Aelredian spirituality.[16] As an heir to a Stoic and biblical vision of the world, Aelred considers the cosmos and all it contains to be the fruit of God's infinite and benevolent love. Therefore the universal order established by divine wisdom is governed entirely by the same laws of love that govern trinitarian life itself. These laws, according to the book of Wisdom,[17] so often referred to in the Cistercian tradition, constitute a principle of *harmony and order*—the order of love, to be precise—by which complementary and reciprocal relationships exist among all beings in such a way that every creature needs all other creatures. A creature can only exist and subsist to the extent that it institutes, with all others, bonds of interdependence and mutual aid, and therefore of charity.

This principle, stated in the very earliest paragraphs of Aelred's first treatise, *The Mirror of Charity*, leads Aelred to affirm that every creature, from the simple fact of its existence, participates not only in the existence of God, but also in three of God's attributes: his nature, his form, and his usefulness. By participating in God's nature, Aelred says, each being is good; by participating in God's form, each creature is beautiful; and by participating in God's usefulness, all living things are also useful,

> by which all in good order [*bene ordinata*] may serve some purpose. He who is responsible for their being is also responsible for their being good, beautiful, and well-ordered. They all exist, because they are from him who is supreme and unchangeable being. All are beautiful because they are from him who is supremely and unchangeably beautiful. All are good, because they are from

16. John R. Sommerfeldt, "The Roots of Aelred's Spirituality: Cosmology and Anthropology," CSQ 38 (2003): 19–26.

17. See Wisdom 8:1: "She reaches therefore from end to end mightily, and ordereth all things sweetly." This supports the Stoic idea, so appreciated by Bernard and Aelred, according to which God established and ordered all things "in measure, and number, and weight" (Wis 11:21).

> him who is supremely and unchangeably good. All are
> well-ordered, because they are from him who is su-
> premely and unchangeably wise. They are therefore good
> by nature, beautiful in form, and well-ordered that they
> may give splendor to the universe itself.[18]

In his treatise *On Spiritual Friendship* also Aelred builds upon this grandiose cosmological vision in his interpretation of the history of the world from its creation at the dawn of time, all the way to its eschatological conclusion and perfect consummation in God at the end of time.

From the start, then, this originary vision of a "universal harmony" as God wished it for the created world, and by virtue of which peaceful bonds of complementarity, reciprocal alliance, and mutual interdependence reigned among all things, drew one and all out of their solitude and isolation: "Therefore, as the highest nature he fashioned all natures, set everything in its place, and with discernment allotted each its own time. Moreover, since he so planned it eternally, he determined that peace should guide all his creatures and society unite them. Thus from him who is supremely and uniquely one, all should be allotted some trace of his unity. For this reason, he left no class of creatures isolated, but from the many he linked each one in a kind of society."[19]

Similarly, the image is completed at the end of time by a prophetic vision of the perfect realization of this design, the day when God, being at last "all in all,"[20] will recapitulate all things within himself and reestablish, through bonds of charity and friendship, that universal harmony and peace that constitute the very structure of the cosmos and that, from the start, he

---

18. Spec car 1.2.4 (Aelred of Rievaulx, *The Mirror of Charity*, trans. Elizabeth Connor, CF 17 [Kalamazoo, MI: Cistercian Publications, 1990], 89).

19. Spir am 1.53 (Aelred of Rievaulx, *Spiritual Friendship*, trans. Lawrence C. Braceland, CF 5 [Kalamazoo, MI: Cistercian Publications, 2005], 65).

20. 1 Cor 15:28; cited in Aelred, Spir am 3.134 (CF 5:126).

willed and desired: "This is that great and wonderful happiness we await. God himself acts to channel so much friendship and charity between himself and the creatures he sustains, and between the classes and orders he distinguishes, and between each and every one he elects, that in this way each one may love another as himself. By this means each may rejoice over his own happiness as he rejoices over his neighbor's. Thus the bliss of all individually is the bliss of all collectively, and the sum of all individual beatitudes is the beatitude of all together."[21]

We emphasize these two corresponding originary and eschatological elements of Aelred's vision because they define a space, an *interim* consisting of the timespan of human history, within which Aelred inscribes humankind's unique ethical responsibility. According to Aelred, humans are given a specific mission to fashion the world in such a way that it increasingly conforms to the divine plan. Their task is to help establish on earth the originary order of harmony, peace, and unity that God himself has structurally and ontologically inscribed in the cosmos at large. They must do so by working to establish bonds of charity and friendship—that is, bonds of reciprocity and mutual complementarity—among all things.

There is much to be said on the subject of the ethical agenda Aelred assigns to humankind. But within the framework of this introduction, we will simply call attention to two significant points. First, by interpreting the Stoic conception of the universe as structurally and originally governed by a cosmic principle of order and harmony through the lens of the Cistercian doctrine of charity, Aelred superimposes "cosmic order" upon "charitable order" and conflates the two. Consequently, far from limiting the application of the Cistercian principle of ordering of and by charity to the domain of human and social relations, Aelred considerably broadens this principle's scope, extending it to the far vaster dimensions of the entire cosmos.

---

21. Aelred, Spir am 3.79 (CF 5:107).

The result of this specifically Aelredian perspective is that humankind's ethical responsibility is not limited to the realm of social and political life. Instead, it includes what we would today call ecology. This perspective therefore also implies respect toward creation and the maintenance of the natural, environmental equilibrium. At first glance, this last remark might seem superfluous, or even anachronistic. It is not, as we shall see later. In fact, when Aelred addresses certain twelfth-century princes of England, he emphasizes the idea that the cosmic equilibrium of the world in which they live—in particular, the fertility of its soil and the absence of natural disasters—derives directly from their moral responsibility. Such a balance, he suggests, is nothing other than the fruitful and beneficial impact on nature of the wise management of public affairs, of the healthy administration of society's temporal goods, and above all of each ruler's constant efforts to promote social justice and civil peace among humans.

The idea that humankind's moral and political responsibility toward the world and society is constitutive of both human and universal history becomes a focal point in Aelred's life and underscores the heart of our principle. We believe it possible and legitimate to transpose onto Aelred's personal life this concept, which he himself globally defined as the ethical goal of political action. We therefore hold that it is also valid to interpret Aelred's entire life, and in particular his multiple engagements in the ecclesiastical and social life of his time, through the lens of this dual principle of cosmic order and ordering through charity, which he himself established as the ontological and structural foundation of the world. In this sense our principle can be stated as follows: as Aelred was led throughout his life to assume increasingly heavy responsibilities, he never ceased contributing, in his own way and within the limits imposed by his monastic vocation, to the establishment of a world order in which peace, harmony, and cohesion held ever greater sway. In short, he never ceased helping the world conform more and more closely to the divine project.

The Perspective of this Biography

From this second principle derives the present biography's unique perspective. Throughout this work we show how Aelred allowed himself to be guided by this moral requirement in all his actions. Little by little as his sphere of influence expanded over time, he applied himself to the wider and wider expansion, as if in larger and larger concentric circles, of that order of charity he had initially sought to establish in his own heart and in his own affective relationships, seeking all the while (as in our first principle) to unify his own life around the person of Christ.

This approach to Aelred's life, starting from the dual principle of personal unification and edification of the world on the foundation of the universal order of charity, affects our tracing the path of Aelred's existence in four ways. The first two go almost without saying; the second two are more subtle and difficult to grasp.

The first remark is self-evident; the second is a direct consequence of the first. In light of the dual principle guiding us, it is clear that to weave the text of Aelred's biography, we must interlace two threads until they become one, despite occasionally emphasizing one or the other according to the events and callings that punctuate Aelred's existence. The first thread is the thread of Aelred's personal life, consisting of those choices that determined his life's general orientation and, in particular, his monastic vocation. But within this vocation, and within the context of the responsibilities successively entrusted to him, the thread of his life was increasingly crisscrossed by the thread of his growing involvement in the temporal affairs of the Church and the society of his time. Such involvement in secular affairs permitted him to orient his personal life and to influence, more or less directly and effectively, the course of history itself.

We demonstrate this pattern in two ways. In local history, we examine Aelred's activities as abbot, including canonical visits to the daughter houses within Rievaulx's jurisdiction. In

England's national history, we consider some of Aelred's historical works. These works unveil Aelred's status as the moral conscience of the Anglo-Norman princes during the last ten years or so of his life (1154–1167) as well as his active contribution to the development of a renewed national consciousness and identity.

The interlacing of these two threads—Aelred's personal life and his engagement in temporal affairs—becomes increasingly indistinguishable as Aelred advances in age and his personal prestige expands into ever-wider zones of influence. Our approach is thus principally, though not systematically, chronological, because of the paucity of precise chronological data on Aelred's life in the primary sources at the historian's disposal—data indispensable for establishing the exact timeline of his writings and life events. This problem is clear, for example, in the *Life*, which shows little concern for such details except for the last year and especially the final week of Aelred's life—time frames for which Walter provides nearly daily health reports, in themselves of great interest to the historian.

We can therefore present only the broad periods of Aelred's life, of which we delineate four, which constitute the different parts of our biography. First there is the time of human and spiritual foundation, from Aelred's birth (1110) until his entrance into Rievaulx (1134). Next comes the time of his monastic instruction (1134) through the earliest responsibilities entrusted to him: first as secretary to and delegate of his abbot in Rome (1142), and then as novice master charged with the instruction of new brothers at Rievaulx (1142–1143). Then follows the time of great pastoral responsibilities within his monastic order. The first of these was his charge as the founding abbot of Revesby (1143–1147); the second was his tenure as abbot of Rievaulx, the monastery of his profession, to which he was recalled in 1147 after the premature resignation of Maurice, Rievaulx's second abbot (1145–1147).

Finally comes the time of maturity. In this time the infirmities of Aelred's old age coincide with his widening influence on the social and political life of an England that, in the aftermath of extended unrest and civil war, was in the process of creating national unity around the person of Henry II. This period covers roughly his fifteen final years, from the date of Henry's ascension to the throne of England until Aelred's death (1153/54–1167). During this period Aelred also composed the majority of his historical works, as well as his masterful commentary on the *Burdens of Isaiah*. The theology implicit in the history permeating the latter work, as has been underscored by its recent editor, Father Gaetano Raciti, is of great political value.[22]

This remark leads us to two final observations.

The link between the two aforementioned methodological considerations—the documentary impossibility of establishing a precise, detailed chronology of Aelred's life and the decision to entwine the dual thread of Aelred's personal life and his progressive engagement in secular affairs—has led us to privilege an existential approach over a more traditional event-based reading. This is not to say that we will not support our discussion with the concrete and real events of Aelred's life. His personal choices, his written works, the community he fashioned, the society and the church on which he sought to leave his mark, are all elements of greater or lesser importance without which his life could not have inscribed itself in time and history.

But through these events and contexts, we strive as far as possible to uncover the man Aelred in all his complexity—his joys and pains, convictions and doubts, hopes and difficulties—animated by the certainty that it is always through actions that a person can be discovered and understood in full human density and depth. Transposing words of John Paul II in *The Acting Person*, "the theme [of our biography] has been

---

22. Gaetano Raciti, "Introduction," in Aelredi Rievallensis, *Homeliae de oneribus propheticis Isaiae, quas recensuit Gaetano Raciti*, Opera omnia 5, CCCM 2D (Turnhout: Brepols, 2005), vii, n. 6.

the person [of Aelred] who reveals himself through action [in other words: his choices, decisions, and the resulting actions], who reveals himself through all the psychosomatic condition-ings that are simultaneously his wealth [in his own singular nature] and his specific limitation."[23]

From this perspective, through which actions (or the more general concept of action) are considered a manifestation and an epiphany of the singular and unique identity of the person, exhaustiveness is out of the question. Only the criterion of representativeness suffices, with each event retained insofar as it renders the person visible to the gaze of the heart.

Similarly, while respecting the chronological sequence sketched earlier, we bring to light various facets of Aelred's personality that, once connected to each other, allow us to draw his full portrait. Mentioning here only the most important fac-ets, we see the man in search of inner unity; the monk engaged in spiritual combat; the novice master, instructor of the heart; the doctor of friendship, in search of rules for establishing con-structive, humanizing affective relations; the abbot, at one and the same time respectful of individuals and attentive to their uniqueness while equally concerned with the formation of a monastic community united in charity and the respect of dif-ferences; the mystic seeking union with God; and finally the counselor of princes, engaged in the social questions of his time.

This existential and personalizing approach to Aelred's life explains our avoidance of detailed descriptions of the various contexts in which Aelred lived, whether sociohistorical (e.g. feudalism), political (e.g. the Anarchy), or religious (e.g. the Gregorian Reform and the Cistercian monastic revival). The reader can easily find detailed information on such matters in more general historical works on the twelfth century. In terms of historical context we provide only information indispens-able for understanding Aelred's life choices.

---

23. Karol Woytyla, *The Acting Person*, trans. Andrzej Potocki (Boston: D. Reidel, 2005), 300.

Sources for Aelred's Life and Engagements; Friendship as the Hermeneutical Key

There remains one consideration. With no intrinsic link to the preceding remarks, this consideration comes nonetheless as their synthetic and prospective reprise. In the work presented here, we offer a synthesis neither of Aelred's spiritual doctrine nor of his monastic theology such as that appearing, for example, in two recent works by John Sommerfeldt[24] or in the classic study of Amédée Hallier.[25] Rather, we propose an existential and personalizing biographical essay. We of course explore aspects of Aelred's spiritual doctrine, which is inseparable from Aelred as a person since it contributes to the physiognomy given him by Cistercian authors of his time such as Bernard of Clairvaux, Guerric d'Igny, and William of Saint-Thierry.

Among these doctrinal elements, we are particularly interested in the principle of spiritual friendship, which gives a unique tonality to both Aelred's monastic teaching and his mysticism.[26] This is not the only aspect that merits attention, but it requires emphasis because, in one way or another, it colors all other components of his doctrine and spiritual theology. Indeed, as Wincenty Polek correctly stresses, this idea can be considered the hermeneutic key *par excellence*, not only

24. John R. Sommerfeldt, *Aelred of Rievaulx: Pursuing Perfect Happiness* (Mahwah, NJ: Newman/Paulist Press, 2005); John R. Sommerfeldt, *Aelred of Rievaulx: On Love and Order in the World and in the Church* (Mahwah, NJ: Newman/Paulist Press, 2006).

25. Amédée Hallier, *The Monastic Theology of Aelred of Rievaulx: An Experiential Theology*, trans. Columban Heaney, CS 2 (Shannon, Ireland: Cistercian Publications, 1969).

26. On this hue of Aelred's mystical doctrine we refer the reader to the article of Michaela Pfeifer, "Trois styles de la mystique cistercienne: Bernard, Guillaume, Aelred," Coll 65 (2003): 89–110. The article originally appeared in Italian as Michaela Pfeifer, "Tre stili della mistica cistercense," in *L'esperienza di Dio nella vita monastica: La nostra risposta alla ricerca dell'esperienza di Dio nella cultura attuale* (Civitella san Paolo: Monastero Santa Scolastica, 1996), 137–65.

of all of Aelred's written work but also, as we have suggested, of Aelred's entire life and all his human engagements.

As Polek writes, "Friendship is . . . the end of everything. It is the end that becomes the goal. It is the goal that becomes the principle of everything. Friendship is the hermeneutical key to Aelred's works."[27] Further on he adds:

> In his reflections, the abbot of Rievaulx attempted to find a complete and panoramic vision capable of explaining the whole history of salvation as the history of friendship and, at the same time, tried to demonstrate this thesis: if the adventure of friendship aims to be the history of true friendship in the fullest sense of the term, that is to say, a friendship lived to the fullest, it must be part of the history of salvation. In Aelredian philosophy, friendship has its own anthropology, its own morality, and its own theology.[28]

Such an affirmation evidently applies in its own right to the two axes of approach described earlier, which serve as our constant interpretive guides. In either the unification of his personal and affective life (our first guiding principle) or his engagement in the social life of his time (our second guiding principle), Aelred sought only one thing—to establish the widest possible, if not universal, cosmic and harmonious order governed by rules of charity and friendship. Indeed, the decidedly Christocentric orientation of Aelred's spirituality, as well as the two extensions of this orientation—his ecclesiology taken as "spirituality of communion" and his eschatology taken as the ending of time and the closing of human history conducted to perfection and salvation—must be viewed from the perspective of an order of charity and friendship to be instituted in the universe.

27. Wincenty Polek, "Teologia dell'amicizia negli scritti di Aelredo di Rievaulx (1110–1167)," *Cistercium Mater Nostra* 2 (2008): 102.
28. Polek, "Teologia," 102.

The Unification of Aelred's Personal Life: Friendship and Christocentrism

Thus the Aelredian ethics of relational and affective life, insofar as those ethics are meant to be lived in the context of personal life and in the framework of friendship, are inconceivable without this Christocentric perspective. Indeed, to appreciate the relevance of such relations, Aelred establishes Christ himself as the sole point of reference. He specifies this as his nearly exclusive objective in the first lines of his *Spiritual Friendship*: to show how all human friendships draw their moral legitimacy solely from the extent to which they refer to Christ, in whom they must find their beginning, their model, and their end (Spir am 1.8). Thus Aelred subscribes fully to the manner in which his interlocutor, Ivo, formulates the question before him, and replies to him in these words: "What statement about friendship can be more sublime, more true, more valuable than this: it has been proved that friendship must begin in Christ, continue with Christ, and be perfected by Christ."[29]

Social Life: Friendship and an Ecclesiology of Communion

This understanding applies similarly to social life. We have already noted that the cosmic order of charity and friendship— which according to Aelred must originally and ideally have structured the life of all human society[30]—rests on the principle of communal property and mutual interdependence, founded in the reciprocity of giving and receiving. Such an order coincides closely with the model proposed by the early church

---

29. Aelred, Spir am 1.10 (CF 5:57).

30. See Aelred, Spir am 1.58. Furthermore, one could also say "naturally," since in the same passage Aelred insists on the fact that "from the very beginning nature impressed on human minds this attachment of charity and friendship" and that it is only from the moment in which sin (covetousness and its derivatives: avarice, jealousy, rivalries, disputes, and hatred) entered into the world that it became necessary to distinguish between charity and friendship.

community as described in the Acts of the Apostles: "And the multitude of believers had *but one heart and one soul*: neither did any one say that aught of the things which he possessed was his own, but *all things were common unto them.*"[31] In other words, Aelred imagines all kinds of social life, whatever its nature (nation, church, family, monastic, or religious community), on the basis of the ecclesiological model *par excellence* offered by the early apostolic community.

At the same time, Aelred also imagines all of these on the model of cenobitic life, which has historically been conceived in continuity with the apostolic community of Jerusalem and organically linked to it as a source and a model. Thus, among monastic society, church, and civil society there is for Aelred no rupture of continuity. Monastic society offers a micro-realization of what the church and civil society are called upon to realize on a larger, universal scale.

Such a transposition of the monastic model to the scale of the church and of the entire universe should not be too surprising. It was a relatively common idea shared by many twelfth-century authors who, with Saint Bernard, dreamed of transforming the world into a vast monastery. On the other hand, as Roberto de la Iglesia has correctly shown in two articles, Aelred's originality lies in the fact that he imagines ecclesiastic and social life on the model of his own monastic experience and, more important, strictly in line with his doctrine of spiritual friendship,[32] whose

31. Acts 4:32. This text is so central that Aelred cites it in each of the three books of his treatise on *Spiritual Friendship*: see Spir am 1.28; 2.21; 2.67; 3.99; and 3.124.

32. On these two points (the "monastic face" of the Church and the doctrine of friendship as the key to Aelredian ecclesiology), see Roberto de la Iglesia, "La comunidad monástica, realización completa de la Iglesia según Elredo de Rievaulx," *Cistercium* 244 (2006): 389–437; "La ecclesiologia monástica de san Elredo de Rievaulx," *Cistercium* 250 (2008): 81–101. In the first of these two articles, specifying what he means by the "monastic face [*rostro monástico*]" that Aelred gives the church, de la Iglesia writes that "the monastic congregation is, for him, like the leavening in a great loaf, the entire Church; not

major ethical characteristic rests on the principle of reciprocity. To neglect reference to this doctrine of friendship would be to deprive ourselves of the key to fully understanding the manner in which Aelred conceives of not only church and societal life, but also his own role therein.

Friendship and Eschatology: An Ecclesiology of Friendship and Christocentrism

The coloring of Aelred's Christocentrism and social ecclesiology (or ecclesiastic sociology) by his doctrine of friendship applies also to his eschatology. The latter is rigorously inscribed at the confluence of these two elements and subsumes their components. We noted this fact in our previous discussion of the ecclesiological aspect of our second principle, citing *Spiritual Friendship* 3.79, where Aelred explains that eternal life consists of the final and perfect realization of the divine plan to establish reciprocity and mutual interdependence between all beings. This realization, he says, will occur once friendship, initially restricted here on earth by "moral necessity"[33] to only a few individuals, is able to pass into all men and women, and from all of them to God, without further limitation:

> When the fear is dispelled that now fills us with dread and anxiety for one another, when the hardship is removed that we must now endure for one another, when, moreover,

---

separate from it but intimately linked to it; like a miniature body of Christ inside the Entire Body; or as archetype and model for the entire Church, as *ecclesiola in Ecclesia*" (Iglesia, "Comunidad," 437). In the second article, he reprises the theme, further articulating the doctrine of spiritual friendship and insisting that according to Aelred the ideal of spiritual friendship is not strictly reserved to cenobitic monastic life alone, but instead is an ideal that must also spread and permeate (*traspasar*) the entire life of the church (see in particular sections 3–4 of the article, pages 92–99, and especially page 98).

33. For the ethical foundation of this restriction of friendship to only a few, here on earth, see Aelred, Spir am 1.58–61 (CF 5:67).

> along with death the sting of death is removed . . . then
> with the beginning of relief from care we shall rejoice in
> the supreme and eternal good, when the friendship to
> which on earth we admit but few will pour out over all
> and flow back to God from all, for God will be all in all.[34]

Thus Aelred's eschatology is in a sense conceived as the ecclesiology of a friendship finally made universal.

Friendship and Eschatological Christocentrism: From the City of Confusion to the City of Peace

To demonstrate that Aelred's eschatology is colored by his
doctrine of friendship in accordance with his Christology, we
turn to one of his last works: his *Homilies on the Burdens of Isaiah*,
and in particular the third homily, which is of capital importance
in this matter. On the frontispiece of this great work, Aelred
sketches what might be called an immense fresco of salvation
history, at the end of which, as on the summit of a high mountain, he plants the standard of the cross. Aelred, like Saint Paul,
uses this cross as the instrument through which Christ, by virtue
of his own obedience, submitted to himself the entire universe—
the sky, the earth, and hell—in order to reconcile it with God:

> Hear blessed Paul describe how the cross weighs down:
> Christ was made obedient to the Father unto death, death
> on a cross. Because of this God exalted him and bestowed
> on him the name above every other name, so that at the
> name of Jesus every knee should bend in the heavens, on
> earth, and in hell [Phil 2:8-10]. See how heaven, earth,
> and even hell itself are subjected to the mystery of the
> cross, and how the Babylonian king's power is every-
> where weighed down, his might emptied.[35]

---

34. 1 Cor 15:28. Aelred, Spir am 3.134 (CF 5:126).
35. Aelred, Oner 3.12 (Aelred of Rievaulx, *Homilies on the Prophetic Burdens
of Isaiah*, trans. Lewis White, CF 83 [Collegeville, MN: Cistercian Publications,
2018], 42).

Thus placed at the culminating point of salvation history, the mystery of the cross becomes in Aelred's eyes the instrument that Christ, come finally to "the fullness of time" (Gal 4:4), was to use not only to judge the world, but above all to liberate it from the powers of evil that oppress it: "Babylon, the city of confusion, used vices and errors to hold the chosen ones in captivity together with those who were condemned. But Babylon would be invaded through the Lord's coming, and would be destroyed by the chosen ones' separation from the condemned."[36]

Affirming that by the cross the entire universe is submitted both to Judgment and to the salutary power of Christ, Aelred assigns to Christ a place analogous to the one already attributed to him in the realm of spiritual friendship. In both cases, whether in terms of personal and relational life or in terms of universal history, Christ is in effect established as the absolute end point toward whom all things must tend and who, ultimately recapitulating all things in himself, gives to each thing its true measure.

Aelred declares that "Jesus, who has both built and restored this spiritual ark, sits there alone in his beauty, without peer. By his gentleness he keeps all lower creatures in order. May he give savor to all of them, fill all with his fragrance, enlighten all, shed upon all his splendor, and bring the whole lower span in a straight line to that single cubit of his love."[37] Similarly, Aelred holds that Jesus is also he who, by his victory over the "City of Confusion" (Babylon), reigns over all of human history to establish over it, in his person, the "City of Peace" (Celestial Jerusalem), building it in the harmony of a world henceforth unified and governed by the rule of a truly universal friendship.

Conclusion

With the preceding remarks on the doctrine of friendship as the global hermeneutical key to Aelred's life and works, we

36. Aelred, Oner 3.5 (CF 83:40).
37. Aelred, Spec car 3.106 (CF 17:296).

have arrived nearly at the end of our introduction. We conclude, however, by formulating one last consideration that permits us to perceive the tensions at play in situating Aelred's life in the context of his doctrine of spiritual friendship.

In the article cited earlier, Polek asks the question of what friendship was for Aelred. We have already cited part of Polek's answer to this question: "Friendship is also the end of everything. It is the end that becomes the goal."[38] But this thought merits fuller citation. According to Polek, friendship

> is a reality that integrates everything. It connects man's world to God's eternity. It is an anthropological category describing humanity's predestination, and a theological idea seeking to explore man's life in God. It is an excellent idea that protects intimacy and assures universality. Friendship is a conception of the individual that, deployed in all its magnificence, must be considered Christianity's greatest contribution to human reflection.[39]

In this description three main tensions stand out: the world of humans and God's eternity, anthropological category and theological idea, intimacy and universality. These in turn lead to this question: throughout his life, is it not precisely this threefold tension that Aelred constantly sought to reduce as much as he possibly could? In other words, taking things inversely, from the narrowest idea to the broadest, following the chronological thread of Aelred's existence, we must ask three questions. First, during his youth, did Aelred not discover the intimate space that the relation of friendship offered to him as a springboard and pedagogical tool that would conduct him progressively to the universality of a love that knew neither limit nor restriction? Second, through his Cistercian monastic vocation, did he not seek to make of his human existence, in all its breadth

38. Polek, "Teologia," 102.
39. Polek, "Teologia," 102.

and all its demands, a space to experience the God who could be known only by and through fraternal love? Finally, subjected to growing pastoral responsibilities, did he not, for the benefit of all, attempt to make of the world and of history a space where, in anticipation of what was to come, every person might have a taste of divine eternity? Did he not attempt to make of the world and history a space in which, little by little, the Creator's plan would be realized, a space that would ultimately be ruled by laws of mutual reciprocity and therefore governed by the principle of an active and universal charity?

We demonstrate these three theses over the course of our biography, proceeding by way of successively larger and larger concentric circles. There will be four such circles. The first circle (treated in part II: "The Time of Human and Spiritual Foundations") is that of Aelred the man and Aelred the monk. The second circle (examined in part III: "The Time of Instruction and First Responsibilities") is that of the monk in the service of his monastic community. The third circle (discussed in part IV: "The Time of Great Pastoral Responsibility") is that of the abbot in charge of guiding his brothers along the paths of the Gospel according to the Rule of Saint Benedict. Last, the fourth circle (considered in part V: "The Time of Spiritual Maturity") is that of Aelred's growing influence on the civil and ecclesiastical society of his country.

Part II

The Time of Human and Spiritual Foundations

Aelred the Man (1110–1134)

Introduction

In this second part of our biography, devoted to Aelred's human and spiritual foundations, we turn our attention primarily to two items particularly important in better understanding Aelred as a person. In this chapter, we examine the historical and religious context of Rievaulx's founding in 1132. Rievaulx was the second Cistercian abbey established in the British Isles[1] and the first English daughter house of Clairvaux. While the abbey may have been the apple of Saint Bernard's eye, it also served Bernard as a bridgehead into Yorkshire, assuring the future expansion of the Cistercian (or Clairvallian) reform into the north of Europe, principally in Scotland and Ireland.[2]

In chapter 3 we consider Aelred's childhood, his first intellectual development, and the circumstances that led him to enter the court of the king of Scotland, first as a page, then as steward. Having established this context, in chapter 4 we explore Aelred's vocation. In particular we examine his 1134 decision to enter the recently founded monastery of a nascent order, which he chose over other institutions both closer to home and of longer standing.

---

1. The first was Waverley, eighth daughter house of Cîteaux, founded in 1129 by L'Aumône.
2. Because of Rievaulx's numerous foundations (see Appendix III).

Chapter Two

The Foundation of Rievaulx
The Context of Aelred's Life

In 1132, Bernard of Clairvaux sent a group of monks to England.[1] At their head he placed his secretary, William, in whom he had every confidence. Their mission was to found a monastery on the banks of the Rye in Yorkshire, drawing its name from the river on whose banks it would be built: Rievaulx. On the way, the group was to present a letter to Henry I, king of England. The letter was all the more imperious and persuasive for its brevity. In this short missive, Bernard instructs the king to welcome as "messengers of God" his followers sent forth "as scouts." He also asks the king, as a faithful vassal, to facilitate their task by providing them with all the aid they might need to bring their project to term. Bernard concludes by saying that God's honor, the king's own earthly glory and eternal salvation, and the kingdom's peace and security all depend on this project. Here is the letter:

> To Henry, the illustrious King of England, that in his
> earthly kingdom he may faithfully serve and humbly

1. This chapter relies heavily on a previously published article: Pierre-André Burton, "Aux origines de l'expansion anglaise de Cîteaux. La fondation de Rievaulx et la conversion d'Aelred (1132–1134)," Coll 61 (1999): 186–214.

obey the king of heaven, from Bernard, styled Abbot of Clairvaux.

In your land there is an outpost [*praeda*] of my Lord and your Lord, an outpost [*praeda*] that he has preferred to die for rather than to lose. I have proposed to occupy it, and I am sending men from my army who will, if it is not displeasing to you, claim it, recover it, and restore it with a strong hand. For this purpose I have sent ahead these men who now stand before you to reconnoiter. They will investigate the situation carefully and report back to me faithfully. Help them as messengers of your Lord, and in their persons fulfill your duties as vassal of their Lord. And may he for his honor, the salvation of our soul, and the health and peace of your kingdom, bring you safe and happy to a good and peaceful end.[2]

The letter unfortunately gives little concrete information on the founding of Rievaulx. But the art with which Bernard drafted it, especially his mix of thematic devices—the image of the hunt,[3] the allusion to the moral code governing the feudal relationships between lord and vassal, and finally the relationship between the eternal and temporal kingdoms—allows a glimpse of the multiplicity and diversity of the social and political stakes involved in such an enterprise. The implications of the hunting metaphor in particular—seeking a prey, tracking it, subduing, capturing, and finally retrieving it[4]—leave the impression of an array of negotiations that must have preceded Rievaulx's founding. We will undoubtedly never know the details of these negotiations, but they imply a close

2. Bernard, Ep 92 (SBOp 7:241); Bernard of Clairvaux, *The Letters of Saint Bernard of Clairvaux*, trans. Bruno Scott James (London: Burns Oates, 1953), 141–42 [#95].

3. [Translator's note: Burton translates the Latin *praeda* "prey" as *une proie* in his translation of the letter, but in the English translation James translates *praeda* with the neutral "outpost."]

4. [Translator's note: Here again, the hunting images appear in the Latin of the letter used by Burton but not in its English translation, which is more strictly military in its terminology (e.g. *outpost, occupy, army, reconnoiter*).]

initial cooperation between Bernard; King Henry; the local bishop, Thurstan; and the land's donor, Walter Espec. Bernard does not name them in his letter, but we know through Aelred that each played a major role in the founding of Rievaulx. Indeed, without them the monastery would never have been built. Although little is known about Thurstan and Walter Espec, we can affirm that they were fully committed to the new, reformative ideas working their way through twelfth-century ecclesiastical and political society.

Thurstan: A Bishop Committed to Reform

Thurstan belonged to that new generation of twelfth-century bishops charged with promoting within their dioceses the moral and spiritual renewal inspired by the eleventh-century Gregorian Reform. Thurstan's apostolic activity as bishop of York from 1114 to 1139 attests to the fact that he did not content himself with the simple role of executor. On the contrary, he committed himself to transmitting those ideas as widely and actively as he could. Numerous pieces of evidence demonstrate this fact, but here we limit ourselves to two. First there is the personal support he brought to the implantation of new religious orders, and Cistercian monasticism in particular, within his diocese. Second is the extreme care with which he oversaw the application of the canonical norms promulgated by the Reform, especially the replacement of married clergy (still widespread in the early twelfth-century Anglo-Saxon church) with clerics living under the discipline of ecclesiastical celibacy. These two points exerted a direct and decisive influence on Aelred's own life choices.

Pastoral Solicitude for New Orders: The Affair of Saint Mary's Abbey in York

Throughout his tenure as bishop, Thurstan demonstrated great pastoral solicitude toward institutions of sacred life and was in particular an ardent protector of new monastic orders.

His solicitude can be seen in the numerous Augustinian monasteries he saw established in his diocese.[5] Additionally, according to Janet Burton, who has closely studied religious establishments in twelfth-century England,[6] Thurstan showed the same solicitude toward the Cistercian Order. His personal appeal led Saint Bernard to send a colony of monks to found in his diocese the soon-to-be prestigious monastery of Rievaulx. While we possess no written documentation—not even the monastery's founding charter—attesting to Thurstan's personal investment in this enterprise, the great esteem in which he held the Order suggests that he indeed initiated the project. As proof we note the pastoral protection he accorded in 1132 to a group of thirteen Benedictine monks of Saint Mary's Abbey in York, who, stimulated by the example of austerity and poverty offered by the newly arrived Cistercian monks then establishing themselves at Rievaulx, in turn sought to promote reform within their own community.

Narrative of the Event: Aelred and Thurstan

This well-known and widely documented[7] event is worth relating for several reasons. First, it certainly must have been the talk of the area, profoundly marking people's thoughts.

5. See Aelred Squire, *Aelred of Rievaulx*, CF 50 (Kalamazoo, MI: Cistercian Publications, 1981), 15–16. The preceding expression comes from Janet Burton's qualification of Thurstan as a "keen patron of the monastic orders" (Janet Burton, "The Foundation of the British Cistercian Houses," in *Cistercian Art and Architecture in the British Isles*, ed. Christopher Norton and David Park [Cambridge, UK: Cambridge University Press, 1986], 26).

6. Janet Burton, "Foundation," 26.

7. In addition to two surviving documents (a passage from Aelred's *The Battle of the Standard*, and a letter from Thurstan to the metropolitan archbishop of Canterbury), an epistolary exchange took place between Saint Bernard and the two protagonists in this affair: Thurstan, bishop of York, and Geoffrey, the abbot of Saint Mary's of York. Only Saint Bernard's letters have been preserved (letters 168, 169, 170).

Second, it casts light on twelfth-century ecclesiastical life. Finally, it must have resonated in Aelred's imagination, because, some thirty years later, he echoed it in his narrative of the *Battle of the Standard*. In this short historical treatise, composed toward the end of his life between 1153 and 1157, Aelred curiously and somewhat self-interestedly inserts a brief history of the expansion of the Cistercian Order in England. In that history, he notes that Rievaulx's founding was the source of an immense swell of emulation, which affected none other than the Benedictine monastery of Saint Mary's of York. Speaking of the installation of the Clairvallian monks in the Rye valley, Aelred writes, "By their reputation for holiness they stirred up many to emulation of the loftiest endeavors, with the result that in a short time they increased beyond counting and founded many communities in both kingdoms, that is, of England and of Scotland." Then, to illustrate his point, he underlines Thurstan's role in the affair:

> Furthermore, in the second year of the monks' coming into England, certain monks of the Church of Blessed Mary at York, admiring Cistercian purity and poverty and relying on the help of the venerable Archbishop Thurstan, abandoned the prosperity and pleasures contrary to monastic simplicity. In great poverty and with wonderful fervor, they set up a monastic community at Fountains. Then uniting themselves more fully to the aforesaid Order of brothers, they too founded many monasteries throughout the island.[8]

Understated, yet somewhat tendentious,[9] this relation of events is largely confirmed by Thurstan's more detailed narrative. In

8. Aelred, Bello 2; Aelred of Rievaulx, *The Battle of the Standard*, in Aelred of Rievaulx, *The Historical Works*, trans. Jane Patricia Freeland, CF 56 (Kalamazoo, MI: Cistercian Publications, 2005), 250–51.

9. A few lines further on, and contrary to historical fact, Aelred effectively declares Rievaulx the first Cistercian monastery in England, though Waverley

fact, as soon as the monks' secession was consummated in December 1132, the bishop drafted a detailed report[10] to his metropolitan, William of Corbeil, archbishop of Canterbury, apparently in order to inform him of the situation. However, Christopher Norton correctly notes that Thurstan's primary goal lay elsewhere, as is clear only at the end of the letter.[11] In effect, Thurstan sought not so much to inform Archbishop William of what had happened in York as subtly to pressure him to use all his authority and legitimacy to support the reformist monks but also, should he have the opportunity, to order Geoffrey, the abbot of Saint Mary's of York, to return to his abbey. The letter containing Thurstan's report is too long to cite fully here, but it reveals his state of mind, and in particular his great and unceasing interest[12] in all the initiatives of renewal permeating his era's religious life.

According to Thurstan, the affair of Saint Mary's of York began on June 28, 1132, when Richard and Gervase, the prior

---

had been founded three years before. However, it never attained the prestige of Rievaulx, thanks, no doubt, to the exceptional personality of Aelred, its third abbot.

10. Specifically letter 439 [Translator's note: From Thurstan to William, archbishop of Canterbury]; M. l'abbé de Charpentier, trans., in Saint Bernard, *Œuvres complètes* (Paris: Vivès, 1866), 2:80–88. This letter, dated at the end of 1132 and known through two separate versions, one long, one short, raises numerous questions for the historian, in terms of both its manuscript tradition and the history of its drafting. For more detail on the discussion, the reader should consult the following excellent study: Christopher Norton, "Richard of Fountains and the Letter of Thurstan: History and Historiography of a Monastic Controversy, St. Mary's Abbey, York, 1132," in *Perspectives for an Architecture of Solitude: Essays on Cistercians, Art and Architecture in Honour of Peter Fergusson*, ed. Terryl Kinder (Turnhout: Brepols, 2004), 9–34.

11. Norton, "Richard of Fountains," 31.

12. This interest is evident even unto the eve of Thurstan's death. We know, thanks to a letter from Saint Bernard, that Thurstan wanted to resign from his episcopal responsibilities in order to end his life in a monastery. In his reply to this request—Letter 319 (SBOp 8:252), dated ca. 1138—Bernard flatly refused to grant the request.

and sub-prior of the Benedictine monastery, supported by eleven other monks, sought out their abbot Geoffrey to inform him of their desire to live in greater conformity with the Rule of Saint Benedict. The abbot, overwhelmed and indecisive, put off his decision until September 8. Confronted with the abbot's temporizing equivocation and above all with the resistance they faced from a large part of the community who remained firmly attached to their acquired privileges, the reformers finally decided to appeal to their bishop. To keep the situation from getting out of hand and to maintain peace in the community, the bishop summoned the abbot and his two officers:

> I heard that Christ's servants wanted to put nothing before the love of Christ, according to the Rule of Saint Benedict.[13] I was afraid of offending the grace of Christ with regard to these men if I did not take care to support their just petition with a bishop's loving care. Indeed, these are a bishop's highest duties: to provide religious tranquility to monks, and to comfort the oppressed in their time of need.[14]

By the end of the interview, Abbot Geoffrey had recognized the legitimacy of the reforms requested by his prior and sub-prior. He agreed to refrain from any further obstruction of their project provided that his council consented to it. It was further agreed that Thurstan would soon come to the abbey to discuss this matter with the community during a conventual chapter. In the meantime, however, the tension between the two opposing parties grew to such an extent that when on the appointed date Thurstan presented himself at the gates of the monastery, he was received with extreme hostility by those opposing reform. Try as he might to explain that he had come

13. RB 4.21 (*RB 1980: The Rule of St. Benedict*, ed. and trans. Timothy Fry [Collegeville, MN: Liturgical Press, 1981], 182–83).

14. For Thurstan's letter to William, see William Dugdale, *Monasticon Anglicanum* (London: Bohn, 1846), 5.295.

solely in the spirit of conciliation to reestablish peace and renew the ties of fraternal charity among the divided brothers, it was useless. Blocked in the exercise of his episcopal authority and the accomplishment of his peace-making mission, he despaired of his cause and threatened to censure the abbey.

This threat unfortunately threw fuel on an already intensifying fire: the monks immediately seized those brothers seeking a more austere lifestyle and cast them into the monastery prison. The latter were saved in turn only by grabbing onto the bishop and begging for protection—both his personal protection and that of the apostle Peter. Then, to avoid any further disastrous developments, they sought refuge with him inside the abbey church, where, all together, they locked themselves in so as to escape the mob justice of the other *"homines abbatiae"* (men of the abbey),[15] who were led to rioting by all this agitation. Thurstan continues: "Since it had been impossible for the monks to reach an agreement, we returned home, taking with us the aforementioned twelve priests and one subdeacon. Many of these men were learned, and all desired equally to follow the Rule fully, as well as their vows and the Gospel."[16]

We have already seen how the story ends: after the brothers spent some weeks residing with Thurstan, he, having been entirely won over to their cause, gave them a domain in the Skell valley, where they could build what would soon afterward become the monastery of Fountains. Furthermore, as Aelred notes, once they were established there, Thurstan helped them to regularize their situation, and in their name he began negotiations with Bernard, who, in 1133 or 1144, agreed to integrate this "wild" brotherhood into his own house.[17]

---

15. Dugdale, *Monasticon*, 5:295.

16. Dugdale, *Monasticon*, 5:295.

17. On this matter see Letter 95 that Saint Bernard addressed to Thurstan, in which he praises the latter for the "zeal for righteousness" (*zelus iustitiae*) and "priestly activity" (*sacerdotalis vigor*) that he showed in defending these poor men deprived of all support (Bernard, *Epistolae* [SBOp 7:244–45]; James, trans.,

Some Lessons from the Event

So ends the narrative. The event is rich in lessons, among which we underscore the following. In the first place it is representative of a certain dissatisfaction, or even a profound malaise, that was scattered throughout Europe in the 1130s and that a good number of old-school Benedictine religious communities felt toward a lifestyle they found if not decadent, at least relaxed. It will be recalled that at the same time, specifically between 1131 and 1133, William of Saint-Thierry was confronted with a similar challenge within the Benedictine congregation to which his monastery in Reims belonged, presiding over three successive chapters at which the very same question of a return to a stricter way of life appeared on the agenda. In this sense, the events of Saint Mary's of York are typical of numerous twelfth-century efforts in religious communities to breathe new life into traditional monasticism.

But this event also demonstrates the attraction and fascination that the Cistercian reform generated, and the speed with which that reform became a nearly exclusive model for imitation for the ecclesiastical community of the time. Thus in his report to Archbishop William, Thurstan's references to Cîteaux's origins and his comparison of the hostility encountered by the monks of York to that faced by Robert of Molesme and his companions are symptomatic.

By its radical tendencies and austere lifestyle, Cistercian monasticism troubled and awakened sleeping souls. So it is

---

Letters, 240 [#170]). We should also underline, on the same subject, Bernard's letter to Geoffrey, the abbot of Saint Mary's of York, in which he reminds Geoffrey that he must not "extinguish the spirit" [*omnino non expedire spiritum velle extinguere*] and must instead encourage those of his sons who wish to do good, and even rejoice in it: "Rather should you take pride in the progress of your sons, because it is written that a wise son is the pride of his father [*Gloriari autem magis oportet in profectibus filiorum, quoniam filius sapiens gloria est patris*] (Bernard, Ep 94 [SBOp 7:243–44]; James, trans., *Letters*, 237 [#168]).

understandable that it was a source of genuine annoyance for some and even provoked a savage resistance. The public epistolary jousting between Bernard and Peter the Venerable around 1124 bears witness to this, as does Bernard's *Apologia ad Guillelmum abbatem*. The latter offered an eloquent argument in favor of a diversified monasticism. It was composed at the urging of William of Saint-Thierry precisely to calm down the controversy and was published at more or less the same time as the exchange between Bernard and Peter, though the precise chronology is unknown. In any case, for many religious institutions seeking a sense of renewal, Cistercian monasticism was an incomparable model for emulation and a source of inspiration whose influence extended well beyond the relatively restricted realm of ecclesiastical circles.

The Saint Mary's of York Affair and its Resonance in Aelred's Heart

Thanks to its powerful identity and to the monastic rigors it sought to bring about without conceding or compromising the values of the century, the Cistercian reform vigorously appealed to many of the era's young people, inspiring their most noble and profound spiritual aspirations. Enamored with the absolute, these youths turned to the writings of Bernard, whose reputation and prestige were growing significantly. In Bernard's writings they found an anthropological and theological education, solidly rooted in the deep loam of biblical revelation and long monastic tradition, assimilated and revisited in depth through an intensely lived personal experience of the divine. It is these roots in personal experience that gave Bernard's doctrines such force of attraction. Indeed, Bernard suggests in both his writings and his own being that there is no personal or human dimension—body and soul, memory, intelligence, and will, spirit, the heart, and its emotions—that should be kept at a distance from men and women's spiritual quest. And yet all these personal and human elements, when

correctly ordered, contribute in their own way to the unification of desire and to the only ends befitting the grandeur and
dignity of humankind: the search for God and our spousal
union with him.

At Yorkshire's Helmsley castle in 1132, when Aelred first
heard of the Cistercian way of life recently established at
Rievaulx and then Fountains, he knew nothing of Bernard's
doctrines. And he probably had no idea that on entering
Rievaulx his exposure to Bernard's writings and teachings
would provide a set of spiritual and intellectual tools to order
his own emotional life and resolve the interior conflict devouring him at the time of his conversion. Similarly, he was far from
suspecting that fewer than ten years later, around 1142, Bernard would use his prestige and authority to press Aelred to
pour out in writing his own spiritual experience, or that *The
Mirror of Charity* would enrich the spiritual heritage later called
The Cistercian School of Charity.

Yet if we are to believe Walter Daniel's testimony (VA 5 and
6), the description Aelred heard at that time of the new life led
by these strange men known as the white monks had a profound and powerful resonance in his heart that acutely aroused
his natural curiosity. His desire thus awakened, Aelred decided
to drop everything and rush to Rievaulx so that he might see
with his own eyes the truth of what he had heard, even though
in his haste, his biographer enjoys telling us, Aelred "speeds
his mount he knows not where."[18]

For now, however, we must go back and consider an event
that occurred in 1114. Aelred was only four years old at the
time, but what happened then must have affected him profoundly. Beyond the immediate repercussions it had on his
family life, the event had multiple long-term consequences
that, in one form or another, determined the direction of his
life. It is probable that in the short term the event played a

18. VA 6 (Walter Daniel, *The Life of Aelred of Rievaulx*, trans. F. M. Powicke,
CF 57 [Kalamazoo, MI: Cistercian Publications, 1994], 99).

decisive role in the choices that Eilaf, Aelred's father, had to make to guarantee the intellectual development of his son and assure him of a future profession. In the long term, these choices were going to place Aelred himself in situations that not only enriched his human experience but, more important, permitted him to make a personal choice of his own, leading him finally to knock on the doors of Rievaulx Abbey.

The Gregorian Reform and New Canonical Norms: The Priory of Hexham

Thurstan belonged to that new generation of English bishops responsible for promoting within their dioceses the moral and spiritual renewal inspired by the eleventh-century Gregorian Reform. In this context, it behoved them to encourage the enactment of new canonical norms promulgated by the Reform. One of these turned out to be particularly painful to apply. In order to eradicate the abuses linked to the existence of married clergy and to relieve the vexing consequences that came along with clerical marriage—in particular the inheritance of ecclesiastical posts and benefits—the bishops were directed to impose the discipline of ecclesiastical celibacy on all candidates for the priesthood and simultaneously to effect the gradual replacement of married clergy with secular or monastic clergy who had submitted themselves to this new discipline. The application of this decree struck Aelred's family very hard, since Eilaf, his father, held a pastoral charge at Hexham church that had been handed down from father to son for at least four generations.[19]

---

19. We refer the reader to the genealogical chart of Aelred's ancestors published in Brian Patrick McGuire, *Brother and Lover: Aelred of Rievaulx* (New York: Crossroad, 1994), 12. This chart was borrowed from James Raine, ed., *The Priory of Hexham: Its Chroniclers, Endowments and Annals*, 2 vols., Surtees Society 44 (Durham: Andrews and Co., 1864), 1:li. See also on this subject David Knowles, *The Monastic Order in England: A History of its Development from the Times of St. Dunstan to the Fourth Lateran Council (940–1216)*

In truth, the decision to replace Eilaf with regular clergy—in this case with two Augustinian canons—had already been made by Thomas II, Thurstan's immediate predecessor in the see of York (1109–1114). But because of Thomas's premature death in 1114, the delicate responsibility of executing the decision fell to Thurstan (bishop from 1114–1139). He therefore compelled Eilaf to step down from his position, sent for a certain Aschatil, canon regular of the priory at Huntingdon, and decreed that henceforth the rule of chastity would be observed at Hexham.[20]

It is easy to imagine[21] the disastrous and dramatic consequences this could bring about. First, psychologically, it was akin to being cut off from one's historical or ancestral roots and falling into escheat. Such was the case for Aelred's father, who was required to renounce a heritage that until then had been considered a family possession. In a certain sense, this change also modified cultural, spiritual, and religious signposts vital to an individual's psychological landscape. Hexham was a church in which the relics of numerous Anglo-Saxon saints were preserved, relics to which Aelred's father was profoundly attached precisely because of his pastoral charge.[22] In short, to ask Eilaf to abandon his

---

(Cambridge: Cambridge University Press, 1976), 228–29; and Maurice Powicke, "Introduction," in Walter Daniel, *The Life of Ailred of Rievaulx*, ed. and trans. F. M. Powicke (Oxford: Clarendon: 1950, 1978), xxxv–xxxvi.

20. In fact, we have two different narratives of the same event: that of Richard of Hexham in his *History of Hexham Church* (*De statu et episcopo Hagulstadensis ecclesiae*, 8–9), and a more irenic version by Aelred himself, in his treatise *The Saints of the Church of Hexham and their Miracles* (SS Hag). See Aelred of Rievaulx, *The Saints of the Church of Hexham and their Miracles*, in *Aelred of Rievaulx: The Lives of the Northern Saints*, trans. Jane Patricia Freeland, ed. Marsha L. Dutton, CF 71 (Kalamazoo, MI: Cistercian Publications, 2006), 87–92. See also Aelred, *Saints of Hexham*, in CF 71:65–107, and Marsha L. Dutton, "Introduction," in CF 71:14–26.

21. We reproduce here almost verbatim a few paragraphs of Burton, "Aux Origines," 200–201.

22. For more detail, see what Aelred himself says of his father in Aelred, *Saints of Hexham*, CF 71:89–91.

charge was to wound the most intimate part of his religious and national identity. It was also to deprive him of his daily bread.

Beyond the loss of spiritual nourishment, the impact was also socio-economic in nature. In this respect, the stakes were especially high since a strict and brutal application of canonical decree promulgated in light of the Gregorian Reform risked the financial ruin of the families concerned. Giving up an ecclesiastical charge effectively meant giving up the revenues that put bread on the table to nourish a family. The heavy resistance and even ferocious hostility that met the Gregorian Reform is understandable. And even when some gave in to the Reform—albeit reluctantly and with bitterness in their hearts—it was not without first demanding the establishment of what would today be called a severance package, or in some cases extorting it. This was what Eilaf effectively did by refusing to renounce the benefits of his position until just a few days before his death—a fact that shows just how much he must have resented what he saw as the profound injustice of the Gregorian decree.

In this context, it is surprising to note that in his version of events, Aelred rather curiously reveals nothing of the family drama it engendered. On the contrary, he goes so far as to pretend that it was his father who took the initiative and went before the archbishop of York to ask that the pastoral charge of Hexham church be conferred to regular clergy. He writes: "Burning with zeal for the house of God, he went to that venerable man, the younger Thomas, archbishop of York, and humbly asked that he commit the church to the canons regular and that he hand over to them himself and his property." He then adds, "When the venerable prelate had agreed to his request, he built with his own hands some buildings suitable for the religious life, but of wood. With the approval of the aforesaid pontiff he first brought into the church at Hexham two brothers of virtuous life, one of whom had passed his life laudably in the church at York, the other at Beverley."[23]

23. Aelred, SS Hag 11 (CF 71:91).

How can we explain the irenic and diluted tone of Aelred's relation of events? There are three possibilities. First, perhaps, there is Aelred's natural temperament, as he was always inclined toward the establishment of peace over the sowing of discord and division. Then there is the fact that he is composing his treatise in 1155, some forty years after the events in question. Obviously by this time things had calmed down. As we have noted, just before dying at Durham in 1138, Eilaf, still in clerical robes, had reconciled with the canons of Hexham and had released to them their due privileges and revenues. Finally, it should be remembered—as Aelred Squire and Marsha Dutton have both hypothesized—that before taking form as a historical treatise, the work in which Aelred recounts these events was probably presented as a homily that the canons regular of Hexham had requested he give on March 3, 1155, for the solemn occasion of transferring the sacred relics (Saints Eata, Acca, Alchmund, Frithubeorht, and Tilbeorht) that were housed there. It is easy to imagine that the liturgical framework in which the historical treatise was written lent itself poorly to the re-awakening of sad memories and the re-opening of old wounds.

Nevertheless, these memories and wounds must have been very real and must have had a powerful resonance for Aelred and his family. The fullness of this resonance can even be measured by means of a confidence Aelred offered in one of his sermons, as well as through an anecdote recounted by Walter Daniel in his *Letter to Maurice*.

In S 70, for the Feast of the Apostles Peter and Paul, Aelred compares himself both to the cripple seated before the Beautiful Gate of the temple who was miraculously healed by Peter (see Acts 3:2) and to the poor Mephibosheth, who, at the age of five, having been dropped from his nursemaid's arms—that is, from the arms of grace—also became disabled (see 2 Sam 9:13 and 4:4):

> *And behold, a person disabled from his mother's womb was carried in* [Acts 3:2]. Who is this *disabled person*? It is clearly me. *Disabled* without a doubt, and therefore too weak to

advance, powerless to climb upward, and unworthy to enter. *For the disabled and blind do not enter the temple* [see 2 Sam 5:8]. I am poor *Mephibosheth, disabled in both feet* [see 2 Sam 9:13]. This is the same Mephibosheth who, when he was five years old, fell from his nanny's arms and was disabled [see 2 Sam 4:4]. How unfortunate I am! I call my unhappiness to mind, I remember my disaster. I fell, I fell from my nanny's arms when I was five years old.

This nanny is grace, who, when I was *small in* my own *eyes* [see 1 Sam 15:17], received me and nursed me. She carried me when I was weak and gave me milk when I was a baby, but she left me when I was five years old. She left me and I fell. She left me because I was five years old.[24]

While it is obviously better to be prudent in any autobiographical interpretation of this passage, it is nonetheless piquant to notice Aelred's insistence on the "age of five years" (stated four times!) as well as the almost precise chronological alignment between this scriptural reference with Aelred's age at the moment of the episcopal decree. It is reasonable to say that at that time he felt the earth beneath his feet fall away and that he was tortured by the vague feeling of betrayal and abandonment. Moreover, it seems plausible that because of this event and the profound repercussions it seems to have had on his emotional life, Aelred felt throughout his existence the ceaseless, visceral need to create binding amical ties. Clearly nothing allows us to affirm this with absolute certainty, but neither does anything prevent us from conjecturing that such a deeply rooted human experience is the source of what would be the very heart of Aelred's monastic spirituality.

As for the anecdote related by Walter, it reveals the rather tense climate in which Thomas's decision, and its execution by his successor Thurstan, was so poorly received by Aelred's father. In fact, Walter writes,

---

24. S 70.23–24 (Aelred of Rievaulx, *The Liturgical Sermons: The Durham and the Lincoln Collections*, trans. Kathryn Krug, Lewis White, and the *Catena Scholarium*, CF 80 [Collegeville, MN: Cistercian Publications, 2018], 270–71).

Again, when he was a little boy he comes into the paternal abode from the games which little boys play with their fellows in places of public resort. His father looking upon him said, "Well, my son, and what stories have you been hearing?" And he: "Father, the archbishop of York died today." The man laughs to hear this, and all the family also, and commenting on Aelred's prophecy with whimsical politeness says, "True, my son, he is dead who lives an evil life." "Not so, my father, in this case," replied the boy, "for on this day he has ceased to breathe and said goodbye to mortal men."[25]

When Walter insists on recounting this brief anecdote, it is above all to emphasize Aelred's precocious gift of prophecy. But for us, its principal interest resides rather in the fact that by reporting the caustic statement of Aelred's father—"True, my son, he is dead who lives an evil life"—Walter, without considering too carefully the weight of what he was writing, allows us to put a finger on just how cruelly Aelred's family, and especially his father Eilaf, were affected by Thomas's decision. Additionally, it might be more accurate to offer a rather more vulgar translation Eilaf's words, hearing instead from his lips something akin to "Really!? Then the devil take him!"

In any case, the institution of ecclesiastical celibacy created a situation so radically new that Aelred's father had probably never even imagined it. It no doubt forced him to modify any plans he might have had for his eldest son's future. In all likelihood, by birthright and family tradition, Aelred should have inherited both his father's curial responsibilities—the keeping of the Hexham church relics—and the related revenues. Supposing Aelred's consent, this paternal plan turned out to be unrealizable. Thus, barely four years old, Aelred saw a door close before him and was forced to follow another path.

---

25. Walter Daniel, "Letter to Maurice," CF 57:151–52. See also Maurice Powicke, "Introduction," xxxv–xxxvi (for historical context); and Aelred Squire, *Aelred of Rievaulx: A Study*, CF 50 (Kalamazoo, MI: Cistercian Publications, 1981), 11.

This being said, Eilaf's decision ten years later, in 1124, to obtain his eldest son's entry into the court of the king of Scotland, turned out to be providential. At the time he certainly could not have measured the numerous and fortunate implications this decision would have on Aelred's life in terms of his personal and affective growth, his cultural and intellectual development, and his religious and vocational orientation. Even if, by personal inclination and temperament, Aelred always remained closely attached to the cultural and mental universe of his ancestors, and even if he never renounced his strongest spiritual roots—in particular a lifelong devotion to those saints honored in his childhood church[26]—the fact remains that Aelred's entry into the Scottish court turned out to be a source of personal enrichment whose importance must not be minimized. His sojourn there broadened his horizons considerably. Those horizons had been rather limited and conservative in the family home where he grew up, but at King David's court, he came into contact with a cultural universe that was entirely new to him—that of the Franco-Normans. Since William the Conqueror's victory over King Harold at the battle of Hastings in 1066, English royal power had passed into the hands of William and his descendants, and therefore, from that time forward, the royal court of England was heavily influenced by Franco-Norman culture.

Because of tight familial ties maintained with the royal family of England, David had been sent there to perfect his intellectual and military education before succeeding his brother Alexander to the Scottish throne in 1124. By coming into con-

---

26. Apart from the short work dedicated to *The Saints of the Church of Hexham and Their Miracles*, Walter Daniel notes in VA 51 that some days before death, as Aelred wrote his testament, he asked among other things that the "relics of certain saints" be brought to him, those that he kept with care in the cell set aside for him in his final days of illness (VA 31). While Walter does not specify the saints in question, it seems reasonable to suppose that they were in fact the relics of those saints he learned to honor in Hexham from his earliest childhood, or perhaps those of Saint Cuthbert. For more detail, see Powicke, "Introduction," xxxviii–xxxix.

tact with David's court, Aelred saw vast horizons open up before him that he had never previously imagined. Here he completed his initial education and discovered numerous aptitudes that greatly aided him to assume the multiple responsibilities later laid upon him. Furthermore, he gained the advantage of an extended network of personal relationships preparing him to play a front-line role in the social, political, and ecclesiastical life of his era. But for the moment, let us return to the founding of Rievaulx in 1132.

Walter Espec: Anglo-Saxon Noble and Donor of the Rievaulx Lands

Until now, we have focused on the role of Archbishop Thurstan of York in Rievaulx's founding. This has allowed us to outline the ecclesiastical context of that community's creation and to uncover Aelred's early familial universe. We pass now to another driving force in the foundation of Rievaulx: Walter Espec, whose role as the donor of the Rievaulx lands is confirmed both by Walter in chapter 5 of the *Life of Aelred* and by Aelred himself in his narrative *The Battle of the Standard*. These two texts allow us a better understanding of the often difficult socio-political context in which Aelred lived the better part of his life.

The Origins of Rievaulx: Walter Espec as Probable Initiator

The precise circumstances of Walter Espec's first contact with the Cistercian Order, and with Saint Bernard in particular, are unknown. Some have hypothesized that Walter might have met Bernard at the court of the king of England, Henry I, when the abbot of Clairvaux came to request Henry's support in the cause of Pope Innocent II.[27] Unfortunately, we have no formal

---

27. Christopher Brooke writes, "It would be tempting to suppose that Walter Espec was at Henry's court at this time, and had himself met Bernard." He continues, "There is, however, no evidence for this; and it really seems more likely that original contact was made more remotely" ("St. Bernard, the

evidence to confirm such a hypothesis. On the other hand, it seems clear that Espec must have remained in fairly close contact with Bernard, at least by letter, even if, again, we have recovered no trace of it. In fact, since Bernard never returned to England, we can surmise that the delicate task of choosing the site for the monks of Clairvaux fell to Espec. But as we know of the special attention Bernard paid to this question, we must suppose that Espec questioned him carefully in order to know precisely what his needs were in this matter.[28]

Walter has left a particularly evocative description of the site. This rich text appears in a passage of the *Life of Aelred* where Walter briefly retraces the circumstances of Rievaulx's founding. We will see later, in our discussion of Aelred's conversion, that this passage allows a glimpse of those aspects of the Cistercian reform that seduced the youth of the twelfth century. For now, it should be noted that in this description Walter insists above all on comparing the monastery to a "cloistral paradise." This comparison is a well-known theme from monastic literature, and one to which Aelred gave a unique hue in *Spiritual Friendship*. In that text, Aelred approached it from a strictly spiritual angle by underlining the way fraternal, communal relationships foreshadow eternal life. More prosaic in his own text, Walter limits himself to the natural geography of Rievaulx and describes the site as a *locus amoenus*, a place of paradisiacal charms:

> Well, as I have said, these holy men [the founders of Rievaulx] reached England safely from their monastic wrestling ground across the sea. They set up their huts near Helmsley, the central manor of their protector, Walter

Patrons and Monastic Painting," in *Cistercian Art and Architecture in the British Isles*, ed. Christopher Norton and David Park [Cambridge: Cambridge University Press, 1986], 15).

28. "However it occurred, Brooke concludes that Walter Espec *must have been very well informed on Cistercian needs before he chose the site*" (Brooke, "St. Bernard," 15–16 [Burton's emphasis]).

Espec, a very notable man and one of the leading barons of King Henry I. The spot was by a powerful stream called the Rye in a broad valley stretching on either side. The name of their little settlement and of the place where it lies was derived from the name of the stream and the valley, Rievaulx. High hills surround the valley, encircling it like a crown. These are clothed by trees of various sorts and maintain in pleasant retreats the privacy of the vale, providing for the monks a kind of second paradise of wooded delight. From the loftiest rocks the waters wind and tumble down to the valley below, and as they make their hasty way through the lesser passages and narrower beds and spread themselves in wider rills, they give out a gentle murmur of soft sound and join together in the sweet notes of a delicious melody. And when the branches of lovely trees rustle and sing together and the leaves flutter gently to the earth, the happy listener is filled increasingly with a glad jubilee of harmonious sound, as so many various things conspire together in such a sweet consent, in music whose every diverse note is equal to the rest. "His ears drink in the feast prepared for them, and are satisfied."[29]

Walter Espec: Loyal Vassal of Henry I, King of England

It is possible that Aelred himself might have succumbed to the charms of such an enchanting locale and that the beauty of the landscape might have influenced his choice even if, as we will later show, more profound existential motivations led him to Rievaulx. In any case, what is important here is that Walter describes Espec as "a very notable man and one of the leading barons of King Henry I." This qualification, reiterated by Aelred, shows Walter Espec as representative of the old Anglo-Saxon aristocracy. At least in part out of political realism following the Franco-Norman conquest, these Anglo-Saxon nobles collaborated

29. Walter, VA 5 (CF 57:98).

with the new governing power, actively supporting its efforts toward territorial unification and political pacification.

Thus, despite Walter Espec's advanced years, and because Henry Beauclerc (the later Henry I) had had the opportunity to appreciate his perfect loyalty and great military valor, Henry honored Espec with important responsibilities in the northern marches of England, assigning him the task of ensuring their security and defending their borders. Within the Yorkshire lands entrusted to his protection stood the castle of Helmsley, located very near the property he would soon donate to the white monks.

Espec's patronage was not limited to the founding of Rievaulx. At the beginning of *Battle of the Standard*, Aelred offers a list of all the religious houses of which Espec was the patron (Bello 2). Indeed, while Aelred begins his narrative by listing the princes engaged in the battle, it is only when he gets to Walter Espec that he inserts a two-part portrait. The first part gives a vivid description of his hero, while the other enumerates Espec's numerous acts of generosity, which Aelred tells us, expressed Espec's great piety:

> Walter Espec was also there. He was an old man full of years, of penetrating intelligence, prudent in counsel, forbearing in peacetime and farsighted in war, always maintaining friendship with allies and faith with kings. He was of great stature, and his limbs were not of excessive size, but suited to such a height. He had black hair, a full beard, an open and free forehead, large and piercing eyes, a very broad face of good proportion, and a voice like a trumpet, which brought a certain majesty of sound to his easy eloquence. He was moreover noble by birth, but nobler still in his Christian devotion.
>
> As he had no children as heirs (though he had no lack of vigorous nephews), he made Christ the heir of all his best possessions.[30]

---

30. Aelred, Bello 2 (CF 56:249).

Then begins the enumeration of the many monasteries founded through Walter Espec's patronage. First mentioned is the non-Cistercian priory of canons regular at Kirkham, later home to Waldef, King David's stepson and Aelred's childhood companion: "In an extremely pleasant spot named Kirkham he founded a monastery of regular clerics, adorning it with many gifts and endowing it with property. Moreover, he turned his castle, his rooms, and his storehouses into dwellings for the servants of Christ."[31] Then come the two Cistercian monasteries Espec founded: Rievaulx, in 1132, and Rievaulx's first daughter house, Wardon, established in 1135 in Espec's native Bedfordshire. Here Aelred speaks of the immense wave of admiration inspired by the founding of Rievaulx, and the founding of Fountains in its wake:

> He also brought to these regions the Cistercian Order, of whose fame England had scarcely heard, with the backing of the renowned King Henry, receiving brothers from the very celebrated monastery of Clairvaux by the hand of Abbot Bernard, holy and beloved of God.
>
> The monks came to England in the year of the Lord's Incarnation 1132 and found a place in a deep valley along the bank of the River Rye, from which the monastery took its name, Rievaulx. By their reputation for holiness they stirred up many to emulation of the loftiest endeavors, with the result that in a short time they increased beyond counting and founded many communities in both kingdoms, that is, of England and of Scotland.
>
> This Walter, not yet satisfied with so many good deeds, founded with the same brothers a well-known monastery in the territory of Wardon.[32]

Two seemingly insignificant details in this long narrative merit special attention, since they allow a glimpse of the political

---

31. Aelred, *Bello* 2 (CF 56:249–50).
32. Aelred, *Bello* 2 (CF 56:250).

context in which Rievaulx was founded, as well as something of Aelred's spiritual physiognomy.

The Political Stakes of Cistercian Expansion in the British Isles

The first detail to be underscored concerns the order in which the Cistercian institutions were founded under Walter Espec's patronage. It is surprising that Walter first founded Rievaulx, in Yorkshire, since one might expect him to have begun with an abbey in his native Bedfordshire, where he bore the title Lord Wardon. Janet Burton, who has closely studied the Cistercian expansion in England,[33] has hypothesized that the answer to this chronological inversion lies in England's twelfth-century political context.

The victory of William the Conqueror over King Harold at Hastings in 1066 had triggered in England a period of political insecurity and instability. The immediate successors to William—his sons William II (1087–1100) and Henry I (1100–1135)—were confronted with two serious challenges. The first was finding a way to merge the local Anglo-Saxon and imported French-inspired cultures. The second was finding the means to guarantee long-term Franco-Norman hegemony among the newly subdued populations. By successfully meeting these two challenges, William's successors concretely reinforced their personal authority over the whole of their English territory.

To achieve these two goals, they had several means at their disposal. The best known, and the most efficient for them, involved reliance on the principles of the feudal social structure. For the sovereign, this meant trusting the administration and military defense of each domain to reliable men who were bound tightly to him by means of matrimonial alliances or other-

---

33. See Janet Burton, "Foundation," 24–39. The information in the following paragraphs is taken from that text.

wise, by way of feudal oath. In some cases, the king could simply evict a member of the old local nobility and replace him with a royal relative promising greater loyalty. Redistributing local power and systematically consolidating territory in this way obviously met fierce resistance from the old Anglo-Saxon nobility thus dispossessed. There followed, therefore, a time of intense difficulty that Janet Burton calls the "tenurial crisis." In this political context, the founding of a monastery in a politically unstable and exposed region such as Yorkshire would prove to be a good strategy. Because the territory was only newly given to Espec, and because of its proximity to the Scottish border, his possession of the land was vulnerable to contest.

So the establishment of a monastery there was for Espec a means of affirming Henry's authority. It allowed Walter to offer his overlord a clear expression of his perfect allegiance and his fervent desire to contribute to the pacification and defense of the country. But in choosing to found a *Cistercian* monastery, he accomplished even more. Because Cistercian monasticism was of French origin and because it conveyed values of spiritual renewal promoted by the Gregorian Reform, we can hypothesize that Espec, guided by a sense of fashion, also sought to offer King Henry "a symbol of 'Normanness.'"[34] He thus ostensibly showed Henry his attachment to the new dynasty's culture and provided, however indirectly, an additional guarantee of his loyalty.

Contested Succession and Civil War (1135–1153/1154)

The second detail worth examining concerns the structure of *The Battle of the Standard.* It is curious that in this narrative Aelred memorialized what could be called the *Exordium Cistercii in Anglia,* even though at first glance such a story appears to be a pointless digression from the main topic. One might

---

34. Janet Burton, "Foundation," 25.

object that the relation of these events has nothing to do with the narrative of a battle. However, this objection holds only if we seek in the narrative the mere reporting of a battle and refuse to see anything other than its anecdotal aspect. But by closely examining the known history of the reception and distribution of Aelred's short historical treatise, Elizabeth Freeman convincingly shows that the text's scope was substantially broader.[35] Aiming toward a political objective, Aelred contributed to the creation of a national and religious collective memory, intended for the era's civil and military authorities as well as for religious institutions then rapidly expanding. The text reminded kings and princes first of their duty to protect ecclesiastical institutions and, second, of the fact that a healthy public administration could be had only by respecting the principles of justice and piety necessary to maintaining peace between peoples and ethnic groups.

The work also reminded clerics both that they must scrupulously guard against the loss of fervor and that they must always emulate their founders' spirit in order to maintain their place in civil society, guarantee their institution's legitimacy, and keep their spiritual autonomy and land assets. Other works composed in the same time frame (1153–1155), notably Aelred's *Genealogy of the Kings of the English*, offer similar admonitions reminding civil princes and religious institutions of their respective duties in the promotion of interactive and complementary relationships that, in Aelred's eyes, were necessary to the smooth functioning of society as a whole. It suf-

---

35. See Elizabeth Freeman, "Aelred of Rievaulx's *De Bello Standardii*: Cistercian Historiography and the Creation of Community Memories," Cîteaux 49 (1998): 5–27. See also Elizabeth Freeman, "The *Relatio de Standardo*: Cistercian Historiography and Multiple Audiences," in *Narratives of a New Order: Cistercian Historical Writing in England, 1150–1220* (Turnhout: Brepols, 2002), 31–54. For a shorter version, see also Elizabeth Freeman, "The Many Functions of Cistercian Histories Using Aelred of Rievaulx's *Relatio de Standardo* as a Case Study," in *The Medieval Chronicle: Proceedings of the First International Conference on the Medieval Chronicle*, ed. Erik Kooper (Amsterdam/Atlanta: Rodopi, 1999), 124–32.

fices for now to note that at the time Aelred began composing
Battle—fifteen years after the events[36]—he probably had more
personal reasons to paint a rapid panorama of the Cistercians'
origins in England and to remind the reader of the context in
which Rievaulx was founded.

To grasp the narrative's more personal aspect, it is worth
glancing at the historical context of the Battle of the Standard
itself. The battle took place on August 22, 1138, in Yorkshire,
at Northallerton, near York and Rievaulx, and was part of the
civil war that tore England apart from December 1135 until
November 1153. With the wreck of the *White Ship* on November
25, 1120, King Henry I lost his only legitimate son, William
Adelin, born to Edith / Matilda of Scotland, sister of King
David. His second marriage, to Adeliza of Louvain, unfortunately provided no male heir. On January 1, 1127, Henry made
all the barons of England swear an oath of loyalty to his daughter Matilda, widow of the Emperor Henry V, and to recognize
her children as his successors. In 1128, Henry married Matilda
to Geoffrey Plantagenet, count of Anjou. Henry made the barons renew their oath to Matilda first on September 8, 1131, and
again on August 2, 1133, some months after the birth of his
grandson and potential successor, the future Henry II.

Two years later, however, on December 1, 1135, Henry I
died, leaving as successor an infant barely two years old. A
regency council was immediately put in place. At this point
certain Anglo-Norman barons, refusing the authority of a
woman—that is, the Empress Matilda, mother of the young
Henry II—recognized William the Conqueror's grandson, Stephen of Blois, as king of England. At the end of December 1135,
Stephen was crowned king by his brother Henry of Blois,

---

36. The dating of this short treatise is subject to discussion. Anselm Hoste
once proposed the years 1155–1157. Dutton, on the other hand, arguing from
the perspective of critical analysis of the text itself, has hypothesized an
earlier date of composition, around 1153–1154, during the transition between
the reigns of Stephen of Blois and Henry II.

bishop of Winchester, but only received homage from the kingdom's magnates in March 1136. This usurpation unleashed a twenty-year period of civil war between Stephen's and Matilda's supporters—including, among the latter, King David I of Scotland and great-uncle of the future Henry II—that ended only with the Treaty of Wallingford in November 1153. The Battle of the Standard, later recounted by Aelred, is one of numerous cruel and destructive battles that contributed to the ruin, confusion, fear, and desolation of England.

At the time the battle took place, Aelred had been at Rievaulx for four years. But one can easily guess the internal resonance the battle must have had for him, since there were men on both sides of the melee whom he knew particularly well and to whom he was emotionally tied in one way or another. The English coalition, defending the interests of Stephen of Blois, included Espec, founder and protector of Rievaulx, whom Aelred had met on several occasions before arriving at Rievaulx. Partisans of the Empress Matilda included Matilda's uncle, King David of Scotland, who had been a second father to Aelred during the ten years he spent in David's service before becoming a monk at Rievaulx. The following touching and eloquent lines from Aelred's *Lament for David, King of Scots*, reflect this attachment:

> I too, though a sinner and unworthy, nevertheless remember your kindnesses, my most gentle lord and friend, which you showered on me from an early age. I remember the grace in which you now for the last time received me, I remember the good will with which you granted all my requests, I remember the generosity that you showed me, I remember the embraces and kisses with which you released me, not without tears, while all those present marveled. I skim over my tears for you; I relinquish my attachment, and I pour out all my spirit. For you I offer this sacrifice to my God. I expend this effort because of your kindnesses. And because this is so slight, my mind will always remember you in the very core of

its being, there where for the salvation of all the Son of the Father is daily sacrificed.[37]

Also in Matilda's army was King David's twenty-five-year-old son, the young prince Henry (1113–1152), three years younger than Aelred. Aelred and Henry were bound by a strong, unwavering friendship that nothing could break despite their very different life choices. Aelred later wrote the following vibrant praise of this prince, companion, and childhood friend, in a famous passage from his *Genealogy of the Kings of the English*:

> Henry, a man gentle and devout, a person of sweet spirit and cheerful heart and worthy in every way to be born of such a father. I lived with him from the very cradle. I grew up with him, boys together, and even when we were both adolescents I knew him. To serve Christ I left him while he was stamping out the flowers of youth, as I did his father, whom I loved beyond all mortals, at that time illustrious in the flower of old age. I left them bodily, but never in my mind or my heart.[38]

Similarly, in *Battle*, Aelred sings Prince Henry's praises, here accenting his friend's military prowess and moral virtues rather than the ties of friendship binding them:

> He was a young man fair of face and handsome in appearance, of such humility that he seemed lower than everyone, of such authority that he was revered by everyone, and so gentle, so pleasant, and so agreeable that he was loved by everyone. He was so chaste in body, so sober in speech, so honorable in all his ways, so diligent in church and so attentive in prayer, so kind to the poor and so resolute

37. Lam D 13; Aelred of Rievaulx, *Lament for David, King of Scots*, in Aelred of Rievaulx, *The Historical Works*, trans. Jane Patricia Freeland, ed. Marsha L. Dutton, CF 56 (Kalamazoo, MI: Cistercian Publications, 2005), 69–70.

38. Gen angl 25; Aelred of Rievaulx, *Genealogy of the Kings of the English*, in *Aelred of Rievaulx, The Historical Works*, CF 56:121.

against malefactors, so respectful toward priests and monks, that he appeared to be a monk in a king and a king in a monk. His prowess was such that no one in this army resembled him in attacking the enemy or in wholeheartedly withstanding the attackers; he was braver than others to pursue, keener to resist, slower to flee.[39]

One can easily understand how Aelred's heart must have ached when men for whom he felt such affection needlessly exposed themselves to almost certain death fighting each other in a fratricidal war that he believed murderous and foolish.

In any case, the question that comes to mind is whether this battle in 1138 gave birth to Aelred's political sensitivity, a sensitivity so great that during his abbacy he was preoccupied with contributing to the development of a society based on principles of peace, justice, and cohesion. The battle played a vital role, no doubt, but one can also surmise that Aelred had begun developing this sensitivity even earlier during his service at the court of King David. One thing, however, is certain. As Walter twice states in *The Life of Aelred*,[40] Aelred was firmly convinced that monasteries could opportunely intervene to stifle fratricidal quarrels and play an important role in the establishment of peace in the land. This is undoubtedly one of the reasons that in writing *Battle* Aelred recounted the origins of Rievaulx, a monastery closely tied to the battle's various participants.

Transition

This overview of the historical context and material conditions in which the monastery of Rievaulx came into being has allowed us to uncover the religious and political environment that awakened Aelred's monastic vocation. In its course we have

39. Aelred, Bello 4 (CF 56:259).

40. About the foundation of Revesby in 1147 (VA 20) and a visit to Dundrennan, daughter house of Rievaulx (VA 38).

encountered figures who played a crucial role in Aelred's adolescent life. It is time now to direct our attention more closely to the ten years from 1124 to 1134 that were so personally and intellectually formative for Aelred, and to the definitive turn his life took at the end of that period. We will do this in two stages. Chapter 3 focuses on Aelred's intellectual development and his time at the Scottish court, while chapter 4 is devoted to the year 1134 and an examination of the personal and spiritual context in which Aelred finally decided to enter Rievaulx.

Chapter Three

Aelred's Intellectual Development and Life at the Scottish Court

Earlier we left the four-year-old Aelred with his father, Eilaf, who, because of the Gregorian Reform's disciplinary norms, was forced to give up his pastoral charge in Hexham church along with the position's revenues in 1114. We noted that Thomas II's episcopal decision, ratified by his successor Thurstan, was a veritable catastrophe for Aelred's family. At the very least it forced Eilaf to rethink his eldest son's future and any plans he may have conceived for Aelred to succeed him at Hexham.

Between this date and his arrival at Rievaulx in 1134, we do not know in any detail what became of Aelred. The period has been appropriately referred to as "the hidden years" of Aelred's life.[1] Various sources tell us that out of concern for his family's material subsistence, Eilaf refused to cede his ecclesiastical benefits and consented to do so only on the eve of his death in 1138, four years after Aelred had entered Rievaulx. But from 1114 until that date, little is known of Eilaf's arrangements for

---

1. This is the judicious title that Chrysogonus Waddell, who died in 2008, gave to one of his last publications: Chrisogonus Waddell, "The Hidden Years of Aelred of Rievaulx: The Formation of a Spiritual Master," CSQ 41 (2006): 51–63.

Aelred, or of the direction he gave to Aelred's education and intellectual development. Nevertheless, we shall attempt to answer these questions as best we can.

We open our inquiry by reading the brief portrait that Jocelin of Furness devotes to Aelred in a passage of his *Life of Saint Waldef*. Of Waldef, who planned to leave his community of canons regular at Kirkham in order to join the Cistercian community of Rievaulx, Jocelin writes these historically valuable lines:

> He also consulted a man revered for his life, habits and teaching, Abbot Aelred, his schoolfellow and very close friend. Aelred was a man born of the best old English stock, who early left his schooldays behind to be raised and educated from boyhood in the court of King David with Henry, the king's son, and Waldef himself. In time he became first a monk of Rievaulx, afterwards abbot. He did not acquire much skill in liberal arts while in school, but yet, by virtue of his own hard work and practice, he achieved the development and refinement of his fine natural talent, and was better cultivated than most who had been fully trained in profane letters. Well versed in the interpretation of Holy Scripture, he left after him to posterity as a perpetual monument splendid books and treatises, written in a magnificent style, filled with edification as Aelred himself was filled with the inspiration of the Spirit of Wisdom and Discernment.[2]

Regrettably, the passage's chronology is imprecise, and much of the information appears to be borrowed from chapter 18 of *The Life of Aelred*. Additionally, the text was written at a comparatively late date, as Jocelin composed his "Life of

2. Jocelin of Furness, "The Life of Waldef, Abbot of Melrose," in "An Edition and Translation of The Life of Waldef, Abbot of Melrose," trans. George Joseph McFadden, dissertation, Columbia University, 1952, 237–38 (Ann Arbor: University Microfilms International, 1952).

Waldef" at the start of the thirteenth century, between 1210 and 1214. Nevertheless, the passage deserves attention, since it brings to light three important details. First, the curriculum of Aelred's intellectual development at school was precipitously interrupted so that he might enter the service of David, king of Scotland. Second, in the wake of this premature interruption, Aelred's natural gifts and lively intelligence enabled him to acquire a knowledge of the liberal arts through rigorous and painstaking self-education. Finally, while at the Scottish court, Aelred's study companions were Waldef and Prince Henry, David's stepson and son. We will examine each of these three points in turn.

A Precipitously Interrupted Education

The first thing "The Life of Waldef" shows is that Aelred had to precipitously interrupt the course of his schooling in order to enter the king of Scotland's household. But as Aelred Squire rightly states, "it is unfortunate that we know in only the most general terms" the circumstances in which this took place.[3] Walter himself, Aelred's biographer, is unable to satisfy our curiosity. Walter abruptly begins chapter 2 of his *Life* by describing Aelred's moral qualities at his entry into royal service, saying nothing of the event's conditions, date, or reasons, reducing us to conjecture alone.

The most likely and commonly accepted hypothesis, a hypothesis never truly contested, is that Aelred's father, Eilaf, called on his vast network of personal relations and took the initiative to have his son admitted to the Scottish king's court. From the moment he was forced to renounce his ecclesiastical charge and relinquish it to regular clergy, Eilaf probably came to the conclusion that Hexham could provide Aelred with no serious future prospects. From that date, Eilaf probably strove

3. Aelred Squire, *Aelred of Rievaulx: A Study*, CF 50 (Kalamazoo, MI: Cistercian Publications, 1981), 12.

to find an alternate situation for his son, and kept a lookout for any favorable opportunity that might present itself. If we take Jocelin of Furness at his word, such an opportunity appeared fairly suddenly and unexpectedly, since, to enter the Scottish court, Aelred had to abruptly abandon his schooling. Jocelin's affirmation indicates first that Aelred had indeed begun some form of schooling and, second, that Eilaf must have been surprised by the opportunity since he had to interrupt Aelred's course of study in order to send Aelred to court.

We know nothing of Aelred's early studies. But according to Maurice Powicke, the first serious Aelredian historian, there is reason to think that after his primary education at Hexham, Aelred "almost certainly"[4] went to Durham's cathedral school to receive a more focused secondary education. Study at Durham permitted him, as Aelred himself attests in the prologue of his treatise on *Spiritual Friendship*, to discover, savor, and appreciate Cicero's work on the same subject: "When I was still a boy at school . . . a volume of Cicero's *On Friendship* fell into my hands. Immediately it seemed to me both invaluable for the soundness of its views and attractive for the charm of its eloquence."[5]

We will return to the powerful role Aelred's childhood discovery of Cicero's *On Friendship* played in his later life. Suffice it to say for now that this statement is the clearest refutation of the belief, encouraged by Aelred himself, that he had not received a very advanced education. In fact, as Squire astutely notes, this book is "not the kind of book that a genuinely illiterate man would be able even to read, much less to enjoy."[6]

More difficult to evaluate is the second question, regarding the event that brought Aelred to interrupt his education to enter the king of Scotland's household. Jocelin of Furness and

---

4. Maurice Powicke, "Introduction," in Walter Daniel, *The Life of Aelred of Rievaulx*, trans. F. M. Powicke (Oxford: Clarendon, 1950, 1978), xc.

5. Aelred, Spir am Prol.1 (CF 5:53).

6. Squire, *Aelred*, 14.

Walter are silent on the matter. But the brief discussion in "The Life of Waldef" gives the impression that Eilaf acted quickly, as if he found himself presented with an opportunity he had to seize immediately lest it slip out of his grasp for good. There is some discussion regarding the nature of this opportunity. With the exception of a single historian, Brian Patrick McGuire, who recently hypothesized that Aelred entered the king of Scotland's household very early, at the age of six or seven, around the year 1116, the majority of historians estimate that Aelred's departure for the Scottish court must have coincided with David's accession to the Scottish throne, after the death of his elder brother Alexander in 1124.

McGuire's proposition is intriguing, since it might explain the reason that Aelred never speaks at all of his mother. However, it fails to take into account the little information we actually do have. Certainly, in the passage from *The Genealogy of the Kings of the English* cited earlier, on which McGuire bases his hypothesis, Aelred claims to have known Prince Henry "from the very cradle."[7] But as Powicke suggests, that could mean simply that "Henry was Ailred's companion at Hexham, and that Ailred was Henry's companion at the royal court."[8] Furthermore, it does not account for the fact that Jocelin specifies that Aelred interrupted the course of his studies to enter royal service *a iuventute*, that is to say, "from his youth" (14–21 years old), and therefore not during his *adulescentia* (the age of puberty, between 12 and 14 years old), and certainly not during his *infantia* (pre-speech infancy), or his *pueritia* (pre-pubescence, between 4 and 12 years old).

If we trust Jocelin's chronology, placing Aelred's birth in 1110, we must conclude that his entry into royal service "from his youth"—beginning at the age of fourteen, or at the latest fifteen—must have occurred around 1124, the year of David's accession to the throne. Indeed this, by all evidence, is an event

7. Gen angl 25 (CF 56:121).
8. Powicke, "Introduction," xxxv.

that must have been fairly unexpected and that must have appeared to Eilaf as a sufficiently rare opportunity to justify his precipitous decision to redirect his son's schooling and development. Without more precise evidence to the contrary, it therefore seems more historically accurate to adhere to the traditional hypothesis that Eilaf took advantage of David's accession to the throne in 1124 to seek entrance for the fourteen- or fifteen-year-old Aelred into the royal household.

An Autodidact Taught by the Holy Spirit[9]

If indeed Aelred interrupted his secondary studies at Durham to enter the Scottish royal household in 1124 near the age of fourteen, then Jocelin of Furness seems justified in affirming that Aelred acquired the better part of his education from self-study rather than from formal schooling, especially in the liberal arts, which were at the time the province of secondary classes.

Jocelin's affirmation is partially supported by various statements Aelred made throughout his life in his writings and sermons. No doubt because he prematurely ended his schooling, Aelred frequently expresses a sharp awareness of what he considers to be significant gaps in his own intellectual development. Thus, perhaps from excess of humility, he tends to beg pardon of his audiences for his so-called lack of culture and near-illiteracy.

9. For more detail on what follows here, see the first part of the following study: Pierre-André Burton, "Aelred of Rievaulx: an Illiterate, or a True Master of Spiritual Teaching?" in *A Companion to Aelred of Rievaulx (1110–1167)*, ed. Marsha L. Dutton (Leuven: Brill, 2017), 197–220, esp. 197–206. Also see Emero Stiegman, "*Woods and Stones* and *The Shade of Trees* in the Mysticism of Saint Bernard," in *Truth as Gift: Studies in Medieval Cistercian History in Honor of John R. Sommerfeldt*, ed. Marsha L. Dutton, Daniel M. La Corte, and Paul Lockey, CS 204 (Kalamazoo, MI: Cistercian Publications, 2004), 321–54. Stiegman comments (331–47) on Bernard's letter to Aelred, found in the English translation of *Mirror* (CF 17:69–72).

The first example of such a statement can be dated to the year 1141 or 1142 when, faced with Bernard's order to draft what was to be his major work, *The Mirror of Charity*, Aelred recused himself on the pretext that he was "inexperienced in writing—illiterate if you will—and tongue-tied as well, not yet capable of lapping milk properly!"[10] Similarly, in a sermon unfortunately impossible to date that Aelred gave before an assembly of clergy at a synod, he began in terms similar to those he used in his letter to Bernard: "I am not wise, I am not a scribe; I am no expert in the law, but a common man and almost unlettered, more like a fisherman than an orator."[11]

Finally, much later in his life, in spring 1163, when he began composing his thirty-one *Homilies on the Prophetic Burdens of Isaiah*, Aelred blended paternal affection for the monks to whom he preached, and with whom he shared all, with humility, by which he admitted his lack of "scholarly mastery," in order to attribute his teachings to the glory of the Lord:

> I recognize my obligation [Rom 1:14] to your progress in all respects, because of my office, of course, but mostly because of my affection for you. But *necessity* also *compels me. Woe to me if I do not preach the gospel* [1 Cor 9:16], especially since I do not doubt that whatever progress I make in spiritual teaching or in understanding of the Scriptures is not so much for me as it is for you, given through me. Nothing should be attributed to my merits, since I am a sinner, nor to scholarly training, since, as you know, I am mostly uneducated; nor to my zeal or diligence, since I am rarely at leisure and frequently busy. Everything, therefore, is from God, entrusted to me and passed on to you, *so that all who boast should boast in the Lord.*[12]

10. Aelred, Spec car Pref B 2 (CF 17:73).

11. S 64.1; Aelred of Rievaulx, *The Liturgical Sermons: The Durham and the Lincoln Collections*, trans. Kathryn Krug, Lewis White, and the Catena Scholarium, CF 80 (Collegeville, MN: Cistercian Publications, 2018), 208.

12. 1 Cor 1:31. Oner 1.10; Aelred of Rievaulx, *Homilies on the Prophetic Burdens of Isaiah*, trans. Lewis White, CF 83 (Collegeville, MN: Cistercian Publications, 2018), 25.

In these few statements, gleaned over the course of Aelred's life, there is some measure of literary artifice belonging to a compositional convention of the time, illustrious examples of which can be found in the writings of Saint Bernard, to begin a work with an entirely rhetorical profession of modesty or admission of unworthiness and inability. But Aelred's tone is stamped with a sincerity that appears all the less doubtful given what we know of his scholastic itinerary.

On the other hand, Jocelin of Furness's statement that Aelred was an autodidact is more questionable. This assertion contradicts one other statement in the same text, according to which, having entered the Scottish king's service, Aelred was not only "raised" (*nutritus*) but also "educated" (*educatus*) with the royal princes.[13] This statement leads us to understand that even if the normal course of his schooling was interrupted, Aelred's arrival at the royal court most certainly did not prevent his pursuing an intellectual development that, while perhaps not a typical academic or scholastic education, allowed him to acquire a significant openness of mind that by its depth and breadth would serve him greatly in the future.

In truth, when Jocelin states that it is not "while in school"[14] but rather "by virtue of his own hard work and practise"[15] that Aelred acquired the core of his liberal arts knowledge, and when he further adds that Aelred "was better cultivated than most who had been fully trained in profane letters"[16]—by which he means more cultivated than those with much longer schooling—it seems that he borrows this drastically abridged assertion from Walter, who had devoted an entire chapter of *The Life of Aelred* to his abbot's intellectual qualities. In that chapter we find the same affirmation that Aelred was not only his own teacher but also that his sharp intellect allowed him to acquire a vaster and more penetrating education than the

13. Jocelin, "Life of Waldef," 237.
14. Jocelin, "Life of Waldef," 238.
15. Jocelin, "Life of Waldef," 238.
16. Jocelin, "Life of Waldef," 238.

one dispensed in the schools. Thus in *The Life of Aelred*, Walter writes, "He had indeed been given, as he retained, natural capacity to a high degree. Of course he retained it, he who, having acquired but little knowledge in the world, knew so much afterwards, and knew so well what he did know."[17]

Walter then enumerates Aelred's areas of knowledge, from the mundane sciences to the liberal arts to the master sciences of theology and Scripture, to the supreme science of mystical knowledge:

> He felt rather than absorbed what the authorities call the liberal arts, by the process of oral instruction in which the master's voice enters the pupil's breast; but in all other respects he was his own master, with an understanding far beyond that of those who have learned the elements of secular knowledge from the injection of words rather than from the infusion of the Holy Spirit. These acquire from their teacher a hazy idea of Aristotelian forms and the infinite reckonings of Pythagorean computation; but he, by the rapidity of his genius flying through the world of numbers and transcending every figure of speech, both real and feigned, knew in the Scriptures, and taught, him who alone has immortality, where there is no number, and dwells in light inaccessible where there is no figure but the very truth which, rightly understood, is the goal of all earthly knowledge.[18]

The reader will have noted that Walter's subtle play on words suggests that if Aelred had such facility in the realm of study that he could dispense with teachers, it is not only because he was naturally gifted with a sharp intellect—though this is certainly true considering the mention of Aelred's "natural capacity" and "genius"—but because his only teacher was, in reality,

17. Walter, VA 18; Walter Daniel, *The Life of Aelred of Rievaulx*, trans. F. M. Powicke, CF 57 (Kalamazoo, MI: Cistercian Publications, 1994), 109.
18. Walter, VA 18 (CF 57:109).

the Holy Spirit. Thus Aelred's biographer opposes two modes of learning—the first by *inieccioni verbi* or "the injection of words" (it is tempting to translate this as "brainwashing") and the other by *infusione Spiritus Sancti*, that is to say, "the infusion of the Holy Spirit." In the first case, science is acquired by the indirect, laborious, and uncertain means of formal instruction; in the second, on the contrary, science is gently infused by the direct, effortless, and certain means of a gift from the Holy Spirit, as Walter describes it. For Walter, there is no doubt that Aelred was the beneficiary of this second means of education, and Jocelin too presents this idea in his own fashion when he states that Aelred was "filled with the inspiration of the Spirit of Wisdom and Discernment [*spiritu sapientiae et intellectus inspirante et eum replente*]" when he composed all of his works.[19]

Walter's and Jocelin's insistence on the role of the Holy Spirit in Aelred's intellectual development and qualities represents a discreet allusion to the doctrine of "learned ignorance" that was widespread in ancient monastic literature and revitalized by the Cistercian and Bernardine traditions. According to this doctrine, erudition acquired through schooling or books ("science" used in a pejorative manner) counts for nothing by comparison with the delectable knowledge of things (called wisdom) to which personal experience alone can lead us. It is precisely this that Walter and Jocelin of Furness suggest. They are not saying Aelred's mind was devoid of all knowledge and intelligence. Indeed, they emphatically underscore the contrary. Rather, they say that Aelred received this knowledge and intelligence from the Holy Spirit, who made of him, as Saint Gregory the Great said of Saint Benedict, a man "instructed with learned ignorance, and furnished with unlearned wisdom."[20]

Their assertion was based on two pieces of evidence. The first was the fact that Aelred had had to interrupt his studies; the second was the number of multiple literary avowals of

19. Jocelin, "Life of Waldef," 238.
20. Pope Gregory I, *Dialogues* (London: Philip Lee Warner, 1911), 52.

ignorance that Aelred sowed throughout his works. It is no doubt this point as well that so attracted Bernard to Aelred's personality and that in 1141–1142 persuaded Bernard to persist in his command to the young, promising monk of Rievaulx to undertake composition of *The Mirror of Charity*. In a letter to Aelred that figures as the prologue to the *Mirror*, Bernard states that while he understands his correspondent's reticence and his "excuses" for refusing the assigned task, it was these very excuses that "fanned . . . the spark of his desire" to see the task executed:

> You pointed out the reasons for your inability, saying that you are little skilled in letters—almost illiterate, in fact—and that you have come to the desert not from the schools but from the kitchens where subsisting peasant-like and rustic amid cliffs and mountains you sweat with axe and maul for your daily bread, where one learns to be silent rather than to speak, where the buskin of orators is not allowed beneath the garb of poor fishermen.
>
> I accept your excuses gratefully, but I feel that they fan still more, rather than extinguish, the spark of my desire.[21]

Contrary to what is all too often believed, there is on Bernard's part not a single shred of anti-intellectualism. We see rather the expression of a solidly anchored conviction, emphasized in his Sermons 34 and 38 on the Song of Songs, that a purely bookish erudition is without interest. At best it is a vain curiosity; at worst it is a proud vanity. In Bernard's view, what saves knowledge is that when it is combined with lived experience it can be used in the service of one's own spiritual edification, in which case it becomes prudence, or it can be used in the service of others, in which case it becomes charity. Bernard insisted that Aelred consent to write the *Mirror*, be-

---

21. Bernard, Pref Ep 2 (Spec car 17:70).

cause he perceived and appreciated in his young English disciple the presence of this subtle alloy—the richness of an authentic spiritual experience, tested in the crucible of internal struggle, combined with the natural finesse of an intellect untainted by the extended, formalized scholarly education provided by a university.

For Bernard, this alloy made Aelred a particularly authentic, convinced, and convincing witness capable of speaking to others' hearts. It also gave him the ability to show, through his own being and personal history, the spiritual relevance and fruitfulness of Cistercian monasticism as a school for charity and a place of authentic, holistic personal development.

At the Court of Scotland

Jocelin of Furness's short text reveals that during Aelred's service with the Scottish king, he became the schoolmate and childhood companion of Waldef, whom Jocelin designates as Aelred's "schoolfellow" (*coalumnus*) and "very dear friend" (*amicissimum*), and Prince Henry, Aelred's junior by four years.[22] Since Walter makes no mention of this information in his biography, this passing statement by Waldef's biographer is of great importance: first because without Jocelin's testimony we would not have known anything of this aspect of Aelred's life at court, and second because it illuminates personal issues related to his life amidst the Scottish royal family. For his father, Aelred's service with the king of Scotland was of social value, since the whole point for Eilaf was to open more promising future professional prospects for his son. On other hand, entering the king's service had a far more personal dimension for Aelred himself, who, on the brink of adolescence, was at an age that opens the heart to deeper emotions and greater friendships. This period at court turned out to be a time of unimaginable

---

22. Jocelin, "Life of Waldef," 237–38.

fertility for his personal development. Indeed, the Scottish court was for Aelred a school of holiness and piety, a school of culture and universality, and ultimately a school of friendship.

We already know, thanks to the passage from the *Lament for David* cited earlier, that Aelred considered the royal household he entered in 1124 as his second family, and David in particular as a second father. What made this family so important in Aelred's life was their piety and the moral virtues of true charity and justice they practiced on a daily basis. According to certain anecdotes recounted in the last chapter of *Genealogy,* it seems that Aelred retained the most poignant memories of these traits. The first story concerns the magnanimity of Malcolm III of Scotland, King David's father, who offered to spare the life of a baron who had plotted to assassinate him; the second concerns the great love for the poor and the lepers shown by Matilda (David's sister and the wife of King Henry I of England), who took it upon herself to care for them personally. David himself, growing up under the influence of such a sister, was not to be outdone. The *Lament,* which in surviving medieval manuscripts appears in abridged form as a chapter of the *Genealogy* right after the dedication to Henry II, attests to this fact.

In the *Lament,* Aelred describes David's strong moral virtues, though he does not endorse all of David's actions. Indeed he criticizes David's leadership of the Scottish army in the Battle of the Standard, pointing out David's responsibility, however indirect, for the depredations committed by his troops during the campaign.[23] Nonetheless, this exception aside, the *Lament* can be read both as a biography and as a eulogy extolling the virtues of the dead king. It is in fact under the two

---

23. The abridged version of the *Lament,* inserted into the body of the *Genealogy,* did not retain any of this passage. It should also be noted that the severity of Aelred's judgment of David here is absent from the narrative of *Battle,* where he hides the king's name. Perhaps he did so because in that work, he sought to preserve a living man's reputation—an obviously unnecessary precaution after the king's death in 1153.

Latin titles of *Vita* or *Eulogium* that the work was handed down to posterity.[24] Thus the *Lament* is intended to show if not King David's piety, at least the exemplary execution of his royal responsibilities as a just, chaste, and humble man, "beloved of God and humans."[25] David was "beloved by God," Aelred explains, "having at the very beginning of his reign at once diligently carried out *the things that are God's*, building churches and founding monasteries," which he richly endowed.[26]

Second, David was "beloved by humans" because of his keen sense of justice, his receptivity to others' complaints, and his patient and pertinent responses to even the most untimely appeals brought before him. Aelred even offers an anecdote regarding an event he personally witnessed: "I saw with my own eyes that once, as he was ready to go hunting, having placed his foot in the stirrup ready to mount his horse, he drew it back at the voice of a poor man demanding that he give him a hearing. Leaving his horse he went back into the hall. He did not return to his purpose that day but kindly and patiently heard the case for which he had been summoned."[27] A little later Aelred adds, "Then if a priest, or a soldier or a monk, a rich person or a poor one, a citizen or a stranger, a tradesman or a rustic spoke with him, he so appropriately and humbly discussed the affairs and duties of each that all thought him concerned only with their own business. And so he sent everyone away delighted and reassured."[28]

---

24. Aelredus Rievallensis, "Liber de uita religiosi Dauid regis Scocie," in *Opera Omnia*, vol. 6, *Opera Historica et Hagiographica*, ed. Domenico Pezzini, CCCM 3 (Brepols: Turnhout, 2017), 78*–90*, 5–21. A title in another manuscript is *Historia de vita et moribus et morte regis Dauid Scocie*. Walter includes this work in his list of Aelred's works in VA 32, referring to it as "a life . . . in the form of a lamentation" (CF 57:120–21).

25. Sir 45:1; Lam D 2; Aelred of Rievaulx, *Lament for David, King of Scots*, in Aelred of Rievaulx, *The Historical Works*, CF 56:48–49.

26. Aelred, Lam D 2 (CF 56:48–49).

27. Aelred, Lam D 4 (CF 56:51).

28. Aelred, Lam D 4 (CF 56:51).

In one of the rare chapters of the *Life* devoted to Aelred's "Scottish period," Walter underscores the fact that Aelred did not precipitously abandon the royal court for Rievaulx, because he wished to benefit fully from David's pious example and to learn "royal virtues" from him, virtues that he would later need:

> As a boy, he was in the service of the King of Scotland, that great, that second David; he was in the world, like good fruit of the true vine, but in thought and will, he was in heaven. Child though he was, he desired no worldly service, but he was willing for a while and in some measure to serve a lord so pure and holy, a man whose life inspired a veneration due to it, a king whose authority gave strength to it. He had great humility, and he was loath to leave the wise prince, so compassionate in the exercise of his power, so chaste in the maintenance of his honor, an example to him of constancy through steadfastness in what is good, and the avoidance through bodily integrity of the pressures of evil desire, fulfilling that precept of the first David, *Depart from evil and do good.*
>
> And, an even better and more profitable reason for this earthly service, he shared the rule of a great king and acquired from the best of leaders the royal virtues which later he was to describe in writing for the consolation of the faithful, and himself found profit in the reading of this consolation, and so did not merely make others bear fruit but himself bore fruit of sweet savor.[29]

The remainder of chapter 2 is in the same vein, detailing the personal and moral qualities Aelred demonstrated during his service at the royal court—absolute loyalty to King David, amiability and courtesy, generosity of spirit joined with patience and prudence, unfailing generosity and accessibility to all, a keen sense of moderation and justice in the managing of

---

29. Walter, VA 2 (CF 57:90–91).

temporal affairs, unwavering attention to peacekeeping, affability and goodwill, extreme emotional sensitivity, simplicity of dress, dignity of function, etc. Walter describes Aelred's spiritual qualities as well, such as his fervor and his attachment to the realities of heaven. In his enthusiasm, Walter goes so far as to claim "that in the hall of kings he was looked upon rather as a monk than as given to the service of the world and the display of office."[30]

When we look at Aelred's conversion more closely, we have to nuance this somewhat excessive affirmation as contradicted by Aelred's own claims. However, it is difficult to deny that through contact with King David and his family, Aelred's time at the Scottish court must have presented him with a true education in piety. From this point of view, it is regrettable that Walter makes no mention, at least in chapter 2 of the *Life*, of a devotion to which Aelred would remain profoundly attached for the rest of his life, and to which he was probably introduced by King David, who had himself received it from his mother, the future Saint Margaret. By this devotion, we are referring to the Scottish royal family's devotion to the True Cross, which in the *Lament* Aelred qualifies explicitly as "a hereditary gift" passed on from Queen Margaret to her sons.[31]

Aelred undoubtedly benefited from the climate of intense piety that reigned in the Scottish royal court. We would like to think that it was also during his youth spent at court, in the devotion to Christ's cross learned from King David, that Aelred acquired at least in part the substance of what would become two central elements of his spirituality and his theology of monastic life. The first of these is the idea of the cross as "the mirror of the Christian,"[32] wherein is reflected both divine

30. Walter, VA 2 (CF 57:91).

31. *quasi munus haereditarium:* Aelred, Lam D 10 (CF 56:63).

32. S 10.30; Aelred of Rievaulx, *The Liturgical Sermons: The First Clairvaux Collection*, trans. Theodore Berkeley and M. Basil Pennington, CF 58 (Kalamazoo, MI: Cistercian Publications, 2001), 180.

charity and the "love of enemies—which is the perfection of fraternal charity."[33] The second of these is the idea of monks themselves as "men who not only adore the cross of Christ but have also made profession on it."[34]

If the Scottish court was a school of holiness and piety for Aelred, it was also a school of cultural openness. To demonstrate this fact we need only briefly recall King David's family origins and matrimonial relations, situated at the crossroads of four different cultures. By his descent, David fused three different cultural backgrounds. His father, Malcolm III, gave him Scottish blood and a Saxon cultural heritage. David's mother, the future Saint Margaret, gave him an English and German cultural heritage, as she was the child of Edward Aetheling, son of the English King Edmund Ironside (treacherously murdered in 1016), and Ealdgyth, daughter of Emperor Henry II of Germany.

To these varied genealogical contributions can be added another cultural connection by way of matrimony. By his sister Matilda's marriage with Henry I (third son of William the Conqueror), David was introduced to the royal English court, where he received a large part of his education, probably living there until his accession to the Scottish throne in 1124. David's presence at the English court allowed him entry into a new universe, immersed in King Henry's Franco-Norman culture. This immersion in the French cultural universe was reinforced in 1113 when King Henry had David married to Matilda, daughter of the Saxon Earl Waltheof of Northumbria, grand-niece of William the Conqueror, and widow of Simon de Senlis, earl of Northampton and of Huntingdon.

---

33. Spec car 3.5.14 (CF 17:231).

34. Aelred, S 10:29 (CF 58:180); see also Spec car 1.5.16; 2.1.3; 2.6.15 (CF 17:95, 164, 173). For examination of the theme of the cross as an essential element of Aelred's spiritual doctrine, see Pierre-André Burton, "Contemplation et imitation de la Croix: un chemin de la perfection chrétienne et monastique d'après le *Miroir*," Coll 55 (1993): 140–68.

Thus when Aelred entered the king of Scotland's service, he was introduced into a cultural melting pot, open to the world and to Europe, where both English and French were spoken. In *The Mirror of Charity* Aelred writes of the broad French and European cultural horizon thus opened to him; in the course of a conversation with one of his novices, he states that "when reading fables that are being made up in common speech about some Arthur—I don't know exactly who—I remember being moved sometimes even to the point of weeping."[35] The statement is a barely veiled reference to the courtly literature of the Arthurian cycle—the best-sellers of the era.

The ten years Aelred spent at the Scottish court from 1124 to 1134 thus opened his heart and mind to broader cultural vistas than those visible in the confined, provincial, and rather conservative milieu in which he had lived until then, in which he would no doubt have been locked away by a father apparently insensitive to the spiritual renewal sweeping through twelfth-century Europe. Further, this prolonged exposure to a decidedly European cultural universe brought at least two great benefits to Aelred's life. First, living in a multi-ethnic Anglo-Saxon and Franco-Norman family must have made Aelred particularly sensitive to both the singular challenge and the immense richness represented by the harmonious cohabitation of individuals of different temperaments and multiple cultural origins. The time spent at the Scottish court in the company of David and his wife Matilda probably convinced Aelred that difficult as it might be, desire for a peaceful cohabitation was not a utopian dream.

Rather, it was possible for individuals and even for entire peoples, however different they might be from one another, to build a truly fraternal world. To put it differently, in the company of King David and his family, Aelred precociously

35. Aelred, Spec car 2.17.51 (CF 17:199).

acquired the "sort of ecumenical passion"[36] of which Gaetano Raciti speaks and which, throughout Aelred's life, "motivated him to work from every angle to abolish or transcend discord, schism, ideological opposition, exclusivism, individualistic compartmentalization, intolerance, and fanaticism, and to promote understanding, compassion, reconciliation, peace, acceptance of differences, receptivity to otherness, the pooling of individual gifts, friendship."[37] Raciti goes on to say that all of this was "from the microrealization of a plan of personalized community in the framework of Cistercian monastic life, to unwavering support for a refounding of the British nation, bringing together the old Celto-Saxon population and the new population descended from the Norman invasion, through the assimilation of each other's values."[38]

Of more immediate importance—difficult as it is to affirm this with certainty since Aelred left nothing conclusive on the subject—is the point that when Aelred came to choose which religious order he was going to enter it was probably the Francophile atmosphere of the Scottish court and the new values promoted there that prepared him to leave behind his native provincialism and inclined him to pass over the local Benedictine and Augustinian institutions, instead choosing the only twelfth-century order with a truly European aspect, embodying better than any other institution the era's spiritual aspirations.

Henry, Waldef, and Simon: The Scottish Court as a School of Friendship

While both a school of piety and universality, the Scottish court was also a school of friendship. As Aelred himself later

---

36. Gaetano Raciti, "Présentation générale," in Aelred of Rievaulx, *Sermons pour l'année I. Sermons 1–14*, trans. Gaetane de Briey (Oka, Canada: Abbaye Notre-Dame-du-Lac, 1997), 17.

37. Raciti, "Présentation générale," 17.

38. Raciti, "Présentation générale," 17.

admitted, his slow and laborious apprenticeship was not initially without error, but in the end it resulted in an understanding of authentic relationships among friends.

When introduced by his father at David's court, Aelred found himself in the company of Queen Matilda's three sons. Two were from her first marriage to Simon de Senlis: Simon, born in 1095, and Waldef, perhaps born in 1103. The third was from her second marriage, to David: Henry, born in 1114, who died in 1152, aged thirty-eight, the year before the death of his father. Of these three, only Henry and Waldef seem to have meant something to Aelred. Of the first, we have already said that Aelred was his constant companion; an unwavering friendship bound them together. The second, Waldef, was according to Jocelin of Furness Aelred's "schoolfellow and very close friend [*coalumnus et amicissimus*]."[39] On the other hand, no one mentions Simon. Whether he received his education elsewhere, perhaps at the English court, is unknown. He seems in any case to have dissociated himself from his stepfather, since during the English Civil War and in particular at the Battle of the Standard in 1138, he did not support David's niece, the Empress Matilda. Instead, he aligned himself with Stephen of Blois, of whom he was the grand-nephew through his uncle Robert de Beaumont, to whom he would remain faithful to the end, even after Stephen's imprisonment.

In the prologue of his treatise on *Spiritual Friendship*, Aelred describes his adolescent discovery of friendship. With the passing of time and the mature perspective of old age,[40] Aelred

39. Jocelin, "Life of Waldef," 238.

40. According to the chronological clues found in this treatise, books 2 and 3 were composed between 1164 and 1167. Book 1 was written much earlier—after 1142, when *Mirror* was written, and certainly before Aelred's election as abbot of Rievaulx in 1147. As for the prologue, we have no precise date, but we can hypothesize that Aelred wrote it at the time he edited his work into its final form, from which we conclude that it is an older, more mature Aelred speaking there.

recounts the experience of his youth—severely, perhaps, but also realistically and without regret. For the benefit of his readers, he sifts that experience through his encounter with Christ and through his monastic life. He does so in part to refer to the "sweetness" of the experience, the happiness attained through loving and knowing one is loved. But at the same time he also does so to measure the experience's limits and imperfections, for, he writes, "even at that time, nothing not honeyed with the honey of the sweet name of Jesus, nothing not seasoned with the salt of the sacred Scriptures, wholly won my affection":[41]

> *While I was still a boy at school*, the charm of my companions gave me the greatest pleasure. Among the usual faults that often endanger youth, my mind surrendered wholly to affection and became devoted to love. Nothing seemed sweeter to me, nothing more pleasant, nothing more valuable than to be loved and to love.
>
> Wavering among various loves and friendships, my spirit began to be tossed this way and that and, ignorant of the law of true friendship, was often beguiled by its mirage.[42]

Thus Aelred's main preoccupation at that time of his life was to seek out "a model to which I could recall my quest for many loves and affections."[43] He found at least part of this model in Cicero's *On Friendship*, whose treatment of the subject, Aelred says, "seemed . . . both invaluable for the soundness of its views and attractive for the charm of its eloquence."[44]

Aelred could not have better expressed the profound admiration he felt on reading this treatise. The statement highlights how essential his discovery of Cicero's work was to his intel-

---

41. Aelred, Spir am Prol.5 (CF 5:54).

42. Aelred, Spir am Prol.1–2 (CF 5:53).

43. Aelred, Spir am Prol.3 (CF 5:53).

44. Aelred, Spir am Prol.2 (CF 5:53). [Translator's note: My ellipsis, to fit the English quotation to Burton's phrasing.]

lectual development and what a milestone it was on his personal and spiritual journey. The book left such an indelible mark on his heart and mind that years later when he wrote his own treatise on *Spiritual Friendship*, he used Cicero's work as a foundation and model. He often cited from Cicero's text, albeit never in a purely servile or scholarly manner. As Giovanni Zuanazzi has pointed out,

> Even when he undertakes the most traditional themes, Aelred is not content to simply repeat other treatments, but instead reworks them according to his own sensibilities, culture, and experience. He does not limit himself to "copying" Cicero. He takes Cicero as inspiration, transforms him, interprets him and, where necessary, completes him with other input. As a result, the philosophical world drawn from Cicero is not diluted in Aelred's text, but rather is renewed, and set, as it were, in the framework of a superior logic.[45]

Alternatively, as Hans-Georg Gadamer states, Cicero's treatise, repeatedly read and reread by Aelred, constituted an inner horizon that, once he became a Cistercian, he constantly illuminated further by "fusing" it with two other horizons his monastic vocation put at his disposal: Scripture, and the spiritual tradition of the church fathers.[46] Aelred himself affirms this clearly, taking pains to underline the eminently existential issues he saw as inherent in such a task: "Musing on Cicero's thoughts again and again, I began to wonder whether perhaps

45. Giovanni Zuanazzi, "Introduction," in Aelredo di Rievaulx, *L'amicizia spirituale*, trans. Giovanni Zuanazzi (Rome: Città Nuova, 1997), 11. See also Gaetano Raciti, "L'apport original d'Aelred de Rievaulx à la réflexion occidentale sur l'amitié," Coll 29 (1967): 77–99. Of particular interest is Raciti's critique (92–93) of Delhaye's opinion that Aelred's work is a text with no real depth or value; see Philippe Delhaye, "Deux adaptations du *De amicitia* de Cicéron au XIIᵉ siècle," *Recherches de théologie ancienne et médiévale* 15 (1948): 107–8.

46. Hans-Georg Gadamer, *Truth and Method* (New York: Crossroad, 1988).

they might be supported by the authority of the Scriptures. But when I read the many passages on friendship in the writings of the holy fathers, wishing to love spiritually but not able to, I decided to write on spiritual friendship and to set down for myself rules for a pure and holy love."[47]

These lines reveal Aelred's extraordinarily open mind and furnish a perfect example of the "Cistercian humanism" that Louis Bouyer so astutely characterized as "a fundamentally Biblical spiritual thought, whose meditation was stimulated and rendered fertile by the Classics"[48]—in this case, Cicero and the ancient philosophical tradition. Furthermore, these lines show that in his spiritual and existential quest Aelred neither neglected nor refused any external contribution provided that it nourished his reflection and aided his progress.

In the end, such intellectual optimism—if it can be qualified as such—was valuable to Aelred in more than one respect. It allowed him to take into consideration what today's moral philosophy calls "the law of graduality." Furthermore, it allowed him never to denounce the experiences of his youth, even those stained with imperfection or sin—the proof of this seen in the freedom with which he speaks of them. Applied to others, it allowed him to receive and welcome everyone, wherever they happened to be in their personal and spiritual journey. And in his reflections on friendship, it allowed him never to negatively judge even incomplete forms of friendship, provided that they remained open to future progress and remained an opportunity for personal growth. It is in this manner, at once so human and so supernatural, that he judges the adolescent and still "carnal" friendships of Saint Augustine's youth. Indeed, for the benefit of his interlocutor, who is in his eyes too inclined to a sort of "supernatural spiritualism,"[49] Aelred audaciously affirms:

---

47. Aelred, Spir am Prol.5–6 (CF 5:54).
48. Louis Bouyer, *La Spiritualité de Cîteaux* (Paris: Flammarion, 1955), 191. This idea appears in the chapter devoted to Aelred.
49. Raciti, "L'apport," 96.

However, if you avoid childishness and dishonesty, and if nothing shameful spoils such friendship, then in hope of some richer grace this love can be tolerated as a kind of first step toward a holier friendship. As devotion grows with the support of spiritual interests, and as with age maturity increases and the spiritual senses are illumined, then, with affection purified, such friends may mount to higher realms, just as we said yesterday that because of a kind of likeness the ascent is easier from human friendship to friendship with God.[50]

Of course, when Aelred discovered friendship with Waldef and Henry at the Scottish court, he had not yet attained the high degree of personal and spiritual maturity that later allowed him to cast upon himself and others such a gaze of compassion and hope. He is, rather, at an earlier, fumbling stage. By his own words, his experience with friendship at that point in his life, despite certain immense joys he felt, left him with ambivalent feelings in a bitterly divided heart:

I was lying rotting and covered over, bound and captive, snagged in the birdlime of clinging iniquity, overwhelmed by the weight of inveterate habits. So I interrogated myself: who am I, where am I, what kind of person am I? I shuddered . . . and trembled at my own effigy. I was terrified at the loathsome image of my unhappy soul. I was displeasing to myself, because you were becoming pleasing to me. . . . The chain of my worst habits bound me, love of my kinsmen conquered me, the fetters of gracious company pressed upon me tightly; above all the knot of a certain friendship was dearer to me than all the delights of my life. I relished the others, the others were pleasing to me, but you more than any.[51]

Further on, Aelred goes so far as to say this profound self-loathing led him to the brink of despair and, in addressing

---

50. Aelred, Spir am 3.87 (CF 5:109).
51. Aelred, Spec car 1.28.79 (CF 17:134).

God, he evokes in thinly veiled terms the temptation of suicide: "Very deep within me was my wound, crucifying, terrifying, and corrupting everything within me with an intolerable stench. Had you not quickly stretched out your hand to me, O Lord, unable to endure myself I might perhaps have resorted to the worst remedy of despair."[52]

We are led to wonder what happened in Aelred's life to cause him such despair and also how we are to interpret such confessions. Before examining these questions, we should consider Squire's warning about taking care to attribute to these words their proper meaning and avoiding the interpretive missteps that are so easy to make when trying to read the inner life of a man so far removed from us in time. Squire holds that despite appearances, and contrary to what the reader may be inclined to believe, Aelred "speaks far less of himself than is often supposed."[53] As a result, his personality presents itself to us as "an enigma," so that to a large extent "the essential interiority of his inner life escapes us."[54]

Thus to better perceive the nature of Aelred's spiritual crisis before entering Rievaulx, which the statements here seem to evoke, it is worth keeping in mind at least two things that clarify these statements from the standpoint of both the Augustinian sources from which Aelred derives them and the human context in which he lived at the time. The two things we must consider are his functions in the royal entourage and the important place that he later occupied.

A Rapid Rise

Aelred entered the royal household around 1124 and, in the company of the royal princes, pursued the intellectual development he had had to interrupt by leaving school. In time, however, he so gained the affection and trust of King David

52. Aelred, Spec car 1.28.79 (CF 17:135).
53. Squire, "Aelred par lui-même," 25.
54. Squire, "Aelred par lui-même," 27.

that according to Walter, David "made him great in his house and glorious in his palace. He was put in charge of many things and was as a second lord and prince over a host of officials and all the men of the court. . . . He was steward of the royal household. Nothing, inside or out, was done without him. He was respected by all in all things and never failed."[55]

Unfortunately we know neither the exact date on which Aelred was appointed steward nor the precise details of the position. Regarding the date, Powicke has advanced the hypothesis that this appointment likely took place "at the earliest in 1131 or 1132, only two or three years before he entered Rievaulx."[56] Aelred was then barely twenty or twenty-one years old. Of course, today that might surprise us, but nothing prevents us from accepting it, since in an era where individuals reached personal maturity at a younger age, it was not at all rare—indeed, far from it—that important responsibilities were confided to very young men. One has only to recall the example of Bernard, who became abbot at the age of twenty-three or twenty-four.

Regarding the position itself, we are luckily a bit better informed. In the prefatory letter addressed to Aelred in *The Life of Saint Brigit of Kildare*, Lawrence of Durham—a childhood friend and perhaps one of Aelred's former teachers—describes the functions exercised by Aelred at the Scottish court in terms similar to those used by Walter. He mentions that Aelred was "*dispensatori domus regiae.*"[57] Powicke's research on this expression led him to assert that the word *dispensator* is a synonym of the Latin *dapifer* and an equivalent to the Anglo-Saxon *disc-þegn* or *steward.*[58] According to Powicke, this term designated a function

55. Walter, VA 2 (CF 57:91).

56. Powicke, "Introduction," xli.

57. Anselm Hoste, "A Survey of the Unedited Work of Laurence of Durham and an Edition of his Letter to Aelred of Rievaulx," *Sacris Erudiri* 11 (1960): 263.

58. Powicke, "Introduction," xl. [Translator's note: In his text Powicke provides two English translations for the term—*seneschal* and *steward*. Burton uses the word *seneschal* in his text. I have opted to use the term *steward* here, since Powicke presents them as synonyms, and since *steward* allows for consistency

normally confided to an "official of second or lower rank,"[59] but one that after the Norman Conquest gave increasing status to its executor in relation to the extent of the powers it conferred.[60] This charge did not, as Aelred might lead us to believe, involve merely working in "the kitchens"[61] (in the strict sense of the term), but instead involved the duties of a general superintendent. That is to say, while he was the administrator of royal goods and therefore directly responsible for the management of the kitchens, he was also the head administrator of the king's financial and economic portfolio as well as, according to Walter, the king's social affairs. This, at least, is what is suggested by Walter's statements when he underscores the quality with which Aelred performed his functions: "Everything done at court was in his keeping, yet he did whatever he did with such mildness that under his just and affable management of affairs there was no unrest, no disturbance among the people."[62]

In any case, as Powicke notes, it seems that Aelred would have been fully aware of the importance of the charge to which he was appointed by King David. When in his twilight years Aelred composed his *Pastoral Prayer*, he recalled that distant time and asked, as abbot, for the grace to be made "the dependable dispenser, the discerning distributor, the prudent provider of all that [God has] given."[63]

---

with the citations from Powicke's English translation of Walter Daniel's *Life of Aelred of Rievaulx*, which also uses the word *steward*.]

59. Powicke, "Introduction," xl.

60. Powicke, "Introduction," xl.

61. Bernard of Clairvaux, Pref Ep 2; "A Letter of Bernard Abbot of Clairvaux, to Abbot Aelred," in Aelred, *The Mirror of Charity*, CF 17:70.

62. Walter, VA 2 (CF 57:91).

63. Aelred of Rievaulx, *Pastoral Prayer*, in *For Your Own People: Aelred of Rievaulx's Pastoral Prayer*, trans. Mark DelCogliano, ed. Marsha L. Dutton, CF 73 (Kalamazoo, MI: Cistercian Publications, 2008), 55. For more information on Aelred's responsibilities as *dispensator* at the Scottish court, see Pierre-André Burton, "Aux origines de l'expansion anglaise de Cîteaux: La fondation de Rievaulx et la conversion d'Aelred: 1128–1134 (I–II)," Coll 61 (1999): 250–54.

As steward of the kingdom, Aelred occupied an important position. Combined with the affection and esteem that David showed him, this position placed Aelred in a delicate situation by raising virulent jealousy against him and exposing him to the retribution of a knight far less fortunate than he. Walter presents this conflict at length, devoting the entire third chapter of the *Life* to it, so allowing him to continue the preceding chapter's description of Aelred's personal and moral qualities, highlighting his patience, charity, humility, largesse of spirit, and forbearance.

The incident similarly allows Walter to emphasize the tightening of the already close bonds between King David and his protégé. On at least two occasions, Walter states that the qualities demonstrated by Aelred in this circumstance "bound him still closer in the bonds of love to his lord the king . . . so that the king increasingly confided in him and entrusted him with business of importance." This confidence, Walter adds, would later be returned to him, since he "began to be so fond of him who did these things that he gave him the first place among his friends, and, as though it had been said to him 'Friend, go up higher,' he was every day loaded with kindness by the humble Aelred as a colleague, praised as his dearest and made to rejoice as his neighbor." Walter then emphasizes how worthy Aelred was of the confidence placed in him, underlining the fact that Aelred had "a fitting name" since, etymologically, the English name *Aelred* is composed of the two Saxon words *all* and *rath*, translated as "all counsel" or "perfect counsel," a quality that earned him his place as royal advisor.[64]

But beyond the purely anecdotal aspect of the narrative and its hyperbolic style, this chapter is worthy of our attention for two reasons. First, from a very general point of view, Aelred's rapid promotion at the Scottish court offers a case study of relatively

---

Other texts discussed in the article, by Aelred or Saint Bernard, provide further insight into this word's meaning.

64. Walter, VA 3 (CF 57:94–95).

common twelfth-century practice.[65] In an era when professional-
ization began to appear in the temporal administration of states
and when, correspondingly, reliance on written documents became more commonplace, princes and kings surrounded themselves with a progressively larger and larger administrative staff
to help manage affairs. This staff consisted largely of clerks—educated men capable of reading and accounting. Most of the time,
this staff was chosen from outside the ranks of the hereditary
nobility, specifically from the most modest social classes. This
type of recruitment permitted princes and kings to take into service not only competent, qualified personnel, but personnel they
could trust, since, being of inferior social rank, they were further
removed from court intrigues and therefore represented no threat
to the prince's or king's power. While not denying the quality of
the relationship between David and Aelred as Walter describes
it, we can theorize that Aelred's rapid advancement was also due
in part to this court context, in which social differences counted
for so much. Aelred's biographer goes so far as to say that had it
not been for Aelred's desire to enter Rievaulx, David would have
honored him with a bishopric (see VA 2).

The second point of interest found in the *Life's* third chapter
is the light it casts on the rivalries that existed even in the heart
of the royal entourage and on the human baseness that resulted
from them. Of course, this reality applies universally to all
environments where ambition and arrivism reign. But its manifestation in chapter 3 of the *Life* is of particular interest as certain
contemporary historians, for example Brian Patrick McGuire,
have sought to base their explanation of Aelred's monastic
vocation on the accusations brought against him by his rival
as reported in this chapter, and in particular on what those accusations might suggest or insinuate regarding Aelred's emotional and sexual orientation. We examine this delicate subject
in the next chapter.

---

65. Some twenty years later at the English court, Thomas Becket had a
similarly spectacular ascent in the service of Henry II. See Pierre Aubé, *Thomas
Becket* (Paris: Fayard, 1988).

Chapter Four

Aelred's Conversion (1134)

In the preceding chapter, we followed Aelred through twenty years of childhood and adolescence.[1] As far as events go, the balance sheet is fairly empty. No dates truly stand out. At most we know that after receiving a primary education, probably at Hexham while living with his parents, Aelred was sent to Durham at an unknown time to continue his studies. These studies were suddenly interrupted in 1124 by Eilaf's opportunity to place his son at the Scottish court. This was Eilaf's hope of guaranteeing Aelred a future otherwise compromised by the execution of the Gregorian Reform's ecclesiastical norms. Aelred's entry into the Scottish king's service—the first major landmark in his journey—allowed him to complete his intellectual development and to discover an aptitude for the administration of temporal affairs. Later, in 1131 or 1132, when Aelred was about twenty years old, King David conferred on him the charge of *dispensator*, or steward.

As for Aelred's personal and spiritual balance sheet, the entries are certainly abundant, but fairly contradictory as well.

---

1. Much of this chapter is derived from Pierre-André Burton, "Aux origines de l'expansion anglaise de Cîteaux: La fondation de Rievaulx et la conversion d'Aelred: 1128–1134 (I-II)," Coll 61 (1999): 248–90; "The Beginnings of Cistercian Expansion in England: The Socio-Historical Context of the Formation of Rievaulx," CSQ 42, no. 2 (2009): 395–411.

The first twenty-four years of Aelred's life were above all a time of intellectual development, marked by a major turning point—his entry into King David's household. This event was to be providential. It offered Aelred the opportunity to live in the bosom of a second family, who would contribute greatly to the molding of his personality. On an intellectual level, Aelred gained an uncommon openness and depth of mind. On a spiritual level he gained an inner life centered on the mystery of the cross; finally, on a personal and emotional level, concurrent to his reading of Cicero's *On Friendship*, he discovered the wondrous joys of that principle. But as we learn from Aelred's own writings, these emotional relationships, intoxicating as they may have been, also filled him with a self-loathing that led him to the brink of despair and the temptation of suicide.

This reality represents a second major turning point even more decisive than the first. The first was, so to speak, purely factual, reorienting Aelred's education without affecting him deeply. At any rate, we have no reason to think otherwise. In contrast, the second turning point represents an existential crisis that shattered Aelred's inner bearings. Violently shaken by this spiritual upheaval, Aelred radically reconsidered the meaning of his life and redirected it, setting it on an unexpected, albeit not wholly new, course. Against expectations—surprising even King David, who had reportedly planned to offer him a bishopric—Aelred decided, apparently out of the blue, abruptly to halt a promising clerical career to enter the monastery of Rievaulx.

This key moment in Aelred's conversion is the focus of the present chapter. The chapter is divided into three parts. First we consider the external circumstances of Aelred's conversion; then we look at how Aelred himself interprets the event; finally we interpret and contextualize these details in relationship to the quest for inner peace, freedom, and unity that led him to enter Rievaulx.

The External Circumstances

The external circumstances surrounding Aelred's conversion are relatively well known, since Walter Daniel devoted chapters 4 through 7 of his narrative to them. We summarize those circumstances here, re-encountering several major figures mentioned earlier in our sketch of the socio-historical and politico-religious contexts of Rievaulx's founding and Aelred's youth at King David's court.

On a date unspecified by Walter, but which must have been around 1134, Aelred, as David's steward, was sent to York to discuss some matter with Bishop Thurstan. We do not know for certain the nature of this matter, but according to Maurice Powicke's hypothesis,[2] it probably pertained to the conflict at that time between Thurstan, the archbishop of York, and John, the bishop of Glasgow. For several years, the latter had refused to recognize the authority of the former as metropolitan of the Scottish dioceses. It does not appear, however, that Aelred's intervention bore any fruit, since in a letter from Pope Innocent II addressed to the two metropolitan archbishops of England, Canterbury and York, we know that despite pontifical injunctions, the recalcitrant bishop had still not yielded in 1136. In itself the event matters little, though in existential terms it represents an early step in Aelred's journey toward his personal vocation.

Indeed Walter reports that on this trip Aelred had the opportunity to see "a close friend of his"—employing the superlative term *familiarissimus*—who spoke to him at length of a group of "white monks by name and white also in vesture,"[3] who for two years had been established at Rievaulx. Some

2. F. M. Powicke, "Introduction," in Walter Daniel, *The Life of Aelred of Rievaulx*, trans. F. M. Powicke (Oxford: Clarendon: 1950, 1978), xliii–xliv.
3. Walter, VA 5 (CF 57:96–97).

have suggested this close friend[4] was none other than Waldef, King David's stepson and, as was noted in the previous chapter, a childhood friend of Aelred. Though this hypothesis cannot be proven, it is neither unlikely nor without interest. Around 1130 Waldef had joined the Augustinian canons regular of Nostel, a Yorkshire priory. Soon afterward, as early as 1134, he was elected prior of Kirkham, an institution of the same order, created around 1121 by Rievaulx's founder, Walter Espec. Waldef seems to have been quickly won over by the ideal of Cistercian life. Driven by the desire to embrace this way of life, he even envisioned an affiliation between his priory and the order of Cîteaux and made overtures to Rievaulx. For unknown reasons, though no doubt at least partially political in nature, these overtures came to nothing, and Waldef, leaving his priory, entered Wardon, a daughter house of Rievaulx founded, again by Walter Espec, in 1135 in Bedfordshire.[5]

Later Waldef crossed Aelred's path again, albeit in very different circumstances. For the moment, if it is indeed to him that Walter alludes in his narrative of Aelred's conversion, we can easily imagine that Waldef, still dazzled by his newly discovered Cistercian life and probably burning with the fervor of a novice, must have painted an enthusiastic picture of what he had glimpsed or heard of the laudable reputation of the monks who had come across the sea from Clairvaux.

Two echoes of this enthusiastic description survive. The first is also in the fifth chapter of the *Life of Aelred,* where Walter enumerates what he considers the most striking features of the Cistercian way of life: poverty, charity, measure and discretion in all things, unanimity and obedience, and separation from the world. The second echo is found in Aelred's *Mirror of Charity*—probably Walter's primary source—where Aelred reproduces a dialogue he had with one of his novices and whose

---

4. Powicke, Introduction, 10, n. 3.

5. For more on Waldef, see Charles Dumont, "Walthéof," *Dictionnaire de spiritualité* (Paris: Beauchêne, 1995), 16:1311–12. Waldef's life is known primarily through Jocelin of Furness's "Life of Waldef," considered in chap. 3 above.

enthusiasm, as Aelred Squire has astutely noted,[6] is a thinly veiled reproduction of Aelred's feelings at the time of his own conversion. The novice explains that he was seduced by several things: the austerity and frugality of Cistercian life, the nocturnal vigils and hard manual labor that allowed him to "mortify [his] members which are on earth,"[7] along with his guilty passions, obedience in all things, a life preserved from all unwholesome idleness, good relations with those outside the monastery (notably the peasants and the poor, who uttered no complaint of mistreatment by the Cistercians), a tranquility and wondrous freedom from worldly tribulations, bonds of unbreakable fraternal charity, an admirable sharing of goods where "what each has is considered as belonging to everyone, and what everyone has to each one," and a life respectful of human well-being and diversity. In short, "to summarize many things in a few words,"[8] it was a life containing nothing contrary to evangelical or apostolic perfection, nothing conflicting with the writings of the church fathers, nothing that contradicted the words of the ancient monk.

Of course it is unlikely that Aelred would have spoken in these precise terms when he entered Rievaulx in 1134. But it is not surprising that barely seven years later, when he wrote this passage in *Mirror,* he included the seed of nearly all the grand themes of his doctrinal teachings and of his preoccupations as abbot. We list here only the most significant ones: the importance of corporal asceticism as an instrument to promote "the growth of charity"[9] or "the ordering"[10] of desires, the building of a fraternal community founded on the tightly connected dual

6. "There is no doubt, he writes, that the enthusiasm for Rievaulx attributed by Aelred to his novice could just as well have been his own" (Aelred Squire, "Aelred par lui-même," Coll 29 [1967]: 28).

7. See Col 3:5. Spec car 2.17.43; Aelred of Rievaulx, *The Mirror of Charity,* trans. Elizabeth Connor, CF 17 (Kalamazoo, MI: Cistercian Publications, 1990), 194.

8. Aelred, Spec car 2.17.43 (CF 17:194–95).

9. Charles Dumont, "Le personnalisme communautaire d'Aelred de Rievaulx," Coll 39 (1977): 129–48.

10. Dumont, "Personnalisme," 129–48.

principles of "a community-based personalism"[11] and "a preferential option for the poor,"[12] the responsibility to build a society based on social justice—no doubt directly inherited from his charge as *dispensator* at the Scottish court—and, finally, overarching the entire list, the constant desire to make peace, harmony, and tranquility reign over all things.

Waldef seems to have described Cistercian life with such fervor that he passed on his enthusiasm to Aelred. From that moment, Aelred had only one desire (VA 6): to see with his own eyes the veracity of what he had been told. On the advice of his friend, he asked Bishop Thurstan's permission and blessing; then, barely taking the time and trouble to return home and say good-bye to his hosts, he jumped on his horse and galloped away, even though, his amused biographer adds, he did not know which way to go. Before nightfall he arrived at Helmsley Castle, home of Rievaulx's founder, Walter Espec, where he stayed the night. They spent the evening in conversation, and, according to Walter, as Walter Espec "told him still more about the life of the monks, Aelred's spirit burned more and more with inexpressible joy."[13] The next morning Aelred visited Rievaulx. The welcome he received touched him deeply. Aelred opened the floodgates of his heart, and "the fountain of tears gushe[d] forth like a deluge flooding the earth."[14]

Aelred's Decision to Enter Rievaulx

This first emotionally charged visit did not have any immediate effect, however. Aelred returned to Helmsley Castle, where he spent another night. The next morning, at dawn, he hastily made his preparations to return to David's court in Scotland. Yet, Walter says, he did not account for "the heat of the Holy

---

11. Dumont, "Personnalisme," 129–48.

12. Gaetano Raciti, "L'option préférentielle pour les pauvres dans le modèle communautaire aelrédien," Coll 55 (1993): 186–206.

13. Walter, VA 6 (CF 57:99).

14. Walter, VA 7 (CF 57:99).

Spirit."[15] Skirting the edge of a hill overlooking the Rye Valley and the monastery, Aelred asked the friend traveling with him if he would like to descend with him in order to visit the place once more. Walter—who claims to have been told this by Aelred himself—asserts that Aelred would never have gone back down again by himself if his friend had not chosen to accompany him. As Charles Dumont has noted, this point is of interest not "for the reasons the biographer gives, but because in the narrative that Aelred would later provide, his decision depended upon a harmony between two wills, a harmony that he would soon and henceforth define as friendship and charity itself."[16]

Following this exchange, which reveals once more the importance and substance of friendship in his life, Aelred went down once more to Rievaulx, where he received a similar welcome to that of the day before. And "since he listen[ed] to their words with an eager and unreserved attention, making them his own with tears as things to be embraced," his interlocutors came to guess Aelred's true intention—to become a monk. This Aelred asked to do in the conviction that he was merely accomplishing his duty (Luke 17:10). Right away "he divided all his goods; he abandoned everything he had [to those accompanying him]. He kept beside him only the one man of his company who was not unwilling to stay."[17]

A Narrative that Raises Questions

Whatever we may think of Walter's narrative, of whom Dumont writes that his "manneristic style contrasts painfully with the simplicity and the rejection of superfluity he sincerely

15. Walter, VA 7 (CF 57:99).

16. Charles Dumont, "Aelred de Rievaulx: Introduction à sa vie et à ses écrits," in *Une éducation du cœur* (Oka, Canada: Abbaye Notre-Dame-Du-Lac, 1997), 207. In his presentation of the episode (VA 7), Walter Daniel speaks only of Aelred's humility in allowing his friend to make the choice, overlooking an essential element of the event—the central role of friendship in Aelred's life.

17. Walter, VA 7 (CF 57:100).

praises,"[18] we should nonetheless recognize its merit in vividly relating the moment of Aelred's conversion. This notwithstanding, the historian is right to question the historical accuracy of Walter's testimony, which can be called into doubt on more than one point. It is, of course, not a question of contesting the fact that this testimony rests, as Walter himself repeatedly asserts, on statements made by Aelred himself, probably near the end of his life when he was in poor health and under Walter's care. But it is hard to know what to make of Walter's portrayal of the abruptness of Aelred's decision to enter Rievaulx.

Marsha Dutton has convincingly shown that such a version of events is at least improbable, if not absolutely unimaginable.[19] To confirm this fact, one has only to consult chapter 4 of the *Life*, where Walter himself, contradicting the continuation of his narrative, presents Aelred already stricken with the desire for religious, or monastic, life. He goes so far as to assert that "fearing to give open expression to his joyful intention, lest he should be disturbed by his fear for his lord and suffer delays [in his mission to York], he concealed his determination" from King David. In other words, even before his departure for York, Aelred seems already intently preoccupied by this question. If we are to believe his biographer, Aelred appears to have never envisioned anything other than a clerical life entirely given to God, since Walter states that King David "every day was more and more considering how to advance him" and that had Aelred not entered the monastery, the king "would have honored him with the first bishopric of the land."[20]

What is new in Aelred's inner deliberations is the question of the precise orientation he would give to his consecrated life.

---

18. Dumont, "Aelred: vie et écrits," 207.

19. See Marsha Dutton, "The Conversion and Vocation of Aelred of Rievaulx: A Historical Hypothesis," in *England in the Twelfth Century*, ed. Daniel Williams (London: Boydell, 1990), 31–49. See also the Spanish translation: Marsha Dutton, "Conversión y vocación de San Elredo de Rievaulx," *Cistercium: Revista monástica* 45 (1993): 307–30.

20. Walter, VA 2 (CF 57:91).

Would he follow the path King David laid out before him, or would he go off in a different direction? On this point we can hypothesize that Waldef's choice to become an Augustinian canon some years earlier in 1130 must have had some effect on Aelred.

In any case, it seems clear that around 1134, Aelred's inner deliberations became so acutely intense that the answer came to him like a "medicine,"[21] as Walter puts it, speaking explicitly of a *remedium medicinali*. Walter does not say what this medicine was for, leaving it to us to elucidate the question—as we will do shortly—using elements we have gleaned here and there. At the least it appears evident that on his departure for York, Aelred was so wrapped up in the inner torment of this question that his three successive encounters—first with his friend Waldef, then with Rievaulx's founder Walter Espec, and finally with the community of Rievaulx itself—shifted his decision definitively toward Cistercian monastic life. There remain however two questions to be addressed. The first is why Aelred chose the Cistercian path over other options. The second is the nature of the ailment to which this life would serve as a medicine. To answer these questions we examine Aelred's own words.

Aelred as Interpreter of His Own Vocation

To understand why Aelred chose a Cistercian life, we fortunately have Aelred's own testimony. In several of his written works, he speaks of this crucial and decisive moment in his life. We have already mentioned two of them: the Prologue to *Friendship*, and *Mirror* 1.28.79. In addition to these two texts, there is also *Formation* 32, as well as 18 and 22, where, like Saint Paul, Aelred speaks in the third person but probably refers to himself ("I know a monk," and "I have known a man").[22]

---

21. Walter, VA 4 (CF 57:96).

22. Inst incl 32, 18, 22; Aelred of Rievaulx, "A Rule of Life for a Recluse," trans. Mary Paul Macpherson, in *Aelred of Rievaulx: Treatises. Pastoral Prayer*, CF 2 (Kalamazoo, MI: Cistercian Publications, 1971), 92–97, 66, 69.

These five texts have already been the object of a detailed study.[23] This is not the place to repeat that examination. It suffices to reiterate that the interpreter of these five texts is confronted with three difficulties requiring prudence, particularly in that Aelred may not speak as explicitly and as clearly as one would be tempted to believe, just as Squire earlier warned.

The first difficulty is psychological and derives from the fact underlined by Xavier Thévenot that any autobiographical conversion narrative has a tendency to proceed through "a Manichean periodization of personal history."[24] This process, he says, demarcates pre- and post-conversion states in the narrator's consciousness and in rhetorical terms translates into "a tendency to blacken his pre-conversion state and to idealize his post-conversion state."[25]

A second chronological difficulty follows the first, notably the temporal distance that separates the actual event from its later narration. *Mirror* 1.79 was written only seven years after Aelred's conversion. This is shorter than the interim between any of the other texts, but it is still rather a long period, as the author had already had time to rework the text internally and submit the recounted experience to several stages of rereading. The four other texts are written far later, dating from the end of Aelred's life—between 1160 and 1162 for *Formation*, and after 1164 for the prologue of *Friendship*. In other words, these texts are heavy with personal experiences, but the recounting is enriched by later experiences that modify, to a greater or lesser extent, the interpretation of each initial experience.

The third difficulty is literary and raises two points. The first point is, as Pierre Courcelle has shown,[26] that Aelred liked to

23. Burton, "Aux Origines," 266–85.

24. Xavier Thévenot, "Conversion chrétienne et changement psychique," in *Compter sur Dieu: Études de théologie morale* (Paris: Cerf, 1992), 273–94. See Burton, "Aux Origines," 265–66.

25. Thévenot, "Conversion," 273–94.

26. Pierre Courcelle, "Aelred de Rievaulx à l'école des *Confessions*," *Revue des études augustiniennes* 3 (1957): 163–74.

reread his own conversion experience through the lens of, and as a reflection of, the *Confessions* of Augustine. In so doing, Aelred poured his own narrative into an expressive literary mold inherited from Augustine. The second point is that having been novice master for two years, Aelred never lost sight of, or wanted to forget, the propaedeutic and pedagogic components his writings could, and indeed should, have. Thus when he apparently speaks of himself with a literary rhetoric giving the appearance of a confession, it is always with a very precise pastoral goal, and he writes the references to his own life into the context of a strict argumentative development. This development provided his readers with lessons Aelred drew from his own experiences, however unfortunate or painful they might be. It thus helped his readers de-dramatize their own errors by showing them that they must never despair of themselves or of God, since divine grace and mercy are stronger than evil and sin, and are always victorious.

To correctly interpret the texts in which Aelred seems to speak of himself, it is important to keep in mind these methodological remarks, which allow us to approach each text through different hermeneutical frameworks and protect us against the temptation of a too-rapid or too-autobiographical reading. Keeping in mind these methodological and precautionary frameworks while examining apparently autobiographical passages in these and other texts, we notice that the general tone and manner in which Aelred re-reads and interprets his own experience years after the fact remain surprisingly consistent. A clear indicator of Aelred's psychological equilibrium in his self-perception and self-appreciation, this consistency allows us to attribute to these different narratives a solid, albeit relative, guarantee of accuracy.

Of these five autobiographical texts, we have already cited the prologue of *Friendship* and the first book of *Mirror*. In these texts, Aelred puts his experience into words and accounts for the existential crisis he underwent at the time of his conversion, a crisis, it appears, that led him to knock on the door of Rievaulx. It falls to us to uncover the nature of this existential crisis.

In the Prologue to *Friendship*, Aelred insists above all on the fact that the relations of friendship in which he was engaged gave him feelings of fracture, dispersion, and, consequently, inner instability: "wavering among various loves and friendships, my spirit began to be tossed this way and that and, ignorant of the law of true friendship, was often beguiled by its mirage."[27] The discovery of Cicero's treatise on friendship permitted him, he says, at least partially to "find a model to which I could recall my quest for many loves and affections."[28]

Without contradicting any of what Aelred later wrote in the Prologue of *Friendship*, *Mirror* 1.79 is even more specific. With a style and lexicon borrowed from Augustine's *Confessions*, Aelred speaks of his past life with no indulgence whatsoever and insists not simply on the feelings of division and inner fracture he had at the time of his conversion but, more important, on their deep resonance in the profound reaches of his heart. What he experienced then, he tells us, led him to feel such an intense disgust for himself that he—note the prefix of intensity for the first two verbs—"shuddered" with horror (*ex-horrui*), "trembled" with fear (*ex-pavi*), and was "terrified" (*terrui*) by his own image. At the end of this same paragraph, he returns to this "wound," which was "very deep within" him, and in similar terms he specifies, "[it] was crucifying, terrifying and corrupting everything within me with an intolerable stench."[29]

To this first trait of self-disgust, Aelred adds the feeling of being a slave to himself and to his passions, "chained" by his inveterate habits, "fettered" by his social relationships, and finally "bound" by "the knot of a certain friendship [that] was dearer to [him] than all the delights of [his] life"[30]—feelings that were undoubtedly the source of this immense disgust.

The last of the three texts in which Aelred speaks of himself in the first person, *Formation* 32, is written in the same Augus-

---

27. Aelred, Spir am Prol.2 (CF 5:53).
28. Aelred, Spir am Prol.3 (CF 5:53).
29. Aelred, Spec car 1.28.79 (CF 17:134–35).
30. Aelred, Spec car 1.28.79 (CF 17:134).

tinian vein as *Mirror* 1.79. But it adds no facts beyond those we have already covered. However, it shows great literary calculation and pastoral orientation as Aelred accumulates the blackest expressions possible into a pitiless crescendo describing the moral degradation in which he wallowed at the Scottish court. Presenting himself in counterpoint to his sequestered sister, he begins by describing their common education. Quickly thereafter, however, he arrives at the moment where their paths diverged. She persevered on the path to piety; he, with bowed head, took the slippery slope of vice along which his youth was to be swept away. Then come the allusions to what Aelred calls the "impure desires" of his youth: a morally lax and loose life, "disgraceful behavior" and "corruption" into which he willingly sank, a "whirlpool of debauchery" that engulfed him, "a cloud of passions exhaled from the murky depths of [his] fleshly desires and youthful folly," leading him to drink from the "sweet cup of love," which truly offered only the "poison of self-indulgence,"[31] etc.

It is probably on the basis of these three texts, or perhaps also having been witness to Aelred's youth, that upon the publication of the *Life*, certain unknown individuals sharply criticized Walter and reproached him—not without reason—for pretending that the future abbot of Rievaulx had lived piously at the Scottish court: Aelred's spiritual fervor was such, Walter writes, that "in the hall of kings he was looked upon rather as a monk than as given to the service of the world."[32]

Under this withering critique, Walter found himself forced to retract the statement. He did so in a letter addressed to a certain Maurice,[33] in which he replied point by point to the

---

31. For these expressions, see Aelred, Inst incl 32 (CF 2:94).

32. Walter, VA 2 (CF 57:91).

33. Known as the *Letter to Maurice*. We have discussed the literary structure of this letter, its importance, and the issues surrounding Walter Daniel's publication of the letter as a preface to the *Life of Aelred* in Pierre-André Burton, "Walter Daniel, un biographe injustement critiqué? À propos de la 'réception' de la *Vita Aelredi*: Entre 'vérité historique' et 'vérité mythique,'"

reproaches directed at him in order to justify the compositional choices he had made. But instead of situating the composition exclusively in the framework of history, as his detractors had done, Walter placed his choices in a strictly literary framework. Thus, when he affirmed in the *Life* that Aelred was considered by the royal entourage "as a monk," his intention, he says, was not, as his detractors incorrectly believed, to imply that Aelred had led a chaste life at the Scottish court. He was simply utilizing synecdoche—designating a thing by one of its parts, or the reverse—as a figure of speech. And, as humility is one of the principal monastic virtues, was he not fully justified to say that Aelred had truly lived "as a monk"? Not, of course, in terms of a perfect purity of moral conduct, but because at the Scottish court he had demonstrated great humility?[34]

This convoluted argument may not be entirely satisfactory from a historical standpoint, but there is one thing worth retaining, as Brian Patrick McGuire has pointed out, that gives us a more precise appreciation of Aelred's personal depth. By replying as he does to his detractors, Walter tacitly acknowledges that Aelred's life at the Scottish court was less honorable than he would have had us believe in the *Life*.

But while admitting this, one must ask if it is appropriate to go even further, as McGuire does, and attempt to identify more precisely and concretely to exactly what Aelred alludes when he speaks of the "impure desires" of his youth or of the "whirlpool of debauchery" engulfing him. This is not a rhetorical question. Attempting to build an argument out of Aelred's own statements, as well as the implications of certain defamatory statements made at the Scottish court reported by Walter in chapter 3 of the *Life*, McGuire insinuates a two-part thesis relating to Aelred's emotional makeup. His principal

---

Cîteaux 53 (2002): 223–68. A shorter discussion can be found in Pierre-André Burton, "Introduction," in Walter Daniel, *La vie d'Aelred, abbé de Rievaulx, La lamentation pour la mort d'Aelred, La lettre à Maurice* (Oka, Canada: Abbaye Notre-Dame-du-Lac, 2003), 26–30.

34. Walter, "Letter to Maurice" [4] (CF 57:154).

thesis is that the friendship in which Aelred found himself "chained" at the time of his conversion was marked with the imprint of homoerotic tendencies. McGuire then proposes, as a corollary to this thesis, that Aelred's decision to enter monastic life was determined by this emotional make up. In other words, monastic life appeared to King David's *dispensator* as the only means at his disposal to reconcile his tendencies with the norms imposed by the Gregorian Reform concerning ecclesiastical celibacy.[35]

It would obviously be off topic to recount the history of the discussions this dual hypothesis has sparked among specialists.[36] Let it suffice to say that these discussions have clearly shown that McGuire's hypotheses are not only unverifiable by historical facts, but are furthermore based on no serious textual or doctrinal foundation.[37] If we limit ourselves solely to known textual documentation, nothing that Aelred says about himself justifies an interpretation along the lines suggested by McGuire; his words—all too vague—have merely the appearance of evidence. The same applies to what Walter tells us. Certainly he shows us that Aelred was the target of slanderous accusations, but as for their content, we know nothing. Therefore it is, to say the least, difficult to draw any conclusions from them.

---

35. Brian Patrick McGuire, *Brother and Lover: Aelred of Rievaulx* (New York: Crossroad Press, 1994), esp. 151. For more detail on this thesis, see Pierre-André Burton, "Aelred face à l'histoire et à ses historiens: Autour de l'actualité aelrédienne," Coll 58 (1996): 161–93, esp. 175–80.

36. Studies of this discussion include Burton, "Face à l'histoire," as well as more recently Ryszard Groń, *"Spór o Aelreda": W poszukiwaniu prawdziwego oblicza Aelreda z Rievaulx* (*The Debate about Aelred: Looking for the True Face of Aelred of Rievaulx*) (Kety, Poland: Antyk, 2005).

37. This has been shown in the following articles: Marsha L. Dutton, "Aelred of Rievaulx on Friendship, Chastity and Sex: The Sources," CSQ 29 (1994): 121–96; Marsha L. Dutton, "Aelred of Rievaulx and the Charge of Sexual Obsession: An Invented History," ABR 47 (1996): 414–32; K. M. Tepas, "Sexual Attraction and the Motivations for Love and Friendship in Aelred of Rievaulx," ABR 46 (1995): 283–307; and K. M. Tepas, "Aelred's Guidelines for Physical Attractions," Cîteaux 46 (1995): 339–51.

The same thing happens if we consider the two passages from *Formation* in which Aelred speaks in the third person referring to a monk or to someone "that he knew." These two texts—especially the first, to which all historians accord a certain autobiographical value—reveal at most the particularly high sensitivity of a man who, apparently right up until the end of his life, struggled bitterly to master the ardor of carnal passions in order to remain chaste and who, at least at the start of his monastic life, declared war on his own body, striving to "deprive it even of what seemed to be necessary"[38] and going so far as to seek "nothing more than what would afflict it."[39]

The five autobiographical passages just considered reveal Aelred's inner dispositions at the time of his conversion and cast light on his decision to enter monastic life at Rievaulx. In these passages we have identified three dominant emotions. First, a feeling of inner division, dispersion, and fracture: Aelred feels tossed about, swept away by the current of his fluctuating affections. Second, the feeling of restraint: he feels a prisoner of himself, of his passions, of his bad habits. Third, he feels ashamed of himself and of the involuntary urgings of the flesh. These three feelings combine and lead him to the edge of the abyss. They filled him, he confesses to us, with a disgust for himself so profound that he was tempted to "resort to the worst remedy of despair."[40]

The expression *pessimum remedium* should not be taken lightly. It obviously echoes the *uotiuumque remedium medicinali* that Walter notes in the *Life of Aelred* (VA 4): Aelred chose a monastic life that he vowed (*uotiuum*) to embrace as a medicinal remedy (*remedium medicinali*). This expression left us unsure what ailment the medicine of monastic life could cure. Aelred's own words provide the answer, revealing a cure for a state of ill-being torturing him from within: "Observing certain things about me, but ignorant of what was going on inside

---

38. Aelred, Inst incl 22 (CF 2:69).
39. Aelred, Inst incl 18 (CF 2:67); see also Inst incl 22 (CF 2:69–70).
40. Aelred, Spec car 1.28.79 (CF 17:135).

me, people kept saying: 'O how well things are going for him! Yes, how well!' They had no idea that things were going badly for me there, where alone they could go well."[41]

In other words, Aelred seems to have arrived at a point of decisive rupture, as Lytta Basset describes it, a "privileged moment"[42] in the existence of a man where, confronted with "a test of excessive pain"[43] and exposed to the experience of "meaninglessness,"[44] he can choose between only two solutions. On the one hand he can aspire[45] to death through the spiral of despair (the *"pessimum remedium"* of which Aelred speaks in *Mirror*). On the other hand, he can open himself to a desire to live that is even stronger than the attraction of death. The latter, in the end, is a desire "in which God appears as the mysterious foundation of all things,"[46] a desire that permits a person to opt for another type of medicinal remedy (*remedium medicinali*) by making life a choice, or even a vow (*uotiuum*).[47]

Here again, this is what Aelred says when he states that he felt so much disgust for himself precisely because he began to love God: "I was displeasing to myself," he writes, "because you were becoming pleasing to me."[48] He completes this thought further on:

> At last I began to surmise, as much as my inexperience allowed, or rather as much as you permitted, how much joy there is in your love, how much tranquility with that joy and how much security with that tranquility. Someone who loves you makes no mistake in his choice, for nothing

41. Aelred, Spec car 1.28.79 (CF 17:134–35).
42. Lytta Basset, *Le Pardon originel* (Geneva: Labor et Fides, 1995), 261.
43. Basset, *Pardon*, 261.
44. Basset, *Pardon*, 261.
45. Basset, *Pardon*, 261.
46. Basset, *Pardon*, 261.
47. "The experience of excessive pain opens out on this privileged moment in which God appears as the mysterious foundation of the value of all things" (Basset, *Pardon*, 261).
48. Aelred, Spec car 1.28.79 (CF 17:134).

is better than you. His hope is not cheated, since nothing
is loved with greater reward. He need not fear exceeding
the limit, since in loving you no limit is set. He does not
dread death, the disrupter of worldly friendships, since
life never dies.[49]

A Quest for Inner Peace, Freedom, and Unity

We are obviously far removed from McGuire's psychoanalytical reading. But we are also a thousand miles away from
the historical reading proposed by Dutton. Certainly, the latter's historical research into Aelred's vocational calling has the
merit of attempting to explain it in the sociohistorical context
of the twelfth century and within the framework of Aelred's
wide network of personal relationships.[50] On the other hand,
the hypothesis she advances, that Aelred chose monastic life
because he was motivated more or less consciously by ambition, has no solid foundation at all. No doubt she can justify it
with a passage from Walter's *Life*. The latter, in effect, echoes
the various slanders targeting Aelred while he was abbot, and
notes that among the slanderers "there are some who think
that ambition brought him to the headship of this house."[51]

Apart from the justification Walter alleges in reply to such
an accusation—suspect in its own right by way of the bias
naturally aroused by envy and jealousy of another's virtue—
the hypothesis of ambition as the primary motivation of
Aelred's decision has absolutely no support whatsoever in the
autobiographical passages of his writings. Furthermore, if that
had truly been the case, it is hard to see why Aelred would
have chosen to leave the Scottish court. The court certainly
offered him ways to otherwise satisfy his ambition that were
more rapid and efficient than choosing a life hidden away in

---

49. Aelred, Spec car 1.28.80 (CF 17:135).
50. Dutton, "Conversion," 31–49, 307–30.
51. Walter, VA 26 (CF 57:115).

the cloister of a monastery. Indeed, it should be reiterated that Walter says that at the time of Aelred's conversion, King David was on the verge of granting Aelred a bishopric (see VA 2).

The reasons behind Aelred's decision to enter Cistercian life must be sought elsewhere and found in a more existential framework. Indeed, if we are at least willing to consider the elements uncovered above as determining factors, it appears that in expressing his desire to embrace monastic life, Aelred had a somewhat brilliant intuition regarding what could offer an appropriate remedy for his inner torment. In short, he expected to find in monastic life the means necessary to recover the inner peace and self respect that he had lost (Spec car 1.28.79). This was a path, of course, that he took by means of corporal asceticism. It permitted him to free himself from the selfish tendencies of the flesh (Inst incl 18) to which he felt enslaved (Spec car 1.28.79). But this path also led him through a progressive ordering of his emotional powers. Thanks to this ordering, he was finally able to unify all his desires by focusing them toward God and thus escape—more definitively than his reading of Cicero had allowed—from a state in which "wavering among various loves and friendships, [his] spirit began to be tossed this way and that."[52]

Thus the twenty-four-year-old youth presenting himself at the doors of Rievaulx sought three things: inner peace, freedom, and unity. His quest would be a successful one. Through his experience and his writings, he gave his quest a universal quality and helped others find their way to life and happiness by following the Cistercian path of love. Let us cross the threshold of Rievaulx and, with Aelred, take on the second period of his life: that of his initial monastic instruction and his first responsibilities within the monastery and the diocesan church of York.

---

52. Aelred, Spir am Prol.2–3 (CF 5:53).

Part III

Aelred's Instruction and First Responsibilities

Monk and Teacher of the Monastic Way of Life (1134–1143)

Introduction

In 1134, after three or four years as King David's *dispensator*, Aelred underwent a major existential crisis, leading, in Lytta Basset's words, to a "privileged moment."[1] In that moment, faced with the apparent ruin of his own existence, the future abbot of Rievaulx discovered God as "the mysterious foundation of all things."[2] This discovery of the foundation of all things in God and the meaninglessness of a life not focused on him as its center of gravity led Aelred to knock unexpectedly on the door of Rievaulx. Saint Bernard's white monks had founded the monastery on the banks of the Rye barely two years previously to implant there the Cistercian way of life, probably at the request of Thurstan, the local bishop.

Aelred's action was animated by a desire for inner liberation, unification, and pacification. Hoping to recover the inner peace that his "lax and loose" life at the Scottish court seems to have cost him, he sought to unify his emotional life and, in so doing, free himself from the chains of bad habits and the weight of guilty passions. Thus began a period of seclusion for Aelred, and a time of spiritual and monastic instruction lasting six or seven years, until 1139 or 1140. The period was marked by immense ascetic efforts, followed by immense intellectual labors. It also led him to compose his master work, *The Mirror of Charity* (1141–1142), and prepared him to assume his

---

1. Lytta Basset, *Le Pardon originel* (Geneva: Labor et Fides, 1995), 261.
2. Basset, *Pardon*, 261.

first responsibilities. Inside the monastery from 1142 to 1143 he served as novice master, to whom the instruction of candidates to monastic life was entrusted, and outside the monastery he carried out a role as an agent, executing delicate and difficult missions assigned by Abbot William. These experiences readied him to lead a group of brothers from Rievaulx who, for the third time in Rievaulx's history, founded a new monastery, this time in Lincolnshire: the abbey of St. Laurence of Revesby, in 1143. Then began a new period in Aelred's life when he served as abbot, first at Revesby until 1147, then at Rievaulx from that date until his death.

For now, having considered Aelred's time of personal and spiritual development, let us pass to the second phase of his existence, as a monk in the service of his monastic community. We proceed in two stages, considering first Aelred's period of monastic instruction up to 1142 (chapter 5), and then the time of Aelred's first responsibilities, from 1142 to 1143 (chapter 6).

Chapter Five

Aelred's Monastic Instruction (1134–1143)

The *Letter to Maurice*, today read as a preface to the *Life of Aelred*,[1] was originally composed to deflect criticism the *Life* received when it entered circulation. In it Walter compiled a cycle of four miracles attributed to Aelred.[2] These miracle narratives were intended to supplement those previously related in the *Life*, meant to exhibit Aelred's thaumaturgical powers. The extent of these powers is shown both in chronological terms corresponding to the stages of Aelred's life[3] and in terms of the elementary matter constituting the nature of things.[4]

---

1. On the question of textual relations between the *Letter to Maurice* and the *Life of Aelred*, see Pierre-André Burton, "Walter Daniel, un biographe injustement critiqué? À propos de la réception de la Vita Aelredi. Entre vérité historique et vérité mythique," Cîteaux 53 (2002): 223–67. For a briefer discussion, see Pierre-André Burton, "Introduction," in Walter Daniel, *La Vie d'Aelred*, trans. P.-A. Burton (Oka, Canada: Abbaye Notre-Dame-du-Lac, 2004), 26–30.

2. Walter Daniel, "The Letter to Maurice" [1]–[4], in *The Life of Aelred of Rievaulx*, ed. and trans. F. M. Powicke, CF 57 (Kalamazoo, MI: Cistercian Publications, 1994), 151–54.

3. One miracle per stage of Aelred's life, according to typical "stages" of the time—early childhood (*infantia*), childhood (*pueritia*), youth (*adulescentula*), and old age (*senectus*).

4. In this case, one miracle for each of the four elements of ancient physics: air, earth, fire, and water.

We have already spoken of the second of these miracles, which occurred during Aelred's childhood when the child Aelred announced the death of Thomas II, the archbishop of York, the man responsible for forcing Eilaf, Aelred's father, to resign his position in the Hexham church. Here it is the third story that interests us. Walter states that it occurred while Aelred was still a postulant residing in the monastery guest house. According to Walter, a great fire had erupted and was destroying the novice wing when Aelred extinguished it by merely tossing upon it "a tankard filled with native English drink."[5]

Even if, as Walter pretends, there is more than one trustworthy eyewitness to confirm this story, the question of its factual truth and authenticity are not so important. What does merit attention is the scope and the symbolism here regarding Aelred's stage of life on the eve of his admission into the novitiate. The fire Aelred would henceforth have to extinguish would not be the one devastating the woodwork and carpentry of a building but, as he suggests elsewhere—allusively in *Mirror*, or explicitly in *The Formation of Recluses*—the burning of the carnal pleasures consuming his rebellious flesh, depriving him of an inner peace to which he aspired with all his heart. Thus, as Aelred states, he hoped to "overcome the inflammation of lust"[6] and master the guilty passions devouring him

---

5. Walter refers to an English alcoholic drink. [Translator's note: Burton's original text surmises beer or whiskey; Powicke's English translation of the *Letter* specifies "cider" further on in the passage. I have retained the ambiguity of the first reference from the start of Powicke's paragraph (Walter, *"Letter to Maurice"* [3]; CF 57:153).]

6. Inst incl 18 (Aelred, *A Rule of Life for a Recluse* 18, trans. Mary Paul Macpherson, in Aelred of Rievaulx, *Treatises; Pastoral Prayer*, CF 2 [Kalamazoo, MI: Cistercian Publications, 1971], 67). [Translator's note: Burton discusses the title of this work on pp. 207–8 below, calling attention to the Latin title *De institutione inclusarum*, or *The Formation of Recluses*, but in his text refers to the work with the title of the French translation *La Vie de Recluse* (*The Life of a Recluse*); the title of the English translation is *Rule of Life for a Recluse* (CF 2). In this book I follow Burton's translation of the Latin title.]

at the start of his monastic life by plunging himself wholly into a radical, rigorous, and indiscreet asceticism.

Several textual examples bear witness to the initial unenlightened fervor that marked Aelred's first steps in monastic life. But Aelred soon recognized that such practices could only lead him to an impasse.

A Novitiate Marked with Great Ascetic Effort

We saw that asceticism occupied an important role in Aelred's monastic life as among the reasons that Aelred chose to join the Cistercian Order. Among the characteristic Cistercian traits that Aelred mentioned and praised was what he called, in his novice's words, the "apostolic dictum," in particular the recommendation of Saint Paul, who enjoined the Colossians to "put to death, then, the parts of you that are earthly" and urged them to avoid "immorality, impurity, passion, evil desire, and the greed that is idolatry."[7] Although Aelred does not cite the second part of the verse, he must certainly have had it in mind.

The fundamentally ascetic motivation for Aelred's vocational calling and the moral preoccupation that accompanies it—the mastery over guilty passions—are consonant with what Aelred says of himself when, regarding his conversion, he evokes the nature of the inner torments he was then suffering. We also find confirmation of these two traits elsewhere in Aelred's writings as well as in Walter's *Life of Aelred*.

Aelred's account in *Formation* 18 is as explicit as it can be. As a mature abbot recollecting in his later years (after the age of fifty) the first days of his monastic life, Aelred recounts the early difficulties and in particular the inflamed zeal with which he "declared war on himself" to be free of "the promptings of nature" that tormented him. He writes, "I know a monk who at the beginning of his monastic life was afraid of threats to his

7. Col 3:5.

chastity from the promptings of nature, from the force of habit and from the suggestions of the wily tempter, and so declared war on himself, was filled with savage hatred for his own flesh, and sought nothing more than what would afflict it."[8]

Among all these "afflictions of the body" intended to suppress even "its simplest movements," Aelred mentions food deprivation: "he weakened his body by fasting," starving it "by depriving it of its lawful due." But as that did not suffice—no more than did tears, prayers, and supplications—he added baths of cold water and, following Saint Benedict's example, "rubbed his body with nettles."[9]

Walter confirms these assertions in his own narrative. He devotes chapters 8–13 of the *Life* to Aelred's initial monastic instruction: reading, meditation, and prayer in chapters 10–11, and then, in chapter 12, manual labor. In the latter Walter underlines the way, despite a delicate physical constitution little adapted to grueling agricultural work, Aelred never spared energy. He put such ardor into his tasks, Walter says, that not only was he able to complete "the labors of stronger and strenuous men," but, further, "His masters" had to exercise vigilance to temper his efforts and "tighten the reins of this most valiant beast of burden of our Savior Christ."[10]

Additionally, the passage in *Formation* where Aelred speaks of the monk who took cold baths is reinforced in the *Life*, which describes the small tank that Aelred built and in which, in his free time and sheltered from others' eyes, he used to "immerse his whole body in the icy cold water" in order to "quench the heat in himself of every vice."[11] The question is whether or not Aelred's efforts succeeded.

For Walter, too preoccupied with showing his abbot's holiness to realize the human and spiritual issues underlying the personal problems Aelred faced, success seems a given. The

---

8. Aelred, Inst incl 18 (CF 2:66–67).
9. Aelred, Inst incl 18 (CF 2:66–67).
10. Walter, VA 12 (CF 57:105–6).
11. Walter, VA 16 (CF 57:108).

intended goal—the pacification of the passions—immediately becomes an established reality in Walter's mind. Whether it was true for Aelred is another issue. More lucid than his biographer, and also more critical of himself, Aelred offers a more mitigated assessment.

The Impasse of Ascetic Excess

If the novice Aelred gave himself over to ascetic excess it was no doubt in good faith, as he was convinced that the various corporeal exercises meant to master his passions—unrelenting physical labor, fasts, and ice-cold baths—would bring him the inner tranquility he desired. But he would soon have to admit that the more he submitted himself to such exercises, the more the peace he sought was aleatory and fleeting, always escaping him in the end. It might be said that Aelred found himself at an impasse, since, as he admits to his sequestered sister, because of such useless and desperate excess he at last found himself in such a state of physical exhaustion that he was forced to moderate his efforts—which then only aggravated his situation: "But when he was forced by weakness to allow himself more, the flesh came to life again and upset the tranquility which he thought he had acquired."[12]

In fact, by the pain of this bitter failure, resulting from a purely voluntary asceticism, Aelred learned to his cost the truth of a severe warning Bernard had addressed to his Cistercian brothers some ten years earlier, around 1124, in his *Apologia*.[13] This warning came at the height of the debate over who most piously observed

---

12. Aelred, Inst incl 18 (CF 2:67).

13. Bernard of Clairvaux, Apo 12, 13; Bernard of Clairvaux, "Cistercians and Cluniacs: St Bernard's Apologia to Abbot William," trans. Michael Casey, CF 1 (Kalamazoo, MI: Cistercian Publications, 1970), 46–50. The dating of the *Apologia*, like the question of its addressees, remains a subject of discussion for historians. But it is largely acknowledged today that Bernard composed the treatise around 1124 at the request of his friend William of Saint-Thierry, to calm tensions in the conflict opposing White Monks and Black Monks on the question of the legitimacy of diverse interpretations of the Rule of Saint Benedict.

the Rule of Saint Benedict: the black monks, who lived "more reasonably [*discretius*]," or the white monks, who observed "more strictly [*districtius*]" and became "more exhausted [*fatigatior*]."[14] The latter were tempted to believe that only a monastic life defined by greater corporeal austerity (in other words, their own) could infallibly guarantee salvation. What illusion and pretense! "How wrong! [*magna abusio*],"[15] Saint Bernard reminds them, for these thoughts are evidence of unbridled pride, and such pretense itself is contrary to the teachings of the apostle of nations. Did he not assure Timothy that only devotion holds a "promise of the life that now is and of that which is to come," while "bodily exercise is profitable to little [1 Tim 4:8]"? In other words, for Bernard, what counts most in the observance of the Rule of Saint Benedict is less the intensity of exterior austerity (more or less corporeal asceticism) than the inner quality of one's life (living in humility and with charity)—*discretius* versus *districtius*. Addressing himself to his Cistercian brothers, Bernard writes,

> By detracting from your brothers, you lose humility in that you exalt yourself; in that you deprecate others, you lose love. These are the better gifts. You wear down your body with many excessive labors and mortify that which is earthly in you with regular severities. Well done. But what if the man whom you condemn for not working may have only a small degree of that which is useful to a small degree [1 Tim 4:8], namely physical work? He may have more than you of that which is of value in every way, that is, piety [1 Tim 4:8]. Who, I ask, follows your Rule better? Isn't it the one who is better? And who is better, the more humble man [*humilior*] or the more exhausted man [*fatigatior*]? Isn't it the one who has learned from the Lord to be gentle and humble at heart [Matt 11:29], and the one who with Mary has chosen the better part, which will not be taken from him?[16]

14. Bernard, Apo 14 (CF 1:51).
15. Bernard, Apo 13 (CF 1:50).
16. Luke 10:41; Bernard, Apo 13 (CF 1:50).

The lesson may seem harsh, but it is worthy for its clarity. In any case, the lesson would bear abundant fruit in Aelred's life.

The Fruits Of Experience

The path of generous but unmeasured corporeal asceticism led Aelred to a bitter and inevitable impasse. He discovered that asceticism in itself could not truly free him of his demons and passions and bring him peace without the accompaniment of an inner process. In other words, he discovered that an outer focus, attempting somehow to exert mastery over the disordered impulses of his body, was insufficient and that it was necessary to dig down to the roots of these impulses to reach them at their source in the emotional depths of his heart. This fundamental discovery was a positive force in Aelred's life, obliging him to make a personal and intellectual paradigm shift whose terms were closely tied to each other. This discovery had repercussions on a pastoral level as well.

First, on a personal level, Aelred's realization of how little peace asceticism really offered him shifted the focus of his struggle from the level of bodily passions to a deeper struggle on the level of his emotional relationships. In fact, he writes once again in *Formation* 18 that in the wake of asceticism and prayers addressed to God, "he was granted some temporary relief but refused lasting tranquility. For while the irregular movements of the flesh died down for a little, his heart was beset with forbidden affections."[17]

This personal paradigm shift in Aelred's private struggle— from an exclusively corporeal view of the question to a more deeply emotional one—pushed him to completely revise his perception of asceticism in spiritual life and integrate into it more relational and emotional aspects. The latter are elements of asceticism that Aelred had up to that point if not totally ignored, at least partially underestimated. By virtue of this

17. Aelred, Inst incl 18 (CF 2:67).

revision, Aelred's asceticism would not only aim to master the passions (a purpose to which asceticism is all too often reduced), but also more broadly to establish correct relationships with himself, with others, and with God.

Accepting Saint Bernard's invitation to seek piety ("which is of value in every way") over ascetic exploits (which "may have only a small degree of that which is useful"),[18] Aelred was led to a profound reflection on asceticism insofar as its purpose must be to help every man and woman "live soberly and justly and godly" (Titus 2:12) in the world and thus support them as they go "looking for the blessed hope and coming of the glory of the great God and our Savior Jesus Christ, who gave himself for us, that he might redeem us from all iniquity and might cleanse to himself a people" (Titus 2:13-14).

Thus concurrently with the personal paradigm shift in his struggle, Aelred was led to undertake an intense intellectual labor focused on integrating the lessons of his experience into the framework of a vast doctrinal synthesis. More precisely, he worked to justify theologically the value of the Cistercian reform from the standpoint of what makes it unique—as a "school of charity" where one learns to order all one's affections according to the "certain measure" that is Christ.[19] The fruit of this intellectual effort is found first in *Mirror*, which we examine fully in the next chapter. Its traces are also found in numerous liturgical sermons, where it appears to have been at the heart of Aelred's experience and struggle in the early days of his monastic life.

We see this, for example, in sermons where Aelred compares entrance into monastic life to a way out of Sheba, that is, a path to inner freedom: that same "three days' journey"[20] that allowed the Hebrews to leave Egypt and escape the slavery and captivity in which Pharaoh had held them. It is an exit from

18. Bernard, Apo 13 (CF 1:50).

19. Aelred, Spec car 3.31.74 (CF 17:272).

20. Aelred of Rievaulx, S 6.17, in *The Liturgical Sermons: The First Clairvaux Collection*, trans. Theodore Berkeley and M. Basil Pennington, CF 58 (Kalamazoo, MI: Cistercian Publications, 2001), 134.

the world, or more exactly from that place of captivity (doubt-less echoing Aelred's life at the Scottish court as he describes it in *Mirror*[21]) where "captives to our vices . . . bound with the chains of the worst habits . . . we were blind and para-lyzed, lying prostrate in the desires of the flesh as on a cot, dissipated and sick and incapable of any good work and ig-norant of the way which leads to life."[22]

Monastic life is thus delivery from a place of captivity, as well as from a place of scourging grace. These places are the crucible of a painful conscience (see S 6.7), where the voice of God began to be heard, of him who "by the grace of his visitation . . . stirred us to indignation at our sins" and "inspired an attachment to worthy emulation,"[23] making us, Aelred says, rise up and take the "most direct way of our Father [Saint Benedict]."[24] Passing "through Christ to Christ,"[25] he goes on, we were led to follow the path that the Rule and all its observances indicate, which under the guidance of Saint Benedict teach us "to offer God spiritual sacrifices, to celebrate the Sabbath spiritually, to build in our hearts a spiritual tabernacle for Christ" in order to become with him "heirs of the Kingdom of Heaven."[26]

Monastic Asceticism and Christian Life: The Monk as Votary of the Cross

These latter statements offer an extraordinary summary of what was, from the time of his novitiate until his dying breath, the most intimate of Aelred's convictions regarding the highly spiritual value of the Rule as a Christian way of life. Intimately

---

21. Aelred, Spec car 1.28.79 (CF 17:134).

22. Aelred, S 4.29–30 (CF 58:115–16). [Translator's note: The first ellipsis is Burton's; the second is mine to fit the English quotation to Burton's phrasing.]

23. Aelred, S 4.30 (CF 58:116). [Translator's note: My ellipsis to fit the En-glish quotation to Burton's phrasing.]

24. Aelred, S 7.6 (CF 58:143).

25. Aelred, S 7.5 (CF 58:143).

26. Aelred, S 6.10 (CF 58:132).

bound together are the principal ideas that guided Aelred throughout his existence and formed the hardened core, so to speak, of his theology of monastic life. For him, being Christian meant following Christ, and following Christ meant being plunged by baptism into the mystery of his death and resurrection, and participating in the mystery of the cross in order to be freed from the slavery of sin. Monastic life is one path of Christian life among many, and living by the Rule is a way of following Christ. Since to follow Christ is to participate in the mystery of his cross, embracing the Rule and its observance as a way of Christian life is at the same time to "take up the cross" and to embrace it as a way of life.[27] In other words, as Aelred asserted, the monastic Rule makes the person who vows to embrace it as a Christian "rule of life" not only one who adores the cross but also far more than that—it makes that person one who has "made profession on it."[28] This short expression sums up in a few words what Aelred had already expressed in much greater detail in *Mirror:*

> To share in the sufferings of Christ means to submit to regular discipline, to mortify the flesh by abstinence, vigils, and toil, to submit one's will to another's judgement, to prefer nothing to obedience, and—to sum up many things in a few words—to follow to the limit our profession, which we have made according to the Rule of Saint Benedict. This is to share in the sufferings of Christ, as our Lawgiver bore witness when he said: *And so, persevering in the monastery until the end, let us share in the sufferings of Christ by patience, that we may deserve to share in his kingdom.*[29]

---

27. Such an idea could not help but speak to the heart of young generations in Aelred's time. This was, in fact, the usual expression designating those who "took up the cross" to go to Jerusalem.

28. A famous expression from S 10.29 (CF 58:180). For a more detailed study of this question, see Pierre-André Burton, "Contemplation et imitation de la Croix: un chemin de perfection chrétienne et monastique d'après le *Miroir,*" Coll 55 (1993): 140–68.

29. See RB 50; Aelred, Spec car 2.15 (CF 17:173–74).

Elaborated soon thereafter, this doctrinal synthesis, centered on communion with the mystery of Christ's passion, had the advantage of joining the Scottish royal family's devotion to the holy cross, transmitted to Aelred by King David,[30] with the best of the ancient monastic heritage offered to Aelred during his initial instruction. The latter included the Rule, of course, but also the teaching of John Cassian on the threefold renunciation of the world and the spiritual combat against the passions and improper thoughts. This classical doctrine always remained for Aelred an uncontested and uncontestable source of inspiration, even if, as it has recently been shown, his own freedom of thought often distanced his ideas from it.[31]

The Summit of Contemplative Life: Theology of the Cross and *Intentio Cordis*

Walter understood that Aelred's personal experience and monastic spirituality were rooted in a theology of the cross, centered on the person of Christ and the mystery of his incarnation, passion, and resurrection. Walter situated Aelred's entire life from beginning to end between two scenes that express Aelred's attachment and adherence to the cross of Jesus.

Walter Daniel's Testimony—Chapters 10 and 54 of The Life of Aelred

Of the nature and the content of Aelred's prayers during his novitiate, Walter writes, "The force of his mind was directed

---

30. See chap. 3 of the present work, devoted to Aelred's time at the Scottish court.

31. For Aelred's free use of ancient sources, and in particular Cassian's ascetic doctrine of the struggle against the passions, see Elias Dietz, "Aelred on the Capital Vices: a Unique Voice among the Cistercians," CSQ 43 (2008): 271–93. On the importance of Cassian as a fundamental and explicit reference in Aelred's writings, see in particular Spec car 3.33.79 (CF 17:277), where Aelred refers his reader to book IV of Cassian's *De institutis coenobiorum.*

where there are no passing things to flow by, no vain things to end in smoke, where the things that perish make no clamor and hurtful things do not take their stand. The whole strength of his mind was poured out like a flood upon God and his Son; it was as though he had fastened to the crucified Christ a very long thread whose end he had taken back as far as the seat of God the Father." Immediately afterward he underlines this fundamental orientation of Aelred's heart: "By this thread I mean the strain and concentrated vigor of his mental being [*intentionem eius; acumen intellectus*]."[32]

Describing a scene from just a few days before Aelred's death on January 7, 1167, which Walter says he observed with great emotion and "inspired awe," he went on to report the unceasing prayer that Aelred, with his eyes fixed on the cross, addressed to Christ:

> For we heard him say again and again, "Hasten, hasten"; and often he drove the word home by calling on the name of Christ in English, a word of one syllable in his tongue and easier to utter, and in some ways sweeter to hear.[33] He would say, and I give his own words, "Hasten *for crist luve*," that is, "For the love of Christ, hasten." When I said to him "What, lord?" he stretched out his hands, as to heaven, and, fixing his eyes like lamps of fire upon the cross which was held there before his face, said, "Release me, let me go free to him, whom I see

32. Walter, VA 10 (CF 57:103). Regarding this "thread," see Pierre-André Burton, "Aelred, tel un second Noé: l'abbé de Rievaulx, un bâtisseur à la recherche de la coudée unique," Cîteaux 52 (2001): 231–318, esp. 284–303.

33. We find here a clear example of the "Invocation of the Name" in twelfth-century Cistercian spirituality. Aelred himself offers examples in his writings. The best-known passage is in the Prologue to his treatise on *Spiritual Friendship*. But the Invocation of the Name is equally attested to by Saint Bernard, for example in his SC 15. Further, Walter's reference to the word *luve* as "easier [*facilius*] to utter, and in some ways sweeter [*dulcius*] to hear" offers some textual support, albeit not definitive, of the attribution to Aelred of the famous "*Dulcis Iesu memoria*" in Charles Dumont, "L'hymne Dulcis Iesu memoria: Le Jubilus serait-il d'Aelred de Rievaulx?" Coll 55 (1993): 233–43.

before me, the King of Glory. Why do you linger? What
are you doing? What are you waiting for? Hasten, for
the love of Christ, hasten."[34]

Evidence in The Mirror of Charity

The intensity of Aelred's gaze upon Christ was a constant
throughout his life. It was the fortunate outcome of his asceticism, a true anchor point, and the theological and spiritual
space *par excellence* that allowed him to reestablish the inner
peace to which he aspired and permitted him to unify his emotional life by freeing it from his shattered desires, thus fulfilling
his deepest hopes at the time of his conversion. Two passages
from *The Mirror of Charity* eloquently attest to this.

Regarding inner peace, Aelred describes a high point of
spiritual experience—the moment when the soul is perfectly
pacified in love of self and the other, and fully unified in the
contemplation of Christ Jesus: "it is thoroughly absorbed by
that ineffable light and unaccustomed sweetness. All that is
bodily, all that is sensible, and all that is mutable are reduced
to silence. The soul fixes its clear-sighted gaze on what is and
is so always and is in itself: on the One. Being at leisure it sees
that the Lord himself is God, and in the tender embrace of
charity itself keeps a sabbath, doubtlessly the sabbath of
sabbaths."[35] A little later Aelred again writes of the *Intentio
cordis*, with Christ in the spiritual ark of the heart, himself the
unification of emotional life; his language remains mystical,
but now also ethical:

---

34. Walter, VA 54 (CF 57:136). A little later, Walter, seeing his abbot on the
brink of death, said to him, "Lord, gaze on the cross; let your eye be where
your heart is" (VA 57 [CF 57:138]). In the preceding chapter he tells of Aelred's
listening to the story of the passion (VA 56 [CF 57:137]).

35. Spec car 3.6.17 (CF 17:232).

There remains yet one place higher than all the others. Jesus, who has both built and restored this spiritual ark, sits there alone in his beauty, without peer. By his gentleness he keeps all lower creatures in order. May he give savor to all of them, fill all with his fragrance, enlighten all, shed upon all his splendor, and bring the whole lower span in a straight line to that single cubit of his love.

He alone in all, he alone above all, both captures our attachment and demands our love. He claims for himself a place in the abode of our heart; not only the most important place but the highest; not only the highest but also the innermost.[36]

Pastoral Repercussions

Aelred was thus enriched by this spiritual experience and by this ascetic and mystic doctrine, conscious of his own difficulties in the realm of asceticism and well aware of the impasses to avoid. He was henceforth able to assume with great humanity and respect for others (for which he would later be reproached) the mission his abbot, William, was prepared to entrust to him—the charge of leading monastic candidates along the paths of Cistercian life at Rievaulx. But as Francesco Lazzari has astutely pointed out, Aelred did this less as a master and more as a witness: "More than a teacher, Aelred is a witness . . . . it is clear that he has experienced the things about which he speaks, that his personal experience is omnipresent, like the source from which flows every thought, every attempt at doctrinal theorization."[37]

But before following Aelred through this stage of life, which made of him a *formateur en vie monastique* ("instructor of monastic

---

36. Aelred, Spec car 3.106 (CF 17:296). For more discussion, see Burton, "Second Noé."

37. Francesco Lazzari, "Il *contemptus mundi* in Aelredo di Reivaulx," Coll 29 (1967): 61–62.

life")[38] and above all an *éducateur des cœurs* ("educator of hearts"),[39] we should mention certain events—notably the death of his father and the Battle of the Standard—that must have touched him profoundly during the period of his own initial instruction and his first years as a monk, and that also must have given direction to his near future, seen in his abbot's early signs of confidence in him.

Two Painful Events (1138)

Already four years into his monastic life, Aelred was deeply affected by these two painful events, both probably occurring in the same year. First came the death of Eilaf. Until the end of his life, he had offered resistance to the episcopal decision of Thomas II and his successor Thurstan to enact the canonical norms decreed by the Gregorian Reform, which relieved him of his curial charge in Hexham and consequently deprived him of the ecclesiastic revenues attached to it. But just before Eilaf's death, Aelred, accompanied by his abbot William, traveled to the monastery of Durham where Eilaf had asked to end his days. There, during this visit—and it may even have been the underlying reason for it—Aelred experienced the joy of witnessing the act by which his father, after a quarter century of conflict (1114–1138), ceded those benefits to the clerics who had succeeded him at Hexham.

The second event that painfully affected Aelred was the Battle of the Standard. The battle took place on August 22, 1138, around Northallerton, about seventy kilometers (forty-three miles) from York and not far from Rievaulx. It represented the English army's reversal of the victory won by the

---

38. Adapted from the title of a classic work on Aelred and Cistercian spirituality: Amédée Hallier, *Un éducateur monastique: Aelred de Rievaulx* (Paris: Gabalda, 1959).

39. Taken from the title of another classic work on Aelred and Cistercian spirituality: Charles Dumont, *Une éducation du cœur* (Oka, Canada: Abbaye Notre-Dame-Du-Lac, 1997).

Scottish troops at the Battle of Clitheroe in Lancashire two months earlier, on June 10, 1138.

In fact, to use Marsha Dutton's well-chosen expression, the Battle of the Standard was "simply"—so to speak—one of the numerous and needlessly destructive and bloody battles that followed one after another from 1135 to 1153/1154. These repeated battles devastated England over the course of an interminable civil war, which, after the death of Henry I, opposed partisans of Stephen of Blois (William the Conqueror's grandson) and partisans of the Empress Matilda (Henry I's daughter and mother of the future king Henry II) in a struggle for the English succession.

There are several possible reasons for this battle's breaking Aelred's heart. Cloistered at Rievaulx, Aelred was a powerless witness to the encounter, incapable of stopping the cruel course of events. Additionally, his beloved protector, King David, as leader of the Scottish coalition, was responsible[40] for the reputed cruelty and barbarity of the army toward the civil populations, indirectly staining his own conscience by his accountability for their actions.

However, all of that is nothing compared to a third point that, like cold steel, must have cruelly cut Aelred to the quick. Sadly, Aelred had to witness a fratricidal war in which he saw rise up against each other not only former friends—thus breaking old alliances[41]—but, even worse, to see pitted against each

40. In the long version that we have of the *Lament for David, King of Scots*, Aelred goes so far as to speak of David's sinning: *Fateor peccavit et noster David*. Aelred of Rievaulx, "Lament for David, King of Scots," in *Aelred of Rievaulx: The Historical Works*, trans. Jane Patricia Freeland, CF 56 (Kalamazoo, MI: Cistercian Publications, 2005), 53.

41. From this point of view, the second discourse in the narrative of Aelred's *Battle of the Standard* is enlightening. It is placed on the lips of Robert the Bruce, who was simultaneously vassal of the king of England and childhood friend of King David. Torn between these two obligations—his feudal oath to Stephen of Blois and his friendship to David of Scotland—Robert intervened as mediator, attempting in vain to avoid the worst. Among the arguments he advances to dissuade David from engaging in a foolhardy battle,

other two of the brothers who had been close to him at the Scottish court. First was the young Prince Henry, who, like his father David, aligned himself with the partisans of the Empress Matilda (for good reason, since David was her maternal uncle and Henry her first cousin). The second was Henry's older half-brother Simon,[42] who, faithful to his Franco-Norman obligations, allied himself to Stephen of Blois, his great-uncle by way of his uncle Robert de Beaumont.

Perhaps his experience as a saddened and powerless witness to this battle at the time of his initial monastic instruction later determined Aelred to push with all his might and moral authority for the reestablishment of national peace once he became abbot. We will never know for certain. What is certain, though, is that the relative political calm that had characterized the end of Henry I's reign and made possible the foundation of Rievaulx a few years earlier was over once and for all.

The period beginning with Henry I's death in 1135 and ending with Stephen of Blois's recognition of Henry II as heir and legal successor to the throne in the treaty of Wallingford signed at Westminster on December 25, 1153, was a period of permanent agitation and civil turmoil. Aelred's monastic life over that span was shaped by the period's turbulent political context and served as the "perfect medium" for Aelred's future vocation as mediator and moral conscience for the princes of his time.[43]

---

he underscores two items relevant here. First he points out that the battle will pit David against former allies, despite the fact that David had always found "their counsel useful, their aid ready, and their allegiance welcome." Second, he points out the risk of seeing the long-standing friendship between him and David ended in death (Aelred of Rievaulx, "The Battle of the Standard," in Aelred of Rievaulx, *The Historical Works,* trans. Jane Patricia Freeland, CF 56 [Kalamazoo, MI: Cistercian Publications, 2005], 261–65).

42. Simon was the older, by the first marriage of David's wife, Matilda of Senlis, not to be confused with King David's sister and the wife of Henry I, Matilda of Scotland, who took the name Edith after her marriage and gave birth to the Empress Matilda (the title she received from her first marriage to Henry V, Holy Roman Emperor).

43. See part V below, on Aelred as the "moral conscience of his time."

Abbot William's First Signs of Confidence (1138–1142)

At the beginning of chapter 14 in the *Life*, Walter speaks of the first responsibilities entrusted to Aelred. There we read the following suggestive lines, echoing what happened some years earlier at the Scottish court:

> While Aelred so prospered in the monastic life his abbot, the lord William, observing his labor and solicitude for the good, determined to admit him to the intimacies of his counsel and to the discussion of matters closely affecting the household of Rievaulx. He discovered that Aelred was ten times as wise and prudent as he had supposed, and that he revealed an unexpected ease in the solution of hard, difficult and important problems. The venerable William had no fears about the good issue if Aelred had early cognizance of a case; for made aware of the facts, he was like a second Daniel in disentangling cases and coming to a prudent decision.[44]

The comparison here between Aelred and the biblical figure of Daniel had already been made in chapter 3 of *The Life of Aelred* and corresponds to the etymological interpretation Walter gives the name *Aelred*. For those who know the story of Daniel as judge of "the chaste Susanna," the comparison's intent is obvious. It underlines the presence of two qualities in Aelred rarely joined in a single person—youth and wisdom (or enlightened discernment). Thus Walter wants his reader to understand that the rare conjunction of these two qualities, which had previously led King David to name Aelred his steward at the Scottish court, is the same as what later led Abbot William to make Aelred a member of his council. Aelred's biographer does not tell us precisely when this occurred, but we can hypothesize that it was early on, perhaps as soon as 1138, and in any case certainly before 1142.

---

44. Walter, VA 14 (CF 57:106–7); Dan 13.

In fact, Maurice Powicke, in his biography of Aelred, draws attention to the probability that in the context of the civil war discussed above, Aelred might have accompanied Abbot William to arrange Walter Espec's surrender of Wark Castle to King David in 1138.[45] We can therefore presume that it is around this date, perhaps even earlier, that William began to "admit him to the intimacies of his counsel."[46]

The Controversy over the Succession of the See of York: Aelred is Sent to Rome (1142)

Events of 1142, however, are known with more certainty. This is the year Abbot William sent Aelred to Rome "on the famous case of the dissension at York."[47] Walter unfortunately offers no detailed information on the exact nature of this "dissension" (*dissensio*) in the *Life*. Luckily this famous case (or *maxima causa*) is widely documented and well known to historians, since it reveals the rise to prominence of Bernard, whom some in the mid-twelfth century began to call "the arbiter of Europe"[48] or "the prophet of the West."[49]

At issue was the unpleasant question of succession to the episcopal see of York.[50] On February 6, 1140, after twenty-five years as bishop and three weeks after resigning the office on January 21, 1140, Thurstan died—the same Thurstan who in

---

45. For more detail, see Maurice Powicke, "Introduction," in Walter Daniel, *The Life of Ailred of Rievaulx*, trans. F. M. Powicke (Oxford: Clarendon, 1950, 1978), xliv–xlv and n. 1; xci.

46. Walter, VA 14 (CF 57:106).

47. Walter, VA 14 (CF 57:107).

48. From Paul Miterre, *Saint Bernard de Clairvaux: Un moine arbitre de l'Europe au XIIe siècle* (Genval, Belgium: Lannoy, 1929).

49. From Robert Vallery-Radot, *Bernard de Fontaines, abbé de Clairvaux: Le Prophète de l'Occident, 1130–1153* (Tournai: Desclée, 1968).

50. See, for example, Powicke, "Introduction," *Vita Ailredi*, xxxvii; Jean Leclercq, *Bernard de Clairvaux* (Paris: Desclée de Brouwer, 1989), 64; Pierre Aubé, *Saint Bernard de Clairvaux* (Paris: Fayard, 2003), 489–92.

1132 had brought Cistercian monks from Clairvaux to found Rievaulx. The majority of York Cathedral's canons elected their treasurer, William Fitzherbert, nephew of the English King Stephen of Blois, as his successor. The election was immediately contested: some suspect that the vote was stained with simony, the worst sin in such matters at the time. Some men—among whom are counted William, abbot of Rievaulx; Waldef, Aelred's friend and prior of Kirkham; and Richard, abbot of Fountains—took the initiative and appealed to the pope to annul the election. Waldef, stepson of King David of Scotland,[51] was proposed as an alternative. The proposal failed to account for opposition from Stephen of Blois, who rejected it. In fact, the tight family ties binding Waldef to the Scottish royal family and by extension to Stephen's rival the Empress Matilda represented too great a threat to Stephen's interests in the north of England. If he had consented to the nomination, he would have exposed himself to the risk of a dangerous collusion between the episcopal see of York and the Scottish royal court. He would furthermore have exposed himself to the very real risk of seeing territory coveted by King David, the target of frequent Scottish incursions, definitively annexed into Scotland. In the face of such an impasse, the northern prelates decided to send a delegation to Rome to resolve the situation. William, abbot of Rievaulx, chose as his representative on this delicate mission Aelred, who, probably because of his intimate ties to at least one of the interested parties, was in a position to take on the role of mediator.

The enterprise seems to have failed, however, since the affair dragged on until 1147 when, after personally intervening before Pope Eugene III, Bernard finally succeeded in placing his own chosen candidate, Henry Murdac, in the position. Murdac was a native of Yorkshire and one of Bernard's former

---

51. Waldef was the second son of Simon de Senlis (d. 1111) and Matilda. After Simon's death Matilda married David, who three years later became king of Scotland.

disciples; at the time of his nomination he had been abbot of Fountains since 1144.

Whatever the result of this thorny question, in which the Cistercians do not seem to have been at their finest and which moreover had repercussions beyond the 1153 deaths of Saint Bernard and Henry Murdac,[52] Aelred returned from Rome enjoying immense prestige. According to Walter, Aelred "expounded the business and brought it to conclusion with such energy, that the esteem and admiration which he won after his return was widespread."[53]

This is not the least of the benefits gained by Aelred in the course of these events. Certainly his journey to Rome permitted him to acquire, or reinforce, a noteworthiness and reputation already well established in both religious and civil circles since his days at the Scottish court. But he also received two other benefits, even more essential to his life—one on departure, the other upon his return.

The benefit of his departure—albeit one not attested to in any available historical sources—is the fact that he passed through Clairvaux, the founding house of Rievaulx, and was therefore able to meet Saint Bernard himself. It is Bernard who, with all the intimidating weight of his authority, encouraged the much younger man to begin drafting *The Mirror of Charity*. The benefit on Aelred's return was probably unexpected: he was entrusted with the initial instruction of candidates for monastic life. Walter reports this with his usual panache:

> It was then that the lord William put him in charge of the novices, to make them worthy vessels of God and acceptable to the Order and even examples of perfection to those who truly yearn to excel as patterns of goodness. This he

52. After Henry Murdac's death, William Fitzherbert was reinstated as bishop by Anastasius IV, successor of Eugene III, who had also died in 1153. Remembered as an exceptional pastor, William was canonized in 1226.

53. Walter, VA 14 (CF 57:107).

did and made good monks of them; some are still alive to testify, as much by the sweetness of their character as by the living voice to his praiseworthy industry. Their manner of life is such that they seem to bear blossoms more dazzling white than the white flowers about them and reveal a yet greater loveliness of incomparable grace.[54]

Leaving aside for the moment the personal prestige that later made Aelred a wise and trusted counselor to princes, it is these two essential benefits—of his departure (his being convinced to compose *The Mirror of Charity*) and of his return (becoming a monastic instructor)—that we will explore in the next chapter.

54. Walter, VA 14 (CF 57:107).

Chapter Six

Teacher of Humanity; the *Mirror of Charity* (1142–1143)

When Abbot William named him novice master in 1142,[1] Aelred was no longer the same twenty-four-year-old who had entered monastic life tormented by a profound existential crisis. That crisis had led him to the brink of despair and finally pushed him to knock at the monastery door in hopes of finding a remedy for his ill-being.

The younger Aelred had been in search of something. He had wished to regain an inner peace that the loose and easy life at the Scottish court had taken from him, and toward that goal he sought appropriate means to unify his scattered desires and put into order what he considered a disordered emotional and relational life. In concrete terms, he sought a rigorously austere and ascetic life that he incorrectly believed would extinguish the burning embers of the passions smoldering in his body, and to which he attributed the origins of his malaise.

Asceticism and austerity—he certainly found them. Indeed, Cistercian monasticism had earned a large part of its reputation from them. In the Order's earliest days this asceticism and austerity frightened many to the point of repulsion, and it was not until 1114 or 1115, when the future Saint Bernard arrived

---

1. See Maurice Powicke, "Introduction," in Walter Daniel, *The Life of Ailred of Rievaulx*, trans. F. M. Powicke (Oxford: Clarendon, 1950, 1978), lvi, xci.

at Cîteaux in all his religious fervor, that reforms initiated by Robert de Molesme and then borne on the shoulders of Saints Alberic and Stephen finally took hold.[2] In other words, upon his arrival at Rievaulx, Aelred found an austere and harsh life made all the more bitter in that the recently founded monastery was suffering from material difficulties.

As a novice, Aelred found something completely different at Rievaulx. His initial monastic instruction immersed him in a long spiritual tradition revolving around the works of three key authors. For the way of life he embraced, there was Saint Benedict's Rule. For a spiritual doctrine to combat the vices, passions, and improper thoughts with which he had arduously struggled by means of extreme asceticism, there was John Cassian's *Conferences* and *Institutes.* Most beloved of all were Augustine's *Confessions,* which, Walter reports, were a valuable and sure guide for Aelred throughout his existence, especially "when he was converted from the world."[3]

Thanks to such masters, and as if in the mirror of their writings and spiritual doctrines, Aelred found the words to unravel and express his own personal and spiritual experience. In particular these masters allowed Aelred to make sense of the stinging impasse to which his unbridled corporal asceticism had rapidly and inevitably led him. Thanks to this life-changing failure, Aelred discovered a major spiritual truth that would mark him forever and henceforth color his personal and humane way of accompanying men and women along the path to sanctification. This truth was that, however important and necessary they might be, ascetic efforts to master the passions are worthless and lead only to impasse if they are not simultaneously

---

2. See for example "Petit Exorde de Cîteaux," in Alessandro Azzimonti, *Les Origines cisterciennes: Les plus anciens textes* (Paris: Les Éditions du Cerf, 1998), 65–66, 67–68; Chrysogonus Waddell, ed., "Exordium Parvum," in *Narrative and Legislative Texts from Early Cîteaux (Cîteaux: Commentarii Cistercienses,* 1999), 199–259.

3. Walter Daniel, *The Life of Aelred of Rievaulx* 42, trans. F. M. Powicke, CF 57 (Kalamazoo, MI: Cistercian Publications, 1994), 128; see also 51.

accompanied by an effort to retrace one's way to the sources of desire. In other words, ascetic effort must include a serious stock-taking of the whole individual. It must include not just the body, but also the soul—and not just the soul in the anthropological configuration of memory, intelligence, and will that the Middle Ages had inherited from Augustine, but also human emotions, a completely new addition to ancient and medieval Christian thinking.[4]

This discovery brought in its wake numerous implications. First, Aelred's discovery as a novice of the emotions' anthropological centrality in the process of inner unification allowed him to proceed to an unqualified reinstatement of the emotions as the locus of inner dynamism or as a spiritual instance essential to the restoration of humankind's resemblance to God's own likeness. Similarly, Aelred discovered for himself, and allowed others to glimpse, the horizon of a reconciliation between the flesh and the spirit, a reconciliation to which he fervently aspired.

Next, in spiritual terms, though closely connected to the anthropological element, Aelred discovered that the best way to integrate the human being's affective instance into the process of inner unification was actually to turn to another person—Jesus. Son of Man, found and beloved in the full depth of his humanity as savior and friend, as the origin and supreme measure of all Love, he was the "beginning, model, and end" of all authentic human affections and relationships. In this way, Aelred gave substance to a spiritual path opened by Bernard, which would enjoy a lengthy posterity:[5] a spiri-

---

4. On this rediscovery of affect as the fundamental instance of spiritual life, see Damien Boquet, *L'Ordre de l'affect au Moyen Âge: Autour de l'anthropologie affective d'Aelred de Rievaulx* (Caen: Crahm, 2005).

5. Among the most famous are Saint Francis, Ludolph of Saxony, and Ignatius of Loyola. On this spiritual posterity, see Charles Dumont, "La méditation selon Aelred de Rievaulx," in Aelred de Rievaulx, *La Vie de recluse. La Prière pastoral*, trans. Charles Dumont (Paris: Les Éditions du Cerf, 1961),

tuality founded on a tender devotion to Jesus' humanity, a spirituality founded on what has rightly been called an "affective Christology."[6] Additionally, Aelred ventured along a path that Bernard certainly knew but had neither fully explored in all its richness nor envisioned as "mounting the steps" to a higher "level."[7] Aelred's path, like Bernard's nuptial mysticism, leads to the most authentic experience of union with God, an experience that allows us to know and resemble him. This trajectory is none other than the path of spiritual friendship. Thanks to his personal experience and to his reading of Cicero, Aelred had felt the value and interest of this path from the time of his sojourn at the Scottish court. But following his conversion and thanks to his encounter with Jesus, he henceforth made it the centerpiece of his monastic doctrine and became its greatest proponent in the history of Christian spirituality.

The path laid out by Aelred, consisting of a tender devotion to Jesus' humanity combined with spiritual friendship as the route to Christian excellence, represents a paradigm shift from the mystical to the ethical. It represents a transformation of the mystical desire for a vision of God (contemplated face to face for eternity) into the ethical aim of "the intentions of the heart [*intentio cordis*],"[8] reaching toward a desire to conform to Christ's likeness for the duration of human history contemplated here

---

republished in Charles Dumont, *Une éducation du cœur* (Oka, Canada: Abbaye Notre-Dame-du-Lac, 1996), 375–96. See also Marsha L. Dutton, "The Cistercian Source: Aelred, Bonaventure, Ignatius," in *Goad and Nail: Studies in Medieval Cistercian History X*, ed. E. R. Elder, CS 98 (Kalamazoo, MI: Cistercian Publications, 1985), 151–78.

6. Anna Maiorino is to our knowledge the first to employ this expression to define Aelred's Christology. See Anna Maiorino, "La christologie affective d'Aelred de Rievaulx," Coll 29 (1967): 44–60.

7. Aelred, Spir am 2.21, 14; Aelred of Rievaulx, *Spiritual Friendship*, trans. Lawrence Braceland, CF 5 (Collegevile, MN: Cistercian Publications, 2010), 75, 73.

8. Aelred, Spir am 3.139 (CF 5:124).

in his humanity, "as if present before us [*sicut praesens*],"[9] "almost beneath our eyes [*quasi sub oculis*]."[10]

From these three paradigm shifts—in (1) anthropology, (2) spiritual life, and (3) ethical action—flows (4) a point of convergence, a principle worth reiterating here since it appears evident in Aelred's theological methodology: there is nothing in the theological reflections or doctrinal discussions in Aelred's works that does not derive from his experience or that is not deeply rooted in it.

This remark is significant for two reasons. First, it shows that Aelred always took care to maintain constant dialogue between experience and reflection—a dialogue by which the former feeds the latter and in which the latter, inversely, dips into the well of the former and finds its validation therein. Second, it shows that Aelred intended his interlocutors to benefit from this dialogue, from the ceaseless coming and going between personal life and doctrinal reworking. This intent is true for those of his time or beyond, for the novices entrusted to him from 1142–1143, or for the readers of *The Mirror of Charity* and his other works.

Composing *The Mirror of Charity* (1142)

When upon his return from Rome Aelred was named novice master, he brought back with him not only Bernard's encouragement, but apparently a direct order to undertake the com-

9. [Translator's note: Burton does not indicate the source of this phrase, though it echoes 1 John 3:2. It does not seem to appear as such in Aelred's writings but refers to what Robert Clark calls a broader "interpretive mode" for meditation: "As early as the twelfth century, Bernard of Clairvaux, Aelred of Rievaulx, and others began to work in an interpretive mode that contributed to the pious practice called affective devotion. It was based on the idea of meditating on the life of Jesus *sicut praesens* ('as if present')" (Robert L. A. Clark, "Spiritual Exercise: The Making of Interior Faith," in *The Oxford Handbook of Medieval Christianity*, ed. John H. Arnold [Oxford: Oxford University Press, 2014], 271–86, here 276).]

10. Aelred of Rievaulx, *The Liturgical Sermons: The First Clairvaux Collection*, S 9.2, trans. Theodore Berkeley and M. Basil Pennington, CF 58 (Kalamazoo, MI: Cistercian Publications, 2001), 155–56.

position of what Walter calls the "best of all his works."[11] Bernard enjoined Aelred to call the work *The Mirror of Charity*, since it would allow the reader "to see as in a mirror what charity is,"[12] "not only because of its worth but also because of the blameworthiness of its opposite, self-centeredness."[13] Walter confirms that the composition of this treatise was contemporary to Aelred's appointment as novice master. Even while giving no date, he indicates that Aelred undertook the task "during this same time."[14]

Moreover, the exchange of correspondence between master and disciple in the form of two published letters (one from Bernard, one from Aelred), and Aelred's care following the suggestion of his correspondent to reproduce this exchange in the Preface to his treatise in order "to spare your modesty,"[15] seem to attest to the fact that Bernard was the "instigator" of the work, as others have written.[16] This exchange between the two men has caught the attention of historians and raises at least three questions.

Question One: Was Bernard the Instigator of Mirror?

The first question is whether Bernard was truly the instigator of *Mirror*. Taking the text of Bernard's letter to Aelred at face value leads us to believe this is the case. A simple list of injunctive verbs employed by Bernard seems to support this— Bernard "asked [*rogavi*]," "ordered [*immo praecepi*]," "adjured [*immo adjuravi*]," and finally "commands [*praecipio*]" Aelred not to "put off jotting [something] down on the excellence of

11. Walter, VA 17 (CF 57:109).

12. Bernard of Clairvaux, Pref Ep 5, in Aelred of Rievaulx, *The Mirror of Charity*, trans. Elizabeth Connor, CF 17 (Kalamazoo, MI: Cistercian Publications, 1990), 71.

13. Aelred, Pref B 4 (CF 17:7175).

14. Walter, VA 17 (CF 57:108).

15. Bernard, Pref Ep 6 (CF 17:71–72)

16. André Wilmart, "L'instigateur du Speculum Caritatis," RAM 14 (1933): 369–94, 429.

charity, its fruit and its proper ordering."[17] However, a closer reading of Bernard's letter to Aelred and of the latter's reply invites us to nuance this first assessment somewhat. When Bernard writes "I command you," telling Aelred to jot down the substance of his "prolonged meditation,"[18] it is clear that the reflections Aelred is enjoined to write are not recent, as is confirmed by Aelred's own reply, where he states that to compose *The Mirror of Charity* he had to pull together scattered reading notes taken over a long stretch of time, some of which he had already included in letters to his most reverend prior, Hugh, then absent from Rievaulx:

> So then, with the goal of undertaking the present work, I have selected material intended for it, some from my own meditations, some as if mine, yet even more mine, because I dictated them from time to time to be communicated to my very reverend prior, Hugh, who is closer to me than I am to myself. Then, inserting these different notes where they seemed to fit in best, I divided the whole work into three parts.[19]

This admission is important, as it permits us to narrow down the role Bernard played in the composition of *Mirror*. While he certainly was the "instigator" of the treatise, it was not in the sense of ordering Aelred to initiate reflection on the topic but in inciting Aelred to gather together reflections begun long before and to organize them for official publication.[20] At the same time Bernard was prepared to offer Aelred the sheltering

---

17. Bernard, Pref Ep 1, 6 (CF 17:69, 71) [emendation in CF 17].

18. Bernard, Pref Ep 6 (CF 17:71).

19. Aelred, Pref B 4 (CF 17:74–75).

20. This question was the subject of a detailed study: Jean Leclercq, "Les deux rédactions de la lettre de saint Bernard à Aelred de Rievaulx," in *Recueil d'études sur saint Bernard et ses écrits* (Rome: Ed. di Storia et Letteratura, 1987), 301–15. See also Jean Leclercq, *Nouveau visage de Bernard de Clairvaux: Approches psycho-historiques* (Paris: Les Éditions du Cerf, 1976), 41–42.

pretext of obedience, thus assuming full moral responsibility for the work.[21]

A Subsidiary Question

This conclusion reopens the debate and raises two other questions. If Bernard was the instigator of *Mirror* in the sense just specified, what incited him to press Aelred so hard, going so far as to multiply injunctions that in his own mind brooked no refusal? Independent of any psycho-historical reading of Bernard's letter to Aelred, it seems, given the content and the persuasive tone with which it was composed, that Bernard had serious reasons for being so insistent. What were they?

A Third Question, No Less Important

This inquiry also raises another related question. It is one thing to see that Bernard ardently wanted *Mirror* published. It is another thing, however, to see that he desired Aelred himself—and apparently no other—to undertake the task. Was there truly no one else who could bring this project to term? Why him and no other, when Aelred admits that he feels unqualified, writing, "when I came from the kitchens [at the Scottish court] to the desert [the monastery of Rievaulx], I changed my place but not my station."[22]

Many questions have been raised by this protestation of humility, and recent inquiries examine exactly how much trust should be accorded to it.[23] Should it be taken at face value, at the risk of gravely misassessing Aelred's true intellectual

21. Bernard, Pref Ep 6 (CF 17:71).

22. Aelred, Pref B 2 (CF 17:74). The bracketed annotations are in Burton's original text and do not appear in the English translation.

23. Pierre-André Burton, "Aelred de Rievaulx: An Illiterate, or a True Master of Spiritual Teaching?" in *A Companion to Aelred of Rievaulx (1110–1167),* ed. Marsha L. Dutton (Leuven: Brill, 2017), 197–220.

aptitudes? Or on the contrary, should one interpret it, as we do, as being at least in part a rhetorical or literary game, a friendly oratory joust between an older, experienced master and a young, very promising disciple?

Whatever the answer is to this question—a question to which we have already attempted to provide some solution[24]—one thing at least is certain. In the same way that Bernard had his reasons for wanting *The Mirror of Charity* to be published, he also had his reasons for wanting Aelred alone to take charge of it, in spite of Aelred's repeated protestations of humility. All that remain for us to uncover, in both cases, are the reasons for Saint Bernard's wishes.

We proceed in three stages. First we attempt to elucidate the question of why Bernard was so intent on *The Mirror of Charity's* publication, and we seek the answer in the context of the Cistercian Order's situation at the time Bernard enjoined Aelred to undertake the task. Then we try to answer the question of why Bernard assigned the task to Aelred rather than to anyone else. The answers to these two questions allow us in the final stage to summarize three key elements that structure Aelred's masterful treatise.

Why *The Mirror of Charity* Was Written: A Second *Apologia*?

The first question to be answered is why Bernard was so intent in demanding that Aelred compose *Mirror*. Charles Dumont examined this question in 1992 in a conference talk with the evocative title "Pourquoi *Le Miroir de la charité* a-t-il été publié?" ("Why was *The Mirror of Charity* published?").[25] He explores at length why it seemed so important to Bernard that

24. Aelred's intellectual development is discussed in chap. 3 above.
25. Charles Dumont, "Pourquoi Le Miroir de la charité a-t-il été publié?" *Coll* 55 (1993): 14–27; republished as Charles Dumont, "Pourquoi Le Miroir de la charité a-t-il été publié?" in *Une éducation du cœur* (Oka, Canada: Abbaye Notre-Dame-Du-Lac, 1997), 237–56.

such a treatise be written without delay. In his reply, he considers the state of the Cistercian Order at the time Bernard gave his directive to Aelred in 1141/1142.

A Brief History of the Cistercian Order in the Twelfth Century

This is obviously not the place to recount the whole history of the Cistercian reform during its mid-twelfth-century expansion. Suffice it to say only that the state of the Order at the start of the 1140s was very different from that of ten or even twenty years earlier. In fact, it was no longer the heroic era of the first legal foundations, during which, in 1119, Stephen Harding submitted the new order's earliest constitutional documents for Pope Callixtus II's approval. Similarly it was no longer the painful, troubled era around 1124, during which certain adherents of traditional Benedictine monasticism launched virulent attacks against the Cistercians, certain Cistercians proudly boasted of the greater austerity of their way of life, and William of Saint-Thierry wisely informed Saint Bernard of the situation's gravity and invited the latter to compose the *Apologia*[26] with a view to calming tensions that risked becoming mutual anathema.

Fortunately, around 1130, attitudes calmed and the undisguised hostility and open rivalries characterizing the preceding decade were no longer to be seen. Now enjoying full ecclesiastical legitimacy thanks to Stephen Harding, and benefiting from a growing influence thanks to the increasing personal prestige of Bernard—then becoming a "beacon for his time"[27]—the Cistercian Order of the early 1130s experienced a period of extraordinary expansion. "Shining like the morning

---

26. On the *Apologia*, see above, chap. 5. For a broader angle of approach, see also Conrad Rudolph, *"The Things of Greater Importance": Bernard of Clairvaux's Apologia and the Medieval Attitude Toward Art* (Philadelphia: University of Pennsylvania, 1990). See also Adriaan H. Bredero, *Cluny et Cîteaux aux XII* *siècle: L'histoire d'une controverse monastique* (Amsterdam: APA-Holland University Press, 1985).

27. After the lovely expression from a hymn for the Feast of Saint Bernard.

star,"[28] the Order was admired by all. Some admired it as a source of internal renovation toward the time-tested way of life of ancient monasticism; others, in new religious orders, admired it as an inspirational model for their own constitutions, as seen for example in the secession of Saint Mary's of York and the founding of Rievaulx. It was also an era when men like the Benedictine William of Saint-Thierry, for example, presided over congregational chapters with the stated goal of promoting within them a course of reforms inspired by Cîteaux. Thus, as Jean Leclercq correctly writes, as far as all these traditional and recent groups were concerned, Bernard played a role first as doctrinal and emotional motivator and second as institutional reformer.[29]

Some ten years later, at the start of the 1140s, when Bernard asked Aelred to compose *Mirror*, Bernard was trying to manage the consequences of such influence. Victim of his success, paying the price of his glory, the Cistercian Order had to deal with an unexpected flood of new recruits. Some requested the complete affiliation of an entire monastic congregation, others sought to integrate the Cistercian reform into their particular abbey, and finally some desired an individual *transitus*, asking permission to leave their current institution in order to enter a Cistercian monastery.

The Challenges Posed by the New Phenomenon of the Transitus

The *transitus* was a new phenomenon that posed enormous challenges. The first was on a canonical level. Until the end of the eleventh century, Western religious life was almost exclu-

---

28. After the title of the bull *Fulgens sicut stella matutina*, issued July 12, 1335, by Cistercian Pope Benedict XII (Jacques Fournier, 1285–1342, former Cistercian monk from Boulbone, then abbot of Fontfroide, elected pope in 1334), who honored the resplendent virtues of his order, "brilliant like the morning star."

29. See Leclercq, *Nouveau visage*, 59.

sively monastic in nature and inspired by Benedictine principles. Religious life had a rather homogenous quality, and it
was therefore easy to pass from one institution to another because the observational differences that might have existed
between institutions were insignificant. When a monk wished
to change religious houses, it sufficed to apply Benedict's principles on the matter, which, accepted by all, required nothing
more than the prior approval of the superiors of the two houses
in question.

But starting in the twelfth century, and for the first time in
Church history, there was such a diversity of institutions and
forms of religious life that it was no longer possible to stick
solely to the instructions furnished by the Rule of Benedict.
Henceforth, other criteria had to be considered, which Bernard,
taught by the experience of his youth and past mistakes, attempted to educe in a treatise composed at the start of the
1140s, his *Book on Precept and Dispensation*.[30] Steering clear of
all formalism and legalism, using his theology of freedom (*On
Grace and Free Choice*) and mysticism (*Sermons on the Song of
Songs*) as a foundation, he addressed the question of monastic
observances and by extension the issue of *transitus*.

But instead of treating the subject with the polemical tone
used in the *Apologia* some fifteen years earlier, Bernard now
considered it from the perspective of a spiritual theologian of
canon law. Thus instead of holding to the "sacramentalizing"
perspective adhered to by Peter the Venerable, who thought
that a monk's mere presence in a monastery was salutary because the monastery was objectively a place of salvation working with an *ex opere operato* efficacy, Bernard deliberately shifted
the focus of the debate. While not excluding this sacramental
perspective, he nevertheless resituated the issue in terms of
personal conscience and showed that in order to adequately

30. Bernard of Clairvaux, "Monastic Obligations and Abbatial Authority:
St Bernard's *Book on Precept and Dispensation*," trans. Conrad Greenia, CF 1
(Spencer, MA: Cistercian Publications, 1970), 71–150.

address the question of monastic observances, it was impera-
tive to establish a close correlation between purity of the Rule
(to be scrupulously observed, albeit with those dispensations
demanded by the principle of charity) and purity of the heart
and conscience (borrowing the image of the "lightsome eye"
from Matthew 6:22) that freely, voluntarily, responsibly, and
joyously embrace the rule.

Saint Bernard's displacement of the question is of considerable importance, because as Françoise Callerot eloquently puts
it, by emphasizing the free commitment of personal conscience,
Bernard established "a pedigree for spiritual discernment."[31]

Thus elevated solely in terms of general principles directing
spiritual discernment, the debate as reformulated by Bernard
was not directly able to resolve another more crucial and existential challenge arising from the context of early monastic instruction. In the wake of the *transitus* phenomenon, the Cistercian
Order was faced with the great difficulties these recruits found
in adapting to Cistercian life. Having embraced Cistercian life
in the wake of a less austere existence, these monks now felt the
hard rigors of the Rule not as a "sweet yoke" and "light burden"
(Matthew 11:30) but rather as a weight too heavy and difficult
to bear. This discomfiture led to criticism, this time from within
the Order itself, of the community's extreme austerity, which
came to be seen as an obstacle to the full development of that
very charity toward which the institution pretended to aspire.

Dumont has proposed the likely hypothesis that, faced with
the threat these internal criticisms represented to the Order,
Saint Bernard felt it urgent to counter them with a firm and
solidly argued reply. In the vein of a second *Apologia*, the reply
was intended to assert the value of Cistercian life on theological grounds by demonstrating, through Scripture, "its per-

---

31. *ses lettres de noblesse au discernement spirituel.* For these considerations,
see Leclercq, *Nouveau visage*, 59; and Françoise Callerot, Introduction to Bernard de Clairvaux, *Sur le précept et la dispense* (Paris: Les Éditions du Cerf,
2000), 21–140. See also Jean-Pierre Torrell and Denise Bouthillier, *Pierre le
Vénérable, abbé de Cluny: Le courage dans la mesure* (Chambray: CLD, 1988).

fect cohesion and the harmonious ordering of its observances, tending toward a single goal: the acquisition of charity."[32]

It seems Bernard wanted specifically to entrust the theological justification of Cistercian monasticism to Aelred. This desire comes out fairly clearly in the letter Bernard wrote to Aelred enjoining him to compose *Mirror*, which can be read as a charge:

> I command you, then, . . . to the extent that these things have been remarked to you in prolonged meditation, not to put off jotting [something] down on the excellence of charity, its fruit and its proper ordering. Thus in this work of yours let us be able to see as in a mirror what charity is, how much sweetness there is in its possession, how much oppression is felt in self-centeredness, which is its opposite, how *affliction of the outer man [afflictio hominis exterioris] does not, as some think, decrease, but rather increases the very sweetness of charity*, and finally what kind of discretion should be shown in its practice.[33]

Aelred fully accepts this charge when in the letter he addresses to Bernard in reply he reveals the outline he will follow in the composition of his treatise: "in the first book my painstaking intention was to recommend especially the excellence of charity, not only because of its worth but also because of the blameworthiness of its opposite, self-centeredness; *in the second book, to reply to the inappropriate complaints of certain people*; and in the third, to show how charity should be practised."[34]

---

32. *sa parfaite cohésion et l'ordination harmonieuse de ses observances vers le but unique de l'acquisition de la charité.* For more on this paragraph and the thesis that *Mirror* should be read as a second *Apologia*, destined to silence internal critics of the Cistercian Order's extreme austerity, see Dumont, "Pourquoi le Miroir?" as well as Callerot, Introduction, 24. See also Pierre-André Burton, "Le Miroir de la charité ou les trois premiers cercles de l'amour," Coll 64 (2002): 80–82. For the last expression, see Dumont, "Pourquoi le Miroir?" 246–47, 339.

33. Bernard, Pref Ep 6 (CF 17:71).

34. Aelred, Pref B 4 (CF 17:75); Burton's emphasis.

Why Bernard So Strongly Desired Aelred to Write *Mirror*

Now knowing why and in what context *Mirror* was composed, we still have to elucidate the second question of why Bernard so fervently wished to entrust its composition to Aelred rather than to anyone else. The question is far from superfluous. Leclercq appropriately posed it in his commentary on Bernard's letter to Aelred. There Leclercq shows how Bernard exercises the full weight of his prestige and moral authority, employing multiple injunctions demanding that Aelred not shelter behind the pretense of an inability to write. Leclercq hypothesizes that Bernard asked Aelred to be the author of *Mirror* because he was sure to find in Aelred a defender of his own vision of monasticism.[35]

This possibility is certainly the case, but it is possible to go a step further and advance two additional motivations behind Bernard's insistence. If one accepts the hypothesis that Aelred passed through Clairvaux on his way to Rome in 1141, one can realistically imagine that he took advantage of this passage to meet Bernard and have a personal interview with him. It is also possible that on this occasion Aelred spoke not only of his own spiritual itinerary, but also of his meditations on the subject of charity and on questions such as how to allay suspicions directed against the Cistercian *conversatio* and its extreme aus-

---

35. Leclercq writes: "In this letter [from Bernard to Aelred], Bernard refutes each of the objections offered [by the young monk of Rievaulx] to refuse [to draft *Mirror*]. Bernard's insistence may have had circumstantial motives, but it must also have more profound and constant motivations. For what reason does he demand of Aelred an obedience that brooks no refusal? What he consciously hopes to obtain is a text appropriate for the benefit of his novices. But are there not also unconscious motivations driving him to desire that Aelred write it? There are many different ways of usefully writing on such a subject. However, with Aelred, Bernard was certain that the work would be in line with what he himself taught, and that it would conform to the ideal of the monastic reform he intended to promote" (Leclercq, "Deux rédactions," 314; emendations by Burton).

terity. Aelred already understood from experience the gravity of these questions, and he must have known they were troubling Saint Bernard's heart and mind as well.

We would like to imagine that it was at this providential meeting with Aelred in 1142 that Bernard acquired the firm certainty that Aelred shared his convictions on an ideal of monastic reform that Bernard himself had been promoting for roughly twenty-five years. But there is more to it than this. Bernard probably also realized that entrusted with the task of defending this ideal of Cistercian life, Aelred would undertake it specifically on the terrain where Bernard had always wanted to situate it—in the realm of experience. To start with, Bernard must have quickly understood that Aelred could only speak from experience. On the one hand this advantage was because Aelred's lack of scholastic university education removed any danger of a bookish delivery of his teachings, a didactic style that Bernard abhorred.

On the other hand, the issue under debate is the very question Aelred had personally confronted from the moment asceticism had become the battleground of his own personal and spiritual struggle. The issue was how to demonstrate that Cistercian asceticism, far from being an obstacle to the development of spiritual life, instead contributes to the individual's inner unification and to the ordering of charity within him.

Thus it is not at all difficult to imagine Bernard's impatience in awaiting Aelred's reply in this debate. In Bernard's eyes, Aelred's answer must have been all the more substantial and forceful for his having come out of such a great trial victorious. Under the circumstances, Bernard's hope must have been great. Aelred's method of theologically grounding Cistercian observances would deliver a decisive blow against all the incriminations that had for years arisen from within the Cistercian Order itself. Consequently, Aelred would manage to silence once and for all the dangerous mutterings that threatened the Order's cohesion and unity.

The Mirror of Charity as a Theological Justification of Cistercian Asceticism

It remains now to show how Aelred attempted to honor Bernard's intimated order. In this third section, we briefly present *Mirror's* key elements and doctrines. *The Mirror of Charity* is a monumental work, whose organic complexity and thematic richness lend themselves to multiple approaches and "infinite" readings. This rich potential derives from several factors, three of which we identify here. The rich potential of *Mirror* comes first from its compositional nature. Aelred presents it as a compilation of scattered notes taken from his reflections over time, as he states in his letter to Bernard. Each of the work's three books presents traces of this fact, traces that appear as seams or joints that Aelred made no attempt to hide. For example, we might consider the long section in which Aelred summarizes in his own slightly scholarly manner the Bernardian doctrine of grace and free will in chapters 11 through 15 of book 1. Even more obvious is the long dialogue between Aelred and a novice, inserted into the heart of Aelred's argumentation in chapters 17 through 20 of book 2, whose seams Aelred himself indicates. Additionally, in book 3 Aelred presents chapters 11 through 17 (*Mirror* 3.11.31–17.40) as a short treatise on different feelings of attraction in which flights of desire originate. Additionally, in chapters 35 and 36 in book 3 Aelred borrows from Bernard's *Book of Precepts and Dispensations* to refute, point by point, the argumentation of a certain letter on the meaning and extent of the monastic profession.

The second element that gives *Mirror* its complexity and makes it a difficult text to read is the fact that it situates itself at the crossing of a threefold preoccupation. It attempts to reply simultaneously to three questions that, while interlaced and complementary, remain distinct from one another, each weighed down by its own problems. In other words, it has three different but interwoven threads of reflection.

First, *Mirror* echoes an eminently personal preoccupation, in that it can be read as the answer Aelred sought to resolve his own inner conflicts. In this sense, *Mirror* illuminates the personal and spiritual path he cut to reconstruct his personal, emotional unity and thus to recover his inner peace and freedom.[36] The trace of this personal preoccupation is found largely, but not exclusively, in book 3 of *Mirror*, which focuses primarily on the development of an affective anthropology.

Second, Aelred inscribes the object of his personal research within the universal framework of every Christian's baptismal vocation, thus situating it in the larger perspective of a theology borrowed from the church fathers (in particular Augustine) concerning the creation of humankind in the likeness of God. This more general concern, grafted and superimposed onto the first, constitutes a second level of reading that principally, though again not exclusively, marks book 1 of *Mirror*.

Finally, a third level of reading centers on the historical context in which *Mirror* was written. We have seen that composition of the work was instigated by Bernard's intense concern that internal criticisms of the austere life he promoted were threatening the Cistercian Order with implosion. In Bernard's eyes, again, the goal of *Mirror* was to silence those criticisms and to furnish a theological justification of Cistercian asceticism based on Aelred's personal experience. In other words, *Mirror* needed to show the Cistercian path as a valid route of Christian conversion for those who took it generously and freely. We know from Aelred himself that he principally, though not exclusively, devoted book 2 to the task of theologically justifying Cistercian life.[37]

Many contemporary readers' difficulties originate when they first attempt to study *The Mirror of Charity* in the tight interweaving and imbrication of these three levels of reading (personal, universal, and particular) and this threefold preoccupation (affective anthropology, baptismal theology, and ascetic and monastic spirituality).

---

36. See chaps. 4 and 5 of this study.
37. Aelred, Spec car, Pref Ep 4 (CF 17:75).

Diverse Hermeneutical Practices

A third element of *Mirror* renders contemporary readers' task even more difficult, Aelred's use of what we may call diverse hermeneutical practices. Taken together, they give readers the impression of penetrating under total darkness into the heart of a dense forest where they rapidly become lost for what seems to be a lack of identifiable landmarks. It is not our intention to present here in detail the various heuristic paths Aelred takes to deal with questions Bernard asked him to examine. We simply point out certain major axes to keep in mind so as to avoid running around in circles. Among the constitutive elements of Aelred's approach, it is important to retain the following points:

In biblical exegesis, Aelred resorts to the method known as "the four levels of scriptural meaning," common to all ecclesiastical and patristic traditions and well explored in the erudite research of Cardinal Lubac.[38] Most important in this biblical exegesis are symbolic readings that transpose what is said in historical terms to meanings tied to spiritual experience. This is particularly true of numerical symbolism (the numbers one, three, and seven occupy a central place in *Mirror*), etymological interpretations of place and personal names, and the interpretive transposition of biblical images and facts. Examples of these include the Sabbath as rest and the three relational spheres (God, one's neighbor, and oneself), Noah's ark as the home of the heart and human affections, the seven-day creation of the world in parallel with moral and spiritual growth (the seven virtues, four cardinal and three theological), the image of circumcision as the passage from covetousness to well-ordered charity, etc.

This symbolic approach, though impregnated with Aelred's style, never strays far from stricter dogmatic and theological approaches with a clearly trinitarian hue and rests on a solid

---

38. Henri de Lubac, *The Four Senses of Scripture*, 4 vols. (Grand Rapids: Eerdmans, 1998).

theology of creation (the contemplation of God the Father, creator of the universe, particularly in book 1), a strong theology of the incarnation (the contemplation of God the Son in his work of redemption, particularly in book 2), and a fervent theology of sanctification (the contemplation of the Holy Spirit, the breath of love, in the work of conversion and unification of the individual, particularly in book 3).[39]

Finally, the work is "irrigated," so to speak, from beginning to end by a nearly constant anthropological reflection centered on the figure of Christ as a man, constituting a moral Christocentrism or a "Christoreferential" ethics, and doubling as a monastic theology. Joining together Christocentric anthropology and monastic theology, Aelred's reflection, like sacramental and baptismal theology, shows that the Cistercian ascetic path contributes effectively and efficiently to the restoration of humankind to the likeness of God. His reflection therefore also demonstrates that the emotional ordering made possible by Cistercian asceticism (anthropology of the *affectus,* or the ordering through charity of the natural dynamism of love and desire) contributes equally to the edification and integral unification of the entire human person.

From a Linear Reading to a Systemic or "Constellated" Reading

Keeping in mind these three levels of complexity (compositional, thematic, and hermeneutical) and the fact that the three interpenetrate one another with a cumulative and mutually enriching effect, it is not difficult to estimate how necessary

---

39. The three-book structure of *Mirror* brings to mind the invitation Aelred addressed in a more mature work (*De Iesu puero duodenni*) to his friend Ivo of Wardon, suggesting that he structure his meditation around three distinct poles, corresponding to the three days Jesus spent in Jerusalem before being found by his parents: contemplating God's power (in the Father), wisdom (in the Son), and goodness (in the Spirit).

a simple linear reading of *Mirror* is in order to acquire an initial overview of the text. However, such a reading remains insufficient if one wants to take into account the multiple networks of meaning woven through it and the internal relationships that each network maintains with the others. We must shift from a linear reading—reading the treatise from the first line to the last—to a different type of reading that we will call "systemic" or "constellated." This approach consists of considering *The Mirror of Charity* as organically structured like a solar system, with a center of gravity or attraction—the question of charity—around which a host of related themes revolve, like planets orbiting the sun. These in turn are rich in their own right with secondary thematic networks, each in its own way forming "constellations of meaning" that pull on each other with varying degrees of power in proportion to their respective zones of mutual influence or their respective degrees of thematic proximity.

Such a reading, even succinctly presented, would be beyond the scope of this biography.[40] However, we point out certain major elements that seem particularly representative of the perspective Aelred brought to his justification and legitimization of the Cistercian way of life.

Aelred's Justification of Cistercian Asceticism

The organic complexity and thematic richness of *The Mirror of Charity* lead us to hypothesize that one must go beyond a simple linear reading of the treatise and undertake an organic, systemic, or "constellated" reading. In the present section we point out four aspects of the banquet to which Aelred invites

---

40. The reader interested in such a reading should consult our own attempt at a joint reading of *The Mirror of Charity* and *Spiritual Friendship*, organized in six complementary circles. See Burton, "Miroir ou trois cercles," 80–104. See also Pierre-André Burton, "Le Traité sur l'amitié spirituelle ou les trois derniers cercles de l'amour," Coll 62 (2002): 197–218.

us, four aspects that are fundamental to appreciating Aelred's justification of the Cistercian way of life on anthropological, spiritual, and theological grounds.

Bernard's principal goal in requesting the composition of *The Mirror of Charity* was to silence once and for all recriminations against Cistercian austerity arising from inside the Order itself in the 1140s. Certain Cistercians, mainly those who had already experienced religious life before joining a Cistercian monastery, judged that austerity excessive. They concluded that, contrary to the Order's officially declared purpose, the "yoke of regular discipline" as experienced at Cîteaux contradicted the aim formulated by Benedict when he instituted his Rule and was far from promoting the development of spiritual life and contributing to the "preservation of charity."[41] Aelred reports this recrimination in the first paragraphs of book 2 of *Mirror*: "But, you say, it is clear that to waste the body away by unremitting vigils, to afflict the flesh by daily toil, and to weaken the strength of one's members by eating very poor food are not only [causes of] not inconsiderable toil, but are *opposed to the charity* you are trying hard to recommend so that, *emptying the mind of all pleasantness, they leave it drained of all spiritual gentleness.*"[42]

Let us consider the full force of this accusation. It struck at the very heart of the monastic institution as proposed by the Cistercian reform, risking a fatal blow to the institution from the moment it questioned the legitimacy of the Cistercian way of life as an authentic path to sanctification. It is easy to understand the urgent need to demonstrate the accusation's inanity; this is what Aelred attempts in *Mirror*, particularly in book 2.

In truth, Aelred's argument is extremely simple, in keeping with the radicality of the way of life that he intends to defend and promote. His reply consists of an affirmation that the yoke

---

41. *RB 1980*, ed. and trans. Timothy Fry (Collegeville, MN: Liturgical Press, 1981), Prol. 47, p. 164.

42. Aelred, Spec car 2.8 (CF 17:168–69) (Burton's emphasis).

of regular discipline is only "a heavy burden, difficult to bear" for anyone who has not yet completely renounced the harness of concupiscence: "I toil, not because I have taken the yoke of Christ upon myself, but *because I have not fully cast off the yoke of self-centeredness.*"[43] Moreover, if this yoke was objectively cumbersome, it is not surprising. Is monastic life not, as Aelred had noted earlier, a manner of communing with the paschal mystery of Christ and therefore participating in the mystery of the cross? And, he writes, "in the cross, of course, there is nothing pleasant, nothing soft, nothing tender, nothing at all delicate as far as the flesh is concerned."[44] Likewise, one who rebels against the austerity of Cistercian life is wrong to do so, he says, since, against the authority of Saint Paul himself, such a one vainly "strives to abolish the cross of Christ."[45]

Inversely, for one who loves and has definitively renounced the yoke of concupiscence, the rigors of regular discipline, however harsh they may be objectively, will no longer subjectively seem a burden to be borne. Regular discipline reveals itself to be like a nest: a place of the true repose of charity and a space for spiritual growth, which gives wings and allows one to rise to the summit of a full life of union with God:[46] "I . . . declare

43. Aelred, Spec car 2.4.7 (CF 17:168). In a similar vein, "those who dispute about the harshness of this yoke perhaps have either not completely cast off the very heavy yoke of concupiscence of the world, or with greater confusion have taken up anew what was once cast off" (Aelred, Spec car 1.30.86 [CF 17:138–39]).

44. Aelred, Spec car 2.8.9 (CF 17:169).

45. 1 Cor 1:17. [Translator's note: The exact English rendering of Burton's biblical reference reads: "For Christ sent me not to baptize, but to preach the Gospel: not in wisdom of speech, lest the cross of Christ should be made void" (1 Cor 1:17). Since the syntax of this verse does not fit Burton's phrasing, I have quoted instead the English translation of Aelred's work, whose idea is the same but whose syntax fits here better (Aelred, Spec car 2.9 [CF 17:169])].

46. The image of the nest of discipline appears at least twice in *Mirror*. First it appears as a place of growth, where the image is associated with the theme of the cross: "Meanwhile let my soul grow wings, Lord Jesus; I ask, let my soul grow wings in the nest of your discipline . . . . Let my soul meanwhile embrace you crucified and take a draught of your precious blood" (Aelred,

boldly that affliction of the flesh is not contrary to the spirit if it is inspired by a healthy intention and if discretion is observed . . . . affliction of the flesh is not contrary, but necessary to the spirit. It does not lessen divine consolation either, but rather, I think, elicits it. So much so that I would estimate that as long as we are in this life these two things, that is, outward tribulation and inward consolation, always balance each other."[47]

The radicalism of this reply might seem surprising. Barely attenuated by the invitation to observe discretion, it seems to take neither human fragility nor corporeal limitations sufficiently into account. In fact, it all moves along as if for Aelred "healthy intention" suffices by itself to unmask "wheeling flattery."[48] It is as if a good inner disposition alone allows one to sustain any form of hardship or corporeal incapacity. Simplistically Aelred states, "this is a toil, not of the flesh, but of the heart, just as it is also evident that the rest about which we speak is one of the heart and not of the flesh, although outward toil is determined by the quality of a person's inward [toil], and it should not be said that there is outward toil if there is not already some within."[49]

Spec car 2.5.16 [CF 17:96–97]). Then it appears as a place of repose, where the image is associated with the yoke of the Lord: "Take my yoke upon you . . . and you will find rest for your souls [Matt 11:28-30]. Look! Here is rest, tranquility, and a sabbath. And you will find rest for your souls, for my yoke is easy and my burden light. Yes, his yoke is easy and his burden light; therefore you will find rest for your souls. This yoke does not oppress but unites; this burden has wings, not weight. This yoke is charity. This burden is brotherly love" (Aelred, Spec car 1.27.78 (CF 17:132–33]). As for the association of the yoke of discipline and Christ's cross, Aelred writes of having "bowed the shoulders of our minds beneath the Gospel yoke," paralleling the idea that a monk is one who "professes the cross of Christ" (Aelred, Spec car 2.1. 4 [CF 17:164]). See also the texts previously cited on this subject.

47. Aelred, Spec car 2.1.9 (CF 17:169–70). [Translator's note: The first ellipsis is mine to fit the English quotation to Burton's phrasing; the second ellipsis is Burton's.]

48. Aelred, Spec car 2.1.3 (CF 17:164).

49. Aelred, Spec car 2.2.4 (CF 17:165).

One should guard against an overly rapid interpretation of these statements, which at first glance seem to have been offered with little sense of subtlety. However, they echo the famous adage of Saint Augustine that "where there is love, there is no labor [*ubi amatur, non laboratur*]."

Furthermore, if Aelred expresses himself here in a radical manner, appearing to tolerate no concession, it is in order to frame his text in spiritual rather than psychological or psychosomatic terms. Because of this purpose, he leads his reader to a fundamental contrast between the governing principles of the spiritual life and the intentionality of desire. It is important not to confuse the concrete, objective harshness of monastic asceticism with the subjective inner dispositions with which such asceticism is spiritually undertaken. This essential distinction prevents us from all too rapidly attributing to the former what is in reality an infirmity of our "intention of the heart [*intentio cordis*]."[50]

It should be noted that Aelred's ideas on the relationship between corporeal asceticism and spiritual disposition would evolve and—no doubt because of his own experience with weakness and an ever-growing compassion toward others—he was led to temper his mindset, which here appears intransigent. Indeed, inspired by the rule of moral discernment established in Gregory I's *Book of Pastoral Rule*, Aelred always sought to join and neutralize, through their respective positive and negative effects, the apparently contradictory forces of "observance without rigidity" and "compassion without relaxation."[51] He thus safeguarded the value and finality of monastic institutions (faithful adherence to the Rule) without in the process ever failing to account for humans' weakness (condescension). He similarly safeguarded the primacy of the person (compas-

50. The terminology is taken from Aelred, Spir am 3:129 (CF 5:124).

51. Aelred, S 3.35 (Aelred of Rievaulx, *The Liturgical Sermons*, trans. Theodore Berkeley and M. Basil Pennington, CF 58 [Kalamazoo, MI: Cistercian Publications, 2001], 103); citing Gregory I, *Book of Pastoral Rule* 2.6.

sion) without in the process ever abandoning the fundamental values of monastic life (severity).

Aelred here walks a thin line. He maintains a balance between extreme moral rigor and excessive laxity at the risk of neglecting the individual and the value of institutional monasticism respectively. Though he moved back and forth between the two, he ultimately, and quickly, came to favor compassion and respect for the individual over moral rigor and absolute adherence to the Rule.

Two pages written by Aelred in different periods but not terribly far apart bear witness to this rapid change of emphasis. The earlier of the two (1141–1142) is found in book 3 of *Mirror*. Here, in keeping with the general rigorous tendency of his treatise, Aelred maintains a reserved stance on the principle of dispensation relative to the common rule:

> We must carefully ward against letting a dispensation—a modification or variation—become in any way destruction. Since the reason for the institution itself is the safeguard of charity and the correction of vices [see RB 47], the dispensation will obviously be reasonable if it furthers this purpose. If, on the other hand, vices are fostered by the dispensation more than by the institution, charity is violated. Even if it may do no harm in itself, the dispensation is surely not without danger.[52]

On the other hand, Aelred takes the inverse position in a sermon for Advent that cannot be dated with any certainty but that, according to a hypothesis proposed by Fr. Chrysogonus Waddell,[53] must have been delivered as early as the period of

---

52. Aelred, Spec car 3.35.95 (CF 17:287), alluding to Gregory I's *Book of Pastoral Rule* 2.6.

53. See Chrysogonus Waddell, "The Hidden Years of Aelred of Rievaulx: The Formation of a Spiritual Master," CSQ 41 (2006): 51–63. Of particular note are pages 53–54, dating the "First Clairvaux Collection," which includes S 3, For the Nativity of the Lord.

Aelred's abbacy at Revesby, between 1144 and 1147. In this sermon, Aelred bases his stance firmly and explicitly on the Gregorian principles of the *Book of Pastoral Rule*. While he does not seek to encourage "self-indulgent relaxation under the guise of accommodation,"[54] he nevertheless seeks to adopt toward others' weakness a pastoral solicitude, a solicitude that he henceforth maintained and encouraged in all of his brothers.

In this light Aelred addresses the "strong" members of his community, who might be tempted to judge their less austere brothers hastily or to criticize their abbot for what might be in their estimation an unacceptable laxity. Even a superficial, commentary-free reading suffices to show the immense shift in Aelred's conception of asceticism and monastic observances over the short period of three or four years:

> You who are strong in religious observance and very quick to embrace all sorts of austerities should be warned not to judge rashly those whom you see tempering their rigor somewhat to the infirmities of the weak. I am entrusted with the care of my brother's body and soul—for I do not love the whole man if I neglect anything belonging to either. If I see him suffering some distress, whether on account of the austerity of the food or of the work or of the vigils—if, I say, I see that he is tormented in body and tempted at heart—for it is extremely difficult for the mind not to be tempted when the flesh suffers grievously—if I see him in such affliction and, although provided with the goods of this world, I shut up my heart against him, how can it be said that God's love dwells in me [1 John 3:17]? Surely, if I always conduct myself according to the rigor of the strong and do not on occasion accommodate myself to the infirmities of the weak, I am running not in the fragrance of Christ's ointments but in the harshness of the Pharisees. They vaunted themselves on their rigorous abstinence and condemned the disciples

54. Aelred, S 3.35 (CF 58:103).

of the Lord, indeed the Lord himself, calling him a glutton and a wine-bibber [Matt 11:19]. What must certainly be guarded against is fostering self-indulgent relaxation under the guise of accommodation. Blessed Gregory's maxim must be observed: observance without rigidity and compassion without relaxation.[55]

In this lengthy passage Aelred opens his heart and reveals the inner disposition of a true pastor, modeled on the likeness of Jesus. But the statements are also prophetic. Walter explains that Aelred "relieved [the infirm] so manfully in their imperfect state," and wrote of his having been "a friend of the sick [and their] physician,"[56] with the result that he was accused of the same charges that had been directed at his master, Jesus, who had been called "a glutton and a wine drinker, a friend of publicans and sinners" (Matt 11:19). His great pastoral solicitude misunderstood—or perhaps envied because of an inner freedom judged excessive by some vis-à-vis the austerities of Cistercian life—Aelred was criticized by certain intransigent and radically rigorous individuals to be "a glutton and a wine-bibber and a friend of publicans,"[57] exactly as in the sermon just cited.

We will take up this question again in the chapter devoted to Aelred's abbacies at Revesby and Rievaulx, since it has recently been revisited by a contemporary historian presenting Aelred as a highly tolerant abbot who accepted even the homoerotic tendencies of his brothers—a presentation based on information given by Walter and on what the historian himself suspects to be Aelred's homosexually tinted psycho-affective orientation. For the moment, though, we return to the essential point of the spiritual implications of Aelred's distinction between the objective harshness of monastic asceticism and the

---

55. Aelred, S 3.35 (CF 58:103).
56. Walter, VA 27 (CF 57:116).
57. Walter, VA 26 (CF 57:115).

subjective inner dispositions that largely determine the way in which a monk experiences and welcomes that asceticism.

Aelred's distinction is of the highest importance, and it is worth examining its originality.[58] The distinction probably owes much to the emergence of individual or personal conscience during Aelred's era. Aelred emphasizes that one's relation with asceticism, or more precisely one's subjective perception of it as a cumbersome burden or a source of inner freedom, is principally a question of one's inner disposition or, as we would say today, a question of intentionality. Aelred calls upon the conscience of his interlocutors and invites them to realign their mindset in view of the choice they must one day make to embrace a life more rigorously disciplined than that of others. That way of life may be rugged, and Aelred's justification of it may seem intransigent. However, Aelred's argument that individuals must look to their own conscience is legitimate and entirely in keeping with Cistercian practices as originally conceived by Bernard himself in the Order's earliest days. Indeed, Father Joël Regnard has convincingly shown that beyond the superficial differences that divided Cistercian and Cluniacs, the question of spiritual conscience was at the very heart of their debate.[59]

The lack of voluntary engagement, and the attendant complaints against the rigors of regular discipline, were perceived by the Cistercians as the sign of a "divided conscience." However, their apparent intransigence (and Aelred's own early inflexibility) regarding this matter was, in reality, commensurate with the total confidence they had in each person's individual conscience and freedom.

From the standpoint of anthropological and ethical reflection, this position marks a considerable shift. The choice of Cistercian monastic life (or, more broadly, any choice) is transformed into

---

58. See Burton, "Miroir ou trois cercles," 90–91.

59. See Joël Regnard, "Le traité du précepte et de la dispense et les origines cisterciennes," Coll 60 (1998): 31–58, esp. 36–37, 40–43.

the anthropological question of the free engagement of one's conscience, thereby constructing an "ethics of the volunteer" as the sovereign criterion and founding norm for judging the morally humanizing value of any decision. This shift would have an irrevocable impact on all later European moral philosophy, and indeed in all areas of human existence.

We have developed three constitutive aspects of Aelred's attempt to legitimize the Cistercian reform: anthropological, spiritual, and theological. These three foci inscribe themselves fairly tightly and directly within the sphere of a general Cistercian spirituality, in close correspondence with the Bernardine doctrines of institutional or juridical-canonical worth and the spirituality or mysticism of monastic observances, as they had been elaborated in Bernard's *Book of Precepts and Dispensations*.

This spiritual and doctrinal connection is readily confirmed by what we call the ethics of the volunteer. Aelred brings this concept into play in *Mirror*, particularly in book 3.36.96–97, which concludes his discussion on the meaning of the monastic profession's formula. Here he masterfully articulates in a single movement all the multiple components—mystical and ascetic, juridical, institutional, and canonical, anthropological, ethical, and pastoral—that lie at the heart of monastic or religious engagement.

The fourth and final aspect involves one of Aelred's own traits, as seen in *Mirror*. The treatise finds its thematic unity in the fact that each of the three books addresses the same question, albeit from different angles as they address diverse manifestations of charity. Book 1 presents charity in the Father's work of creation, book 2 shows it in the Son's work of redemption, and book 3 illustrates it the Holy Spirit's sanctifying actions. All three books present these manifestations of charity from a perspective that is both common and differentiated. They offer a spiritual pedagogy of humankind's return to God, or the restoration of humankind to its resemblance to God's likeness, by the single trinitary path of love of self, love of one's neighbor, and love of God.

The Augustinian- and Bernardian-inspired approach of book 1 of *Mirror* is essentially cosmic and anthropological. Book 2, devoted to defending the Cistercian path, proposes a more ascetic and spiritual trajectory. Finally, book 3 returns to the anthropological angle of book 1, now developing it with an element unique to Aelred's thought. When Augustine sought to demonstrate that man as a spiritual being resembled the likeness of God more than did any other creature, he based the resemblance on the three principal faculties of the soul, which from that time on were to be classic in Christian and patristic anthropology—memory, intelligence or reason, and will.

To these three faculties Aelred added another, insisting more than any of his contemporaries on the primordial importance of humans' affective dimension—in other words, the natural dynamism of desire that runs through their being. For Aelred, this dynamism is a gift from God and therefore a "good of the soul" that is always good in itself.[60] Such dynamism presides over all the inner forces that drive men and women to act, even before the discernment of reason and the consent of the will come into play. In a word, Aelred develops a fundamentally positive affective anthropology, unique in its class and truly exceptional for its time.

The application of this idea to the field of human relations occupies nearly the entirety of book 3 of *Mirror*. This development of the human being's affective authority leads Aelred to consider whether on the road to personal sanctification one must consent to the natural "spontaneous, pleasant inclination of the spirit toward" another human being[61]—and if so, to what degree. Such reflection brings him to enumerate certain rules and principles destined to clarify moral discernment in matters of relationships and affect: for example, the principle of universality (to love all people), coupled with the principle of order or hierarchy (establishing a system of priority),

60. Aelred, Spec car 3.7.20 (CF 17:234).
61. Aelred writes, "Attachment is a kind of spontaneous, pleasant inclination of the spirit toward someone" (Spec car 3.11.31 [CF 17:241]).

founded on the dual principles of ethical proximity (to love those who are close to me in life) and affective proximity (to love those who are dear to my heart).[62] Above all, this reflection drives Aelred to show that if friendship is a privileged emotional relationship between two people, and one that they experience spiritually, it can play an inestimable role in the mystical life of union between humans and God as love.

This is certainly Aelred's most personal contribution to Cistercian and, more broadly, Christian spirituality. Such friendship constitutes an "ascent [that] does not seem too steep,"[63] and, moreover, one that contributes to elevating all human society through love. This elevation is so great that spiritual friendship can legitimately be posited as the true preparation, and a "horizon" in historical time, for all human relational ethics. It can also be posited as a true anticipation, or a "horizon" and "destination point," of all human history, ultimately to be completed in Christ.[64]

All of these points are extremely important, permitting us to elucidate the personal orientation that Aelred later applied to his abbatial charge as pastor of a monastic community (chapter 7 below) and to his public engagement in the socio-political life of his era (chapter 8). For the moment, however, we examine his tenure as novice master.

Aelred: Novice Master and Instructor (1142–1143)

Written in a troubled period while the Cistercian Order was on the verge of implosion, *Mirror* poses a fundamental question that goes far beyond its specific historical context. The question is that of the articulation of the institution and the individual,

62. For more detail on all of the above, see Pierre-André Burton, "Aelred, tel un second Noé: l'abbé de Rievaulx, un bâtisseur à la recherche de la coudée unique," Cîteaux 52 (2001): 231–318, esp. 257, 268–69.

63. Aelred, Spir am 2.14; 2.18–21; 3.133 (CF 5:73, 74–75, 125–26).

64. Aelred, Spir am 1.51–61; 3.79–80; 3.134 (CF 5:65–67, 107, 126). For more detail, in particular on friendship and its temporal order, see Burton, "Amitié ou trois cercles," 211–16.

one always difficult to balance. In this case, the former category is monastic institutions, whose integrity must be safeguarded in all their exigence and rigor, while the latter centers on the full respect owed to individuals by reason of their uniqueness and possible, often very real, weaknesses.

The preceding section demonstrated how Aelred resolves this tension in general anthropological and theological terms, following in the footsteps of Bernard in his *Book of Precepts and Dispensations*. His thought on this question evolved considerably over a very short span of time. He always sought to maintain a reasonable balance between the two polar opposites, condemning the full extremes of both rigorism and laxism. Nevertheless, he initially held strong views that hewed closely to intransigence as he tenaciously defended institutional rigor. Yet he subsequently came to attenuate these views as he progressively privileged a more respectful attention to the needs of the individual, which took form in his pastoral practice.

There were three distinct but mutually complementary branches in this aspect of Aelred's life. The question of the relationship between the institution and the individual exists on three different levels. First it appears in the link established between the individual and the community. In this case, the link is the individual's initial training, intended to help him assimilate the common values of a community and integrate him into the group.

This relationship has two other levels, examined in later chapters. Aelred's concern is not limited to the articulation of the individual and the community. Beyond that, he promotes the insertion of this community of individuals focused on common values into the larger community of faith, so that an ecclesiastic dimension is added to the individual and community elements. By virtue of this dimension, any monastic community, considered as an *ecclesiola* or "small local Church cell," is called upon to be a place of fraternal communion but later to become, for the Church as a whole, what Aelred called the exemplar, or the "near-sacrament of cordial harmony,"[65] that should reign between brothers. In other words, from the instruction of individuals, who were at the heart of the first articulation in being integrated into the community, the second articulation edifies an ecclesiastical community called to be the Body of Christ and the mysterious incarnation of the communion of saints. We examine this second concern below regarding Aelred's abbacies at Revesby and Rievaulx.

Aelred then added a third component to these first two elements, about the instruction of individuals and the edification of a brotherly community as the Body of Christ. This component is the role of the church and specific ecclesiastical communities in civil society and in the building of a just and peaceful world. In other words, he adds a final political dimension to the personal, communal, and ecclesiastic elements. We examine this dimension below regarding Aelred's role as the moral conscience of his time.

For now we linger on the first of the three elements just mentioned, which relates to Aelred's responsibilities as novice master. The discussion has three parts. First, we consult Walter's testimony, which confirms the shift in Aelred's conception of monastic life as Aelred relinquished the somewhat narrow and intransigent rigor of his early thought, marked by personal concerns with asceticism and the mortification of his passions in favor of an increasingly generous pastoral concern for the well-being and equilibrium of each human being. We then consult Aelred's own conception of and approach to his charge. Finally, we briefly consider the space that Aelred as the doctor of spiritual friendship allotted to affective interpersonal relationships—and specifically to friendship—in the process of others' spiritual and personal instruction.

---

65. Christian de Chergé, *Invincible espérance*, 164, cited in Christian Salenson, *Christian de Chergé: Une théologie de l'espérance* (Paris: Bayard, 2008), 142.

Testimony in The Life of Aelred, *or the Emblematic Value of a Triptych*

Walter devoted few chapters of his biography to Aelred's time as novice master—a mere five chapters in all (chapters 14–18). This group of chapters includes Aelred's journey to Rome in 1142 (14), the ice-water baths Aelred took as a novice to "quench the heat in himself of every vice" (16), the drafting of *Mirror* (17), and a long presentation of Aelred's knowledge and intellectual abilities (18).

One might be tempted to say that Walter's treatment of this period is too brief to enlighten us about Aelred's pastoral function as novice master. This is not entirely true, however, for in the midst of this five-chapter group, in chapter 15, Walter inserts a colorful narrative to which he provides a two-part continuation in chapters 22 and 28, relating what must be considered Aelred's first miracle. While not the first in chronological terms, since Aelred had already accomplished two miracles before entering Rievaulx,[66] it is his first miracle realized within the limited framework of the *Life*. The true merit of this narrative resides in the fact that the miracle involves the intersection of two complementary elements that, like an illuminated manuscript, illustrate the manner in which Aelred dealt with challenges presented to him in terms of both pastoral practice and doctrinal reflection at the moment he began to write *Mirror*.

In *Mirror* Aelred offered a justification of Cistercian life, argued on ascetic and theological principles and intended as a reply to the incriminations of those in the Cistercian community who complained of the Order's excessive austerity. The miracle that Walter reports, painted over three verbal panels (chapters 15, 22, and 28), is meant be read in parallel with

---

66. The first of these dates from Aelred's early childhood, and the other from the start of his novitiate, but Walter recounts them not in the *Life* but in the "Letter to Maurice."

this problem and is therefore offered as an exemplum. With these three miniature narrative paintings, Walter shows how Aelred sought through pastoral solicitude to save the at-risk vocations of novices previously instructed elsewhere who had difficulty adjusting to the ascetic demands of their new Cistercian way of life.

The Symbol of Aelred's Pastoral Practice: Aelred as Man of Compassion and Mercy

In chapter 15 of the *Life*, Walter recounts that when for an entire day one of Aelred's novices fled the monastery, Aelred hid that fact from his abbot. The novice, says Walter, was a secular cleric with an unstable mind, "always staggering about, now here, now there, from one thing to another, shaken like a reed by the wind of his changeful will." Severely put to the test by all of this and finally falling prey to "his evil thoughts," the cleric decided, despite Aelred's "counsel of salvation," to execute "the unlawful thing" he had conceived, that is, to abandon a monastic life, for which he now felt such an aversion.[67] Presenting the tormented novice as a foil to Benedict, the veritable sage, "knowingly ignorant and wisely unlearned,"[68] Walter specifies that "unknowingly ignorant [*inscienter nescius*]" and "shallowly unconstructed [*insipienter indoctus*]"—lacking depth of wisdom and the edification of learning—the novice left the monastery.[69]

---

67. Walter, VA 15 (CF 57:107–8).

68. Gregory I describes Benedict in these words in the prologue to book 2 of his *Dialogues: scienter nescius et sapienter indoctus*: Gregory I, *Dialogues* (London: Philip Lee Warner, 1911), 52.

69. Walter, VA 15 (CF 57:108). [Translator's note: Because of differences between the French and English translations of *The Life of Aelred*, I have inserted the clarifying phrase regarding Aelred's "depth of wisdom" and "edification of learning" to render the English version of the text compatible with Burton's semantic analysis of the French version.]

This unstable monk appears on at least two other occasions in the *Life*. The first is in chapter 22, about Aelred as abbot at Revesby; the second is in chapter 28, when he was on the threshold of his second abbacy, at Rievaulx. Each occasion is tied to a major stage of Aelred's life as a Cistercian monk. It is natural to wonder whether Walter wished to present the unstable monk as a living symbol of his abbot's pastoral practices and solicitude, and wished thereby to show, against those who would reproach him for those traits, the abundant fruits of perseverance that Aelred's practices and solicitude nurtured. We like to think that to be the case and recommend reading the text this way.

In chapter 15, Walter attributes the miraculous return of this monk to Aelred's prayer and the "pact" he makes with God: "All day long, after [the unstable monk] had passed through the outer enclosures of the monastery, he wandered aimlessly about the woods until, shortly before sunset, he came to the road by which he had left and suddenly found himself again within the monastic wall." The remainder of the story is nothing more than a transposition to Aelred of the emotions felt by the father in the parable of the prodigal son (Luke 15:11-32). This approach allows Walter to affirm that Aelred was truly a man of compassion and mercy (*motus vir misericordiae et miseratus*): a "merciful man, . . . distressed . . . and in pity for the fellow," and, at the end of the chapter, "a man of mercy."[70]

The First Reprise: Chapter 22 of the Life, or the Infinite Kindness of a Father

Chapter 22 is a sequel to chapter 15. Walter recounts that this same monk, probably one of the group of monks sent with Aelred to found Revesby, "was once again caught in the fire

---

70. Walter, VA 15 (CF 57:107–8). [Translator's note: My ellipses, to fit the English quotation to Burton's phrasing.]

of his former instability."[71] Walter here goes into greater detail than in chapter 15, affirming that the monk's instability derives from a fundamental incapacity to endure the rigors of the Order: "In this same time the same brother to whom I have referred above, he whose soul Aelred had begged God to give him, was again caught in the fire of his former instability, and wished to leave the monastery. Coming to the Abbot he made his application in these terms: 'Lord, my inconstancy is not equal to the burden of the Order.' "[72] Then follows the enumeration of all that in the cleric's eyes makes the Cistercian burden so difficult to bear: long vigils, heavy manual labor, bad food, rough clothing, restrictive obedience, and finally, on top of everything, a frustrated longing for the world's emotional pleasures:

> Everything here and in my nature are opposed to each other. I cannot endure the daily tasks. The sight of it all revolts me. I am tormented and crushed down by the length of the vigils, I often succumb to the manual labor. The food cleaves to my mouth, more bitter than wormwood. The rough clothing cuts through my skin and flesh down to my very bones. More than this, my will is always hankering after other things, it longs for the delights of the world and sighs unceasingly for its loves and attachments and pleasures.[73]

Aelred's reply, while a direct continuation of chapter 15, raises the ante. As superior of Revesby, he can no longer have recourse to dissimulation as he had had as novice master. On the other hand, while he "enters his chamber to pray" and as "the most pious father pours out lamentations for his son, and mourns for the wanderer," he also has two other remedies to apply—fasting, which he is ready to endure even unto death,

71. Walter, VA 22 (CF 57:112).
72. Walter, VA 22 (CF 57:112).
73. Walter, VA 22 (CF 57:112–13).

and, above all, a softening of Cistercian austerity that must have provoked indignation in the dogged supporters of unwavering rigor, for whom it would have been absolutely unacceptable: "I am prepared to give you better food to eat and softer raiment and to grant you every indulgence allowable to a monk, if only you will persevere and bring yourself to live with me in the monastery."

But, as in chapter 15, the monk is once again adamant: "I would not stay, he replied, though you gave me all the wealth of this house." He insists on putting his plan immediately, albeit vainly, in motion:

> The fugitive comes to the gate, hastening to get away, but at the open doors he felt the empty air as though it were a wall of iron. Again and again he tries with all his might to break through and get out, but every effort was in vain and willy-nilly he gets no farther. At last, in intense rage he takes hold of the hinges of the gate with both hands and, stretching out his leg, tries to put one foot forward, but in no way did he contrive to reach even the boundary.[74]

Walter attributes this miracle to the power of Aelred's prayer, while Aelred gives all the credit to God's compassion for the unstable monk.

Compensation for Great Perseverance—the Secret Joy of a Loving Father

From the perspective of the *Life's* literary structure, chapter 28 is chronologically situated on the threshold of Aelred's abbacy at Rievaulx and probably should be read as the crowning glory in the wake of chapters 15 and 22. Walter's major concern in this chapter is to show the gifts of prophecy and premonition with which Aelred was blessed. The premonitory vision recounted in

---

74. Walter, VA 22 (CF 57:113).

this chapter concerns the impending death of the same unstable monk who had been the focus of chapters 15 and 22.

This chapter reports incidentally that Aelred sent this brother (who in the meantime had finally embraced his monastic profession) with other monks from Rievaulx to Swineshead Abbey, also known as Hoyland. Perhaps by assigning him to this expedition, Aelred estimated that the brother, having overcome his numerous hesitations, had now attained an inner stability sufficient to make him an expert witness on the Cistercian reform. Or, if the monk was still tormented and once more tempted to leave the monastery, perhaps Aelred wanted to allow him a change of scenery or, better still, to offer him a monastic experience he might find stimulating and thereby encourage him to persevere. We will never know Aelred's thinking, since Walter says nothing about the pastoral motivations leading Aelred to this decision. On the other hand, the mission assigned to this group of monks is a specific one. Founded in 1134 by the Benedictine abbey of Furness, Swineshead had asked in 1147 to be incorporated into the Order of Cîteaux. For this to happen, the monks of Swineshead had to be introduced to Cistercian practices. This instructional task was assigned to the abbey of Rievaulx, probably by the general chapter at Cîteaux. At that point Aelred, who had just been elected abbot, selected the unstable monk to be part of this group of monastic instructors.

At the end of this mission, when the monks sent to Hoyland were preparing to return to Rievaulx, Aelred, waiting for their return, had a premonition of the unstable monk's impending death. When he was informed of the monk's arrival at the gate of Rievaulx the next day, Aelred rushed to greet him with the warmest of welcomes. There then follows a dialogue revolving around a misunderstanding, mixing humor and friendly jests. The disciple teases his abbot about monastic life, which he describes as a "a death without end which the cloistered always endure," and from which, once more, he wishes to take his leave in order to visit his family, while the master, for his part, announces to his disciple that not much time remained before the latter will die in the presence of his abbot.

Persuaded by Aelred's words, the monk consented to reenter the confines of the monastery. At this, Aelred "rejoiced beyond belief and began to celebrate in his heart a glad, though hidden, feast."[75] Stingy with his explanations, Walter does not, unfortunately, tell us the source of this joy. However, he says enough to indicate that Aelred's joy must have come from the fact that after his premonitory dream, he was now certain that this monk he had had to protect single-handedly throughout his monastic life would run no further risk of straying. With the monk once more in the safe harbor of the monastery, and soon to die there, barely ten days later, Aelred no longer feared for the monk's salvation.

The Honey of Holiness Mixed with the Milk of Compassion

This narrative triptych brings to light a pastoral attitude that was so constant from the moment Aelred was appointed novice master through the remainder of his life that it left an indelible personal mark on the two other ministries assigned to him—first as superior at the founding of Revesby, and later as the abbot of Rievaulx. This pastoral attitude is the same one that he described in a sermon for the nativity of the Virgin Mary, commenting on a verse of the Song of Songs.

Regarding the dual image he reads in Song 4:11—"honey and milk are under your tongue"—Aelred explains that the honey, made from so many different flowers, should be considered a particularly appropriate symbol for the holiness of life, composed as it is from so many different virtues. Similarly, he continues, the milk should be considered both a symbol of maternal love, since a mother gives it to her children to nourish them, and a symbol of compassion, since in giving the milk to

---

75. Walter, VA 28 (CF 57:117).

her children she must bend toward them, exactly like him who out of compassion for another bends before that one's weakness. Aelred concludes that it is of greatest importance that the two always be offered together, for fear that compassion offered without holiness be perceived implicitly as "indulgence [*remissio*]."[76]

It is within this framework that Aelred always defined his own pastoral practice. As Walter clearly illustrates, Aelred never failed to offer his mercy and compassion to the weakest members of his community. He did so at the risk of exposing himself to criticisms from his more radically minded brethren. Yet like the father of the prodigal son in the gospel of Luke, Aelred was animated by an invincible hope that led him to believe such demonstrations of compassion were the means of saving vocations on the road to perdition. At the same time, he was saddened, even tormented, on occasions when this hope was dashed, even going so far as to compare such situations to a persecution.[77]

In any event, as many of his liturgical sermons indicate, Aelred never missed an opportunity to mix the "milk of compassion" with the "honey of holiness"—in other words, to remind everyone, the weak and the strong,[78] in season and out of season, of both the great ascetic demands implicit in the monastic vocation and the high ideals of holiness, charity, and

76. Aelred, S 23.19–20 (CF 58:324–25).

77. See §18 of S 26, for the Feast of All Saints (CF 58:359): "It is a grave persecution to have everyone's care, to bear everyone's sorrow, to be saddened when someone is sad, to be afraid when someone is tempted. Again, what an intolerable persecution it is that sometimes befalls us when one of those whom we nurture and care for and love as our own flesh and blood is so overwhelmed by the devil that he even departs from us or lives so perversely and prodigally that we have no choice but to expel him from our midst."

78. See for example S 26.46–47, encouraging the weak so they do not despair and encouraging the strong so they do not hesitate to push themselves harder (Aelred, CF 58:368).

spiritual intimacy with Christ toward which that vocation guides those who embrace it.[79]

In another sermon—S 24, for the Nativity of Holy Mary—Aelred presents his pastoral ministry in the same, albeit slightly modified and colorful, way. Here he speaks to candidates for religious life who experience difficulties entering the monastery because doing so forces them to resist or renounce the powerful attraction of personal and emotional relationships. Aelred suggests that those candidates counterbalance their "physical attachments" by turning their eyes to Christ, and that they "reflect on him as father, mother, brother, friend. As father, because he instructs us; as mother, because he comforts us and nourishes us with the milk of his sweetness; as brother, because he has taken flesh from our flesh; as friend, because he has shed his blood for us."[80] It does not seem out of place to imagine that in attributing these four relational forms to Jesus, Aelred was merely transmuting into the likeness of Christ the very thing he continuously tried to be in his pastoral

---

79. The sermons in which Aelred returns to this question are numerous. He often underlines the spiritual fertility of "exercises" in monastic asceticism, including the corporeal (vigils, labor, fasting, silence) and the spiritual (compunction, reading, meditation, liturgical prayer). These exercises, he says, purify "the eye of the heart," darkened by vices that "prevent it from seeing the purity of the true light for which it should yearn" (S 24.41 [CF 58:342]). See also the following numerous, but not exhaustive, examples: S 26, for the Feast of All Saints, evoking Gen 27:27-28, regarding the "abundance of grain [wisdom], wine [contemplation], and oil [charity]" produced by monastic asceticism (S 26.33–35 [CF 58:364–65]); S 19, for the Assumption of Saint Mary, alluding to the gospel of Martha and Mary (Luke 11:38-42) and proposing a healthy alternation between corporeal and spiritual exercises (S 19.18–31 [CF 58:268–74]); S 21, for the Assumption of Saint Mary, commenting on Prov 31:13, referring to the strong woman who "sought wool and flax" in order to show the indispensable complementarity between these two types of exercise (S 21.35–45 [CF 58:300–304]); and S 8, for the Feast of Saint Benedict, commenting on Exod 35:20-29 (the institution of "cities of refuge") to show how each ascetic exercise proposed by monastic life can offer an appropriate remedy to different temptations (S 8.13–17 [CF 58:151–53]).

80. Aelred, S 24.31 (CF 58:338).

relationships with the brothers entrusted to him as both novice master and abbot. We shall consider this more closely by examining how Aelred conceived of and executed his responsibilities as novice master.

The preceding paragraph underlines how Aelred perceived himself in his pastoral charge, following Christ's example as an educating father, a comforting mother, a burden-sharing brother, and a self-sacrificing friend ready to give his life and his all to those entrusted to him. In the discussion that follows, we emphasize two of the four traits that seem particularly characteristic of Aelred in his role as novice master, being careful, however, not to lose sight of the four traits throughout the chronological periods. Here then, we speak primarily of Aelred's role as an educating father and a selfless friend, saving our examination of the other two traits—the comforting mother and the burden-sharing brother—for the portion of this biography devoted to Aelred's time as abbot.

Aelred's Testimony: An Educator, a Comforter, a Brother, and a Friend

The first of the four images is well known. It was made famous by the title of a work by Amédée Hallier, who spoke of Aelred as a "monastic educator," an expression that Dumont echoed when he gave the title *Une éducation du cœur* ("an education of the heart") to a collection of studies devoted to the affective spirituality of Bernard and Aelred.[81]

Aelred rarely speaks explicitly about his role as novice master, and when he does so, it is always indirectly, through treatises written at someone else's request. Three works in particular draw our attention. First is *Mirror*, now examined from the narrow aspect of a passage in book 2, in a dialogue with one of his novices. After that come two later treatises—*The Formation of Recluses*, and a meditation on the pericope of Jesus

---

81. Dumont, *Éducation*.

as a boy, *On Jesus at the Age of Twelve*. The first of these two treatises, intended for Aelred's recluse sister, was probably written between 1160 and 1162, while the second, requested by Ivo of Wardon, one of Aelred's older novices, was drafted during the years 1153–1157. The three works share a thematic unity allowing them to be grouped in the context of Aelred's methods of monastic instruction. We could have included Aelred's treatise *On Spiritual Friendship* with these three texts as well. However, it is better to save discussion of that work until later, when we discuss the second element of Aelred's pastoral physiognomy, Aelred as friend.

Aelred quickly came to grips with the dual purpose of the educational task entrusted to him by Abbot William in 1142.[82] Within the framework of Cistercian cenobitic monastic life, instruction focused on two complementary and inseparable goals. The first and more important was to provide each person's human formation; the second was to ensure that each person thus formed be integrated as a full member of a group constituting itself as a community of brothers. In a way, the formation of individuals can only be conceived in terms of its openness to those brothers and its ability to assimilate them into the community that they are to build.

From his first days as novice master, Aelred acquired an acute awareness of this communal end to the initial instruction of the person. He shows this awareness by a particularly telling expression in *Mirror*: "Not long ago, when a certain brother renounced the world and entered our monastery, our most reverend abbot entrusted him to me, meager fellow that I am, for his formation in regular discipline."[83] The expression that Aelred uses here underlines both elements just noted—the

82. All that follows is based on Pierre-André Burton, "Aelred prédicateur. De la visée à la vision ou l'art d'apprendre à regarder avec les yeux dans la tête," in Aelred of Rievaulx, *Sermons pour l'année 3. Sermons 29–46*, trans. Gaetane de Briey (Oka, Canada: Abbaye Notre-Dame-du-Lac, 2002), 7–31.

83. Aelred, Spec car 2.17.41 (CF 17:192–93).

formation of the person and integration into a community—with the one clearly subordinated to the other. It is notable that in the first place, it is a question of transmitting regular discipline to someone, that is to say, in its true sense, to initiate him in the use of all of the instruments that monastic life puts at his disposal and whose use is codified by a rule and intended for a specific "spiritual art"—in this case the one proposed by the Rule of Saint Benedict—and a common *conversatio morum*.

The verb *initiate* literally means "to admit (someone) into" (*in*-itier), and it is appropriately applied to the act of transmitting knowledge. This is all the more pertinent since it is a question of "*intro*-ducing" someone (again with the idea of "admission into") to the practices of monastic "disciplines"—a word that derived from the verb *discere*, "to learn." Thus initiation involves transmitting to the candidate the values tied to monastic life, whose progressive assimilation, interiorization, and appropriation will allow him to share a common conscience and consciousness with his brothers, focused on the same life ideal. It is specifically in this sense that one can say that the initial instruction is systematically directed toward integrating the individual into a community and that, beyond this integration, it aims at the edification of that community.

On the other hand, it is clear that the quality of a community so edified will depend heavily on the quality of each of its constituent members. Thus before even thinking about constructing a specific community, one must take great care in the formation of the individual. Such training can only take place through an apprenticeship in those same "regular disciplines" of which we just spoke. In this context we see the full dimensions of Aelred's chosen expression. Aelred does not conceive of the transmission of values or the initiation of the individual person exclusively in terms of instruction, as if it were a mere question of transmitting simple data or know how. If that were the case, Aelred would no doubt have used a verb such as *docere* or *instruere*, reflecting the attitude of the simple disciple who allows himself to be instructed (*discere*).

However, Aelred never uses either of these verbs, preferring another term, one that can also, of course, connote teaching simply as the transmission of knowledge or a skill, but whose full meaning is far broader. Aelred literally affirms that a brother was entrusted to him by his abbot "for his formation in regular discipline,"[84] using the Latin word *instituendus (disciplinis regularibus instituendus)*. On close consideration, this expression can be taken in two different but complementary ways. Aelred shows himself to be profoundly convinced of the eminent value of monastic discipline in terms of both instructing and structuring individuals so that they might grow in human dignity. He believes this to such an extent that the very act of *institution* consists of both establishing (by the term's Latin etymology) individuals in their personal identity and using regular observances as an institutional tool (by the term's connotation as community) specially adapted to this end.[85] In short, instructing someone in monastic life is to "institute" him in this dual manner.[86]

Although this conception of monastic instruction dates from the very start of Aelred's pastoral ministry as novice master,

84. Aelred, Spec car 2.17.41 (CF 17:192–93). [Translator's Note: Burton's analysis focuses on the French translation *instituer* of the Latin *instituendus*, which is most closely but not exactly echoed by *formation* in the English translation. I therefore added more explicit references to the Latin than appear in Burton's text, since these are necessary in English to follow Burton's analysis.]

85. [Translator's note: The parenthetical references are my own, again because the English translation of Aelred's Latin does not parallel the French translation used by Burton.]

86. For the grammatical explanation of this double translation, see Burton, "Aelred prédicateur," 19, n. 3. It should be noted in passing that this is still the case today. The Cistercian Order's *Ratio institutionis* presents the role of initial instruction: "The experience of centuries expressed in the Rule of St. Benedict as well as in the legislation of the Church and the Order have provided for a gradual initiation into the monastic way of life. The various stages that comprise this initiation are meant to assist the candidates to grow as human beings" (*Ratio Institutionis: Guidelines on Formation. Order of Cistercians of the Strict Observance*, acc. June 2, 2017, http://www.ocso.org/formation/ratio-institutionis/).

we emphasize it because it informed Aelred's efforts at ordinary instruction, as transmitted to us through his liturgical sermons all the way through his abbacy. Indeed there is not a single sermon in which Aelred does not strive in some way to demonstrate the spiritual value of each monastic observance as an instrument specifically ordained for the integral growth of the human person and his integration into a fraternal community. We provided an example of this fact earlier when we mentioned the delicate concoction Aelred took great pains to prepare for his brothers in that subtle mixture composed of "the honey of holiness" and "the milk of compassion." However, to avoid erroneously truncating Aelred's framing of his teaching role, we add a third element that shows its full breadth.

To introduce this third element, we return to a particularly suggestive image at the start of book 1 in *Mirror*. This image comes at the conclusion of the first section of the treatise (*Mirror* 1.1–16) as Aelred sketches out a vast three-part fresco of human history. The first part consists of the creation of the world, with creatures bearing the indelible three-faceted imprint of the divine Creator (for all creatures, "nature, form, and usefulness,"[87] and for the reasoning creature, "memory, understanding, and love or will"[88]). The second consists of the unfortunate consequences of the original "withdrawing"[89] from God that broke, albeit not irrevocably, the beautiful harmony of the universe that God had intended (the multiple disorders of the world, humankind "disfigured" and unable to enjoy the full fruits of his three faculties of love, understanding, and memory, and with an existence "out of phase" with their divine origin). The final part consists of the path to redemption and therefore, for humankind, the road to a possible "restoration"[90] allowing them, if they take it, to recover their original beauty. For Aelred, as a

87. Aelred, Spec car 1.2.4 (CF 17:89).
88. Aelred, Spec car 1.3.9 (CF 17:92).
89. Aelred, Spec car 1.4.11 (CF 17:92).
90. Aelred, Spec car 1.5.14 (CF 17:94).

Christian and monk, this path to "renewal"[91] (allowing human-kind to restore the resemblance to God that sin had caused them to lose) necessarily passes through the mediation of Christ cruci-fied, contemplated, and imitated through all of his days, and it coincides exactly with the path of monastic discipline.

This coincidence between the cross of Christ, baptismal life, and the profession of monastic life leads Aelred to introduce an image in which the path of monastic discipline, defined as communion with Christ crucified, becomes a "nest." That is, in line with the idea of instruction as an act of institution, mo-nastic life is a space of human and spiritual growth: human because through monastic observances humans are able to recover their innate dignity, and spiritual because in following that path, they embrace Christ crucified,[92] imitating Christ in being and action. Aelred takes up one by one each of the three spiritual faculties that constitute humans in the likeness of God—memory, reason, and will:

> Meanwhile let my soul grow wings, Lord Jesus; I ask, let my soul grow wings *in the nest of your discipline* . . . . Let my soul meanwhile *embrace you crucified* and take a draught of your precious blood. Let this sweet meditation meanwhile fill my memory, lest forgetfulness wholly darken it. Let me meanwhile judge that *I know nothing* but my Lord, and him crucified, lest empty error lure my knowledge from the firm ground of faith. May your won-drous love claim all *my love* for itself, lest worldly self-centeredness engulf it.[93]

The ethical Christocentrism (or Christocentric ethics) of monastic life presents itself in Aelred's writing as in the writing of more or less all the Cistercian fathers, as a transformative mystique of contemplation or, alternatively, as a mystique of conformity to Christ, in which the one who contemplates Jesus

91. Aelred, Spec car 1.5.14 Title (CF 17:94).
92. Aelred, Spec car 1.5.16 (CF 17:95).
93. Aelred, Spec car 1.5.16 (CF 17:95–96).

is called to become similar to him whom he contemplates. Aelred associates two distinct elements of Augustinian spirituality—Saint Paul's image of Christ as the Head of the church's Body, and Saint John's image of Christ as the way. In so doing, he evokes Ecclesiastes 2:14 and exhorts his brothers to avoid imitating the fools who "walk in darkness," but rather to follow the example of wise men with "eyes in their heads" who always keep their gaze on Christ (Christ the Head) and walk toward his light (Christ the way):

> Whoever does not know how to keep the works of our Lord always before the eyes and to regulate life, actions, and words is a fool. He walks in darkness and does not know where he wanders, because he does not follow the light. The one who is wise, however, always has his eyes in his head, that is, in Christ. Therefore that one goes on the way in the light and knows where he ought to put the foot of his works, because he follows the light of truth.[94]

This to say that Aelred's moral teaching, like that of his master, Saint Bernard, is always oriented toward a mystical imitation of Christ, a mysticism of union and conformity in love of human and divine will.[95] This mystical orientation of

94. S 30.17; Aelred of Rievaulx, *The Liturgical Sermons: The Second Clairvaux Collection,* trans. Marie Anne Mayeski, CF 77 (Collegeville, MN: Cistercian Publications, 2016), 9.

95. In *Mirror,* the most beautiful theological and trinitary expression of this mysticism of the conformity of wills by and through love is found in book 2.18.53: "To join one's will to the will of God, so that the human will consents to whatever the divine will prescribes, and so that there is no other reason why it wills this thing or another except that it realizes God wills it: this surely is to love God . . . . The will of God is itself his love, which is nothing other than his Holy Spirit by whom charity is poured out into our hearts. It is an outpouring of divine charity and a coordination of the human will with, or certainly a subordination of the human will to, the divine will. This happens when the Holy Spirit, who is the will and love of God, and who is God, penetrates and pours himself into the human will. Lifting it up from lower to

Aelred's moral and spiritual doctrine was clearly perceived by a contemporary of Aelred's, Abbot Gilbert of Hoyland. Interrupting his commentary on the Song of Songs to lament Aelred's death and praise his preaching, Gilbert uses the dual image of milk (as nourishment given to children) and wine (of contemplation or spiritual ecstasy) to underline how Aelred's discreet but ever-present mystical elevation was never far from his interpretation of Scripture, and to show how the latter served as a springboard for the former:

> He did not search out some tasteless subtlety which pro-
> vides matter for wrangling rather than instruction. Busy to
> gather a knowledge of morals, he stored it in the well-
> fashioned cells of his words. He was prudent in mystical
> discourse which he reserved for the perfect. He abounded
> in milk-clear teaching for the salvation and consolation of
> little ones, yet he often slyly mixed with it the wine of a
> merry and sparkling diction. This is the truth. His milk was
> as potent as wine. His simple teaching and milk-clear ex-
> position often swept his listener's spirit unaware into the
> intoxicating transport of a mind beside itself. Hence one
> addicted to this drink could rightly say: "I have drunk wine
> with milk" [Song 5:1]. Indeed he knew how to mix wine
> deftly in milk and to dispense either one in the other. He
> chose material easy to work with, but you could feel in his
> words the passion of inebriating grace. He was endowed
> with a ready understanding but a passionate affection![96]

---

higher things, he transforms it totally into his own mode and quality, so that
cleaving to the Spirit by the indissoluble glue of unity, it is made one spirit
with him [1 Cor 6:17]" (Aelred, Spec car 2.53 [CF 17:200–201]). This theological
affirmation finds expression in the field of action (or practical theology) when
Aelred shows how the contemplation of Jesus crucified as a man (the love of
God) is a source of unification for a person's affective forces in the love of
oneself and of one's neighbor, leading all the way to "the tender embrace of
charity itself" (Spec car 3.5–6.13–17 [CF 17:232]).

   96. Gilbert of Hoyland, *Sermons on the Song of Songs, III*, trans. Lawrence
C. Braceland, The Works of Gilbert of Hoyland, CF 26 (Kalamazoo, MI: Cistercian Publications, 1979), 497.

Whatever the value of this testimony, which parallels Walter's more grandiose affirmations on Aelred's qualities as a writer and preacher,[97] what should be taken from this long discussion is that for Aelred, monastic instruction extends far beyond the simple dialectic between individual and community, however rich that dialectic might be. Such a dialectic remains unsatisfactory if we are fully to understand the role that Aelred, in the context of preceding tradition, assigned to monastic initiation. Indeed, if we limited ourselves to this sole dialectic, we would remain on a strictly horizontal plane, similar to that of a mere naturalistic or sociological perspective. But the issue of Christian initiation is far more serious, since, without disregarding the social necessity of submission to a common rule (in this case regular disciplines), this initiation targets above all a spiritual transcendence: stimulating the freedom to generously embrace a way of life (the disciplines) that will allow growth in humanity in the very heart of a personal relationship with God, or, more specifically, with Christ.

Thus a monk's initial instruction must not merely be "to assist the candidates to grow as human persons" but also to grow "as disciples of Christ."[98] To use an expression borrowed from Saint Paul, initial instruction seeks to ensure that "Christ be formed in [them]."[99] In other words, the instruction performed here implies "a slow initiation" to what Dom Denis

---

97. See in particular chap. 18 of *The Life of Aelred,* in which Walter states that even if Aelred "despised the vain pursuit of eloquence and preferred the pure, undiluted truth . . . he did not convey any impression of uncouthness in expression, but had at his command all the resources of splendid eloquence and a noble flow of words. He was ready and easy in speech, said what he wished to say and said it well" (CF 57:110).

98. *Ratio institutionis* (17) of the Order of Cistercians of the Strict Observance. *Ratio institutionis (English),* www.ocso.org/.

99. According to Gal 4:19, the biblical verse at the heart of Guerric d'Igny's spiritual doctrine; see Annie Noblesse-Rocher, *L'Expérience de Dieu dans les sermons de Guerric, abbé d'Igny (XIIᵉ siècle)* (Paris: Cerf, 2005), which the Order of Cistercians of the Strict Observance reprises by placing its "Guidelines on Formation" under a seal inspired by a similar verse from Saint Paul: "Called

Heurre, following in Saint Benedict's footsteps, has called the constant preference for Christ.[100] Literally, to "in-itiate" someone consists in helping him to "*enter-into* the impossible [of God] that has become possible, into the unimaginable that has become everyday: to live in God as God lives in us."[101]

Considering instruction from this perspective, Heurre further underscores the idea that "*such an initiation must extend beyond* the framework of the novitiate,"[102] since "to learn the mores of God, lived in perfect humanity,"[103] "an *entire lifetime* [is] necessary."[104] Thus, in keeping with Heurre's writing, we can add, in a sense, that monastic life becomes "*in its entirety an initiation.*"[105] This is also to say that monastic instruction or initiation implies a process that engages not only the newly professed, but the entire community, which "continues to initiate itself whenever it incorporates a new brother."[106]

With this in mind, it is easier to understand the aptness of the remark once made that a mere two years as novice master were enough for Aelred to retain a novice-master mindset throughout his life as abbot. This being established, we can formulate three aspects of monastic education as applied by Aelred first as novice master, then later as abbot. These elements of monastic education intersect along two axes, one

---

to be transformed into the image of Christ (2 Cor 3:18)" (*Ratio*, http://www.ocso.org/formation/ratio-institutionis/).

100. Inspiration for the following lines comes from Denis Heurre, "L'initiation monastique aujourd'hui," *Liturgie* 98 (1996): 165–90, esp. 181–82.

101. "la préférence constante pour le Christ"; "*entrer-dans* l'impossible [de Dieu] qui est devenu possible, dans l'inimaginable qui est devenu quotidien: vivre en Dieu comme Dieu vit en nous" (Heurre, "Initiation," 181–82).

102. "*une telle initiation ne peut donc que déborder* le cadre du noviciat" (Heurre, "Initiation," 181–82).

103. "pour apprendre les mœurs de Dieu vécues en parfaite humanité" (Heurre, "Initiation," 181–82).

104. "la *vie entière* [est] nécessaire" (Heurre, "Initiation," 181–82).

105. "*tout entière* initiatique" (Heurre, "Initiation," 181–82).

106. "ne cesse de s'initier elle-même quand elle s'incorpore un nouveau frère" (Heurre, "Initiation," 181–82).

horizontal and one vertical. The horizontal axis is anthropological and social. Here we encounter individuals to be instructed and a community to be assembled. Along this axis, individuals are initiated into a specific form of living, organized according to a "rule of life" (a *conversatio morum,* or "regular discipline"), enabling them to integrate themselves easily and harmoniously into a fraternal community that they are called upon to build together.

But the construction of this community of free individuals is itself organized according to a higher plan, which alone can provide it with its true dimensions. Indeed, individual and community must henceforth situate themselves along the vertical axis, which is teleological and theological in nature. This axis represents the ultimate goal of such individual education and community building, consisting of a common spiritual quest allowing both the individual and the community together to become a residence or throne for God, worthy of receiving him. Thus with each individual bearing Christ within him, the combined community of individuals forms the very body of Christ.

A Program of Monastic Instruction: The Formation of Recluses *and* On Jesus at the Age of Twelve

Two works offer testimony to this vast program of monastic instruction, which we now examine in order: *The Formation of Recluses,* and the meditation on the evangelical pericope of Jesus found in the temple (Luke 2:41-52). Two elements attest to the fact that *Formation* aims at the holistic instruction of the human person in the sense defined above. First there is the work's title. Different renderings into major European languages (French, Italian, Spanish, and English) translating the title simply but inadequately as "Life of a Recluse" (French and Spanish), or, more precisely but no less inadequately, as "Rule(s)" (plural in Italian, singular in English) "of Life for *a* Recluse" (English) or "for Recluses" (Italian), must not delude us. None of these translations takes into account the meaning of the Latin title that Aelred gave to his treatise. Of course, the manuscript tradition causes us to take pause, as it offers the titles *De vita inclusarum* ("On the Subject of the Life of Recluses") or *De institutione inclusarum* ("Rules of Life of / for Recluses"), which justify to an extent the different translations just mentioned. But Dumont, following André Wilmart, Anselm Hoste, and Edmond Mikkers, has convincingly shown that the earliest title of the treatise must have been *De institutione inclusarum*, an expression that must be translated not solely in a descriptive sense ("Rules of Life") but instead in a more active manner, while nevertheless including the descriptive element: "À propos de l'institution ou de la formation des recluses" ("On the Institution or Formation of Recluses").[107]

The second element showing that *Formation* is intended for the holistic human and monastic instruction of recluses (and in a broader sense, if one considers the recluse as a symbol of the soul, for the instruction of every monk or nun[108]), is the structure of the work. The treatise is composed of three rela-

107. See Charles Dumont, Introduction, in Aelred of Rievaulx, *La Vie de recluse, La Prière Pastorale*, trans. Charles Dumont (Paris: Éditions d'Occident, 1961), 11, n. 1.

108. A point that seems confirmed by the first words of the second part of the treatise, in which, no doubt following the example of the first words of the Rule of Saint Benedict, Aelred no longer addresses his sister the recluse alone (as in the first part, where he states that he is replying to her request), but rather to any soul aspiring to a solitary life: "But now, whoever you may be who have given up the world to choose this life of solitude, . . . listen to my words and understand them" (Inst incl 14). Aelred of Rievaulx, "A Rule of Life for a Recluse," in Aelred of Rievaulx: *Treatises: Pastoral Prayer*, trans. Mary Paul Macpherson, CF 2 (Kalamazoo, MI: Cistercian Publications, 1971), 62. From this point of view, we diverge somewhat from Damien Boquet's reading, which seems—to our mind incorrectly—to reduce the intended audience to women alone: "Here [in *Formation* and in contrast with *Mirror* and *Spiritual Friendship*], the abbot [of Rievaulx] proposes a specifically feminine spiritual itinerary, or even a privileged path to salvation for women." Aelred, according to Boquet, "does not at any moment envision community as a means to spiritual actualization for women" (Damien Boquet, *L'Ordre de l'affect au Moyen Âge. Autour de l'anthropologie affective d'Aelred de Rievaulx* [Caen: Crahm, 2005], 273).

tively autonomous parts, each targeting one of the three components of human nature according to Pauline anthropology. First the corporeal element of the body is seen in the edification of behaviors, with the formation of the "outer man" through "bodily observances" governed by a way of life and a daily regimen fixed by rules (§§1–13). Then there is the psychical component of the soul, seen in the instruction of "the inner man" through the moral edification of the individual (§§14–28). Finally there is the spiritual element proper of the heart, formed through the mystic edification of feeling through the transformative contemplation of Jesus' life (§§29–33).

Aelred himself summarizes these three parts in the conclusion to his treatise. To his sister he writes:

> You have now what you asked for: rules for bodily observances [*corporales institutiones*] by which a recluse may govern the behavior of the outward man [*exterioris hominis mores componere*]; directions for cleansing the inner man from vices and adorning him with virtues [*formam praescriptam qua interiorem hominem vel purges a vitiis, vel virtutibus ornes*]; a threefold meditation to enable you to stir up the love of God in yourself, feed it and keep it burning.[109]

The focus of our work does not allow a detailed analysis of a text long attributed to other authors (Saint Augustine or Saint Anselm), however considerable its influence on the history of Western spirituality.[110] We therefore limit ourselves to a few

---

109. Aelred, Inst incl 33 (CF 2:102).

110. Any reader interested in these questions should refer to Dumont's introduction to the treatise's French translation, published in Sources chrétiennes. The third section in particular (Dumont, Introduction, *La Vie*, 32–36) is devoted to the treatise's spiritual posterity (notably its influence as a source of other rules of life written in a similar vein, and the influence of the affective meditational method proposed by Aelred on the *devotio moderno* and Ignatius of Loyola's *Spiritual Exercises*). The reader should also consult Domenico Pezzini's substantial and remarkable introduction to his own Italian translation of the treatise: Domenico Pezzini, "Introduzione," in Aelred of Rievaulx, *Regola*. Of particular interest is the fourth part, on the work's circulation,

remarks relative to the instructional angle from which we approach the work. To this end, we begin by presenting the text's content as Aelred describes it in the quotation above. Taking at face value this summary along with the final lines of each of the two first parts, we might initially believe that we are faced with a treatise composed of three distinct parts all independent of each other, each written in isolation, which Aelred then later combined into a single work.

This hypothesis has been proposed by Marsha Dutton.[111] She suggests that Aelred first composed a treatise on contemplative life corresponding to what would eventually become the second and third parts of the *Rule of Life for a Recluse*. It was only later that he wrote what appears to be, in the accepted form of the treatise, the first part, which is to say a "rule of life." More specifically "disciplinary" in nature, this rule of life could have been composed to remedy a certain scandalous situation appearing in the chronicles of female monastic institutions of the time and in which Aelred himself was deeply engaged as an outside ecclesiastical counselor.[112]

---

where, revealing the work's success even among the lay readership, Pezzini draws attention to the existence of two Middle English translations of the treatise, from the 13th and 14th centuries, to which he devotes a detailed study within the framework of a theoretical essay on medieval translation practices and techniques (Pezzini, "Introduzione," *Recluse*, 90–107). See also on this subject Domenico Pezzini, "Two Middle English Translations of Aelred of Rievaulx's *De Institutione inclusarum*: An Essay on Varieties of Medieval Translational Practices," in *English Diachronic Translation. Atti del VII Convegno Nazionale di Storia della Lingua Inglese Ministero per i bene culturali e ambientali*, ed. Giovanni Iamartino (Rome: Quaderni di Libre e Riviste d'Italia, 1998), 81–95.

111. Marsha L. Dutton, "Getting Things the Wrong Way Round: Composition and Transposition in Aelred of Rievaulx's *De Institutione Inclusarum*," in *Heaven on Earth: Studies on Medieval History IX*, ed. E. Rozanne Elder, CS 68 (Kalamazoo, MI: Cistercian Publications, 1983), 90–101.

112. We allude here to a sad affair of a rape that took place in a convent of Gilbertine nuns near York and to which Aelred himself refers in a brief historical narrative, "A Certain Wonderful Miracle." There is currently no French translation of this short work. For the English translation, see Aelred of

Such a thesis is obviously worthwhile in terms of historical contextualization, but in our opinion it does not sufficiently take into account other internal and external aspects of the treatise that suggest its unity of composition. In the introduction to his Italian translation of *Formation*, Pezzini has advanced arguments to this effect, affirming that "we must read the *Rule* as a text that, in its author's own mind, *possessed a unity and a structure* making it a work composed in the manner in which it presents itself to us today."[113] Thus, he says, it is possible that the "summary" we cited earlier—presenting the treatise in three parts—was not written by Aelred but rather by a later copyist, who sought to make the structure of the treatise more apparent. In any case, from the first paragraph of the treatise addressed to his sister, Aelred specifies that although he would distinguish between the questions at issue—on the one hand a rule of life "most useful in forming the exterior man," and on the other the moral directives to cleanse the soul of its vices and imbue it with virtues—he would nevertheless be led, "whenever it seems helpful, [to] blend the spiritual with the corporeal."[114] He would also do the inverse when, speaking in the second part on moral virtues (specifically virginity-chastity, *discretio*, humility, and charity), he would not fail to add practical recommendations. That is to say that, in Aelred's mind, these elements are indissociably dovetailed.

To these first two arguments advanced by Pezzini, we would like to add at least two others, more external to the text. When Walter enumerates Aelred's publications, he specifically

---

Rievaulx, "A Certain Wonderful Miracle," in Aelred of Rievaulx, *The Lives of the Northern Saints*, trans. Jane Patricia Freeland, ed. Marsha L. Dutton, CF 71 (Kalamazoo, MI: Cistercian Publications, 2006), 109–22. We will later return to this treatise when we examine Aelred's engagement in the ecclesiastic and political life of his era (chap. 9 below).

113. Domenico Pezzini, "Introduzione," in Aelred of Rievaulx, *Regola delle recluse*, trans. Domenico Pezzini (Milan: Paoline, 2003), 73.

114. Aelred, Inst incl 1 (CF 2:44).

mentions the treatise that Aelred wrote "to his sister, the chaste virgin who was a recluse, in which he traced the course of this kind of profession, from the ardor of entrance into the same to its perfection." However, he speaks of it as "*a* book [*unum librum*]," which certainly must have significance since just further on, he refers to Aelred's *Dialogue on the Soul*, this time identifying it as *three* books. We might surmise that Walter would have done the same if *Formation* had been composed of three distinct parts.

The other, more serious argument relates to the general anthropological remark we formulated at the start. To accept that *Formation* was composed of two originally independent parts is to lose sight of a fundamental aspect of the ancient and medieval monastic anthropology that Aelred inherited according to which humankind consists of a whole whose diverse parts (body, soul, heart, and, for Aelred, imagination and emotion), are distinguishable in the different role each has to play, but nevertheless so tightly connected through reciprocal implication that it is unthinkable to consider them as autonomous. David N. Bell highlights this point in his article "From Molesme to Cîteaux: The Earliest 'Cistercian' 'Spirituality.' "[115]

Bell roots his argument in three general characteristics of medieval spirituality: spirituality as a synonym for moral progress, spirituality as the expression of experiential theology, and exterior action or asceticism as the manifestation of inner piety and the key to spiritual life. He establishes a parallel between these elements and the three successive foundations on which Cistercian spirituality is built. But we can also see these points in parallel with the three-part structure of Aelred's *Formation*, appearing as mystic union with God in part 3, moral edification and the acquisition of virtues in part 2, and outward ac-

---

115. David N. Bell, "From Molesme to Cîteaux: the Earliest 'Cistercian' 'Spirituality,' " CSQ 34 (1999): 469–82. The article also exists in a Spanish version: David N. Bell, "De Molesme a Cîteaux: la primera 'espiritualidad' 'cisterciense,' " *Cistercium* 218 (2000): 317–33.

tions and the rule of monastic observances in part 1. Not only
do these elements interpenetrate each other, but each of them
also contributes in its own way to the edification of the individual, in terms of both instructing him or her as a person and
making him or her a full member of a consciously chosen community of values, destiny, and persons. Thus Bell's conclusions
regarding early Cistercian spirituality apply fully to Aelred's
spiritual writings as well—and in particular to *Formation*:

> The earliest Cistercian spirituality therefore was a spiri-
> tuality of action, a spirituality centered on the conquest
> of the Goliath of vice by the David of virtue. It was also a
> spirituality of praise, in which the Creator of virtue was
> praised by the body in manual labor, by the mind in *lectio
> divina* and *meditatio*, and by the spirit in the liturgical and
> communal celebration of the *opus Dei*. It was a spirituality
> solidly based on the Rule of Saint Benedict—a *disciplina
> regularis*—although the Rule on which it was based was,
> naturally, a Rule amended and adapted to the social and
> cultural conditions of the late eleventh and twelfth centu-
> ries. And it was a spirituality that endeavored to achieve
> what the Rule itself was designed to achieve: the amend-
> ing of vices and the preservation of ordered charity.[116]

Bell specifies that "none of the essential principles of what
are commonly conceived as *Cistercian* spirituality—devotion
to Christ and his mother, the note of affective tenderness, charity, prayer, asceticism, poverty, simplicity, meditation, contemplation—are uniquely Cistercian; what makes them Cistercian
is their interconnection, individual emphases, and balance
within that tradition."[117] On reading *Formation*, we clearly find
that the text's roots plunge deep into this humus of monastic
tradition, and that the text bears witness to the interpenetration
and interconnection of its constituent parts on various levels.

116. Bell, "From Molesme," 480.
117. Bell, "From Molesme," 481.

Indeed, Aelred assimilates and transposes into mystical principle the philosophical concept that "like can only be known by like"[118] and that it is impossible to see God or unite with him unless one becomes like him. And since "God is charity" (1 John 4:8, 16), one must become like him through charity. To become charity oneself, there is no other path than to live a life of charity, which implies an unending struggle against all manner of passions (Cassian's *Institutiones*) and in particular against the forces of covetousness, which are contrary to charity (*Mirror*). Such a struggle takes place through a reordering of desire and affective powers, that is, through a moral conversion and the acquisition of virtues in themselves only possible through a combination of discipline (i.e. rules and observances) with what we termed earlier the "transforming contemplation" of Christ's life: "Become that which you contemplate."

The three books of *Formation*, so different in content (asceticism, morality, mysticism), and yet so complementary, lay out the path of this movement toward the formation of Christ in the individual. An expression used by Aelred, inspired by Bernard's Sermons 45 and 50 on the Song of Songs, sums this up, opening and closing part 3 of *Formation*. Aelred begins the section devoted to the "threefold meditation" by reminding the reader that "while Mary drank from the fountain of divine love" ("the sweetness tasted by the spirit" and "inner dispositions" or *affectus mentis*), the love of God nevertheless only finds its perfect expression in Martha (the "practice of virtues" and the "performance of works" or *effectus operis*).[119] Aelred concludes his discussion of this triple meditation similarly:

> These, sister, are some seeds of spiritual meditation which
> I have made it my business to sow for you concerning the
> memory of Christ's boons in the past, the experience of

118. Aristotle, *On the Soul. Parva Naturalia. On Breath*, trans. W. S. Hett, Loeb Classical Library (Cambridge, MA: Harvard University Press, 1957), 23.
119. Aelred, Inst incl 29 (CF 2:79).

things present, and the expectation of what lies in the future. . . . Meditation will arouse the affections, the affections will give birth to desire, desire will stir up tears, so that your tears may be bread for you day and night until you appear in his sight and say to him what is written in the Song of Songs: "My Beloved is mine and I am his."[120]

There is no need to belabor this point. We shall simply point out in conclusion that if this treatise is deeply rooted in nourishing soil comprised of ancient monastic traditions and early Cistercian spirituality, it nevertheless also contributed in its own right, along with the works of Bernard and the other fathers of Cîteaux, to making the personal interiorization inherent to all Cistercian spirituality more psychological and above all more theological.[121]

It should also finally be noted that the substance of the work's anthropological and spiritual doctrine, however differently it may be formulated, appears in numerous sermons written by Aelred. By way of example, we might consider S 32, for the Purification of Mary, whose doctrinal importance will be evident to anyone.[122] In this sermon, Aelred guides his reader from a spirituality of vigilance, guarding against the senses, to a spirituality of desire, a nuptial mysticism through the joining of wills. He does this by recentering the flights of the heart (*affectus*) on the person of Christ. In this process, Christ is contemplated as redeemer (memory of the past), remunerator (memory of the future), and creator and Lord (memory of the present) so that, from this recentering toward the inner self and toward Christ, all human action receives its outward form.

120. Song 2:16; Aelred, Inst incl 33 (CF 2:102). [Translator's note: My ellipsis, to fit the English quotation to Burton's phrasing.]

121. This latter remark is inspired by Bell, "From Molesme," 481–82.

122. For a study of this sermon, the reader should consult Philippe Nouzille, *Expérience de Dieu et théologie monastique aux XIIe siècle. Étude sur les sermons d'Aelred de Rievaulx* (Paris: Les Éditions du Cerf, 1999), esp. 182–91. The reader should also see Burton, "Aelred of Rievaulx: An Illiterate?" 206–16.

Another example of this recurrent doctrine would be Aelred's long meditation on the gospel scene in which Jesus is found in the Temple of Jerusalem: *On Jesus at the Age of Twelve*. It is to this text that we now turn our attention.

Jesus at the Age of Twelve: *A Pamphlet "Sent from the Library of his Heart"*[123]

It may seem out of place, or perhaps paradoxical, that we should present here, in the framework of our reflections on monastic instruction as Aelred conceived it, a commentary devoted to the Lucan narrative of Jesus found in the Temple. In the first place it departs from our chronology. As best as can be determined, the treatise was written before 1160. Its composition can probably be narrowed down to between 1153 and 1157 or, according to Pezzini, possibly even to between 1154 and 1155.[124] The work belongs therefore to a later period of Aelred's life and is thus posterior to his tenure as novice master. One might also find the discussion paradoxical since, in this pamphlet addressed to Ivo (a young monk from Wardon[125] for whom Aelred felt great affection), Aelred seems to offer nothing more than a fairly unoriginal commentary on

---

123. Walter, VA 32 (CF 57:121). In our presentation of this treatise, we draw heavily from the following works: Anselm Hoste, Introduction, in Aelred de Rievaulx, *Quand Jésus eut douze ans*, trans. Joseph Dubois (Paris: Éditions du Cerf, 1987); Domenico Pezzini, "Introduzione," in Aelredo di Rievaulx, *Gesù dodicenne. Preghiera pastorale* (Milan: Paoline, 2001); Dumont, Introduction, *La Vie*.

124. For more on these time frames, see Pezzini, "Introduzione," *Gesù*, 27; see also Hoste, Introduction, *Jésus*, 13–14. The foundation for determining this chronology can be found in Walter's *Life of Aelred*, which states that Aelred composed this treatise before his health dramatically deteriorated and therefore before he was permitted to withdraw to a cottage, starting in 1157 (VA 32).

125. Wardon, also known as the abbey of Sartis, as Walter Daniel calls it (VA 8 [CF 37:101]), is the first of the daughter houses established by Rievaulx (in 1135–1136) under the patronage of Walter Espec, the founder of Rievaulx (see discussion in chap. 2 above). A certain Simon, who was Aelred's novice master, was sent there to establish it. As Simon was still alive after Aelred's

a well-known pericope. Thus, as he had so often done in his liturgical sermons, Aelred frames his work in the purest tradition of patristic and medieval exegesis and proposes a reading of the scriptural passage based on the three traditional levels of biblical meaning: the literal (Iesu §§1–11a), the allegorical (Iesu §§11b–18), and the moral (Iesu §§19–32).

In reality, these two objections crumble under their own weight. They fail first because we read at the end of the Lucan pericope that "Jesus advanced in wisdom and age and favor before God and men" (Luke 2:52). Additionally, the objections fail because Aelred holds this verse to be the entire point of the Lucan narrative, and on this foundation he builds a vast commentary whose last two parts reveal two main, interwoven, lines of interpretation.

The first of these, found principally in the second part of the treatise (the allegorical commentary, *allegorice*), and echoed in Aelred's thirty-one *Homilies on the Prophetic Burdens of Isaiah*, focuses on the concept of universal history. Through the symbolism of the three-day search for the missing boy Jesus (Iesu 13–18) it shows the three ages of the church (preaching to the nations and persecutions, conversion of princes and heresies, and the era of the church fathers and the cooling of early Christian fervor), as well as "an image of its full destiny"[126] until the cosmic ending of all human history in the person of Christ, who, finally victorious over all divisions, will recapitulate all things in himself, reuniting as one people Jews and pagans, and establishing peace between them.

The second line of interpretation, running throughout the treatise, though most explicitly in part 3, is devoted to the moral interpretation of the pericope (the *secundum moralem sensum*). This interpretation positions the reader in the framework of a universal personal history and shows through the symbolism of the number twelve (Jesus' age in the narrative)

---

death, Walter was able to question him and integrate his testimony into chap. 8 of the *Life*, detailing Aelred's novitiate.

126. Hoste, Introduction, *Jesus*, 19.

218 Aelred's Instruction and First Responsibilities

the different stages of a person's human, moral, and spiritual growth (Iesu 19–21) until the time when Christ has been perfectly formed in that person and can then access the summit of contemplation (Iesu 22). At that moment, in symbolic parallel to Jesus' three days in the Temple, one can discover the power, wisdom, and goodness of God (Iesu 23–29).

These considerations on the final two parts of the treatise, in contrast with a superficial reading of Aelred's literal commentary in part 1, show that Aelred's pamphlet provides much more than a simple sentimental effusion intended, in conjunction with the "seeds of devout meditation and holy love,"[127] to stimulate Ivo's inner devotion or to fuel a surge of affection for Jesus' humanity. On the contrary, this treatise, despite its modest length, opens immense insight into certain aspects of his theology. On a personal and spiritual level, the work reveals Aelred's theology of spiritual life, based on the formation of Christ in the soul of the individual. On a universal and cosmic level, the work reveals Aelred's theology of the history of salvation, based on the world's configuration in and adherence to Christ.[128]

For now, however, we concentrate on the first of the two interpretative lines—the one that makes Aelred's commentary a veritable "letter of [spiritual] instruction addressed to a young monk"[129] and "a treatise on the sacramental grace of the mysteries of Christ, infusing man with a resemblance to the Word."[130] Here again, however, we limit ourselves to four

127. Iesu 1; Aelred of Rievaulx, "Jesus at the Age of Twelve," trans. Theodore Berkeley, in Aelred of Rievaulx, *Treatises, Pastoral Prayer*, CF 2 (Kalamazoo, MI: Cistercian Publications, 1971), 3.

128. These concepts of a theology of spiritual life and a theology of history are taken from Pezzini, "Introduzione," *Gesù*, 49.

129. *"lettre de direction (spirituelle) adressée à un jeune moine"* (Dumont, Introduction, *La Vie*, 10).

130. *"traité de la grâce sacramentelle des mystères du Christ, infusant en l'homme la ressemblance du Verbe"* (Anselm Le Bail, Unpublished notes, cited in Hoste, Introduction, *Jésus*, 20).

remarks.[131] The first two are general and theological: the theology of the incarnation and the sacraments and, more broadly, the sacramentality of Jesus' life. The second two remarks are more specific. The first of these shows the doctrinal cohesion of the commentary's third part with the three-part structure of *Formation*, within the context of human and spiritual monastic instruction. The other, anecdotal yet no less important, deals with the addressee of the treatise. This last point shows the incomparable role that relations of friendship played in Aelred's literary production, and in particular the space that friendship occupied for Aelred in the frameworks of monastic instruction and the larger realm of spiritual life.

The Theological Foundation of the "Formation of Christ in the Soul"

The first point to underline is the theological foundation for the treatise's principal theme: the formation of Christ in the soul. As Hoste has stated, "the relationship Aelred establishes between the phases of spiritual progress in the believer's soul and Christ's bodily growth is not based on a superficial analogy. Rather, it is founded on the common patristic doctrine of the restoration of God's likeness in man, or the deification of human nature, through the incarnation of the Word."[132] In other words, the parallel reading Aelred proposes between the spiritual growth of the believer's soul in part 3 and Jesus' corporeal growth in part 1 rests on a fundamental element of incarnation theology, common to all Christian theology, according to which the Word is made flesh (or God is made man) so that, in turn, humankind can participate in God's nature. Indeed Cistercian spirituality, and Aelred's

131. For more detail, especially on the sources, influence, and diffusion of the treatise, as well as its attribution to other authors, the reader should consult the various French and Italian introductions cited earlier.
132. Hoste, Introduction, 19.

in particular, fully assumes this patristic theological tradition. But it highlights even further the fact that participation in God's nature occurs through the transformative contemplation of Christ's humanity. This gentle devotion toward that humanity leads to conforming one's entire being to his person, a concept that Dumont has called "a spiritual phenomenon of supernatural mimetism."[133]

The theological and spiritual weight of this affirmation is so substantial that Aelred repeats it in all three parts of his short treatise. As early as the fourth paragraph, he affirms that "this is the beginning of this conversion, a spiritual birth as it were [*quasi spiritalis cujusdam nativitatis initia*], that we should model ourselves upon the Child [*ut conformemur Parvulo*]." He concludes the passage by evoking Ephesians 4:13: "For just as the Lord Jesus is born and conceived in us, so he grows and is nourished in us, until we all come to perfect manhood, that maturity which is proportioned to the complete growth of Christ."[134] Similarly, at the very beginning of part 2, in an Augustinian and Johannine vein overflowing in its spirituality, he writes,

> Now this God of ours, eternal, outside time, unchangeable, in our nature became changeable and entered time, in order to make the changeableness which he took upon himself for our sakes the way for changeable men, men within time, to enter into his own eternity and stability; so that in our one unique Savior there should be the way by which we might mount on high, the life to which we might come, and the truth which we might enjoy. As he himself said: "I am the way, the truth and the life."[135]

---

133. "*un phénomène spirituel de mimétisme surnaturel*" (Dumont, Introduction, *La Vie*, 25). Dumont himself borrows the expression from Léon de Connick, "Adaptation ou retour aux origines. Les Exercices spirituels de saint Ignace," *Nouvelle revue théologique* 70 (1948): 927.

134. Aelred, Iesu 4 (CF 2:7–8).

135. John 14:6; Aelred, Iesu 11 (CF 2:15).

Aelred reprises this principle in its full scope at the start of part 3. Addressing Ivo directly, Aelred significantly tells him, "Now I must come back to you, my dearest son, who have resolved to model yourself on Christ and follow closely in Jesus' footsteps."[136] Then begins the moral commentary on the Lucan pericope, in which Aelred strives to show the route that Ivo's own spiritual progress had taken, through three main metaphorical stages. This first is Bethlehem, the stage of conversion and renunciation of the world. The second is Nazareth, the stage of slow growth in spiritual maturity and grace owed to an unwavering struggle against vice, and to the progressive acquisition in twelve steps, each corresponding to a year, of the spirits in Isaiah 11:2-3 (fear, piety, knowledge, fortitude, counsel, understanding, wisdom) and the cardinal virtues in Wisdom 8:7 (sobriety, prudence, justice, strength). The virtues of this second stage are no less present in the ancient philosophical tradition cited by Saint Paul, for example in Titus 2:12, mentioning temperance, justice, and devotion. The third and final stage is arrival in Jerusalem, the stage of spiritual perfection and contemplation.

In the foregoing, it is easy to identify recurrent themes of Aelred's ordinary instruction, as they were previously formulated in *Mirror*, or as they appear in certain sermons, even if he expresses them differently according to their context. The theme of virtue acquisition compared to the seven days of creation appears in the first book of *Mirror* (Spec car §§90–97). Aelred cites the Pauline reference from Titus 2:12 at least once in each of the three books, developed most extensively in book 3 (Spec car §§74–75). Similarly, in S 24, for the Nativity of Saint Mary, he offers a parallel reading between the stages of spiritual growth and Christ's genealogy as presented in Matthew (S 24.6–48). This parallel reading is in keeping with Johannine and Augustinian spirituality ("Christ the way" for the former,

136. Aelred, Iesu 19 (CF 2:25).

and *in via ad patriam* for the latter), as Aelred treats the three series of fourteen generations as so many rungs by which Christ descended to us and which we, in turn, must climb from the starting point of Jesus' humanity in order to reach him in the hope of participating one day in his divinity (see in particular S 24.7). Aelred had already presented this latter point in S 7, for the Feast of Saint Benedict, where he invited his listeners to pass from Christ to Christ—that is, from Jesus' humanity to Jesus' divinity—by the strait and narrow path proposed by the Rule of Saint Benedict, leading directly to Christ (S 7.5). These examples among others demonstrate the Christocentrism of Aelred's spiritual doctrine.

Sacramental and Liturgical Theology, or the Sacramentality of Jesus' Life

Philippe Nouzille has already explored Aelred's treatment of this topic extensively in his study of the monastic theology and spiritual experience in Aelred's liturgical sermons,[137] so we here offer merely a few summary remarks. Aelred's insistence (and that of Cistercian spirituality) on the contemplation of Christ's humanity as the necessary passage to the restoration of the divine likeness in humankind rests on two complementary elements. On the one hand, it assumes the Christological and soteriological principle according to which Jesus, being both God and man—or as Saint Paul says, "the image of the invisible God" in whom "dwells the whole fullness of the deity bodily" (Col 1:15; 2:9)—is simultaneously "the way and the truth and the life" (John 14:6) and the supreme "form" (Phil 2:6) that humankind is invited to imitate in order to recover its original dignity.

On the other hand, the idea also assumes the ethical principle according to which the process of *reformatio* into Christ's

---

137. Nouzille, *Expérience.*

likeness through a *conformatio* to his humanity (the Christological principle just noted) only realizes itself through a process of increasingly perfected identification with Christ's human existence. By virtue of this identification, the latter becomes the literal model for humans to imitate so that they might recover their lost likeness, a concept Nouzille has qualified as "Christological exemplarism."[138]

This Christological exemplarism allowing one to pass, as Dutton has stated, from "intimacy to imitation,"[139] manifests itself in two primary ways. First, it manifests itself in the "sacrament of [Jesus'] body and blood,"[140] the supreme memorial of the Eucharist, and more broadly in all the liturgical celebrations. The role of these celebrations, as Aelred explains in S 9, for the Annunciation of the Lord, is to "re-present now" (*re-praesentatio*) the mysteries of his birth, passion, resurrection, and ascension.[141] One anthropological result of this re-presentation is that "that wondrous loving-kindness, that wondrous gentleness, that wondrous charity that he showed for us in all these, will always be fresh in our memory."[142] On a theological level, the result of this re-presentation is that, as in the threefold meditation of *Formation*, our faith might be fortified "whenever we hear with our ears and almost see beneath our eyes what Christ suffered for us [memory of the past], and what he gives us in this life

138. Nouzille, *Expérience*, 304.
139. Marsha L. Dutton, "Intimacy and Imitation: The Humanity of Christ in Cistercian Spirituality," in *Erudition at God's Service: Studies in Medieval Cistercian History, XI*, ed. John R. Sommerfeldt, CS 98 (Kalamazoo: Cistercian Publications, 1987), 33–70. The article is spotlighted and nuanced in Nouzille, *Expérience*, 137–51, 304. Nouzille correctly shows that is it unnecessary to force the tension between the two terms for, as he says "the two go hand in hand, the imitation of Christ having as its purpose intimacy with Christ, and intimacy leading to imitation" (*Expérience*, 145).
140. Aelred, S 9.1 (CF 58:155).
141. Aelred, S 9.2 (CF 58:155). The same text is found, nearly word for word, in S 26, for the Feast of All Saints (S 26.3 [CF 58:354–55]).
142. Aelred, S 9.2 (CF 58:155).

[memory of the present] and what he promises us after this life [memory of the future]."[143]

But to live the reality and experience of Christ's transforming presence,[144] Aelred proposes, next to the more objective way of the liturgy, is an equally important but more affective way. This second way is the path of meditation that, through imagination and contemplation, permits the individual to see Gospel scenes with "the eyes of [the] heart [*ante oculos cordis*]"[145] and to make oneself virtually a present participant in the events themselves—to make oneself "contemporary" with those events, as it were.

We shall not belabor the contemporaneity with contemplated events through which Aelredian meditation is realized and made effective and which, according to Nouzille and Inos Biffi, constitutes Aelred's originality in this domain.[146] Nor shall we insist on the consequent displacement, from a spiritual perspective, of strict Christocentrism toward a pneumocentric parallel to the imitation of Christ. We will simply underline the capital but often neglected place that Aelred reserves within his spirituality for the contemplation of Christ's humanity. This contemplation confers an almost sacramental aspect, so to speak, on each event in Jesus' life, as well as on each of

---

143. Aelred, S 9.2 (CF 58:155–56).

144. Nouzille establishes a tension within this double form of presence (memory and imitation) between what he calls "présence" (with an "é") and the neologistic "presance" (with an "a"). For more on this see his treatment of liturgical representation (Nouzille, *Expérience*, 146).

145. Aelred, Iesu 1 (CF 2:4).

146. Nouzille, *Expérience*, 143. Nouzille cites Inos Biffi, "Aspetti dell'imitazione di Cristo nella letteratura monastica del secolo XII," *La Scuola Cattolica* 96 (1968): 150, n. 2; 451. Biffi cites in turn Inos Biffi, "Bibbia et liturgia nei sermoni liturgici di Aelredo di Rievaulx," in *Bibbia et spiritualità: Biblioteca di cultura religiosa*, ed. Cipriano Vagaggini and Gregorio Penco (Rome: Paoline, 1967), 517–98. Regarding the act of *re-praesentatio* as constituting liturgical celebration and meditation, the latter text speaks of a "re-evocation, [not] detached, but committed, engaged" (Biffi, "Bibbia," 567).

his attitudes and inner dispositions (hunger and thirst, suffering and pain, fatigue and labor, joy and sadness, anguish and fear, love and friendship, and many others). This sacramental aspect exists because, *patiens et compatiens,* having assumed our human condition and espoused our human feelings, and "purged of the leavening of iniquity,"[147] Christ, the "bread without leavening," is in a position to transform them from within.[148] Christ thus gives them a truly soteriological value.

The Doctrinal Continuity Between Formation *and* Jesus at Twelve

A third aspect of Aelred's commentary on the gospel scene of *Jesus* is the surprising doctrinal continuity between this treatise and *Formation* on the question of monastic instruction. For Aelred, again, such instruction consists of three elements linked by a dynamic circularity, on which rests the tripartite structure of *Formation,* based on ascetic, moral, and mystical elements. The ascetic element consists of life discipline or external rules and observances, the moral component consists of the struggle against vice and the acquisition of virtues, and the mystical dimension consists of union with God through conformity with and imitation of Christ. This structure is reproduced in miniature in the third part of *Jesus,* Aelred's commentary on the Lucan narrative. In this work the tripartite structure is based on the three principal phases of Jesus' childhood. Jesus was born in Bethlehem, grew up in Nazareth, and finally at the age of twelve went to Jerusalem. In Aelred's treatise Bethlehem corresponds to the beginning of spiritual life, consisting of the renunciation of the world and the self, the "casting off" implied by this renunciation, and the struggle against temptation. Nazareth corresponds to the time of growth and the formation of virtues in the soul, which

147. Aelred, S 12.11 (CF 58:197).
148. Aelred, Spec car 3.39.110 (CF 17:299).

advances along the path of spiritual asceticism. Finally Jerusalem corresponds to "the heights of luminous contemplation," where the soul "abounds in delights through the sweetness of what it tastes spiritually."[149]

In these three phases of Jesus' life it is not difficult to recognize the three dimensions of human and spiritual instruction underlined earlier. To instruct people is to institute them as persons, that is, to establish their ethical "form." And to establish people's ethical form is to pass them evenly through the twofold mediation of monastic institutions. This mediation consists on the one hand of an ascetic component, embracing a way of life regulated by outward observances, and, on the other hand, of a mystical component, through which they arrive at "adult perfection, or the fullness of the age of Christ" (Iesu 4) by embracing Jesus and modeling themselves entirely on his person.

To demarcate the stages of this spousal path leading to union with Christ, Aelred relies on three passages from the Song of Songs—a point that, to our knowledge, has never been fully discussed by other commentators, not even by the most perspicacious Pezzini. For the first phase, Aelred refers to Song 2:12— "the voice of the turtledove has been heard in our land"[150]—where the song of the turtledove evokes the plaintive moans of the solitary soul who, harshly tested by the apparent absence of the Lord, pines for his presence. For the second phase, he makes reference to Song 2:11-12, where the past winter is the symbol of temptations and of initial struggles finally overcome, and the flowers symbolize the virtues that begin to bear fruit: "Winter has passed away, the rains have abated and gone. Flowers have appeared."[151] Finally, for the last stage, Aelred cites Song 4:7— "You are wholly beautiful, my friend, and there is no spot in

149. Aelred, Iesu 19 (CF 2:26).
150. Aelred, Iesu 20 (CF 2:28).
151. Aelred, Iesu 20 (CF 2:28).

you."[152] This passage he uses to symbolize the wholly purified soul, henceforth ready to contemplate its spouse, "comely of aspect beyond the sons of men"[153] in the secret recesses of the heart and the intimacy of prayer. In other words, as described both here and in *Formation* (Inst incl 33), this contemplation takes place at the highest level of experience, where the soul, invited to "rise up, hasten,"[154] can say "I have found him whom my soul loves, I have held him fast and I will not let him go,"[155] appropriating the words of the definitive and conclusive meeting of *Formation*: "My Beloved is mine and I am his."[156]

This sequence of scriptural quotations from the Song of Songs is not insignificant. We cannot help but wonder if Aelred was consciously alluding to it at the end of *Formation*, six or seven years after the composition of *Jesus at Twelve*. While we cannot affirm this guess definitively, we would like to think it so, insofar as precious little was left to chance in the rhetoric of the Cistercian fathers. In any case, intended or not, this sequence is another indicator of the remarkable continuity between the two treatises, a point confirmed by one further element.

In our presentation of *Formation*, we showed that Aelred introduced the third part of his treatise, proposing his triple meditation on the past, present, and future, with an admonition not to allow one's contemplative life to wither under the simple impulses of affection or devotion (Mary's *affectus mentis*) but, on the contrary, to give it substance by means of works or action (Martha's *effectus operis*). This same recommendation is found in Aelred's meditation on the story of Jesus' recovery in the temple, though not at the beginning but at the end, and not in the guise of the classical figures of Martha (action) and Mary (contemplation), but rather wrapped in inverse and more original traits of

152. Aelred, Iesu 20 (CF 2:27–28).
153. See Ps 44:3; Aelred, Iesu 22 (CF 2:30).
154. Song 2:9-10; Aelred, Iesu 22 (CF 2:30).
155. Song 3:4; Aelred, Iesu 22 (CF 2:30).
156. Song 2:16; Aelred, Inst incl 33 (CF 2:102).

Jesus' dual obedience. This dual obedience is seen on the return trip to Nazareth (Iesu 30–31), during which Jesus submits to the authority of two masters—Mary, whom Aelred interprets as "mother charity,"[157] and Joseph, as "the Holy Spirit."[158] In an advantageous complementarity of maternal and paternal functions (respectively the inspiration of charity and the works of the Holy Spirit), these two masters "by an eternal law command us not wholly to neglect the contemplation of God for the sake of our neighbor's welfare, nor again to neglect our neighbor's welfare for the delights of contemplation."[159] And reading this prescription in the context of both a subordinate under the authority of his superiors and someone with a pastoral charge who must submit himself to the needs of those dependent upon him (certainly thinking of his own case), Aelred writes, in the style of Saint Bernard's *Sermons on the Song of Songs* 49–50,

> But if the love of repose leads the soul's feelings to murmur against such necessities, as if to say, "Ought I not to concern myself with my Father's business?" none the less the reasoning spirit considers that Christ died in order that he who lives may not live for himself. And he goes down with them in subjection to them. The man who goes down with such a foster-father and such a mother need have no fears. The man who is led by God's Spirit to put himself on the same level as his inferiors out of charity will be happy to go down. With these as my leaders I will gladly go down even to Egypt; only, if they lead me there, may they bring me back again, if they make me go down, may they make me come up again. Gladly will I submit myself to such masters, gladly will I put my shoulder to any burden they may lay upon me, gladly will I welcome the yoke they may make me bear, well aware that their yoke is sweet and their burden is light.[160]

157. Aelred, Iesu 30 (CF 2:37).
158. Aelred, Iesu 31 (CF 2:38).
159. Aelred, Iesu 31 (CF 2:38).
160. Aelred, Iesu 31 (CF 2:38).

This text reveals Aelred's own journey from novitiate under the painful and heavy "yoke" and "burden" of regular discipline (*Mirror*) to the time of this commentary's composition, when the yoke and burden of abbacy were henceforth borne with joy (a word repeated three times). By the time of his abbacy, Aelred was led, like Christ, no longer to live for himself, but to die and give his life for those entrusted to his care, being thus submitted to them, obeying their needs and their expectations, ready to go down with them even to Egypt, the land of slavery. Apart from Saint Paul, who wished to be "an anathema from Christ, for my brethren: who are my kinsmen according to the flesh" (Rom 9:3), and who wanted to share in the weakness of the weak, to win over the weak, and to become everything for everyone in order to save at least a few (1 Cor 9:19-22), it is likely that no one had ever pushed pastoral solicitude so far. This solicitude, however, led Aelred, as novice master and as abbot, to live his pastoral ministry under the seal and in the image of the imitation of Christ as friend, who showed what it was to "lay down his life for his friends" (John 15:13). For the moment, it led him to honor Ivo's request.

The Commentary's Recipient: The Role of Friendship in Aelred's Works

The final consideration regarding Aelred's commentary on the gospel pericope of Jesus in the temple concerns the incomparable role that friendship played in Aelred's literary production. This consideration prepares for the role of friendship in monastic instruction as conceived and lived by Aelred.

Historians have often underlined, as we have done regarding *Mirror*, the almost instinctive repugnance Aelred felt toward writing. Dumont asserts in his introduction to *Formation* that "the abbot of Rievaulx did not compose voluntarily,"[161] and he enumerates all the works Aelred wrote at the behest of others.

---

161. Dumont, Introduction, *La Vie*, 10.

These include *Mirror, Friendship, Formation,* the *Homilies on the Burdens of Isaiah,* and finally *Jesus.* Was this a simple literary fiction, or the sincere expression of unfitness? It matters little. Dumont continues: "the fact remains that Aelred awaits the stimulus of an audience or a correspondent, who gives to his works a direct and lively tone and renders them, in the final analysis, more universal than so many anonymous writings whose ideal is to abstract themselves from these contingencies."[162]

However pertinent, the remark does not get to the bottom of the matter and ultimately only finds its justification in the pastoral dispositions animating Aelred's heart. If in fact, after hesitation and prevarication, Aelred finally agreed to write, it is because he perceived a debt of charity in the request from which he could not extract himself, a pastoral emergency that demanded all his attention, or human and spiritual stakes that he could not ignore.

In the case of *Jesus,* a treatise that Walter said Aelred "sent . . . out of the library of his heart"[163] to his friend Ivo, and in which he offered the best of himself, it is clear, as Hoste has written, that the treatise was composed "under the inspiration of friendship."[164] But let us not be mistaken. Certainly the composition of the treatise originates, above all, from "a spontaneous, pleasant inclination of the spirit"[165] that Aelred felt for a disciple and friend to whom he had been intimately bound by affection for some ten years. In other words, it was a bond existing since Aelred had had the opportunity to converse with Ivo on the nature, origin, and cause of friendship during a visit Aelred made to Wardon after becoming abbot of Rievaulx in 1147.

To appreciate the warm affection Aelred felt for Ivo, one has only to read the Prologue of *Jesus at Twelve,* or the beginning of book 1 of *Friendship.* Indeed, these two texts do not simply

162. Dumont, Introduction, *La Vie,* 10.
163. Walter, VA 32 (CF 57:121).
164. Hoste, Introduction, *Jésus,* 14.
165. Aelred, Spec car 3.31 (CF 17:241).

reveal the paternal tenderness with which Aelred enthusiastically welcomed Ivo's request.[166] They also allow us to glimpse the monastic qualities of humble discretion and introspection that Aelred immediately discerned in the heart of his avid young disciple, as well as Aelred's own more profound reasons for accommodating these requests. To cite only the opening exchange of the first dialogue of *Friendship*, Aelred replies to his disciple's request as follows: "I shall gladly comply. I am delighted to see that you are not prone to empty and idle talk, that you always introduce something useful and necessary for your progress."[167]

Such a reply is obviously important, for in honoring the request of his disciple, Aelred was driven not only by the warm affection he felt for Ivo, but also by the desire to oversee Ivo's personal growth and to help him along his spiritual path. In other words, the reply reveals the second of what Aelred considered the two constituent components of friendship. The first component is the exquisite tenderness and human appeal that make up its charm and delight, while the second component is the moral legitimacy and spiritual value that provide friendship with all its seriousness and integrity. The latter component consists of the impulse described earlier, from which spiritual friendship derives. This impulse—as Aelred highlighted in *Mirror* and in *Friendship* (2.19–20)—binds together on the one hand a "spontaneous, pleasant inclination of the spirit toward someone"[168] or a general *affectus*, and, on the other hand, "a rational attachment,"[169] or a more specific *affectus* or *spiritus rationalis*. The former consists simply of an *affectus* in the

---

166. In *Jesus*, Ivo requests "seeds of devout meditation" on this gospel that might stimulate his love for Jesus (Iesu 1.1 [CF 2:3]); in *Friendship*, he requests the favor of conversing freely with Aelred on each of his visits to Wardon (Spir am 1.3 [CF 5:56]).

167. Aelred, Spir am 1.4 (CF 5:56).

168. Aelred, Spec car 3.11.31 (CF 17:241).

169. Aelred, Spec car 3.12.33 (CF 17:242).

generic sense of the term.[170] The latter derives from the moral reflection by which a person strives for the good—either one's own, through personal conversion, or that of another, through pastoral solicitude in the framework of spiritual friendship. Both of these goods are achieved through a common search for "agreement in things human and divine, with good will and charity."[171]

The Pastoral Prayer *and* On Spiritual Friendship

Examining *Mirror* and its correlation to *Formation* and *Jesus*, and considering certain liturgical sermons, we have demonstrated that the instruction received by novices under Aelred's tutelage rests on three complementary elements, existing in a dynamic and circular tension. The first is a personal and ascetic component, entailing individual conversion and the adoption of an outward way of life. The second is a social and ethical component, involving the insertion of the individual into a community of values and other people, along with the acquisition of virtues, and in particular the cardinal virtues. The last is a mystical element consisting of a union with God by way of an ethical imitation of and an identification with the person of Christ contemplated in his humanity, leading to a way of action, thus coming full circle back to the ascetic element.

We have shown, from Aelred's mode-based standpoint, that instruction proceeds from a two-faceted inward movement: a movement deriving from reason (or the *affectus rationalis*), and an impulse deriving from the will, or the loving heart. The first is reflected in the paternal solicitude of a pastor who seeks to edify those entrusted to him. The second is reflected in the

170. As Aelred defined it in Spec car 3.11.31.

171. This is Cicero's definition of friendship, which Aelred adopts as an anthropological and ethical foundation for his own spiritual friendship; see Spir am, where this definition appears for the first time (Aelred, Spir am 1.11 [CF 5:57]).

example of Christ as friend, by which the pastor offers his life for those he loves, as it leads him to "be everything for everyone" and "to be weak with the weak."

Finally, we have shown that according to Aelred, the conjunction of this dual movement of reason and the heart defines spiritual friendship, in the sense that it constitutes spiritual friendship's two principal qualities and provides spiritual friendship with human, moral, and spiritual value. It now remains to demonstrate how spiritual friendship, as a mode of instruction, colors Aelred's pastoral mission and how as the content of instruction it contributes to the human and spiritual development of the individual, serving as a springboard or step toward the perfection that allows humankind to achieve a state of holiness by progressively tightening the union of divine and human wills.

The Pastoral Prayer, *or the Mirror of a Pastoral Soul: The Abbot as Pastor and Friend*

When we cited the thirty-first paragraph of Aelred's S 24, for the Nativity of Saint Mary, we noted that by Christ's interposed likeness, Aelred offered a composite sketch of what he tried to be as a pastor, first as novice master and later as abbot of Revesby and Rievaulx. He there underscored four things that a pastor must be for his brothers: a father, a mother, a brother, and a friend.

We have already emphasized the first of these traits: the role of pastor as educator, whose mission is first to form and edify individuals (in particular as novice master), and then to form and edify a community (in particular as abbot). Our reading of *Formation* and *Jesus* shows the degree to which the first trait is confirmed in Aelred's relations with his sister and Ivo. Aelred worries over each one's spiritual progress and makes it a point of honor to oversee the edification of each one's entire being. However, this reading also demonstrates an overlap with the second trait: Aelred's affection for his sister and his friendship with Ivo.

The extent to which this conjunction of affection or friendship unfolds in service to the edification of the individual is examined in the next section, concerning the role of spiritual friendship in the individual's instruction. For now we note merely that friendship tints Aelred's conception of the pastoral mission with what is perhaps a unique color. We see a testament to this in that jewel of medieval spiritual literature, *The Pastoral Prayer*.[172] As the sole existing manuscript shows, Aelred's prayer was "composed and used by him [*ab eo composita et usitata*],"[173] which no doubt explains the fact that, preciously "kept as a family heirloom,"[174] the text was not distributed beyond the walls of Rievaulx until Wilmart discovered it and revealed its existence to the public in 1925.[175]

172. For all that follows, we refer principally to Anselm Hoste, "Introduction à la Prière pastorale," in Aelred de Rievaulx, *La Vie de Recluse. La Prière pastorale*, ed. and trans. Charles Dumont (Paris: Éditions du Cerf, 1961), 173–82; Domenico Pezzini, Introduzione to the *Preghiera pastorale* in Aelredo di Rievaulx, *Gesù dodicenne. Preghiera pastorale* (Milan: Paoline, 2001), 131–36; Marsha L. Dutton, Introduction, in *For Your Own People: Aelred of Rievaulx's Pastoral Prayer*, ed. Marsha L. Dutton, trans. Mark DelCogliano, CF 73 (Kalamazoo, MI: Cistercian Publications, 2008), 1–33; Aelred of Rievaulx, "*Oratio pastoralis*: A New Edition," ed. Marsha L. Dutton, CSQ 38 (2003): 297–303; Marsha L. Dutton, Introduction to "*Aelred of Rievaulx: The Pastoral Prayer*," CSQ 37 (2002): 453–59.

173. Aelred, *Orat*, CF 73:37. The manuscript containing *The Pastoral Prayer* (Cambridge MS. Jesus College, 34), which comes originally from Rievaulx's library, dates from the end of the twelfth or beginning of the thirteenth century. It is a compilation of texts. The indication that Aelred composed this prayer for his personal use is written in a later hand, from the fourteenth or fifteenth century, and comes after a thirteenth-century indication, also in another hand, that specifies that the prayer's text was "meant for prelates and especially abbots [*propria praelatorum maxime abbatum*]" (Dutton, Introduction, CF 73:10). For the editorial history of this text, see Dutton, "Aelred of Rievaulx's *Oratio*," 297–303, esp. 299–302.

174. The expression is used for the first time by André Wilmart, "L'oraison pastorale de l'abbé Aelred," RBen 37 (1925): 266, cited in Hoste, Introduction, 178.

175. The prayer does not figure on Walter's list of Aelred's works (VA 32 [CF 57:120–22]).

When Aelred committed this prayer to parchment, he was apparently in the twilight of his life. Dutton, in her two introductions to *The Pastoral Prayer* (2002 and 2008), tentatively advances the hypothesis that Aelred might have composed the text of the prayer at the very start of his abbacy, after 1143. But this hypothesis seems to have been put forward only to better support the commonly accepted later dating of the work that places it in the last decade of Aelred's life, between 1160 and 1167.[176] Apart from Dutton's arguments, Hoste's suggestion that the prayer contains a number of "ideas developed [by Aelred] previously in his sermons, [but which] appear to have come spontaneously into his mind,"[177] also seems to plead in favor of a later dating. Having noted this, Hoste concludes that it is "in a sense"[178] legitimate to consider Aelred's *Pastoral Prayer* "a synthesis of his spiritual life."[179]

As Pezzini suggests, it is not unreasonable to think that in this concise masterpiece Aelred brought together the most characteristic traits of his personality in such a way that he leaves us, as if looking through a mirror, "a true and authentic portrait of his paternal soul, of his compassionate heart, of his confidence and self-abandonment in the arms of Christ."[180]

---

176. For the prayer's dating, Dutton speaks of the "sixties," although she leaves the question open (Dutton, "Aelred: Prayer," 457–59). Elsewhere, she suggests that *Prayer* could have an autobiographical tint (Dutton, Introduction, *For Your Own People*, 8). Pezzini places the composition of the work very broadly "near the end of Aelred's life" (Pezzini, Introduzione, *Preghiera*, 131). He proposes 1166 in his chronology of Aelred's works (Pezzini, Introduzione, *Preghiera*, 10). Less precisely, Hoste indicates the range of 1163–1166 (Anselm Hoste, *Bibliotheca Aelrediana: A Survey of the Manuscripts, Old Catalogues, Editions and Studies Concerning St. Aelred of Rievaulx* [Steenbrugge: Nijhoff, 1962], 39).

177. Hoste, Introduction, *Prière*, 12.

178. Hoste, Introduction, *Prière*, 12.

179. Hoste, Introduction, *Prière*, 12.

180. Pezzini, Introduzione, *Preghiera*, 132–33. In a similar vein, Dutton notes that *Prayer* is "usually read as a portrait of its author" (Dutton, Introduction, *For Your Own People*, 17). Further on, however, she nuances this affirmation by rightly underlining that, even if this prayer can truly be considered as an

Indeed, nearing the end of his life, Aelred places himself under the Lord's gaze, to whose light he confides the most intimate feelings of his heart, either regarding himself and his acute awareness of his weakness and limitations vis-à-vis the abbatial charge he was called to fulfill, or regarding the brothers entrusted to him and his acute awareness of his multiple duties and responsibilities toward them.

In this respect, Dutton has better than anyone brought to light the sharp perception Aelred had of himself and of his responsibilities. In her 2008 introduction, she attempts to bring out the various overlapping and complementary biblical and Benedictine images he employs to communicate in different contexts. On the one hand he uses these images to speak to the community entrusted to him, comparing it to a flock, a family, or a people. On the other hand he uses them to define his abbatial mission: first as a father figure looking out for the material needs of his community with prudent discernment like a good *dispensator*, then as a Solomon-like shepherd responsible for wisely guiding them (*ducere*) and protecting them against the multiple dangers of vice and sin, and finally as a king responsible for instructing (*docere*), governing (*regere*) firmly, fairly, and gently, and edifying (*aedificare*) the community while maintaining respect for each individual.[181] As Dutton has rightly noted, each time Aelred uses one of these images, he effectively

---

"uncurtained window" into the heart and soul of its author or as a "powerful window into his view of the abbot's role," we must nevertheless guard ourselves against a superficial and exclusively autobiographical reading (Dutton, Introduction, *For Your Own People*, 26, 29). She adds, "The work cannot be read as transparently autobiographical," and "Aelred's work is less autobiographically transparent than has often been thought" (Dutton, Introduction, *For Your Own People*, 27, 29). On the autobiographical value of various passages from Aelred's writings, see the relevant remarks made above.

181. On this sequence of four abbatial roles, see Aelred, Orat 7 (CF 73:49–53). While admitting that he is not up to the task, Aelred enumerates these roles one after the other, presenting himself as "this blind leader [*caecus ductor*], this untaught teacher [*indoctus doctor*], this ignorant guide [*nescius rector*]," and asking Jesus to help him in the task of edifying his brothers (Aelred, Orat 7 [CF 73:51]).

reads his mission through the mirror and by the light of the true king and shepherd of his people, Christ himself.[182]

It is regrettable, however, that among these images describing Aelred's vision of his abbatial mission, Dutton does not mention that of "friend." In fairness, the word *friend* does not appear explicitly anywhere in *Prayer*. However, the reality of this image, included among those of the abbot as king and shepherd, is subtended throughout the entire *Prayer* and is, so to speak, constantly present in Aelred's thought. Care must be taken, however, not to project contemporary meanings on the term, and we must keep in mind, as we stated on the subject of S 24, for the Nativity of Saint Mary, and paragraph 31 of *Jesus at Twelve*, that Aelred uses this word the way Saint John's gospel does, affirming that the greatest love is to "lay down his life [*animam suam ponere*] for his friends" (John 15:13). We will return to this verse from John's gospel, as well as the two subsequent verses, since Aelred reserves a privileged place for them in his conception of spiritual friendship. What matters here is that Aelred sees Christ as a model to imitate as abbot, and therefore, just as Jesus gave his life for his friends, the abbot must similarly give himself entirely for his brothers, an idea that Aelred presents in paragraph 7 of *Prayer* in words more eloquent than any commentary:

> You know my heart, O Lord: whatever you have given to your servant, it is my will that it be expended upon them in its entirety [*totum impendatur illis*] and entirely spent on them [*totum expendatur pro illis*]. Still more, may I find happiness in being utterly spent for them [*ipse libenter impendar*; see 2 Cor 12:15]. Let it be done in this way, my Lord, let it be done in this way! All my feeling,

182. For more on Aelred's modeling of his abbatial mission on Jesus "the good shepherd" (John 10:11-14, and RB 2.7-10), see Dutton, Introduction, *For Your Own People*. Dutton states that "in both roles the abbot is above all to imitate Jesus" (Dutton, Introduction, *For Your Own People*, 18). She adds that Aelred's abbatial ministry effects in him "a self-conscious *imitatio Christi*" (Dutton, Introduction, *For Your Own People*, 21–22; see also 23).

all my speaking, all my rest and all my work, all my action and all my thought, all my success and all my hardship, all my death and all my life, all my health and sickness— all that I am, all that gives me life, all that I feel, all that I discern [see S 68.1]—let all this be expended upon them in all its entirety and entirely spent for their benefit, for the benefit of those for whom you yourself did not consider it unworthy to be utterly spent.

O Lord, teach me, your servant; teach me, I beseech you, through your Holy Spirit, how I can spend myself for them and how I can expend myself entirely for them. Through your indescribable grace, O Lord, enable me patiently to support their weaknesses, to have compassion on them lovingly, and discerningly to help them. Let me learn, let your Spirit teach me, to console the sorrowing, to strengthen the fainthearted, to set the fallen upright, to be weak with the weak, to be indignant with the scandalized [2 Cor 11:29], to become all things to all people in order to win them all [1 Cor 9:19, 22]. Grant me a true and right way of speaking and an eloquence of mouth to build them up in *faith, hope, and love*, in chastity and humility, in patience and obedience, in fervor of spirit and devotion of mind [*devotio mentis*].[183]

The similar words that Aelred spoke to his brothers one Pentecost, when the illness that would soon carry him off had eased into an unexpected remission, demonstrate the extent to which Aelred sought to fulfill his abbatial responsibilities by living as a good shepherd, in Jesus' likeness, and how he tried unto his final breath to live up to this idea by devoting himself body and soul to the cause of his brothers and to the edification of his community:

I acknowledge my debt, because whatever I live, whatever I taste, and whatever I perceive is yours. I do not consider it safe for my soul to live any longer for myself,

183. Aelred, Orat 7 (CF 73:49–51).

but rather for you, to whom, through whom, and because of whom I have been called back from nearly the threshold of death. And behold, the spirit is willing, but the flesh is still weak [see Matt 26:41]. Yet affection outweighs weakness and charity outweighs faintness of heart. The weakness of the flesh has been despised to a degree, and the spirit, trusting in the power of your prayers, which it has already experienced, cannot be kept from devoting itself to you.[184]

The words Aelred addressed to his community assembled around him just ten days before his death confirm these thoughts. Bequeathing to his brothers the few personal objects in his possession (a glossed psalter, Augustine's *Confessions*, the gospel of Saint John, some relics, and a small cross), he expressed, as Walter reported, a characteristically acute awareness that his entire person belonged to his brothers: "Behold, I have kept these by me in my little oratory and have delighted in them to the utmost as I sat alone there in times of leisure. 'Silver and gold have I none' [Acts 3:6]; hence I make no will, for I possess nothing of my own; whatever I have and I myself are yours."[185]

Aelred's intense pastoral side is shown above all by the indelible mark left by it in the memory of his brothers long after his death. One has only to think of Walter, whose testimony here, contrary to what might be imagined, cannot be suspected of bias because of its confirmation by the slightly later testimony of another monk, Matthew of Rievaulx, who died around 1215. Generous with superlatives in his biography, Walter declares in a loud, clear voice that Aelred was "a peerless man" and "a fine and prudent shepherd."[186] Matthew, choir master of Rievaulx at the end of the twelfth century, echoes Walter and affirms in a collection of documents

---

184. Aelred, S 68.1; Aelred of Rievaulx, *The Liturgical Sermons: The Durham and the Lincoln Collections*, trans. Kathryn Krug, Lewis White, and the *Catena Scholarium*, CF 80 (Collegeville, MN: Cistercian Publications, 2018), 244.

185. Walter, VA 51 (CF 57:135).

186. Walter, VA 44 (CF 57:129).

preserved after his death that Aelred was the *"pius pastor rievallense."*[187]

We return to Aelred's pastoral side in the next part of our biography, exploring in detail Aelred's abbacies at Revesby and Rievaulx. There we will complete the portrait of Aelred begun here, as a pastor seeking to be not only a father and a friend to the members of his community, but also a mother and a brother. But for the time being, it remains to show how for Aelred friendship contributes to the integral spiritual growth of the individual. In so doing we shed light on the role friendship played in his personal life as well as the role he assigned it in the unification and affective education of the person in human and monastic instruction.

Spiritual Friendship *as an Instrument for Individual and Monastic Instruction*

As Aelred Squire has rightly noted in his biography of Aelred, we can never know in detail all the personal and human issues involved in the origins of a work such as *Spiritual Friendship.*[188] On the other hand, in even a first reading of the text one thing immediately jumps out that has been underscored unanimously by those who have examined Aelred's life, and that is the great importance friendship held throughout Aelred's existence. Friendship colors all the events of that existence and confers on them what Squire refers to as a "hidden meaning."[189] Thus he affirms that the need for friendship was "in many ways the oldest of his [Aelred's] conscious spiritual needs, and probably the plan of the book goes back a long way in his religious life."[190]

---

187. This testimony was brought to light by Wilmart in 1940. He discovered the collection and identified Matthew of Rievaulx as its author (cited in Hoste, Introduction, *Jésus*, 12, n. 10; Hoste, Introduction, *Prière*, 181, n. 4).

188. Aelred Squire, *Aelred of Rievaulx: A Study*, CS 50 (Kalamazoo, MI: Cistercian Publications, 1981), 111.

189. Squire, *Aelred*, 111.

190. Squire, *Aelred*, 99.

We have demonstrated the relevance of these notions to the time Aelred spent at the Scottish court. It was in this period, as he states in the Prologue to *Friendship*, that he discovered Cicero's treatise on friendship and profited from it to order his life. It was also during this period that he developed strong and enduring friendships, especially with King David's son, the young prince Henry, but also with David's two stepsons, Simon and Waldef. We have seen the value Aelred attached to these friendships in his personal life as well as the inertial effect they had on his life choices. It was these friendships that at the time of his conversion, Aelred said, held him back and prevented him from immediately answering the inner call exerting its own powerful pull on him from the moment Waldef became an Augustinian canon.

From this point of view, the historian cannot help but notice the surprising, if not paradoxical, contrast between what Bede Jarrett has called "the beauty of his friendships," which were "the beauty of his life,"[191] on the one hand, and, on the other, the extremely rigorous asceticism into which the young Aelred launched himself headlong. One has only to recall the ice-water baths, probably inherited from some ascetic tradition of his native Celtic culture, that Aelred habitually took, unbeknownst to others, in a small purpose-built brick chamber.[192]

Of course, in this matter it is appropriate to point out the vast and rich monastic heritage Aelred inherited from diverse

---

191. "The beauty of his life is the beauty of his friendships; for him they made his life, they helped him to understand life, they gave life the only value it ever had for him" (Bede Jarrett, "Saint Aelred of Rievaulx," in *The English Way*, ed. Maisie Ward [London: Sheed and Ward, 1933], 87).

192. See Walter, VA 16. The story is confirmed by Aelred himself in Inst incl 18. Dumont rightly points out that "the space occupied by chastity and his struggles seems exaggerated" and that "the excessive rigors of corporal mortification, proposed [by Aelred] as an infallible remedy . . . must not be taken without a grain of salt" (Dumont, Introduction, *La Vie*, 13). On the Celtic origins of this type of asceticism, see Squire, *Aelred,* 124. Squire refers the reader to the Venerable Bede's *Life of Saint Cuthbert* and Reginald of Durham's *Life of Saint Godric*. Godric is of particular interest, since he was a friend and contemporary of Aelred.

sources and tendencies. This heritage certainly gave his ascetic doctrine what Squire calls a "true complexity."[193] The historian is left with the delicate task of reconciling these two contrasting aspects of Aelred's personality. On the one hand, there is "the shining human goodness"[194] that radiates from him and is beautifully reflected in his friendships, while on the other hand there is "Aelred's inclination to value the more extreme and violent forms of bodily asceticism."[195]

One might be tempted to seek an explanation within Aelred's psycho-affective structure, relying on the hermeneutical means and resources that developments in the human sciences put at our disposal nowadays. As we underscored in our general introduction, many scholars of the 1980s and 1990s, especially those across the Atlantic, have attempted to go down this psychoanalytical path, reading Aelred's life through the lens of a supposed homosexual orientation. This hypothesis generated significant discussion among Aelred specialists. It is not within the purview of the present study to relate that discussion in all its details. This has already been done in an excellent 2005 study by Ryszard Groń,[196] who put into perspective both the hypothesis itself and the issues involved in the debates over Aelred's psycho-affective identity. In so doing Grón was able to demonstrate that these discussions had value on two levels.

First, they demonstrated the absurdity[197] of such a debate in and of itself. Among other things it is steeped in the error of

---

193. Squire, *Aelred*, 127. Squire mentions Celtic asceticism along with Jerome, Cassian, Palladius, and Gregory the Great, whose tendencies toward exaggeration in the realm of corporal asceticism were attenuated thanks to the measure and moderation of the Rule of Saint Benedict.

194. Hoste, Introduction, *Jésus* 12.

195. Squire, *Aelred*, 127.

196. Ryszard Groń, "The Debate about Aelred. Looking for the True Face of Aelred of Rievaulx: A Summary," Appendix B in *Spór o Aelreda. W poszukiwaniu prawdziwego oblicza Aelreda z Rievaulx* (Kety, Poland: Antyk, 2005), 167–84. See also what we have already said on this topic in chap. 1 of the present study.

197. Grón, "Debate," 182.

anachronism. Second, and more positively, the discussions drove scholars to reorient their studies toward more constructive and fundamental aspects of Aelred's spiritual doctrine. In fact, these debates underlined the fact that scholars must not impose too exclusive or excessive an autobiographical reading on texts in which Aelred seems to speak openly of himself. Of course, as Squire has correctly stated, the fact that Aelred never sought to hide either his personal difficulties or his constant efforts to resolve them "is a mark of uncommon bravery of spirit."[198] But if Aelred had the courage to evoke his personal experiences and difficulties, it is not because he was moved by some self-indulgent tendency toward spiritual exhibitionism—a sin against which he ceaselessly exhorted his brothers to guard themselves.[199] If he speaks of his own experiences and difficulties, it is because—as the majority of historians now agree—he was gifted with an uncommon innate pedagogical sense. This sense allowed him to put himself in another's shoes.[200] Driven by a pastoral desire to lead his brothers to God, Aelred was convinced that in the realm of moral conversion, revelation of the factors that allowed him to order and unify his own life—his personal experience both with human weakness and with God's divine mercy— would benefit others confronted with the same human needs and the same spiritual challenge to unify their own lives.

198. Squire, *Aelred,* 111.

199. So in a sermon for the Purification of Saint Mary, Aelred speaks of the confession of sins and the pleasure that some may find in recalling them and relating them to others in order to boast of them (Aelred, S 33.29–30 [CF 77:44–45]).

200. In S 33.5, Aelred writes that "the one who speaks ought not to reflect so much on what he feels in himself as on what others may feel in themselves. For people listen willingly when what they hear from another they also find in themselves" (CF 77:37). It is hard to imagine a better way to express the pedagogical value of shared experience, when that of the speaker can serve as a mirror for his readers and listeners, allowing them to find their own experience and to recognize themselves in him, not with the intent of finding pleasure in others' gazes on him, but with the hope of helping them.

Without minimizing the very real tension between the charm of his friendships and the rigors of his austerity, and without re-constituting at any cost Aelred's psycho-affective makeup, as we could probably not do in any event, we here show that if at the start of his monastic life Aelred believed that corporeal asceticism could channel what he called the "this way and that"[201] of his affective life, he very quickly realized that he did not need to repress the natural temperament leading him spontaneously to create bonds of friendship. On the contrary, thanks to his readings and to his two principal instructors—Abbot William and novice master Simon, who showed great generosity of spirit by having confidence in him and encouraging him in his quest—Aelred learned that he could find strength in his personal qualities and natural aspirations. He also learned that he could legitimately consider friendship, which to that point had been a source of delight in his worldly life, not as a chain impeding his progress, but rather as a most reliable ally in his step-by-step efforts to attain his goal. Friendship was a means to the human and spiritual unification of his being through the perfection of charity.

To put it another way, if Aelred realized and remained convinced that asceticism had a role to play in the necessary mastery of a disordered affectivity's centrifugal tendencies, he was also able to temper the excesses of asceticism toward which his native culture and his own inclinations pushed him. He was thus able to avoid the pitfalls of excessive rigor, which might have broken him body and soul if he had not successfully integrated into it the grace of friendship, whose authentic spiritual and monastic value he recognized.

There is unfortunately no space here to retrace the evolution of Aelred's thought on the question of friendship from the timid, prudent affirmations advanced in *Mirror* to the confident proposal of a solid, synthetic doctrine of friendship as a privi-

201. Aelred, Spir am Prol.2 (CF 5:53) (*inter diversos amores et amicitias fluctuans*).

leged instrument of individual and monastic instruction in the three dialogues on *Friendship*. As we have done for *Mirror*, and again at the risk of oversimplifying, we merely point out certain elements that seem particularly pertinent to our discussion. We begin by correcting two commonly held misconceptions regarding Aelred's doctrine of friendship.

When Aelred's spiritual doctrine on friendship is mentioned, two commonly accepted but completely erroneous notions spring to mind. It is important to cast aside these misconceptions immediately so as to avoid further skewing or misunderstanding of Aelred's ideas on this matter.

God Is Not Friendship

The first of these misconceptions concerns the idea that Aelred, adapting a verse from the first letter of Saint John (1 John 4:16—"God is charity [*caritas*]") to his own purposes, claimed that "God is friendship."[202] This expression appears at the end of the first dialogue on friendship, in *Friendship* 1.9, when Aelred and Ivo, his young disciple and friend from Wardon, discuss the definition that should be given to friendship. But when this phrase is quoted, it is generally reproduced out of context. Those citing it neglect to specify that it comes from the lips of Ivo and does not represent a firm affirmation, but rather a working hypothesis expecting confirmation, or at least validation, from the master to whom Ivo poses the question. Aelred, however, refuses to offer either—not because he does not feel up to the task, but rather because he is impelled to refuse for two reasons.

The first argument is that no such expression appears anywhere in the Bible, and thus Scripture does not offer Aelred any foundation on which to base a confirmation of this idea. The

---

202. Dumont drew attention to this error in Charles Dumont, "Le personnalisme communautaire d'Aelred de Rievaulx," in *Une éducation du cœur* (Oka, Canada: Abbaye Notre-Dame-Du-Lac, 1997), 329.

second argument appears far more serious in that it revolves around not only a theological conception of God himself, but also the doctrinal coherence of Aelred's definition of friendship. Starting with the etymology of the word *friend*, which in Latin derives from the verb *to love*,[203] Aelred asserts that friendship is to be considered first as a particular form of love, that is to say, according to the definition he had already given in *Mirror* (3.8–20), "Now love is an attachment of the rational soul [*quidam animae rationalis affectus*]. Through love, the soul seeks and yearns with longing to enjoy an object."[204] However, shortly thereafter, Aelred specifies that friendship is also "that virtue . . . through which by a covenant of sweetest love our very spirits are united, and from many are made one."[205]

What prevents Aelred from asserting that "God is friendship" is that even if there is a natural and undeniable connection between charity and friendship, providing continuity from one to the other—both are, indeed, forms of love—there exists nevertheless a degree of difference preventing either form of love from being reduced to the other. According to Aelred's definition, friendship is an elective and selective relationship, since the bond is typically formed between two people who to the exclusion of all others (selection) feel toward each other spontaneous tenderness and affection (election). This understanding makes the field of friendship much narrower than that of charity, which by its universality gathers in its embrace the full spectrum of human relations, independent of feelings of particular affection.

In other words, to state that "God is friendship," as Ivo suggests, would be to place unacceptable limits on God's love.

---

203. [Translator's note: *amicus* / *amare*. This derivation applies to Romance languages in general, including the French *ami* / *amour* as it appears in Burton's original text. The discussion loses something in English without some explanation, since the same derivation does not apply.]

204. Aelred, Spir am 1.19 (CF 5:58).

205. Aelred, Spir am 1.21 (CF 5:59). [Translator's note: My ellipsis to fit the English quotation to Burton's phrasing.]

Such limits are contrary to Scripture, which states the opposite—that the love of God, who reigns over the universe with wisdom, gentleness, and strength, extends from one end of the earth to the other (see Wis 7:30–8:1) and embraces all people indiscriminately, whether good or evil (see Matt 5:45). Thus, according to Aelred, to avoid unduly restricting the length and breadth of God's love, it is better to refrain from asserting that he is friendship and instead to limit oneself to the teachings of Scripture that declare that he is charity.

Friendship Is Not the Most Perfect Form of Charity

The second idea commonly attributed to Aelred's doctrine of spiritual friendship is that Aelred considered friendship to be the most perfect form of charity. It is true that some of his remarks, such as certain passages from *Spiritual Friendship*, taken out of context and isolated from his overall thought, present the charm, beauty, and privileges of friendship with a dazzling lyricism that might lead the reader to believe that he considers friendship to be the highest and most perfect form of charity. One example appears in *Friendship* 2.18–20, when he explains to Gratian by a comparison with charity the "special prerogative" enjoyed by friendship:

> But do note briefly that friendship is a step toward the love and knowledge of God. In friendship, indeed, there is nothing dishonest, nothing feigned, nothing pretended. Whatever does exist here is holy, unforced, and genuine. This is also characteristic of charity.
>
> But thanks to a special prerogative, friendship outshines charity in this, that among those who are mutually bound by the bond of friendship, all things are experienced as joyful, secure, pleasant, and sweet. Through the perfection of charity we have perfect love for many who are a burden and a bore to us. Although we consult their interests honestly, without pretense or hypocrisy but truthfully and voluntarily, still we do not invite them into the intimacies of friendship.

> In friendship, then, we join honesty with kindness, truth with joy, sweetness with good will, and affection with kind action.[206]

This text should be considered alongside two other passages: *Friendship* 3.3 and *Mirror* 3.48, where the comparison with charity is made in similar terms as Aelred contrasts friendship's *prerogative* with charity, which he says proceeds solely from the impulse of reason. Charity, he says, represents obedience to the divine commandment of love that obliges us to love others whoever they may be. Friendship too proceeds from reason and from the same divine commandment to love others, but it also joins to this an affection or attraction that spontaneously inclines a person toward someone.

The prerogative of friendship thus harmoniously joins affection and reason. It preserves the advantages of both (charm and sweetness for the former, honesty and a fertile obedience to the rule of love for the latter), without their respective disadvantages (the danger of disordered affection for the former, and bitterness toward the commandment obliging us to all others, even those for whom we have no personal feelings). Such a prerogative must not deceive us. Obviously, Aelred comments on the perfection unique to the love of friendship. But it is important to see that for Aelred, who is faithful to the teachings of Scripture and in particular of the gospels, the perfection of friendship, so real in its own domain, does not correspond at all to the perfection of charitable love in the gospels. Indeed, the love involved in friendship is limited in its breadth by two restrictions. Insofar as that love derives from friendship, it only concerns those toward whom we are inclined (*affectus*); insofar as it is qualified as spiritual, it is limited again to those with whom one shares the same life ideal of the pursuit of good. In opposition to that, truly charitable Christian love does not know the limits of human feeling, since, being perfect (that is, resem-

206. Aelred, Spir am 2.18–20 (CF 5:74–75).

bling the divine love touching all people, good or evil) and modeled on Jesus' love (seen even in his prayers for his executioners), this form of love naturally extends ever outward, step by step, in larger and larger concentric circles. This expansion continues until it embraces the infinite spectrum of human relations, including in its embrace all people, even our enemies.[207] Thus according to Aelred, spiritual friendship is too limited in its scope ever to be considered the "summit of fraternal charity."[208] Only love of our enemies, which takes love to its most extreme limit, can merit this praise.[209]

This conclusion leads Aelred to consider the role of friendship in two ways. First he considers it as a *sub specie aeternitatis*—that is, as a protological divine project for humanity and its definitive and total eschatological fulfillment at the end of time. On the other hand, he also considers it as a *sub specie historiae vel humanitatis*—that is, as humanity's present, concrete, but partial realization in time and human history. Aelred makes this distinction clearly in the first dialogue in *Friendship* (1.51–61) when he discusses with Ivo the question of friendship's origin.

Friendship as a Principle of Cosmic Harmony

In book 1 of *Spiritual Friendship*, when Ivo asks Aelred about the origin of friendship (Spir am 1.50), Aelred reintroduces a philosophical principle he had previously stated at the start

207. On the breadth of charitable love without limits, see in particular *Mirror*, with its images of the heart as an inn (Spec car 3.2.7–10 [CF 17:225]) and as Noah's ark (Spec car 3.38.103–6 [CF 17:294–96]). See *Mirror* as well for the idea that the perfection of charitable love is only attained when, in the likeness of God (who "makes his sun rise on the bad and the good") or in the likeness of Christ's love (who prays for his executioners), it embraces all people, including our enemies (Spec car 1.31.87 [citing Matt 5:45] and Spec car 3.5.14–16 [CF 17:140; 231–32]).

208. Aelred, Spec car 3.4.10 (CF 17:228).

209. See Charles Dumont, "L'amitié spirituelle dans l'école de charité," in *Une éducation du cœur* (Oka, Canada: Abbaye Notre-Dame-Du-Lac, 1997), 370.

of book 1 of *Mirror* (1.2.4–7). Here he ponders the divine act of creation and, specifically, the traces that the creator of the cosmos left behind. He notes three of them, each coinciding with one of God's properties. First there is existence, by virtue of which the cosmos, as God's creation, is part of God's very being. The two other properties—beauty and goodness—are of greater interest, since, according to Aelred, they derive from the principles of order and utility that govern the entire universe. Indeed he rereads ancient philosophy in the light of a biblical theology of creation holding that every creature in the universe occupies a unique and particular place in space and time. Each thing, he says, so long as it remains in its assigned place and does not trouble the established divine order, contributes in its own way to maintaining harmony and peace in the cosmos and therefore, along with all other things, participates in the divine beauty that all existing things reflect through the harmony among them. Similarly, since no thing is self-sufficient but instead relies on all others for its very existence, every creature possesses a certain utility and thus reflects some part of divine goodness.

Ordering the cosmos and generating its beauty, these principles of order and utility lead to an important consequence that Aelred did not lay out explicitly in *Mirror*. That consequence, which he some years later spelled out in *Friendship*, is that by virtue of these two principles, and through the original plan of creation, relationships of reciprocity and mutual dependence naturally exist among all things. Such a state of "alliance" or even "society" among things makes it evident, he says in S 112, on the Feast of the Chair of Blessed Peter, that "in the compassion of loving-kindness," God causes the strong to care for the weak.[210] Thus Aelred writes in *Friendship*, "Therefore, as the highest nature he [God] fashioned all natures [the principle of existence], set everything in its place, and with

---

210. S 112.13; Aelredi Rievallensis, *Sermones LXXXV–CLXXXII*, ed. Gaetano Raciti, Opera Omnia vol. 4, CCCM 2C (Turnhout: Brepols, 2001), 150.

discernment allotted each its own time [the principle of order]. Moreover, since he so planned it eternally, he determined that peace should guide all his creatures and society unite them. Thus from him who is supremely and uniquely one, all should be allotted some trace of his unity. For this reason, he left no class of creatures isolated, *but from the many he linked each one in a kind of society* [the principle of mutual utility]."[211]

This principle of all things being linked "in a kind of society" provides Aelred with numerous practical theological applications, both in terms of his theological conception of communal life and ecclesiology of communion, and in terms of a general social and political theology. Aelred later refers to this universal society, or this reciprocity and mutual dependence, with the word *friendship*, as he did not do in *Mirror*, either because he lacked the audacity to do so at the time of its composition, or because his thought did not achieve that degree of maturity until two decades later, when he wrote *Friendship*.

In any case, and contrary to common belief, when Aelred speaks of friendship he is not speaking primarily of sentimental human affection. Obviously he neither rejects nor scorns such affection—far from it. It is this affection, he says, that gives to human friendships their charm and sweetness. But he focuses here on an entirely different element, a vast ontological dimension broader than sentimental affection. Developed from this ontological dimension, Aelred's concept of friendship—belonging to the origin of all things and, through the divine will of creation, to the very structure of the cosmos and the essential nature of things—is built upon a universal cosmic foundation. Moreover, this ontological and cosmic conception of friendship leads him to say to Ivo, "In my opinion, nature itself first impressed on human minds the feeling of friendship."[212]

Thus, according to Aelred's vision of the cosmos as the originating principle of all things in the heart of the divine project

211. Aelred, Spir am 1.53 (CF 5:65).
212. Aelred, Spir am 1.51, 58 (CF 5:65, 67).

of creation, friendship is the source of the charm, beauty, and harmony of the world, because friendship's specific and exclusive purpose is to make possible and to establish relations of social alliance among all creatures. That is to say that friendship creates natural and spontaneous (*affectus*-based) relationships of reciprocity, mutual dependence, and free exchange. By virtue of these relationships, and in keeping with Augustine's adage, the gifts belonging to each are the gifts of all (*singula omnium*), and the goods of all belong to each (*omnia singulorum*). Thus nothing and no one would ever feel deprived or frustrated, since everything is placed in common and none ever has exclusive and personal possession of any thing.[213]

But Aelred, reinterpreting original sin, reports that this beautiful divine project was shattered when "after the fall of the first human, with charity growing lukewarm," jealousy, cupidity, and avarice crept in between creatures. This development allowed private interest to dominate the common good and consequently created the miseries and misfortunes of disputes, rivalries, hatred, and suspicion.[214]

This fact had two consequences, according to Aelred. First, in terms of eschatology, the perfect accomplishment and realization of the initial divine project, which he discusses in *Friendship* 3.79–80, is postponed until the end of things. Second, in terms of human history and ethical life, it becomes necessary to distinguish charity, which is due to all people, good or evil, from friendship, which he says is given only to those for whom one feels a "stricter bond of love."[215] Furthermore, it became

---

213. Dumont notes that Augustine's *Tractates on the Gospel of John* (32.8) are the source of this adage (Dumont, "L'amitié dans l'école," 370). Dumont also attempted to list all the principal occurrences of this adage in Aelred's works, from Spec car 2.17.43 through Anima 3.47 (Dumont, "Le personnalisme," 129–48). He showed this adage to be a leitmotif of Aelred's thought. See our later discussion of Aelred's view of communal life.

214. Aelred, Spir am 1.58 (CF 5:67).

215. Aelred, Spir am 1.59 (CF 5:67).

necessary to regulate things by "law and precept" so that true friendship might not be confused with baser relationships bearing only its outward appearance. Thus only those friendships maintained through a mutual search for goodness and a common desire for moral perfection would be qualified as *spiritual*. Aelred thus concludes that "the authority of the law sanctioned the friendship that nature had established and use confirmed."[216]

Aelred's vision of the cosmos and history—from their divine origin, to the "interim" of original sin and our present condition, to their consummation at the end of time—might be considered naive. Aelred rereads human history from the perspective of the entropic principles of the degradation and "cooling off" of friendship / charity (see Matt 23:12), which, from its original universality, is subsequently reduced to an infinitely smaller space. Nevertheless, such a vision allows Aelred to provide human friendship with its true spiritual pedigree. Because it is, so to speak, sandwiched between the protological origin of things and the eschatological end of things, spiritual friendship as felt and experienced in the present time is in effect graced with an initiatory or pedagogic value as well as a quasi-sacramental dimension.

The Prefatory Value of Friendship as a Stair, Rung, or Springboard to God's Love

Spiritual friendship has first of all a prefatory value. Aelred states this fact repeatedly. In *Friendship* he affirms five times, and in nearly identical terms on each occasion,[217] that friendship presents itself as a "stair," a "rung," or a "springboard" that makes it possible, by way of a certain analogy (or by the law of graduality, so dear to contemporary moral theology) to pass more easily from the imperfect love that binds us to a friend toward the love that unites us with God: "As devotion

---

216. Aelred, Spir am 1.60–61 (CF 5:67).
217. Aelred, Spir am 2.14; 2.20–21; 3.87; 3.127; 3.132–34.

grows with the support of spiritual interests, and as with age maturity increases and the spiritual senses are illumined, then, with affection purified, such friends may mount to higher realms, just as we said yesterday that because of a kind of likeness the ascent is easier from human friendship to friendship with God himself."[218]

Indeed, as Dumont explains, by means of the total conformity of feeling and will,[219] our friendship for a brother or sister allows us to glimpse and to a certain extent prepares us to experience the love of God—that is to say, a perfect and total adhesion to his will, since, by analogy, this friendship too, as Aelred had previously affirmed in *Mirror* 2.18.53,[220] is characterized by a similar union of wills and a similar conformity of feeling and way of life.[221]

218. Aelred, Spir am 3.87 (CF 5:109).

219. Aelred takes Cicero's and Sallust's ideas as the foundation for developing his own definition of friendship. For Cicero, friendship is "an accord in all things, human and divine, conjoined with mutual goodwill and affection" (*De Amicitia* 20 [Cicero, *De Amicitia*, in Cicero, *De Senectute, De Amicitia, De Divinatione*, trans. William Armistead Falconer (Cambridge, MA: Harvard University Press, 2001), 131]). For Sallust, friendship is "to have the same desires and aversions" (*The War with Catiline* 20.4 [Sallust, "The War with Catiline," in Sallust, *The War with Catiline, The War with Jugurtha*, trans. J. C. Rolfe, rev. John T. Ramsey (Cambridge, MA: Harvard University Press, 2013), 53]).

220. In one of the high points of the treatise, Aelred describes the adhesion of human will to divine will, which, in the end, leads us to be "one spirit" with God (1 Cor 6:17): "To join one's will to the will of God, so that the human will consents to whatever the divine will prescribes, and so that there is no other reason why it wills this thing or another except that it realizes God wills it: this surely is to love God" (Aelred, Spec car 2.18.53 [CF 17:200]).

221. See Charles Dumont, "L'amour fraternel dans la doctrine monastique d'Aelred de Rievaulx," in *Une éducation du cœur* (Oka, Canada: Abbaye Notre-Dame-Du-Lac, 1997), 335–47, esp. 346–47. See also in this volume Dumont, "L'amitié dans l'école," 359–73, esp. 364: "The experience of friendship is for Aelred the human experience of a harmony of wills and consequently an experience of the love of God, which is harmony with divine will. Doing God's will is charity and spiritual perfection."

Aelred's idea that there is a true analogy between friendship and the love of God, allowing the former to be a springboard to the latter, is the fruit of his meditations on chapter 15 of Saint John's gospel, so dear to his heart, and of Saint Ambrose's interpretation of it in his treatise *On the Duties*. John's gospel presents Jesus' affirmation that "You are my friends, if you do the things that I command you" and specifies in the same context that his commandment is to "love one another, as I have loved you," that is, in giving one's life for those that one loves (John 15:12-14).

Aelred follows up on this idea from the gospel of John by building upon Saint Ambrose's thought, viewing friendship as a form of "twofold education." In the first place, he says, friendship allows us, through the object of our love, to raise ourselves up to the love of God (objective genitive), since to love God is to observe his commandment, and his commandment is to love one's neighbor. In the second place, friendship teaches us, considering the modality of our love, to love as God himself loves us. That is to say that it leads us to love our brothers and sisters so much that we would give our lives for them. Thus we begin this process with "the easiest" love, love of those to whom we are most tightly bound by "the pleasant bond of spiritual friendship,"[222] after which we subsequently raise ourselves step by step to the most difficult love, the love of our enemies.

Thus based on Christ and on the "form [*forma*]" or the "model [*exemplar*]" that Ambrose offers,[223] friendship becomes the ideal space in which "I train my heart to love everyone,"[224] and where, to use Aelred's terms, "All this begins with Christ, is advanced through Christ, and is perfected in Christ. The

222. Aelred, Spec car 3.39.110 (CF 17:298–99).
223. That is, the model Ambrose presents of Christ who provides "a model of friendship," a recurrent idea throughout book 3 of *Friendship*, in particular 3.5, 69, and 83.
224. *j'exerce mon cœur à aimer tout le monde* (Dumont, "L'amitié dans l'école," 370).

ascent does not seem too steep or too unnatural, then, from Christ's inspiring the love with which we love a friend to Christ's offering himself to us as the friend we may love."[225]

This idea that the love of Christ and the charm of fraternal love are inextricably linked is so dear to Aelred that he repeats it toward the end of *Friendship* (3.127). He emphasizes that charity presents itself as a ladder by which one can climb toward Christ's embrace and the dazzling regions of divine love, or by which one can descend toward love of one's neighbor and the sweetness of fraternal charity. But by connecting friendship to Christ as the source and form of fraternal charity, Aelred imperceptibly changes thematic register. Henceforth he no longer situates his discourse solely in the pedagogical realm of human friendship as the school of charity or as the practical school where little by little one learns to love as God loves, but instead adds to it a quasi-sacramental dimension.

The Quasi-Sacramental Dimension of Friendship: Christ as Head and Christ as Body

In Aelred's eyes, friendship always must assume the ancillary role of a preparatory school for perfect charity. But from the moment he links friendship to Christ as its source and its model, friendship is suddenly called upon to become much more than a simple springboard permitting men and women to attain the summit of perfect love. It simultaneously becomes the sacramental sign of a larger reality. To use Dumont's words, friendship becomes "the visible expression of our ideal of divine love."[226]

In truth, Aelred had already glimpsed the sacramental dimension of friendship in 1142–1143 while composing *Mirror*. It may be that some were already openly reproaching him at that time for according too much importance to the role of friendship in his own monastic life and in the framework of

---

225. Aelred, Spir am 2.20 (CF 5:75).
226. Dumont, "L'amitié dans l'école," 362.

initial instruction. Or it may be that a certain delicate sensitivity allowed him to foresee the criticisms and objections that would eventually be addressed to him on this subject. We will obviously never know for sure. On the other hand, one thing is certain. Very early on, from the time of his novitiate, Aelred felt the need, if only for himself, to seek a solid foundation that would give friendship a spiritual legitimacy and, through this legitimacy, to justify the importance he accorded to it in his personal life.

Nothing attests better to how essential friendship was to monastic life for Aelred than the eulogy he inserts at the end of the first book of *Mirror* to celebrate the memory of his friend Simon, taken too soon from this world. At the time of his conversion Aelred had found in Simon a guide, a support, and above all what he called a "model for my life [*exemplar vitae meae*]" and a "harmonizer of my conduct [*compositio morum meorum*].''[227] The expression is worth noting, since what he says of his friend in book 1, he says again of Christ in book 3. There he compares the heart of man to Noah's ark, specifying that therein resides Christ, who, like Aelred's friend, "keeps all lower creatures in order [*componere*]" and "brings the whole lower span in a straight line to that single cubit of his love.''[228]

Identifying his friend with Christ through the parallel in their roles—to be a "reference point" (that is, a form, an archetype, an exemplar, a standard or cubit as unit of measure) permitting Aelred to "order" his affections and his way of life—paves the way for the development of all the future doctrinal developments he lays out in *Friendship*. In particular, it allows an audacious use of Ambrose's interpretation of chapter 15 in John's gospel, according to which Christ gives through his person "the model of friendship," an affirmation only timidly suggested in

227. Aelred, Spec car 1.34.98–114, here 1.109 (CF 17:154).
228. Aelred, Spec car 3.38.103–6, here 106 (CF 17:296). [Translator's note: The French translation from which Burton works says "harmony" rather than "order."]

Mirror 3.107–10. Relying on the example given by Paul and Philemon (Phlm 20), Aelred shows in effect that it is entirely legitimate "in this present life . . . to enjoy those who are linked to us more intimately and more closely by the pleasant bond of spiritual friendship."[229] With his remarkable theological sense, Aelred established this legitimacy on the basis of the "Christological exemplarism" underscored earlier in Nouzille's work. Drawing practical anthropological conclusions from his theology of the incarnation, Aelred posits that because of Jesus' full assumption of the human condition, Jesus' entire life took on a sacramental value and became for us a sign of our humanity, transformed and saved by his own.

After first advancing the salutary sacramentality of Jesus' life as a general principle, Aelred soon applied it to spiritual friendship. Indeed, he justified his teaching on spiritual friendship by explaining that "even though all the disciples were cherished by the sweetness of supreme charity," it was to one alone that Jesus "accorded . . . a prerogative of yet more intimate affection," of such a kind that this one "would be called that disciple whom Jesus loved." He goes on: "Lest someone think that this very holy sort of charity [friendship; *caritatis sacratissimum genus*] should seem reproachable, our Jesus himself, lowering (Himself) to our condition in every way, suffering all things for us and being compassionate towards us, transformed it by manifesting his love. To one person, not to all, did he grant a resting-place on his most sacred breast in token of his special love."[230]

While this statement is solidly supported by a theology of the incarnation, Aelred presents it only with extreme caution, employing it as a sort of preemptive attacking strategy. Aelred's manner of expression ("Lest someone think that this . . . should seem reproachable") underscores his advancement of the idea only as a means to parry the objections that might be raised

---

229. Aelred, Spec car 3.39.110 (CF 17:298–99). [Translator's note: My ellipsis, to fit the English quotation to Burton's phrasing.]

230. Aelred, Spec car 3.39.110 (CF 17:299). [Translator's note: The parenthetical clarification "(Himself)" appears in the English translation.]

against him. Indeed, he would not truly be able to propose the idea freely until the twilight of his life. Being a later development of his thought,[231] the idea does not even appear in book 1 of *Friendship*,[232] but only in books 2 and 3, which he almost certainly wrote after 1164, in a more mature state of mind.[233]

In the two later books, Aelred affirms that spiritual friendship is simultaneously a pedagogical tool in the service of fraternal charity and the sacrament of union with Christ, despite the church fathers' traditional mystical commentary on Song of Songs 1:1 as the expression of a nuptial union between the soul and God, audaciously going so far as to interpret this verse in this manner: "Hence a friend clinging to a friend in the spirit of Christ becomes one heart and one soul with him. Thus mounting the steps of love to the friendship of Christ, a friend becomes one with him in the one kiss of the spirit. Sighing for this kiss, one holy soul cried out, 'let him kiss me with the kiss of his mouth!' "[234]

---

231. The date of the first dialogue's composition is unknown. Aelred must have written it before 1160, since that is the date of Ivo's death. The majority of historians agree nevertheless that Aelred must have composed it relatively soon after his rise to the abbacy of Rievaulx in 1147. But a more precise date cannot be established. This hypothesis relies on the fact that at the very beginning of book 2, Aelred explains to his new interlocutor, Walter, that "many years have passed since the pages disappeared on which I had recorded his [Ivo's] questions about spiritual friendship and my answers" (Aelred, Spir am 2.5 [CF 5:71]). For him to have lost this text, one must assume an extended lapse of time between the composition of the first dialogue and the moment when the two others were drafted. Unfortunately no evidence allows us to determine the exact length of the intervening period.

232. Except, it must be said, in the form of a desire for explanation expressed by Ivo at the very start of the dialogue: "I want to be more fully taught about the right kind of friendship between us, which should begin in Christ, be maintained according to Christ, and have its end and value referred to Christ" (Aelred, Spir am 1.8 [CF 5:57]). Aelred did not explicitly answer the question, however, until books 2 and 3.

233. For this chronological overview, see Gaetane de Briey, Introduction, in Aelred de Rievaulx, *L'Amitié spirituelle*, trans. Gaetane de Briey (Bégrolles-en-Mauge: Abbaye de Bellefontaine, 1994), 13.

234. Song 1:1; Aelred, Spir am 221 (CF 5:75).

Aelred reprises this affirmation at the end of book 3 in almost the same terms, but without the explicit citation of the Song of Songs: "Thus rising from that holy love with which a friend embraces a friend to that with which a friend embraces Christ, one may take the spiritual fruit of friendship fully and joyfully into the mouth, while looking forward to all abundance in the life to come."[235]

This last point, postponing "all abundance" until "the life to come," is important. It introduces the last significant element of Aelred's spiritual doctrine of friendship. Friendship is for him, as just seen, not only the instrument and sacrament of a mystical union with God. It is also an instrument and sacrament of the reality to come. In the former case, friendship is in a way related to Christ as Head, insofar as Christ is its source, origin, and foundation. In the latter case, on the other hand, friendship is related to the Christ as Body and must be edified through a communal fraternity that is called upon to build itself on sharing and communal possession of gifts. This is how friendship is lived on a smaller scale. In this sense spiritual friendship, as Aelred conceives it, becomes the partially realized sign and expression, or sacrament, of an eschatology of hope.[236]

This explanation means that in Aelred's eyes friendship is a space of universally anticipated spiritual solidarity in which the breadth of human history and the original project of a humanity perfectly configured to correspond to the divine model of the Holy Trinity—that is, a reconciled humanity in which reciprocity and mutual dependence among all beings come to life in the joy of freely "giving and receiving" (Phil 4:15)—are already partially but truly realized. In this sense, spiritual friendship carries us into an eschatological hereafter not found in any place, and situated beyond the present time.

---

235. Aelred, Spir am 3.134 (CF 5:126).

236. "eschatologie de l'espérance," an expression borrowed from Christian de Chergé. The discussion that follows is inspired by Christian Salenson's commentary in his work *Christian de Chergé*, 16.

However, through spiritual friendship, this hereafter is one that is already being lived within the limits of time. This also means, from an eschatological perspective, that spiritual friendship can never be an end in itself for Aelred. Rather, it is directed toward an objective and an end that transcends it and gives to it its ultimate and plenary purpose: the formation here on earth of a community of brothers, united in charity. Already anticipating the communion of saints in the life of the world to come, this community realizes here and now, within the confines of history itself, the restoration of humanity to the divine image in the unity of individuals through charity.[237]

Aelred had already intuited this idea of friendship, related to ultimate ends and as a partially realized anticipation in the present time of the world to come, in the first book of *Friendship*[238] and even in some of his sermons.[239] But there he expressed it imperfectly, only giving it full expression in the veritable spiritual testament of *Friendship's* final two dialogues.

In book 2, Aelred expresses this idea through the analogy of the kiss as an exchange and mingling of the "same breath," which, in the "watermark" image of the early apostolic community, realizes spiritual unity among a multitude of individuals as well as union with God:

> Now the spiritual kiss belongs to friends who are bound
> by the one law of friendship. This takes place not through
> a touch of the mouth but through the attachment of the
> mind, not by joining lips but by blending spirits, while
> the Spirit of God purifies all things and by sharing himself

237. This discussion is directly inspired by Charles Dumont, "Chercher Dieu dans la communauté selon Aelred de Rievaulx," in *Une éducation du cœur*, 275–308. Of particular note is the section "Le paradis retrouvé" (Dumont, "Chercher Dieu," 288–89).

238. See on this point Aelred, Spir am 1.51–61 (CF 5:65–67) on the historical origin of friendship.

239. For example, S 8, for the Feast of Saint Benedict. Also worth noting in the same vein are the texts indicated in Dumont, "Chercher Dieu," 275–308.

pours in a heavenly flavor. This kiss I would aptly name the kiss of Christ, which he offers, however, through the lips of another, not his own. He inspires in friends that most holy affection, so that to them it seems that there exists but one soul in different bodies, and so they may say with the prophet, *see how good and how pleasant it is for brethren to live in unity.*[240]

Aelred's fullest expression of this idea, however, occurs in book 3 of *Friendship*. The first instance is in 3.79–80, where Aelred replies to one of Walter's objections. Walter is prepared to believe that it would perhaps be better to live without friends in this world given how high and demanding the ideal proposed by his master is. "Nonsense!" replies Aelred:

> This is that great and wonderful happiness we await. God himself acts to channel so much friendship and charity between himself and the creatures he sustains, and between the classes and orders he distinguishes, and between each and every one he elects, that in this way each one may love another as himself. *By this means each may rejoice over his own happiness as he rejoices over his neighbor's. Thus the bliss of all individually is the bliss of all collectively, and the sum of all individual beatitudes is the beatitude of all together.* There no thoughts are concealed and no affections disguised. The true and eternal friendship that begins here is perfected there. Here it belongs to the few, for few are good, but there it belongs to all, for there all are good.[241]

Aelred reprises this idea in the closing words of the final paragraph of the treatise, marking what Aelred himself assures us is evidence of the sovereign good *par excellence*: "When the fear is dispelled . . . , when the hardship is removed . . . , when . . . the sting of death is removed . . . then with the

---

240. Ps 132:1; Aelred, Spir am 2.26 (CF 5:76–77).
241. Aelred, Spir am 3.79–80 (CF 5:107). Emphasis Burton's.

beginning of relief from care we shall rejoice in the supreme
and eternal good, *when the friendship to which on earth we admit
but few will pour out over all and flow back to God from all, for God
will be all in all."*[242]

There is at least one foundational idea to be retained from
this passage. What we have just presented of friendship's eschatological aim, in the context of spiritual and monastic life,
tends to highlight the extreme importance of fraternal communal life as the sign and sacrament *par excellence* of a friendship
meant to become, or in accordance with the divine plan of
original creation to re-become, universal. Consequently, what
is often underappreciated is that, as Dumont has stated, Aelred's
conception of spiritual friendship reveals that the ultimate goal
of all charity, asceticism, and monastic discipline is nothing less
than to make possible the restoration of the entire universe on
the sole basis of a friendship finally become universal once
more.[243] This also means that in Aelred's eyes the edification of
a truly fraternal community, first in one's own monastery and
then within civil society at large, was not simply one pastoral
priority among others. As his spiritual influence grew over time,
the creation of such a community based on reciprocity and mutual dependence as the body of Christ (Eph 1:22-23) and as a
sign of the unity of all things in God (1 Cor 15:28) was the most
vital and urgent aspect of Aelred's abbatial ministry.

In the first two parts of this biography we have scrutinized
two "first circles" of Aelred's life. In part II we considered the
time of human and spiritual foundations, or Aelred the man
and the monk, and in part III we examined the time of instruction and early responsibilities, or the monk in the service of
the monastic instruction of his brothers. Around these two

242. 1 Cor 15:28; Aelred, Spir am 3.134 (CF 5:126). Emphasis Burton's.
[Translator's note: The third ellipsis is mine, to fit the English quotation to
Burton's phrasing; the others are Burton's.]
243. See Dumont, "Chercher Dieu," 307, adapted.

circles appear two additional, larger concentric circles. On the one hand there is the time of Aelred's great pastoral responsibilities, when as abbot of Revesby (1143) and of Rievaulx (from 1147 on) he was charged with conducting his brothers along the paths of the Gospel in order to build with them a fraternal community according to the Rule of Saint Benedict. On the other hand, there is the time of spiritual maturity, when, beginning with the accession of Henry II to the throne of England in 1154, he progressively extended his spiritual influence and his desire for universal harmony and peace across the civil and religious society of his time.

These two new, larger concentric circles are examined in parts IV and V.

Part IV

The Time of Great Pastoral Responsibilities

Abbot and Pastor

(1143–1147, 1147–1154)

Introduction: Searching for Unity
Asceticism and Charity
by Way of Friendship

What remains to be shown is that for Aelred, all temporal human history is inscribed in this cosmic and universal in-between time (*interim*), and, consequently, that this history can be interpreted as that of humankind's ceaselessly redoubled anticipatory efforts to inscribe the kingdom yet to come within the limits of time. Additionally, this chapter shows that Aelred's pastoral activity as the head of his monastic community, as well as his political engagements in his external relations with secular princes, was already informed by his developing doctrine of spiritual friendship.

To put it another way, beginning near the 1150s, in his pastoral practice as abbot and in his role as counselor to secular princes, Aelred's sole aim was to build and edify all human communities on the same spiritual and theological foundations that anchored and legitimized interpersonal spiritual friendship, albeit transposed to a grander scale—first within his own monastic community, then across the multicultural and multiethnic English nation.

Aelred expended such effort and energy to turn Revesby and Rievaulx—the former from 1143 to 1147, the latter from 1147 until his death—into communities of authentic fraternal life, because he believed they were called to offer a theological and political model on which all manner of ecclesiastic or civil social life should be built. In theological terms, this model rested upon the concept *ecclesiola in Ecclesia*, a miniature image of the reality that is the church, the body of Christ, a part of the entire Body.[1] In civil terms, as Gaetano Raciti states, this model rested on the microrealization of a project of communal personalism able to serve as a "new foundation for the British nation" at the end of a civil war that had devastated the nation from 1135 to 1153.[2]

Reserving the final part of our biography for the examination of this socio-political dimension of Aelred's conception of friendship, we devote the present part of our study solely to the ecclesiological dimension, showing how Aelred envisioned his pastoral role as abbot and how he devoted himself to the edification of a community that it might become the sacramental sign and anticipation of the kingdom yet to come. We preface this discussion in chapter 7 by presenting the thread of historical circumstances in which Aelred was called to his abbatial charge. This main ecclesiological discussion constitutes the central focus of chapter 8, at the end of which we point out signs of Aelred's awakening awareness of the social and political role that as abbot he would increasingly be called upon to assume in civil society. We thus establish the first indications—principally theological, ecclesiastical, and spiritual—of the reasons for Aelred's personal involvement in secular affairs. We then enter the final part of our biography, which follows Aelred's political engagements and public stances, what Alberic Stacpoole called "the public face of Aelred."[3]

1. See Roberto de la Iglesia, "La comunidad monástica, realización concreta de la Iglesia, según Elredo de Rievaulx," *Cistercium* 58 (2006): 389–437. See also Roberto de la Iglesia, "La ecclesiología monástica de san Elredo de Rieval," *Cistercium* 60 (2008): 81–102.

2. "microréalisation d'un projet de personnalisme communautaire . . . refondation de la nation britannique" (Gaetano Raciti, "Présentation générale," in Aelred of Rievaulx, *Sermons pour l'année I. Sermons 1–14*, trans. Gaetane de Briey [Oka, Canada: Abaye Notre-Dame-du-Lac, 1997], 17).

3. Alberic Stacpoole, "The Public Face of Aelred," *The Downside Review* 85 (1967): 183–99, 318–25.

Chapter Seven

Key Events

Foundation of Revesby (1143) and Election at Rievaulx (1147)

Rievaulx Under Its First Abbot, William (1132–1145)

Probably after preparing the new English foundation in 1130 and then realizing it on March 5, 1132, Saint Bernard placed it under the direction of William. Bernard's appreciation of William's capabilities appears in the fact that as early as 1119, just one year after William's arrival at Clairvaux, Bernard made William his secretary and close collaborator. His subsequent choice of William as the founder of Rievaulx seems to have been a particularly judicious decision. William was a native of Yorkshire, and, having received part of his intellectual education at York, he must certainly have been familiar with the ecclesiastical and political networks of that English metropolis. One can easily imagine that as the first Anglo-Saxon recruited to enter Clairvaux (even before Henry Murdac, who went there in 1125[1]),

---

1. The career of Henry Murdac, also a native of Yorkshire, is well known. After a brilliant start to a professorial career as master of the cathedral school of York, he was finally convinced by Saint Bernard, probably around 1125, to renounce his profession and join Bernard at Clairvaux, since, Bernard said, "you will find much more labouring amongst the woods than you will ever

William, present in the time of Clairvaux's active growth and engaged in an imagination-defying recruitment effort,[2] inspired Bernard to found a monastery in England and to entrust all the preparations to his secretary, even before sending him at the head of a twelve-monk colony to found the abbey.[3]

The choice of William turned out well. In the space of a dozen years, from Rievaulx's founding in 1132 to his death in 1145, he turned the monastery into a flourishing community of more than three hundred people. Among these was Aelred. Having entered Rievaulx in 1134 while the first buildings were probably still made of wood,[4] Aelred was elected to succeed

---

amongst books. Woods and stones will teach you what you can never hear from any master" (Ep 106 [SBOp 7:265–67]; *The Letters of Saint Bernard of Clairvaux*, trans. and ed. Bruno Scott James [London: Burns Oates, 1953], 155–56 [#107]).

2. One has only to think of the diverse houses founded by Clairvaux one after the other in the space of only a few years, each of which required a colony of at least twelve monks (see the following note). Here we mention only the daughter houses: Troisfontaines (1118), Fontenay (1119), Foigny (1121), Igny (1126), Reigny (1128), Ourscamp (1129), Bonmont (1131), Cherlieu (1131), Longpont (1132), Rievaulx (1132), Orval (1132), Vaucelles (1132), Vauclair (1134), Buzay (1135), Chiaravalle (1135), Eberbach (1135), La Grâce-Dieu (1135), and Hautecombe (1135). For the chronology, see for example, Pierre Aubé, *Saint Bernard de Clairvaux* (Paris: Fayard, 2003), 681. For the genealogy and filiation of Clairvaux, see Ivan Gobry, *Les moines en Occident. Tome 5. Cîteaux* (Paris: François-Xavier de Guibert, 1997), 559.

3. On the minimum number of twelve monks required for the foundation of a new monastery, see *Summa Cartae Caritatis*, 9, on the construction of abbeys: "A new abbot is not to be sent to a new place without at least twelve monks, or without these books: psalter, hymnal, collectary, antiphonary, gradual, Rule, missal; nor without having first constructed these places: oratory, refectory, dormitory, guest quarters, gatehouse—so that they may straightaway serve God there and live there in keeping with the Rule" ("Summa Cartae Caritatis," in *Narrative and Legislative Texts from Early Cîteaux: Latin Text in Dual Edition with English Translation and Notes*, ed. and trans. Chrysogonus Waddell [Cîteaux: *Commentarii Cistercienses*, 1999], 408).

4. Walter Daniel's narrative in his *Letter to Maurice* §3 seems to attest to this fact in recording that Aelred, on the eve of entering the novitiate, put out a

William in 1147. Gifted with numerous personal and spiritual attributes, notably in economic management, William rapidly attracted the attention of new donors, expanding the monastery's land assets and consolidating the monastery's economic foundation.[5]

Additionally, benefiting from Rievaulx's proximity to numerous stone quarries (seven of which have been identified by historians and archaeologists), William showed his architectural competence by beginning, probably with the help of Geoffrey of Ainai, a first wave of stone construction for the cloister buildings, including what are today the remains of the monastery's west wing (the lay brothers' wing).[6] It would fall to Aelred to complete the work during the twenty years of his

---

fire that was consuming the building (Walter Daniel, "The Letter to Maurice," in *The Life of Aelred of Rievaulx*, trans. F. M. Powicke, CF 57 [Kalamazoo, MI: Cistercian Publications, 1994], 152–53).

5. For the history of Rievaulx's land assets and economic development, see Janet Burton, "The Estates and Economy of Rievaulx Abbey in Yorkshire," Cîteaux 49 (1998): 29–94. See also Emilia Jamroziak, "Rievaulx Abbey and its Patrons: Between Cooperation and Conflict," Cîteaux 49 (1998): 59–71. For a broader history of Rievaulx and its architecture, see Peter Fergusson and Stuart Harrison, *Rievaulx Abbey: Community, Architecture, and Memory* (New Haven: Yale University Press, 1999). See also Christopher Norton, "Richard of Fountains and the Letter of Thurstan: History and Historiography of a Monastic Controversy, St. Mary's Abbey, York, 1132," in *Perspectives for an Architecture of Solitude: Essays on Cistercians, Art and Architecture in Honour of Peter Fergusson*, ed. Terryl Kinder (Turnhout: Brepols, 2004), 9–34. Norton argues that Rievaulx knew its greatest period of territorial expansion only after Aelred's election as abbot in 1147.

6. The importance of William's role as an "architect, founder and director of works" ("*architectus . . . et fundator et ductus*") is confirmed by Matthew, Rievaulx's precentor, who so describes William in his *Vita Beati Willelmi*, a work he composed at the start of the thirteenth century (around 1220). On this topic, see Fergusson and Harrison, *Rievaulx Abbey*, 45–58, esp. 45. As for the possible presence and assistance of Geoffrey of Ainai at Rievaulx, see Fergusson and Harrison, *Rievaulx Abbey*, 50, 55. Historians consider Geoffrey, a monk of Clairvaux, to have been one of the most important master builders and leaders in early Cistercian architecture. His presence has been noted at

abbacy, adapting the buildings' dimensions in relation to the monastic community's growing numbers.

Finally, most of Rievaulx's direct affiliates were founded during William's abbacy—four out of five monasteries in all.[7] First, in 1135 or 1136 Melrose Abbey was founded in Scotland, reclaiming the name of an ancient Scottish monastic site. Melrose was founded under the patronage of King David himself, the king who was like a father to Aelred during his ten-year sojourn at the Scottish court. David's stepson Waldef, Aelred's childhood friend, became abbot of Melrose in 1148. The same year, Rievaulx founded her second daughter house, Wardon, in Bedfordshire under the patronage of Walter Espec, who had offered Rievaulx its first lands. Simon, Aelred's novice master, was sent to be Wardon's abbot.

The Founding of Revesby (1143)

Seven years later, in 1142–1143, following a severe, life-threatening illness, William de Roumare addressed the monks of Rievaulx and proposed his protection for the founding of a monastery in his county of Lincolnshire. Roumare had recently been appointed count of Lincoln (1140) by King Stephen of England,[8] and his proposal, according to the chronicler Orderic Vitalis,[9] was perhaps intended to make up for his libertine youth and dissolute life. In any event Revesby, the third daughter house of Rievaulx, was born. Revesby was also called Saint Lawrence since, as Walter explains, the abbey was built on a

---

numerous construction sites affiliated with Clairvaux, including Rievaulx, Clairvaux, Vauclair, and Fountains.

7. For a succinct presentation of the houses founded by Rievaulx, see David H. Williams, "The English Cistercians in the Times of St. Aelred, Abbot of Revesby (1143–1147) and of Rievaulx (1147–1167)," *Cistercium Mater Nostra* 2 (2008): 13–30.

8. No doubt for fear of losing in Roumare a substantial ally in his war against the Empress Matilda (discussed in the second part of this biography).

9. Orderic Vital, *Histoire de Normandie* (Paris: Guizot, 1826), 4:414.

site where a church devoted to this saint already existed (VA 2). Now the time had come for Aelred to follow in the footsteps of his novice master. Employing the imagery of maternity so dear to the early Cistercian spiritual tradition and so important to Aelred, Walter writes that "the house of Rievaulx conceived a third daughter in her womb and showed signs that the time of her labor was drawing near. And when she gave birth, the midwives chose Aelred as bearer and nurse of the latest lusty addition to the family, declaring that, nourished by the milk of his solicitude, it would quickly grow into a stout child."[10]

Although Aelred had been novice master at Rievaulx for barely two years (1142–1143), his masterful monastic and doctrinal synthesis in *The Mirror of Charity* propelled him forward, with the result that at the age of thirty-three he was appointed to preside over a newly founded house. But this appointment would last only four years, from 1143–1147, for events at Rievaulx moved faster than anyone could have imagined. In any case, shortly before his departure for Revesby, Aelred had the pleasure of receiving his childhood friend Waldef—son of David's queen, Matilda of Senlis—in Rievaulx's novitiate. Waldef had become an Augustinian canon regular in 1130 and no doubt helped awaken Aelred's religious vocation, directing him towards the Cistercian life.

Just after Revesby's founding, King David spoke to Abbot William once again, seeking a group of monks to found a second Cistercian monastery. The result was the establishment of Dundrennan Abbey in Galloway, in southwest Scotland. Later, three years before his death, Aelred traveled here to comfort a daughter house threatened by fratricidal struggles between rival princes.

Rievaulx later founded a fifth daughter house, Rufford Abbey, in Nottinghamshire, south of Yorkshire. Rufford's first abbot was Philip de Kyme, and its patron was Gilbert de Gant,

---

10. Walter Daniel, *The Life of Aelred of Rievaulx*, trans. F. M. Powicke, CF 57 (Kalamazoo, MI: Cistercian Publications, 1994), 110, chap. 19.

brother-in-law and rival of William de Roumare. Gilbert was a loyal ally to Stephen of Blois, fighting at his side against the Empress Matilda during the English civil war (1135–1153). When Rufford was founded in 1147, Abbot William of Rievaulx had already been dead for two years. But his successor, Maurice of Durham, who completed the process of founding Rufford, certainly benefited from the immense pastoral zeal generated after the death of William, who was unanimously recognized as an exceptional being, blessed by God, and venerated by his brothers as a saint.

The brief obituary that Walter devotes to William in *The Life of Aelred* attests to William's reputation in his commemoration of his actions:

> While the venerable father Aelred shone in the magnificent radiation of these and many other miracles and virtues, death, *the last enemy* [1 Cor 15:26], closed the life on earth of the lord William, abbot of Rievaulx. His life is indeed to be blessed, for *the Lord gave him his blessing and confirmed his covenant on his head* [Sir 45:24]. From him, as from an inexhaustible well, streams of the religious life have watered those who have come after him, and to this day they flow and overflow in full measure in the house of Rievaulx and in her daughters, grateful and pleasant to drink, wholesome and of unfailing efficacy to lave those who are weak.[11]

The fact that after his death, as an exception to early Cistercian law, William was buried in the chapter house of the monastery also attests to this reverence. Still more significant is that one hundred years later, around 1250, William's brothers, driven by a surge of devotion, exhumed his body and placed his remains in a reliquary intended for public veneration.

11. Walter, VA 24 (CF 57:114).

The Brief Abbacy of Maurice of Durham (1145–1147)

Shortly after William's death, the brothers of Rievaulx gathered in the chapter house to elect his successor. They chose their cantor, Maurice of Durham, a man of great intellectual and spiritual merit who, according to Walter, enjoyed an excellent reputation for piety. Before joining Rievaulx in around 1138, Maurice had been a monk in Durham Cathedral's Benedictine monastery, a major center of profane and theological culture in northeast England. As subprior there, Walter reports, Maurice had been appreciated for his immense cultivation: "called by his companions a second Bede; and truly in his day, by his pre-eminence both in life and learning he alone could be compared with Bede."[12]

Maurice was abbot at Rievaulx for barely eighteen months. In 1147 Henry Murdac, abbot of Fountains since 1144, was elected to the archiepiscopal see of York and selected Maurice as his successor at Fountains. However great were Maurice's personal and spiritual qualities, he did not possess Murdac's aptitudes for the administration of temporal affairs. Crushed under the weight of his pastoral charge, Maurice resigned three months later, returning temporarily to Rievaulx before retiring permanently to another unidentified monastery. There he died, four years before Aelred's death, apparently still enjoying the esteem of his contemporaries.

The circumstances surrounding Maurice's resignation are not clear. Walter, who says Maurice's abbacy lasted two full years, fails for unknown reasons to mention that Maurice had been called upon to succeed Murdac as abbot of Fountains. Perhaps Walter felt it was not worth mentioning such a short tenure at Fountains, or perhaps he did not want to stain Maurice's reputation for piety. *The Chronicle of Fountains* (*Narratio de fundatione*), however, explicitly records that Murdac asked Maurice to succeed him and that Maurice withdrew from the

12. Walter, VA 25 (CF 57:115).

position after three months.[13] Walter is alone in specifying that Maurice resigned because he found the responsibility too heavy, and it is doubtful that that was the only reason. Janet Burton has suggested that Maurice's resignation could have been connected to a profound discord between Maurice and Murdac. The latter was known for his intransigence, and it seems that he may have wanted to keep his hand in the affairs of Fountains, as in fact he did during the abbacy of Maurice's successor, Thorald, who we know resigned precisely for this reason.[14]

However brief his abbacy at Rievaulx, Maurice was nonetheless able to initiate preliminaries for the founding of Rufford. Similarly, before leaving for Fountains, he had just enough time to sort out the thorny litigation between Rievaulx and the Savigniac priory of Byland. The problem arose from the fact that the two monasteries were located on opposite sides of the Rye Valley. Located only a few miles apart, they not only risked property disputes, but monks in each monastery could so well hear the bells of the other that their daily schedules interfered with each other. To resolve the conflict, one of the two monasteries had to move. Fortunately for the monks of Rievaulx, the integration of the Savigniac congregation into the order of Cîteaux in 1147 made the solution easier. Byland Priory was moved elsewhere, and Rievaulx thereafter claimed sole possession of the lands on both sides of the valley, solidifying its land base.

Rievaulx's rapid demographic increase during William's abbacy (1132–1145) allowed the community to found four daughter houses in only twelve years: Melrose and Wardon in 1135–1136, then in 1143 Dundrennan and Revesby, the latter founded by William de Roumare. Aelred, who had until then been novice master at Rievaulx, was sent to be the first abbot.

---

13. See Burton, "Rievaulx Abbey: The Early Years," in *Perspectives for an Architecture of Solitude*, ed. Terryl N. Kinder (Turnhout: Brepols, 2004), 50, citing the *Chronicle of Fountains*.

14. Burton, "Rievaulx Abbey," 50 and n. 27.

From Revesby (1143) to Rievaulx (1147): Aelred's First Steps
As Abbot

Walter devotes five chapters of his *Life* to Aelred's four-year
abbacy at Revesby, in chapter 19 relating the founding of the
monastery and Aelred's selection as abbot, and in chapters 20
to 23 highlighting that "the holy father made miraculous progress" there, leading to an illustrious reputation. Chapter 20
thus shows that the extraordinarily rapid growth of Revesby
in both recruitment and economic development directly resulted from Aelred's prestige. According to Walter, Aelred's
reputation during this time had spread so far, both within
Lincolnshire and throughout the kingdom, that he attracted
the favor of princes and bishops: "As he sweats in exhausting
and endless labors on behalf of his tender little flock, he is
comforted by God and made glad by his manifold blessing.
His fame runs through the whole countryside [see Luke 4:37].
Bishop, earls, barons venerate the man and the place itself, and
in their reverence and affection load it with possessions, heap
gifts upon it and defend it by their peace and protection." A
little later, Walter adds, "And so the servant of the Lord, greatly
beloved by all in the province, indeed by the whole realm and
most of all by the king, made his house rich and fruitful.
Within, the religious life waxed every hour and grew day by
day; without, possessions increased and gave a regular return
in money and means for all kinds of equipment. For God was
in that house and the Lord blessed it greatly."[15]

Two details in Walter's account of Aelred's abbacy at
Revesby deserve particularly close attention. The first is socio-
political in nature:

> The bishop orders him . . . to accept grants of land from
> knights in generous free-alms, and he obeys, since he had
> realized that in this unsettled time such gifts profited
> knights and monks alike, for in those days it was hard

---

15. Walter, VA 20 (CF 57:110–11).

for any to lead the good life unless they were monks or members of some religious order, so disturbed and chaotic was the land, reduced almost to a desert by the malice, slaughters and harryings of evil men. And so he desired that that land, for which almost all men were fighting to the death, should pass into the hands of the monks for their good; and he knew that to give what they had helped the possessors of goods to their salvation, and that, if they did not give, they might well lose both life and goods without any payment in return.[16]

This detail might seem surprising today. At the time, however, it was nothing extraordinary; it is a perfect reflection of what we now know of the general political situation in England at the end of the eleventh century and the first half of the twelfth. Again, historians agree that this period is characterized on the one hand by great social and political instability following the Norman Conquest and subsequent territorial redistribution[17] and, on the other hand, by the civil war that from 1135 to 1153 drained England and made prosperity impossible. In other words, this detail offers a glimpse of the political issues involved in founding a monastery as an "instrument of pacification." Walter underlines this issue one more time when in chapter 38 he mentions the founding of Dundrennan in Scotland.

The second detail meriting close attention in chapter 20 of Aelred's *Life* is pastoral. In chapter 19 Walter compares the role of abbot to that of a nursing mother and presents Aelred's mission as offering the "milk of his solicitude"[18] to his community in order to assure its rapid growth. In chapter 20, he

16. Walter, VA 20 (CF 57:111).
17. See "The Political Stakes of Cistercian Expansion in the British Isles" in chap. 2 above, which, largely on the basis of Janet Burton's work, discusses the tenurial crisis following the Norman Conquest, in part characterized by the eviction of those members of the Anglo-Saxon nobility hostile to William the Conqueror and by the replacement of those dispossessed by those in favor with the new authority.
18. Walter, VA 19 (CF 57:110).

extends this image, complementing it with a paternal dimension by comparing the community of Revesby to a woman and its pastor to Aelred, her husband:

> There was no sterility there, for our Jacob begot twins by both Leah and Rachel [Gen 29:15-30], as he preached fear and justice to the monks [*activis et officialibus*] and impressed the duties of prayer and love upon the brothers [*contemplativis et claustralibus*], saying to the former, "Fear the Lord, ye his saints, for there is no want in them that fear him [Ps 34:10]," and to the latter, "They who dwell in your house, O Lord, shall be always praising you."[19]

Walter goes on to illustrate these two traits of Aelred's pastoral charge with three miracles. The first, in chapter 21, involves the miraculous healing of Aelred's subprior, stricken by a cardiac ailment. The second, in chapter 23, also tells of the miraculous healing of a lay brother, a skilled artisan who loses the use of a hand following a serious work accident. The third, sandwiched between the other two, perhaps to emphasize its importance, is the narrative of the solicitude of Aelred in triumphing over the instability of a monk whom he had previously helped as novice master at Rievaulx.[20]

Aelred thus confidently guided the young community of Revesby and oversaw its harmonious development for four years; no one could have foreseen that he would soon have to leave it. But when in 1147 Maurice of Durham, the second abbot, was called to Fountains as the new abbot, the conventual chapter of Rievaulx gathered to elect a new abbot. In accordance with Cistercian law and the customs of the time, they selected a brother who had originally been a member of their monastery: Aelred. His election opened a twenty-year period of prosperity for Rievaulx and began the longest segment of Aelred's life ever spent in the same place and exercising the same function.

---

19. Ps 84:5; Walter, VA 20 (CF 57:111).
20. See chap. 6 above.

Rievaulx (1147–1167): A Narrative of Private or Political Life?

This twenty-year period indelibly marked the Rievaulx community and probably contributed more than any other to make it a prestigious and never-to-be-forgotten abbey. When Aelred had originally arrived there in 1134, just two years after its founding, much work was needed to construct the monastery and develop the community, but when he left ten years later for Revesby, Abbot William had already achieved several significant goals: abundant recruitment, consolidation of the abbey's land assets, and the beginnings of construction in stone. Nonetheless, when Aelred returned to lead Rievaulx four years later, in 1147, he still faced enormous responsibilities. Over time these responsibilities became even larger because of his increasing role in the contemporary affairs of civil society, particularly after 1153.

Walter Daniel's Choice: Narrating Private Life

Aelred's abbacy at Rievaulx can be divided into two periods of more or less equal length, as Walter makes clear. He bounds his narrative with a number of chronological markers, so suggesting that Aelred's twenty-year abbacy at Rievaulx was comprised of two ten-year periods, the first from 1147 to 1157 (chapters 27 and 30 of the *Life*), and the second from 1157 to 1167 (chapters 31 to 60). The latter period, in turn, falls into two sub-periods. The second of these, beginning in chapter 40, showcases the four final years of Aelred's life.

The framework Walter used derives from Aelred's private life and is primarily medical in nature. He increasingly imposed this organization in the *Life's* final twenty chapters, offering an almost day-by-day evolution of Aelred's state of health before his death.[21] This structure is consistent with

---

21. For a detailed study of the structure of the *Life of Aelred* and its chronological markers, see Pierre-André Burton, "Introduction," in Walter Daniel, *La Vie d'Aelred*, trans. P.-A. Burton (Oka, Canada: Abbaye Notre-Dame-du-Lac, 2004).

Walter's project, as he undertook the composition of the *Life* with the goal of refuting two accusations directed at Aelred in the context of his election as abbot of Rievaulx, reported in chapter 26 of the *Life*.

The first accusation holds that Aelred rose to become head of Rievaulx through personal ambition. Walter dismisses this accusation, qualifying such calumny as the fruit of jealousy and envy on the part of Aelred's rivals. In the following chapter he refutes the second accusation, which appears briefly at the end of the chapter. First he reports Aelred's characterization as "a glutton and a wine-bibber and a friend of publicans" (Matt 11:19). But also, the complaint goes on, having shown himself a friend of publicans and "a friend of the sick, the physician who used to relieve them,"[22] Aelred is accused of being lax regarding others' weaknesses. Against this second accusation Walter positions his refutation along two defensive lines. First he insists on Aelred's pastoral virtues in order to show that Aelred wanted to make his monastery a true place of mercy (in particular in chapter 29). Second, and more emphatically, Walter gives a detailed description of Aelred's state of health. In proceeding this way, Walter's insistence on Aelred's failing health contributed effectively to accomplishing his authorial goals, incrementally showing that, contrary to the accusations, Aelred was never a relaxed or self-indulgent monk. The proof as Walter presents it lies in the austere regimen that Aelred never ceased to maintain, even against the advice of his doctors, though his health, as he became ever more debilitated, would certainly have allowed him to moderate his rigor.

An Alternative: A Politically Based Narrative

As pertinent as it may be, Walter's approach in the *Life* fails to satisfy the historian's expectations, as it leaves the public

---

22. Walter, VA 26 (CF 57:116).

and political dimensions of Aelred's life largely untouched. An alternative approach, intended to highlight the public and political aspect of Aelred's personality, bases the narrative on other chronological landmarks taken from external events that had a profound impact on Aelred's life. From this point of view, the year 1153–1154 was a pivotal year in Aelred's life and in the general history of the era. Until then, Aelred had confined himself to playing a secondary role in historical events. But starting that year, things began to change. He progressively moved from the role of supporting actor to leading man, so to speak, or in any event one among several such at the time, moving into a position to direct the course of history or at least bend its trajectory.

In terms of the limited arena of local history, the 1153 deaths of King David of Scotland and Walter Espec, Rievaulx's founder, preceded the year before by that of David's son, Prince Henry, inevitably conferred a new prestige upon Aelred, moving him into center stage. As a direct witness and actor in events that shaped public and ecclesiastic affairs for almost a quarter century, from 1130 to 1153, he became for younger generations the living memory of recent history and the guardian of its continuity.

In terms of England's social and political life, 1153 was decisive in the signing of the treaty of Wallingford, which ended the more than twenty years of civil war between the partisans of Stephen of Blois and those of the Empress Matilda and her son Henry II. It is certainly no coincidence that in 1153 Aelred began to publish his first major historical works. Apart from his *Lament for David, King of the Scots*, a commemorative piece in which he mourns the death of his "second father," and his brief narrative of *The Battle of the Standard*, there was also his notable *Genealogy of the Kings of the English*. These three treatises, each in its own way, can be said to mark Aelred's official entry into political life, since through them Aelred seized the opportunity presented by the new sociopolitical context to present himself as a counselor of princes, and in particular of King Henry II.

That year saw an important change in church history as well, since in less than a month's time, two of the era's most prestigious religious figures passed away. Both were Cistercians who had dominated the social, political, and ecclesiastical life of the decade preceding their deaths. They were Eugene III, elected pope in 1145 and deceased on July 8, 1153, and Bernard, whose dazzling influence had been seen from as far back as the 1130s, who died on August 20 that year.

All these factors indicate that Aelred's abbacy at Rievaulx must have reached a major turning point not in 1157, with the decline of his health midway between his election as abbot and his death, as Walter suggests, but rather in 1153–1154, with his first public interventions as a political counselor. The study of Aelred's political activities comes in the final part of our biography, offering an overview of Aelred's long abbacy.

A Broad-Brush Summary of Aelred's Abbacy at Rievaulx: Compassion and Mercy

Immediately after recounting Aelred's election as abbot of Rievaulx and refuting the slanders directed at Aelred, in chapter 28 Walter tells of the death of the unstable monk, of whom he had already written twice before. In the context of hagiographic strategy, this narrative plays a dual role, allowing Walter to connect the three great periods of Aelred's monastic life—as novice master at Rievaulx, as abbot at Revesby, and finally as abbot of Rievaulx—and to show the true continuity between them. At the same time, the narrative allows Walter to introduce two chapters presenting the general balance sheet of Aelred's abbacy. In this accounting, Walter notes that at Aelred's death Rievaulx had more than six hundred brothers, monks and lay-brothers combined, and that even so the monastery was able to meet the economic needs of a multitude of brothers, with enough left over to provide for subsequent generations. Further, he suggests that Rievaulx's demographic growth and economic development during Aelred's abbacy were the result of Aelred's unceasing pastoral solicitude—simultaneously fraternal, paternal, and maternal—toward all.

Outside of the laconic note affirming that Aelred's "material legacy was great enough, under prudent management, to feed and clothe a still greater number, and to leave something over for their successors,"[23] Walter says almost nothing else about Rievaulx's economic growth during Aelred's abbacy. We have already identified the reason: concerned above all with defending the reputation of his abbot from the point of view of the latter's austerity, such a question never entered his mind.

Other scholars have already treated this question. We here simply underline two points. First, Janet Burton has noted that while William's abbacy contributed to consolidation of the monastery's earliest land assets, Rievaulx experienced its greatest period of territorial expansion under Maurice and, especially, Aelred. Because under Maurice the priory of Byland was moved elsewhere, Rievaulx was able effectively to lay sole claim to the lands on both sides of the Rye Valley. Janet Burton has also highlighted two other important facts concerning the growth of land assets during Aelred's abbacy. One is that this growth became significant only after Henry II's accession to the English throne in 1153–1154—proof positive of the close link between political context and the prosperity of monasteries. The other is that this growth was probably tied to the networks of relationships Aelred maintained with Scotland (the "Scottish network") and with the cathedral of Durham (the "Durham network").[24]

The second important point about Rievaulx's economic development concerns the monastery buildings. When Aelred had arrived at Rievaulx in 1134, the buildings were primarily made of wood; a first wave of stone construction began under the direction of Abbot William. The modern-day remains of the monastery's west wing date from this period. As William's

23. Walter, VA 30 (CF 57:119).
24. See Janet Burton, "Rievaulx Abbey," 50–53.

successor, Maurice was abbot too briefly to leave any mark in this domain. It is therefore principally Aelred's abbatial initiatives that brought about the construction and expansion efforts that effected the near completion of the abbey. With a few notable exceptions such as the abbey church, rebuilt in the second quarter of the thirteenth century, and a few other elements either destroyed or reworked, the monastery's present-day ruins reflect the amplitude of Aelred's undertakings.[25]

Nevertheless, while Aelred's solicitude as abbot led to the construction of a stone-built monastery, Aelred focused more on his own spiritual growth, making his heart, as Walter describes it, "a house of perfection."[26] Above all, he strove to build up his community, to make it a place of true fraternal life and of sacramental communion as well as a visible anticipatory sign of the kingdom yet to come.

25. For details on Aelred as builder see Fergusson and Harrison, *Rievaulx Abbey*, 59–68.
26. Walter, VA 40 (CF 57:127).

Chapter Eight

Aelred

A Master Architect Building a Community

When Aelred was named novice master in 1141–1142 by his abbot, William, he was only about thirty years old and had barely nine years of monastic life under his belt. But from the time of his entry at Rievaulx, he had come quite a long way, both personally and intellectually. Personally, in terms of his own inner unification, he managed to move progressively beyond the anthropological body-soul dualism that had limited his perspective at the time of his conversion and that, as a result of personal and cultural tendencies, had automatically pushed him toward a rigorous, almost intransigent asceticism. But two aspects of Aelred's initial monastic experience during his novitiate moderated this first impulse. The first was the salutary failure of his unilaterally and excessively ascetic approach to monasticism. The second was his assimilation of the broad, open monastic teachings dispensed by his mentors. These facets of his early experience allowed him to bring back to the center of his spiritual quest a second fundamental element of his personality—the natural capacity, perhaps even the vital need, for the bonds of friendship in his interpersonal relationships. Consequently, as a novice master Aelred aligned himself with the spiritual doctrine of Saint Bernard on the ordering of human affectivity through charity, while enriching that doctrine by reintegrating the whole of human affectivity as an essential component in Christian and monastic spirituality.

In the wake of this rich initial spiritual experience and his first doctrinal synthesis in *The Mirror of Charity*, Aelred was sent to be the first abbot of Revesby. This appointment, much like his election to the abbacy of Rievaulx four years later, was providential. Both events forced him to broaden his perspective, since as abbot he would be led to transpose his spiritual doctrine of community edification—initially the fruit of his personal experience of inner unification, later elaborated to serve for the monastic instruction of other individuals—to a much larger scale.

It is this broader perspective—leading from the individual, to others, to the group as a whole, and leading from personal instruction to the edification of a community of brothers—that we now examine, proceeding in two main steps. The first step completes our sketch of the way Aelred envisioned, lived, and expressed his abbatial ministry, focusing on two new images. Alongside the figure of the abbot as friend and father, we consider that of the abbot as mother and brother. The basis for our discussion is two-faceted: Aelred's words, taken from his liturgical sermons, and a comparison of the fruits of that examination with those derived from Walter's words. This comparison allows us to proceed to the second main step—to pursue our inquiry by uncovering fundamental characteristics of the monastic community as Aelred imagined it and tried to construct it.

The Multidimensional Nature of Abbatial Ministry

The Pastoral Prayer best attests to Aelred's sharp awareness of his duties and responsibilities as abbot. *Prayer* was not only a major text of medieval spiritual literature but the perfect mirror of Aelred's pastoral heart. However, *Prayer* is far from being the only text in which Aelred offers a glimpse of his conception of his role as abbot and pastor of a community. Additionally, in numerous sermons, in conjunction with a common lesson for his brothers, he inserts reflections that shed light on one facet or another of his abbatial mission.

In S 24.31, For the Nativity of Holy Mary, Aelred invites his brothers to see Christ as a father who educates, as a friend who gives his life for those he loves, as a mother who consoles and nourishes with the milk of his sweetness, and as a brother who, being flesh of our flesh, has shared in the fragility of our human condition. These four traits of Christ as man are the fruit of a tender devotion toward Jesus' humanity re-developed in twelfth-century spirituality, and in Cistercian spirituality in particular. These traits allow Aelred to paint the portrait of a pastor acting "according to the heart of God." He painted this portrait first for himself as abbot, but also for whoever else might occupy a position of pastoral obligation—in particular priests and bishops. Thus these traits, typically in groups of three, appear in various liturgical sermons whenever Aelred speaks of the figure of the shepherd or pastor.

Moses and Saint Benedict: Being a Brotherly Participant in a Common Condition

A prime example of such a sermon is S 56, for the Feast of Saint Benedict, in which Aelred presents the patriarch of Occidental monks, and therefore indirectly of abbots, as a father, teacher, and leader.[1] First he shows him as a father (*pater*), because through the Gospel he begets monks through Christ Jesus.[2] Then he treats Benedict as a teacher, because through him, having entered the school of self-offering (*scola*

---

1. Aelred of Rievaulx, *The Liturgical Sermons: The Durham and the Lincoln Collections*, trans. Kathryn Krug, Lewis White, and the *Catena Scholarium*, CF 80 (Collegeville, MN: Cistercian Publications, 2018), 2–3.

2. This is precisely the manner in which Walter presents his relationship of spiritual filiation with Aelred. Aelred was the one, Walter writes in the first chapter of *The Life*, "*who begot me to the life* [e.g, following the Rule] of Saint Benedict through the Gospel of God and showed himself a father to the brethren" (Walter Daniel, *The Life of Aelred of Rievaulx*, trans. F. M. Powicke, CF 57 [Kalamazoo, MI: Cistercian Publications, 1994], 90).

pietatis), the monk progresses in wisdom, justice, and grace. Finally Aelred shows Benedict as a leader (*dux*), because, placed under Benedict's guidance and under the Rule, the monk is led out of Egypt and the slavery of sin to make his way progressively toward the Promised Land of spiritual freedom found in Christ.[3] Expanding upon this symbolism, which presents monastic life as a path of liberation from slavery in Egypt, Aelred compares Benedict to Moses and thus refines his portrait of the true shepherd by highlighting three new criteria that justify entrusting the abbot with a pastoral charge. First, the personal experience of temptation teaches the shepherd to have compassion for others. Then spiritual love stimulates pastoral solicitude. Finally the inner life of contemplation purifies discernment so that the shepherd may guide others by preceding them along the path:

> One who is worthy to be put in authority over others is the one whom the *sting of temptation* has tormented, whom the *heat of love* has set on fire, whom the *splendor of contemplation* has illuminated. Temptation instructs one in compassion; love, in solicitude; contemplation, in discretion [*ad discretionem*]. I confidently commit myself to your care, Father Benedict, you who have learned in your temptations to be compassionate toward my infirmities, who, burning with the fire of charity, know how to be present to my neediness, who, illumined by the knowledge of God, know how to meet my doubts. Go before me now, my blessed leader, along the way that you yourself have chosen: I am ready to follow you wherever you will go.[4]

In this text Aelred establishes a link between pastoral solicitude or spiritual love on the one hand and the personal experience of temptation on the other. Aelred thus advances the idea

---

3. On the theme of the Rule as the instrument of spiritual liberation, see the earlier discussion in chap. 6 above.

4. See Luke 22:33; 9:57. Aelred, S 56.6 (CF 80:119).

that the only person who can be a true pastor (exhibiting the paternal aspect) and come to the aid of others (exhibiting compassion or the maternal aspect) by guiding them with judicious counsel is the one who has first been tested by temptation and has proven himself able to overcome it. In other words, three of the four aspects of the pastoral charge as Aelred states them in S 24 are presented as complementary. The compassionate and consoling maternal aspect cannot truly be effective, he shows, unless preceded by the fraternal aspect of shared human weakness. And the two of these together qualify an individual to be the pastor or shepherd of others, giving insightful counsel defining the paternal aspect. Thus only one who, through a capacity for compassion, acts as a mother of mercy can be a true pastor in the mold of Moses or Benedict.

But, Aelred insists, only one who is a brother in humanity, who has acquired this capacity for compassion through his own experience with human weakness and through an awareness drawn from his own misery, can ever be such a mother of mercy. He affirms this point most explicitly in his presentation of Peter and Paul as the two pillars of the church in S 18, for the Feast of the Holy Apostles Peter and Paul: "because they were to be the *Fathers of the Church* and the *doctors to cure the sick* [the paternal aspect], *in order to know how to have compassion on the infirmities of others* [mercy and the maternal aspect], they *first experienced infirmity in themselves* [the experience of every person's "misery," representing the fraternal aspect]."[5]

We must not think for a moment that these are empty words for Aelred. One reason Aelred seems so contemporary to us,

---

5. Aelred of Rievaulx, *The Liturgical Sermons: The First Clairvaux Collection*, trans. Theodore Berkeley and M. Basil Pennington, CF 58 (Kalamazoo, MI: Cistercian Publications, 2001), 256. A similar passage appears in *Jesus at the Age of Twelve*, where Aelred states that the pastor must "remember the weak" (Aelred of Rievaulx, *Jesus at the Age of Twelve*, trans. Theodore Berkeley, in *Aelred of Rievaulx: Treatises. Pastoral Prayer*, CF 2 [Kalamazoo, MI: Cistercian Publications, 1971], 370).

despite the nine centuries separating his time from ours, is that, gifted as he was with a largely innate pedagogical sense and animated by a sharp pastoral concern, Aelred readily evokes his own personal experiences and the spiritual difficulties he had to overcome. In that way he gives his readers the impression that they are in the presence of a brother who, sharing in their own experience of weakness, is sensitive to the troubles in their hearts.

One of the finest examples of this heart-to-heart, brother-to-brother communion can be found in a sermon in which Aelred presents himself as the crippled beggar before the Beautiful Gate of the temple,[6] expressing his need for his brothers' compassion and begging alms of mercy from them.[7] Aelred here uses this confession of personal weakness to exhort those of his brothers most advanced in spiritual life to show such compassion not only toward him, their abbot, but also toward all the weakest members of their community.[8]

Giving One's Life for the Flock: The Pastor as Mother and Friend

A pastor's experience of human weakness awakens in his heart the awareness that he is not stronger, better, or above others, but on the contrary, with them fraternally. Aelred does not simply reveal the source of this compassion, which binds together mercy and the shared condition of misery in the experience of human frailty and the trials of temptation and sin. He also reveals that from this source flows mercy, manifesting itself downstream in the unconditional gift of the pastor's self, offered fully to his brothers. In particular SS 63 and 64 attest

---

6. See Acts 3:2. On this assertion's possible root in an event from Aelred's early childhood, see part II of this work, in particular the discussion of Eilaf's forced resignation as guardian of Hexham's church.

7. Aelred, S 70.23 (CF 80:270–71).

8. Aelred, S 70.40 (CF 80:276).

to this point. Each of these sermons was delivered before a synod of priests, and for Aelred these were prime occasions to present his pastoral ideal.

In S 63 Aelred inquires why Jesus, appearing on the lake shore after his resurrection, asked Peter the same question three times: "Do you love me?" (John 21:17). Astutely, and with a certain humor, Aelred superimposes the figure of Peter upon that of Samson and explains, before what must have been an amused and breathless audience, that he sees therein strands forming a single, slender, solid cord, the uniting of three qualities that must constitute the love of every priest and pastor. The first of these is prudence (*prudens*), which, based in discernment (*discretio*), allows the pastor to avoid the evils afflicting his subordinates and prudently remove those ills. The second is sweetness (*dulcedo*), which allows the pastor to bear others' weaknesses with compassion (*compassio*). The last is strength (*fortitudo*), which, forbearing in nature (*longanimitas*), allows him to tolerate their disorder with magnanimity.[9]

The statement brings to mind Aelred's words in S 56, which contain two of these three elements, discernment (or informed judgment) and a merciful compassion exhibited through patient forbearance toward others' weaknesses. The statement here in S 63 is different, however. In this sermon, instead of exploring the path of mercy from the standpoint of participation in a common human condition, Aelred brings together three Johannine texts. Associating the figure of the pastor with that of Christ as friend and that of the good shepherd,[10] Aelred demonstrates that he who shows a love that is "prudent, gentle, and strong"[11] toward those entrusted to his care resembles Christ. As Christ gave his life for us, so does the shepherd for his sheep (see John 10:11). Thus Aelred exhorts pastors similarly to devote their entire lives to the service of their brothers (see

---

9. Aelred, S 63.7, 26 (CF 80:197, 204–5).
10. Aelred, S 63.23–24 (CF 80:203–4).
11. Aelred, S 63.7 (CF 80:197).

1 John 3:16). This, he says, is no different from the concept of *friend*, since, as Saint John reminds us, "greater love than this has no man, that a man lay down his life for his friends."[12] Aelred also evokes the apostle Paul to underline the all-consuming love, the pastoral zeal, and the attention to others' needs with which every priest must be filled: "those who love do not spare their money, indeed would not spare even their own lives. Listen to a certain good shepherd (I am speaking of Paul): he says, 'I will most gladly spend and be utterly spent for your sakes.' Love also, each of you, and you will not hesitate to do the same."[13]

"All to All" or Mercy as the Pastor's Crown

Aelred holds this aspect of the pastoral role—a love that extends to the total gift of oneself and that adapts to the needs of all—in such high esteem that he makes it practically the sole theme of a sermon that he gave for the feast of the apostles Peter and Paul.[14] Several passages from this sermon are worth citing. We highlight a few paragraphs (S 71.29–33) in which Aelred compares the apostle Paul to the innkeeper to whom the good Samaritan (Jesus) entrusted the man he discovered by the side of the road, wounded and abandoned, so that he might care for him, and who spent far more than the two pieces of silver given to him for this purpose (see Luke 10:29-37). Thereafter, although "free as to all," he sought to make himself "the servant of all, that I might gain the more" (1 Cor 9:19), to become weak with the weak, to become "all things to all men, that I might save all."[15] There follows (S 71.32–33) praise for Paul, vibrating with Aelred's immense admiration for this incomparable pastor, whose heart burns with such love that

---

12. John 15:13. On this theme, see chap. 6 of the present work.

13. See 2 Cor 12:15. Aelred, S 63.25 (CF 80:204)

14. S 71, on the Feast of the Apostles Peter and Paul (CF 80:277–90).

15. 1 Cor 9:22. Aelred, S 71:31 (CF 80:288).

he sees therein "the seat of goodness, the courtyard of mercy, and the throne of charity,"[16] echoing what he wrote a few lines earlier: "What, I ask, is more precious than this soul? He seems to go about the entire world as though with open arms of charity, an exposed heart of goodness, and a generous bosom of compassion. Like that hen in the gospel that gathers its chicks under its wings [see Matt 23:37], he seems to gather together Greeks and foreigners, the wise and unlearned, in the expanded breast of his love."[17]

Aelred then introduces spiritual paternity (begetting, instructing, strengthening) and maternity (nourishment and compassion) as two major images characterizing pastoral ministry, along with their lesser counterparts, friendship (giving oneself freely) and fraternity (the desire to share each individual's condition by making oneself all to all). Thus he continues:

> He would give birth to some, nurse others already born with a sweet cup of milk, and strengthen others who were fully grown with solid food [Gal 4:19; 1 Cor 3:1-2]. In pain with the first, cooing at the second, and coming down to the last, he seems to be a storehouse of divine wisdom. He himself plays the role of mother, nurse, and guide. You should view him as higher than everyone in his sanctity, lower than everyone in his humility, on the same plane with everyone in equality, and among everyone in charity.
>
> Someone who was in pain saw nothing but tears from Paul; someone else rejoiced, and Paul was glad with him [Rom 12:15]. Another person was sick, and the compassionate doctor Paul attended to him. He worked together with everyone, suffered with everyone, took delight in everyone [1 Cor 12:26]. "Who is weak, he said, and I am not weak? Who is scandalized, and I do not burn?"[18]

16. Aelred, S 71.37 (CF 80:290).
17. Rom 1:14; Aelred, S 71.32 (CF 80:288).
18. 2 Cor 11:29; Aelred, S 71.32–33 (CF 80:288–89).

This charity even manifested itself, Aelred says, in the art with which Paul exercised his ministry of fraternal correction, for the desire to amend others is in itself a proof and an act of love. If charity results in being severe with someone, it is only because charity inspires in us a hope for that individual and the belief that he or she can be corrected (see S 71.36). At the same time—in contrast with Peter's passionate but less enlightened zeal when Jesus had to ask him to resheath his sword—Paul demonstrated extreme tact in executing the delicate task of correcting others: "There was a rumor of fornication among the Corinthians, and of such a sort that was not found among the pagans: someone taking his father's wife [1 Cor 5:1]. Paul said to them, 'What do you want? Shall I come to you with the rod, or in charity and a spirit of gentleness?' " (1 Cor 4:21). Aelred concludes, "What sort of person do we think he is, my brothers, what kind of man, offering himself to the chaste and threatening the incestuous with nothing but the rod? Charity does not know the sword, of course; it is unaware of iron."[19]

Thus the virtue of mercy is the principal robe in which the pastor must clothe himself, the crown that must adorn his head, as Aelred affirms again in S 64, addressed to a synod of priests. After having compared the four elements of an Old Covenant priest's liturgical vestments (see Exod 28:39-42) to the four cardinal virtues (temperance, justice, fortitude, and prudence), Aelred wonders if they are enough, and then answers his own question:

> Certainly they are sufficient if they have the oil of *holy anointing* poured over them [see Lev 10:7]. For it is neither becoming nor expedient for a priest to be without oil. Oil, indeed, signifies mercy. And who is the priest who does not want mercy to be shown to him? "Blessed are the merciful for they shall obtain mercy" [Matt 5:7]. Who is there among us, my brothers, who is sufficiently washed,

19. Aelred, S 71.33 (CF 80:289).

sufficiently adorned with these virtues? What hope have we, except in the oil of him whom God the Father *has anointed with the oil of gladness above his fellows*? [Ps 44:8]. May you also have the oil of mercy and loving-kindness poured over you, so may you neither buy the *sinner's oil* [Ps 140:5] nor try to borrow like the foolish virgins [see Matt 25:8-9] from those who will rebuke you, but give in abundance and abound in giving, and may the bounty of holy anointing [see Lev 10:7] build up whatever you fall short of in terms of washing or vesture. And since it is the nature of oil to be borne upon the top of all liquids into which it is poured, may you experience with regard to this spiritual oil what is written, *The compassion of the Lord is upon all his works* [Ps 144:9]—so that thus crowned in mercy and compassion [Ps 102:4], you may come with happiness to him who with the Father and the Holy Spirit lives and reigns, God forever and ever. Amen.[20]

The Ideal toward which Aelred's Loving Heart is Bent

We could continue indefinitely citing passages of Aelred's liturgical sermons revealing his conception of pastoral ministry. They all would confirm the four principal facets we have highlighted: paternity and maternity, fraternity and friendship. Or, inversely, they might allow us to bring still others to light.[21] But at this point in our discussion, it is more important to focus on the fact that by proposing such an ideal to his audience, Aelred was not offering empty words. He knew only too well, as Benedict had taught (RB 2.11–13) and as his personal experience had convinced him, that anyone who received the

20. Aelred, S 64.25–26 (CF 80:217–18).

21. See, e.g., Aelred, S 17, for the Feast of the Holy Apostles Peter and Paul (S 17.5–8), where Aelred speaks of three categories of monks—the "cloistered" (who have no specific charge), the "officials" (who have been charged with a specific responsibility within the monastery), and the "superiors" (who are responsible for better organizing community life)—and identifies the role of and trials faced by monks in each category (CF 58:247).

title of abbot had to guide his disciples by the example of his actions even more than by his words.

Thus by vocation and the abbatial charge entrusted to him, by conviction and an innate sense of his responsibilities, and by consciousness of his own limitations and personal weaknesses, as expressed in *Prayer*, esp. §§6–8, Aelred sought constantly to live up to the ideal that he proposed, doing so to the extent that his own abilities and the grace of God allowed him. The passages of *Prayer* that demonstrate this effort echo the words in his sermons.

Like Solomon (see 1 Kgs 3:4-14), Aelred expresses an awareness of his own limitations and asks that God grace him with discernment so that he can wisely govern the flock entrusted to him:

> My God, you are well aware of my stupidity [see Ps 68:6], and my weakness is not hidden from you. And so, sweet Lord, I ask to be given not gold or silver or jewels, but rather wisdom so that I may know how to guide your people. O font of wisdom, send her forth from the throne of your glory so that she may be with me, toil with me [see Wis 9:10], work with me, speak with me, and bring my thoughts and my words, all my undertakings and decisions, into harmony with your good will, to the honor of your name, for their progress and my salvation.[22]

Aelred then reveals his desire to be, like Saint Paul and following Christ, a friend and good shepherd, simultaneously "all to all," a brother among brothers. He expresses his wish to give himself completely to each one, a friend who spends himself without keeping accounts:

> You know my heart, O Lord: whatever you have given to your servant, it is my will that it be expended upon

---

22. Aelred of Rievaulx, *Pastoral Prayer* 6, in *For Your Own People: Aelred of Rievaulx's Pastoral Prayer*, trans. Mark DelCogliano, CF 73 (Kalamazoo, MI: Cistercian Publications, 2008), 49.

them in its entirety and entirely spent on them. Still more, may I find happiness in being utterly spent for them [see 2 Cor 12:15]. Let it be done in this way, my Lord, let it be done in this way! All my feeling, all my speaking, all my rest and all my work, all my action and my thought, all my success and all my hardship, all my death and all my life, all my health and sickness—all that I am, all that gives me life, all that I feel, all that I discern—let all this be expended upon them in all its entirety and entirely spent for their benefit, for the benefit of those for whom you yourself did not consider it unworthy to be utterly spent. O Lord, teach me, your servant; teach me, I beseech you, through your Holy Spirit, how I can spend myself for them and how I can expend myself entirely for them.[23]

He then asks, again emulating Saint Paul, for the maternal graces of mercy and compassion in order to bear others' weaknesses in patience and to bring all of his brothers closer to Christ by the gentleness and justice of his teachings:

Through your indescribable grace, O Lord, enable me patiently to support their weaknesses, to have compassion on them lovingly, and discerningly to help them. Let me learn, let your Spirit teach me, to console the sorrowing, to strengthen the fainthearted, to set the fallen upright, to be weak with the weak, to be indignant with the scandalized [see 2 Cor 11:29], to become all things to all people in order to win them all [see 1 Cor 9:19 and 9:22]. Grant me a true and upright way of speaking and an eloquence of mouth to build them up in *faith, hope, and love*, in chastity and humility, in patience and obedience, in fervor of spirit and devotion of mind [*devotio mentis*].[24]

Furthermore, in keeping with the recommendations of Benedict, who invites all abbots to "convince, entreat, rebuke" (2 Tim 4:2), and who encourages them to "show the sternness

23. Aelred, Orat 7 (CF 73:49–51).
24. Aelred, Orat 7 (CF 73:51).

of a master [*dirum magistri*], the affection of a father [*affectus patris*]" (RB 2.23-24), Aelred asks also for the paternal grace to correct his brothers, while respecting the character of each (see RB 2.31-32):

> And because you have given them this *blind leader* [see Matt 15:14], this untaught teacher, this ignorant guide, teach the one you have put in a teacher's position, lead the one you have commanded to lead others, guide the one you have appointed as a guide—if not for me, then for them! Therefore teach me, sweet Lord, to admonish the disturbed, to console the fainthearted, to support the weak [see 1 Thess 5:14], and to *accommodate* myself *to each one's character*, disposition, inclinations, aptitude, or simplicity, according to the place and time, as seems best to you.[25]

Finally, as if he feared being misunderstood, Aelred returns to his desire to be seen by his brothers as one among them, a brother useful in charity and obedient in humility:

> Our God of mercy, *hear me*—for their sake! I pray to you for their sake, compelled by the duty of my office, urged on by my attachment to them, yet quickened with joy when I contemplate your kindness. You know, sweet Lord, how much I love them, how I have poured out on them all that I can from the depths of my being, how my heart melts over them. You know, my Lord, that I do not order them around harshly [see Ezek 34:4] or out of an overblown sense of my authority. You know how I want to *profit them* in love *rather than to preside over them* [see RB 64.8], to be placed in a humble position below them but also to be held in affection among them as one of them [*quasi unus ex illis*].[26]

---

25. Aelred, Orat 7 (CF 73:51).
26. Aelred, Orat 8 (CF 73:53); citing Sir 32:1.

This desire to be considered *quasi unus ex illis* is so profoundly anchored in Aelred's heart that he went so far as to propose the idea to secular princes of his time as a veritable *forma vivendi*—that is, as a model of government. We see a fine illustration of this when, in the course of the moral portrait he paints of Edward the Confessor, Aelred reprises this phrase from the Scriptures to encourage Henry II, the addressee of *The Life of Saint Edward*, to show toward all his subjects the same humility and accessibility that his illustrious predecessor had acquired from his constant meditation upon this biblical verse.[27]

Walter's Testimony

We have already considered Aelred's statements to uncover four facets characterizing the way in which he envisioned and lived his abbatial ministry. Of these, two are major (paternity and maternity), and two minor, though no less essential (fraternity and friendship). All are in one way or another intrinsic to the principle of mercy. Now we examine Walter's testimony to the abbatial ministry of the man he served for many years as secretary and nurse. His work substantially corroborates the presence of these four traits in Aelred's sketch of a true pastor's spiritual physiognomy, showing that at least in Walter's eyes Aelred's life corresponded as perfectly as possible to that ideal.

---

27. "In all these things the blessed man was not inflated by human renown. Deeply acknowledging God's goodness toward himself, he pondered steadily this saying of Wisdom: *Have they made you a prince? Do not let it go to your head, but be among them like one of themselves* [Sir 32:1]. Keeping this pattern of living [*formam vivendi*] before him, he comported himself as the equal of the domestic servants, humble to the priests, pleasant to the people, compassionate to the suffering, and generous to the needy" (Aelred of Rievaulx, *The Life of Saint Edward, King and Confessor*, in *Aelred of Rievaulx: The Historical Works*, trans. Jane Patricia Freeland, CF 56 [Kalamazoo, MI: Cistercian Publications, 2005], 142).

Like a Father: The Nourishing Father, the Master,
and the Physician

Walter emphasizes four components of the abbot's paternal role, the first being begetting. From the first chapter of the *Life*, Walter refers to Aelred as the one "who begot me to the life of Saint Benedict through the Gospel of God and showed himself a father to the brethren."[28] This image takes on full consistency in chapters 19 and 20, when in narrating the founding of Revesby Abbey, Walter states that his superiors chose Aelred so that he might preside over the destiny of this house and so that he might be its "bearer [*gerulum*]" and "nurse [*nutricium*]."[29] At the same time, he compares Aelred to the patriarch Jacob and the community of Revesby to Jacob's two wives, Rachel and Leah, who became mothers of Jacob's children (VA 20). The monastic community thus becomes by analogy and conjugal symbolism the maternal womb in which conception takes place.

The second paternal component Walter emphasizes is teaching, with Aelred a master who instructs and corrects. He mentions this educational function several times in the *Life*, beginning as early as chapter 20, where he states that the children born of these unions of Aelred and Revesby—that is, the monks begotten in the community—were instructed by Aelred's preaching. In chapter 46, he illustrates that this preaching included an element of fraternal correction and the development of moral conscience. In other words, Walter shows the instructional task as completing the portrait of the father as teacher, accompanying two other traits associated with the pastor's physiognomy. Through fraternal correction and the development of the heart that it entails, he says, the

---

28. Walter, VA 1 (CF 57:90).

29. Walter, VA 19 (CF 57:110). [Translator's note: Burton's French translation rendered these terms differently, with *gerulum* as *tuteur* (tutor) and *nutricium* as *père nourricier* (foster father).]

educational task takes on a medicinal function. The teacher becomes after a fashion a physician who cares for and heals souls as well as bodies. Furthermore, the subtle tact with which Aelred assumes this corrective role in a sermon given in chapter, inviting his brothers to examine their lives and improve them, reveals the maternal tenderness he cultivated with respect to his children.

Walter attests to Aelred's possession of these traits in his *Lament for Aelred*, composed immediately following his abbot's passing: "Did any sick person appeal to Aelred and not immediately sense his healing gifts? Was he not an eminent sophist with no equal who, by the abundance of his words and a flood of aimiable speech revealed maladies of minds? This education in charity [*educatio caritatis*] was so close to us that it approached the richness of a mother's milk for her sons and undeviatingly displayed the grace of a responsible father."[30]

Traces of these qualities also appear in the *Life* itself. The miracle narratives marking the work (specifically chapters 21, 23, 34, and 36) revealed the medicinal function of Aelred's abbatial ministry. But more important in this context is Walter's description of the Rievaulx community as the "mother of mercy." For Walter, Rievaulx was a place of compassion and healing, where, under Aelred's paternal governance, whoever came found not only a refuge, but also the fraternal support necessary to remake himself:

> He turned the house of Rievaulx into a stronghold for the sustaining of the weak, the nourishment of the strong and whole; it was the house of piety and peace, the abode of perfect love of God and neighbor. Who was there, however despised and rejected, who did not find in it a place of rest? Whoever came there in his weakness and did not

30. Walter Daniel, *Lament for Aelred*, in *The Life of Aelred of Rievaulx*, trans. Jane Patricia Freeland, in Walter Daniel, *Vita Aelredi*, CF 57 (Kalamazoo, MI: Cistercian Publications, 1994), 142.

find a loving father in Aelred and timely comforters in the brethren? When was anyone, feeble in body and character, ever expelled from that house, unless his iniquity was an offence to the community or had destroyed all hope of his salvation? Hence it was that monks in need of mercy and compassion flocked to Rievaulx from foreign peoples and from the far ends of the earth, that there in very truth they might find the peace and "the holiness without which no man shall see God" [Heb 12:14]. And so those wanderers in the world to whom no house of religion gave entrance came to Rievaulx, the mother of mercy, and found the gates open, and entered by them freely, giving thanks unto their Lord.[31]

Several lines later, Walter ascribes words with a similar effect to Aelred himself, tirelessly pursuing his task as "instructor in charity," in response to possible criticism for the warm welcome he accorded to any presenting themselves at the gates of Rievaulx:

Aelred would say "Do not, brother, do not kill 'the soul for which Christ died' [1 Cor 8:11], do not drive away our glory from this house. Remember that 'we are sojourners as were all our fathers' [1 Chr 19:15], and that it is the singular and supreme glory of the house of Rievaulx that above all else it teaches tolerance of the infirm and compassion with others in their necessities. And 'this is the testimony of our conscience,' that this house is a holy place because it generates for its God sons who are peacemakers. All"—he would continue—"whether weak or strong, should find in Rievaulx a haunt of peace, and there, like the fish in the broad seas, possess the welcome, happy, spacious peace of charity, that it may be said of her, 'Whither the tribes go up, the tribes of the Lord, unto the testimony of Israel, to give thanks to the name of the Lord.' There are tribes of the strong and tribes of the

31. Walter, VA 29 (CF 57:117–18).

weak. The house which withholds toleration from the weak is not to be regarded as a house of religion. 'Your eyes have seen me, yet being imperfect, and in your book all shall be written.' "[32]

Like a Mother: Mediator of Mercy and Compassion

This ministry of maternal mercy and compassion, allowing Aelred to welcome his brothers and sympathize with each one's needs, is also testified to by Jocelin of Furness in his biography of Waldef, King David's stepson and Aelred's childhood friend. In the midst of his presentation of the friendship between Aelred and Waldef, Jocelin adds the following moral portrait of Aelred: "he was a man who brought out the best in everyone [*optime morigeratus*], gifted in the world's wisdom [*sapientia seculari praeditus*], witty [*facetus, facundus*], good and jolly company [*socialis et jucundus*], liberal and discreet [*liberalis et discretus*]. He was, what is more, gentle and patient [*mansuetus et patiens*] and most compassionate [*valde compatiens*], beyond all his fellow-prelates, of the infirmities of others, whether bodily or moral."[33]

In the exercise of an abbatial ministry, such patience and compassion had numerous implications. As Gilbert of Hoyland says in his eulogy for Aelred, these qualities rendered Aelred impervious to all impulse toward anger:

> He was lucid in interpretation, not hasty in his speech. He questioned modestly, replied more modestly, tolerating the troublesome, himself troublesome to no one. Acutely intelligent, deliberate in statement, he bore annoyance with equanimity. I remember how often when

32. Walter, VA 29 (CF 57:118), citing Ps 139:16.
33. Jocelin of Furness, "The Life of Waldef, Abbot of Melrose," in "An Edition and Translation of The Life of Waldef, Abbot of Melrose," trans. George Joseph McFadden, dissertation, Columbia University, 1952, 237–38 (Ann Arbor: University Microfilms International, 1952).

someone of his audience rudely interrupted the course of his instruction, he stopped speaking until the other had fully exhausted his breath; when the gushing torrent of untimely speech had ebbed away, he would resume his interrupted discourse with the same calmness with which he had waited, for he both spoke and kept silent as the occasion demanded. Quick to listen, slow to speak, but not slow to anger. How is he to be described as slow to anger? I would rather say he was not in the race![34]

This statement confirms Walter's report of Aelred's final words to his brothers at the time of his death:

I have lived with a good conscience among you [see 1 Cor 4:4; 2 Cor 1:12], for as I lie here, as you see, at the point of death, my soul calls God to witness that, since I received this habit of religion, the malice, detraction or quarrel of no man has ever kindled feeling in me against him which has been strong enough to last the day in the domicile of my heart. I have always loved peace and the salvation of the brethren and inward quiet. By the grace of Christ I have commanded my spirit that no disturbance to the patience of my mind should survive the setting of the sun.[35]

Aelred's capacity to bear with patience and compassion the infirmities of each of his brothers explains the second Aelredian characteristic to which Walter testifies. He affirms that so great were the dimensions of Aelred's heart, and so unequaled his gentleness, that during the seventeen years Walter lived under Aelred's leadership, he never once saw Aelred expel anyone from the monastery. Moreover, he adds, during this same pe-

---

34. Gilbert of Hoyland, *Sermons on the Song of Songs, III*, trans. Lawrence C. Braceland, The Works of Gilbert of Hoyland 3, CF 26 (Kalamazoo, MI: Cistercian Publications, 1978), 496 (S 41.4).

35. Walter, VA 50 (CF 57:134–35); see Eph 4:26; RB 4.73.

riod only four monks attempted to leave, and Aelred managed to convince all of them, "save one follower of Satan,"[36] to return to the monastery.[37]

The third consequence of Aelred's greatness of heart is probably the least expected. At the very least, it contrasts starkly with the spirit of solicitude so vital to early Cistercian spirituality. It is the existence at Rievaulx of fraternal colloquia or, as we would say today, community dialogues, which Charles Dumont has highlighted.[38] Walter mentions these several times in *The Life of Aelred*. However, chapter 31 in particular, which introduces the final ten years of Aelred's life, enumerates the special dispensations, with the consent of the Cistercian general chapter, taken to permit Aelred to spare his inexorably deteriorating health. Among these dispositions, Walter mentions the existence of a small "cottage"—literally a "mausoleum" (also called a *cubiculum*, a point to which we will return)—which Aelred had built for his convenience close to the infirmary[39] but which, over time, became more and more a focal point of Rievaulx's community life. Walter asserts that "this cottage was, indeed, a great source of consolation to the brethren, for every day they came to it and sat in it, twenty or thirty at a time, to talk together of the spiritual delights of the Scriptures and of the observance of the Order."

This chapter ends with the highly revealing and significant image of Aelred's maternal heart: "There was nobody to say to them, 'Get out, go away, do not touch the abbot's bed'; they

36. Walter, VA 31 (CF 57:120).

37. This passage recalls the unstable monk who, thanks to Aelred's pastoral solicitude, ended his life in Aelred's arms (see Walter, VA 15, 22, and 28).

38. Charles Dumont, "Chercher Dieu dans la communauté selon Aelred de Rievaulx," in *Une éducation du cœur* (Oka, Canada: Abbaye Notre-Dame-Du-Lac, 1997), 295–302.

39. On the existence and location of this "cottage" see the archaeological study of Peter Fergusson, "Aelred's Abbatial Residence at Rievaulx Abbey," in *Studies in Cistercian Art and Architecture*, ed. Meredith P. Lillich, CS 167 (Kalamazoo, MI: Cistercian Publications, 1998), 5:41–56.

walked and lay about his bed and *talked with him as a little child prattles with its mother.*"[40]

This aspect of Aelred's pastoral practice, particular to him and apparently contrasting with the dictates of early Cistercian legislation,[41] may seem surprising to some. Independent of this institutional aspect, this pastoral practice raises multiple questions. Certain historians, such as Gaetano Raciti, have wondered where Aelred's sensitivity and attention to the weaknesses and limitations of others originated. The answer to this first question seems obvious and is suggested by a number of Aelred's liturgical sermons, which we have already considered in terms of the exercise of spiritual paternity. One point on which Aelred insisted was that those whom God destined for a position of pastoral responsibility should have first passed through the crucible of temptation, so that the experience of their own weakness made them more understanding of others' weaknesses. Thus Raciti rightly asserts that the source of Aelredian compassion is a fundamental spiritual attitude rooted "in the humus of his natural gifts," as well as in "his experience of conversion and the rereading of the events of his youth in

---

40. Walter, VA 31 (CF 57:120).

41. Dumont hypothesizes that a statute promulgated in 1152 by the Cistercian general chapter of Cîteaux and reiterated two years later explicitly "targeted the abbot of Rievaulx for the colloquia taking place on his visits to other monasteries and for those taking place in the infirmary" (Dumont, "Chercher Dieu," 302). If this hypothesis is correct, it means that the practice of engaging in such dialogues began before the deterioration of Aelred's health, in other words before 1157. It could even be, as Aelred's *Spiritual Friendship* seems to indicate, that these dialogues began all the way back at the beginning of his abbacy early in the 1150s, or even that they took place while he was occupying the post of novice master in 1142 and 1143—a post in which his inclination toward and aptitude for interpersonal dialogue were already well known. On this latter point see Gabriel Ghislain, "À la recherche de la réponse juste: un novice interroge son père maître," Coll 55 (1993): 78–109. See in particular the first paragraph of the first section, "L'art du dialogue" (Ghislain, "À la recherche," 81).

light of the divine *dispensatio* accorded to him"[42]—in other words, his own experience with God's mercy.

This being the case, the second question that immediately comes to mind is how to explain the maternal aspect with which both Walter and Aelred affectively tint this attitude of compassion. To provide an appropriate reply to this question we must take into account various levels it implies, in symbolic and psychological-anthropological terms as well as in the theological terms of Christology and Mariology as they jointly pertain to medieval and Cistercian spirituality.

From Mother to Friend: From Mary to Christ

To grasp the maternal aspect of Aelredian compassion, two levels of meaning have to be considered: one anthropological, the other theological. The anthropological aspect offers few difficulties, but the theological aspect requires much more attention. In anthropological terms, the symbolic division of paternal and maternal roles emphasized by contemporary psychology must be taken into account. The paternal role is mainly one of structuring the individual by means of a "transcendent third party" and essentially consists of imposing a framework of fundamental laws, rules, and restrictions. Conversely, the maternal role tends more toward welcoming, openness, tenderness, gentleness, and compassion. It is clear that as abbot and through the "magisterial" functions implied by this position, Aelred assumed the paternal role of structuring individuals, with the maternal role being assumed primarily by the Rievaulx community as a "womb-like space of conception." The proof of this is Walter's reference to the abbey under Aelred's direction, and not to Aelred himself, as the "mother of mercy."[43] In other words, we can only speak of the maternal

---

42. Gaetano Raciti, "L'option préférentielle pour les pauvres dans le modèle communautaire aelrédien," Coll 55 (1993): 199.

43. Walter, VA 29 (CF 57:118).

aspect of the abbatial charge by way of analogical transposition (or in a derived and second—but not secondary—manner). That is, the abbatial charge itself is maternal only to the extent that the abbot assumes a ministry of compassion and mercy as an integral part of his overall duties.

Truly to appreciate the analogical character of the abbatial charge's maternal aspect, we must abandon the strictly anthropological perspective of the abbot's functions and situate our discussion within the realms of theology and spirituality. Fortunately, though perhaps without even fully realizing it, Walter opens the way for this approach in chapter 50 of the *Life*. Here, with great emotion, he transcribes Aelred's final words to his brethren some ten days or so before his death, stating that at the end of their visit, all present began to weep profusely, especially at the moment "when he, weeping, said to us, 'God who knows all things knows that I love you all as myself, and, as earnestly as a mother after her sons, I long after you all in the [heart] of Jesus Christ.' "[44]

By explicitly linking the maternal aspect of his abbatial ministry ("as earnestly as a mother after her sons, I long after you all") to "the affection of Jesus Christ" (Phil 1:8), Aelred provides a solid Christological foundation for that maternal aspect. At the same time, he inscribes the maternal aspect within the framework of a broader medieval spiritual tradition that emphasized two things. First was a tender devotion to the humanity of Christ, seeing in Jesus the Word made flesh and the "sacrament" of sweet and merciful divine compassion toward humanity, and emphasizing the contemplation in Christ of a mother who offered humankind the milk (see Heb 5:12-13 and

44. Phil 1:8. Walter, VA 50 (CF 57:135). [Translator's note: The English translation of *The Life of Aelred* gives "I long after you all in the bowels of Jesus Christ." The French translation, provided in Burton's original text, gives "heart" in place of "bowels." I have opted to replace the English *Life's* expression with "heart," since the term "bowels" does not lend itself as explicitly or as logically to Burton's follow-up discussion of affection.]

1 Cor 3:2) of his own salvational humanity—food for infants—before subsequently offering humankind the more solid food derived from the contemplation of his divine nature. This particular devotion to Jesus as mother, widespread in the twelfth century, is well known to historians of spirituality.[45] Cistercian authors beginning with Saint Bernard himself became highly qualified ambassadors of the idea. Early on, they joined the figure of Mary to this devotion, in whom they contemplated the "Mother of Mercy" (*Mater misericordiae*), that is, literally, the Mother of the one who *is* Mercy, Jesus in his humanity.[46]

Similarly, on the basis of this three-pronged convergence between anthropology, spirituality, and theology, Suzanna Greer Fein correctly asserts that beyond the three principal feminine figures in the gospels—Mary of Bethany, contemplative and figure of filiation; the Virgin Mary, mother of Jesus and figure of maternity; and finally Mary Magdalene, wife and figure of spousal union—Aelred's perception of maternal function flows preeminently from his contemplation of Christ on the cross. As he tells his sister, the recluse: "On your altar let it be enough for you to have a representation of our Savior

45. See for example Caroline Bynum, *Jesus as Mother: Studies in the Spirituality of the High Middle Ages* (Berkeley: University of California Press, 1982).

46. Bernard's "Sermon on the Sunday in the Octave of the Assumption," which presented Mary as the mother of all tenderness and the mediator before the Mediator, can be read in light of the theology of the incarnation (developed in SC 20). Here Bernard explains that when the invisible God sought to make himself visible in the flesh and live as a man among humankind, "he wanted to recapture the affections of carnal men who were unable to love in any other way, by first drawing them to the salutary love of his own humanity, and then gradually to raise them to a spiritual love" (Bernard of Clairvaux, *On the Song of Songs II*, trans. Kilian Walsh, CF 7 [Kalamazoo, MI: Cistercian Publications, 1976], 152). For Aelred, see e.g. a sermon on the Assumption referring to the "throne of [Mary's] grace" and describing her as "the mother of mercy" (S 74.28 [CF 80:319]). See also his S 75, "On the Birth of Blessed Mary," where he again compares the body and soul of the blessed Virgin Mary to a throne "on which [Jesus] arranges and pays out the riches of his mercy in charity" (S 75.4, 16 [CF 80:319]).

hanging on the Cross; that will bring before your mind his Passion for you to imitate, his outspread arms will invite you to embrace him, his naked breasts will feed you with the milk of sweetness to console you."[47] That is, she must nourish herself spiritually from the contemplation of Jesus' mercy, made manifest by his humanity crucified and sacrificed.[48]

In other words, if there is a source to Aelredian compassion, it lies in Aelred's personal experience with divine grace at the time of his own conversion. On the other hand, as Raciti rightly states, the veritable archetype of Aelredian compassion resides in Aelred's rereading and reinterpretation of this same event "in stimulating contact with and illuminated by the fertile radiance of the mystery of redemption," as Aelred contemplates it, with very Bernardian accents, through the passion of Christ. Son of God he may be, yet he took upon himself "the likeness of sinful flesh" (Rom 8:3) in order to learn compassion through his suffering. Or, rather, Christ sought to gain first-hand knowledge of humankind's wretched and miserable condition in order to learn mercy based in this shared experience.[49]

Proceeding from what he calls "the transformative interpenetration of Christic and human experience" that he sees in Aelred, Raciti underscores the idea that through "Inspiration, lucidity, perseverance in the application [of maternal compas-

---

47. Aelred, Inst incl 26 (CF 2:73); on this passage see Marsha L. Dutton, "Christ Our Mother: Aelred's Iconography for Contemplative Union," in *Goad and Nail: Studies in Medieval Cistercian History, X,* ed. E. Rozanne Elder, CS 84 (Kalamazoo, MI: Cistercian Publications, 1985), 21–45.

48. Suzanne Greer Fein, "Maternity in Aelred of Rievaulx's Letter to his Sister," in *Medieval Mothering,* ed. John Carmi Parsons and Bonnie Wheeler (New York: Routledge, 1996), 147.

49. Raciti, "L'option préférentielle," 201. Raciti comments on an unedited sermon by Aelred for the Feast of Saint Benedict. For the Bernardian source, see *The Steps of Humility and Pride* 3.6–7, where, in his audacious exegesis of the letter to the Hebrews (Heb 2:17; 5:8), Bernard offers Christ as the model of compassion and mercy, he who *"pati voluit ut compati sciret, miser fieri ut misereri disceret . . . experimento."*

sion toward his brothers, the abbot of Rievaulx] drew them out of a meditation both theological and affective on the debasement, diminution, and annihilation of the Word made flesh, in which he contemplates in Jesus Christ the ontological crystallization of divine condescendence toward man."[50] The Christological basis of Aelredian compassion in the mystery of kenosis and the merciful heart of Jesus allows us to understand why friendship and fraternity were two fundamental elements of an abbot's functions as Aelred envisioned them. But it also allows us to see that they flow directly toward the maternal aspect of pastoral ministry.

One of friendship's essential traits consists in giving one's life for those one loves (see John 15:13). In light of this trait, Christ's compassion, which led Jesus to "empty himself" of himself (Phil 2:7) and become poor though he was rich so that by his poverty we might become rich (see 2 Cor 8:9), is the expression *par excellence* of the gift of oneself and therefore the expression of perfect friendship. Walter offers a marvelous illustration of the close connection between compassion and friendship as gift of self—to the point of emptying oneself of oneself—in the way Aelred assumed his abbatial ministry. This appears in chapter 51 of the *Life*, where Walter records Aelred's last testament to his brothers:

> After this he ordered to be brought to him his glossed psalter and the *Confessions* of Augustine and the text of John's Gospel and the relics of certain saints and a little cross which had belonged to Henry, archbishop of York, of good memory, and he said to us, "Behold, I have kept these by me in my little oratory and have delighted in them to the utmost as I sat alone there in times of leisure. 'Silver and gold I have none' [Acts 3:6], hence I make no

50. Raciti, "L'option préférentielle," 201, 202.

will, for I possess nothing of my own; whatever I have
and I myself are yours."[51]

Reading this text, one could wonder if it is pure fiction, entirely invented by the author, or an exact account of events and
a faithful transcription of Aelred's words. We will never know
for certain. Two clues lead us to believe, however, that Walter's
testimony is trustworthy and that perhaps, without recounting
events with absolute accuracy in every detail, Walter was at
least closely inspired by what Aelred himself did say or write
in other circumstances. There is an obvious spiritual kinship
between Aelred's final words as Walter reports them and the
substance of certain passages from *The Pastoral Prayer*—especially paragraph 7—in which Aelred expresses his desire to
spend himself entirely in the service of his brothers.

Similarly one sees the verse from the Acts of the Apostles,
"Silver and gold I have none," cited in the middle of the chapter. Such a discreet clue is more difficult to interpret, but it is
not too far a stretch to hear two echoes of this thought. The
first is in paragraph 6 of *Prayer*, where Aelred appropriates
Solomon's prayer and asks God not for gold or silver (alluding
to both Acts 3:6 and Rom 3:4-14), but only wisdom, in order
better to guide the flock entrusted to him.[52]

The second is in his S 70, on the Feast of the Apostles Peter
and Paul, commenting on the episode of the crippled beggar
who, seated at the Beautiful Gate of the temple, begs mercy
from passersby.[53] In his commentary on this passage, as a
pastor Aelred identifies with the apostle Peter, who, unable to
give gold or silver that he does not have, offers what he does
possess—salvation in Jesus' name. At the same time, Aelred
identifies with the invalid and seeks to present himself before
his brothers as a crippled beggar in need of their mercy. It is

51. Walter, VA 51 (CF 57:135).
52. See Orat 6 (CF 73:49).
53. Acts 3:2.

difficult to say which of these two facets of Aelred's sermon is more admirable.

In any case, if one interprets the verse from the Acts of the Apostles in chapter 51 of the *Life* in light of Aelred's commentary in S 70, the entire chapter gains a new depth of meaning. When Aelred affirms before his brothers that he "has neither gold nor silver" to bequeath to them, but only the little he does possess along with his person, he leaves them the greatest heritage of all: his twofold experience of mercy, comprised of the mercy he ceaselessly offered to all through his identification with the apostle Peter and the mercy he himself received, through his identification with the cripple in Acts 3:2.

From Compassion to Fraternity: The Fraternal Aspect of Compassionate Ministry

Because of its Christological foundation, then, pastoral ministry as Aelred lived it is based on an intrinsic link between maternal compassion and friendship as gift of self. The same type of link exists between compassion and fraternity. As a disciple of Bernard, Aelred knew that there was no compassion other than that rooted in the shared experience of suffering: *com-* (with) plus *passion* (suffering). Bernard states in fact that compassion is the reason for the incarnation, as Christ sought to experience humankind's misery (*miser fieri*) in order to learn mercy (*ut misereri disceret*). What is true of Christ in his relationship with humankind applies equally to relationships between humans: there is no true charity but that founded on the principle of fraternity. By identifying with the cripple in S 70.23–24, Aelred demonstrated that even as an abbot he was no stranger to his brothers' condition. Similarly in *Prayer*, he expressed his desire "to be held in affection among them as one of them."[54]

54. Aelred, Orat 8 (CF 73:53).

On both a Christological and spiritual level we must evaluate Walter's insistence on how much Aelred needed to feel surrounded by his brothers.[55] Certainly before accepting this spiritualizing or theologizing interpretation of the facts, the historian has a right to wonder first about the human foundations of this need and to seek deeper reasons for it in Aelred's personal history. Again, the events of 1114, when the bishop of York had taken the church of Hexham from Aelred's father and handed it over to Augustinians, probably had a great impact on Aelred and may well have left him with a feeling of abandonment and insecurity, for which he later sought to compensate by multiplying friendships, even at the risk of dispersion and fragmentation. Indeed, twenty years later, at the time of his conversion, he came to a bitter awareness of this result through painful experience.

However accurate this affective and psychological reading of the facts may be, based as it is on relatively tenuous clues, it is far more important to note that Aelred's desire to establish friendships followed him throughout his life, well after his conversion. This fact may explain why as abbot Aelred subsumed and ordered this desire in his Cistercian vocation, transforming it into an effort greater than that of any other Cistercian abbot of his generation to build around himself a fraternal community.

Building a Fraternal Community, or Aelred's Mystical Pluralism

As Aelred's personal history and innermost aspirations probably made him need to feel surrounded by brothers united in common affection to a greater degree than any other abbot of his generation, this need may have furnished Aelred with

---

55. Walter's chap. 31 tells of the gathering of twenty or thirty brothers in Aelred's "mausoleum," and in chap. 50 he reveals Aelred's sense of fraternal life as seen in the tiniest details of his life, reporting Aelred's final conversation with his brothers, in which he asked their permission to die as, he says, he had previously asked permission to travel from the monastery.

the major guidelines for his community-building project and led him to spend himself freely to build a fraternal community founded on charity through the bond of peace. There is no dearth of textual documentation to support such a reading of the facts, which seem principally personal and affective in nature. Frequently cited in this regard is a passage from book 3 of *Friendship*, where Aelred recounts to Gratian and Walter the story of an experience he had had while passing through the cloister of the monastery. Watching the brothers there, he says that he felt as if he had been transported to "the fragrant bowers of paradise." He then explains to them the reason for this feeling:

> I marveled at the leaves, blossoms, and fruits of each single tree . . . .[56] Finding not one soul whom I did not love and, I was sure, not one soul by whom I was not loved, I was filled with a joy that surpassed all the delights of the world. Indeed as I felt my spirit flowing into them all [*sentiebam meum spiritum transfusum in omnibus*] and the affection of all coursing through me [*et in me omnium transmigrasse affectum*], I could say with the prophet, "See how good and how pleasant it is for brethren to live in unity."[57]

This text is a godsend for the historian, for Walter, who personally participated in the discussion, recalls just such conversations in the *Life*, where he recounts the events at the end of Aelred's life, as when he recalls the brothers' frequent assemblies:

> The second night after he had received the sacrament of the holy oil . . . . All of us came together in one, not doubting of the father's passing to God, and vying with each other in pious zeal in ministering to his needs in his

56. The image of the trees should be read as each brother and his respective virtues. [Translator's note: My ellipsis, to fit the English quotation to Burton's phrasing.]
57. Ps 132:1; Aelred, Spir am 3.82 (CF 5:108).

weakness. There were now twelve, now twenty, now forty, now even a hundred monks about him; so vehemently was this lover of all of us loved by us. And he indeed, whose memory is blessed forevermore, himself counted this the greatest of all blessings, that he should be chosen by God and men to be so well beloved.[58]

But chapter 56 of the *Life* is the most eloquent in its thematic parallel to both this passage and Aelred's earlier description of the cloister. Walter situates the event on January 11, 1167, on the eve of Aelred's death. Aelred is once more surrounded by nearly all the brothers of the community, reading him the narrative of the passion. Despite his weakness and inability to speak, Walter says, Aelred participated in the reading, allowing all his emotions to show through the movements of his hands or the expressions on his face. Walter then adds a further significant detail showing the mutual affection uniting the brothers of Rievaulx to their abbot and the unanimity of hearts and sentiments—one might almost say the "communication of properties"—that reigned among them: "As the reading proceeded you could see in all joy and grief running together, smiles and tears, the voice of exaltation and the sighs *as from one mouth, at one time, the same in all and all in each, on communal procession* [*Eadem in omnibus et onmia ex singulis in rem quam publicam progredi*]."[59]

The vocabulary employed in this last expression differs somewhat from that which Aelred borrows in his description of the cloister. There he speaks of "flowing" and "coursing" (*transfundere* and *transmigrare*), while in the *Life* Walter speaks of things following in "communal procession" (*in rem publicam progredi*). But the spiritual kinship between the two passages is obvious. Thus it is clear that Walter intended to suggest that

---

58. Walter, VA 53 (CF 57:136). [Translator's note: My ellipsis, to fit the English quotation to Burton's phrasing.]

59. Walter, VA 56 (CF 57:137). The emphasis is Burton's.

Aelred's desire to build a fraternal community joined in mutual affection and communion of feelings was not a mirage or an unachievable utopia. Rather, he indicates that Aelred had truly transformed that desire into a concrete reality within the community of Rievaulx.

This conclusion, though, creates two dangers. It might lead us to believe that through the fraternal relationships he encouraged within his community, Aelred sought only to fulfill his own unmet affective needs. Of course we know through Aelred's own accounts how much his friendships meant to him before entering Rievaulx and how as a monk he made friendship an instrument of spiritual growth at the heart of his monastic life. But to consider the question only from this angle reduces his community-building project to human and affective dimensions, whereas his project was much broader than that.

The second reason to move beyond a simple psycho-affective approach to the question is connected to the first. It derives from the fact that adherence to this approach risks confusing a Christian or monastic community with a mere group of friends and thus, as Dumont has written, to reduce Aelred's community-building project to the rather limited proportions of a "small community of likeable people,"[60] founded not on the supernatural principle of a divine calling, but solely on the natural principle of mutual co-option.

In other words, we must avoid the illusory fusion of two distinct but complementary elements. There is certainly the element of fraternal and communal charity, meant to be universal and extended to all, but there is also the element of friendship, which, while being a "very holy sort of charity [*caritatis sacratissimum genus*],"[61] remains limited charity with a doubly restricted application. First it is limited to those toward whom we feel a "spontaneous, pleasant inclination"

---

60. Dumont, "Le personnalisme," 327. On the same issue, see Dumont, "Chercher Dieu," 305.

61. Aelred, Spec car 3.39.110 (CF 17:300).

(i.e., the *affectus*, or the affective dimension of friendship), and second, in the case of truly spiritual friendship, it is limited to those with whom a "mutual search for goodness" (i.e., the *consensus*, or the ethical dimension of friendship) is possible.

Moreover, even if Aelred's statements contain some ambiguity, sometimes giving the impression of not distinguishing among members of his community, as if he considered them all his friends, he well knows the risk of confusion between the two elements. He is conscious of the need to maintain a clear distinction between charity and friendship, as he shows when, after affirming that he felt loved by all and that he similarly loved them all in return, he feels obliged, almost regretfully, to reply negatively to Gratian's question: "We are not to assume, are we, that you have received into your friendship all those whom you so love and by whom you are so loved?"[62] Aelred then explains that friendship consists of communicating one's secrets and aspirations, and that it would be inappropriate to do so with many of those he loves, "since they are not old enough, mature enough, or discreet enough for such intimacies."[63]

Aelred's hesitation between a desire to make everyone his friend and the healthy and realistic assessment that such universal friendship is a practical impossibility might appear inconsistent and illogical. But this is not so. One must bear in mind that Aelred projects upon all interpersonal relationships the light of cosmic and universal friendship that shines on all things in accordance with the Creator's original plan, whose perfect realization is anticipated at the end of historical time, something true both of interpersonal relationships involving one-on-one friendships and of the fraternal charity constituting communities.

Situated between protological origins and eschatological ends, the fraternal and communal aspect of monastic life is theologically conceived of by Aelred on the three-part model

---

62. Aelred, Spir am 3.82 (CF 5:108).
63. Aelred, Spir am 3.83–84 (CF 5:109).

offered by intratrinitarian life (that is, the trinitarian theology of the communication of properties), Christ's life and redemption (a theology of the incarnation as one person of two natures), and monastic life's first historical realization in early apostolic community life as seen in Acts 2:42, 4:32-35 (the ecclesiology of communion and the sharing of gifts).[64] The ethical duty and prophetic necessity inherent in the communal aspect of monastic life, as Aelred views and desires it, make it the imperfect but partially realized manifestation in historical time of what will be in the kingdom yet to come. In that kingdom, where everything is recapitulated in Christ, there will no longer be any need to distinguish friendship from charity, since "the friendship to which on earth we admit but few will pour out over all and flow back to God from all, for God will be all in all."[65]

According to Raciti, viewed in eschatological terms, this twofold "dépassement" (overflow) or "assomption" (assumption) of fraternal relations into the context of community personalization and human friendship constitutes "Aelred's original contribution to western reflections on friendship."[66] We must now examine this principle's practical implications.

Theological Shifts and Implications

As the human dimension of Aelred's desire to build a fraternal community is insufficient, a complete understanding of his project requires framing it in a much larger, more theologi-

---

64. That is, through his incarnation and passion, Christ made himself like us in order to clothe us in his own dignity. This theme is seen in particular in S 12, "For the Feast of Easter," where Aelred comments on Isaiah 28:21: "*That he may accomplish his work* [of salvation], *his alien work* . . . his work was foreign to him" (S 12.13 [CF 58:198]).

65. Aelred, Spir am 3.134 (CF 5:126).

66. This is the title of his article: Gaetano Raciti, "L'apport original d'Aelred de Rievaulx à la réflexion occidentale sur l'amitié," Coll 29 (1968): 77–99.

cal[67] context, derived from a threefold shift—trinitarian, Christological, and ecclesiological—through which he extends the temporal limits of human friendship and community life ever closer to the infinite eschatological horizon awaiting at the end of history.

This theological and eschatological shift is immediately perceptible in the image of the cloistral paradise toward the end of *Friendship*. What remains to be seen are the numerous practical implications that this "transfiguration of friendship"[68] brings to communal life and to the fraternal relationships that comprise it. Some of them we have already glimpsed in Aelred's seeking to educate his brothers' hearts and shape his community's life according to the model of the feelings in his own heart, configured according to the model of Christ as the Good Shepherd.

Mercy and Compassion toward the Community's Weakest Members

The most obvious and important of these traits is mercy, the pastor's compassion toward the community's weakest members. Aelred developed these characteristics in himself to a high degree, and he ceaselessly sought to stimulate their growth in the hearts of his brothers. For example, in closing S 70, on the Feast of the Apostles Peter and Paul, he exhorts the strongest members of his community to "carry" their weaker (or "lame") brethren:

67. [Translator's note: Modern English appears to have only one term, "theological" where modern French maintains two expressions, *théologique* (for ideas or concepts relating or pertaining to theology) and *théologal* (for ideas or concepts having God as their object). Although English examples such as "theologal virtues" dating as late as 1610 appear in the *Oxford English Dictionary,* current usage in English seems to authorize "theological" alone. Since Burton does not oppose the two terms, I have opted to use "theological" in all cases.]

68. Dumont, "Le personnalisme," 325, after Raciti, "L'apport original," 81–86.

What should we do, then, about the disabled person, whose legs are slack and whose feet are weak [Acts 3:7]? These are the ones who are disabled in both feet [see 2 Sam 9:13], who abandon the physical without rising to the spiritual, the murmurers, the complainers [Jude 16], those who love their own will rather than God's. They are lazy in their work, inclined to what is empty and idle, slack in the Order's discipline, frivolous with their words, bitter in silence, ready to deal out wrongs but impatient to suffer them.

O dear brothers, you who are spiritual [Gal 6:1] and perfect, carry those who are like this, carry the disabled, carry them, I beg you [Acts 3:2]. Bear them with your advice and comfort, with your encouragement and corrections, but above all with your prayers. May those who are disabled receive this offering from those already beginning to enter the temple [Acts 3:3], until by the voice of your prayer and the invocation of Christ's name, their legs and feet grow strong [see Acts 3:6-7]. May they thus rise up by confessing and walk by progressing; may they leap by being fervent and cheerful in everything, so that one day they too may enter with you, walking and leaping and praising God [Acts 3:8], who lives and reigns, forever and ever. Amen.[69]

Walter provides a similar detail later in the *Life*, pointing out that if some brothers were inclined "to reprove in angry commotion some silly behavior,"[70] Aelred did not hesitate to tactfully correct them, reminding them that a Christian community that disdains to support the weak is not worthy of being called a religious house:

All . . . whether weak or strong, should find in Rievaulx a haunt of peace, and there, like the fish in the broad seas, possess the welcome, happy, spacious peace of charity, that it may be said of her, "Whither the tribes go up, the

69. Aelred, S 70.39–40 (CF 80:276).
70. Walter, VA 29 (CF 57:118).

tribes of the Lord, unto the testimony of Israel, to give thanks to the name of the Lord" [Ps 122:4]. There are tribes of the strong and tribes of the weak. The house which withholds toleration from the weak is not to be regarded as a house of religion.[71]

Apart from the means of showing support for the weak proposed in S 70—counsel, encouragement, exhortations, reprimands, prayers—Aelred sets forth another, joining two other characteristics of his conception of communal life: the sharing of gifts, and the complementarity of the blessings accorded to each person.

The Sharing of Gifts and the Complementarity of Blessings: The Image of a Gathering of Angels

These traits are like two sides of the same coin, as Aelred points out more than once in his exegesis of the Augustinian adage by which the gifts proper to one belong to all (*singula omnium*), just as the gifts of all belong equally to each one in particular (*omnia singulorum*).

Singula omnium

The first aspect of this gift-sharing principle derives directly from the Aelredian theology of creation, according to which every creature, by its simple existence, participates in the very being of God and shares to some extent in God's beauty and goodness (Spec car 1.4–6). In his eighth sermon, for the Feast of Saint Benedict, Aelred explains that the "goodness" of things and the virtue of God's merciful plan, which "causes each person to need the other,"[72] mean that every creature possesses

---

71. Walter, VA 29 (CF 57:118). [Translator's note: My ellipsis, to fit the English quotation to Burton's phrasing.]

72. Aelred, S 8.10 (CF 58:150).

a certain usefulness toward all other creatures in such a way that all are called upon to contribute, each in its own way, to the splendor, beauty, and harmony of the whole universe. Should any creature try to withdraw itself from this system of mutual utility, the equilibrium of the entire world would be damaged. Aelred then transposes this concept of the overall plan of creation to the level of community life. For him, no ability or thing a person possesses belongs solely to that person (*singula*), but must be contributed to the common good (*omnium*). Otherwise one risks depriving one's brothers of something to which they are entitled and on which they should be able to depend. Therefore, anyone who knowingly acts otherwise and, through "laziness or inattention," jealously withholds efforts owed to all, "is guilty of fraud."[73]

Omnia singulorum

For Aelred, the divine distribution of things and of the world, engaging every creature and person to contribute to the good of all, is both a means of preserving humility (for one cannot be self-sufficient if one has need of others) and of increasing charity (as one places oneself in the service of others from whose gifts one benefits). However, it is also a means of making visible a complementarity of blessings that welds together all creatures in a single communion, creating unity among them. This is the second aspect of the Augustinian adage adopted by Aelred—the gifts thus placed in common (*omnia*) immediately become the goods of each (*singulorum*).[74]

To speak of this aspect of community life, one could certainly use the vocabulary of trinitarian theology and, transposing to the realm of fraternal relationships what is proper to the Trinity, employ the analogy of a "communication of properties." Aelred, however, uses the more concrete language of

---

73. Aelred, S 26.46 (CF 58:368).
74. For these three traits, see Aelred, S 8.10 (CF 58:150).

images. In S 8, for the Feast of Saint Benedict, Aelred presents
two important images. The first, borrowed from the book of
Exodus, speaks of the construction of the tabernacle Moses
raised through contributions brought to him by the children
of Israel (Exod 35:20-29) according to the particular gift each
had received from God (see 1 Cor 7:7). Aelred explains that
this tabernacle should be understood not by the letter but by
the spirit and applied to the monastic community, composed
of a multitude of brothers constituting a single "temple of
God."[75] A similar transposition of the text's spirit regarding
that which each individual contributes to the building of that
temple is also valid, applying not only to material goods, such
as cowls and robes, but also, far more importantly, to "our
strengths and spiritual gifts."[76]

The second image, immediately following the first, is borrowed from the Pauline theology of the "mystical body of
Christ," constituting the entire church and the whole of any
particular church community. Aelred feels authorized to affirm
that "whatever any one person does belongs to all and whatever
all do belongs to everyone," because Paul himself in his Epistle
to the Romans encourages him to do so. Quoting Paul, Aelred
explains the connection: "*just as the members of a single body do
not all have the same function,*" yet, as the Apostle says, "*The many
are one body in Christ, they are each members of one another.*"[77]

Practical Consequences

Aelred outlines a twofold practical consequence of this idea,
applicable to the fraternal life of his community. It presents
itself both as an infallible remedy to those swollen with pride
in their God-given gifts and as a way to appease those feeling
envy, jealousy, or suspicion over the perceived lack of a par-

75. 1 Cor 3:17. Aelred, S 8.3 (CF 58:148).
76. Aelred, S 8.9 (CF 58:150).
77. Rom 12:4-5. Aelred, S 8.11 (CF 58:150–51).

ticular gift or the supposed unjust deprivation of a favor offered to another. He reminds the former that the gifts they received were given to them for the good of all; he reminds the latter that through the sharing of gifts, they can consider the perfection of others as their own (S 8.10; see also S 26.46–47).

The second practical consequence Aelred derives from this Pauline principle concerns the extent of its application. He points out at least four different areas of relevance.

The first area, unsurprisingly, is the mutual support the brothers are asked to provide one another and, in particular, the support the stronger members of the community owe to the weaker ones. It is clear that the doctrine of particular gifts communicated to all is a particularly effective means of aiding others of lesser strength. Aelred explains this idea at the conclusion of S 26, for the Feast of All Saints, comparing the monastic community to a "holy fellowship" of angels: "They have such unity and concord among themselves that, although some are inferior and others superior, nonetheless through their unity whatever belongs to each is the common property of all and whatever belongs to all the property of each."[78] For Aelred, what applies to the relationships among angels between the inferior and the superior applies by analogy to the relations that ideally govern connections of mutual aid within the heart of the community. Provided that they are not guilty of laziness or inattention, he advises, "let those who may be sickly and weak and therefore cannot do as much as others, not be saddened or despair," for those who received the gift of engaging in more manual labor, prayer, fasting, or vigils, have received that gift "not for themselves alone but for the sake of those who cannot do as much."[79]

Similarly, in S 8, for the Feast of Saint Benedict, Aelred advances the same argument to account for the diversity of vocations (lay brothers or choir brothers) within the community.

78. Aelred, S 26.45 (CF 58:368).
79. Aelred, S 26.46–47 (CF 58:368).

He invites the former not to complain of chanting and keeping vigil less than the latter, and the latter not to complain of working less than the former: "For very truly I say that whatever any one person does belongs to all and whatever all do belongs to everyone."[80]

Although Aelred does not say so, this principle could extend to the diversity of vocations and of functions within the community. For the cloistered, who have no material charge, this responsibility means being faithful to the various observances of regular life (work, abstinence, vigils, and *lectio*). For the obedientiaries (cellarers, porters, and guest-masters) it means generously, charitably, and mercifully providing for the material needs of all. For the *prelati* (the superiors) it means organizing (literally "ordering") community life with such discerning judgment that all can assume without complaint the tasks assigned to them; the *prelati* also prevent regular discipline from becoming relaxed through excess of freedom.[81] He exemplifies this idea in S 17, for the Feast of the Holy Apostles Peter and Paul, comparing the monastic community to a castle that must be defended against the assaults of vice and where, for the safety of all, each monk must loyally defend the post assigned to him—that is, the role he fulfills in the community.[82]

Because of the complementarity of status for lay brothers and choir brothers and their function, which for the obedientiaries means imitating Martha and for the cloistered imitating Mary, and because, as Dumont says, "it is in the community that personal limitations are overcome *in* the community,"[83] Aelred promotes a healthy pluralism within the community that takes into account its general welfare along with the par-

---

80. Aelred, S 8.11 (CF 58:150–51).
81. Aelred, S 8.5–11 (CF 58:148–51).
82. Aelred, S 17.4 (CF 58:246).
83. The expression comes from Charles Dumont, "L'équilibre humain de la vie cistercienne," in *Sagesse ardente* (Oka, Canada: Abbaye Notre-Dame-du-Lac, 1998), 27.

ticular welfare of each person considered individually. Thus the communal social equilibrium created by his exhortation that individual brothers not steal that which belongs to all (*singula omnium*) is balanced against a personalization that respects the needs and individual equilibrium of each community member (*omnia singulorum*) as far as the smooth operation of the whole allows.

Again, S 8, for the Feast of Saint Benedict, expresses it best. Here Aelred compares each of the principal monastic observances[84] to the six cities of asylum selected by Moses (see Num 35:11-15). He encourages each of his brothers to focus most on those observances in which he finds the most abundant grace, for experience shows, as he himself is aware, that "no one possesses equal grace in all exercises."[85] Aelred could never have advanced such an assertion in theoretical terms nor have promoted such pluralism within his community in practical terms without the conceptual foundation of his cosmological doctrine of a universe founded on harmony and complementarity.

Only Aelred's particular genius allowed him fully to exploit the Augustinian adage *omnia singulorum, singula omnium*, directing its practical consequences toward the ordering of community life. His original contribution in this matter can be assessed by three different measures.

A Subtle Equilibrium

Shedding light on what he calls Aelred's "preferential option for the weak," Raciti has emphasized the fact that in promoting this option in his community, Aelred did not seek to "realize a simple atmosphere of human indulgence or to establish a regime of peaceful coexistence between strong and weak." He instead forcefully insists that this option, and the governance

---

84. E.g, the three *corporalia* (labor, vigil, fasting) and the three *spiritualia* (reading, prayer, meditation).
85. Aelred, S 8.17 (CF 58:153).

it implies, is in reality infused with "a great theological breath"[86] that confers upon Aelred's perspective not only sociological value but also an eminently theological element. Similarly, expanding on Dumont's concept of "community personalism,"[87] Raciti again underscores that "Aelred's community-building design establishes what one could broadly qualify as 'mystical pluralism,'" and that there, in the end, one finds oneself at a "nerve-center of his thought, at a major interchange on the broad highway of his monastic doctrine."[88]

Inspired by the Rule of Saint Benedict—which encourages the abbot to be "all things to all" (1 Cor 9:19, 22) in order to adapt himself to each individual's temperament (RB 2.32; see Aelred, Orat 7)—and even more inspired by a theology of creation permeated by the spirit of Augustine—*singula omnium, omnia singulorum*—Aelred founded his community on the basis of a delicate and difficult balance in which the development of individuals was closely and reciprocally articulated with the building of a communal space conceived as a place of exchange and the sharing of personal gifts. On the one hand, he aimed for the development of the individual to stimulate the generous contribution of each one to the common good, establishing a community-based personalism. In return, the communal space encouraged the individuals' mutual respect of each other's personal limitations, with those limitations to be overcome by each member sharing his own gifts, thereby establishing a community of persons.

This was of course a delicate and difficult equilibrium. Between the two poles of individual and community, a constant tension and a permanent play of opposed forces left Aelred walking a narrow path with pitfalls on each side, one that demanded uncommon skill in governance. The first pitfall consisted of the danger of considering the individual's unique-

---

86. Raciti, "L'option préférentielle," 203.

87. Charles Dumont, "Le personnalisme communautaire d'Aelred de Rievaulx," Coll 39 (1977): 129–48.

88. Raciti, "L'option préférentielle," 203.

ness as the sole measure of community life, so sliding from a perfectly legitimate respect for each person into an idiorhythmism losing sight of the common good of all through the "desolidarization" of the fraternal community itself. This pitfall presented the risk of excessive individualism and the dictatorship of the self-sufficient ego.

The second pitfall, no less dangerous, was the mirror-image opposite of the first. The necessary effort to guarantee cohesion and unity within the group risked mutating into the desire to impose the sole measure of a common norm or common rule on all members, with no consideration for the diversity of temperaments. The desire to safeguard the common good at all costs could confuse unanimity of hearts with unanimity of external observances, risking communitarianism and the dictatorship of the common good, so dissolving the individual within the community.

The whole history of religious and monastic life is permeated by this tension. That life has never ceased to oscillate between the two poles, creating its two principal forms: cenobitism, which emphasizes community, and eremitism, which emphasizes the individual. From this point of view, the diverse and more or less successful reforms of Western European religious and monastic life in the eleventh and twelfth centuries represent the multiple attempts to resolve this tension. Some, such as the Carthusian reform, emphasized the eremetic element. Others, such as the renewal of canonical life by the Premonstratensians and others, emphasized the community element. Still others, including the Cistercian reform, attempted to reconcile the two paths into one, along which a harmonious equilibrium could be progressively established between the solitude of personalism and the shared life of community.

Admiration was the response of William of Saint-Thierry when on visiting Clairvaux he viewed in great wonder this subtle combination of solitude and communion: "Their love was well ordered and made that vale full of men into a solitary place for each of them, because their life was so well ordered— for just as if one person is in disorder, even when alone, so that person is inwardly disturbed, so where unity of spirit and a rule of silence govern a multitude, solitude of heart and an orderly life defends each one."[89]

Over time, the Cistercians attempted to inscribe this effort within the framework of their legislation, so that this ideal of equilibrium between communion and solitude, the respect of the individual and the building of a fraternal community, lasted for centuries. After an unfortunate period during which it was forgotten—roughly from the post-French-Revolution Cistercian restoration until the 1969 statute "Unity and Pluralism"—it regained its importance in the current *Constitutions of the Order of Cistercians of the Strict Observance*, approved in 1990, as for example in Constitutions 14 and 16. Explicitly inspired (as is true for at least for the first of these) by Aelred's spiritual doctrine, these *Constitutions* clearly and firmly reinforce the dual principle he emphasized, according to which the Cistercian community is a community of graces and individuals, wherein, "with reverence for the human person created in God's image" (Const 16.3), "each brother is to contribute to the upbuilding of fraternal relations especially by sharing with others the spiritual gifts he has received by God's manifold grace" (Const 14.1), by applying himself "according to the character, training and age" (Const 14.2) proper to him, and living in conformity with "the equilibrium . . . . essential to the Cistercian way of life"[90] under the guidance of an abbot whose mission it is "to discern and moderate everything so that each brother may grow in the Cistercian vocation."[91]

89. William of Saint-Thierry, Arnold of Bonneval, and Geoffrey of Auxerre, *The First Life of Bernard of Clairvaux*, trans. Hilary Costello, CF 76 (Collegeville, MN: Cistercian Publications, 2015), 41.

90. [Translator's note: My ellipsis, to fit the English quotation to Burton's phrasing.]

91. *The Constitutions of the Order of Cistercians of the Strict Observance* 14.2, 2005, Order of Cistercians of the Strict Observance, accessed June 2, 2017, http://www.ocso.org/index.php?option=com_docman&Itemid=122&lang=en.

The Monastic Community as "Ecclesial Body of Christ"

If Aelred was able to maintain an equilibrium between community and individual, it is because instead of simply keeping the two polar elements in tension and balancing himself on the narrow path between the precipices, he considered those elements to be two pillars of the same arch, converging toward a single keystone, where the two opposed forces cancel one another out and together allow the whole structure to remain upright. This keystone, the unique point of convergence toward which Aelred's entire community-building effort is oriented, is none other than the person of Christ. The person of Christ must be formed first within each monk individually in such a way that each becomes in his own right a member of the same body—that of Christ. Then, as if in one single motion, the person of Christ must be built into the substance of the community as a whole so that, thus integrated into a single body, the individual members constitute together an *ecclesiola*, a small church with one heart and one soul forming, with Christ the Head, his entire Body.

Of course, when Aelred speaks of dual aspect of Christ's formation—the personal aspect (*in anima*) and the community aspect (*in Ecclesia*)—he typically presents them separately, insisting on one or the other of the two elements. But he does so without ever losing sight of either.[92] In this way, he does

---

92. For the personal aspect (*in anima*), see S 8, for the Feast of Saint Benedict, where, inspired by a passage from the Epistle to the Romans, Aelred bases his conception of the monastic community as a place of communion, mutual support, and sharing, in the Pauline doctrine of the Church as the body of Christ: *The many are one body in Christ, they are each members of one another* (Rom 12:5) (Aelred, S 8.11 [CF 58:150–51]). For the community aspect (*in Ecclesia*), Aelred takes inspiration in S 26 from Acts 4:32 to affirm the unity of the community: "Each and every one of you, before you came here, had one soul, which was his alone. You converted to God and, behold, the Holy Spirit, that heavenly fire which our Lord sent to earth and willed to burn, inflamed your hearts, set your souls aflame[, and] from all your hearts and all your souls made one heart and one soul" (S 26.43 [CF 58:367]). In both cases, the two

more than simply accept the spiritual inheritance of his illustrious master, Bernard of Clairvaux, and of the latter's disciple, Guerric of Igny, enriching each with the other. Rather, he significantly extends their range and opens a path that is fully consonant with theirs. But this path is at the same time entirely original in synthesizing Bernard's and Guerric's ideas.

Beyond Saint Bernard: From Intermonastic Ecumenism to Intracommunity Pluralism

Aelred relies first on Bernard's thought. By emphasizing the principle that each person's limitations can be overcome within the community by the sharing of individual gifts (the Augustinian *omnia singulorum*), Aelred organized his community's internal life in such a way that the individuality of each person could be welcomed and respected. By ordering community life in terms of individual respect, and therefore placing communal life in the service of individual growth, he legitimized the possibility of differentiated ways of living one common monastic grace by adapting it to each person's temperament, within a single uniform community. In so doing, he appropriated a principle set forth by Bernard in his *Apology* roughly a half century earlier, around 1124, when—in order to relax tensions opposing traditional Benedictine monasticism and the new Cistercian monasticism—he proposed a legitimate diversity in the interpretation and application of the Benedictine Rule.

But instead of restraining the application to a healthy pluralism among different monastic traditions, as Bernard had,

---

aspects are present, but in differing proportions. One exception, however, occurs in S 84, on the Nativity of Holy Mary, the last in the Durham collection. This sermon is unfortunately incomplete, but it promised to be all the more worthwhile since, in its last surviving lines, Aelred expresses his intention to examine these two elements together while adding yet a third—to show that God resides not only in the community aspect of the church and in the personal aspect of each faithful soul, but also, cosmically and politically, in the world (S 84.7 [CF 80:437]).

Aelred extended the idea to the interior of the community in order to create a legitimate "intracommunity pluralism," whose spiritual posterity is today inscribed at the heart of the OCSO *Constitutions*. This migration from one area of application to another—from Bernardian intermonastic ecumenism to Aelredian intracommunity pluralism—like the profound theological and spiritual continuity that exists between them, manifests itself in Aelred's citing the same biblical passage and the same images as Bernard had. But where Bernard had used these passages and images, in Raciti's words, "to found and justify the existence of a plurality of monastic orders living by diverse legitimate interpretations of the Rule," Aelred used them, again in Raciti's words, "to envision that pluralism within the Cistercian community itself, as a personalist community of mystical participation."[93] This idea evokes the patriarch Joseph's coat of many colors (see Gen 37:3), "without seam, woven from the top throughout" (John 19:23), which Bernard used in chapters 3 and 4 of the *Apology* to speak of the diversity of monastic ways of life within the church and which Aelred reprised for diversity within a particular monastic community.

At the end of his article on Aelred's preferential option for the weak, Raciti cites an unpublished sermon attesting to this passage from one area of application to the other. The connection between two other sermons, in which Aelred transposed his statements on the incarnation of the Word in S 9 to the community of brothers in S 59, confirms this transition. In S 9, for the Annunciation of the Lord, Aelred begins with the affirmation that just as God made a garment of skin to cover the nudity of "Adam the disobedient," he similarly covered "the most holy flesh of our Savior" with Joseph's "many-colored tunic." In other words, he says, God adorned the Lord Jesus with "the complete variety of virtues." Passing immediately to the moral sense of this image (S 9.32–33), Aelred invites each

---

93. Raciti, "L'option préférentielle," 204. See also Pierre-André Burton, "Aux origines de Cîteaux d'après quelques sources écrites du XIIe siècle: Enquête sur une polémique," Cîteaux 48 (1997): 209–29.

of his brothers to strip away the garment of skin in which Adam was clothed—that is, "the works of darkness"—and to put on the many-colored tunic that is Christ himself (see Gen 37:3; Rom 13:12-14) by donning, like him, "*compassion, kindness, humility, gentleness, patience.*"[94] These are a selection of virtues or inner dispositions among a multitude of others.

Later, in S 59, for the Annunciation of the Lord, Aelred specifies that it is not necessary for all to be equally or identically clothed in all of these virtues, because within the community each person, according to his own gifts, is called to shine in some one virtue rather than another. One may be humble, another patient, yet another chaste, and so on.[95] In other words, he suggests that donning Christ is not an entirely individual matter, but rather a vocation to be realized together, as it is by joining together and using the unique gifts of each individual that the many-colored coat of Christ is woven.

From the Spiritual Maternity of the Soul to the Spiritual Maternity of the Community

Aelred's technique of extending Bernard's ideas on the formation of Christ to a "personalizing community pluralism" applies equally well to the ideas of Guerric of Igny, former master of the cathedral school of Tournai. Now, however, he uses them in the opposite order, beginning with the second part of the Augustinian adage that "what belongs to each belongs to all" (*singula omnium*).

Inspired by the pioneering 1935 study of Deodatus de Wilde, Annie Noblesse-Rocher has drawn attention to the central importance of the theme of Christ's formation in Guerric's spiritual theology. In particular she highlights the logical coherence of the six sermons of Guerric's homiletic collection

94. See Col 3:12. Aelred, S 9.30–33 (CF 58:166).
95. Aelred, S 59.25 (CF 80:160–61).

that deal explicitly with this question, especially the Marian and baptismal elements of this examination.[96]

The Marian element of Christ's formation in Guerric's writing resembles that of Bernard and many fathers of the church before him. Guerric argues that if Christ's formation consists above all in the incarnation of the Word made flesh, then Mary's divine maternity with respect to Christ extends far beyond him to include maternity with respect to the church. As he explains in his First Sermon for the Assumption, Mary, "being the blessed Mother of Christ . . . is the mother of the Life by which everyone lives"—that is, "when she brought it [Jesus' life] forth from herself she in some way brought to rebirth all those who were to live by that Life," so that she also gives birth to all Christians, members of the single body of Christ that is the church. Guerric continues: "She who is the only virgin-Mother, she who glories in having borne the Only-begotten of the Father, embraces that same Only-begotten of hers in all his members and so can be truly called *Mother of all* in whom she recognizes her Christ to have been formed, or in whom she knows he is being formed."[97] Clearly this is to say that the divine maternity of Mary is twofold and entirely Christic in nature. Mary is certainly the mother of Jesus, the Word made flesh, she who gives birth to the ecclesial Christ as Head. But her maternity is not limited solely to the birth of her only Son in the broadness of time. Rather, it is coextensive with all history, extending to the entire church, which comprises the whole body of Christ.

In his second sermon for the Annunciation, Guerric extends this affirmation about the role of Mary to the incarnational mystery of the formation of Christ in time and in the historical mystery of the church as body of Christ, and emphasizes that if Mary is indeed the only person worthy of bringing the only

---

96. Annie Noblesse-Rocher, *L'Expérience de Dieu dans les sermons de Guerric, abbé d'Igny (XIIᵉ siècle)* (Paris: Les Éditions du Cerf, 2005), 209–73, esp. 237–38.

97. S 47.2–4; Guerric, *Liturgical Sermons*, vol. 2, trans. Monks of Mount Saint Bernard Abbey, CF 32 (Spencer, MA: Cistercian Publications, 1971), 168–69.

Son of the Father into the world, giving him the flesh of her flesh, it was not a privilege strictly reserved to her alone.[98] In a sense, by reason of baptism, every Christian is called upon to share in her vocation and "conceive him whom creation cannot contain,"[99] and thus every Christian is closely associated with her maternity: "Now that you may know more fully that the Virgin's conception has not only a mystical [*non solum mysticum*] but also a moral sense [*sed et moralem*], what is a mystery for your redemption [*sacramentum ad redemptionem*] is also an example for your imitation [*exemplum tibi ad imitationem*]." This means that, like Mary, every Christian participates in the mission of conceiving the Word.

This conception takes place first, of course, in one's heart through faith and by means of hearing and obeying the Word. After a brief hesitation Guerric also audaciously adds that it also takes place in one's body: "if you will faithfully receive the Word from the mouth of the heavenly messenger you too may conceive the God whom the whole world cannot contain, conceive him however in your heart, not in your body. And yet even in your body, although not by any bodily action or outward form, nonetheless truly in your body, since the Apostle bids us glorify and bear God in our body" (see 1 Cor 6:20). Further on he continues: "Behold the unspeakable condescension of God and at the same time the power of the mystery [of the conception of the Word] that passes all understanding. He who created you is created in you, and as if it were too little that you should possess the Father, he wishes also that you should become a mother to himself."[100]

This theological affirmation is unquestionably an audacious one, as comes out even more clearly because of Guerric's moment of hesitation. Thanks to this affirmation, Guerric confers an eminently Marian dimension on the baptismal vocation, as

98. Guerric, S 2:43–45 (CF 32:5–6).
99. Guerric, S 2:45 (CF 32:6).
100. Guerric, S 2:44–45 (CF 32:6).

every Christian is called, like Mary and with Mary, to give birth to Christ in himself and give him flesh. On the other hand, Guerric curiously appears to establish no intrinsic and explicit link with his affirmation in the previously examined sermon for the Assumption. Passing silently over the ecclesial dimension of Christ's spiritual maternity, Guerric limits himself to the moral and personal dimension of Christ's formation in the soul, inviting each individual to become the mother of Christ. He invites each to open his ears to the divine word: "Open to the Word of God an ear that will listen. This is the way to the womb of your heart for the Spirit who brings about conception; in such fashion are the bones of Christ, that is the virtues, built up in the pregnant womb."[101]

In his own sermons, Aelred makes this fundamentally moral dimension of Christ's formation in each Christian's soul his own. All of his ascetic and mystical doctrine points in this direction. But in contrast with Guerric, who seems not to have had this idea, Aelred never dissociates that element from the ecclesial or community element. Instead he considers the formation of Christ in the soul—what Guerric presents as giving consistency to virtues that are the "bones" of Christ—to be far more than an individual or personal matter. In the literal sense of the term,[102] it is a com-*mun*-al *munus*: a "charge" (*munus*) that each individual must assume first on a personal level, but also a "charge" that is taken on by all brothers together.

The idea of propping up the personal dimension by referencing the community appears clearly in Aelred's S 59. Like Guerric in his second sermon for the Annunciation, Aelred speaks in S 59 of the ethical aspect of Christ's formation in the soul, and he too insists that this formation occurs through the

---

101. See Eccl 11:5. Guerric, 2:45 (CF 32:7).
102. See Denis Heurre, "Vie commune et transcendance," Coll 71 (2009): 124–43. Heurre valuably explores the various levels of meaning contained in the expression *communal life*, based on the etymology of the Latin *communis* (138–42).

development of virtues in each individual, but with a different image. He abandons Guerric's anatomical image of bones in favor of the arboricultural image of an orchard made up of different species of fruit trees. While Guerric considers the growth of virtues only from the individual perspective, with each individual responsible for developing in himself Christ's skeletal structure through the cultivation of virtues, Aelred emphasizes the communal aspect of this process. Just as the fruits each tree bears according to its species result in the creation of a unique orchard, so the various virtues each brother brings according to his individual qualities and aptitudes make the community.

This image brings to mind Jacob's coat of many colors, woven in one piece, since the two images are thematically similar. Both emphasize the fertile tension between the diversity of individuals with their qualities and the unity of the community, and both stress personal contribution toward the common good. But the second image, of the orchard, offers an additional element of which Aelred takes full advantage. This image suggests the celestial garden or Paradise, allowing Aelred to transpose what he had already asserted regarding spiritual friendship to monastic life in community. Like spiritual friendship, but on a much larger scale, this life offers itself as a cloistral Paradise, a space as much as a way of life, which allows humankind to return to Adam's original condition:

> The repose of the cloister is a physical [Lat *corporalis*] paradise—indeed it is fairer to my mind than the Paradise in which Adam was placed [Gen 2:15], and not inferior to it. In this paradise the individual brothers are like fruitful trees, bearing rich crops of the different virtues: one is more lowly in humility, another more illustrious in charity, another stronger in patience, another more becoming in chastity, another more hardworking at manual labor, another more at rest in silence and tranquility, another more abounding in tears and compunction, another brighter in reading and meditation. I consider this paradise preferable

to that from which the first man was expelled, both for its rich yield of fruit and for its spiritual beauty.[103]

From the Cloister to the World: Institutional and Social Issues

Thus, buttressing the two elements of monastic development—the person and the community—on the keystone that is the formation of Christ either in its individual moral dimension or in its communal, ecclesial dimension, Aelred both adopted and extended the dual teachings of Bernard and Guerric in his own way. On the basis of the Augustinian adage (*omnia singulorum, singula omnium*), Aelred was able to develop a conception of community life that simultaneously involved the "personalizing intracommunity pluralism" inspired by Bernard and the "communal personalism" inspired by Guerric. Ordering the community in terms of the individual (*Ubi Ecclesia, ibi Christus*) and the individual in terms of the community (*Ubi Christus, ibi Ecclesia*),[104] Aelred avoids the dual pitfalls of collective absolutism through an excessively uniform communitarianism, and of personal absolutism through an excess of differentiated individualism. Moreover, thanks to the give and take he consistently maintains between individual and communal life, he builds a community in unity and harmony through the bonds of peace and charity. Dumont shows the fruitfulness of this dual interaction when he describes Aelred's community-building project:

> The unity realized through charity and harmony transcends the inequality of rank or capability, as well as the diversity of gifts, in a manner unrelated to egalitarianism, which, inspired by envy, seeks to make everyone be and act like everyone else. It is sufficient to know that the gifts,

103. Aelred, S 59.25 (CF 80:160–61).
104. For these two expressions, see Timothy Radcliffe, *Pourquoi donc être chrétien?* (Paris: Cerf, 2005), 237.

the virtues, and the strengths of each are given to each
for others; it is also necessary that each one believe he
possesses all these qualities simply by reason of his relationship to the community.[105]

One may easily ask how Aelred elaborated such a community-
building project, which sets so much importance on the individual, when in order to recognize and validate each person's
identity he had to break with a widespread medieval social ideol-
ogy holding that the individual did not truly exist as such and
only had substance to the extent that he was bound in a tight
network of relationships and subordinated to the collective,
which effectively absorbed him, so that each one was subject to
rather than subject.[106] Three converging factors made this conception of personal, social, and communal reality possible.

The first factor is cultural. It is difficult to circumscribe the
multiple and complex elements at issue. However, despite dis-
agreements about the extent, the period, and the intellectual
concepts involved in the phenomenon of the development of
the person, individual, or inner self, most historians hold that
the twelfth and thirteenth centuries (and perhaps the latter half
of the eleventh century) in the Western Middle Ages experienced
a major shift in the discovery and progressive emergence of the
notion of the individual. This movement, simultaneously intellectual, cultural, and spiritual, gave birth to a "new humanism,"[107]
sometimes referred to as "Christian Socratism." The twelfth-

105. Dumont, "Le personnalisme," 316.

106. We refer here to the familiar historical theory of the three medieval
ordines (*oratores-bellatores-laboratores*) defined by socio-professional status,
providing each individual a social place and role.

107. There is abundant technical literature on this question. See, e.g.,
Edouard-Henri Weber, *La personne humaine au XIIIe siècle* (Paris: Vrin, 2002);
Walter Ullman, *The Individual and Society in the Middle Ages* (Baltimore: Johns
Hopkins University Press, 1967); Colin Morris, *The Discovery of the Individual:
1050–1200* (Toronto: University of Toronto Press, 1987); and Aron Gourevitch,
La Naissance de l'individu au Moyen Âge (Paris: Seuil, 1997). In particular, this

century Cistercians were the movement's most engaged promoters and most illustrious representatives.

The second factor is contextual, related to the history of the Cistercian reform. In our examination of *The Mirror of Charity* and Bernard's reasons for insisting that Aelred not shrink from writing the work, we underscored that by around 1140 things had greatly changed since the Order's founding, so that the Cistercians had to defend the values of their *forma vivendi* not against external attack but against internal criticisms. In a way, victim of its own success, the Cistercian Reform saw itself submerged by a wave of protest that, probably originating from monks instructed in less austere forms of monastic life, called into question the soundness of its asceticism. One can reasonably conclude that Aelred, sensitive to this new situation, tried through his spiritual doctrines to contain the risk of rupture threatening the integrity of the rapidly expanding Order. In addition, he must also have sought through his teaching to safeguard the unity of his own community, in which he may have sensed factionalism. Some, perhaps from the founding generation still burning with its initial fervor, remained attached to the protest-oriented values that had inspired the Cistercian reform. Others with a weaker temperament, perhaps the new recruits and those monks arriving from less austere monastic congregations, sought a loosening up of Cistercian asceticism.

Finally a third, personal, factor contributes to Aelred's theoretical and practical elaboration of a pastoral project for his community and brothers. Throughout his abbatial ministry, Aelred never ceased to exhibit attention to the well-being and needs of each person according to the diversity of individual gifts and temperaments. Furthermore, he opened wide the arms of his compassion to welcome the weaknesses and limitations of others. He had these traits because early in his own

---

discussion is highly influenced by a masterful biography of Saint Louis: Jacques Le Goff, *Saint Louis* (Paris: Gallimard, 1995), 499–508.

life—probably around 1132–1133 at the time of his conversion at age twenty-two or twenty-three—he had not only gained an acute awareness of his own personal limitations, human weaknesses, and sins, but had also felt the dazzling, overwhelming experience of divine mercy.

Additionally, Aelred always took care to relate the individual to the community, with the view that the first was unable to subsist without the other, while the second found its cohesion and unity only through the willing contribution of each individual to the common good. This concern was due to his personal experience and the central place that friendship occupied in his life from before he entered Rievaulx. Friendship allowed him to discover the joys and human fruitfulness of a relationship founded on the principle of exchange and reciprocity, based simultaneously on a fundamental harmony of wills, the affective union of hearts, and the sharing of property. Enriched by the experience of human friendships before his conversion, and at the same time conscious of their limitations and the pitfalls to which they exposed him, Aelred strove to clarify the meaning of friendship and to purify its nature.

In his youth, before becoming a monk, he had sought this clarification and purity by passing the idea of friendship through the sieve of Cicero's treatise *On Friendship*. After entering Rievaulx, he sought it in the teachings of the holy Scripture and the church fathers. This was a labor-intensive intellectual and spiritual investigation that allowed him to develop a synthesis unique in the history of Christian spirituality. He firmly rooted friendship's unity in the Pauline theology of the Body of Christ, its unanimity in the Lucan ecclesiology of communion, and its affectivity in the Johannine spirituality of friendship in Jesus' heart. He thus showed that it was spiritually possible and theologically legitimate to apply principles of individual friendship to the broader realm of interpersonal relationships within the monastic community, provided that the sole source for both was the formation of the Body of Christ on a moral level for individuals, and on an ecclesial level for the community.

The Monastic Community as a "Cloistral Paradise,"
the "Sacrament of Salvation"

The transposition of the values of individual friendship to
the edification of a monastic community led Aelred to magnify
the space of community life across the horizon embracing the
three dimensions of time. Turned toward the past, that life
offers itself, as in his S 59 for the Annunciation as a "cloistral
paradise," as a restoration and improvement upon the Adamic
condition prior to the Fall. Oriented toward the future, that
life anticipates the kingdom yet to come, the place where
Aelred, in his first sermon for Advent, sees the accomplishment
of Isaiah's famous prophecy announcing and contemplating
the arrival of a new harmonious and peaceful world, where
"the wolf shall dwell with the lamb and the leopard shall lie
down with the goat; the calf and the lion shall graze together,
and a little child shall herd them."[108] This accomplishment
occurs, Aelred says, "in a far more beautiful and better way"[109]
than among animals.

The fact that this social, community-based reading of Isaiah's vision appears in the very first sermon of the First Clairvaux Collection of Aelred's homilies is highly significant.
According to Chrysogonus Waddell it is very probable that
the homilies contained in the first Clairvaux collection were
given by Aelred between 1143 and 1147, when he took on his
first abbatial charge at Revesby.[110] In contrast with Saint Bernard, and outside of the series of thirty-one *Homilies on the
Prophetic Burdens of Isaiah*, Aelred does not seem ever to have
personally assembled his homilies into organically structured
collections, so there is no edition revised, corrected, and

108. Isa 11:6.
109. Aelred, CF 1.32 (CF 58:68).
110. Chrysogonus Waddell, "The Hidden Years of Aelred of Rievaulx: The
Formation of a Spiritual Master," CSQ 41 (2006): 51–63.

approved by him.[111] It is therefore risky to formulate any hypothesis on the intentions presiding over the arrangement of these sermons into a collection. The risk is even greater given that the common usage of respecting the pre-established conventional order of the liturgical year was probably followed by the compiler, who is likely to have been a monk of Rievaulx.[112] It is therefore not surprising that the sermons begin with Advent.

Nonetheless, it is possible to imagine that the compiler wanted it to be this sermon rather than another (for example, the second in the series, also a sermon for Advent), to appear first in the collection, as if he had noted, or perhaps even wanted to emphasize, its programmatic character. This hypothesis is obviously unverifiable. On the other hand, one thing is certain. Aelred's perception of the monastic community as a restoration of the prelapsarian condition and as an anticipation of eternal

111. See Gaetano Raciti, the great contemporary compiler and editor of the collections of Aelred's liturgical sermons, in his introductions to the critical edition of Aelred's sermons: Gaetano Raciti, Introduction, in *Aelredi Rievallensis Opera omnia*, CCCM 2A and 2B (Turnhout: Brepols, 1989–2012), 2A:v, 2B:v. Regarding questions raised by the parallel existence of several drafts of certain sermons, see Raciti, Introduction, CCCM 2A:v–vi, nn. 2, 3. See also Gaetano Raciti, "Deux collections de sermons de saint Aelred—une centaine d'inédits—découvertes dans les fonds de Cluny et de Clairvaux," Coll 45 (1983): 165–84; Gaetano Raciti, "Une allocution familière de saint Aelred conservée dans les Mélanges de Matthieu de Rievaulx," Coll 47 (1985): 267–80, esp. 272. See also C. H. Talbot, "Aelred's Sermons: Some First Drafts," *Sacris Erudiri* 13 (1962): 153–92. Talbot was the first to draw attention to this phenomenon of double recension (long and short) for Aelred's liturgical sermons, so conferring on the manuscript tradition, as Raciti has said, a character that is "riche et bigarré" (rich and colorful) (Raciti, "Allocution," 272).

112. See Raciti, Introduction, CCCM 2A:vii. Raciti suggests that this collection was probably put together shortly after Aelred's death, for the benefit of the Clairvaux community (hence the name of the collection). On the other hand, he does not hypothesize about the compiler's identity. It is tempting to think it was the work of Walter Daniel, who, in chap. 18 of the *Life*, affirms that Aelred's writings were "preserved for posterity by the labor of my own hand" (CF 57:110). However, nothing allows us to confirm this.

life was also firmly planted in the present, as a concrete realization of the entire church's vocation to be a sacrament of salvation in and for the world.[113] That is, to use the terms of the Second Vatican Council's constitution, *Lumen gentium*, the church's vocation is to be "sign and instrument both of a very closely knit union with God and of the unity of the whole human race."[114] Envisioned this way as the miniature realization of Christ's body within his Body, the monastic community becomes much more than Roberto de la Iglesia's "archetype or model for the Church as a whole,"[115] but rather a veritable ideal for society, valid for every human community, including the multi-ethnic English nation comprised of Anglo-Saxon and post-Conquest Franco-Norman elements.

Unable to make a monk or nun out of every man and woman—as he would have liked—Aelred holds that of all paths to holiness open to Christians, the monastic life is the surest path.[116] He strives to extend beyond the narrow limits of the cloister the influence of the community-building model by which he sought to edify his own monastic community. This desire to fashion civil society on the model of the early

113. On this theme, see Roberto de la Iglesia, "La comunidad monástica, realización concreta de la Iglesia, según Elredo de Rievaulx," *Cistercium* 58 (2006): 389–437. See also Roberto de la Iglesia, "La ecclesiología monástica de san Elredo de Rieval," *Cistercium* 60 (2008): 81–102.

114. *Dogmatic Constitution on the Church, Lumen Gentium, Solemnly Promulgated by His Holiness Pope Paul VI on November 21, 1964*, 1.1, acc. June 2, 2017, http://www.vatican.va/archive/hist_councils/ii_vatican_ council/ index.htm.

115. Iglesia, "Comunidad," 437.

116. Of course this assertion needs to be nuanced. Nonetheless, it is a conviction Aelred shares with many other authors of the medieval period. See Aelred, S 83, on the Nativity of Holy Mary, in which he concedes that "All the ways of life and orders that have been established in the holy Church," principally religious life and marriage, offer themselves as authentic ways of following "in the faith of the cross," after which he hastens to add "But . . . all are not of the same security" (S 83.4 [CF 80:426]). The best way, in Aelred's eyes, is complete renunciation of the world. [Translator's note: My ellipsis, to fit the English quotation to Burton's phrasing.]

church's communal life (the *vita apostolica*), establishing it on the ethical and ecclesiological foundations of spiritual friendship, clarifies to a large extent Aelred's concrete political engagements, beginning with his concern for engaging in peacemaking works during his first abbacy at Revesby. But this preoccupation also explains the public stances marking the final period in his life, in particular beginning around 1153–1154, a date that represents a major turning point. At this time he composed his first historical treatises, as if, immediately following the passing of some of the most prestigious figures of the preceding generation,[117] he became aware that he was living the pivotal moment not just between two reigns, but between two eras. As a privileged witness of this passage from one world to another, he felt obliged to become the moral conscience of the new generation and especially of the new king, the young Henry Plantagenet. In this way he could keep the memory of the recent past, troubled by nearly twenty years of civil war, and at the same time bring hope to civil authorities, secular princes, and an entire nation that had for so long aspired finally to see a world at peace.

These points should establish the tight correlation between two facets of Aelred's personality that contemporary historians have only begun to explore in the last fifteen years. These are Aelred's public face, consisting of the political role he probably assumed in the civil society of his time and of his work as a historiographer, the latter facet a strategic element serving the former. It is this correlation that we examine more closely in part V, about the fourth and final period of Aelred's life, the period of the world and history.

---

117. To cite only those with whom Aelred was closely connected, Bernard of Clairvaux, Pope Eugene III, King Stephen of England, King David of Scotland, and Walter Espec, all of whom died between 1152 and 1154. Less well known, but no less dear to Aelred's heart, was Prince Henry, son of King David, who died in 1152.

Part V

The Time of Spiritual Maturity
Aelred, the Moral Conscience of His Time (1153/54–1167)

Introduction:
From Babylon to Jerusalem

Among the multiple facets in Aelred's portrait, historians have until recently highlighted those relating to his personality as a man, his vocation as a monk, and his twofold pedagogical and pastoral mission—both as a novice master educating individuals and as an abbot serving as the guide and shepherd of monastic communities. At the same time, considerable effort is being made in translations and critical editions of Aelred's works to make them more accessible. This effort has principally involved his ascetic and mystical treatises[1] and his immense homiletic production.[2] The body of the latter, currently consist-

---

1. Assembled in 1971 in a single volume (CCCM 1).

2. These can be broken down as follows: the "First Clairvaux Collection," twenty-eight sermons included in PL 195, and the "Second Clairvaux Collection," eighteen sermons discovered by Raciti in 1982, making a total of forty-six sermons, numbered 1 to 46 in Raciti's critical edition published in CCCM 2A; the "Durham Collection," thirty-two sermons edited in part by C. H. Talbot in 1952 and completed by Raciti, numbered 47 to 78 in the critical edition in CCCM 2B; a single sermon also discovered by Raciti, from a compilation of works gathered by Matthew of Rievaulx, numbered 79 in CCCM 2B; the "Lincoln Collection," five sermons, again discovered by Raciti, numbered 80 to 84 in CCCM 2B; and finally the "Reading-Cluny Collection," ninety-eight sermons also discovered by Raciti, in CCCM 2C. One more sermon, in the fifteenth-century "Peterborough Manuscript" (Central Library, unnumbered) and discovered in 2005 by Peter Jackson, which preserves the text of Aelred's sermon at the transfer of Saint Edward the Confessor's relics to Westminster on October 13, 1163, can also be added to the list (Peter Jack-

ing of 182 or 183 sermons, has grown considerably since 1982 thanks to Father Gaetano Raciti's discoveries in various libraries.[3] Taking advantage of this valuable translation and editing work, numerous scholars, mainly Anglo-American and Franco-Belgian but also recently Italian and to a lesser extent Spanish, have explored diverse facets of Aelred's rich spiritual doctrine. These scholars have established in more detail its connection to what we know of Aelred's life and personality and to his historical context.

We have followed this existential and doctrinal path in the first three parts of the present study, tracking it across the span of Aelred's life and responsibilities. Illuminated by his spiritual doctrine, we have shown three larger and larger concentric circles, each one corresponding to a principal period of his life. The first, the "circle of the man," extends from Aelred's birth in 1110 to his monastic conversion in 1134 and includes a presentation of the twelfth-century's socio-cultural and politico-religious context (part II, chapters 2–4). The second, "the circle of the monk," extends from 1134 to 1143 and covers the period of Aelred's initial monastic instruction and his first responsibilities within the monastic community, especially as an educator (part III, chapters 5–6). The third, "the circle of the abbot," covers the final twenty-five years of Aelred's life from 1143 to 1167. Within this circle we survey the events that led to Aelred's abbacy and examine Aelred's doctrine regarding his conception of his abbatial charge, wholly devoted to building a fraternal community (part IV, chapters 7–8).

---

son, "*In translacione sancti Edwardi Confessoris:* The Lost Sermon by Aelred of Rievaulx Found?" CSQ 40, no. 1 [2005]: 45–83).

3. See Gaetano Raciti, "Deux collections de sermons de saint Aelred—une centaine d'inédits—découvertes dans les fonds de Cluny et Clairvaux," Coll 45 (1983): 165–84. See also Gaetano Raciti, "Une allocution familière de S. Aelred conservée dans les mélanges de Matthieu de Rievaulx," Coll 47 (1985): 267–80.

To successively navigate each circle, we intertwined general anthropology and spiritual theology into something resembling Ariadne's thread. An anthropological perspective shows that across the three circles Aelred moves from the individual in search of inner unity (the circle of the self as object or "me") to the individual unified both humanly and affectively through personal friendships (the circle of the self as subject or "I"), and then from the individual to the community (the circle of the self joined with others or "we"). In the latter circle we saw how, following the Augustinian principle *singula omnium, omnia singulorum,* Aelred invited his brothers to weave interpersonal relationships into a network of sharing and exchange, a network that allowed them to build a place of increasingly extensive communion and reciprocity to serve as a precursor to eternal life. Similarly, from the perspective of theology and Aelred's own life experiences, all three circles are connected by the doctrine of friendship. Aelred conceived the human experience of friendship as an authentic spiritual path to personal affective unification and community edification by means of charity and in the person of Christ, the cornerstone. In the process, Aelred demonstrates the theological roots of his idea of monastic life as an ethical space in the individual and an ecclesiological space in the community for the formation of Christ.

In favoring this doctrinal and existential approach we have largely, and intentionally, left aside Aelred's public face. Walter, Aelred's earliest biographer, has been unfairly criticized by contemporary (primarily English and American) historians for doing that. Modern scholarship, however, is only beginning to shed light on Aelred's active efforts, from 1153 onward, to influence public affairs and the course of history by engaging personally in social and political matters in the wake of his country's civil war.

We now turn our attention to the political dimension of Aelred's personality, so entering the fourth circle of Aelred's theological and spiritual synthesis. Moving beyond the cloister,

Aelred passes from building a monastic community as a model for all communal life to the construction of a civil society that is a Jerusalem-like city of peace rather than a Babylon-styled city of confusion. Aelred's historiographic and hagiographic works gradually exhibit a more unified vision of history and the world, oriented toward their ultimate ends in the person of Christ. Aelred progressively develops a mystic and cosmic theology of history through his last great work, the thirty-one *Homilies on the Prophetic Burdens of Isaiah*.

We proceed in two phases. First, chapter 9 considers Aelred's social and political engagements as glimpsed through Walter's *Life of Aelred* and Aelred's own historiographical works. In so doing, we reflect on issues relating to Aelred's historiographical practice. These reflections permit us in chapter 10 to broaden our study and lay the foundations of what can be called a "cosmic mysticism of history" based on the *Homilies on the Prophetic Burdens of Isaiah* and related texts.

Chapter Nine

Aelred's Social and Political Engagements

The Iconic Value of The Life of Aelred

Testimony relating to Aelred's social and political engagements is relatively sparse, and contemporary historians have often reproached Walter, his first biographer, of having almost completely ignored this part of Aelred's life. True though that may be, the accusation is unfair and only partially valid. It is unfair because it does not adequately take into account Walter's intended compositional and editorial goals, which were to invite the reader "to move beyond appearances"[1] and "to have him pass, as through a mirror, from the *historical truth* of Aelred's life to his *spiritual and ethical truth*, from the *description* (of events) to the *icon*, from the *visible* to the *invisible*."[2]

In other words, Walter is less interested in events than in their meaning. They reveal the deepest parts of Aelred's personality and offer a model monk and abbot. Even if the histo-

---

1. Pierre-André Burton, "Introduction," in Walter Daniel, *La Vie d'Aelred*, trans. Pierre-André Burton (Oka, Canada: Abbaye Notre-Dame-du-Lac, 2004), 25.

2. Burton, Introduction, 30. See also Pierre-André Burton, "Walter Daniel, un biographe injustement critiqué? À propos de la réception de la *Vita Aelredi*. Entre vérité historique et vérité mythique," Cîteaux 53 (2002): 223–67. Additionally, see chap. 1 of this book.

ricity of events themselves retains its importance—for Walter is fully aware that the believability of his narrative and of his portrait of Aelred depends on historical precision—it is nevertheless true that Walter does not seek to offer a historically critical biography. Rather, he invites the reader to contemplate an icon, a window opening on the invisible. He strives to create an account that is representational rather than exhaustive. It is easy to understand that in the historical thread of Aelred's life, Walter proceeded selectively, retaining only those *gesta* most representative of the aspects of Aelred's personality that he wished to bring into relief. With this approach, the historical facts related play more or less the same iconic role as certain objects depicted in a painting, whose presence in the portrait suffices to suggest the identity of the portrait's subject.

This general principle guiding the composition of an iconic tableau or a hagiographic narrative such as *The Life of Aelred* obviously applies to Aelred as a public figure and the role he played in the society of his time, which was no doubt more important than it appears at first glance. Instead of sketching that public life as fully as we might have liked, Walter selected and related events that he thought evoked Aelred's public face and role. Thus, to reproach Walter for mostly passing over the public and political dimension of Aelred's life is not only unfair to him, but a conclusion drawn from a superficial reading. Such a reading is incomplete in its failure to account adequately for the work's genre. Although that genre's pretensions to combine event-related historicity and exhaustivity are not entirely absent from the work, Walter treats them as secondary to his primary intention: to offer a life model worthy of imitation (VA 1).

Walter's Portrait of Aelred as the "Peaceful" and the "Peace-Maker"

In one of the rare chapters of the *Life* devoted to the ten-year period Aelred spent at the Scottish court, Walter underlines King David's contribution to the personal and moral development of the man who was to become Rievaulx's most prestigious abbot. Indeed, Walter states that it is under David's influence and guidance, and sharing in David's temporal responsibilities, that Aelred learned "the royal virtues which later he was to describe in writing for the consolation of the faithful," and that Aelred "himself found profit in the reading of this consolation, and so did not merely make others bear fruit but he himself bore fruit of sweet savour."[3] Among these "royal virtues," Walter emphasizes one in particular: Aelred's sharp sense of moderation and justice in the management of temporal affairs in order to guarantee peace and the common good: "Everything done at court was in his keeping, yet he did whatever he did with such mildness that under his just and affable management of affairs there was no unrest, no disturbance among the people. He set the foot of justice and walked in the paths of peace where truth could suffer no violence."[4]

Here, perhaps inspired by Psalms 85:11-14 and 34:14-15, Walter links three key words: *justice* and *truth* leading to *peace*. These three concepts furnished Aelred with an ethical foundation for all his actions in administrative practice. Aelred's superiors, and Abbot William in particular, saw when Aelred arrived at Rievaulx that he already possessed in abundance the virtues of justice and truth and a great motivation to see peace reign over all; they probably soon came to him for counsel on varied and often confidential issues. In 1142 they even entrusted him, along with several Cistercian abbots, with a diplomatic mission to Rome to settle the question of succession to the episcopal see of York.[5] However, only once Aelred became abbot was he finally able fully to demonstrate his diplomatic abilities and show that his political and social engagements had the single source of justice and truth, and the single goal of peace, as Walter underlines on two occasions

---

3. Walter Daniel, *The Life of Aelred of Rievaulx*, trans. F. M. Powicke, CF 57 (Kalamazoo, MI: Cistercian Publications, 1994), 91, chap. 2.

4. Walter, VA 2 (CF 57:91).

5. Walter, VA 14 (CF 57:107). For details, see chap. 5 of this book.

in the *Life*, recounting Aelred's peacemaking works among the people surrounding Cistercian monasteries.

The Founding of Revesby

The first of these two narratives concerns the 1143 founding of Revesby in Lincolnshire, entrusted to Aelred by his peers. Walter relates that beginning with this date Aelred's reputation began to spread beyond the narrow horizon of monastic and ecclesiastical circles, stretching out into civil and political arenas of the kingdom of England. The local bishop, Alexander of Lincoln—one of the nephews of Roger, bishop of Salisbury, who had previously been the influential chancellor of King Henry I and King Stephen of Blois[6]—invited Aelred to participate in diocesan synods and requested that he participate in the instruction of secular clergy: "To preach to the clergy . . . to bring priests to a better way of life."[7] What lies behind these words is Alexander's intention that Aelred represent a religious movement fully informed by the ideas of Gregorian reform, instituting or even imposing them in his own diocese.

6. Of unknown origin (perhaps from Caen or Avranches) and no doubt of low birth, Roger was noticed by the future Henry I, who took him into service first as a chaplain, then probably as seneschal. Shortly after becoming king in 1100, Henry named Roger chancellor of England in 1101 and entrusted the reign to him while Henry was in Normandy from 1123 to 1126. Roger became bishop of Lincoln on August 11, 1107. On Henry's death in 1135, Roger played a major role in rallying the barons and clergy of the kingdom to the cause of Stephen of Blois against the Empress Matilda, daughter of Henry I, whom in 1126 Henry had designated to succeed him. Roger's actions gained him Stephen's gratitude and allowed Roger to bring two of his nephews into the government: Nigel, bishop of Ely from 1133 to 1169, and Alexander, bishop of Lincoln from 1123 to 1148. In 1138 all three earned the jealousy of several barons of the kingdom, who accused them of plotting against the king and rallying to Matilda's cause. They escaped royal justice thanks only to a vehement protest from Henry of Blois, the bishop of Winchester and brother of King Stephen, who demanded their reinstatement.

7. Walter, VA 20 (CF 57:111). [Translator's note: My ellipsis, to fit the English quotation to Burton's phrasing.]

Walter also states that during this period Aelred increasingly
gained the affection and veneration of civil and military authorities—the counts and barons of the region—as well as of
the local population of Lincolnshire (VA 20).

Where did this influence originate? According to Walter, it
came from Aelred's miracles, which made him famous. But
above all, Aelred's influence came from his efforts to make
peace through what might be called a "strategy of ecclesiastical
geography" or a "policy of monastic estate expansion." To our
secularized, twenty-first-century eyes, these concepts may
seem curious, even scandalous. But for his part, Aelred, apparently counseled by his bishop, who ardently encouraged
him, seems to have had no qualms at employing such policies.
He was firmly convinced that by pursuing such policies more
than any other means he was adding to the common and individual well-being of all concerned, thereby contributing to
the salvation of local potentates, to the material security of the
monasteries, to the social and political stability of the region,
and to the general economic prosperity of the country as a
whole, as Walter explains:

> The bishop orders him . . . to accept grants of land from
> knights in generous free-alms, and he obeys, since he had
> realized that in this unsettled time such gifts profited
> knights and monks alike, for in those days it was hard
> for any to lead the good life unless they were monks or
> members of some religious order, so disturbed and cha-
> otic was the land, reduced almost to a desert by the mal-
> ice, slaughters and harryings of evil men. And so he
> desired that that land for which almost all men were fight-
> ing to the death should pass into the hands of the monks
> for their good, and he knew that to give what they had
> helped the possessors of goods to their salvation and that,
> if they did not give, they might well lose both life and
> goods without any payment in return.[8]

8. Walter, VA 20 (CF 57:111).

Considering these beneficial political and social consequences of Revesby's founding, it is easy to understand why immediately after this passage Walter notes that Aelred was "greatly beloved"[9] by the king of England. Although Walter does not establish a direct link between Aelred and Stephen, it nevertheless seems probable that Stephen's affection for Aelred[10] was linked to Aelred's efforts to calm the social upheavals draining the country, bringing much-needed aid to the king. This aid was all the more valuable given that from the moment of his accession to the English throne after Henry I's death in 1135, Stephen had been hard pressed to establish his own political legitimacy, which was widely contested because he had seized power against the express will of the late King Henry. As a result, the supporters of the Empress Matilda, Henry's designated heir, and in particular her uncle, King David of Scotland, and his allies, considered Stephen a usurper, to be ousted at all costs.

In this context of high political tensions and civil war, Stephen needed whatever support he could find, and Aelred's help, however limited, was of inestimable value, if only because of its substantial symbolic impact. Stephen must have been well aware of the affection that bound Aelred to the Scottish royal family. Though it may have cost him greatly, Aelred did not hesitate to cut these ties. A much greater good was at stake, one worth any sacrifice, even if it meant renouncing affections that were dear to him. The greater good in question was the political stability and the civil peace of the kingdom.

9. Walter, VA 20 (CF 57:111).

10. In the introduction to the re-edition of the English translation of the *Life*, Marsha Dutton proposes the alternate hypothesis that Aelred's biographer is guilty of a chronological error in this case, and that he jumps the gun, placing royal affection for Aelred in Stephen's reign, when in reality this royal favor exists only after 1153–1154, during the reign of Henry II. This is obviously possible, but it detracts nothing from the remarks that follow regarding Aelred's peace-making political engagements (Marsha L. Dutton, Introduction, in Walter Daniel, *The Life of Aelred of Rievaulx*, trans. F. M. Powicke, CF 57 [Kalamazoo, MI: Cistercian Publications, 1994], 34).

Several years later, around 1153, when Aelred wrote his own account of the Battle of the Standard,[11] he had the opportunity to express his recognition of Stephen's political legitimacy and to explain this choice, which went against his natural and heartfelt affections. He did so not theoretically, in a treatise of political theology argued on the basis of what should constitute a just war. Rather he did it narratively, in the form of a drama placing the historical participants on a stage and placing words in their mouths. As Marsha Dutton has shown, Aelred did this not with the goal of offering a precise relation of events as they took place or reporting the participants' words as they truly were spoken, but instead with the purpose of spotlighting human, social, and ethical issues,[12] as well as what Marie Anne Mayeski has identified as spiritual and theological issues.[13]

This question is essential to understanding the theology of history of Aelred's historiographical works. For the moment it suffices to note three elements that explain why, in the context of Revesby's founding and later events, Aelred made the rational choice contributing to the general welfare and social peace rather than the affection-based choice promoting his personal interests by cultivating the ties binding him to the Scottish royal family. The first element relates to Aelred's bitter memory of the terrible depredations committed by the Scottish troops[14] during the campaign leading up to the Battle of the

---

11. On the historical events of the battle, see chap. 2, in "Contested Succession and Civil War (1135–1153/1154)."

12. Marsha Dutton, "Introduction," in *Aelred of Rievaulx: The Historical Works*, trans. Jane Patricia Freeland, CF 56 (Kalamazoo, MI: Cistercian Publications, 2005), 26.

13. Marie Anne Mayeski, "*Secundum naturam*: The Inheritance of Virtue in Aelred's *Genealogy of the English Kings*," CSQ 37 (2002): 221–28. Mayeski notes that the narrative and historical texts of the Middle Ages, including hagiography among other genres, should be considered as spaces allowing doctrinal and theological reflections.

14. For a vivid description of these depredations, see the French translation of *La Bataille de l'Étendard*: Pierre-André Burton, "Le récit *La bataille de l'Étendard* par Aelred de Rievaulx: présentation et traduction," Cîteaux 58 (2007): 29–30.

Standard, for which he was never able to forgive King David. Even if the latter had not directly ordered these actions, he had tolerated them. So Aelred committed himself to preventing such atrocities in the future, even while relegating his own friendships to a level of secondary importance. The second element inclining Aelred to support King Stephen rather than the Scots united around Matilda is that in Aelred's mind, Stephen had justice and right on his side in taking up arms in self-defense and in order to protect the English people against the cruelty of enemy troops. His cause was right because his legitimacy was, if not uncontested, at least uncontestable, as Aelred affirms clearly and forcefully in his narrative account of the Battle of the Standard through the discourse he places on the lips of Walter Espec, Stephen's lieutenant and commander in chief of the king's army in the battle:

> Do we distrust the cause? But we are not undertaking an unjust war on behalf of our king, who has not invaded a kingdom not rightfully his, as enemies falsely claim, but has accepted it as an offering, he whom the people sought, the clergy chose, the pope anointed, and apostolic authority confirmed in his kingdom.
>
> But to be silent concerning the king for a moment, no one surely will deny that we are right to take up arms for our country, that we fight for our wives, for our children, and for our churches, warding off an impending danger.[15]

The third element explaining Aelred's decision relates to King David himself, the head of a Scottish coalition defending the cause of the Empress Matilda. According to Aelred, David's decision to take up his niece's cause and raise troops—unscrupulous barbarians at that—to fight against Stephen, the legitimately established king, was not only contrary to the principles

---

15. Bello 3; Aelred of Rievaulx, "The Battle of the Standard," in *Aelred of Rievaulx: The Historical Works*, trans. Jane Patricia Freeland, CF 56 (Kalamazoo, MI: Cistercian Publications, 2005), 254.

of right and justice, but went against the interest of his own kingdom and the general course of history. In fact this decision presents itself as the unjustified disavowal of an alliance with the Anglo-Norman court, from which David had greatly benefited, as he owed his own power to it. Aelred reminds him of this fact through the words of Robert de Brus, David's childhood friend and Stephen's vassal, sent to David on an unsuccessful diplomatic mission to dissuade him from engaging in battle:

> Against whom are you raising arms today and leading this immense army? Surely against the English and the Normans! O King, have you not always found their counsel useful, their aid ready, and their allegiance welcome? Therefore I ask you, my lord, have you found such fidelity in the Scots that you can safely dismiss the counsel of the English for yourself and your people and deprive yourself of the aid of the Normans, as if the Scots alone sufficed even against the Scots?
>
> This reliance on the Galwegians is new to you. Today you are attacking with arms those through whom you have until now ruled, beloved by the Scots and terrible to the Galwegians. Do you think then, O King, that the heavenly Majesty will with equanimity see that you are intent on destroying those through whom you procured the kingdom for yourself and your people and security for your kingdom? With what troops and what auxiliaries did your brother Duncan crush the army of Donald and recover the kingdom that the tyrant had usurped? Who restored Edgar your brother, indeed more than a brother, to his kingdom if not . . . [16] our army? You yourself, O King, when you sought from your brother Alexander the part of the kingdom that your brother Edgar left you at

---

16. [Translator's note: My ellipsis. The English translation includes the word "to" here, which appears to be a typographical error. Robert is arguing that it was the English army ("our army") that restored Edgar to the Scottish throne, not that Edgar was restored "to" the English army.]

his death, obtained what you wanted without bloodshed through men's fear of us.

Remember last year, when you earnestly sought the help of the English against Malcolm, the heir of his father's hatred and persecution? How happy, how swift, and how prompt to help, how willing to face danger were Walter Espec and many of the other English barons when they hastened to you at Carlisle! Recall how many ships they fitted out, what arms they brought, what young men they provided. Recall how the enemy terrified all your men until they took Malcolm himself, once he was betrayed, bound him once taken, and handed him over once bound.[17]

These wise words inviting David to agree to terms would come to naught, smothered by the open opposition of William Fitzduncan, one of King David's nephews and the primary instigator in the war against Stephen. But Robert's words reveal Aelred's constant primary concern: to preserve peace and understanding among nations at all costs, for the good of the civil populations.

Dundrennan: "Aelred the Peace-maker," or a New Solomon

In 1143, Rievaulx founded the abbey of Dundrennan in Galloway, under the patronage of King David. At one point—Walter places the event sometime between 1157 and 1163[18]—Aelred was asked to go to Dundrennan because the community was endangered by fratricidal rivalries of "the petty king of that land [who was] incensed against his sons, and the sons

---

17. Aelred, *Bello* 6 (CF 56:261–63).

18. As Maurice Powicke and Dutton indicate, Walter seems to confuse Aelred's three known trips to Scotland, which occurred in 1159, in 1164–1165, and in 1166. The Dundrennan episode related in VA 38 corresponds to the first of these journeys (see note below). See Maurice Powicke, "Introduction," in Walter Daniel, *The Life of Ailred of Rievaulx*, trans. F. M. Powicke (Oxford: Clarendon: 1950, 1978), xciv, 45, n.1; Dutton, "Introduction," CF 57:81.

[who were] raging against their father and each other." Unfortunately, Walter gives no information on the events, political stakes (a revolt against the Scottish king's authority), or individuals involved.[19] He simply states, no doubt to keep Aelred center stage, that "the king of Scotland could not subdue, nor could the bishop pacify, their mutual hatreds, rancor, and tyranny." If Aelred's biographer is to be believed, the situation had reached its tipping point. With the civil population facing pillage and massacre, only Aelred's diplomatic intervention could stop things from getting worse. But Aelred succeeded: "Aelred the peacemaker met them all and, with words of peace and goodness, bound together the angry sons by a firm peace in a single bond of affection. He eagerly urged their veteran sire to put on the monastic habit and by his marvelous admonishment bent him to that course."[20] In fact, after Fergus surrendered in 1160, one year before his death, he entered Holyrood, a monastery of Augustinian canons that David had founded in 1128 near Edinburgh.

The peace established by Aelred was short-lived, for in 1174, Fergus's two sons rebelled again against Scottish authority and, at the Battle of Alnwick in July of that year, took prisoner King William the Lion, Malcolm IV's brother, who had succeeded him in 1165. But for Walter, it was enough to know that Aelred's mediation had been crowned with success to grant him the prestigious title of "peacemaker," etymologically assimilating him with the famous king of Israel, Solomon.[21]

19. The petty king was Fergus of Galloway (d. 1161). He sought to take advantage of the weak position of the young Sottish king, Malcolm IV (King David's eldest grandson, who, at the age of twelve, succeeded David in 1153), and break away from his authority. Fergus's sons were Gilbert and Uchtred. The local bishop of the diocese of Whithorn was named Christian.

20. Walter, VA 38 (CF 57:125).

21. Walter establishes the same parallel in his "Letter to Maurice," where he underlines Aelred's extreme patience and forbearance with respect to a brother who had just thrown him into a burning fireplace (CF 57:157–58).

Walter's attribution of this title to Aelred on the basis of an event occurring almost at the end of his life, which parallels the events of Revesby, when Aelred had barely begun his abbatial ministry, implies that all of his abbacy was marked by an unwavering desire to promote peace and justice. It is of course regrettable that Walter limited himself to these two vignettes, but he was not writing modern critical history. Rather, he wrote the history of Aelred's life as if painting an icon. He thus no doubt judged it unnecessary to say more about Aelred's political involvement. The only addition he makes to this material is his inclusion among Aelred's works listed in chapter 32 of the *Life* of the wide range of civil and ecclesiastical figures with whom Aelred had corresponded, a list that included the pope, the kings of France, England, and Scotland, the archbishops of Canterbury[22] and York,[23] all the bishops of England, and "the most distinguished men in the Kingdom of England," with a special mention of the earl of Leicester, the Franco-Norman Robert II de Beaumont, known as "Le Bossu" ("Robert the Hunchback," 1104–1168), who became seneschal and chief justiciar of Henry II upon his accession to the English throne in 1154.

Unfortunately for historians, with the exception of the letter Aelred wrote to Saint Bernard in 1142/1143 regarding the composition of *The Mirror of Charity*, none of this correspondence remains. This is either because Aelred, unlike his master Bernard, judged it useless or unnecessary to preserve it, or because, if he or his secretaries bothered to compile it, the

---

22. Theobald of Bec from 1139 to 1161, then Thomas Becket from 1162 to 1170.

23. After Thurstan's death (Thurstan was archbishop from 1119 to 1140; see part II of this book), William Fitzherbert was elected in 1143, then deposed in 1147 by the Cistercian Pope Eugene III. From 1147 to 1153 the post was held by Henry Murdac, Saint Bernard's disciple and the former abbot of Fountains. William Fitzherbert was reelected and reinstated in 1153 by Pope Anastasius IV, after which Roger de Pont-l'Évêque held the post from 1154 to 1181.

collection was lost. To know Aelred's public face, the historian is reduced to examining other medieval sources, including, of course, Aelred's own historical works. Their dedications, when they exist, and their content reveal the wide spectrum of Aelred's socio-political and ecclesiastical relations and concerns. They also reveal how tightly connected these relations and concerns are, both in the general mentality of the time and in Aelred's mind.

Aelred's Historical Works: Aelred as the Moral Conscience of His Time

It has often been noted that among twelfth-century Cistercian authors, Aelred is remarkably original in the wide range of literary genres to which he contributes. He alone among them composed historical works, a total of seven in all. Contemporary historians tend to divide these works into two groups.

Four of Aelred's historical works address England's civil and political history. Two of those—*The Battle of the Standard*, *The Genealogy of the Kings of the English*, and *The Life of Edward, King and Confessor*—share the common feature of having been dedicated to kings of England, namely Stephen of Blois and his immediate successor, Henry II. The *Lament for David, King of the Scots* is a special case, as it is without explicit dedication. It was composed immediately after the death of King David in 1153. But shortly thereafter, in 1153 or 1154, Aelred himself integrated it into his *Genealogy of the Kings of the English* in such a way that in its present state the text of the *Lament*, immediately preceded by a dedicatory letter to Henry II, constitutes the first chapter of the full *Genealogy*.

The second group of historical works consists of three more modest texts that focus on England's ancient and contemporary religious and ecclesiastical history. The first book in this group is *The Life of Ninian, Apostle of the Southern Picts*, which credits Ninian with the seventh-century founding of Whithorn diocese in Scotland. The second book, a homage to the region in which Aelred was born and spent at least the first four years of his life, is *The Saints of the Church of Hexham and their Miracles*. These saints' relics were kept in Hexham's church for three generations under the curial care of Aelred's father and forefathers. The third work is a brief narrative entitled *A Certain Wonderful Miracle*, also known as the *Nun of Watton*. This work relates the sad moral tale of events that troubled the peace of Watton Priory, a community of nuns founded in 1120 by Gilbert of Sempringham with the support of his bishop, Alexander of Lincoln, and some Cistercian guidance. Gilbert had created the priory for seven girls for whose education he had taken responsibility, but in 1148 he expanded it to include a branch of canons regular. They were responsible for the nuns' spiritual guidance, while lay brothers were responsible for aiding them with material tasks.

An Entry into Politics?

An essential point gives each of these works its own hue and furnishes an important key to its interpretation, preventing a superficial reading of the works as simple anecdotal narratives, or as insipidly pious literature with neither depth nor substance, emanating from a naive mind too inclined to believe in miracles.

Aelred wrote all of these works after 1153, the watershed year in English history when, on December 25, the Treaty of Wallingford was signed in Westminster, finally bringing an end to the civil war that had for twenty years pitilessly burned and bloodied the kingdom of England. This year opened a new era in which all eyes were turned toward Stephen's designated successor, the son of the Empress Matilda, the young Prince Henry Plantagenet, the future Henry II. As Dutton has noted, Henry had suddenly become "the kingdom's hope."[24] It was expected that he would bring about better times by establishing his reign on the solid foundation of mutual understanding and concord, of peace and

24. Dutton, Introduction, CF 56:7.

justice, and with an orientation toward prosperity and the common good. In short, a people disappointed for twenty years pinned all their aspirations on Henry. In this troubled and expectant context, anyone with an even remotely authoritative voice attempted to influence the new king, aiming to direct the course of public affairs toward a brighter horizon.

It is significant that Aelred chose to publish his first historical treatises in a context of political transition, and that he dedicated them to Stephen of Blois or to Henry II. In so doing, he manifested his intention to be one of the voices counseling the young king, to help him assume the enormous political responsibilities now resting upon his shoulders. Aelred thus sought to enter the political realm and, to the extent his religious condition allowed it, play an active role in the social life of his country. Through his historiographical activity, Aelred became engaged in history in the making.

Aelred as Historian and Counselor of Princes

Aelred had certain credentials that authorized him to counsel King Henry through his historiographical work. Dutton has already pointed out some of these.[25] Among those are the fact that Aelred probably benefited from an encouraging family environment where the study of history was held in high esteem. Indeed, Aelred's paternal grandfather, Eilaf, and great-grandfather, Alfred, were both nicknamed "Larwa" (or "Lareow," Master) because of their erudition. Additionally, Aelred's primary education at Hexham, and his probable secondary education at the cathedral school of Durham, were also likely to encourage his interest in history, especially since the Venerable Bede's memory was revered at Durham. Bede had originally

---

25. Dutton, Introduction CF 56:31–32. See also Marsha Dutton, "A Historian's Historian: The Place of Bede in Aelred's Contributions to the New History of his Age," in *Truth as Gift: Studies in Cistercian History in Honor of John R. Sommerfeldt*, ed. Marsha L. Dutton, Daniel La Corte, and Paul Lockey, CS 204 (Kalamazoo, MI: Cistercian Publications, 2004), 407–48.

been a monk of Jarrow, but his relics rested in Durham cathedral. He was of course considered to be the greatest historian of the English people and the definitive reference for English history. For any aspiring historian, Bede was an indispensable model.[26]

It is easy to imagine that, bathed in this long tradition of culture and erudition so characteristic of medieval Northumbria, Aelred naturally developed a taste for history and a vocation as a historian.[27] However, that fact does not explain why he felt authorized to use his interest in history and talents as a writer to engage in the moral and political education of the young King Henry. The motivations for this decision must be sought elsewhere. Here we can advance three possibilities, all more or less personal to Aelred, before going on to uncover more political and institutional motivations.

The first motivation that comes to mind, and the least significant of the three, has to do with the fact that not long after entering Rievaulx, Aelred was called upon to serve as novice master for a period of two years. From this moment on, his pedagogical mission became almost second nature to him, as he maintained a ceaseless concern for the material and spiritual education of both individuals and communities. The earliest beneficiaries of his pastoral and educational attentions were of course his brother monks and the monastic communities entrusted to his care. But he no doubt came to conclude that it would detract nothing from those efforts if he expanded them in the service of a wider cause: the education of a prince and the edification of English society.

Two additional, more serious, motivations also explain Aelred's belief that he had the right to address Henry as a counselor, and even to speak to him as an equal. As before entering Rievaulx, Aelred had been steward of the king of

---

26. On Bede's importance as source, model, and guide, in particular for Aelred, see Dutton, "Historian's Historian," 411–22.

27. For more on this point see Aelred Squire, "Historical Factors in the Formation of Aelred of Rievaulx," Coll 22 (1960): 261–82. Squire presents an impressive overview of Northumbria's long tradition of culture and historical erudition.

Scotland, participating in the daily administration of the kingdom, he must there have gained practical experience about what was expected of a reigning prince and been informed about the prince's social, civil, and military responsibilities. Perhaps because of that experience he felt he could offer informed advice to an inexperienced king.

Finally, in playing the role of counselor to Henry, Aelred was able to speak his heart. Through the blood lines of Henry's mother, the Empress Matilda, the young Henry was the grandnephew of King David of Scotland. At the time of his accession in October 1154, Henry had been fatherless for three years;[28] when David died on May 24, 1153, Henry lost not only his great-uncle but also a significant military ally and an important source of political support. Had David lived longer, he would no doubt have continued to offer Henry aid and counsel, as he probably had in the past. Aelred's memory of his youth at the Scottish court and the debt of gratitude he owed David may have led Aelred to render affectionate homage to David and to feel obligated to offer Henry, even at a distance through his historiographical work, the same fatherly attention and tutelage that he himself had received from David from 1124 to 1134.[29]

The Four Works of Civil History in Their Historical Context

In the year 1153, the figures involved in on-going events did not yet know that it would be a decisive year in England's civil and political history. For more than fifteen years, supporters of

---

28. Henry's father, Geoffrey V, count of Anjou ("Geoffrey the Fair"), died on September 7, 1151.

29. Underlining the strong bond that must have existed between Henry and his maternal granduncle is the fact that David himself knighted Henry at Carlisle on Pentecost Sunday, 1149. In the prefatory letter addressed to Henry in *Genealogy*, Aelred reminds Henry of this fact, noting that it had sealed an even deeper and firmer spiritual kinship between them than their blood ties, thereby obliging and morally binding Henry to a life befitting this heritage. On the theological and spiritual issues, see Mayeski, "*Secundum naturam*," 221–28.

the Empress Matilda had pursued a war of attrition against the supporters of King Stephen, who in 1135 had taken advantage of the tensions dividing the Anglo-Norman nobility to seize power. Years of seemingly endless warfare[30] had led to what everyone expected to be a pitched battle between the two armies in 1153 near Wallingford, on the banks of the Thames. But the battle never happened. Certain noblemen, weary of the interminable and devastating civil war, argued the futility of ceaseless conflict and succeeded in convincing the king to open negotiations with Henry Plantagenet, count of Anjou and Maine and duke of Normandy. These negotiations led to a truce.

But the country had to wait for the August 17, 1153, death of Eustace of Burgundy, the king's son and an ardent opponent of any agreement, before discussion could resume in a climate conducive to establishing a deeper accord. At the end of these diplomatic exchanges, though, the parties arrived at a peace agreement bearing the name of the averted battle, the Treaty of Wallingford. The king readily subscribed to this peace, as he already saw his power dwindling beside Henry's, which was on the rise.

Signed and ratified on December 25, 1153, at Westminster Abbey, the treaty stipulated among other things that Stephen would remain on the throne until his death, but also that he would make Henry his adoptive son and recognize him as legal heir and successor. At the beginning of 1154, both men met once again at Oxford, before the assembled English nobility. There they swore loyalty to Duke Henry and recognized him as Stephen's successor. Ten months later on October 25, 1154, Stephen died, and Henry II acceded to the throne, without opposition. Peace had finally returned.

In this time of transition from 1153 to 1154 Aelred wrote his first three tightly linked historical works, probably composing

30. On this turbulent period of English history and the anarchy that characterized the reign of Stephen of Blois, see Edmund King, *The Anarchy of Stephen's Reign* (Oxford: Oxford University Press, 1994); David Crouch, *The Reign of King Stephen: 1135–1154* (Harlow: Longman, 2000).

them in the following order: *The Battle of the Standard*, the *La-ment for David, King of the Scots*, and *The Genealogy of the Kings of the English*. The timing is of course not mere coincidence. Aelred Squire suggests that the political events of 1153, combined in the same year with the death of King David, encouraged Aelred to extend his attention beyond local and regional affairs and think in broader national, even supranational, terms, going so far as to tie the destiny of England to that of Scotland.[31]

Beyond Anecdote: The Narrative of The Battle of the Standard

Aelred's *Battle of the Standard* is well known. At first glance it appears unimpressive. Aelred anecdotally relates his memories of the battle he helplessly and bitterly witnessed not far from Rievaulx in 1138. Aelred was particularly affected by this battle, which opposed friends, kinsmen, and brothers[32] as well as involving people in both camps who were personally dear to him. On the English side was Walter Espec, founder and patron of Rievaulx, an English dignitary whom Aelred had met on multiple occasions during the time he served as David of Scotland's steward. Wholly devoted to Stephen's cause, Walter was commander of the Anglo-Norman army. On the Coalition side, supporting the Empress Matilda, were Matilda's maternal uncle, David, who had played such an important role in Aelred's development, and Prince Henry, who was Matilda's first cousin, David's son, and a friend from Aelred's youth.

Unfortunately, nothing in this short treatise allows us to determine the date of its composition, its expected audience,

---

31. Aelred Squire, *Aelred of Rievaulx: A Study*, CS 50 (Kalamazoo, MI: Cistercian Publications, 1981), 87.

32. Also present were the two half-brothers Henry and Simon, respectively son and stepson of King David, who joined opposite sides, the former taking up the cause of his cousin the Empress Matilda, and the latter taking up the cause of King Stephen.

or Aelred's authorial intentions. We can do no more than hypothesize, extrapolating from the few clues offered to us by the text itself and by the history of its distribution.[33] Until recently, historians have held that the treatise must have been composed at the very beginning of Henry II's reign. Following Anselm Hoste's lead, they have estimated that Aelred composed the work somewhere between 1155 and 1157. More recently, Dutton hypothesized that the work was composed a few years earlier and rightly suggests that "Aelred wrote it while Stephen was still king, though perhaps with an eye to Henry's imminent succession,"[34] that is, between August 1153 and October 1154, "at the turning point between two dynasties."[35] Dutton's hypothesis is based on the fact that, in the narrative of the battle, Aelred places a discourse in Walter Espec's mouth defending Stephen, justifying the king's taking up arms against Matilda as an act of self-defense and as a way of protecting the English people from atrocities committed by Scottish troops.

Still, we can narrow the window of composition even further. While Aelred explicitly defends the king of England, he never names either King David or his son Henry. Similarly, and in contrast with his treatment of David in the *Lament for David* (at least in the long version), Aelred refrains from too sharply criticizing King David's willingness to take command of an army whose cruelty was well known to him and by ex-

---

33. For more on the questions of intent, audience, and distribution, see Elizabeth Freeman, "Aelred of Rievaulx's *De Bello Standardii*: Cistercian Historiography and the Creation of Community Memories," Cîteaux 49 (1998): 5–27; Elizabeth Freeman, "Multiple Meanings for Multiple Audiences: Aelred of Rievaulx's *Relatio de standardo*," in *Narratives of a New Order* (Turnhout: Brepols, 2002), 31–54; Elizabeth Freeman, "The Many Functions of Cistercian Histories Using Aelred of Rievaulx's *Relatio de Standardo* as a Case Study," *The Medieval Chronicle, Proceedings of the 1st International Conference on the Medieval Chronicle*, ed. Eric Kooper (Amsterdam-Atlanta: Rodopi, 1999), 124–32. See also Dutton, Introduction, CF 56:24–31, and Burton, "Bataille," 6–41.

34. Dutton, Introduction, CF 56:24.

35. Dutton, Introduction, CF 56:29.

tension his tacit approval of the army's depredations. Reading *Battle* in conjunction with the *Lament*, one gets the impression that Aelred seeks at all costs to preserve King David's honor and reputation. As weak as it may be, this detail could be the clue indicating that Aelred composed his narrative of *Battle* while King David was still living, thus before May 24, 1153.

These thoughts on *Battle's* composition date offer some indirect indication of the work's probable audience and of the author's intent. It seems evident that Aelred sought to address David I, king of Scotland, Stephen, king of England, and perhaps even Stephen's successor Henry, intending to remind them of their responsibilities toward the peoples entrusted to their care and of their practical and ethical duty to establish a reign of national cohesion and supranational *entente*, founded on the pursuit of justice and peace leading to the common good, rather than on their own personal interests. In composing an anecdotal treatise of little apparent importance, Aelred uses the concrete example of the event and its actors to illustrate the social and political challenges faced by post-Conquest and post-Civil-War England.[36]

This political and ethical reading of the work is justified by numerous textual elements in the narrative. For now we will underline only one such element, on which all the others depend. As Dutton has rightly noted, of all Aelred's historical treatises, *Battle* is the one that most clearly manifests his vision of what makes a historian, and in which he best expresses his conception of the historian's role.[37] Through the discourses placed in the mouths of Walter Espec on the English side and of Robert de Brus on the Scottish side, Aelred twice underscores the importance of rereading the events of the past. According to him, history is an indispensable discipline, on which the interpretation of present and possible future events must be

36. See Burton, "Bataille," 6–41, esp. 20. The text presented here reprises the principal ideas of that article.

37. Dutton, Introduction, CF 56:24, 32.

based in order to avoid a view of things too anchored in the short term. This is a significant part of government's ethical responsibility in its administration of temporal affairs. That is, he says, we must avoid the temptation "to neglect the memory of what is past and the thought of the future solely for the sake of the present"[38] and instead make the effort "to conjecture from the past to the present and from the present to the future."[39]

In other words, for Aelred, knowledge of history has three inseparable components: sapience, politics, and religion (or spirituality). It is the sapiential component of historical knowledge that helps princes and kings in their task of discernment and analysis of present events. This analysis in turn grants them the wisdom to engage in the political component of action, governing with measure and prudence. They are successful in the latter to the extent that they govern through the religious or spiritual component of piety and respect for divine law, with a view to establishing in the world the order desired eternally by God.

These connections between wisdom and historical knowledge, between historical knowledge and political responsibility, and finally between political responsibility and ethical practice leading to the establishment of divine order in the world are merely implied in *Battle*. Aelred later reiterated them more clearly and in greater detail, in *Genealogy*. There again, as in *Battle*, he placed discourse in another's mouth, this time that of King Edgar the Peaceful. This later redevelopment of the idea shows its real importance to Aelred, and indicates that the civil and political authorities of his time constituted the target audience of his historical works.

It would be an error, however, to reduce the significance of *Battle* to the sapiential-political connection. Thanks to the innovative approach combining what is known of the author's intentions with the history of the work's reception and the

38. Aelred, Bello 6 (CF 57:261).
39. Aelred, Bello 3 (CF 57:251–52).

history of its distribution in manuscript, Freeman[40] has shown that the work is situated through the joining of two audiences, lay and religious. Consequently, the narrative is open to at least two different yet complementary levels of interpretation, one political and the other more specifically religious.

The latter reading is confirmed by the fact that *Battle* was conserved not only in two manuscript compilations of historical texts but also, curiously, in a manuscript presented as a collection of pious works, showing that the work must have been read from a spiritual perspective. Such a reading is borne out by the text itself, where, at the very beginning, the reader encounters a brief historical overview of Cistercian expansion in England in the first third of the twelfth century, with the monastery of Rievaulx presented, with some bias, as the mother of all other Cistercian houses in England. This passage seems at first glance a digression unrelated to the work's narrative.

But Freeman holds that the passage confirms that Aelred intended the work to be read not only by princes and kings as a reminder of their political responsibilities but also by the monastic world of his time, so that the apparent digression is really not one. She argues that the passage is part of Aelred's global historiographic project of setting forth a threefold collective memory, at once national, familial, and monastic. The collective memory is national by way of the text's political component and its praise of Norman greatness in its address to the Anglo-Norman nobility then in power. It is familial by its emphasis on the role that Walter Espec, one of the major figures of the narrative, is shown to play in the foundation of numerous religious houses and of Rievaulx in particular. Finally, it is monastic by way of the history of Cistercian origins related therein and the fact that Aelred addresses the passage directly to the monks of Rievaulx to remind them of the nobil-

---

40. This discussion is based on articles and books by Freeman mentioned in earlier footnotes: Freeman, "*De Bello*," 5–27; "Multiple Meanings," 31–54; and "Many Functions," 124–32.

ity and prestige of their monastery's origins and history. Through this prestigious history, he encourages them to live up to the monastery's past glory and stimulates their desire to imitate the fervor and ideals of their predecessors' way of life. Finally, by addressing this single treatise both to a noble lay readership and to his brother monks, Aelred probably sought to move beyond the threefold collective national, familial, and monastic memory to provoke a dialogue among the different readerships and to raise the text to a transversal and universal level.

The text is transversal in that it reminds all three targeted audiences—kings and princes (Stephen, Henry, and David), local civil and military authorities (Walter Espec), and religious houses (principally Rievaulx)—of their responsibilities toward each other, a reminder all the more important given the frequently divergent nature of the three parties' interests.[41] The text is also universal in allowing a glimpse beyond the bonds of alliance or personal interest that might prevail to bind people together on a local, regional, or even national level, to the one bond that surpasses every other by its excellence and its ability to hold all men and women together—the moral and spiritual bond of piety and holiness. By virtue of this bond, all things are subordinate to God, and it is therefore the duty of every person, each according to his "order"—king or prince, lay or clergy—to carry the cross of Christ[42] as a banner in all endeavors.

By shifting his narrative from a simple anecdote to a more general ethical reflection on the civic duties and responsibilities of the three orders of medieval society, Aelred engaged in what Freeman and other historians have called a new mode, or a new "historiographical tendency," in this time period. On the one hand, this tendency responded to a growing interest among the lettered public for oral and written history. On the other

41. For example, during his own abbacy Aelred found himself after Walter Espec's death in 1153 at odds with Walter's successors, who contested the donations made by their uncle to religious houses, Rievaulx among them.
42. Aelred, Bello 3 (CF 56:257).

hand, the tendency responded to the concerns of two socially distinct groups, sometimes in conflict, sometimes cooperating, but always mutually influential. The first of these groups was the Anglo-Norman nobility, both high and low, in search of political legitimacy and a myth of origins—a group narrative establishing a sense of collective identity and glory—on which to base it. The second of these groups was the clergy, pressed by the urgent need to guarantee both spiritual and financial permanence and integrity of their monastic establishments.

Through his narrative in *Battle*, Aelred's genius as a historiographer and historian resides in the fact that he was able to understand the concerns of these two rather particular and divergent groups. He satisfied the national sentiment of the one and responded to the concerns of the other while managing to subsume both (probably because of his belonging to an international religious order) into a universal, ethical, and religious framework.

Often barely traced, or more often simply suggested, all the elements we have identified in *Battle* were later reprised and elaborated on by Aelred himself in his other historical works, frequently enriched with further nuances. But as Dutton has rightly indicated,[43] Aelred's method and fundamental concern would always remain the same. Aelred sought neither to develop a systematic philosophy or theology of history nor to encumber himself with general, abstract, theoretical principles. Instead he took real people and events from distant or recent history and, in biblical fashion, offered them to kings and princes as a mirror, an instrument of practical discernment and of political government serving to edify all civil and religious society. In short, as his other historical treatises confirm, he made the study of history a wisdom-based discipline, indispensable for the healthy administration of public affairs and the just conduct of peoples and nations.

43. Dutton, "Introduction," CF 56:24, 34.

The Lament for David, King of the Scots:
A Three-Dimensional Work

Thanks to the treaty of Wallingford, which finally brought an end to the long period of anarchy plaguing England since 1135, many people must have met 1153 as a pivotal year, rich in promise and full of hope for a better future. For Aelred, however, it was also a year laden with painful emotional trials. In the space of a few months, he saw the deaths of many of his dearest friends. Henry, a friend of his youth and crown prince of Scotland, died in 1152. Then Walter Espec, founder of Rievaulx, died in 1153. Less than a month later, on July 8, Pope Eugene III died, followed on August 20 by Bernard, who had exercised a powerful influence on Aelred's early monastic life, in particular as the driving force behind his becoming a writer of spiritual works.[44]

Perhaps most significant of all was the death on May 24, 1153, of David of Scotland, who had been a second father to Aelred, overseeing his personal and intellectual growth through the ungrateful age of adolescence and to whom Aelred owed more than can be said.[45] As he later wrote to Henry II, in the dedication to *Genealogy*, Aelred was deeply saddened by David's death: "I have brought together in short form his life and character, not as history [*historiando*] but as lamentation [*lamentando*], as now love, now fear, now hope, and now grief alter my feelings."[46]

This statement is of great importance in accounting for certain issues related to this work. First, it explains the constant

44. See chap. 6 of the present work, in particular the subsection "Why Bernard so Strongly Desired Aelred to be its Author."

45. On David's role in Aelred's adolescence, see chap. 3 of the present work.

46. Pref H; Aelred of Rievaulx, *Genealogy of the Kings of the English*, in *Aelred of Rievaulx: The Historical Works*, trans. Jane Patricia Freeland, CF 56 (Kalamazoo, MI: Cistercian Publications, 2005), 43.

hesitation in the manuscript tradition regarding the title: sometimes a *Lament*, a *Life*, or, more rarely, a *Eulogium*. Aelred's
biographer is perhaps himself in part responsible for this hesitation since when he enumerates the complete list of Aelred's
works, he uses Aelred's own terms when he states that Aelred
"published a life of David, king of Scotland, in the form of a
lamentation."[47] An even more fundamental reason for the hesitation derives from the history of the text itself. Initially, the
Lament was no doubt composed for its own sake, originating
as it did in Aelred's grief at David's death. It must have circulated in this form, at least at first, as a work in its own right, at
one and the same time a *Lament* for the deceased king and a
Eulogy to honor his memory. But shortly thereafter—sometime
after the signing of the Treaty of Wallingford on December 25,
1153, and before the official accession of Henry II on October
25, 1154—Aelred integrated it into *Genealogy*. This latter text
is a more complex work, which, according to the text's prefatory epistle, Aelred dedicated to the man who was then merely
the "Duke of the Normans and Aquitanians, and Count of the
Angevins," but who was soon to be king.[48] The *Lament* became
the first chapter of a much broader historical treatise and thus,
without losing any of its initial meaning, gained additional
value through a change in its genre. The text ceased to be a
simple lamentation, in both the strict sense of the term and
with respect to its audience, which was originally limited to
Aelred himself and perhaps those close to the Scottish royal
family. Instead it became far more: a *Life*, which Aelred inserted
like a precious jewel into a work destined to serve a far grander
purpose.

Before examining this question in greater detail, let us pause
a moment to consider another element unique to the manuscript tradition of the *Lament*. Apart from the fact that Aelred
framed the text differently in two successive presentations—

47. Walter, VA 32 (CF 57:120–21).
48. Aelred, Ep H, in Gen angl (CF 56:41).

first as a stand-alone work, then as an integral part of a broader historical treatise—the text of the *Lament* circulated in two different forms. It circulated first in a long unabridged version, then in a dramatically abbreviated version shortened by two thirds. The long version, edited for the first time in London in 1780 by John Pinkerton under the title *Eulogium*, then re-edited in 1889 by W. M. Metcalfe, is not completely unknown. However the short version, published by Roger Twysden in 1652 and reprinted in 1855 by Jacques-Paul Migne in the Patrologia Latina, is the most widely read today.[49] The very existence of this shorter version raises numerous questions that were impossible to answer so long as we had no reliable critical edition of the *Lament,* and of the *Genealogy* of which it became a part.[50] Among the sections omitted from the abridged version is a passage in which Aelred reproaches David for the sin of commanding Scottish troops at the Battle of the Standard. A detailed side-by-side comparative study of the two versions is required to draw any conclusions on the differences between them. But the detail that we have just pointed out allows us to at least conjecture that the abridged version was intended to preserve King David's honor.

The text of *Lament* has dual layers of meaning derived from its two successive framings. Better yet, it can be understood as having cumulative or expanded meaning, with the initial sense of the stand-alone work being after a fashion absorbed rather than erased by its recontextualization in the larger work. Considered independently of its later insertion into *Genealogy,* one thing is certain about *Lament*: it is above all an act of filial

49. For technical details on the manuscript tradition of the *Genealogy* and the *Lament,* see Dutton, Introduction, CF 56:13, 35–37.

50. [Translator's note: Burton's discussion relies on PL vol. 195 of the Patrologia Latina. As translator, I have quoted solely from the Cistercian Publications edition. Since his book appeared in 2010, Domenico Pezzini's critical edition of Aelred's historical works, including *Genealogy,* has appeared in CCCM 3 (Turnhout: Brepols, 2017).]

piety in which Aelred, giving free rein to his grief at the death of King David, commemorates all the kindnesses for which he owes David gratitude, as is made clear at the work's beginning: "The holy and devout King David has passed from this world. Although he has found a place worthy of such a soul, his death requires a lament from me [*planctum nobis indicit*]. For who would not mourn [*lugeat*] for a man so necessary to the world, now freed from human affairs [*rebus humanis*], except one who resents peace and success [*pacem et progressum invidere*] in human affairs [*rebus humanis*]?"[51]

Aelred reprises the idea in his conclusion:

> I too, though a sinner and unworthy, nevertheless remember your kindnesses, my most gentle lord and friend, which you showered on me from an early age. I remember the grace in which you now for the last time received me, I remember the good will with which you granted all my requests, I remember the generosity that you showed me, I remember the embraces and kisses with which you released me, not without tears, while all those present marveled. I skim over my tears for you; I relinquish my attachment, and I pour out all my spirit. For you I offer this sacrifice to my God. I expend this effort because of your kindnesses. And because this is so slight, my mind will always remember you in the very core of its being, there where for the salvation of all the Son of the Father is daily sacrificed.[52]

In the style of a psalmist, Aelred does not dwell on his own sadness. From the very first lines of the *Lament*, he invites everyone, "young men and maidens, aged and young," to join his mourning and to weep, not so much for the deceased but for themselves, because, he explains, with David's death the world has lost a man of great worth and an exemplary model,

51. Aelred, Lam D 1 (CF 56:45).
52. Aelred, Lam D 13 (CF 56:69–70).

"who lived not for himself but for everyone, caring for everyone, providing for the welfare [*salus*] of everyone: a teacher of morals [*rector morum*], an examiner of crimes [*censor scelerum*], an encourager of virtues [*virtutum incentor*]," a man whose "life was the model of humility [*forma humilitatis*], the mirror of righteousness [*iustitiae speculum*], the exemplar of chastity [*castitatis exemplar*]."[53]

Thus with three carefully chosen words—*forma, speculum, exemplar*—Aelred shifts the *Lament* to an entirely different register, from a lament for a lost friend (*planctus pro amico defuncto*), abundant in medieval literature,[54] to a song of praise and glory memorializing an illustrious and beloved king (*eulogium ad memoriam et gloriam illustrissimi ac amicissimi regis*). But at the same time, because it is a memorial to one man's exemplary conduct (sinner though he may have been, as Aelred readily acknowledges), the *Lament* also attempts to motivate all to live according to the example offered therein.

Aelred emphasizes three virtues in particular to form the main canvas on which he paints the *Lament*: chastity, justice, and humility. These three moral qualities bring to mind the life model Saint Paul proposes to Titus when he recommends that the latter "live temperately [*sobrie*], justly [*juste*], and devoutly [*pie*] in this age" (Titus 2:12). Aelred himself regularly proposed this model to all, regardless of station or vocation, throughout his works, beginning with *Mirror* (e.g., 2.56; 3.56, 74). It was for Aelred not only an ideal of holiness, but also a standard for

---

53. Aelred, Lam D 1 (CF 56:45–46).

54. For example, Saint Bernard's lament for the death of his brother Gerard (S 26 on the Song of Songs), Aelred's weeping for the death of his friend Simon in *Mirror* 1.98–114, or Walter Daniel's *Lament for Aelred*, written just after his abbot's death (Bernard of Clairvaux, *On the Song of Songs*, vol. 2, trans. Kilian Walsh, CF 7 [Kalamazoo, MI: Cistercian Publications, 1976], 58–73; Aelred of Rievaulx, *The Mirror of Charity*, trans. Elizabeth Connor, CF 17 [Kalamazoo, MI: Cistercian Publications, 1990], 147–59; Walter Daniel, "Lament for Aelred," trans. Jane Patricia Freeland, in *The Life of Aelred of Rievaulx*, CF 57 [Kalamazoo, MI: Cistercian Publications, 1994], 140–46).

measuring moral rectitude. In a sense, the *Lament* becomes an illustrated general guide to practical moral theology.

But the thematic importance of the *Lament's* ethical component, striking on even a first reading, must not completely overshadow the work's more discreet political component. Aelred wrote the *Lament* immediately following David's death, in a social and political context rich with future possibilities but also terribly uncertain. In supranational terms, the Battle of Wallingford had been avoided, but the eponymous treaty had not yet been finalized. Furthermore, simply in terms of Scotland itself, the situation was worrying. No one knew what would become of the country after David had lost his only son, Prince Henry, the year before and had designated as heir to the throne the eldest of his grandsons, Malcolm IV, who was barely twelve years old. In addition, the clans over whom the latter was to reign tended to be unruly, given to inter- and intra-ethnic quarrels (as was especially true of the Galwegians), and resistant to all efforts to centralize authority.[55]

In light of this situation, people were legitimately worried and wondered if the young Malcolm would be able to deal with these challenges. In particular, they wondered if he would be able to fend off adversaries and rivals who, from the moment of his accession just three days after his grandfather's death and before the funeral had taken place, would take advantage of his youth to contest the succession and attempt to take the crown.

Aelred must have been fully aware of the threats building up around the young king like a storm about to burst. This concern is no doubt the reason for which almost midway through the

---

55. Three years after his accession to the Scottish throne, Malcolm had to deal with the revolt of King Fergus of Galloway, who took advantage of Malcolm's weak position after Henry II laid claim to Cumbria and Northumbria, two counties subordinate to the English crown, which Malcolm had inherited from his father and grandfather and for which he owed homage to the king of England.

long version of the *Lament* Aelred seeks to preempt any political agitation by speaking to the Scottish people and trying to impress on them that the best way to honor the dead king's memory was to stand together in "mutual concord"[56] and offer support, homage, and fidelity to his grandson. This concord itself, he adds, is the most effective way to guarantee the integrity of the national territory and prevent the risk of invasion:

> What then will you give him for all that he has given you [see Ps 115:12]? You assuredly have some persons in whom to repay him. You certainly have some in whom to give thanks in his stead, some to whom you can repay the good things he deserved. You have him in his grandsons, from whom divine providence has taken their grandfather's help so quickly, perhaps for no other reason than that your faith may be tested [*probari*] and your thankfulness tried [*experiri*]. They are not of age, of course, but the age of a king is reckoned by the faithfulness of his servants [*milites*]. Pay to the sons what you owe the father. May they find you grateful for the favors you received! Above all, may the peril of the English teach you to trust in kings and to preserve [*servare*] mutual concord among yourselves, lest strangers devour your country [*regio*] before your eyes and it be *forsaken as in a hostile wasteland* [Isa 1:7].[57]

This passage adds a third dimension to the *Lament*. The first of these was personal, as Aelred wept over the death of one who was most dear to him. The second was moral, offering to all a standard by which the ethical value of actions could be measured according to the three criteria of sobriety (or temperance and chastity), justice, and piety (or humility). This added third dimension is political, inviting the Scottish clans to stand

---

56. Aelred, Lam D 8 (CF 56:60).

57. Aelred, Lam D 8 (CF 56:60–61). We thank Marsha Dutton for drawing our attention to the importance of this passage. See Dutton, Introduction, CF 56:13.

together in national unity, encouraging them to rally around their new king in order better to resist external threats.

But the text's three dimensions do not exhaust all possible readings of the *Lament*. The fact that Aelred integrated the work into the broader *Genealogy*, and the fact that he addressed this treatise to another reader, King Stephen's designated successor, Henry Plantagenet, both enrich the *Lament* with additional layers of meaning that detract nothing from the foregoing readings and create a cumulative effect that brings further unanticipated nuances to the text.

The Genealogy of the Kings of the English: *At the Confluence of Familial and Moral Lineages*

If Aelred's dedicatory epistle addressed to Henry Plantagenet is to be believed, the death of King David was not long past when Aelred began his composition of *Genealogy*. But it is possible that the work was nearly completed and that Aelred was simply applying the finishing touches. If this is not the case, it is difficult to explain how Aelred seems to have simply inserted the *Lament* as the *Genealogy's* inaugural chapter without any thought to integrating it more harmoniously into the totality of the work.

In fact, if the structure of the *Genealogy* in its final state is closely considered—a brief prefatory letter to Henry Plantagenet, followed by the *Lament*, and finally the *Genealogy* proper— one notices an enormous disproportion between the two primary elements of the treatise. The *Lament*, which in its long version accounts for more than a third of the work (twenty-six out of seventy-eight pages in the English translation), is devoted solely to King David, while the *Genealogy* proper, which accounts for the remaining two-thirds (fifty-two out of seventy-eight pages in the translation), concerns no fewer than eleven kings, from Aethelwulf to Edward the Confessor, with vignettes of varying lengths for each one, running anywhere from a few lines to as many as ten pages. Moreover, the text of the *Genealogy* alone, excluding the *Lament*, consists of these eleven vignettes inserted between connected and coherent opening and closing chapters. The first chapter begins by presenting Henry's genealogy in ascending fashion from his mother, the Empress Matilda, to Adam, and then again in descending fashion from Adam to King Egbert. To this second list Aelred links the first of his eleven vignettes, devoted to Aethelwulf, son of Egbert; he closes with the last Anglo-Saxon king before the Norman Conquest of 1066, Edward the Confessor. The last chapter of the *Genealogy* echoes the first, returning to the Empress Matilda and the Scottish royal family in order to show Henry's connection through Matilda to the English royal family. The discussion of the Empress Matilda in the connected and coherent opening and closing chapters evokes, however briefly, the figure of her uncle, King David of Scotland. Aelred could have expanded these chapters with a more developed presentation of David, without needing to tack on the *Lament* itself as a kind of textual patch. But Aelred might have opted against this solution, choosing instead to juxtapose the two texts.

The first reason for that decision was literary and chronological. It is possible that at that time of David's death in May 1153, the text of the *Genealogy* was already in progress, perhaps even near completion. Aelred could easily have considered it preferable to keep the work's proportions and integral harmony intact rather than altering the text's balance and shuffling the internal organization. This explanation would explain his choice simply to attach the *Lament* to the *Genealogy*, even with the resulting quantitative imbalance.

From a chronological point of view, this hypothesis would mean that Aelred had started composition of the *Genealogy* even before David's death. In that case, David's death would have temporarily interrupted work on the *Genealogy*, which Aelred would complete only after writing *Lament*. This order of composition would have allowed him to publish the treatises together as a single work. In other words, it is easy to imagine that the drafting of the *Genealogy* and of the *Lament* are entwined and that their composition was almost simultaneous, despite the possibility that Aelred had begun the *Genealogy* slightly before starting the *Lament*.

Regardless of the chronology, which in the end is a fairly secondary issue, Aelred certainly had another more fundamental reason in mind for joining these two texts. In writing them, Aelred could have simply left the *Lament* and the *Genealogy* as autonomous works without joining them into a single treatise. The fact that he chose to link them shows that doing so had its own purpose and meaning. It is easy to imagine that apart from the sadness he felt at David's death, he must also have perceived the event as a fortunate coincidence that could serve his historiographic project as he composed *Genealogy*.

The prefatory letter opening the *Genealogy* makes it clear that Aelred intended the work to be read by Henry Plantagenet. This and other textual clues in the *Genealogy* make it clear that as Aelred was writing, Henry had already been designated as successor to King Stephen but had not yet ascended to the throne. The titles for Henry used in the work are explicit: from the prefatory letter all the way to the final lines of the last chapter, Aelred never refers to Henry as king. Otherwise, he enumerates every title Henry already holds: "the glory of the Angevins," "the protector of the Normans," and "the ornament of the Aquitanians," or, literally "Duke of the Normans and Aquitanians and Count of the Angevins."[58] When Aelred alludes to Henry's royal status, he refers not to present reality but to what is yet to come. The prefatory letter refers to Henry as "the hope of the English," and the final chapter refers to him as the "heir to England."[59] In other words, when Aelred addresses the *Genealogy* to Henry, he is speaking to someone who is not yet king but is preparing to becoming one. We argue that it is precisely because Henry was not yet in power that Aelred believed it worthwhile to offer him the *Lament*. In the

58. Aelred, Gen angl Ep H (CF 56:42, 41).
59. Aelred, Gen angl Ep H 26 (CF 56:42, 121).

portrait of his great-uncle and the praise of his royal virtues, Henry would find a particularly eminent model to follow, one that might inspire his own exercise of power so that, in the wake of the long civil war, he would be up to the challenge of fulfilling the hope he embodied for the English people.

By proposing King David as a model for imitation, Aelred hoped Henry would inherit the entirety of David's virtues. In the prefatory epistle he explains this hope:

> as I consider from whose lineage you take your origin, I give thanks to the Lord my God that in exchange for such as these such a son has dawned upon us like a new burst of light, in whom the virtues of all your ancestors have come together. Yet I rejoice most of all that the spirit of the most Christian king David has rested upon you. Hence I believe that it was by an act of Divine Providence that his most pure hands girded you with a knight's sword; through his hands may Christ's grace have poured into you the virtue of his chastity, humility, and loving-kindness.[60]

This goal means that attaching the *Lament* to the *Genealogy* enriched the initial meaning of both works. Thus, beyond the personal, moral, and political levels of meaning in the *Lament*, an additional level emerges from the work's recontextualization, becoming, in Squire's terminology, a veritable "mirror for kings."[61]

The same thing applies to the *Genealogy*. The work's original structure of eleven vignettes sandwiched between connected, coherent opening and closing chapters, suggests that its principal aim consisted of legitimizing, however tenuously, Henry's accession to the English throne by virtue of his bloodlines. Aelred shows, by way of Henry's mother, the Empress Matilda,

---

60. Aelred, Gen Ang Ep H (CF 56:42–43).
61. Squire, *Aelred*, 88.

that Henry was directly connected to the pre-Conquest English royal family through his maternal great-grandmother Saint Margaret of Scotland (d. 1093), the granddaughter of King Edmund Ironside (r. 1016) and the great-niece of King Edward the Confessor (r. 1042–1066).

Moreover, through the literary structure of the *Genealogy* alone, either by the length of each vignette or by the place each one occupies within the treatise, Aelred emphasized the portraits of two kings. The first of these is "the very devout King Alfred" (r. 871–899),[62] who is the subject of the second and longest of all the vignettes, accounting for ten pages in the English translation, or just under one-eighth of the entire work. The second of these is King Edgar the Peaceful (r. 959–975), whose nine pages in the English translation are barely shorter than those devoted to Alfred. The second vignette is notable in its placement at the center of the work and in Aelred's inclusion there of a lengthy five-page speech, of immediately obvious importance. For Henry's edification Aelred enumerates through Edgar's voice a list of the distinct responsibilities of the civil and ecclesiastical authorities,[63] along with the relationship that must exist between those authorities if they are to guarantee national peace and stability. In other words, Aelred places a list of Henry's future responsibilities before him, no doubt Aelred's second goal in addressing the *Genealogy* to him. From this perspective, it is interesting to note the thematic continuity between this work and *Battle;* as in *Genealogy,* Aelred reprises certain themes already presented in *Battle,* but more substantively.

In the discourse credited to King Alfred,[64] Aelred reflects on the nature of a just war. Similarly, in the vignette devoted to King Edgar, he emphasizes the need for those in power to

---

62. Aelred, Gen angl 76 (CF 56:76).

63. Anachronistically one might think in terms of the relationship between state and church. However, strictly speaking, the concept of the nation-state did not yet exist in the twelfth century.

64. Aelred, Gen angl 8 (CF 56:82–83).

devote themselves to serious study of the Holy Scripture and of history, in particular church history, if they wish to exercise justice equitably among all people regardless of station and to promulgate ordinances and decrees in accordance with divine law. If necessary, he says, they should even seek instruction in these fields from learned men.[65] In fact, Aelred explains, it is from God that princes receive their authority, and it was God who placed at their feet all they possess, to ensure that all things on earth be subject to him. Significantly, he allows King Edgar to enunciate this doctrine at the beginning of "Edgar's Speech to the Clergy":

> Since the Lord has been so great as to bestow his mercy on us, most Reverend Fathers, it is right that we should respond to his innumerable favors with appropriate deeds. *We do not possess the land by* our *own sword, nor has* our *own arm saved* us, but his *right hand* and his holy *arm, since* he *has been pleased with* us [Ps 44:3]. It is only right, then, because *he has subjected all things under our feet* [Ps 8:6], that we should subject our souls to him and that we should take care that those whom he has put under us not be slow to put themselves under his laws.[66]

Edgar's voice thus reiterates the doctrine of the two swords, albeit with substantial modification.[67] The duty of the prince, or the sword of Constantine, is to support ecclesiastical authority, or the sword of Peter. He must collaborate closely with the

65. Aelred, Gen angl 16 (CF 56:97).
66. Aelred, Gen angl 17 (CF 56:98).
67. As Elizabeth Freeman notes, the difference between the traditional dualist version of this doctrine, involving two distinct and separate powers, and the Cistercian version, with a rich, optimistic vision of the church and civil society, united by the bonds of charity, was a new reading that rejected the implied separation to encourage a greater collaboration between the ecclesiastical and royal spheres of power (Elizabeth Freeman, "The Timeless Nation: Aelred of Rievaulx's *Genealogia regum Anglorum*," in *Narratives of a New Order* (Turnhout: Brepols, 2002), 55–87, chap. 2.

church—without, however, interfering with internal church affairs[68]—so as to establish the order of charity desired eternally by God throughout all society.

Aelred's efforts to instruct Henry in the political obligation of a prince toward the church and his simultaneous reminder of the limits of his power relative to the church was not an altogether innocent act. The revival of the Investiture Controversy[69] in the international arena, as well as such dramatic events in England ten years later as the open conflict between Henry II and Thomas Becket,[70] former chancellor become archbishop of Canterbury, clearly showed the necessity and urgency of Aelred's insistence. Beyond the apparent simplicity of a chronological-biological or historical-genealogical overview, for Aelred *Genealogy* takes on an ecclesio-political dimension.

68. Aelred underlines this point in his discussion of "The Very Devout King Alfred," whom he praises for having imitated the Emperor Constantine— "something now rarely found on earth"—in believing "that a king's great dignity had no power at all in the church of Christ" and in refraining from attempts to "govern priests by his laws" (Aelred, Gen angl 6 [CF 56:78]).

He also expresses this view in the tenth *Homily on the Prophetic Burdens of Isaiah*, comparing the ecclesiastical and royal orders to the sun and the moon: "O, how fitting were these two lights . . . . The king and priest confined themselves to their spheres: the king's power served only the peace and tranquility of his subjects, and with his wisdom and teaching, the priest was on guard to drive the darkness away from souls and pour in the light of truth" (Aelred, Oner 10.9 [CF 83:96–97]).

69. The Concordat of Worms, signed in 1122 by Pope Callixtus II and the Emperor Henry V, stipulated among other things that the Holy Roman Emperor accept the free election of bishops by cathedral chapters and renounce investiture by "ring and staff." Difficulty of application led to a rebounding of the conflict as early as 1154 during the reign of Emperor Frederick I and lasting until the death of Emperor Frederick II in 1250. Even if the affair concerned only relations between the pope and the Holy Roman Empire, it nevertheless rapidly affected the church in England, where Henry II intended to retake control of the English clergy's privileges, which he thought hindered the exercise of his authority.

70. The conflict resulted in Becket's voluntary exile in November 1164, followed by his assassination on December 29, 1170.

Freeman is quite right in recognizing this point, but doesn't go far enough.[71] In fact, while the responsibility Aelred lays upon Henry is essentially political, it goes beyond a solely social quality and takes on a cosmic quality as well. For Aelred, it is the responsibility of princes to ensure the general harmony of the world and the equilibrium of the entire universe (*harmonia mundi*), through the healthy administration of public affairs and proper management of temporal goods. He enunciates this view fairly clearly on two occasions in the vignette devoted to King Edgar. If Edgar deserved the sobriquet "the peaceful," Aelred suggests, it is because in his wise administration of the kingdom, he efficiently established a fully reconciled world in which all things—including even natural elements such as the sun, the sea, and the earth—contributed in their own ways to the good of all other things and to the beauty of the whole: "While he was reigning, the sun seemed to be more fair, the waves of the sea more peaceful, the earth more fruitful, and the face of the whole kingdom with its abundant beauty more lovely."[72] In the next chapter Aelred attributes to Edgar a speech recalling with joy the days of Saint Dunstan (d. 988): "O, then truly blessed the church of the English, which the integrity of innumerable monks and virgins adorned, which the devotion of the people, the self-discipline of the soldiers, the impartiality of the judges, and the fruitfulness of the land made glad! The most blessed king rejoiced that in his time his order had found the nature of all things, as people showed forth the righteousness they owed to God, the earth the fruitfulness it owed to the people, and heaven the mild weather it owed to earth."[73]

Some might consider this a naive view of things. However, Aelred reveals an astute theological, sociopolitical, and

71. Freeman notes that Aelred presents "a clear religio-political agenda in addition to its apparently simple chronological and biological agenda" (*Narratives of a New Order*, 65).
72. Aelred, Gen angl 16 (CF 56:96).
73. Aelred, Gen angl 17 (CF 56:103).

cosmological intuition. He shows that political, civil, and secular authority (the political aspect), collaborates with God (the theological aspect), on a mission to institute justice in the world (the social aspect). In so doing, they contribute to a world-wide ecological equilibrium, according to the era's naturalistic vision of things. More precisely, given Aelred's theological/teleological perspective, civil and secular authority works with God toward the establishment (or rather the re-establishment) of the original order and harmony among all things in the universe (the cosmic aspect), eternally desired by God.

To put it another way, for Aelred politics is indissociably tied to a theological cosmology of creation and a spirituality of communion through social ethics. These combined elements bear the indelible mark of a general Cistercian spirituality, seeking to establish all things in the order of charity (or the Bernardine *ordinatio caritatis*), along with the ineffaceable mark of Aelred's own voice seeking to institute the order of the world (*harmonia mundi*) on the basis of universal friendship's cosmic ethics, at all times embracing all human and material realities. This conformity and coincidence of times brings together present human history, the time of origins and divine creation, and the divine eternal time of endings, restoration, and re-establishment of all things, "so that God may be all in all."[74]

Aelred's grand, ambitious vision of the secular prince's mission is retranslated through a dual image frequently found in his works. Princes' role, and the direction they should give to the course of history, is to lead the world out of Babylon, the "city of confusion," symbolic of the historic human condition, into Jerusalem, the "vision of peace," symbolic of a saved and redeemed humanity, which every wisely administered Christian nation is called upon to anticipate within its civil society.

---

74. 1 Cor 15:28. For more detail on this threefold temporal relationship (protology-present history-eschatology), see chap. 6 of this book, in particular the subsections "Friendship as a Principle of Cosmic Harmony" and "The Prefatory Value of Friendship as a Stair, Rung, or Springboard to God's Love."

Building the city through the active pursuit of peace must therefore be every prince's top priority. This task begins by moving beyond personal interest to establish bonds of solidarity and alliance among individuals, especially those connected by the natural ties of blood. Aelred reminds Henry of this responsibility by taking advantage of recent events, in particular the death of King David, at the time of whose death, his three grandchildren had already been orphans for a year. They were also Henry's cousins. Recalling Henry's blood ties to David, Aelred encourages Henry to take David's three grandsons under his care:

> From Henry came Malcolm, William, and David, heir to his grandfather's name.[75] May God have mercy on their childhood, and may you too be merciful, whom divine loving-kindness has established as the most noble head of your whole people. May your holy gaze, your loving heart, and your effective action be upon them in all their necessities. They are orphans, left to you by their grandfather, who loved you above all people; you will be a helper to these your wards, for you are in age more mature, in hands stronger, and in feeling more experienced than they.[76]

However, after emphasizing this familial solidarity and the natural genealogical continuity of blood between Henry and his cousins, Aelred immediately reinforces this purely natural genealogical bond with a moral one. This moral bond is based in blood ties but also transcends them, making Henry's connection to his cousins on the basis of his moral lineage even stronger than that derived from his familial lineage.

In other words, in composing Henry's *Genealogy* both as a literary work and as a life history, Aelred shows the legitimacy

---

75. Aelred is speaking here of Henry of Scotland who, from his marriage with Ada de Warenne, had three sons who succeeded each other on the Scottish throne: Malcolm IV (r. 1153–1165), William I (William the Lion, r. 1165–1214), and David (d. 1219). Aelred mentions them in Lam D 9 (CF 56:60–62).

76. Aelred, Gen angl 26 (CF 56:122).

of Henry's reign, of course based on his bloodline, but also based on Henry's inheritance of the combined virtues of his predecessors, making him worthy in his own right of eternal memory among men and women, provided that he imitate them in every aspect of his own life:

> I, moreover, as I end this book beg my God that as a gift of his mercy your way of life should be such—your acts so holy, your life so chaste, your mind so free of avarice, so free of pride, so ignorant of cruelty, so humble and pleasant toward the poor, so devoted to the worship of God—that we may have something worthy of eternal remembrance to transmit to posterity about you by this ministry of letters.[77]

The *Genealogy* as a work does more than simply show Henry's genealogical legitimacy or, as a mirror for princes, to remind Henry of his political duties. It is above all a life history, a "genealogy of virtue"[78] that places Henry, as an agent responsible for his actions, in an ethical lineage and makes him an indispensable link between past and future generations, guaranteeing the continuity of human history on the path toward its final end.[79]

With this in mind, it is easy to understand why Aelred attached the *Lament* to *Genealogy*. By publishing them together,

---

77. Aelred, Gen angl 27 (CF 56:122).

78. Freeman, Narratives, 61. See also Francis Ingledew, "The Book of Troy and the Genealogical Construction of History: The Case of Geoffrey of Monmouth's *Historia regum Britanniae*," *Speculum* 69, no. 3 (1994): 694.

79. For more detail on the biological, socio-political, and subjective components of the individual's genealogical filiation, see Marc-Alain Ouaknin's remarks, where, inspired by Abraham Neher, he opposes Chronos, the Greek god of time who devours his children, to the Jewish *Toledot*, the book of generations or descendants, which preserves time by removing it from the realm of fatality and transforming it into history, conferring upon humankind responsibility and freedom in the face of its own destiny (Marc-Alain Ouaknin, *Bibliothérapie: Lire, cest guérir* [Paris: Seuil, 1994], 365–66).

Aelred kept the *Genealogy* from being too exclusively legitimist or nationalist in nature, by emphasizing only the familial and political legitimacy of Henry's reign in England, instead adding to it a more universal element. In preceding the *Genealogy* with a *Lament* that eulogized David, Aelred was able to show that the familial genealogy, however important it may be, must be reinforced by a moral lineage. The right to reign must always be founded upon the prince's bloodline in conjunction with his virtues.

Further, Aelred's situating Henry at the confluence of a dual heritage of blood and virtue, each dependent upon the other, gives an additional layer of meaning to *Genealogy*. As Marie Anne Mayeski has indicated, the *Genealogy* can be read not only for political and ethical meaning, but for theological meaning as well.[80] She shows that *Genealogy* is permeated by Aelred's belief that every person has inherited from Adam both a natural inclination toward sin (the doctrine of original sin), and a rational soul (the doctrine that humankind was created in God's image). The latter gives each person a natural propensity toward virtue that counteracts his sinful inclinations and is transmitted from generation to generation, inherited from one's ancestors.

Genealogy's function as a theological and eucharistic memorial thus becomes clearer. The work is meant on the one hand to maintain Henry's sense of obligation to his ancestors for having passed such a heritage on to him and thus to nourish in him a feeling of humble gratitude toward them. But it is also meant to encourage him to live up to this inheritance. As Aelred writes in the opening chapter of the *Genealogy*, "To know that one has been bequeathed nobility of blood from the finest on both sides is a great incentive to acquiring habits; one is always ashamed to find a noble mind become ignoble in

---

80. Much of what follows is owed to Mayeski, *"Secundum naturam,"* 223–24, 227.

renowned offspring. And for bad fruit to spring from good stock is contrary to nature."[81]

Ten years later, Aelred provided Henry with a similar reminder when he dedicated to him what would become the most popular and widely read of all his historical works, *The Life of Saint Edward, King and Confessor*.[82]

The History of England Meets the History of Salvation: Aelred's *Life of Edward*

After a reign of over twenty-three years, the last of the great Anglo-Saxon kings to rule over England before the Norman Conquest, King Edward, died on January 5, 1066. Edward was married to Edith, daughter of Godwin, count of Wessex, one of the most influential and powerful princes of England. They unfortunately had no children, and that lack of issue had two major consequences.

The first, political and dynastic in nature, deeply affected England for years afterward. Without an heir, Edward's death led to a war that pitted against each other Edward's designated successor, William, Duke of Normandy, and Godwin's two sons Harold and Tostig, brothers to Queen Edith and so brothers-in-law to the late king, both of whom laid claim to the throne. The subsequent events are well known. The day after Edward was buried in Westminster Abbey on January 6, 1066, Harold seized power and had himself crowned king of England. Nine months later, on September 25, Harold defeated his brother Tostig, who was killed at the battle of Stamford Bridge, near York. Victorious, Harold immediately turned south with his weakened army to confront his rival William, who, with the support of Pope Alexander II, had landed in England with an army of seven thousand men. On October 14, the two armies

---

81. Aelred, Gen angl 1 (CF 56:71).

82. Aelredus Rievallensis, *Opera Omnia*, vol. 7, *Opera Historica et Hagiographica: Vita Sancti Ædwardi Regis et Confessoris*, ed. Francesco Marzella, CCCM 3A (Brepols: Turnhout, 2017), 85–181.

met at Hastings, where Harold was killed, bringing his nine-month reign to an end. The way was then open for William to be crowned king on December 25, 1066.

William's coronation marked the start of a Norman dynasty in England, which for three generations remained separate from the previous dynasty and thus lacked genealogical legitimacy. Even more serious from a social perspective was that William removed the local aristocracy from the kingdom's most important civil and ecclesiastical charges in order to replace them with members of his Norman entourage. In so doing, William created political tensions and explosive animosities between the conquerors and the conquered. A little less than a century later, between 1161 and 1163, during which time Aelred undertook the composition of his *Life of Edward*, this situation had not fundamentally changed. On the contrary, it had become even worse because of the long civil war that Henry Plantagenet's accession to the English throne in 1154 finally brought to an end. This political and social background helps to unravel the multiple issues at play in *The Life of Edward*.

The fact that Edward's marriage to Edith of Wessex was childless had a second major consequence related to his collective representation after his death and its place in hagiographic production, national memory, and the ideal of royal holiness that were all built up around that image. Aelred himself contributed in no small part to the process. The complexity of this question, however, demands further explanation.

The Hagiographic Figure of Holy King Edward; the Genealogy of Aelred's Life of Edward[83]

Soon after his death, King Edward became an object of veneration. Several factors contributed to the rapid development

---

83. For more details, see Domenico Pezzini, "The Genealogy and Posterity of Aelred of Rievaulx's *Vita sancti Eduardi regis et confessoris*," in *The Translation of Religious Texts in the Middle Ages: Tracts and Rules, Hymns and Saints' Lives* (Berne: Peter Lang, 2008), 333–72. See also Domenico Pezzini, "Aelred

of such hero worship. The first is that Edward's reign from 1042 to 1066 was situated between two particularly troubled periods—the Danish invasion led by Canute the Great and the Norman Conquest led by William of Normandy. His own twenty-four years on the throne were by contrast generally perceived as a time of peace and prosperity. However, some suggest that the favor he accorded to his Norman entourage aroused the resentment of Danish and Saxon nobles and provoked the growth of an anti-Norman party centered around his future father-in-law, Godwin of Wessex.

The second reason for King Edward's great popularity derives from his image in the collective memory as a king far more concerned with his salvation and with giving aid to the poor than with material self-interest or the governance of the kingdom. Indeed, he largely left the latter task to his father-in-law, Godwin, who was the true executor of power in the kingdom, as were his sons after him.

In terms of strict historical reality, Edward left an image of himself as "a weak ruler and a pious man,"[84] as Pezzini writes. However, he adds that for both political and religious reasons, this image was progressively modified over time as the narrative of Edward's life was written and re-written, with the result that his reputation as a pious king[85] and the ideal of

---

of Rievaulx's *Vita sancti Eduardi regis et confessoris*: Its Genesis and Radiation," *Cîteaux* 60 (2009): 27–76. The discussion here considers only the question of genealogy, leaving aside issues of posterity.

84. Pezzini, "Aelred's *Vita*," 28.

85. Matthias Lemoine has made a subtle distinction between Edward as a "saint roi" or a "roi saint" (a pious king or a holy king) regarding possible interpretations of Edward's title of "Confessor." According to Lemoine, these interpretations unite and go beyond the notions of either pious royalty or a holiness that is not specifically royal: "The function of 'confessor' is a sort of perfect step toward royal holiness that goes beyond and unites pious royalty and a holiness that is not specifically royal. It transcends the priestly character of the former and the monastic character of the second" (Matthias Lemoine, "Le moine et le saint roi. La qualité de confesseur dans la *Vita Edwardi*

"royal holiness"[86] he represents are in reality more literary construct than historical fact.

The first step in this long process of "memory creating holiness," beginning as early as 1066 and maybe even during the future Saint Edward's lifetime, was taken by an anonymous author, probably a monk from Westminster Abbey, gathering a collection of anecdotes relating the remarkable events and deeds of Edward's life and the miracles that occurred near his tomb after his death. The work, mingling poetry and prose, consists of two apparently heterogeneous books and is complex in both its form and structure. It was published under the title *The Life of King Edward Who Rests at Westminster*.[87] The first book offers a chronicle contemporary to the events related in the text, whose curious protagonists are Queen Edith (Edward's wife) and the House of Wessex. The second book, independent in structure and different in form, brings an inexplicable and radical change in perspective, concentrating exclusively on the figure of Edward, as the author attempts to prove Edward's holiness through various miracle narratives.

Pezzini, expanding on the ideas of Frank Barlow, editor of this early Life of Edward, suggests that the difference in tone between the two books may be tied to the anonymous author's desire to focus his reader's gaze on happier realities—the memory of a reign of peace and prosperity, and consideration of the holy king's beatitude—in the wake of the "miserable collapse of the Saxon monarchy"[88] and the tragic war of succession between Edward's brothers-in-law and the Norman invasion

---

d'Aelred de Rievaulx," Coll 68 [2006]: 227). This article is an abridged version of Lemoine's master's thesis directed by Damien Boquet: Matthias Lemoine, "Saint Édouard, roi et confesseur dans la *Vita* d'Aelred de Rievaulx," thesis, Université de Provence, 2005.

86. Pezzini, "Aelred's *Vita*," 28.

87. Frank Barlow, ed. and trans., *The Life of King Edward Who Rests at Westminster*, 2d ed. (1962; Oxford: Clarendon Press, 1992).

88. Pezzini, "Genealogy and Posterity," 336.

into which England was thrown immediately following the death of the heirless king. At the same time, the anonymous author sought to disengage Edward from all responsibility for the disastrous events following his death by building around him the image of a holy king who lived in perfect chastity, thus transforming the royal couple's sterility into a virtue, and who on his deathbed foresaw the sad future of his kingdom, so depicting him as a prophet and therefore a saint. In this way, the author inaugurated around Edward a hagiographic tradition of holiness, initially articulated along three principal axes: thaumaturgy, virginity, and prophecy. The thaumaturgical element was soon confirmed by miracles at his tomb. And at the exhumation of his remains in 1102 to transfer his relics elsewhere, his body was found intact, a sign taken as incontrovertible proof of the king's perfect continence.

If the anonymous *Life of Edward* is essentially a work of history, the *Life* written in 1138 by Westminster prior Osbert of Clare identifies itself from the very first lines as hagiographical.[89] Osbert undertook the composition of this second *Life* at the request of his superiors. The prefatory letter dedicating the work to Cardinal and Pontifical Legate Alberic of Ostia states that the work's aim is to obtain the canonization of King Edward. The author joins two other aims to this one, one political, one economic. Politically, he seeks to assure the consolidation of King Stephen's fragile and contested royal power by placing him under the protection of his holy predecessor. Economically, he seeks to guarantee the religious and financial interests of Westminster Abbey by the presence of the relics of a recognized saint.

But the cardinal-legate refused to make a pronouncement on the matter and advised Osbert to present his request in person to Pope Innocent II. Diplomatically and politically, this was

---

89. Marc Bloch, "La vie de St. Édouard le confesseur par Osbert de Clare," *Analecta Bollandiana* 41 (1923): 5–131. For more detail on this work, its author, and its aims, see Pezzini, "Genealogy and Posterity," and Pezzini, "Aelred's *Vita*."

not the best moment to do so. Under the pretext that they had plotted against him, King Stephen had had the bishops of Lincoln and Salisbury arrested. Moreover, the Empress Matilda, daughter of King Henry I, was considered the legitimate heir to the throne. Osbert's enterprise therefore failed, but it had the merit of creating a literary work that soon served as the basis for the *Life of Edward* that Aelred was asked to write.

The Papal Schism of 1159: Alexander III, Victor IV, and the 1161 Canonization of King Edward

As Pezzini writes, although the canonization of King Edward was refused to Osbert in 1138, it was by contrast "rather easily obtained" twenty-three years later under Henry II,[90] who had sent a petition to Alexander III supported by several English bishops and the two pontifical legates then in England. Practically all medieval sources speaking of Edward's canonization underline the fact that it was awarded to Henry in gratitude for his rallying to Alexander's cause against his rival, the anti-pope Victor IV, who had been supported only by Emperor Frederick Barbarossa. This diplomatic element aside, Henry's request was motivated by political factors largely identical to those that had previously led Stephen to make the same request. Henry was seeking to assure his reign's dynastic legitimacy by placing it under the national patronage of a holy king, "in whom a symbol of union could be seen between Saxons and Normans in an uninterrupted line of succession."[91]

Edward was canonized on February 7, 1161; two years later, on October 13, 1163, his relics were solemnly transferred. For this event, the abbot of Westminster, Lawrence of Durham, who desired that Osbert of Clare's *Life of Edward* be completely rewritten, called on the literary talents of his close kinsman, Aelred, abbot of Rievaulx. He also asked that Aelred write a

90. Pezzini, "Genealogy and Posterity," 334.
91. Pezzini, "Genealogy and Posterity," 340.

sermon for the translation,[92] one that, as Walter reports, afterward served as a lesson for the Office of Vigils on the saint's feast-day.[93]

When Aelred began composing the *Life of Edward* at Lawrence's request, he was no longer a newcomer to the genre of hagiographic literature, as ten years earlier he had written a *Life of Ninian*. Nor was he a newcomer to the subject of King Edward, to whom he had devoted the brief and final royal vignette of *Genealogy*.[94] However, by both this *Life's* size and the numerous issues it involves—Aelred's practical historical methodology in the interpretation and rewriting of events, in addition to his addressing political and religious issues—the *Life of Edward* is unique among Aelred's historical works.

The first notable item is the difference between the epithets accorded to Edward in the *Genealogy's* vignette and those in the *Life of Edward*. The title of *Genealogy's* vignette refers to him as "Saint Edward, King, Confessor, and Virgin"[95] (*de sancto Eduardo, rege, confessore ac virgine*). Curiously, however, the passage presents the king's virginity only obliquely, regarding the problems of succession resulting from his lack of issue and his designation of Edgar Aetheling as successor. Inversely, and just as curiously, Aelred subsequently dropped virginity from among Edward's epithets, entitling the later work *The Life of Saint Edward, King and Confessor* (*Vita sancti Eduardi, regis et confessoris*).[96] In contrast, he devoted the entire eighth chapter

92. This sermon was long believed to be lost. However, in 2005 Peter Jackson discovered what is probably this sermon in a fifteenth-century manuscript collection of texts related to Saint Edward, conserved in the Central Library of Peterborough, England (Peter Jackson, "*In translacione sancti Edwardi Confessoris*: The Lost Sermon by Aelred of Rievaulx Found?" trans. Tom License, CSQ 40 [2005]: 45–82).

93. Walter, VA 32 (CF 57:121).

94. Aelred, Gen angl 20 (CF 56:113–15).

95. Aelred, Gen angl 20 (CF 56:113).

96. Aelred, Vita E Title (CF 56:123). On the removal of the epithet *virgin* and the absorption of that quality into the word *confessor*, see Lemoine, "Le

of the *Life* to an interior dialogue showing the conflict between the king's desire to remain chaste and his royal duty to guarantee dynastic continuity by having children.[97] This question raises certain literary implications in terms of Aelred's "recrafting"[98] of Osbert of Clare's *Life of Edward*. Pezzini has pointed out three such implications.[99] The first has to do with the way Aelred enriches Osbert's work by adding new miracle narratives, later to be counted among the most famous in Edwardian iconography. The second is more significant, relating to the work's political angle. Unlike Osbert's *Life*, Aelred's *Life of Edward* centers on a crucial topic already seen in the *Genealogy*: presenting Henry as "the kingdom's hope,"[100] as a providential man chosen by God to build the "house of England" in peace. In other, parallel, terms Aelred offers Henry a model of holiness and good governance through the narrative of Edward's life.

The third and final of Pezzini's implications relates to the stylistic and literary quality of Aelred's *Life of Edward*. Even if such assessments are difficult to make objectively, Aelred's work is remarkable in its fusion of two separate styles, falling halfway between the primarily historical style of the anonymous *Life of Edward* and the decidedly hagiographic style of Osbert's *Life*. Aelred's work effectively blends history as the "narration and interpretation of events in the light of divine providence"[101] and hagiography as the "illustration of the

moine et le saint roi," 41. Lemoine suggests that the title *virgin* was eliminated as being too restrictive, being of interest to a limited monastic public while obscuring traits of greater interest to a lay public, such as the peace, justice, and prosperity that had characterized Edward's long reign.

97. Aelred, Gen angl 8 (CF 56:145–49).

98. I take this term from Katherine M. Yohe, "Aelred's Recrafting of the Life of Edward the Confessor," CSQ 38 (2003): 177–89.

99. Pezzini, "Genealogy and Posterity," 335–36.

100. [Translator's note: I here use expressions that Burton quoted earlier to express the same idea, from Dutton, Introduction, CF 56:7.]

101. Pezzini, "Genealogy and Posterity," 334.

mirabilia worked by God in the lives, virtues and miracles of the saints."[102] Combining these two approaches allows Aelred to avoid both the dry presentation of purely historical facts and the dubious "magical" appeal of an exclusive focus on miraculous phenomena. More than this, Aelred's excellence in the art of the short narrative, his fine sensitivity to all that is human, and the quality of his interpersonal relationships all allow readers to feel personally engaged as emotional participants in the narrative's events.[103]

History, Memory, and Politics: Issues Raised in Aelred's Life of Edward

Until now we have focused on the literary and authorial history of the three early Lives of King Edward—the anonymous *Life* and those of Osbert and Aelred—in an effort to show, thanks to Pezzini's studies, Aelred's contribution to the progressive and evolutionary construction of collective memory surrounding Edward as a figure of holiness. It now remains for us to look at the text from another perspective in order to address other issues raised in Aelred's *Life*, showing how his methodology of practical history revolves around three interconnected axes, in which the history of Edward's holiness and the collective memory, building a national consciousness, contribute to the implicit formation of a political theory based on cooperation between civil and religious authorities. This implicit political theory, intended for the ethical instruction of princes, shows Aelred to be once more the counselor of kings

---

102. Pezzini, "Genealogy and Posterity," 334.

103. This quality of writing is also found in the third part of *Formation of Recluses*. By evoking sensory perceptions, Aelred invites his sister to be touched by the gospel scenes described. For more on Aelred's narrative art, see for example Pezzini, "Genealogy and Posterity," 343–45. See also Yohe, "Recrafting," 177–89, esp. 189. Yohe's work presents a comparative analysis of Osbert's and Aelred's narratives.

and his *Life of Edward* to be a "mirror of princes." On the other hand, it is also intended as a means of constructing a universal and cosmic theology of history, in which the *Life* becomes the centerpiece of salvation history on the path to salvation's achievement. The extent to which these different issues are interconnected appears in passages from the *Life* where Aelred rewrites and reinterprets facts previously offered by his two predecessors.

Chapters 6-8 in the Life of Edward: *From Royal Sterility to a Vow of Conjugal Chastity*

King Edward's dying without descendants was one of the historical causes for the fall of the Anglo-Saxon monarchy following his death. This absence of descendants allows at least two explanations. The first and more obvious of the two consists of supposing that the lack of issue was simply the result of the royal couple's biological sterility, an interpretation that Robert Wace put forth in the *Roman de Rou* (1160–1174).[104] The second explanation derives from a spiritual and monasticizing rereading of the facts, by which the king was without issue at his death because he had made a vow of perfect chastity, even within marriage. As Pezzini has shown, authors of the various lives of Edward progressively developed this interpretation: the first *Life's* anonymous author touches lightly on it, then Osbert of Clare gives it more consistency, and finally Aelred gives the explanation its full substance.

Aelred augments the narrative by dramatizing Edward's spiritual struggle, showing him torn between his personal inclination for a vow of chastity and his royal duty to guarantee dynastic continuity with offspring. He augments this explanation by situating the dilemma in a larger perspective, through which by his life of piety (Vita E 6), justice (Vita E 7), and tem-

---

104. This detail is taken from Lemoine, "Le moine et le saint roi," 41, n. 30.

perance, shown by his virginity (Vita E 8), Edward becomes a model of holiness for Henry II, conforming in every way to the Pauline ideal of Christian life (Titus 2:12) already shown in *Genealogy*.[105] In the Prologue to the *Life* addressed to Henry, Aelred reminds the king—as he had done implicitly in the *Genealogy*—that while he had legitimately inherited royal power through his family bloodline, that inheritance was by itself insufficient and had to be confirmed and supported by a moral nobility. Such moral nobility derived, Aelred says, from both the blood of his ancestors and their holy lives. Therefore, at the end of this prologue, Aelred says to Henry, "You have assumed the kingdom of your great ancestor . . . . May you commend yourself frequently to his prayers, commit yourself earnestly to his protection, and strive to imitate his sanctity so that you may obtain eternal happiness with him."[106] Thus in commemorating Edward's life and rewriting and re-interpreting his sterility or virginity, Aelred suggests to Henry that beyond blood, the legitimacy of his kingship derives from a history of holiness, exemplified by his venerable precursor, Edward. Henry must strive to live up to that example in order to establish ethical as well as biological continuity with his past.

Chapters 29–30 in the Life of Edward: *Prophecy of Collapse or Vision of Recovery?*

Aelred conceived the legitimacy of Henry's authority on the basis of a bloodline that also bore the authenticating seal

---

105. Pezzini, "Genealogy and Posterity," 341–43. Pezzini notes that chaps. 6–8 of the *Life of Saint Edward* form a coherent subsection, but he fails to indicate that they offer an implicit illustration (in reverse order) of Saint Paul's recommendation to Titus "to live temperately (*sobrie*), justly (*juste*), and devoutly (*pie*)."

106. Aelred of Rievaulx, *The Life of Saint Edward, King and Confessor*, trans. Jane Patricia Freeland, CF 56 (Kalamazoo, MI: Cistercian Publications, 2005), 127. [Translator's note: My ellipsis, to fit the English quotation to Burton's phrasing.]

of a holy way of life. He was aware of the importance of this genealogical base, especially in the context of contested royal power, extending since the beginning of the Norman dynasty, which had held the English throne since the death of both Edward and his successor Harold Godwinson and the seizing of power by William of Normandy, all of which took place in 1066. After William's conquest, for three generations there was no dynastic continuity between the new Franco-Norman kings (William II, Henry I, and Stephen of Blois) and the last two Anglo-Saxon kings, Edward and Harold. But when Henry II took the throne in 1153–1154, the situation changed. Through his mother, the Empress Matilda; his grandmother, Queen Maud; and his grandmother, Saint Margaret, herself the daughter of Edward Aetheling and grand-daughter of Edmund Ironside, Henry finally re-established continuity with the Anglo-Saxon dynastic bloodline broken at Edward's death. This reconnection created a more solid foundation for the Franco-Norman monarchy's rule.

The new situation following Henry II's accession permitted Aelred to reinterpret King Edward's prophecy regarding the future of his kingdom, though in the process he bent the facts somewhat in his reconstruction of events.[107] Edward's biographers report that just before his death, Edward recounted a vision he had while sleeping of a tree cut off at the root but one day miraculously "restored to its old root—compelled by no human hand, driven by no necessity—and, with its sap restored, [that] flowers again and bears fruit," becoming a source of "comfort in this [present] tribulation and a remedy

---

107. This has been noted by numerous contemporary historians, in particular Dutton in her study on Aelred's two miniatures in the 14th-century Dublin manuscript (Trinity College 172), which includes *The Life of Edward* among other works (Marsha Dutton, "Aelred historien: deux nouveaux portraits dans un manuscrit de Dublin," Coll 55 [1993]: 209–30, esp. 212–13). For an English translation, see Marsha Dutton, "Aelred, Historian: Two Portraits in Plantagenet Myth," CSQ 28 (1993): 112–43.

of the trouble we have foretold."[108] Aelred's two predecessors, the anonymous author and Osbert, interpreted this prophecy as a *revelatio impossibilitatis*: simultaneously an announcement of the irreparable collapse of the Anglo-Saxon dynasty, seen in the cut-down tree, and a sign of divine punishment for uncured evils.

In contrast, Aelred rejected this interpretation and intentionally[109] read the prophecy as an announcement of England's future recovery by showing that the vision had finally been realized in the person of Henry II—an interpretation obviously impossible for his two predecessors, whose versions of the *Life of Edward* were written respectively before Henry's birth and during his childhood. Aelred explains that because of Henry's family ties to both Anglo-Saxon and Franco-Norman bloodlines (by his mother and maternal grandmother for the former, and by his mother and paternal grandfather for the latter), Henry joins (*conjugens*) and creates a unity between the two lines (*de duobus unum faciens*)—like a cut-down tree reflowering on its original roots—"joining the seed of Norman and English kings,"[110] realizing in his very person the unity of the pre- and post-Conquest dynastic branches:

> The tree flowered . . . . And then it bore fruit when our Henry rose from it like the morning star, joining the two peoples like a cornerstone [*velut lucifer matutinus exoriens, quasi lapis angularis utrumque populum copulavit*]. Now certainly England has a king from English stock, and it has bishops and abbots from the same race; it also has princes, the best soldiers, too, who have been brought

---

108. Aelred, Vita E 29 (CF 56:205–6).

109. On this point, see Aelred's transition at the end of Vita E 29, relating the previously accepted interpretation and preparing for his own reading of the facts in chap. 30.

110. Aelred, Vita E 30 (CF 56:208).

forth from the union of the seed of both races, for honor to some and consolation to others.[111]

Such a rereading of Edward's prophecy reveals Aelred's practical historiographic methodology and aims. As Aelred had already stated in his first historical treatise, *Battle*, there is more to history than simply relating the most important facts. It is up to the historian to pull out the hidden meaning of events and discern what is most useful for orienting future action. In other words, for Aelred, being a historian means illuminating the present (here, the reign of Henry II) with the light of the past (Edward's prophetic vision) in order to offer the agents of present history (Henry and the composite Saxon-Norman and civil-religious elite coalescing within the English nation) a concrete guide for behavior. By subtly superimposing layers of meaning, underpinned by a discreet but clear scriptural allusion to the mystery of reconciliation used by Paul in Ephesians 2:14-22, Aelred simultaneously addresses the English people and their king. He invites the former to move beyond the cultural, ethnic, and political factors dividing them since the Norman invasion and to hear the call to national unity (*de duobus unum faciens*; see Eph 2:14). He encourages the king to take stock of his political obligation to be in his person and his actions both the guarantor and the artisan of this slowly growing national unity (*quasi lapis angularis*; see Eph 2:20).

Thus Aelred's historiographical practice consists of three complementary features. The primary function of his historical writing remains, of course, a memorial of past events. But in three ways it is much more than this. First, the historian's memorialization of the past is a political act, participating in the edification of a national collective consciousness by stimulating each individual's sense of belonging to the same group. Second, writing history is also an ethical act in that the historian

---

111. Aelred, Vita E 30 (CF 56:208–9). [Translator's note: My ellipsis, to fit the English quotation to Burton's phrasing.]

contributes to the development of the king's conscience by laying out the king's responsibility to work actively toward establishing peace throughout his kingdom. Finally, overarching the political and ethical aspects, writing history is an eminently theological act in which the particular history of a people (in this case the Anglo-Norman nation) and the singular mission of a king (Henry II) are re-read in the light of Christ or, more precisely, interpreted in the light of the mystery of universal reconciliation realized through the cross.

By his interpretation of past events, consideration of the present, and anticipation of future realities, Aelred reads history on two theological levels, one cosmic, the other Christological. His reading is cosmic in interpreting the history of the English nation, whose two branches are reconciled thanks to Henry, as a privileged moment in the overall history of salvation, in a fashion preparing and anticipating in the present the recapitulation of all things in the Body of Christ. His reading of history is also Christological in that by the peace-making role he assigns to Henry, he invests Henry with a messianic mission that analogically and almost sacramentally assimilates him into the person of Christ,[112] who, encompassing the entire history of humanity, reconciled all things in himself, "in one body, through the cross, putting . . . enmity to death" (Eph 2:17).[113]

Aelred thus in various passages of the *Life* eloquently reaffirms the king's Christological function as God's steward or lieutenant, acting in historical time *in persona Christi*, as well

---

112. Pezzini and Lemoine have both pointed out the royal figure's messianic and quasi-sacramental aspect, but have failed to note the Christological foundation (the Pauline doctrine in Eph 2), so essential from the point of view of Aelred's theology of the history of salvation (Pezzini, "Genealogy and Posterity," 335, n. 18; Lemoine, "Le moine et le saint roi," 45, 223). John Bequette shows how Aelred presents King Edward as an *alter Christus* (John Bequette, "Aelred of Rievaulx's *Life of Saint Edward, King and Confessor*: A Saintly King and the Salvation of the English People," CSQ 43 [2008]: 17–40, esp. 35).

113. [Translator's note: My ellipsis, to fit the English quotation to Burton's phrasing.]

411 of Aelred's Social and Political Engagements

as his cosmic function of re-establishing peace between peoples and in so doing anticipating the advent of God's reign on earth.

The King's Function as Steward of Divine Creation Collaborating with Ecclesiastical Authority

The historian's work is always more than just a memorial act for Aelred. It is also a theological act that inscribes the course of worldly history within the context of salvation history and therefore aims to interpret present events as moments in a long-term history moving toward its eschatological end in Christ.[114] In correlation with this theological and Christocentric re-reading of events, understanding their course from the perspective of their end in Christ, the historian's work also includes an ethical aim. Through the theological interpretation of historical events, the historian sets the present-time agents of those events, notably princes and kings, face to face with their political responsibility. It is the responsibility of these agents to govern justly and thereby to contribute to the advent of God's reign or at least to make possible its partial realization by establishing the harmony and peace of heaven among men and women on earth.

In keeping with the biblical theology of creation, Aelred holds that every human being is God's steward, but he emphasizes the importance of this role for kings and princes. This emphasis is best illustrated in chapter 5 of the *Life*, where, in terms comparable to those already seen in *Genealogy* on the subject of Edgar the Peaceful, Aelred speaks of the "universal jubilation [*communis laetitia*]"[115] of the cosmos. This jubilation, clothed in the joyous mantle of harmony, peace, and equilibrium, is a happy reflection of the ordering of the world and

114. Regarding this inscription of English history in a universal salvation history or "God's eternal plan of salvation," see Bequette, "Aelred's *Life of Edward*," 17–40, esp. 22.

115. Aelred, Vita E 5 (CF 56:140).

nature by Edward's governance, oriented toward establishing
peace among all people:

> What joy there was then for the English, what universal
> jubilation [*communis laetitia*], when they saw restored
> their ancient felicity and things they had bewailed almost
> without hope; in Edward the people received their lost
> peace, the chief men their renown, and the church its
> liberty. The sun rose and the moon stood still in its orbit
> as Edward was crowned with glory and honor. The
> priests shone with sagacity and sanctity; the monasteries
> were strengthened in all their observances [*omni religione*];
> the clergy stood firm in their duty [*stabat in officio suo*] and
> the people in their rank [*stabat in gradu suo*]. It seemed
> that even the land was more fruitful, the air healthier, the
> sun brighter, and the waves of the sea calmer, since, when
> a peaceful king rules for a long time, everything comes
> together in a single bond of peace [*in uno vinculo pacis
> omnia convenirent*]. Then there will be nothing pestilent
> in the air, nothing tempestuous at sea, nothing unfruitful
> on land, nothing unruly among the people.
>
> The report of this felicity, as Edward began to govern,
> was carried to certain neighboring kingdoms. Kings
> and princes, moved by admiration at such a shift in
> affairs [*pro tanta rerum mutatione*], were happy to enter
> a pact [*foedus inire*] with such a king, to join him in
> friendship [*amicitias jungere*], and to establish peace
> [*pacem componere*].[116]

John Bequette has recognized the importance of this passage; his commentary articulates its various aspects. He underlines that in Aelred's presentation, "Edward's sanctity is
such that his moral rectitude *sets aright* both the institutional
and natural situation of his kingdom. His reign is thus *a fore-
taste of the goal of salvation history*."[117] This is an excellent way

---

116. Aelred, Vita E 5 (CF 56:140–41).
117. Bequette, "Aelred's *Life of Edward*," 24 (Burton's emphasis).

to show how Aelred nests the various levels of historical decryption: ethical and spiritual (through the king's moral rectitude and holiness), political and cosmic (by reference to the world of humankind and ecology), and historical and eschatological (by the representation of present time and final ends). One thing, however, can be added to Bequette. While the space opened by the tension between history and eschatology is certainly filled in by the political sphere, that space is above all illuminated by Aelred's doctrine of spiritual friendship. In the directional sense of history moving toward eschatological ends, the political figure's role is to anticipate and bring about the reign of God in the present. Inversely, looking back from eschatological ends to the present, the reign of God must already be instituted within creation, itself awaiting deliverance (see Rom 8:18-25), thanks to the wise administration of temporal affairs intended to establish mutual relations of peace, justice, reciprocity, interdependence, and cooperation among all things.

As Wincenty Polek has stated, Aelred offers "a complete and panoramic vision"[118] of friendship allowing the entire history of salvation itself to be be read as the history of friendship. He goes on to specify, from a reversed perspective, "if the adventure of friendship aims to be the history of true friendship in the fullest sense of the term, that is to say, a friendship lived to the fullest, it must be part of the history of salvation."[119] Thus he rightly concludes, "In Aelredian philosophy, friendship has its own anthropology, its own morality, and its own theology."[120] It is important to reiterate that Aelredian friendship also has its own cosmology and its politics.

We cannot overemphasize the extent to which the political task of establishing peace in the world, and more broadly in the cosmos, resembling the image of the peace that reigns in

---

118. Wincenty Polek, "Teologia dell'amicizia negli scritti di Aelredo di Rievaulx (1110–1167)," *Cistercium Mater Nostra* 2 (2008): 102.

119. Polek, "Teologia dell'amicizia," 102.

120. Polek, "Teologia dell'amicizia," 102.

God, is constitutive of the royal function Aelred assigns to Henry through the mirror of Edward the Confessor's holiness. In the passage above from the *Life*, Aelred shows Edward's influence on neighboring kingdoms and concludes by asserting, "what the holy Scripture says of Solomon is recognized as appropriate to blessed Edward: '*All the kings of the earth sought to see his face and to hear his wisdom.*'"[121]

Aelred also underlines, however, that to be a true steward cooperating with God in his creative work and in the establishment of his reign on earth, kings and princes must work in close collaboration with religious authority. He further insists that this collaboration must reflect a respect for the autonomy of local church authority and, above all, obedience to the pope. He had already stated this principle of cooperation between the two swords of Gregorian theory in his discussion of Edgar the Peaceful in *Genealogy*, declaring that during the time of naval maneuvers that Edgar organized each year, circumnavigating the British Isles, he surrounded himself with bishops and learned men that they might instruct him on the subject of divine law and the holy Scriptures, thus to be better able to create just laws.[122]

This principle of cooperation finds its fullest expression, however, in *The Life of Edward*. Although at first glance the narratives comprising the work seem to be simple anecdotes, they are in reality practical examples of that cooperation, a stylistic technique typical of Aelred's writing. These narratives highlight what Bequette has rightly called a "Petrine covenant,"[123] whose aim is to shed light on royal authority's dependence on the Apostolic See of Rome. Aelred astutely found a particularly eloquent symbol of this dependence in the close tie between Edward and Westminster Abbey. Edward had contributed to the restoration of the abbey with funds from his own treasury, originally earmarked for his planned pilgrimage to Rome. And

121. 2 Chr 9:23; Aelred, Vita E 5 (CF 56:141–42).
122. Regarding circumnavigation, see Aelred, Gen angl 16 (CF 56:97). On the two swords, see Gen angl 17 (CF 56:100).
123. Bequette, "Aelred's *Life of Edward*," 24.

he asked to be buried in the abbey. Consequently, it became symbolically his own abbey. Westminster Abbey, placed under the holy patronage of the Prince of the Apostles and simultaneously connected to the king, thus became a point of contact between heaven and earth or, more precisely, between God and the people of England.[124]

The Investiture Controversy and the Constitutions of Clarendon: What Freedom for the Church?

The relationship between God and the kingdom constitutes one of the major themes of Aelred's treatise,[125] beginning with the numerous narratives of Edward's healing miracles. One question, constant throughout the history of the church but particularly delicate in the twelfth century, was that of the church's freedom in naming bishops. Known in imperial lands as the Investiture Controversy, this conflict was also of concern in relations between the English Church and royal authority. But in England, the conflict took form in the Constitutions of Clarendon, a collection of sixteen articles promulgated by Henry II on January 30, 1164, shortly after the publication of *The Life of Edward*. The articles were supposedly drafted with the intent of returning to judicial customs that had been in effect under the reign of Henry I, from the time of the Concordat of London, signed in 1107 by Anselm of Bec, archbishop of Canterbury. But in reality, the articles were clearly meant to restrict the principal privileges acquired by the English clergy during the Anarchy, under Stephen of Blois, before the reign of Henry II. Above all, the articles were intended to extend royal jurisdiction over both the church and civil law and to limit papal influence in English civil and religious affairs, notably by giving the king direct control over the selection of new prelates.

---

124. The connection between King Edward and Westminster Abbey, and by extension between the king and the Holy See, is highlighted in Bequette, "Aelred's *Life of Edward*," 24–31.

125. See Bequette, "Aelred's *Life of Edward*," 27.

This story's unfortunate and dramatic conclusion is well known. When Henry asked the bishops of the kingdom to approve the Constitutions, all of them did so, including Thomas Becket, former chancellor and Henry's close friend. However, once named archbishop of Canterbury on June 3, 1162, Becket radically changed his position, thereafter opposing the king and instead supporting the position of Pope Alexander III on matters of religious politics. As soon as he had received the pallium in Tours in 1163, he undertook execution of a plan he had conceived to free the English Church from the restrictions that he had previously helped to create. In January 1164, when Henry asked the bishops to sign the new legislation, Becket categorically refused. The price of his intransigence, which became more insistent over time, was his voluntary exile in France, beginning November 2, 1164, to escape the king's wrath.

Finally, after buying enough time to free himself from the threats of Holy Roman Emperor Frederick I, Alexander III threatened Henry with a writ of excommunication in 1170. Henry, concerned by this eventuality, strove to find some middle ground that would allow Becket to return to England. On July 22 a peace accord was finally concluded at Fréteval, and on December 3, after six years of exile, Thomas disembarked at Sandwich. Two days later he returned to his cathedral. But the reconciliation was short-lived. On December 29, 1170, after a new disagreement and a misunderstanding—an outburst of Henry's exasperation interpreted as an order—Thomas was assassinated at the foot of the altar in Canterbury Cathedral by four Anglo-Norman knights of Henry's entourage: Reginald FitzUrse, Hugh de Morville, William de Tracy, and Richard le Breton.

At the time of Becket's murder, Aelred had been dead three years. But it is highly probable, as some have reasonably asserted,[126] considering how great were Aelred's desire for

---

126. See Brian Patrick McGuire, *Brother and Lover: Aelred of Rievaulx* (New York: Crossroad, 1994), 72. See also Lemoine, "Le moine et le saint roi," 225, n. 37.

peace and his moral authority, that if he had still been alive at that time the murder would never have been committed. In any case, we must keep in mind historical context and remember that *The Life of Edward* was composed between 1161 and 1163. In 1159, Henry had expressed support of the papal candidacy of Alexander III, and on Feb. 7, 1161, Alexander had canonized Edward, before the great crisis opposing Henry and his former chancellor, the archbishop of Canterbury, beginning on October 11, 1163.[127] This context is important because it raises the question of whether Aelred foresaw Henry's inclination toward political and religious absolutism and the disastrous consequences of a conflict born almost before his eyes that grew successively more bitter until it reached its fatal conclusion. Aelred was too knowledgeable about English history not to realize that once William I came to power in 1066, the English monarchy had begun to show increasing desire for sole governance of the kingdom's affairs, leaning more and more toward political and religious absolutism. Aelred's knowledge of history and his analysis of its general tendencies also provided context for his understanding of the human heart, an understanding too deep for him not to have guessed the potential explosiveness of a collaboration between two personalities jealous of their respective prerogatives—one so proud of his royal authority, the other infatuated with his episcopal order's rights.

In any case, whether Aelred glimpsed the potential drama of the situation or not, he would not have failed to insist on the necessity of a close collaboration between civil and ecclesiastical powers, specifically one respecting the Church's freedom as the *sine qua non* of the proper governance of public affairs. He had emphasized this abundantly in *Genealogy*. Dutton has studied the *Genealogy* from this perspective and shown precisely how through the figure of Bishop Dunstan, presented as King

127. By an ironic twist, this was just before the solemn transfer of King Edward's relics two days later on October 13.

Edward's counsellor, Aelred illustrated the social, political, and even cosmic fertility of cooperation between the king and religious authority.[128] She presents Aelred's purpose as twofold. First, Aelred underlines the idea that the mere presence of an expert and trusted ecclesiastical advisor can guarantee a king's success in all areas of his life and all his undertakings. Second, on a more personal level, Aelred expresses his own desire to assume for Henry the same role that Dunstan had at the court of his illustrious predecessor, Edgar.[129]

But let us return to Aelred's central concern for collaboration between civil authority and ecclesiastical hierarchy, in particular the corollary issue of church freedom in the naming of bishops. For Aelred these issues are so fundamental that he returns to them in various forms on numerous occasions in *The Life of Edward*. Two chapters linked to these questions deserve attention.

Chapter 27 of The Life of Edward: *The Ring of Saint John or "The Wedding Ring of England"*

The first of these chapters concerns one of the most celebrated scenes of *The Life of Edward*, one that was to play a considerable role both in the collective memory of the English people and in the progressive development of what has been called the Plantagenet myth. Here Aelred recounts that in the name of Saint John, for whom Aelred had a special devotion, two pilgrims returning from Jerusalem returned to the king a ring that he had previously, while on his way to the consecration of a church dedicated to Saint John, given as alms to a beggar.[130] Dutton has

---

128. Marsha Dutton, "*Sancto Dunstano Cooperante*: Collaboration between King and Ecclesiastical Advisor in Aelred of Rievaulx's *Genealogy of the Kings of the English*," in *Religious and Laity in Northern Europe: 1000–1400: Interaction, Negotiation, and Power*, ed. Emilia Jamroziak and Janet Burton (Turnhout: Brepols, 2007), 183–95.

129. Dutton, "*Sancto Dunstano Cooperante*," 193.

130. Aelred, Vita E 27 (CF 56:196–200).

written a brilliant study of this scene, and in particular of the miniatures in the Trinity College Dublin manuscript.[131] There is not space here to examine in detail the various layers of meaning discussed in Dutton's analysis. Suffice to say that from the perspective of the present study, the scene offers remarkable political and religious signification of two main kinds.

The first significance is symbolic and social in nature and has to do with the fact that in Anglo-Saxon culture, the lord presented a ring to his vassal to signify their alliance and to symbolize their respective and mutual duties and obligations as lord and subordinate. For the king, these obligations included feeding and protecting his people, and the arrival of Christianity expanded these to include defending (*stabilitor*) and developing (*auctor*) the Christian faith. The second is liturgical and religious in nature; it has to do with the fact that in the coronation rite, the presentation of the Sovereign's Ring (often called "The Wedding Ring of England") is of great importance. Tradition holds that this is the same ring that Edward gave to the Evangelist and that was returned to him by the two pilgrims. For a long time this rite signified the continuity of the English monarchy from King Edward on. The fact that in Aelred's narrative the ring is given by Edward "for the love of Saint John"[132] and then returned to him in the name of the Evangelist is intended to remind Henry II of his role as intermediary, signifying to him that however great a lord—a "ring giver"—he may be on earth, he is no less the vassal of the apostle John and thus a citizen of heaven. Consequently, the ring proclaims the king's power and his sovereignty over his people and at the same time subordinates him to God, making the king as much a subject as a lord.[133]

In other words, whether it is a question of the theory of the two swords (whose presence is particularly felt in *Genealogy*), the Petrine pact (relating to Westminster and Saint Peter), or

131. Dutton, "Aelred historien," 209–30.
132. Aelred, Vita E 27 (CF 56:197).
133. See Dutton, "Aelred historien," 209–30, esp. 220–25.

the Wedding Ring of England (that is, the ring given to Saint John the Evangelist), Aelred's political logic is consistent. He emphasizes that the king's position in society is that of a mediator, a go-between, or one might even say a *pontiff* (*ponti-fex*: bridge-builder), becoming in his very person the link between heaven (specifically Saints Peter and John, from whom he holds authority over his people) and earth, defending the Christian faith and governing the nation by divine law and in the name of God, as God's steward or lieutenant (literally "place-holder").

There is one more thing to add that Dutton fails to mention, no doubt because it was not the object of her study. It is significant that Aelred places the scene of the ring under Saint John's patronage, and that he specifies that when Saint John identifies himself to the two pilgrims before handing them the ring, he affirms, "I am John, apostle and evangelist, *the disciple whom Jesus loved.*"[134] As Aelred made reference to this same verse in *Mirror* (3.39.110) to establish the evangelical and Christian legitimacy of spiritual friendship, it is not unreasonable to hypothesize that in referring to the same verse here, he discreetly suggests that the king's political mission is related to the doctrine of spiritual friendship, and that the former is strengthened when exercised in light of the latter. This would confirm the idea proposed earlier, expanding upon Polek's work, that friendship also has politics.

Chapter 36 in The Life of Edward: *Saint Wulfstan, or the Freedom of Episcopal Elections*

The second narrative deserving attention on the subject of the Church's freedom relates to Saint Wulfstan, bishop of Worcester from 1062 to 1095. The story Aelred eloquently relates illustrates the delicate question of the Church's autonomy

---

134. John 13:23; Aelred, Vita E 27 (CF 56:199).

in episcopal elections and the proper relationship to be established between civil and ecclesiastical authority. The episode revolves around the prelate's unjust removal from office by William I and his subsequent reinstatement by King Edward's miraculous post-mortem intervention.

As Lemoine has shown, the narrative should be read as a criticism of William the Conqueror and his intervention in Church affairs.[135] On a second level, the text should also be read as a warning to Henry II not to overstep his royal prerogatives, for doing so would be unjust and despotic. Instead, he must maintain a respect for the Church's freedom in the exercise of his authority. Lemoine further points out that in contrast to Becket, whose intransigence led to his exile and death, Aelred's temperament leads him to position himself as a moderate partisan of Gregorian reform. This positioning leaves him standing on a political and religious middle ground where he defends the Church's freedom in the choice of ecclesiastical leaders without denying the king's right to have a say in the ecclesiastical life of his kingdom—for example, intervening at the end of the process, as Edward did in Wulfstan's case, to approve an ecclesiastical election.

Aelred's Historiography and England's National Politics: Political History as Salvation History

In the two preceding sections, we dwelt on Aelred's four works of civil and political history. *Battle of the Standard*, *Lament for David*, and *Genealogy*, into which Aelred quickly inserted the *Lament*, all date from the same period of 1153–1154. *The Life of Edward, King and Confessor*, was written ten years later in 1161–1163. The ten-year chronological gap is reflected in the typological and symbolic manner in which Aelred positions Henry II, to whom he dedicated three of these works. Though

---

135. Lemoine, "Le moine et le saint roi," 224–25.

Battle has no dedication, in the prefatory letter introducing the combined *Lament* and *Genealogy* Aelred presents Henry II as "the hope of the English" (*spes Anglorum*),[136] while the preface to the *Life of Edward* presents Henry as "the consolation of all England" (*totius Angliae consolationem*).[137]

This difference in presentation cannot be explained entirely by the fact Henry was not yet king when Aelred composed the *Lament* and *Genealogy* and that Henry was king when Aelred wrote the *Life of Edward*. The difference has to do in part, and perhaps even principally, with the fact that in 1163 the political and socio-religious context had changed. The English people's general hopes and expectations for Henry's reign as he was preparing to take the throne, while unrealized, as events after 1163 show, had become more focused. In the historical treatises dedicated to Henry, Aelred seems to have assigned himself the task of enumerating Henry's duties and obligations as king through the example of his illustrious predecessors, particularly David of Scotland and the sainted Edward the Confessor. By honoring his predecessors, succeeding them and following their example—that is, by his familial and moral heritage—Henry could become in his own right the veritable "consolation of his people."

Aelred's historical writing thus goes beyond simple memorialization and becomes a political and ethical enterprise. It is political to the extent that he seeks to demonstrate Henry's legitimacy and, on the basis of this legitimacy, to build a collective national consciousness uniting the English people around their sovereign. It is also ethical since, while establishing Henry's genealogical legitimacy by bloodline, Aelred reminds Henry that bloodline alone is insufficient, that it must be coupled with a moral legitimacy consisting of just governance aimed at the common good. Thus the establishment of a collective national consciousness intended to create a rela-

---

136. Aelred, Gen angl Ep H (CF 56:42; CCCM 3:3).
137. Aelred, Vita E Prol (CF 56:127; CCCM 3A:88).

tionship of reciprocity and alliance between the king and his people is joined in Aelred's historical writing with the ethical instruction of princes, and of Henry in particular.

Furthermore, Aelred expresses Henry's political responsibility to realize national unity and cohesion, both physically and morally, in his very person, through genealogy and through a pious life, referring to him with the metaphor of the unifying and architectural function of the cornerstone (*lapis angularis*)— a barely veiled allusion to the mystery of reconciliation through the person and cross of Christ (Eph 2:14-22). Henceforth, he pushes his readers to consider his historiographical work not only as a political and ethical act, but above all as a theological act. By identifying the person of Henry with that of Christ (i.e., as an *alter Christus*), Aelred encourages the Christological reading of English political history, from the perspective of Christ's reconciling mission of salvation. At the same time, Aelred leads us to read English political history eschatologically, as one particular moment in a larger universal history marching toward its final end in God, "who will be all in all" (1 Cor 15:28).

To put it another way, England's history, as Aelred writes it, is inscribed as one particular moment within the course of universal salvation history—the latter a divine work striving toward the universal reconciliation of all things in and through the person of Christ. Because of the king's role as intermediary, England's national history is not simply a static instant in universal history, but rather a dynamic baton passed along through it. Consequently English history is a human instrument placed in God's hands for the execution of his universal plan of salvation, in which all history, from the creation to the recapitulation of all things in Christ, tends to build up the world on the foundation of an eventual universal and cosmic friendship, anticipating the kingdom of God in humanity's present time.

Aelred expresses this Christocentric and eschatological reading of human history on route to its ultimate consummation in numerous, almost infinite ways. He shows how Henry, in his historical and temporal mission as God's lieutenant and an *alter Christus*, participating in Christ's messianic function and ministry of reconciliation, is called upon to realize within himself the unity of the human race. Certain themes deserve renewed emphasis here. Far from being mutually exclusive, they are complementary and can be envisioned as larger and larger concentric circles as if, with time, Aelred's perspective became progressively broader, until it approached infinity. Thus in *Battle*, a work with no designated addressee even if one can imagine that it was addressed to the Scottish and English peoples, Aelred seeks above all to end the violence of a civil war whose principal victims were civilian populations. Similarly, he promotes a certain social cohesion by which laity and clergy might live in harmony through justice and mutual respect, without threatening each other's way of life or financial situations. In the *Lament*, composed immediately after the death of David of Scotland, Aelred addresses the Scottish people more directly and strives even harder to guarantee national political cohesion by engaging the various Scottish clans to unite around their princes. In *Genealogy*, as in the *Life of Edward*, Aelred maintains this concern for national political cohesion while enriching it with other aspects raising it to a higher level. Taken together they show a progression[138] of traits to be reconciled and united in the person of the king:

- personal life: moral rectitude and piety, imitation of royal virtues;

- political legitimacy: an inherited bloodline (descending and ascending genealogy), and inherited virtues (*sequi naturam*);

- political life: national cohesion of a people rallied around its prince; a supranational union of peoples through a

---

138. We limit ourselves here to those aspects already noted in our discussion.

bicultural king of Anglo-Saxon and Franco-Norman origins;

- social life: respect for social justice and the common good; religious freedom and ecclesiastical autonomy;

- English national history: the hope of a people (*spes anglorum*) concentrated in the person of the king who promises "consolation" (*totius Angliae consolatio*);

- religion and salvation history: human history as the partial, anticipatory realization of the kingdom;

- cosmic and universal history: the descent of heaven to earth (symbolized by the Abbey of Saint Peter at Westminster or the Petrine pact) through the harmonization of all things; the pure reflection in nature of the wise administration of public affairs; reading history in light of the doctrine of spiritual friendship.

What all these elements have in common is the mediating, quasi-pontifical bridge-building function of the royal mission, allowing the secular prince who faithfully executes that mission to connect the present-time breadth of human history to God's eschatological salvational plan. This function establishes and maintains a close but flexible collaboration between civil and religious authorities, symbolized in Saint John's ring. In this collaboration, each order must be respectful of the other's authority and freedoms, as expressed in a moderate interpretation and application of the Gregorian theory of the two swords. On this matter, Becket's radical, intransigent position serves as a contrasting counter-model.

Of all these facets, and in the close articulation between civil and ecclesiastic authority, we have emphasized more than any other thing the king's mission to aid the Church as *stabilitor* and *auctor* of Christian faith, and as God's lieutenant and steward bringing heaven to earth. It remains for us to examine the second side of Aelred's historical writings, exemplified in his three treatises devoted to ecclesiastical history.

Church and Society: Aelred's Three Treatises on Religious History

In discussing Aelred's four treatises on English civil and political history, we examined him in the role of counselor to princes that he seems to have assigned to himself beginning in 1153–1154. That year marked a turning point in his personal life, in English history (the end of the Anarchy), and in European history at large (with the deaths of Pope Eugene III and Bernard of Clairvaux). At a stroke, having reached middle age and the peak of his abilities, the forty-three-year-old Aelred found himself thrust into the front line of the day's events. As a living repository of recent history and witness to the birth of a new era beginning with the accession of Henry II to the English throne, Aelred was no doubt eager to contribute to the shape of things to come. He had been enriched by his experience as King David's young steward, and he was strengthened by the personal ties binding him to the Scottish court. Similar strong ties, through marriage, bound the Scottish court to the English court.

Consequently, Aelred felt he could legitimately claim the right to address the new king, on relatively equal terms. By dedicating his 1153 *Lament-Genealogy* to Henry, Aelred came out of his monastic shell to make his official entry into politics. Ten years later, in 1163, Henry's nature was becoming clearer, and the political landscape was slowly shifting toward absolute monarchy and a more hardened approach to problems facing it, as may be seen in the open conflict between the king and his former chancellor, now become archbishop of Canterbury. No doubt aware of the dangers threatening the precarious balance between civil and religious institutions in this context, Aelred seized the opportunity to write an eminently political narrative under cover of a hagiographic exterior: *The Life of Saint Edward, King and Confessor.*

Between these two dates—1153 and 1163—Aelred wrote three works focused on ancient and recent church history: *The Life of Ninian, Apostle of the Southern Picts* (probably in 1154), *The Saints of the Church of Hexham and Their Miracles* (probably in 1155), and finally the more anecdotal text, *A Certain Wonderful Miracle*, also known as *The Nun of Watton* (written probably in 1165–1166). Of all Aelred's works, these have until recently received the least scholarly attention[139] because, compared to Aelred's ascetic and mystical treatises, his homilies, and his large-scale historical works, these three relatively short treatises have been considered minor works. This also explains the fact that until 2017 there was no critical edition or translation to any modern language with the exception of the English-language version translated in 2006 by Jane Patricia Freeland and placed in historical context by Dutton.[140]

Our approach to each text is twofold. First we identify certain key ideas in terms of Aelred's historical method and his theology of history. These remarks complement those formulated at the end of our discussion of Aelred's political histories. Then we expand our perspective to examine the portrait of the church and society as Aelred paints them throughout his seven historical treatises, with clarifications from certain liturgical

139. The only study published [before 2017] on the three works together is Aelred Squire, "Aelred and the Northern Saints," Coll 23 (1961): 59–69. Dutton's studies from 2006 thus fill a significant gap in scholarship relating to Aelredian hagiography. The following pages owe much to Dutton's work. [Translator's note: As Burton's book was published in 2010, editions and studies available after that date were of course unavailable to him and so do not feature in this translation of his book. For more recent studies on these works, see the bibliography on pages 561–82 below.]

140. Aelredus Rievallensis, *Opera Omnia*, vol. 6, *Opera Historica et Hagio-graphica*, ed. Domenico Pezzini, CCCM III (Brepols: Turnhout, 2017); *Aelred of Rievaulx: The Lives of the Northern Saints*, trans. Jane Patricia Freeland, ed. Marsha L. Dutton, CF 71 (Kalamazoo, MI: Cistercian Publications, 2006). This work offers an English translation of *The Life of Ninian* (34–63), *The Saints of the Church of Hexham* (65–107), and *A Certain Wonderful Miracle* (102–22).

sermons. We then proceed to chapter 10, where we consider the full scope of Aelred's spiritual doctrine as condensed in his commentary on the Burdens of Isaiah.

The Life of Ninian: *A Model of Episcopal Holiness*

With *The Life of Ninian*, we leave England for southwest Scotland as Aelred relates the life of Ninian (360?–432), the apostle of the Picts and founder of the episcopal see at Whithorn in Galloway.[141] There, at the request of Count Fergus of Galloway and with the help of King David I of Scotland, Rievaulx established its fourth daughter house at Dundrennan seven centuries later, in 1142, under the direction of its first abbot, Dom William.

Nothing concrete is known of the circumstances that led Aelred to compose this short hagiographic narrative. All we do know, thanks to the enigmatic indications furnished in the work's Prologue, is that the text was written at the request of someone Aelred refers to as "my dear friend,"[142] who was probably a bishop. According to the Prologue, the addressee sought a work from Aelred that would fulfill a desire expressed by "the clergy and people of [the] holy church who hold in extraordinary affection this saint of God under whose patronage

---

141. See *Vita Niniani*, CCCM 3:218*–52*, 111–34. There are three known manuscripts of this text. The work was edited for the first time in 1789 by Johannes Pinkerton on the basis of the twelfth-century Oxford, Bodleian MS Laud Misc 668. It was then re-edited in 1874 by Alexander Penrose Forbes, who used the Pinkerton edition in conjunction with one of the two manuscripts in the British Museum in London: the thirteenth-century MS Cotton Tiberius D.III. In 1899 it was again re-edited by W. M. Metcalfe, again using the Pinkerton edition, adding the Office for the Saint's Feast Day, taken from the Aberdeen Breviary. For more on this, see Marsha Dutton, Introduction, in *Aelred of Rievaulx: The Lives of the Northern Saints*, trans. Jane Patricia Freeland, CF 71 (Kalamazoo, MI: Cistercian Publications, 2006), 31–32.

142. Aelred, Vita N Prol (CF 71:35).

they live."[143] Thus most historians agree that Aelred must have composed the work at the request of the bishop of Whithorn to celebrate some particularly important event in the life of his diocese. On the other hand, opinions vary on the nature of the event itself and also, therefore, on the date of composition and the addressee's identity. Two hypotheses have been formulated on this matter.

The first, and the more widely accepted of the two, is that *The Life of Ninian* was written in 1154 at the request of Christian, the new bishop of Whithorn, on the occasion of his episcopal ordination on December 19 of that same year. If we adhere to this hypothesis, it would be easy to consider this opuscule as the second panel of a diptych, the first being the *Lament*, composed just after King David's death in May 1153. In the *Lament*, Aelred addresses the Scottish people, urging them among other things to rally around the late king's three sons, as for Aelred this was the best way to parry threats of English aggression. By contrast, in *The Life of Ninian*, a more experienced Aelred instead addresses the bishop of that politically and socially troubled region,[144] offering him counsel and a pastoral course of action according to the model provided by Gregorian reform.

Brian Patrick McGuire, however, has hypothesized that the narrative was really written earlier, in 1128, during a period in which Aelred, still discovering the joys of the Scottish court and the friendships to be found there, was not yet thinking of a monastic life. If we were to accept this hypothesis, this would mean, as McGuire states, that *The Life of Ninian* was "one of the first products of Aelred's pen,"[145] a sort of exercise in scholarly Latin composition in the form of a hagiographic narrative modeled after the Venerable Bede's writing, meant to put his education to the test.

143. Aelred, Vita N Prol (CF 71:36).
144. See our earlier discussion of Walter, VA 38.
145. McGuire, *Brother and Lover*, 42–45.

This hypothesis is seductive. Despite Aelred's recurrent protestations of humility or ineptitude throughout his works, this hypothesis frames Aelred as a singularly gifted young man of precocious intellectual and literary qualities.[146] Furthermore, the hypothesis is supported by certain historical facts. If we agree to advance the composition date of *Ninian* to Aelred's premonastic period, 1128 presents itself as a likely date. This is the date that the former episcopal see of Whithorn (*Candida Casa*), originally established by Saint Ninian and destroyed in the early ninth-century Danish invasions,[147] was finally restored. And so it is also the date that the first bishop of the re-established diocese, Gille Aldan, was invested by Thurstan, who as archbishop of York was also historically the metropolitan bishop of the former Anglo-Saxon kingdom of Northumbria, where Whithorn was located.

At that time, Aelred had been in King David's service since the latter's accession to the throne four years earlier. During those four years, David had been able to appreciate the personal and intellectual qualities of the man he would eventually appoint as his steward. Thus it is not unreasonable to imagine that the newly designated bishop of Whithorn was aware of Aelred's literary reputation[148] and so sought the services of the promising

146. Aelred Squire has noted that in literary terms, *Ninian*, "one of Aelred's most purely literary compositions, is written in the rhythmic Latin whose technique . . . Aelred had certainly mastered" at the cathedral school of Durham (Squire, *Aelred*, 115–16). For more on the Durham cathedral school as a center of historical and literary studies in the tradition of the Venerable Bede, see the beginning of the present chapter. Squire also adds that *Ninian* "is the work of a meticulous and sophisticated author" (Squire, *Aelred*, 116). [Translator's note: My ellipsis, to fit the English quotation to Burton's phrasing.]

147. The last-known bishop of Whithorn before its restoration was Beadwulf, who died after 803. Probably because of the calamitous times, he was not replaced after his death.

148. McGuire notes the dedicatory letter that Lawrence of Durham addressed to Aelred while the latter was still at the Scottish court, attached to the *Life of Saint Brigid,* which Lawrence had just re-worked (McGuire, *Brother*

young man to compose a new *Life of Ninian* that would, as Aelred tells us in his Prologue, "draw the life of this illustrious man out of rustic speech, as if bringing it from a kind of darkness into the light of Latin eloquence" that it truly deserved.[149]

Any assumption that *Ninian* was composed in 1128 requires that we account for two elements whose coincidence becomes a determining factor in interpreting the larger meaning of this work. In 1128, when the former episcopal see of Whithorn was being restored, King David had barely begun his reign. It is conceivable that in addition to its obvious pastoral and ecclesiastical aims, the re-establishment of this see had a twofold political purpose. First, in strictly local, Scottish, terms, it allowed David to affirm his *dominium* over a region where the centralized authority of the king of Scotland had always struggled to take hold. Second, in terms of international diplomatic relations with England, it allowed David to show his desire to avoid English influence, a point that appears confirmed by the fact that the bishop investing Gille Aldan was not the archbishop of Canterbury but rather the archbishop of York.

Read in this context, *Ninian* becomes a key component of the young Scottish king's political strategy. Anachronistically, David would have used Aelred's portrayal of the holy episcopal figure of Saint Ninian as a bishop adhering to the principles of Gregorian reform to assert and strengthen his authority vis-à-vis his English neighbor, King Stephen, and the petty kings of certain "uncivilized" regions of Northumbria such as Galloway.

As seductive as it is, McGuire's hypothesis that *The Life of Ninian* was written in 1128 raises an important question. Without doubting that Aelred was a young man of rich potential (something his future would prove without question), or that he showed that potential early on (in this case, at the age of

---

and Lover, 43). For an easily accessible edition of this letter, see Squire, "Historical Factors," 272–73.

149. Aelred, Vita N Prol (CF 71:35–36).

eighteen), one must wonder if this hypothesis does not give Aelred more credit than he deserves. Even supposing that he was precociously gifted (as is reasonable) or that early in life he demonstrated an intense interest in the political and ecclesiastical affairs of his time (again, perfectly reasonable, since barely two years later King David entrusted to him the stewardship of his kingdom), we know through Aelred himself that during this same period and the few years between 1128 and 1134 before his entry at Rievaulx, his principal interest did not lie in administrative questions. Having discovered the joys of friendship, and then seeing his friend Waldef's entry into a community of Augustinian canons, he began internally debating far sharper and more personally important questions. On the one hand, there was the ordering of his affective life, and on the other the general direction he would give to his life as a whole.[150] In such a context, can one really imagine an eighteen-year-old Aelred writing the *Life of Ninian*?

Pastoral and Theological Issues in The Life of Ninian

When Aelred began composing *Ninian*, he had little in the way of reliable historical information at his disposal. First there were a few bits and pieces provided by the Venerable Bede in a short passage on Ninian in his *Ecclesiastical History of the English People*, which Aelred cites in his own Preface.[151] Aelred also mentions another source, unidentified to this day, written in a lesser language, perhaps archaic Latin or a vernacular tongue: "So it is that barbarous speech obscured the life of the most holy Ninian, which the sanctity of his way of life and his glorious miracles commend, and the less it pleased readers, the less it edified them."[152]

---

150. For additional detail, see the discussion of Aelred's conversion in chap. 4 above.
151. Aelred, Vita N Pref (CF 71:37–38).
152. Aelred, Vita N Prol (CF 71:35).

As Squire has noted, this lack of source material left Aelred free to refashion Ninian as he saw fit, anachronistically "reading back into the past" and using Ninian's life to reflect twelfth-century issues: "Ninian had been a simple missionary, and Aelred's picture of him as the founder of a diocese divided into parishes is inspired by the desire to discover in the past a justification for the ecclesiastical re-organization characteristic of the reign of King David of Scotland."[153]

That being said, Mayeski's brief but detailed analysis of Aelred's Prologue to *Ninian* has convincingly shown[154] that the work's author did not just stylistically embellish an earlier, poorly written work. Nor did Aelred simply clothe Ninian in twelfth-century bishop's vestments, as anachronistic as was his promotion of Gregorian reform. By the complex interplay of images offered in the Prologue, centered on the multiple linguistic and theological implications of the vestment as metaphor and of the symbolic antinomianism of light and darkness, Aelred "reveals his understanding of what a hagiographical narrative is and, by extension, what the task of a theological narrator requires."[155] To use Aelred's own words, this role is "to save from oblivion and perpetuate in memory the example of a more perfect life for the edification of posterity," thus

153. Squire, *Aelred*, 116. Squire alludes here to paragraph 6 from book 1 of *The Life of Ninian*, in which Aelred describes how Ninian—following the example of Saint Martin, evangelist of the Gauls and uncontested model of evangelism—administered his diocese by first destroying pagan religious sites, then ordaining priests, investing bishops, distributing various ecclesiastical charges, and finally dividing the country into fixed parishes (Aelred, Vita N, 48–49).

154. Marie Anne Mayeski, "Clothing Maketh the Saint: Aelred's Narrative Intent in the *Life of Saint Ninian*," CSQ 44, no. 2 (2009): 181–90.

155. Mayeski, "Clothing," 181. The expression "theological narrator" comes from what is called "narrative theology," as opposed to "dogmatic theology." The latter develops its theological discourse on the basis of concepts, while the former does so on the basis of historical narratives, as in the majority of the books in the Bible. Hagiography as a literary genre falls firmly into the realm of narrative theology.

operating in the temporal modalities of the past, present, and future.[156] Or, to rephrase it in Mayeski's terms, Aelred's efforts to give *The Life of Ninian* a linguistic makeover "will not merely decorate the saint's life; it will make that life a more effective tool for the sanctification of those who will hear, read, study, and memorize the *vita* he writes."[157]

In this sense, *The Life of Ninian* appears as "a pastoral document, with all of the purposes, theological and devotional, that are essential to good pastoral work."[158] It is, of course, first and foremost a pious and devotional narrative, whose literary beauty not only stimulates affection for the saint but also incites the reader to imitate the saint's virtues and the holiness of his way of life. At the same time, Aelred adds a new dimension to his text relative to prior hagiographic practice in presenting his text as a moral reflection on the power of language as a space of discovered truths hidden behind external realities. Finally, and directly in line with the theology of incarnation so dear to Cistercian tradition, Aelred presents his text as a theological instrument designed to show that the history of salvation, far from ending with revelation and biblical history, continues throughout time through the lives of the saints.

Aelred's understanding of his hagiographic role as narrative theologian and theological narrator must be understood in light of these three main elements of *Ninian*—devotional literature, ethics of language, and theology of history—as he metaphorically describes them in the work's Prologue. The hagiographer's task, Mayeski writes, is to tell the story of saints and illustrious people in such a way that "he may reveal the inner truth accurately, that he may, in fact, make the inner truth present."[159] The hagiographic writer must strive "to reveal not only the truth but also the beauty of what God reveals, and to

156. Aelred, Vita N Prol (CF 71:35).
157. Mayeski, "Clothing," 185.
158. Mayeski, "Clothing," 184.
159. Mayeski, "Clothing," 189.

do so in a language that matches or approximates that beauty as closely as possible."[160]

These pastoral and theological issues relating to Aelred's *Life of Ninian* need to be kept in mind as they will apply to Aelred's other religious histories—*The Saints of the Church of Hexham and their Miracles* and *A Certain Wonderful Miracle*—which share several of *The Life of Ninian's* themes. To better understand these themes, a few general preliminary remarks on the narrative's structure and content are in order.

Apart from the Prologue, whose addressee is unnamed, and the Preface, in which Aelred acknowledges his debt to the Venerable Bede and another unnamed source, *Ninian* consists of two books of unequal length. In classical style, the first and more extensive of the two books contains twelve short vignettes of varying lengths; it is presented as a narrative of Saint Ninian's life from his birth to his death, peppered with accounts of various miracles Ninian performed. The second book, still in keeping with the conventions of the genre, presents three vignettes recounting his posthumous miracles. The text closes on a doxology in the style of Saint John, ending the work, even though, as Aelred writes, there is no end to Ninian's miracles: "These do not cease to shine forth even in our own day, to the praise and glory of our Lord Jesus Christ, who with the Father and the Holy Spirit lives and reigns forever and ever."[161]

It may be that the holy traits Aelred emphasizes in Ninian's life derive from a recollection[162] of his own charge as steward of the Scottish court, for he readily presents the apostle of the Picts as the wise and loyal steward of God. This emphasis occurs in several ways. First, he presents Ninian as a bishop wholly devoted to the ecclesiastical ideal of Gregorian reform.

---

160. Mayeski, "Clothing," 189.
161. Aelred, Vita N 15 (CF 71:63).
162. This requires accepting, as we do, that *The Life of Ninian* was written after 1154.

Not only is he shown to be loyal to the Catholic faith and the Roman see, having made in his youth the pilgrimage *ad limina Pauli et Petri apostolorum* in order to instruct himself in the faith,[163] but he is also shown to have great concern for the rigorous administration of his diocese, organizing it on a territorial basis through the creation of parishes and distributing the curial charges required to ensure its proper management.[164] Completing this trait is Ninian's emulation of Saint Martin, apostle of the Gauls, whom Ninian visited in Tours during his return trip to England.[165] Following Martin's example, Ninian applied himself to the eradication of pagan religions. To accomplish this, he built churches such as the first-known Christian edifice constructed of stone in the British Isles, which became the cathedral church at Whithorn and which Ninian placed under the patronage of Martin upon learning of Martin's death.[166]

But while Aelred shows Ninian as a wise apostolic administrator of the territory entrusted to his pastoral care, he also portrays him as no less a faithful dispenser of divine grace— something far more important in Aelred's eyes. Thus Aelred underlines two traits that mirror the manner in which he perceived his own pastoral charge as abbot of Rievaulx. The first is a concern for the intellectual, moral, and spiritual development of the whole person. The second is the generous dispensation of God's mercy to the weak and the sinful. Aelred eloquently illustrates both traits by recounting that the population adopted the habit of entrusting their children to Ninian so that he might instruct them in sacred letters.[167] As a good disciple of Saint Benedict, Ninian willingly took on this responsibility through both formal instruction and the example

163. Aelred, Vita N 1–2 (CF 71:40–42).
164. Aelred, Vita N 6 (CF 71:48–49).
165. Aelred, Vita N 2 (CF 71:42).
166. Aelred, Vita N 3 (CF 71:44).
167. Aelred, Vita N 10 (CF 71:54–55).

of his life. It is not surprising to find here the same Pauline verse Aelred had used twice in the *Life of Edward* to describe the holiness of life to which princes should aspire: "By wholesome discipline he drove out the faults that are usually found at that age and instilled the virtues by which they might live humbly, justly, and devoutly."[168]

The narrative then continues with the story of a young man who, having committed a grave fault, took flight in a coracle to escape punishment from Ninian, first taking the staff on which Ninian leaned for support. This act turned out to be fortunate, since the staff ultimately saved him from certain death when the boat began to capsize. But in Aelred's narrative theology the story is symbolic—the cane is in reality the quasi-sacramental sign of the divine and salvational power with which people of God are invested. More than this, the cane is the sacramental sign of the presence of Christ the Savior himself, manifested in his saints. Aelred explicitly asserts this reality as his narrative's lesson, insisting that it was Christ himself who acted through Ninian as intermediary, exclaiming, "Yours are these deeds, O Christ!"[169] Aelred repeats this idea again, slightly modified, in recounting Ninian's final posthumous miracle just before the closing of the work, a closing that opens the deepest meaning of the work as a whole: "They returned to their homes healed, to the glory of Ninian, to the praise of God working wonderfully in his saints [see Ps 67:36]."[170]

If we interpret this last sentence in terms of Aelred's narrative theology, it appears to be another way of stating, as in the case of the king's messianic function as cornerstone and *alter Christus*, that the work of salvation does not end with biblical

168. Titus 2:12; Aelred, Vita N 10 (CF 71:54); see Aelred, Vita E 14, 18 (CF 56:168, 176).
169. Aelred, Vita N 10 (CF 71:55).
170. Aelred, Vita N 15 (CF 71:62). Dutton has noted the importance of this part of the narrative but has not drawn out all of the passage's possible theological consequences (Dutton, Introduction, CF 71:12).

history or with the life of the historical Jesus. Rather, it continues throughout human history, provided that men and women cooperate faithfully with God, as sacrament of his current and active presence. This is, after all, what Jesus' words to his disciples on the eve of his death lead us to think—words that Aelred cites to support his argument: "Whoever believes in me will also do the works that I do [John 14:12]."[171] In other words, the moral theology of holiness Aelred proposes through the model of Saint Ninian is raised to the prestigious and glorious rank of a theology of history conceived of, and experienced as, a theology of the incarnation continued.

Such an idea is a fine program for a bishop who by the pastoral zeal he exhibited in the service of his flock did more than just serve and cooperate with God. Aelred calls Ninian "the bridegroom's friend [John 3:29], to whom the heavenly bridegroom [God] entrusted his bride [the Picts], and to whom he had revealed his secrets [John 15:14-15] and opened his treasures [Col 2:3]." More than this, Aelred calls that soul "beloved," as in the Song of Songs (Song 2:10), like a dove who "wept with those who were weeping, was weak with the weak, and burned with indignation with those who were cast low [see 2 Cor 11:29]," declaring that Ninian was now invited to share the eternal repose of a divine contemplation that nothing could henceforth disturb.[172]

In reality, Vita N 11 is a veritable double-weave cloth of interlaced scriptural citations, focusing in particular on those from the Song of Songs, a phenomenon not occurring in any of Aelred's other historical works,[173] bearing the watermark of

---

171. Aelred, Vita N 10 (CF 71:55).

172. Aelred, Vita N 11 (CF 71:56–58).

173. Dutton points out that *Ninian* is the only historical work in which Aelred quotes from the Song of Songs. However, here again, she fails to note the profound ties between these references and Aelred's spiritual doctrine of friendship in its broadest sense, which, beyond its affective component, also includes an eminently pastoral component (Dutton, Introduction, CF 71:13).

themes dear to Aelred's heart. These begin with his vision of pastoral responsibility, which makes the pastor a friend in Christ's image. Thus Aelred projects his own conception and practice of abbatial ministry onto Ninian's episcopal ministry.

History's Memory: The Saints of the Church of Hexham as Spiritual Exercise

Aelred's treatise on *The Saints of the Church of Hexham and Their Miracles* brings us to a new landscape, though not necessarily a new horizon. We leave behind the distant Scotland of the fourth and fifth centuries, that heroic time when the episcopal see of Whithorn was founded, and return to England. Aelred introduces us to Hexham, where he spent his earliest years until the age of four (1114), and possibly even until the age of fourteen (1124), though the latter cannot be asserted with any certainty. But as we change location, we remain in the same religious and cultural universe so characteristic of medieval hagiography, which sometimes irks us twenty-first-century readers, given our inclination to disbelieve the abundant miracle stories that so delighted our ancestors.

We focus here on the principal theological and narrative considerations formulated in our discussion of *The Life of Ninian*. In *The Saints of the Church of Hexham*, as in *Ninian*, Aelred again engages in what Mayeski calls "narrative theology," in which the story and the miracle it contains become the exterior literary shell through which the reader must break in order to access the theological lesson within.[174]

---

174. Aelredus Rievallensis, *De Sanctis Ecclesie Haugustaldensis et Eorum Miraculis*, CCCM 3:179*–217*, 75–110. The *Saints of the Church of Hexham* is preserved in four manuscripts. It was first edited by Mabillon in the 1672 *Acta Sanctorum ordinis Sancti Benedicti* (*Secula Tertia, Pars Prima*, 204–20), based on a twelfth-century manuscript preserved at Oxford (MS Laud. Misc. 668). It was then re-edited with other documents in 1864 by James Raine, from the same manuscript, in *The Priory of Hexham: Its Chroniclers, Endowments, and*

On March 11, 1155, Richard, prior of Hexham's community of Augustinian canons, ordered the solemn translation of relics preserved there. Aelred's father, Eilaf, had been the vigilant guardian of these relics until 1114, when the archbishop of York decided to replace the tradition of parish priests in the church at Hexham with Augustinian canons.[175] On this occasion Richard turned to Aelred—perhaps because of Aelred's faithful attachment to his native parish and its saints,[176] or perhaps because Aelred already enjoyed great prestige as the abbot of Rievaulx—to grace the ceremony with his presence and to give the day's homily. According to Maurice Powicke and Aelred Squire, this homily served as the early core[177] of the work that Aelred later expanded and polished into the form that has come down to us today.

Squire states that of all Aelred's historical works, *Hexham* is "the least perfect in form,"[178] but he also argues that its "lack of the final touches of sophistication gives its message a special piquancy,"[179] for instead of directing itself toward an erudite and cultivated public, the work resounds with "the basic reli-

---

Annals, Surtees Society 44 (Durham: Andrews and Co., 1864), 1:173–203. A recent English translation, "The Saints of the Church of Hexham and their Miracles," appears in Aelred of Rievaulx, *The Lives of the Northern Saints,* trans. Jane Patricia Freeland, CF 71 (Kalamazoo, MI: Cistercian Publications, 2006), 65–107. A survey of the publication history appears in Dutton's Introduction to the book, pp. 31–32. See Squire, "Aelred and the Northern Saints," 58–68. Also of interest are the few pages devoted to this work in Squire, *Aelred of Rievaulx,* 112–15. See also Dutton, Introduction, CF 71:14–20.

175. On the events of 1114, notably the archbishop of York's decision to replace all the married clergy in his diocese with unmarried clergy, in conformity with the canonical edicts of Gregorian reform, see chap. 2 above.

176. The saints are all bishops interred in the Church of Saint Andrew in Hexham: Eata (d. 685), Acca (d. 733), Frethbert (d. 767), Alchmund (d. 781), and Tilbert (d. 789).

177. The homily became the Prologue to the current text. See Aelred, *Saints of Hexham,* 65–68.

178. Squire, "Aelred and the Northern Saints," 61.

179. Squire, "Aelred and the Northern Saints," 63.

gion of the common people who must be given things they can touch and handle."[180] In other words, Squire suggests that the treatise's external, formal imperfections, including its more or less scattered organization as a patchwork of disparate pieces,[181] should be interpreted as a conscious textual reflection of the work's intended public: the common people, possessed of little culture and no interest in learned theological discourses, but who wanted reassurance of the continuing and effective protective presence of their venerated saints.

Aelred's own words seem to support this view of the text's purpose and intended readership. He asserts that the saints whose relics are preserved at Hexham "never cease to heap new miracles on old [*antiqua miracula novis cumulare non cessant*]"[182] and that in relating those miracles, he has four objectives: "to increase the devotion of those serving here [*ut sibi servientium semper augeatur devotio*], to assure their hope [*spes certificetur*], to nourish their love [*caritas nutriatur*], and by the sight of present gifts to confirm their expectation of future ones [*de perceptione presentium munerum, firma sit exspectatio futurorum*]."[183] This declaration of intent is important in shedding light on Aelred's methodology and revealing additional components in his religious histories not present in his civil and political histories.

---

180. Squire, "Aelred and the Northern Saints," 64.

181. Aelred's treatise gives the impression of a poorly aligned piece of marquetry work, in which two frameworks collide: on the one hand are the various miracle narratives, and on the other a narrative of the translation of the relics, upon which is superimposed a family history, relating the role of Aelred's forebears in the restoration of the church of Hexham after the ravages of the eighth- and ninth-century Danish invasions (Aelred, SS Hag 11 (CF 71:87–95). For additional detail, see Squire, "Aelred and the Northern Saints," 61–63. Squire describes the work's content with a particular focus on the narrative's points of rupture and transition.

182. Aelred, *Saints of Hexham*, 66.

183. Aelred, *Saints of Hexham*, 66.

*Memory of the Past as an Exercise in a Theologically Based
Spiritual Life*

In presenting his objectives in *Hexham*, Aelred superimposes
one of these goals on top of three complementary aims. The
first we have seen from as early as Aelred's first history, *The
Battle of the Standard*, probably written two years earlier, in
1153. Already in that text Aelred asserted that the historian's
work was to read present events in light of the past, in a way
that anticipates the future. The same idea appears in *Hexham*
when Aelred reminds his audience that "the just will be remembered forever [Ps 112:6]," so evoking the past before stating further on that "the sight of present gifts [*de perceptione
presentium munerum*]" should "confirm their expectation of
future ones [*firma sit exspectatio furturorum*]," evoking the
present and future.[184] The novelty of this assertion derives to
some extent from the present time of human history, where
"anticipation of the future" appears as an instrument of governance and administration of temporal affairs, an application
of the cardinal virtue of prudence and foresight. However, the
assertion's novelty additionally derives from the eschatological
perspective linked to eternity, where "future gifts" refer to the
promise of the life to come. While the perspective is strictly
moral in *Battle*, it expands to become theological in *Hexham*, a
point underlined by Aelred's explicit reference to the three
theological virtues: augmenting devotion or faith ("*semper
augeatur devotio*"), giving certainty to hope ("*spes certificetur*"),
and nourishing love or charity ("*caritas nutriatur*").

This change represents a considerable shift in perspective.
By inscribing the act of memorialization (in this case of the
saints and their past and present benevolence) within the
framework of theological life, Aelred radically transforms this
act. It becomes not only an ethical act or an instrument of governance (that is, a way of ordering actions) but also, above all,

---

184. Aelred, Hexham Prol (CF 71:66).

a theological act and an exercise in spiritual life. This aspect of memorialization is similar to the method of meditation that Aelred proposed to his sister the recluse five or six years later, between 1160 and 1162, in the third book of the treatise dedicated to her.[185] The method he proposes there also revolves around a threefold meditation: memory of the past by way of the *recordatio* of God's good acts through Jesus' life (*Formation* 29–31), memory of the present through the *experientia* of divine grace acting in one's present life (*Formation* 32), and consideration of the future as in the *consideratio* of the Last Judgment and beatitude promised to those who love God (*Formation* 33).

In both *Hexham* and *Formation*, Aelred's objective is the same: to stimulate his readers' confidence in the benefits of divine grace by showing that it is always at work and that it manifests itself in the life of everyone through the protective thaumaturgical acts of the saints. This idea is so important that Aelred repeats it at least twice more in *Hexham*, citing, as in *Ninian*, the Septuagint version of Ps 67:36: "God is wonderful in his saints [*Mirabilis Deus in sanctis suis*]."[186] This idea has two significant implications.

History as a Quasi-Sacramental Act: Historic Memory and the Continued History of Salvation

The first consequence corresponds directly to what we said previously regarding *The Life of Ninian*. To memorialize the saints' lives is to commemorate the continued action of God in human history, to show that the saints are faithfully cooperating with God as sacraments of his continued and active presence, and to demonstrate that their lives should be read (*legenda hagiographica*) as a moment in the one and only universal history of salvation, which, beginning with biblical history and revealed

---

185. For more detail on the *The Formation of Recluses*, see the discussion in chap. 6 above.

186. Hexham 6, 12 (CF 71:80, 99); Vita N 7 and 15, cited above (CF 71:50, 62).

by Scripture, continues to unfold in time, yesterday, today, and forever. To memorialize the saints is to show that there is no rupture between past, present, and future, and that through their lives the history of all humanity marches forward toward its ultimate end.[187] Thus Aelred considers the historian's work a quasi-sacramental act showing the continuity of salvation history and making the eternal present of divine salvation visible to the eyes of faith. Aelred suggests this in his treatment of Bishop Wilfrid in his Prologue to *Hexham*:

> it happened that after his death all of his people had recourse to him in this church, *as if to someone who was alive* [*ad eum quasi ad viventem confugerent*]. They consulted him in all their needs *as if he were present* [*in omnibus necessitatibus suis quasi ad praesentem consulerent*], and in troubles and distress they did not so much ask for his help as demand it [*non tam peterent quam exigerent*]. The most holy bishop, well disposed to their devotion and faith, was always present to those who called on him, generous to those who asked of him, consoling to the sad, helpful to the struggling, and supportive to the wretched—to such an extent that after his bodily presence was gone his spiritual grace flowed forth to them the more richly [*adeo ut subtracta praesentia corporali, uberius illis gratia proflueret spiritalis*].[188]

The second remark is connected to the one just made regarding the aid given by the saints to those who confidently invoke them and leads to a symmetrical corollary to what was said concerning Aelred's three civil histories: *Battle*, *Lament* plus *Genealogy*, and *The Life of Edward*.

When we examined these three treatises, we noted that their political component consisted of a reminder to princes and

---

187. Mayeski states that the narratives of saints' lives constitute "a theological genre, not only similar to the scriptures but, indeed, a continuation of them." She further adds that "the lives of the saints continue the essential story of salvation begun in Scripture" (Mayeski, "Clothing," 182, 184).

188. Aelred, Hexham Prol (CF 71:67–68).

kings of their civil and religious responsibilities. Princes' civil responsibility was to establish peace and justice in the societies and nations they governed. Their religious responsibility as *alter Christus* was to collaborate with God and orient the present toward the future—that is, to transform the present world into an anticipation or foreshadowing of the world to come. Through their mediation and their political mission, kings and princes of the world (or at least of Christian states) are called upon to cooperate with heaven in such a way that the divine work of salvation is at least partially realized here on earth.

In *Hexham*, as in *Ninian*, Aelred presents a perspective that is inverse yet symmetrical and complementary to the one just described. By focusing on the saints' past lives and reminding the reader that the saints work ceaselessly for the present benefit of people, Aelred shows that heaven now collaborates with earth. That is, he shows how through the saints' quasi-sacramental mediation and intercession for the good of humankind, God continuously accompanies men and women with his saving presence and helps the saints to liberate them from the chains that bind them, so that "we may freely run on the way of the Lord's commands."[189]

Aelred emphasizes these two traits of liberation and collaboration from the first miracle narrative in *Hexham*. In this narrative, a young man falsely accused of theft and condemned to death is miraculously freed from his chains at the last minute by Saint Wilfrid. However, Aelred adds that although the liberated man verbally invoked the name of Wilfrid alone, the other saints of Hexham also cooperated in the miracle[190]—a point neither fortuitous nor gratuitous. Aelred emphasizes that this cooperation must be thought of exponentially: not only as the collaboration of one particular saint with humankind, but the collaboration of all the saints together for the benefit of men and women.

---

189. Aelred, Hexham 1 (CF 71:69).

190. "Although he had named only the most blessed Wilfrid in his hour of death, no one supposed that the other saints who rest in this present church were not co-workers in this miracle" (Aelred, Hexham 1 [CF 71:69]).

In short we see here two inverse but complementary movements. In the civil histories, the movement is upward from earth to heaven, or from present history toward a future eternal life. In *Ninian* and *Hexham*, the movement is downward from heaven to earth, thanks to an active and shining communion of saints who illuminate present time from above.

We shall now determine whether this symmetrical movement reminiscent of Jacob's ladder is also present in Aelred's third ecclesiastical history, *A Certain Wonderful Miracle*. This brief narrative also relates a tale of liberation; in this sense we can assume hidden connections between this work and the other two treatises.

A Certain Wonderful Miracle: *"That . . . I Might . . . Not Remain Silent Concerning the Glory of Christ"*[191]

Of Aelred's seven historical treatises, *A Certain Wonderful Miracle*[192] is the shortest. It is also the least well known and the least studied by contemporary historians.[193] Only one known

191. [Translator's note: My ellipsis, to fit the English quotation to Burton's phrasing.]

192. The earlier common title was *The Nun of Watton*, or *De sanctimoniali de Wattun*, frequent among early editors of the text. It was used by Roger Twysden in his 1652 *Historiae Anglicanae Scriptores X* (2:337–422), and later by Migne in PL 195:789–96. The only extant manuscript containing the text bears the somewhat vaguer title, reproduced from the work's prologue, of *A Certain Wonderful Miracle* (*De quodam miraculo mirabili*). [Translator's note: The work is also known as *La Moniale de Watton* in French, and *The Nun of Watton* in English. Since *A Certain Wonderful Miracle* is the title of the most current English translation, echoing the critical edition, I use that title here.]

193. [Translator's note: Aelredus Rievallensis, "De quodam miraculo mirabili," CCCM 3:253*–*69; 135–46. Before this 2017 edition of the work, it had no critical edition.] For an English translation, see Aelred of Rievaulx, "A Certain Wonderful Miracle," in *Aelred of Rievaulx: The Lives of the Northern Saints*, trans. Jane Patricia Freeland, CF 71 (Kalamazoo, MI: Cistercian Publications, 2006), 109–22. In his biography, Squire devotes barely two pages to it (Squire, *Aelred of Rievaulx*, 117–18). He essentially limits himself to reproducing what he had

copy of this brief narrative, a mere seven columns in Migne's PL, still exists. It is found in a twelfth-century manuscript (Cambridge MS, Corpus Christi College 139), a collection of texts concerning the history of Hexham. In all probability the manuscript was compiled for a readership living in the environs of Hexham or, at the very least, for some religious community interested in Hexham's history, no doubt the community of Augustinian canons of Hexham Priory itself.

A similar conclusion must also be drawn regarding the addressee of the work. The text's publication was limited, to say the least, and it appears in a collection of texts devoted to the history of Hexham. It is therefore reasonable to think that it must have been a more or less private note addressed to a cleric emotionally attached to the community of Hexham,[194] and at any rate a dear friend, since Aelred refers to him as "most beloved father [*pater amantissime*]"[195] and "my dearest friend [*karissimo meo*]."[196] It is to this person that Aelred believed he

---

already written on the work in his previous article: Squire, "Aelred and the Northern Saints," 67–68. It was not until the 1990s that historians began to pay greater attention to this narrative, among them G. S. Daichman, "Misconduct in the Medieval Nunnery: Fact, Not Fiction," in *That Gentle Strength: Historical Perspectives on Women in Christianity,* ed. Linda L. Coon, Katherine J. Haldane, and Elisabeth W. Sommer (Charlottesville: University of Virginia Press, 1990), 97–117; Marsha Dutton, "Crime, Vengeance, and Miraculous Deliverance in the Gilbertine Monastery at Watton" (presentation, The General Theological Seminary Faculty Association, New York, November 1998); Marsha Dutton, "*A Certain Wonderful Miracle*: The Nuns of Watton and Aelred's Hagiographic Vision" (presentation, International Medieval Congress, Leeds, 1996); Marsha Dutton, Introduction, CF 71:1–37, esp. 20–26; Elizabeth Freeman, "Nuns in the Public Sphere: Aelred of Rievaulx's *De Sanctimoniali de Wattun* and the Gendering of Authority," *Comitatus* 17 (1996): 55–80.

194. Without being geographically near since, in the Epilogue, Aelred states that his addressee is "far removed from this region [*longe ab his partibus remoto*]" (Aelred, *Miracle,* CF 71:122). This would suggest that the addressee is far from the place where events took place, which is in Yorkshire or Northumbria.

195. Aelred, Mira Prol (CF 71:109).

196. Aelred, Mira Epil (CF 71:122).

"should reveal [*credidi revelandam*]"[197] the story that "should be written [*scribendum putavi*]"[198] of "a thing wonderful and unheard of in our time [*rem mirabilem et nostris saeculi inauditam*]," which in part he had "seen with [his] own eyes [*ex parte propriis oculis viderim*]" and which for the rest was reported to him by individuals worthy of confidence.[199]

Some historical context helps to reveal what was so wonderful about the event Aelred considered it important to relate, as well as the reasons he felt that he should tell the story.[200]

The Gilbertine Order and the Watton Community

Gilbert of Sempringham[201] founded a community at Sempringham in 1130–1131 with the approval of Bishop Alexander of Lincoln. Sempringham was a hamlet in Lincolnshire where Gilbert had been born and served as parish priest. His community consisted of seven young women, with whose education he was entrusted. Soon after the community's founding, he consulted with William, abbot of Rievaulx. At William's suggestion, Gilbert added a group of lay sisters and then lay brothers to his community to aid the nuns with their daily needs and chores. By 1139, the small community of Sempringham had grown and was able to expand to the Lincolnshire island of Haverholm, near Sleaford. This first foundation was later followed by numerous others, principally in Lincolnshire but also in Yorkshire.

In 1148, because of the growth of his congregation, Gilbert requested that his houses be affiliated with the Cistercian

---

197. Aelred, Mira Prol (CF 71:109).

198. Aelred, Mira Epil (CF 71:122).

199. Aelred, Mira Prol (CF 71:109).

200. In these passages Aelred twice uses the gerundive (translated with *should*) to underline his obligation or duty to recount the tale (Aelred, Mira Prol and Epil [CF 71:109, 122]).

201. For more detail, see Brian Golding, *Gilbert of Sempringham and the Gilbertine Order* (Oxford, UK: Oxford University Press, 1995).

Order, then at the height of its prestige. When he visited Cîteaux and presented his request to the Order's abbots assembled there in general chapter, they declined his request.
Returning to England, he decided to attach to each community
of nuns a group of canons regular, living in accordance with
the Rule of Saint Augustine, to serve as almoners and spiritual
directors to the sisters. It was this situation of nuns and canons
living in the same monastery that led to the sad and indecent
affair about which Aelred wrote.

The Narrative of a Dual Deliverance

The event occurred in the Priory of Saint Mary at Watton,
one of the two communities of his order that Gilbert had established in Yorkshire. This monastery was founded around
1150 in the vicinity of York under the patronage of Eustace Fitz
John. Shortly after its founding, Henry Murdac, archbishop of
York (1147–1153), placed a four-year-old girl there (*quaedam
puella quatuor ut putabatur annorum*), and asked the sisters of
the community to raise her.[202] Difficulties began during her
adolescence. The girl's heart began to long for love, while at
the same time she had "no love of religion, no concern for
order, no sense of the fear of God [*nullus ei circa religionem amor,
nulla circa ordinem sollicitudo, circa Dei timorem nullus affectus*]."[203]
What happened next was predictable. A lay brother, called to
perform some service, was introduced into the part of the community normally reserved for the nuns. He noticed the young
sister, seduced her, raped her, and then ran off. The affair came
to light shortly afterward when others noticed the young nun
was pregnant. Furious and inflamed with "the zeal of God
although not according to knowledge [*non secundum scientiam*;
Rom 10:2]," says Aelred,[204] her sisters put her in chains, had

202. In the material sense of the word, since Aelred speaks only of nourishing (*nutrienda*), not educating the girl.
203. Aelred, Mira 2 (CF 71:112).
204. Aelred, Mira 7 (CF 71:116).

the guilty brother brought to them, and forced him with his own hands to cut off the organ with which he had committed his sin.[205]

It is at this point that the "wonderful thing" occurred. The late archbishop, Henry Murdac, who had earlier entrusted the young girl to the nuns of Watton, appeared twice in a dream to the young sister in irons, enjoining her to recite certain psalms. These might have been, as Dutton suggests, the seven penitential psalms (Pss 6, 31, 37, 50, 101, 129, and 142).[206] In any case, when the time came for her to give birth the girl suddenly found herself, to the great amazement of all the nuns, miraculously no longer with child and liberated from one of the two fetters that had held her feet. Having learned of these events, Gilbert of Sempringham came to Watton and then went to Rievaulx to inform Aelred of the affair, ask his counsel, and press him to return to Watton with him. Aelred agreed to this request. When one of the Watton nuns asked him if they should reattach the fetter to the girl's foot, Aelred opposed it, declaring that to do so would be "cruel [*importunam*] and indicative of a lack of faith [*quoddam indicium infidelitatis*]. We should rather expect [*exspectandum potius*] and hope [*sperandum*] that he who freed her from the other would also release her from this one that still held her."[207]

After this Aelred returned to his monastery, where a few days later he received a letter from Gilbert informing him that the girl was finally freed from the second chain that had held her captive and seeking Aelred's counsel on what should be

---

205. [Translator's note: Burton has "forcent le jeune religieux à couper *de ses propres mains*" (emphasis added) (Pierre-André Burton, Aelred de Rievaulx (1110–1167): *Essai de biographie existentielle et spirituelle* [Paris: Cerf, 1010], 504). In the English translation, it is the young sister who is forced "to cut off his manhood with her own hands" (Aelred, Mira 7 [CF 71:117]). The Latin reads *Adducitur . . . illa malorum omnium causa, datur ei in manibus instrumentum, ac propriis manibus uirum abscidere inuita compellitur* (CCCM 3:142).]

206. Dutton, Introduction (CF 71:119).

207. Aelred, Mira 11 (CF 71:121).

done. Aelred's brief reply is inspired by Scripture and the figure of Saint Peter: "What God has cleansed you must not call common [Acts 10:15], and her whom he has loosed [*absolvit*] you must not bind [*ne ligaveris;* see Matt 16:19]."[208] Aelred's narrative closes on these words. They are followed only by a brief epilogue a few lines long. We must now show why the abbot of Rievaulx sought to relate this event. The answer to this question is delicate and involves two levels of meaning. One is explicit, based on what Aelred himself says in the Prologue and Epilogue. The other is implicit and gleaned only by reading between the lines.

Showing That "The Lord Is Pleased With Those Who Fear Him [Ps 146:11]"[209]

This story centers on two occurrences of deliverance. First, the young nun of Watton is delivered from an unwanted pregnancy, the unfortunate consequence of an act in which she was more victim than guilty. Second, the young woman is also miraculously freed from her chains and from the punishment her fellow sisters had cruelly inflicted upon her. In other words, by telling this story, Aelred emphasizes God's work of liberation. Aelred has already underscored this point in the opening miracle narrative of *Hexham*. The novelty of the present narrative has to do with the fact that the beneficiary of this liberation is not an innocent person accused of theft, but a young woman at least partially guilty of sin. In this sense, the liberation appearing in *Miracle* is greater because it involves the forgiveness of sins signified by the physical delivery from pregnancy, as well as a release from the punishment inflicted by human justice signified by the fetters falling from the girl's feet.

What Aelred shows above all is how the full extent of divine mercy manifested itself in the life of the young nun. This is

208. Aelred, Mira 11 (CF 71:122).
209. Aelred, Mira 11 (CF 71:121).

precisely the reason for which it was so important for him to recount these events, as he explains from the very beginning of the Prologue: "To know and yet hide [*tegere*] the Lord's miracles, the clear signs of his divine loving-kindness [*manifesta divinae pietatis indicia*], is an aspect of sacrilege [*portio sacrilegii est*]."[210] Intended to show "the glory of Christ,"[211] "the whole treasury of mercy [*omnes thesauri misericordiae*],"[212] and "the ever-merciful loving-kindness of Christ [*misericordissima pietas Christi*]" toward sinners,[213] Aelred's narrative also inspires confidence in the idea that however great a sinner one may be, one must "never despair of the goodness of him who so exercises justice as not to forget mercy."[214] Inspiring this hope is therefore the narrative's goal for, to use the Prologue's terms, "to deprive everyone of what can console people of the present [*praesentibus ad consolationem*], instruct those who come afterward [*ad aedificationem posteris*], and increase the devotion of all [*omnibus ad devotionem*] is shameful."[215]

To make clear that "*the Lord is pleased with those who fear him* [Ps 146:11]"[216] and to stimulate sinners' confidence in Christ's great mercy are the two principal goals of *A Certain Wonderful Miracle*. However, underlying this repeatedly stated twofold objective are numerous implicit issues.

Implicit Issues in Miracle: *The Watton Narrative as Exemplum*

Aelred's treatment of the Watton miracle, then, focuses primarily on making manifest the extent of divine mercy and

210. Aelred, Mira Prol (CF 71:109).
211. Aelred, Mira Epil (CF 71:122).
212. Aelred, Mira 8 (CF 71:118).
213. Aelred, Mira 8 (CF 71:117).
214. Aelred, Mira 8 (CF 71:118).
215. Aelred, Mira Prol (CF 71:109).
216. Aelred, Mira 11 (CF 71:121).

stimulating sinners' confidence in it. In this sense it can be considered an exemplum, a parable with a theological or doctrinal lesson. The lesson here is that no one is excluded from Christ's generously granted forgiveness of sins. But beyond this clearly stated goal, hidden pastoral and institutional questions are also present in the work.

Pastoral Issues: Justice and the Zeal of God "According to Knowledge" and Mercy

The most obvious of these issues is a pastoral one. It appears through three scriptural quotations already identified in passing. By insisting on the young nun's miraculous twofold deliverance, and by interpreting it as a sign of divine mercy, Aelred adopts an opposing position to the punitive attitude of the Watton community. He thus reproaches the community in two ways. In condemning the young girl and inflicting the cruel punishment of fetters, the excessively severe community rejects Jesus' own example and instead privileges justice over mercy, a point that is underlined by the reference to the Epistle to the Romans, through which Aelred praises the nuns' zeal in avenging God's tarnished honor, while simultaneously reproaching them for having done so with no discretion, for "having the zeal of God although not according to knowledge [*non secundum scientiam*; Rom 10:2]."[217]

This rebuke is all the sharper for Aelred's opening to the narrative, where he states that the Watton community, both at that time and in the past, had a great reputation for the quality of its religious observances as well as for the high degree of mystical experience attained by a number of the sisters. The lesson seems obvious, even if Aelred leaves it up to the reader to infer it. No matter how faithful a monastic community is to its religious observances, or how many of its members exhibit

---

217. Aelred, Mira Prol (CF 71:109).

mystical graces, it is all for nothing if charity, the greatest of all virtues, is absent, especially in the matter of mercy toward the weakest and most sinful.

In truth, this is a lesson seen before. It resonates perfectly with Aelred's conception of his own pastoral ministry, a conception underlined by his biographer, who writes that Aelred made Rievaulx "the mother of mercy."[218] But this is not the only pastoral lesson that can be taken from these events. There is a second, that having attained a high degree of perfection in religious observances does not mean that a religious community can place justice ahead of divine mercy. This judgment appears clearly in the two Petrine verses (Acts 10:15 and Matt 16:19) on which Aelred bases his final advice to Gilbert: "What God has cleansed you must not call common, and her whom he has loosed [*absolvit*] you must not bind [*ne ligaveris*]."[219] This indeed cuts short all pretension that human justice supersedes divine mercy.

This lesson has two other consequences. The first has to do with what could be called the Petrine character of a superior's pastoral ministry. In *Miracle*, Aelred indicates that the fundamental role of pastors or superiors is to contribute to God's work by becoming ministers of mercy. That is, they are to authenticate through their pastoral authority the liberating action of grace in the hearts and lives of men and women. The second consequence is an extension of the foregoing and completes Aelred's concern with cooperation between heaven and earth. We have indicated that across Aelred's various historical works there exists an upward and downward movement between the two. Seen mostly in the civil histories, the upward movement makes manifest political authorities' collaboration in God's work of creation, making present time, or the city of humans, a foreshadowing of the world to come. Most prevalent in the religious histories, the downward movement reveals

218. Walter, VA 29 (CF 57:118); see Aelred, Mira 8 (CF 71:118).
219. Aelred, Mira 9 (CF 71:122).

the benevolent presence of Christ through the saints' mediation in people's everyday lives, or the mystery of the communion of saints crossing the boundaries of time through God's eternally present saving actions over the course of history. In the Watton narrative, Aelred shows that in reality these two movements, far from being opposites, are joined to one another. The benevolent actions of the saints toward humans—in this case Henry Murdac's miraculous intervention on behalf of the girl—show God's mercy toward sinners and thus represent a downward movement. This downward movement is authenticated and certified through the intermediary of pastors' Petrine ministry; in this case Aelred's final judgment represents an upward movement confirming the downward one.

Such considerations allow us to understand much better two areas that could be held separate and distinct, but that Aelred tightly interweaves. On the one hand there is history perceived in the sequence of events, that is, unfolding in time and experienced by men and women as it progresses toward its final end. On the other hand, there is historical narrative, the result of the historian's reading and interpretation of these events and integrating them into a coherent story.

The first of these two areas—history advancing toward its final end—contributes a broader perspective to Aelred's theology of history, since in the miracle of Watton we can see the full extent of the complementarity Aelred uses in building a world, from beginning to end, on the foundation of universal friendship. This said, it will be shown in the next section that this combined upward and downward movement does not end with cooperation between heaven and earth, but extends also into the framework of human social life and the various orders of which it is comprised.

The second area—Aelred's methodology—consists of the element of narrative theology highlighted earlier in Mayeski's work. The articulation of this area with the first has been highlighted by Dutton: "The narrative is for Aelred not an essentially moral or exemplary one, but rather a historical account:

the story of God's action in human time and space."[220] We can convert this into an assertion that, for Aelred, the historian's work is to bring to light the acting presence of God in the historical framework of human space and time. The question is heavy with implications both in terms of a general theology of history (history as hagiography or the history of the saints) and in terms of Aelred's spiritual rereading of biblical history (the *lectio divina* as an act of transposition). For now we focus on drawing out additional issues implicit in Aelred's Watton narrative, in particular those concerning institutional rather than pastoral questions.

Institutional Issues: Integration of the Sexes, Freedom, Vocation, and Pitfalls to Avoid

Aelred does not explicitly address institutional issues in *Miracle*, but the attentive reader cannot fail to spot them. At least three such issues are implicit to the story. In an unpublished study[221] Dutton hypothesizes that *Miracle* was composed in the context of a serious institutional crisis that the Gilbertine Order underwent during the 1160s, following, on the one hand, a revolt by the lay brothers, and on the other accusations brought against the order for sexual impropriety between nuns and canons. The narrative is therefore a disculpatory text, forming part of a larger corpus of epistolary exchanges intended to defend the Gilbertine congregation's reputation. This

---

220. Dutton, "Historian's Historian," 441. Of note is Dutton's pertinent distinction between story (narrative) and history (events), which unfortunately does not exist in French, since in both cases the word *histoire* is used. That said, one must not exaggerate the opposition Dutton appears to establish here between moral and exemplary value on the one hand and historical value on the other. We would argue that far from excluding each other, these two elements complement each other, the former being subsumed and integrated into the latter the moment Aelred begins to write a hagiographic narrative. This is part of Aelred's unique genius as a historian and as a theologian: that he crafts the framework of a narrative theology from a theology of history.

221. Dutton, "Wonderful Miracle."

objective is reflected by numerous details within the narrative—for example, the care Aelred takes to underline the quality of the Watton nuns' regular life and Gilbert's extreme and constant vigilance (*vigilantissimus sensus in custodia disciplinae*) against all occasions of sin (*ad excludendam vitiorum materium*), along with the multiple precautions he took (*tot tam exquisita machinamenta*). But however explicitly Aelred vouches for the Gilbertine Order's good reputation, an event like that occurring at Watton could only constitute a vigorous invitation to greater prudence for the founder and the superiors of this integrated congregation. And Aelred's narrative, while far from being an explicit and pitiless condemnation of this form of religious life, nevertheless does present itself as a warning against the very real risk of abuses and deviant behavior.

This is no doubt the main institutional issue present in Aelred's opuscule. But two other less apparent issues are connected to it. The first concerns the fact that at the request of their bishop, Henry Murdac, the nuns of Watton took responsibility for a four-year-old girl. The subsequent events at Watton show the risks involved when individuals are institutionally placed into a religious community before the age of reason and without having any religious vocation. Thus, through his narrative, Aelred rebels indirectly against the common medieval practice (and one that, in other forms, was still in effect up until more recent times)[222] of bringing relatively young children into religious institutions for education in the secret hope that some of them might ultimately have a religious vocation. In other words, the story of the young nun of Watton should be

---

222. For the Middle Ages, one has only to think of Aelred's contemporary, Suger (d. 1151), who entered the abbey of Saint Denis around 1090 at roughly ten years of age, or the example of Hildegarde of Bingen (1098–1179), placed at the age of eight in a Benedictine convent, probably Disibodenberg, in Germany. We might also mention the thirteenth century's Saint Gertrude of Helfta, placed in a Benedictine monastery at the age of five. For more recent times, it is natural to think of the boarding school tradition, so prevalent in a good number of Benedictine and Cistercian monasteries of the nineteenth and twentieth centuries.

458 The Time of Spiritual Maturity

read as Aelred's fervent plea to respect a person's inalienable freedom in matters of religious vocation, a respect that would require institutions to admit only persons of a sufficiently mature age as candidates for a religious life.

There is finally a third institutional issue present in Aelred's opuscule. In relating the tragic story of the young nun brought into the monastic community of Watton at too early an age, Aelred indirectly suggests that nuns are unsuited to serve as educators and nursemaids. In other words, Aelred makes it clear that a monastery can be many things, but certainly not a nursery school.

We do not gratuitously assert the foregoing as implicit lessons in Aelred's brief work. It will be recalled that in the spiritual guide addressed to his sister the recluse, some time after the narrative of the miracle of Watton,[223] Aelred explicitly recommends to his sister, "Never allow children access to your cell. It is not unknown for a recluse to take up teaching and turn her cell into a school [*cellam suam vertunt in scholam*]"[224] and thereby run the risk of facing "worldly and sensual temptations, and amid them all what becomes of her continual remembrance of God?"[225]

The History and the Portrait of the Church through Aelred's Liturgical Sermons

Throughout our presentation of Aelred's seven historical works, we have progressively laid out the methods and concerns evidenced in Aelred's historical praxis, showing that this

---

223. *Formation* is typically dated between 1160 and 1162. *Miracle* was probably composed a bit later, around 1165–1166, at the time when the young heroine of the story must have reached the age of puberty.

224. Aelred of Rievaulx, "A Rule of Life for a Recluse," in Aelred of Rievaulx, *Treatises. Pastoral Prayer*, trans. Mary Paul Macpherson, CF 2 (Kalamazoo, MI: Cistercian Publications, 1971), 49.

225. Aelred, Inst incl 4 (CF 2:49).

praxis takes the form of a narrative theology of history. This narrative theology is methodologically inseparable from a reading of events intended to uncover within them the acting presence of God in the unfolding of time and to show within that unfolding the march of human history as the achievement of the divine plan to recapitulate all things in the person of Christ.

Such historical praxis has numerous consequences, of which we here point out two. The first relates to the quasi-sacramental nature of history; the second, an extension of the first, relates to the art of reading biblical history (*lectio divina*) as a mirror of universal history. In chapter 10 we discuss the more global view of Aelred's work as a mystical cosmic history.

The two most noted contemporary historians studying Aelred's work, Dutton and Freeman, have each shown, one from a theological perspective and the other a sociological angle, that Aelred's historical work bears the imprint of a new sensibility in the conception and writing of history. This new sensibility, which appeared in the twelfth century, is one that Aelred himself may well have helped to spread.

According to Dutton, expanding on an earlier study by Marie-Dominique Chenu,[226] this new praxis is characterized by the "awakening of an active awareness of human history,"[227] by virtue of which the twelfth century represents a "turning point between the ahistorical worldview of the past and a new age alert to the reality and theological significance of human history."[228] Dutton has convincingly shown that this passage from one conception of history to the other manifests itself in Aelred's writing in two ways. The first of these is by the growing attention Aelred paid to the interaction between events and an insistence on the connections between the three temporal

226. Marie-Dominique Chenu, "Theology and the New Awareness of History," in *Nature, Man and Society in the Twelfth Century*, trans. Jerome Taylor and Lester K. Little (Chicago: University of Chicago Press, 1968), 162.

227. Dutton, "Historian's Historian," 410.

228. Dutton, "Historian's Historian," 411.

modalities of past, present, and future. For Aelred, writing history is no longer simply a matter of preserving knowledge of the past or edifying his readers through *exempla* of moral value. Henceforth, historiography will also involve showing that events are the fruit of a "process of time" or the result of a "historical connection" tying the past to the present.[229] In this sense, historiography consists of drawing out the causal links between events and showing the interdependence of the present and the past.

Additionally, the new twelfth-century conception of history that Aelred helped create had a second consequence relating to the manner in which it is written. Historiography would not involve only the articulation of past, present, and future; it would also involve discovering, within this chain of events, traces of God's acting presence in human space and time. Again building on Chenu's work, Dutton states that in the same way that some in the twelfth century began to study cosmology in order to better understand the place of humans in the universe, others cast their gaze on human life in a world that changes through time and space in order to uncover God's actions in the world. This contributed to "a new integration of *history* with *theology*, centering in the development of the lives of men and women in human time and in God's interaction with humans within temporal processes."[230]

We have seen such a focus manifest itself in Aelred's work through his effort to show multiple networks of mutual dependence and cooperation linking heaven and earth, God and humankind, in downward and upward movements. The downward movement consists of divine benevolence, the mediation of Christ, and the communion of saints, while the upward movement consists of the cooperation of princes with ecclesiastical authorities, and the king as *alter Christus* or mediator between God and man. Furthermore, through his doc-

---

229. Dutton, "Historian's Historian," 440.
230. Dutton, "Historian's Historian," 442.

trine of spiritual friendship, understood in its fullest sense as a cosmic principle of universal harmony, Aelred also managed to integrate history and cosmology—an idea unique in twelfth-century theological reflections.

To put it another way, the historian's work becomes for Aelred a multidimensional theological act. In this act historical narratives tend toward reading events as the advent of God and his reign in the world, simultaneously including several things. Such readings include first a theology of Creation, that is, a cosmology or a history of the universe. Next they contain a theology of history, or the presentation of human history in its social and political dimensions as the space in which celestial Jerusalem is foreshadowed and realized. Third, these readings involve a theology of the incarnation, or the history of humankind as the continued chronicle of the salvational mediation of Christ and the saints. Finally, we see in these readings a theology of redemption, or history in its progressive march toward its final end and toward the recapitulation of all things in Christ.

In a word, by passing from historical event to historical narrative, Aelred transforms histori-ography, the recounting of historical events in written form, into a hagi-ography, recounting of the story of divine holiness and salvation revealed and made manifest through events in the unfolding of human historical time. As Philippe Nouzille[231] has rightly stated, historiography and hagiography become at one and the same time philocalic: epiphany or theophany of divine beauty in the world and in the faces of humans, called upon to be formed with ever-increasing transparency "in the likeness and image" of Christ, the primordial sacrament, "in which the fullness of divinity dwells corporally."[232] Thus the act of writing history is

---

231. The reader should consult the section "Philocalie" in Philippe Nouzille, *Expérience de Dieu et théologie monastique au XIIe siècle* (Paris: Les Éditions du Cerf, 1999), 317–23.

232. Nouzille, *Expérience*, 318, 320, which discusses the philocalic and sacramental components of Aelred's historiography. There Nouzille expands

framed in the mystery of the incarnation itself and is inseparable from Cistercian devotion to Christ's humanity.[233]

This framing of historiography allows Aelred to assert the
ontologically sacramental character of all reality, including
both creatures and history. First, it includes creatures from
vertical and horizontal perspectives. Vertically, through the
right of creation, every creature points to its origin by its participation in the very being, beauty, and goodness of God, or
what Nouzille calls "the gift received."[234] Horizontally, through
this goodness that is the usefulness accorded to each creature
for the benefit of all others, each creature points to all others
by the duty of mutual reciprocity, or what Nouzille calls "the
gift given."[235] What holds true for creation as such also holds
true by analogy for human history. This interim diachronically
points toward its origin and its end. Synchronically, as a particular moment in human history, it becomes a temporal sequence entrusted to humans for their use. Through wise
government and the just administration of material goods and
political space, men and women can establish in society the
very order of charity desired eternally by God. Thus directing

---

on the ideas of Hans Urs von Balthasar and speaks of an aesthetic that derives
from a theological ontology by virtue of which every being draws its beauty
from its conformity with and participation in the Word, as *forma* and *species*.

233. For more on this point, see: Nouzille, *Expérience*, 320. Also important
is Freeman's demonstration that for Cistercian authors, and especially for
Aelred, there is such a close tie between their affective theology (as seen in
their tender devotion to Christ's humanity) and the field of historiography
"that the two areas can be most profitably investigated in tandem" (Freeman,
Introduction, to *Narratives of a New Order* [Turnhout: Brepols, 2002], 13).

234. Nouzille, *Expérience*, 320.

235. Nouzille, *Expérience*, 320. On this theme, the reader should also see
Spec car 1.2.4–5, where Aelred describes the original beauty of all creation in
its native order (all things "well-ordered that they may give splendor to the
universe itself [*bene ordinata ad ipsius universitatis decorem*]"): "in as far as each
thing in the universe keeps its proper place, time, and measure, all are in
excellent order [*in quantum in ipsa universitate unaquaeque res convenientem sibi
et locum, et tempu, et modum obtinet, optime ordinata sunt*" (Aelred, CF 17:89, 90).

the movement of the world toward its final end, they can build and foreshadow the City of God in present time.

Two points emerge from all we have just said. It is appropriate once more to reformulate these two interconnected points. The first concerns Aelred's work as a historiographer. It is evident that this work goes beyond the simple act of memorializing the *res gestae* of the past and is instead an eminently theological act of interpretation intended to frame events in the long history of salvation, which, from original creation to the recapitulation of all things in God, embraces every era in time by passing through the human mediation of history's agents. The second point, related to the first, concerns the fact that in order to give himself up to such a theological interpretation of events, Aelred employs the general hermeneutical key of the Cistercian doctrine of the ordering of all things through charity, albeit broadened to the larger dimensions of society and history. This doctrine, originally developed in the ascetic and mystical context of the spiritual anthropology of conversion, is one Aelred made uniquely his own as he personally and progressively assimilated it into the framework of his own spiritual theology of a universal and cosmic friendship.[236]

Lectio Divina *as Transposition; Biblical History Read as a Mirror of Universal History*

These two points relative to the hermeneutics and theology of history in Aelred's civil and religious narratives are of great

---

236. On these two points, Freeman states that the Cistercians' historical writings "are relevant to, and inextricably linked with, the Cistercians' broader spirituality and daily communal life" and that the tie between Cistercian historiography and Cistercian spiritual concerns (specifically a theology of fraternal communal life) is so tight that it offers "a means of entry into the sometimes ambiguous histories and, also, a greater appreciation of just how broadly the order's famous cenobitic theology (such as the doctrines of charity and friendship) permeated all areas of Cistercian life" (Freeman, *Narratives*, 14–15).

importance since they concern not only Aelred's historiography but also his reading of biblical accounts in the Old and New Testaments. In his "Art of Reading" Revelation, Aelred employs an "art of transposition" closely tied to the four-level scriptural interpretation of the church fathers' exegetic practice, as masterfully described by Father Henri de Lubac.[237] However, Aelred's use of this exegetic method is, if not unique, at least personal and easily identifiable.

Our discussion of this type of biblical exegesis is limited to two particularly fruitful lines of inquiry relating to the art of historical transposition by which Aelred interprets biblical narratives either as a mirror of personal spiritual experience, wherein the stages of biblical history correspond to stages of growth, or as a mirror of the universal history of humanity. Examples from Aelred's vast body of homilies illustrate these two elements.

Reading Scripture as a Mirror of Personal Spiritual Experience: Sermons 24, 6, 20, and 27

The first historical transposition in Aelred's reading of Scripture, and also the most frequent in his homilies because of his desire to edify his brothers morally, involves tracing parallels between the stages of biblical history and the stages of a monk's spiritual growth. The most representative example of this pattern appears in S 24, for the Nativity of Saint Mary, from the First Clairvaux Collection,[238] where Aelred comments on Christ's genealogy as reported in the gospel of Matthew (Matt 1:1-17). This genealogy is divided into three successive sequences of fourteen generations, showing the stages through which humans must pass spiritually in order to ascend to

---

237. Henri de Lubac, *Exégèse médiévale: Les quatre sens de l'Écriture* (Paris: Aubier, 1959–1964).

238. Aelred of Rievaulx, *The Liturgical Sermons: The First Clairvaux Collection*, trans. Theodore Berkeley and M. Basil Pennington, CF 58 (Kalamazoo, MI: Cistercian Publications, 2001), 327–45.

Christ: "I think we should take these three groupings as three states in which are all those who want to ascend these steps to the place from which Christ descended to us."[239] Aelred then details the three successive sequences of fourteen generations before transposing them (S 24.23–47) into the realm of monastic experience, starting with renunciation of the world, moving through mastery of the passions along with prayer and inner pacification, and ending in the transformative vision of God, with the whole process supported by the impetus of desire. Aelred shares his perspective and goal with that of the Cistercian fathers of his time: the formation of Christ within the individual's soul. And indeed, he reiterates this point in the sermon: "Here and now, then, brothers, let us ascend. And let us begin from Christ and let us arrive at Christ. Let us begin from Christ as a human being, and let us arrive at Christ where he is one with the Father on high."[240]

That said, when Aelred asserts that "the Evangelist aimed not only at this—simply showing us the father from whom Christ was born and letting us know his human lineage—but also that we might derive spiritual fruit from his physical ancestry," he demonstrates that as an attentive reader of the Scripture, he is fully conscious of the process he puts in motion.[241] He tells his audience that in composing Christ's genealogy, the evangelist, not wanting to overstep the numerical framework of three sequences of fourteen generations (S 24.5), found himself forced to modify his presentation of the course of history, and so "he omitted from his enumeration some fathers and sons who belong to this lineage."[242] Aelred would not have been much of a historian had he not noted this detail. At the same time, the remark only makes clearer his keen awareness of his own role as an interpreter and of the spiritual, hermeneutical key he uses to engage in that role.

---

239. Aelred, S 24.10 (CF 58:330).
240. Aelred, S 24.16 (CF 58:332).
241. Aelred, S 24.4 (CF 58:328).
242. Aelred, S 24.5 (CF 58:328–29).

We could compile one example after another of this type of interpretation in Aelred's sermons. We see one example in S 6, for the Feast of Saint Benedict,[243] where he compares the Jews' three-day march into the wilderness to make a sacrifice to God (Exod 8:21-23) both to spiritual life's renunciation of self, sin, and one's own will, and to Benedict's first four degrees of humility. Another example comes in a different "sermon for the Feast of Saint Benedict,"[244] in which he compares stages of the conquest of the Promised Land to the principal trials of spiritual life and the struggle against evil thoughts.[245]

Finally, there is an example in the more complex S 27, for the Feast of All Saints,[246] which shows Aelred's virtuosity in this technique. In the second part of this homily (S 27.11–20), Aelred discusses the eight beatitudes according to the gospel of Matthew (Matt 5:1-10). He draws a parallel between the beatitudes and the six days of Creation as well as the principal virtues and works of monastic life—humility, study of Scripture, struggle against evil thoughts, strength and patience, fraternal charity and compassion. From an explicitly spiritual and mystical perspective, the goal of the whole comparative process is once more to lead the individual, in time, to be "cre-

243. Aelred, S 6 (CF 58:129–41).

244. S 54, in Aelred of Rievaulx, *The Liturgical Sermons: The Durham and the Lincoln Collections*, trans. Kathryn Krug, Lewis White, and the *Catena Scholarium*, CF 80 (Collegeville, MN: Cistercian Publications, 2018), 85–103.

245. On the importance of this sermon, in which Aelred appropriates the monastic spiritual theory of the struggle against evil thoughts (Evagrius, Cassian, Saint Gregory the Great), see Elias Dietz, "Aelred on the Capital Vices," CSQ 43 (2008): 271–93. Parallels to this comparison can be found in some of Aelred's other sermons; e.g., in S 75, on the Birth of Blessed Mary, he splits biblical history from Abraham to Jesus into six periods (Aelred, S 75.17 [CF 80:344]). Similarly, S 56, for the Feast of Saint Benedict, contains a reprise of monastic life's three-part renunciation of self, vice, and will (see Cassian's *Third Conference: On the Three Sorts of Renunciations*), with Aelred comparing it to the three-stage march of the Jews through the desert—from Egypt to the Red Sea, from the Red Sea to the Sinai Desert, and from the Sinai Desert to Jordan (CF 80:117–25).

246. Aelred, S 27 (CF 58:370–79).

ated, or rather re-created, to the image of God" (S 27.19), to lead him or her, in terms of eternal life, to come "to rest and peace of mind," where "servile fear is banished to be succeeded by filial love [see 1 John 5:21]" (S 27.20), and where also "from being a servant one becomes a son of God, so that one may rest in God and God in oneself" (S 27.20).

Reading Scripture as a Mirror of Universal Human History: SS 76 and 77, for All Saints

Aelred's second transpositional way of reading Scripture— or of biblical history read as a mirror of human history—is less common in Aelred's homilies than the first, but its importance should not be underestimated. Two representative examples can be found in SS 76 and 77, for the Feast of All Saints, in the Durham collection.[247] They are closely connected insofar as they both center on the same guiding principle—the list of the twelve patriarchs presented in the book of Numbers (Num 2:3-31)—in order to paint a broad-brush picture of church history in four successive periods, while at the same time providing a summary description of the church's four-part internal constitution.

In S 76, Aelred relies on the letter of the book of Numbers to explain that the people of Israel made up of twelve tribes in four army divisions should be considered a foreshadowing of the spiritual Israel that is the church (S 76.7). Having posed this hermeneutical transposition, from the letter to the spirit of the text, from biblical to church history, and from the people of Israel to the ecclesiastical community,[248] Aelred specifies that

---

247. Aelred, CF 80:357–68, 369–77.

248. Aelred finds the epistemological legitimacy of this reading in Scripture itself, in the writings of Saint Paul, whose first Epistle to the Corinthians he cites (here as in S 76.7)—"All this happened to them as an example, and they have been written as a warning to us" (1 Cor 10:11)—along with two other Pauline verses: "the letter kills: but the spirit quickens" (2 Cor 3:6), and "what things soever were written were written for our learning" (Rom 15:4).

the four divisions comprising the army of Israel correspond respectively to the four periods of the church (S 76.9): the call (Christ's preaching), the trial (the first persecution in Jerusalem and dispersal of the church), the consolation (the conversion of kings beginning with the peace of the church), and finally the end time, which will begin with the coming of the Antichrist (the end of the world).

Having established this pattern, Aelred relies on the etymology of Hebrew names to examine each of the four periods one by one, in terms of the moral and ecclesiastical signification of the three tribes mentioned in each army division/historical period. The first is the apostolic body: apostles and disciples gathered around Christ in faith (Judah: confession), hope (Issachar: recompense), and charity (Zebulun: strength). The second consists of the martyrs, characterized by oblivion of present reality and desire for future reality (Reuben: vision), constancy supported by the certainty that sadness will change to joy (Simeon: fulfillment of sadness), and the torments to which the martyrs are subjected (Gad: trial).

Then comes the third period. For the purposes of this study it is the most interesting since, in contrast with the others, Aelred considers it coexistent with the entire history of the church, from the end of the persecutions until the end of time. This consideration allows him to provide his audience with a socio-religious description of the church's three distinct and complementary orders: the doctors who direct and govern the world (Ephraim: fruitfulness), the religious who renounce the world and "forget what is earthly in favor of the celestial, what is temporal in favor of what is eternal, what is human in favor of what is divine" (Manasseh: forgetfulness; S 76.26), and the lay people engaged in worldly life (identified by Aelred as married men and women: *conjugati*), who, possessing "temporal goods," have a mission to "use them moderately, manage them prudently, and distribute them mercifully [*temporalia sapienter distribuere*]" (Benjamin: the right hand; S 76.28). The fourth period consists of those whom Aelred calls "a very strong squadron of the perfect" (S 76.29) and coincides with the end of the world's temporal history, or the Antichrist's final persecution of Christ's church. In this period are found the last three tribes, representing mercy (Dan: judgment), suffering persecution for justice (Asher: the blessed), and charity (Naphtali: growth).

Leaving aside the millenarian and apocalyptic tone Aelred gives to the fourth and final period of universal history, which would demand its own extensive examination beyond the scope of the present work, Aelred presents that history from three perspectives. Apart from the perspective of Judgment, which is traditional when speaking of final ends, or the end of time and history, Aelred adds two other perspectives, representative of his entire theological doctrine and bearing his particular stamp.

The first pertains to his ecclesiology and the second to his theology of history. Aelred joins the two under the "sign" of Christ and the cross, the space in which all history is completed and recapitulated. In fact, when he speaks of "Asher, that is, blessed" (S 76.31), he immediately underlines that this identification concerns not a specific, isolated group, like Catharism's view of the "perfect," for example. Rather, it concerns the multitude of the faithful who together, and thus with an ecclesiastical character, unite to form Jesus' seamless tunic (see John 19:23) and receive from him their perfection by placing themselves under the sign of a more glorious triumph, the banner of the Cross: "Blessed, truly blessed are those in whom Jesus' cloak, now woven from many faithful believers, will be completed with the sign of a more glorious victory" (S 76.31). But at the same time he takes advantage of the etymology of the name *Naphtali* and adds that all of human history, through the church and by virtue of "a kind of inner breadth of charity"[249] stronger than death, is drawn toward the fullness of communion with

---

249. Aelred, S 76.31–32 (CF 80:368).

Christ from which nothing, neither life nor death, can ever separate it (see Rom 8:38-39).

The sermon ends with this grandiose vision. In keeping with his consistent desire to edify the conscience of his listeners, Aelred specifies that this symbolic reading focused on universal history must be coupled with a second reading, a "reflection on how this pertains to moral teaching" (S 76.33). He writes that "we too have our time periods, in which, divided by squadrons, we celebrate our spiritual watch around God's tabernacle" (S 76.33). But "because the hour has already passed" (S 76.33), he chooses to address this question on another occasion in S 77.

In this sermon, Aelred employs the same principle of hermeneutical transposition from the letter of the text and history to the spirit of religious experience. He also employs the same interpretive technique based on the etymology of proper nouns[250] as in S 76. But instead of relying on the passage from the book of Numbers that served as the basis for that sermon, he here uses the list of the twelve tribes of Israel, enumerated in a different order, from the passage in the book of Revelation read on All Saints' Day (Rev 7:4-8). This passage recounts the vision of the 144,000 from all the tribes of Israel, 12,000 per tribe. On the other hand, as the book of Numbers no doubt suggested to him, Aelred divides the twelve tribes into groups of three in this sermon as well, placing the groups under the four principal chiefs: the Apostles (Judah, Reuben, and Gad), the Martyrs (Asher, Naphtali, and Manasseh), the Confessors (Simeon, Levi, and Issachar), and finally the Virgins (Zebulun,

---

250. He adds to this the symbolism of numbers: four for those who are in the world (the four natural elements, the four points of the compass, the four cardinal virtues), forty for those who renounce the world (Jesus' forty days in the desert, the forty days of Exodus, etc.), and a hundred for those who govern the world (the number hundred being the symbol of perfection and therefore of contemplation and the necessary perspective needed to make just decisions). This description corresponds to the third period described in S 76.

Joseph, and Benjamin). Finally he gives a moral interpretation to each of the twelve tribes, with the tribe name corresponding to a virtue, except in the case of the fourth category, where all three names refer to the virtue of chastity and its necessary inner dispositions. This apparently incomplete sermon, missing at the very least the final doxology, ends on an ecclesiological note comparable to that found in S 76. But instead of using the image of the tunic here, he now turns to the image of progeniture, implying that the twelve tribes/virtues constitute together the Body of Christ: "the offspring of the true Israel, namely, of our Lord Jesus Christ."[251]

Opening a View To Infinity: Toward a Mystical Theology of History

The texts just examined are no doubt sufficient evidence of the theological and spiritual importance of Aelred's rereading of biblical history. Aelred's interpretations allow him to broadly open his audience's view of biblical and universal history to the infinity of their eschatological ending in the person of Christ. Aelred contributes two elements to this eschatological ending. The first is personal, in that from the perspective of a tropological and moral reading of biblical history, he shows how Christ is individually formed in each person. The second is ecclesiastical and social, in that his rereading of universal human history in its march toward God through the mirror of biblical accounts shows that in the diachronic succession of multiple periods of time as well as in the synchronic interdependence of the various orders constituting society in any given moment, Christ takes bodily form in humanity as a whole through the images of the tunic and progeniture.

Thus in terms of human and social (i.e. ecclesiastical and civil) history, Aelred transposes to a grand scale the same ideal

---

251. Aelred, S 77.25 (CF 80:376).

of the "gift received" and the "gift given"[252] that he sought to realize within the monastic community of Rievaulx.[253] This ideal consisted of edifying a community unified in the bonds of charity and friendship through the common ownership of goods and the reciprocity of talents. Individuals called (reflecting an element of personal baptism) would come together (reflecting a communal, ecclesiastic element) to form a single Body in the Person of Christ. The Christocentric component of this formation, in terms of present time, is simultaneously ethical for the individual and political for the community, the church, and society. In terms of final ends, the Christological component is also cosmic, through the recapitulation of all things and history in and through Christ. In S 76 in particular, Aelred places this recapitulation of all things in Christ under the grand victorious sign of the cross. The major consequence of this emphasis is that Aelred's is a mystical and eschatological theology of history centered on Christ. Aelred's theology of history, in the end, is a cosmic mystery of the Cross itself.

252. Nouzille, *Expérience*, 320.
253. See part IV, chap. 8 of this book.

Chapter Ten

Toward a Mystical Theology of History, or the Cosmic Mystery of the Cross of Christ

When Edward the Confessor died in 1066 and William of Normandy landed in England to take the throne usurped by Harold, Edgar Aetheling (1051–1126) was forced to flee and find refuge in Scotland. Edgar was son of Edward the Exile (nephew of the Confessor, appointed heir only to die just before the Confessor) and grandson of King Edmund Ironside. With him into exile Edgar had taken his mother, Agatha of Hungary, and his two older sisters, Cristina (1050–1090) and Margaret (1045–1093). Cristina became a nun and then abbess of Wilton in 1086. Margaret married the king of Scotland, Malcolm III (r. 1058–1093) in 1170, bearing several children, including the future queen of England, Edith or Matilda (wife of Henry I), and three sons who would succeed each other as kings of Scotland: Edgar (r. 1097–1107), Alexander (r. 1107–1124), and finally David (r. 1124–1153). Queen Margaret was canonized by Pope Innocent IV in 1251.

When Aelred arrived at the Scottish court in 1124, Margaret had been dead for thirty years, but everything still breathed her presence. She and her husband had modernized Scotland's administrative structures while at the same time re-Christianizing a countryside completely disoriented by the Danish invasions of the eighth through the tenth centuries. According to certain passages from Aelred's *Lament for David, King of the Scots* and *Genealogy of the Kings of the English*, Margaret left an indelible mark on the hearts and lives of her children. She led a model Christian life, which inspired them in their own conduct, and they were all intensely pious and devoted to caring for the poorest members of society. As an example of this, at the end of *Genealogy* Aelred recounts the incident in which Queen Matilda kissed a leper's feet (Gen angl 24), based on David's own account. From whom would she have learned such a gesture of charity and compassion if not from her holy mother, Margaret? Similarly, at the end of his own life, David requested that his mother's reliquary cross be brought to him to adore. His mother had brought this cross from her native Hungary and had "passed [it] on to her sons as a hereditary gift,"[1] a sign of particular devotion to the cross of Christ, shared no doubt by the entire Scottish royal household.[2]

It is in this climate of fervent charity and intense piety that Aelred spent the ten most significant years of his youth and experienced an essential part of his personal and intellectual development. According to Walter, insofar as Aelred shared temporal responsibilities with King David, in the future that turned out to be providential: under the king's guidance, Aelred learned "the royal virtues which later he was to describe in writing for the consolation of the faithful."[3] It is reasonable to extend Walter's assertion regarding Aelred's intellectual development to the realm of his spiritual and reli-

1. Aelred, "Lament for David, King of the Scots," in *Aelred of Rievaulx: The Historical Works*, trans. Jane Patricia Freeland, CF 56 (Kalamazoo, MI: Cistercian Publications, 2005), 63.

2. Or even, as Aelred suggests in the same passage, by the entire Scottish people, as the cross, he writes, was "held no less in awe than in love by the scottish people" (Aelred, Lam D 10 [CF 56:64]).

3. VA 2; Walter Daniel, *The Life of Aelred of Rievaulx*, trans. F. M. Powicke, CF 57 (Kalamazoo, MI: Cistercian Publications, 1994), 91.

gious development as well. Even if much of Aelred's religious and spiritual development came from his own family—he came from a long line of priests, after all—it is not unreasonable to think that David's family also contributed by encouraging in him a powerful attachment to the cross of Christ.

In the end, however, whether Aelred inherited that devotion from his family or discovered it later in David's household is really of little importance. What is important to note is that what could have remained a simple pious devotion eventually became the core of a larger doctrinal development that led Aelred to integrate the mystery of the cross as the centerpiece or the cornerstone of his entire theological synthesis.

We first noted the presence of this integration in the framework of Aelred's monastic and baptismal theology, centered on the Christian's and the monk's conformity with the person of Christ and the mystery of the cross. We need only recall here the famous apology of the cross found in his S 10, for Palm Sunday: "Our order is Christ's cross . . . do not depart from the cross of Christ . . . do nothing against the cross of Christ . . . . In this way you will beyond any doubt follow Christ to the place where he went from his cross . . . . Christ's cross . . . is our glory, our life."[4]

Aelred's histories also contain a discreet trace of his theology. By expanding our investigation to Aelred's homilies and uncovering his method of interpreting biblical history, we confirmed its importance. The thematically similar SS 76 and 77 are significant in this regard. It is however only in a later

---

4. [Translator's note: The final ellipsis is mine to fit the English quotation to Burton's phrasing; the other ellipses are Burton's.] Aelred of Rievaulx, S 10.26–32, in *The Liturgical Sermons: The First Clairvaux Collection*, trans. Theodore Berkeley and M. Basil Pennington, CF 58 (Kalamazoo, MI: Cistercian Publications, 2001), 180–81. For the baptismal element of this doctrine, see S 22, for the Nativity of Holy Mary, which compares religious life and married life to boats placed at men and women's disposal, allowing them to cross "the sea of the present world" and to go to Christ by the "profession [of faith] in Christ's cross" (S 22.3–5; CF 58:307).

work, his collection of thirty-one *Homilies on the Prophetic Burdens of Isaiah*, Aelred's most mature work, that Aelred gave his theology of history its broadest and most definitive expression, centered on the mystery of the cross and the recapitulation of all things in Christ. The first section of this chapter presents this work. We then expand our perspective by turning our attention to those chapters in the *Life of Aelred* that recount the last years of Aelred's life, seeing there how Walter offered his readers the portrait of a veritable mystic, a man resembling Christ through full participation in the mystery of the cross.

The *Homilies On the Prophetic Burdens of Isaiah*

Thanks to the dedicatory letter opening the work, we know the circumstances that led Aelred to compose this monumental collection of thirty-one *Homilies on the Prophetic Burdens of Isaiah*.[5] Aelred explains to his addressee, Gilbert Foliot, bishop of London, that he had had the opportunity to offer to his brothers gathered in conventual chapter a sermon devoted to the explication (or *disputatio*) of the eleven burdens prophesied by Isaiah.[6] This then evolved into a fuller discussion, as Aelred states: "Although I once discussed the prophetic burdens of Isaiah briefly [*summatim et breviter*], touching on each of them in the gathering of the brothers, many asked me to address them at greater length [*prolixius prosequi*]. And so I yielded to the desire of those whose progress I am bound to

5. Walter's list of Aelred's works in VA 32 provides an incorrect count of the number of these sermons as thirty-three, though this number could be correct if Walter was intentionally counting two pieces that Aelred added to the final edition of the text as front matter: the dedicatory letter to Gilbert Foliot and the "Sermon for the Coming of the Lord," from which the work originated. For more on these two items, see below.

6. The sermon, for Advent, is the first one in the Durham Collection and S 47 in the continuous numbering scheme proposed by editor Gaetano Raciti in Aelred of Rievaulx, *Aelredi Rievallensis Opera Omnia 2: Sermones*, ed. Gaetano Raciti, CCCM 2B (Turnhout: Brepols, 1989–2012), 3–16. Aelred himself placed it at the beginning of the *Homilies on the Prophetic Burdens of Isaiah*.

serve [*servire profectui*]." It is this enormous biblical exegesis, undertaken after that sermon to his brothers, that Aelred sends to his friend Gilbert, whom he asks that "your authority [*auctoritas*] may confirm me when I have perceived rightly, the truth [*veritas*] may shine forth for me by your teaching when I vacillate, and your holy severity [*severitas*] may correct me when I stray."[7]

The Work's Addressee (Gilbert Foliot) and Period of Composition (April 1163 to April 1164)

Apart from Aelred's desire to pass his work through Gilbert's "consideration and discernment [*abritrium discretionis*],"[8] the fact that he identifies Gilbert as "bishop of London" is important. This reference allows us to determine fairly precisely the date of the collection's composition. Gilbert Foliot was a monk of Cluny, probably born the same year as Aelred, in 1110. He served as abbot in the Benedictine monastery of Gloucester from 1139 to 1148 before becoming bishop of Hereford from 1148 until 1163. After this, he became bishop of London, a post he held until his death in 1187. This means that Aelred's composition of the thirty-one *Homilies* came sometime after the spring of 1163. Furthermore, in the collection's twenty-third homily, Aelred mentions as a contemporary fact the schism that had divided the Church beginning in 1159 with the dual pontifical elections of Pope Alexander III and the antipope, Victor IV. As Victor died in April 1164, by this date Aelred must have completed the composition of his collection of sermons.

This said, Aelred specifies in the dedicatory letter that he knows Gilbert has numerous demands placed upon him by his pastoral charge, so if he imposes on Gilbert by requesting his critical examination of the work, it is because "I have heard, most blessed father, that among the countless tasks that either

7. Aelred, Oner Ep 6 (CF 83:3).
8. Aelred, Oner Ep 6 (CF 83:3).

the royal majesty's authority or the needs of pastoral care impose on you, you are a cultivator of wisdom [*cultorem sapientiae*], a friend of peace [*quietis amicum*], eager for spiritual knowledge [*spiritalis scientiae studiosum*], and attentive to reading, and, among the sweet delights of prayer, you lighten the trouble of encroaching cares by frequent meditation [*crebra meditatione*] on the Holy Scriptures."[9] Further, he adds that he hopes to win the friendship of one whose humility and goodness he had occasion to witness during a journey to London, where, he notes, citing Psalm 20:4, Gilbert had welcomed him with "the blessings of sweetness."[10]

Unfortunately, Aelred does not say anything more about this journey to London and his meeting with Gilbert. Perhaps it was on April 28, 1163, the day of Gilbert's investiture as bishop of London. Or perhaps it was later that same year on October 13, at the solemn transfer of Saint Edward the Confessor's relics to Westminster, which Aelred seems to have attended. Or perhaps it was under other circumstances. This will never be known. On the other hand, there is reason to speculate that the two men had known each other for a long time before that. Supposing—and this is not at all certain—that Gilbert was the son of Robert Foliot, it is difficult to see how they would not have crossed paths at some point prior to 1163, since Robert served as steward to David while David was still count of Huntingdon—a post Aelred later occupied once David became king of Scotland.

In any case, in 1163, several things brought the two men together. They were of the same age, having been born (probably) in the same year. Both were also monks—one Cluniac, one Cistercian—and so they shared, albeit in different forms, a common vocation and ideal of life. Both men were also called upon to assume important ecclesiastical charges in the kingdom of England and beyond. And although their responsibilities differed, these important posts made them both prominent

9. Aelred, Oner Ep 2 (CF 83:1).
10. Aelred, Oner Ep 2 and 8 (CF 83:1, 3).

figures and voices of authority. Gilbert was an abbot, and later bishop of London and King Henry II's confessor. Aelred, too, was an abbot, but of a monastery at the head of a large number of daughter houses throughout England and Scotland, a point that gave him an incomparable prestige and influence.

That said, beginning in 1163 many other things must have also contributed to bringing the two men together. Coming immediately to mind is the political and religious conflict between Henry II and Thomas Becket, archbishop of Canterbury, which lasted from 1163 until its well-known and dramatic ending. With this in mind there is no doubt that Gilbert, who was close to the king,[11] must have had a political position similar to that of Aelred, with both men steering away from Becket's intransigent attitude. And if over the course of his ecclesiastical career Gilbert was apparently torn between various loyalties and wavered from one to the other—at one moment supporting Stephen, at another supporting Matilda and the future Henry II—it is precisely because like Aelred, and for the good of all, he was primarily concerned with establishing a lasting peace. This reading appears confirmed by Gilbert's role as mediator throughout the conflict that opposed the king and his former chancellor. Gilbert ceaselessly came and went at all levels, whether between King Henry and Becket, between the English primate and the English bishops, or between Pope Alexander III and his archbishop.

Of course, it is true that when Aelred completed the composition of his commentary, probably in the spring of 1164, the rupture between Henry and Becket was not definitive. This

---

11. Some believe that it was at Henry II's own request that Gilbert was promoted to bishop of London (at the time when he was bishop of Hereford) and confessor to the king. Two points support this. First, on a personal level, this promotion constituted a "consolation prize" for losing out on the archbishopric of Canterbury, for which Gilbert had been seriously considered as a candidate (he had been a close collaborator of Theobald of Bec, who held the post before Becket). Second, on a political level, by naming Gilbert to this post, Henry would have sought to create a power that would counterbalance Becket's influence.

would only come a bit later in November 1164, when Thomas chose exile in France. But if in April 1164 the storm had not yet broken, the sky was nevertheless darkening, and lightning was violently scorching the horizon. In January 1164, Becket had gathered all his strength to resist the king's desire to force the English episcopate to sign the Constitutions of Clarendon, severely limiting the judicial power that ecclesiastical authorities had until then exercised. Becket had even, as a supreme insult, presented himself before the court flaunting his archiepiscopal crosier. Foliot reproached him for this: "If the king were to brandish his sword . . . as you now brandish yours, what hope can there be at making peace between you?"[12]

Thus from the beginning of 1164, the political and religious climate in England had deteriorated considerably since four months earlier in October 1163, when King Edward's relics were transferred to Westminster and Aelred himself was putting the finishing touches on *The Life of Edward*. This social, political, and religious background must be kept in mind when reading and interpreting the thirty-one *Homilies on the Prophetic Burdens of Isaiah*.

"For the Coming of the Lord"[13]: *The Burdens as a Mirror of Personal Spiritual Struggle*

As Aelred states, the thirty-one homilies devoted to the burdens prophesied by Isaiah originate in a sermon he delivered to his brothers gathered in conventual chapter. Relying

---

12. Cited in W. L. Warren, *Henry II* (Berkeley: University of California Press, 1973), 487. The reproach is an obvious allusion to the Doctrine of the Two Swords. [Translator's note: My ellipsis, to fit the English quotation to Burton's phrasing.]

13. [Translator's note: Burton refers to this sermon throughout his discussion as S 47, using Raciti's numbering as found in CF 80. As the discussion in this chapter refers to *Burdens*, however, I quote from the sermon as it appears there, with the title "For the Coming of the Lord" (Adv: CF 83:5–21).]

on his frequently used method of interpretation through etymological and symbolic meanings of Hebrew names found in the Scriptures, and aiming at the moral and spiritual edification of his brothers by breaking "the barley loaf"[14] of the Word with them, Aelred briefly comments on each of the eleven burdens announced by Isaiah in his collection of prophecies (Isa 13–24). This symbolic and spiritual commentary constitutes the core of the sermon. It covers just over half the text (twenty-five of forty-four paragraphs) and is positioned centrally in the sermon.[15]

The paragraphs following that core (Adv.38–41) show the sermon's moral orientation, asking each member of the audience to "look carefully at yourself" (Adv.38) and consider his own conduct; they also allow Aelred to elaborate on the main thread of his discussion, specifying that "the very order in which the burdens are presented is not lacking in mystery [*non vacat a mysterio*]" (Adv.42). This order corresponds to the successive stages of spiritual growth, leading from the initial struggle to overcome covetousness to, finally, the full flowering of fraternal charity that allows each person to bear various burdens, such as moral and physical infirmities (see RB 72.5), with and for his brothers.

The sermon's first and last paragraphs (Adv.1–11, 44) complete the essentially ethical perspective of the work's trajectory by giving it a theological and clearly Christocentric aspect. Aelred shows it to be Christ himself who, by virtue of his salvational humanity and through an abundance of mercy, first carried the burden of human infirmities (Adv.3) in order to free men and women. He thus fulfilled the prophecy of Isaiah that *On that day his burden will be taken away from your shoulder*

---

14. Aelred, Oner Adv.38 (CF 83:20). The image of breaking "the bread of the Word" is commonly used by twelfth-century Cistercian abbots in speaking of their pastoral responsibility to nourish their brothers through commentary on the Scriptures. See, e.g., sermons of Saint Bernard and Guerric of Igny.

15. Oner Adv.12–37 (CF 83:9–18)

and the yoke from your neck, and the yoke will rot from the oil (Isa 10:27) (Adv.7). Then Aelred rhetorically interrogates his audience, to incite them to sing the praises of divine mercy:

> Consider, if you will, what God is, and why he laid aside such majesty, why he emptied himself of such power, why he weakened such strength, why he brought low such loftiness, why he made a fool of such wisdom [see 1 Cor 1:20-31]. Is this human righteousness? Far from it. *Everyone turned aside, all were made useless; there was no one who did good* [Ps 13:3]. What then? Did he lack anything? Not at all. *His is the earth and its fullness* [Ps 49:12]. Or did he by chance need us for something? By no means. He is my God, and he does not need my goods [Ps 15:2]. What then? Truly, Lord, it is not my righteousness, but your mercy; not your lack, but my need. For *you said, "Mercy will be built in the heavens"* [Ps 88:3]. This is clearly so, for wretchedness abounds on earth. Therefore, of your first coming, *I will sing to you of mercy, Lord* [Ps 100:1].[16]

Then Aelred explains, again with the prophet Isaiah (Isa 10:26), that Christ made possible this liberation of humankind by means of his cross, beginning with a reference to the king of Assyria:

> Listen to what the prophet had just said: *The Lord will raise the scourge over him according to the blow of Midian at the rock of Horeb, and his rod over the sea, and he will raise it in Egypt's path.* For after the devil, who is *the king of all the children of pride* [Job 41:25], was scourged and beaten, *the Lord* raised his rod over the sea and raised *it in Egypt's path.*
> The sea is the world, the rod is the cross, and Egypt's path is that *broad and wide way* [Matt 7:13] *that leads to death* [Prov 12:28]. Thank you, Lord Jesus, for raising your *rod over the sea*, for laying low the pride of the world before your cross and subjecting *powers and principalities* to it [Col 2:15]. Truly, Lord, your cross weighs down the

16. Aelred, Oner Adv.5 (CF 87:6).

world's waves; it calms persecutions' storms and lessens temptations' hurricanes. You also raised your cross *in Egypt's path*, blocking *the wide road that leads to death* and pointing out the narrow, constricted way *that leads to life* [Matt 7:14].[17]

Aelred addresses a final question to his audience: what will humans do with the work of salvation realized in Christ's first coming (i.e., the mystery of the incarnation)? Will they neglect the "time of mercy,"[18] which opens the "way that leads to life,"[19] neglecting the temporality of present history or of their own history at the risk of having to fear "the time of Judgment,"[20] the day when, at his second coming, Christ will return in glory to judge the world? Or, on the contrary, from this time forward, will they both embrace mercy and fear Judgment, so that they "may be found devout [*devotus*] here, and free from care [*securi*] there, by the favor of our Lord"?[21]

This sermon echoes themes common to Aelred's other writings and is rich in its use of spiritual and doctrinal concepts borrowed from the oldest patristic traditions, especially the works of Jerome and Augustine, as well as from the most authentic Cistercian school of spirituality, to which Aelred himself belonged.

Christ as the Key to Scripture, the "Cornerstone, Beginning, and End" of Spiritual Life

One must not be fooled by the apparent simplicity of the sermon "For the Coming of the Lord" that opens *Burdens*. With a surprising economy of technique, Aelred demonstrates mastery in the art of the spiritual and moral transposition of the

17. Aelred, Oner Adv.7–8 (CF 83:7).
18. Aelred, Oner Adv.10 (CF 83:8).
19. Aelred, Oner Adv.8 (CF 83:7).
20. Aelred, Oner Adv.44 (CF 83:20).
21. Aelred, Oner Adv.44 (CF 83:21).

letter of the Scriptures. He employs a few simple exegetic processes, including the etymologic and symbolic meaning of words, and an attention to detail in the text such as the order in which the sermon formulates its points. Additionally, his hermeneutics is solidly rooted in the interpretive tradition of the church, which holds Christ to be the key to all the Scriptures. He excels in the art of reading all human existence through the mirror of Scripture and reciprocally reading Scripture as a mirror that sheds light on all human experience. In this way, the full sense both of Scripture and of every human being is discovered, each thanks to the other, with Scripture destined to be "Christified" in the idea of Christ as the end of all existence, and Christian life itself becoming the space of a spiritual struggle. In the homilies he shows that this struggle, in Christ and through his grace, or through him as the source of life, allows all human existence to establish charity by following "the example of the Lord's passion and cross,"[22] that is, by following Christ as the way or the cornerstone.

This idea is of course not new to Aelred. It lies at the heart of his first treatise, *The Mirror of Charity*, in which he examines the question of how to pass from the dis-order of covetousness to the harmonization of humankind's inner emotional forces. Only the image used differs here. In *Mirror*, the approach was somewhat static, relying principally on the image of repose in its three complementary forms—the love of God and Jubilee (the repose of the fiftieth year), love of one's neighbor and Pentecost (the repose of the fiftieth day), and love of self and Sunday sabbath (the repose of the eighth day). In the sermon "For the Coming of the Lord," the representation, which relies on the image of the burden, is more dynamic, involving an eleven-stage process.

Throughout the sermon, Aelred implicitly plays with two possible meanings for the term *burden*. The Hebrew term *massa*

22. Aelred, Oner Adv.9 (CF 83:8).

can mean "burden" (in Latin, *onus*, according to Saint Jerome's translation) as well as "oracle" or "prophetic pronouncement" (in Greek, *orasis*, according to the Septuagint translation). This semantic ambivalence leads Aelred to propose two complementary interpretations. The first of these dominates the sermon and affirms that the term *burden* designates primarily the "weight of a thing to be carried." This is the definition Aelred applies: "And what is a *burden* except a kind of weight that pulls the soul down to the earth, making it pay attention to base things and ignore the things above?"[23] And because he privileges this interpretation, Aelred describes each burden enumerated by the prophet Isaiah as a weight to be carried.[24]

The second, more discrete interpretation, appears only allusively, notably near the end of the sermon in the synthetic reprise of the various burdens described. This time the word *burden* does not signify the nature of the weight to be carried, but rather "the burden of damnation,"[25] to which are exposed those whose disorderly moral conduct allows them to be crushed by or even completely transformed into their various burdens.[26] But Aelred never develops this interpretation in detail, probably for two intrinsically connected reasons. The first is that his abbatial responsibility led him to focus above all on forming his brothers' moral conscience in order to help them order their conduct in the present, instead of threatening them with future punishments for possible deviant behaviors.

23. Aelred, Oner Adv.10 (CF 83:8).

24. For example, he describes the burden of Babylon as "cupidity," a "burden that weighs down many . . . . It burdens its wretched victims in three ways: by labor, by fear, and by pain" (Oner Adv.12 [CF 83:9]). [Trans: The ellipsis is mine, to fit the English quotation to Burton's phrasing.]

25. Aelred, Oner Adv.41 (CF 83:19). Aelred similarly uses expressions such as "weight of punishment [*pondus poenarum*]" (Adv.23) or "burden of punishment [*onus poenae*]" (Adv.25) throughout the text (e.g., CF 83:13, 14).

26. For example, the burden of Egypt, designating the darkness in which men and women walk, where discernment is difficult, is the punishment that weighs on those who themselves become darkness.

The second is that in correlation with the ethical aims of personal edification, Aelred develops a highly positive and optimistic conception of human historical time as "the time of [divine] mercy."[27] That is to say that he develops a conception of human history as an intermediate space, or *interim*, in the old Cistercian vocabulary. God offers people this interim to provide them a path of personal conversion, the dominant theme of the sermon. God also offers this interim—as Aelred discreetly suggests in his treatment of Isaiah's eleventh and final burden, "the beasts of the south,"[28] the symbol of the Holy Spirit's gifts—as a path to edifying a fraternal community founded on charity (seen in the idea of mutual support) and the sharing of the gifts given by the Holy Spirit for the good of all.[29]

The dual edification of individual and community returns to an idea that is constant in Aelred's cenobitic monastic teaching, where he aims toward the personal ethics of Christ *in anima*, as well as the communal religious formation of Christ *in Ecclesia*.[30] But this two-pronged formation of Christ expands in the thirty-one subsequent homilies, which develop its subject matter in detail. A first step, heavily laden with meaning, appears immediately. By placing at the head of his collection the sermon from which it originated, Aelred indicates that everything in the thirty-one homilies will complete and enrich what was present in the original. Readers find themselves looking at a diptych whose two panels, however disproportionate they may be to each other, are intended as complementary. In a word, Aelred's thirty-one *Homilies on the Prophetic Burdens of Isaiah* show that the formation of Christ does not just represent baptismal theology as it occurs in the individual

27. Aelred, Oner Adv.44 (CF 83:20). [Translator's note: The term *divine* appears in Burton's original text but does not appear in the English translation.]

28. Aelred, Oner Adv.33 (CF 83:16).

29. Aelred, Oner Adv.36, 37 (CF 83:17–18), in the second case citing 1 Cor 12:7-27.

30. For more detail see "Building a Fraternal Community" in chap. 8 above.

(*in anima*) and the ecclesiology of communion as it occurs within a community (*in Ecclesia*). Rather, it also represents a cosmic theology occurring within history itself (*in historia*).

The Formation of Christ in Anima *and* in Ecclesia; *the Formation of Christ* in Historia

In the thirty-one *Homilies on the Prophetic Burdens of Isaiah* that Aelred composed in 1163–1164, his global theological perspective does not change: it remains focused on the formation of Christ. What does change is the scale of that perspective. Nothing from the introductory sermon is cast aside or superseded. On the contrary, he incorporates into it everything from universal history (*historia*) and the individual human condition (*anima*) to the constitution of historical societies (*ecclesia et societas*), to paint an immense fresco of salvation history, dominated by Christ's cross and recapitulated in his person. We have shown this for the first two facets: the formation of Christ *in anima* and *in Ecclesia*. We now examine it in the context of all human history.

As the collection of thirty-one homilies is a work of monumental proportions, we limit ourselves to three remarks serving as a point of departure for a more detailed study of the collection.[31] The first remark is brief, concerning the collection's content. The second is more technical, relating to Aelred's exegetic method, which, while maintaining a certain continuity with that used in the "Sermon on the Coming of the Lord," distinguishes itself through an infinite multiplication of meaning. The third and final remark involves Aelred's theological

---

31. Of all Aelred's works, the *Homilies on the Prophetic Burdens of Isaiah* has drawn the least attention from scholars, partly because until recently (2005) there was no reliable critical edition of the work. Apart from a few rare articles treating specific aspects of the collection (we found only three, albeit of very high quality) there exists no study of the entire collection. Such a study would be a worthwhile and promising undertaking.

and Christological reflections and returns to the issue of the recapitulation and ending of history in Christ through the cross. Supporting texts show that this understanding is a fundamental key to the reading of Aelred's works and to an understanding of his "cosmic mystery of history." Thanks to a rapid examination of the *Dialogue on the Soul*, which Aelred wrote at the very end of his life (1165–1166), we can see that this mystery encompasses even the afterlife.

The Collection's Content and Interpretation: The Encounter Between Christ and the World

Again, the collection of homilies contains thirty-three pieces: the prefatory letter to Gilbert Foliot, the "Sermon on the Coming of the Lord," which drew the request that Aelred continue his commentary on the eleven burdens of Isaiah, and finally the thirty-one homilies themselves. In contrast to his original sermon, which briefly examines the eleven burdens one after the other, in the homilies Aelred only discusses the first three, so the work can be subdivided into three sections of unequal length: a set of nineteen homilies devoted to the "burden of Babylon" (Isa 13:1-22), followed by a shorter set of three homilies on the "burden of the Philistines (Isa 14:28-32), and finally a set of nine homilies devoted to interpreting the "burden of Moab" (Isa 15:16). The spiritual and doctrinal richness as well as the thematic diversity of these thirty-one homilies discourages even a succinct presentation of the content. We limit ourselves here to a brief general remark.

In the homilies Aelred abandons the exclusively moral approach characterizing the "Sermon on the Coming of the Lord" and expands his commentary to a vaster scale. The three burdens presented in the homilies cease to symbolize merely the stages of spiritual edification in communal charity considered as the formation of Christ *in anima* with a view to forming Christ *in Ecclesia*. Explicated on the same basis as the etymological interpretation of Hebrew names borrowed from Jerome, these three burdens now become the symbol of nations all together or of various individual peoples. Aelred explains this interpretation twice, doing so when he passes from one burden to the next. In the twentieth homily, for example, the first of the three homilies devoted to the Philistines, he states that under the name of *Babylon* (signifying "city of confusion") the prophet envisioned the world in general, characterized by the confusion reigning there, and largely divided between the chosen and the damned. He adds, however, that with the burden of the Philistines, the prophet passes "from genus to species,"[32] with each separate burden (*singula onera*) corresponding to a particular nation (*singularum gentium*). Since the word *philistine*, Aelred says, translates as those *"falling down from drink,"*[33] we must understand that "this refers to the Jews," since they are in effect "drunk on the letter of the law as though on old wine," and they refuse to slake their thirst in Christ, who offers in his person the wine of a new covenant.[34]

Similarly, in Homily 23, Aelred passes from the burden of the Philistines to the burden of Moab. Here he exploits the etymological meaning of the term *Moab*, meaning *"from the father, or paternal water,"* to show that this burden "means the wise of this world or the *world's wisdom* itself."[35] This wisdom is certainly a good in itself, since it proceeds from God and has permitted men and women to learn many human and divine truths (see Rom 1:18-23). Unfortunately, they have misused it for their own profit and deflected it from its fundamental purpose—the knowledge of God, to which all other knowledge must be subordinated[36]—and have gone so far as to combat

32. Aelred, Oner 20.1 (CF 83:191).

33. This meaning is taken from Jerome, *Livre de l'interprétation des noms hébreux*, 6.12.

34. Aelred, Oner 20.2 (CF 83:191).

35. Aelred, Oner 23.4 (CF 83:221). Jerome, *Livre de l'interprétation*, 8.17.

36. Aelred compares this deflection of understanding, which he says fails to respect the "rightful order [*ordo non legitimus*]" of knowledge, to an incestuous (*quasi ex incestu*) use of it (Oner 23.3 [CF 83:221]).

the true wisdom of God, which is Christ's cross, "unto the Jews indeed a stumbling block, and unto the Gentiles foolishness" (1 Cor 1:17-25).

These three elements combined—Babylon / nations, Philistines / Jews, and Moab / wisdom of the world—constitute Aelred's principal interpretation throughout the homilies. Indeed, each time Aelred addresses the relationship between Christianity and the world, though he examines it from three different angles, he first considers the place of Christianity within human society in general, or Babylon. He then demarcates the modality of the Christian faith's dialogue with Judaism, or the Philistines. Finally, he considers the relationship between the "Wisdom of God"[37] with the world and its ambient culture or its specific individual cultures. In other words, he no longer focuses exclusively on the question of Christ's formation in the soul (*in anima*) or in a Christian community (*in Ecclesia*). Rather, he focuses on the larger question of Christ's presence and formation in human societies and at the heart of human history.

This is a considerable change in scale, since from this point on Aelred reflects on all human history, from the covenant that God sealed with the Jewish people, through the mediation of Christ the Head (the incarnation) and Christ the Body (the church and Christian nations), all the way through the universal recapitulation of all things in God. This third component of Aelred's approach, however, the formation of Christ *in historia*, does not exclude the two preceding ideas of the formation of Christ *in anima* and *in Ecclesia*. On the contrary, this third component superimposes itself on the other two in such a way that the principal interpretation will come to graft itself onto a whole series of secondary meanings that Aelred will enucleate almost infinitely. From this perspective the collection's first homily turns out to be of capital importance, since as a general introduction it gives a fairly theoretical presentation of Aelred's theological and methodological assumptions.

---

37. Aelred, Oner 23.3 (CF 83:221).

The Infinite Multiplication of Meaning through Fragmentation

As the *Homilies* can be read in terms of a general interpretation relating to the formation of Christ in history, along these general hermeneutical lines Aelred branches off into a series of secondary interpretations, as he explains in the first homily of the collection, thus giving it a programmatic value in serving as both a declaration of intent and an exposition of his method. His intentions are clear, as he had already explained them in the prefatory letter addressed to Gilbert. However, he reiterates them in the first homily (Oner 1.10–11) and specifies that in all things (*per omnia*) he feels a great obligation to ensure his brothers' progress, less because of the charge (*officium*) entrusted to him than because of the affection (*affectum*) he bears them. Thus despite his own lack of academic knowledge (*scholastica disciplina*)—indeed he calls himself "mostly uneducated [*paene illitteratus*]"—and despite a schedule that allows him little free time (*raro in otio, crebro in negotio*), he cites Saint Paul (1 Cor 9:16) and states that he feels the necessity to evangelize. This urge is especially the case, he says, when he himself makes progress "in spiritual teaching or in understanding of the Scriptures,"[38] for he is fully aware that such enlightenment is not for his benefit alone, but for the good of all those to whom he has an obligation. His brothers' growth in the knowledge of Scripture, "the source of all instruction,"[39] must permit them to follow the path of wisdom leading from the "deformity" resulting from sin and making humans "like the foolish beasts [Ps 48:13]"[40] to the most perfect form, one resembling Christ / the wisdom of God, for which every rational being was created (Oner 1.2–3).

Aelred's exegetic task is therefore to take from Scripture all that seems fit to nourish the spiritual and theological life of humankind and to teach faith, create hope, and inspire love (Oner 1.3–4). And because his task is thus destined to instruct

---

38. Aelred, Oner 1.10 (CF 83:25).
39. Aelred, Oner 1.3 (CF 83:23).
40. Aelred, Oner 1.3, 2 (CF 83:23, 22).

people in the three domains of faith, hope, and charity, the Holy Spirit "prudently [*tanta prudentia*] established [*ordinavit*] Scripture, [and] arranged it to be broad enough [*capax*] for countless meanings [*sensus; sententiae*]." A source of ever-new readings (*semper recens, semper quadam renovatione*), capable of both stimulating understanding and warding off weariness, Scripture is able to fulfill needs that are as varied as individuals and their circumstances, as it "reveals some meanings to one person and others to another [*istas uni, illas alteri*]."[41]

Having thus founded the legitimacy of an "infinite" reading of the Scriptures, Aelred specifies at the same time that by offering his commentary on "a small part" (*quandam portiunculam*) of the book of Isaiah, he makes no pretense of having created an original work; rather he is simply putting a few exegetic "crumbs" at the disposal of others (see Matt 15:26), which he himself has gathered up from beneath the table of others' ideas. Thus he will "repeat what they said, if not differently [*alia dicere*], at least in another fashion [*aliter repetere*]," at the most bringing "to light just as God provides what they passed over as obvious [*manifesta*] or insignificant [*minima*], gathering seeds from their reasoning."[42] Put simply, Aelred means to frame himself in the interpretive tradition of the church fathers. This is probably why in the next paragraph he allusively enumerates the four principal levels of meaning of the Divine Word as understood by the patristic tradition: the literal or historical sense, the Christological sense, the moral sense, and finally the eschatological sense.[43]

41. Aelred, Oner 1.2 (CF 83:23).
42. Aelred, Oner 1.7 (CF 83:24).
43. Aelred, Oner 1.8 (CF 83:24). The last three levels of meaning (all apart from the literal or historical meaning) correspond to the three components of theological life outlined earlier by Aelred, which Scripture is meant to nourish. Scripture teaches what we should believe (faith in Jesus), what we should hope (blessed expectation of eternal life and eschatological meaning), and what we should love (moral meaning).

Despite his words, Aelred quickly veers away from the interpretive tradition he intends to follow. He detaches himself in particular from the principal source of his own commentary, Jerome.[44] As Lewis White has shown, Jerome is usually satisfied with a univocal interpretation of the biblical passages or expressions he examines.[45] This is the case with the two main terms that Aelred considers at length in his collection: the proper name *Babylon* and the noun *burden*. In contrast with Jerome, who gave these terms an exclusively negative meaning (for *Babylon*, the "city of confusion," to which the righteous do not belong, and for *burden*, a weight or punishment that crushes only the reprobate), Aelred shows that these two terms are laden with semantic ambivalence that the commentator must bring to light. He thus expands on the interpretation he had cautiously begun in the "Sermon on the Coming of the Lord." The word *Babylon*, for example, which the "Sermon on the Coming of the Lord" designated as the burden of greed, signifies the entire world.

Aelred explains that the term *Babylon* can be translated as "confusion." Therefore, *Babylon* symbolically designates the world, since the world itself is a place of general confusion: "the world is surely the place where all things are confused. Here the good live with the wicked, the chosen with the condemned. Here the grain is with the chaff, the oil with the dregs,

44. Apart from Jerome's direct influence, the question of Aelred's sources for the *Homilies* has never been studied in depth. However, some useful information can be found in Thomas Renna, "Aelred of Rievaulx and Isaiah," in *The Joy of Learning and Love of God: Studies in Honor of Jean Leclercq*, ed. E. R. Elder, CS 160 (Kalamazoo, MI: Cistercian Publications, 1995), 253–68. For an index of authors Aelred cites in the Homilies, identifying the external sources and numerous internal parallels with Aelred's other texts, see Aelred, ed. Raciti, CCCM 2D:362–86.

45. Lewis White, "*Bifarie itaque potest legi*: Ambivalent Exegesis in Aelred of Rievaulx's *De Oneribus*," CSQ 42, no. 3 (2007): 299–327; repr. CSQ 52, no. 4 (2017): 395–423.

and the wine with the seed."[46] But as if this first confusion were not enough, Aelred complicates things and confuses his reader. First he asserts that "we usually understand Babylon as only being the city of the wicked with their king, to which city none of the chosen belong." Then he adds, in apparently contradictory fashion, that in reality the reprobate consist of three groups. The first are those who participate in the actions and society of the elect, the second keeps separate from these actions and communion, and the third consists of those who have passed on from their bodily existence and have been delivered to their eternal torment.[47]

Similarly, among the elect there are also three groups: "some have not yet been called, such as Jews [the Philistines] or pagans [Moab]. Others are called but not justified, such as Christian sinners. Others are justified, but not yet glorified, such as the saints still subject to the miseries of this life."[48] Finally, he distinguishes among three complementary meanings in the word *Babylon*. The first is social, designating "all humanity, in which the same errors and vices entangle both the chosen and the condemned." The second is personal or moral, designating the depraved and impenetrable heart of those who are prey to their vices and passions. The third is eschatological, designating "that society of the condemned for whom eternal confusion is prepared."[49]

Aelred proceeds by the successive splintering and fragmentation of words into multiple levels of meaning. The phenomenon becomes even more clear in his treatment of the word *burden*. In the "Sermon on the Coming of the Lord," he was satisfied to give to this word a single and general meaning, that of "a kind of weight that pulls the soul down to the earth, making it pay attention to base things and ignore the things

46. Aelred, Oner 1.17 (CF 83:27).
47. Aelred, Oner 1.18 (CF 83:28).
48. Aelred, Oner 1.19 (CF 83:28).
49. Aelred, Oner 1.20 (CF 83:28).

above."[50] He adds only one more thing to this general definition. While at first glance the word *burden* designates a weight to be carried, it can also designate the "weight of punishment" to be endured when someone's behavior morally ties him to the nature of the burden described. But in the *Homilies*, Aelred infinitely multiplies the process. One burden "weighs down some but does not crush them [*premere sed non opprimere*]," a different burden "crushes others but does not weigh them down [*opprimere sed non premere*]," while another "both weighs down and crushes [*simul et premere et opprimere*]."[51] Furthermore, a burden can also be, in an active sense, something by which one imposes a weight upon someone else or, in a passive sense, something by which a weight is imposed upon oneself.[52] Additionally, a burden is a weight that in certain cases leads to the lowering of some [*depressio*], while in other cases it can lead to the raising up and freeing [*liberatio*] of others.[53] Finally, as for the word *Babylon*, the word *burden* can have a social or collective meaning, applying to everyone, a moral meaning pertaining to individuals, or an eschatological meaning relating to the weight of eternal punishments.[54]

It goes without saying that an interpretive method whereby successive splintering[55] and infinite fragmentation establish "ambivalent exegesis"[56] as a fundamental interpretive principle may well have surprised and disoriented Aelred's readers. This

---

50. Aelred, Oner Adv.10 (CF 83:8).

51. Aelred, Oner 1.15 (CF 83:27).

52. Aelred, Oner 1.16 (CF 83:27).

53. Aelred, Oner 1.14 (CF 83:26).

54. Aelred, Oner 1.20 (CF 83:28).

55. The expression "splintered reading" [Translator's note: "Lecture aux éclats" in the French], borrowed from Marc-Alain Ouaknin, has been applied to Bernardian exegesis. See Pierre-André Burton, "Une lecture 'aux éclats' du Cantique des cantiques. Les enjeux de l'herméneutique biblique selon saint Bernard. Un commentaire du *Sermon 23 sur le Cantique*," Cîteaux 57 (2006): 165–241. The expression also applies to Aelred's *Homilies*.

56. White, "*Bifarie itaque*," CSQ 42:306.

is no doubt the reason that Aelred felt it necessary to present the "new method" in detail to his dumbfounded audience.[57] What remains to be considered is the reason that he adopted this interpretive method, which, beneath the appearance of a traditional reading that Thomas Renna refers to as "somewhat old-fashioned even in his own day," presented itself "in structure, content, and purpose" as a "major shift" from the exegetic practices of his predecessors and contemporaries.[58]

From the "Splintered" Reading of Scripture to the "Splendored" Truth of Christ

As we have just shown, Aelred engages in a splintered reading of the Scriptures, proceeding by a successive and nearly infinite fragmentation of terms. While not entirely original to him, since he may have been inspired by the works of Bernard, who in certain cases uses the same process,[59] the method is nonetheless sufficiently innovative for us to consider the question of Aelred's goals in employing it so abundantly and masterfully in the *Homilies*. We offer several hypotheses here, borrowing certain ideas from White, who laid an excellent foundation in his previously mentioned article, *"Bifarie itaque potest legi:* Ambivalent Exegesis in Aelred of Rievaulx's De Oneribus."

The first reason for the use of this approach is pastoral. If Aelred infinitely multiplies the meanings of the Scriptures, it is because he is convinced that the Scriptures have something to say to everyone, regardless of personal situation. Thus his role as exegete involves providing each passage of the Scriptures with a range of interpretations broad enough that the Scriptures become a source of inspiration from which every individual can satisfy personal needs.[60] Here Aelred applies

---

57. White, *"Bifarie itaque,"* CSQ 42:312.
58. Renna, "Aelred and Isaiah," 261, 256–57.
59. This is shown in detail in Burton, "Lecture aux éclats."
60. Aelred, Oner 1.3 (CF 83:23). See White, *"Bifarie itaque,"* CSQ 42:310–13.

to the spiritual exegesis of the Scriptures that same sharp pastoral sense he demonstrated throughout his two abbacies and that led him to push to great extremes his efforts to adapt to and satisfy the personal needs of each one of his brothers.

A second reason, however, no doubt led Aelred to engage in a "splintered reading" of the Scriptures. White indicates that Aelred's multi-faceted reading of the Scriptures "provides a glimpse into his worldview"[61] and, furthermore, reflects his perception of the human condition. According to White, if Aelred's interpretation of the burdens of Isaiah is ambivalent, it is because the world itself is ambivalent.[62] Confusion reigns throughout the world, just as a multitude of burdens bear down on people, threatening to overwhelm them, placing them in a delicate and perilous situation. White calls this our "human predicament,"[63] as these burdens can in effect lead to either salvation or perdition.

White examines the ambivalence of the world and the human condition from the perspective of its moral and theological importance.[64] In moral terms, he says, Aelred's presentation of people inhabiting an ambivalent world, of people faced with salvation or damnation, is meant to lead his readers to repentance and conversion, and to remind them that there is always reason for hope, since divine mercy is greater than human misery. From this perspective Renna, despite a tendency to minimize the universal scope of Aelred's *Homilies*, is correct in stating that the work has above all a practical impact.[65] Far from providing mere "classroom exercises on technical points of exegesis," Aelred "intended his listeners to apply his exhortations to everyday concerns."[66]

61. White, "*Bifarie itaque*," CSQ 42:299.
62. White, "*Bifarie itaque*," CSQ 42:316.
63. White, "*Bifarie itaque*," CSQ 42:314.
64. White, "*Bifarie itaque*," CSQ 42:313–19.
65. Renna, "Aelred and Isaiah," 261.
66. Renna, "Aelred and Isaiah," 257.

In theological terms, the consequences are just as significant. By underlining the ambivalence of the human condition in a world marked by confusion, Aelred draws attention to the unfathomable twofold mystery of divine election (i.e., predestination) and providence. From the moment God shines his brilliant light on both the righteous and the sinful here on earth, human destiny remains both unknowable and infinitely open to the possibility of salvation so long as one lives.

Aelred's Own Ambivalent World and Quest for Unity

This confused, divided, and uncertain vision of the world might seem dark, but it bears the mark of Aelred's personal experience.[67] Aelred knew all too well the cost of a spiritual battle waged simultaneously on four fronts—against the flesh, against the powers of evil, against worldliness, and against God himself (Oner 13.28–37). This battle, however advanced one may be in spiritual life, allows no rest until the burden of the multiple necessities weighing on one's corporal condition are laid down. In fact, Aelred himself had trodden many difficult paths to attain the inner unity to which he had aspired from the time of his conversion in 1134.

Reading the collection in light of Aelred's personal experience, and therefore in light of spiritual experience in general, reveals that the three periods of church history he identifies, as well as the three burdens he discusses, correspond either to the vices against which men and women must struggle or to the three stages of individual spiritual growth. The three periods as he presents them are the apostolic period, the time of persecution, and the post-Constantine period of princely conversion, while the three burdens are Babylon as the world, the Philistines as the Jews, and Moab as the culture or wisdom of the pagans. The corresponding vices against which one must

---

67. White, *"Bifarie itaque,"* CSQ 42:319–22.

struggle are greed, vainglorious pride, and vain curiosity, while the three stages of individual spiritual growth are conversion and renunciation of the world, penitence and renunciation of the self and self-will, and contemplation of and union with God. This interpretation, privileging the ethical component of the *Homilies'* monastic instruction and spiritual theology, connects to Aelred's main authorial intent.

But however massive the evidence may be in favor of such an approach, it must never obscure the fact that Aelred employed this interpretive method of infinite splintering and fragmentation in order compositionally and exegetically to reflect the confusion of the world in which he lived. We need only recall the numerous lines of social, cultural, religious, and political fracture that deeply marked twelfth-century England as well as Europe as a whole. These diverse fractures, noted throughout the present study, made Aelred's era a troubled one. England suffered the chaos of dynastic quarrels and an interminable civil war, and was exposed to painful social changes as Franco-Norman and Anglo-Saxon culture collided. At the same time, difficult ecclesiastical changes occurred, as church governance became increasingly centralized and reforms of religious institutions took place.

Through his commentary on the burdens of Isaiah and through his authorial style, Aelred offers the reader a glimpse of the chaos of a torn and divided world—but not simply because his personal circumstances had exposed him to it, leading him to feel its effects in his flesh and in his heart. More important, this evocation of a chaotic world torn by history allows him to show a divine and universal reconciliation realized through Christ, seen in three ways. First, it is seen in Christ's assumption of the human condition, or the mystery of the incarnation and the first coming. Second, it is seen in the intermediary coming of the church itself, ideally aided by the civil authorities of Christian nations (by the principle of the Two Swords), whose temporal mission it is to assemble all humanity with Christ into a single Body, until the day at the end of time when God, "all in all," recapitulates all in his Son. Ultimately, it is seen in Christ's second coming in glory and Judgment—that is to say the day at the end of time "when all things shall be subdued unto him, [and][68] the Son also himself shall be subject unto him that put all things under him, that God may be all in all" (1 Cor 15:24-28).

We shall not here insist further on the political theology or the ecclesiology underlying the role of the church in civil society, or on Aelred's concept of fraternal life in an ecclesiastical community. We instead here emphasize the theology of history that derives from the three comings of Christ. The succession of these three moments places Christ at the center of Aelred's theology of history, a grandiose vision that contemplates all things in Christ, who is "that very Truth in which all things are and which is in all things," in whom resides "nothing false [*nihil falsum*], nothing doubtful [*nihil ambiguum*], nothing deceitful [*nihil deceptorium*],"[69] and in whom "all things past, present, and future are true and truly are, [and in whom][70] future things are no different from past, nor the present from past or future, but all things are always and in the same way together."[71]

In truth, this vision of a world truly unified and fully harmonized in the sole Person of Christ is not unique to the *Homilies*. It appeared previously in book 3 of *Mirror*, where novice

68. [Translator's note: My bracketed alteration, to fit the English quotation to Burton's phrasing.]

69. Aelred, Oner 2.15 (CF 83:35).

70. [Translator's note: My bracketed alteration, to fit the English to Burton's phrasing.]

71. Aelred, Oner 2.14 (CF 83:34). This passage refers to what Aelred qualifies in Homily 2 as an "intellectual vision." This "intellectual vision" appears on numerous occasions in Aelred's works as well as in Walter Daniel's *Life of Aelred*. See especially Aelred's *Dialogue on the Soul* (Anima 3.50), which applies it to Saint Benedict, who in the light of inner contemplation saw the whole world gathered under a single beam of sunlight (see Gregory I, *Dialogues II* 35.6). For a detailed analysis of "Sermon Two on the Burdens of Isaiah," see Guglielmo Scannerini, "Mistica o Misticismo? Un approcio patristico ad Aelredo di Rievaulx," Analecta 54 (2002): 134–85.

master Aelred spoke of Christ as the summit of the heart's spiritual ark, where "by his gentleness he keeps all lower creatures in order."[72] Similarly it is present in certain sermons and in *Spiritual Friendship*, whose final words quote 1 Corinthians 15:28.[73] But Aelred never elsewhere gave the idea the same theological scope and substance as in the *Homilies*. Indeed, in almost every page of the collection the reader can find a trace of this cosmic and Christocentric vision of the entire universe's being harmonized in God through Christ's mediation. In the *Homilies*, Christ appears as he who at the beginning and ending of time realizes the unity of all things to recapitulate them all in himself—individuals and communities, the history of peoples and nations, and the entire cosmos. At the very start, in the prefatory letter to Gilbert Foliot, Aelred provides the vision's ontological and anthropological foundation. If Christ can realize this recapitulation of all things, he says, it is because, by virtue of the mystery of the incarnation and his dual divine-human nature, all contrasts come together in his person:

> This love brought heaven to earth's level and planted the Lord of heaven in earthly members, so that the Word became flesh and dwelt among us. This love pulled God down and raised humanity up. Thus, as though on a kind of middle ground [*quasi in quodam medio*], wretchedness and mercy could meet, strength could unite itself to weakness, the Word and the soul could be in one flesh, and, among these three, there could be one person, both God and human being. What is lofty, then, that love does not pull down, or what is base that it does not lift up, making them one in himself? Conserving rather than confusing each nature's properties, with the soul so wonderfully serving as a mediator, he joined heaven to earth, God to flesh, and spirit to dust.[74]

72. Aelred, Spec car 3.106; Aelred of Rievaulx, *The Mirror of Charity*, trans. Elizabeth Connor, CF 17 (Kalamazoo, MI: Cistercian Publications, 1990), 296.
73. Aelred, Spir am 3.134 (CF 5:126).
74. Aelred, Oner Ep.3 (CF 83:2).

Having established this foundation, Aelred begins his commentary proper[75] in the third homily and shows the historic means by which Christ realized this harmonious and universal unification: the mystery of the cross and the passion, "unto the Jews indeed a stumbling block, and unto the Gentiles foolishness" (1 Cor 1:23), a sign *"placed for the ruin and resurrection of many in Israel, and as a sign who will be contradicted* [Luke 2:34]." It is also a sign raised *"over the dark mountain* [Isa 13:2], thus teaching the entire world to submit to the Lord's cross."[76] Through the rest of the collection, Aelred's ambition is to show how through the hazardous history of peoples, cultures, and religions (the presence of Christ *in historia*) and through the stages of each individual's spiritual growth (the presence of Christ *in anima*), the power of the cross cuts a path to victory through all obstacles to the universal reign of Christ. Two homilies in particular merit particular attention on this point.

In the fourteenth homily, dealing with the formation of Christ *in historia per Ecclesiam*, Aelred uses Isaiah 14:1 to evoke the conversion of the Jews to Christianity: *"the Lord will take pity on Jacob and will still choose from Israel, and he will make them rest on their own soil: and the foreigner will be joined to them and will cling to the house of Jacob."* He had made this same point several years before in an extraordinary page of his commentary *On Jesus at the Age of Twelve.*[77] In Homily 14, Aelred offers

---

75. The first two homilies are technical and programmatic in nature. The first lays out the nature and goals of Aelred's exegetic method, and the second specifies the character of the "prophetic vision" as well as the mystical aim or "vision" of his own project.

76. Aelred, Oner 3.10 (CF 83:41–42).

77. According to Domenico Pezzini's chronology in *Gesù dodicenne,* this treatise was composed roughly ten years before the *Homilies.* Regarding the passage in question, see Jesu 2.13–15 on the conversion of the Jews to Christianity, and Jesu 2.16–17 for the conversion of the pagan nations. Regarding the former, Aelred exclaims that the day when this occurs ("at the end of three days," that is, at the end of centuries), is a "longed-for time [*tempus desiderabile*], when Israel shall know its God and come trembling to David its king, when both peoples shall give themselves a single head and go up from

a beautiful vision of universal reconciliation in *"one God, one faith, one baptism* [see Eph 4:5]":[78]

> the nations will hasten to be joined to them, taking up the same faith. . . . It seems to me that the prophecy describes the mutual love with which the Jews and Gentiles will capture each other, as though embracing one another with arms of love. Of this capturing Paul says, *Receive us* [2 Cor 7:2] . . . . when, just as the gentile faithful will draw the Israelite people to the church's breast by the net of holy preaching, so too these converts will subjugate many from the Gentiles to Christian laws by both word and example.[79]

---

the land" (Iesu 2.15; Aelred of Rievaulx, "Jesus at the Age of Twelve," in *Aelred of Rievaulx, Treatises. Pastoral Prayer*, trans. Theodore Berkeley, CF 2 [Kalamazoo, MI: Cistercian Publications, 1971], 19–20). A little later it reads, "the voice of joy and exultation will resound in the tents of Jacob, when at the end of the world the true Joseph [meaning Christ] is recognized by his brethren, and the people of the Jews, like the aging father, are told that he is alive" (Iesu 2.17 [CF 2:21]). Additionally, the prodigal son (meaning both the Gentiles, or non-Christian cultures, as well as heretics, who in Aelred's time were identified with the Cathars) will also be welcomed into the tent of God (Iesu 2.17 [CF 2:22]). Historians such as Aelred Squire have wondered whether the passages in Aelred's works describing the conversion of the Jews are not in some way related to his contact with the large Jewish community living in York at the time (Squire, *Aelred of Rievaulx*, 141–42). Whatever the case, it should be noted that Aelred is not the only twelfth- or thirteenth-century Cistercian to consider the subject, see, e.g., Aelred's compatriot John, abbot of Forde (1145?–1224?), author of a monumental 120-sermon commentary on the Song of Songs. John's attitude is paradoxical in that he appears strict regarding the *sensus judaicus* (essentially a critique of a purely literal interpretation of the Scriptures) but also full of hope for the conversion of the Jews and their integration into the sole people of God, bringing Church and Synagogue together (David N. Bell, "*Agrestis et infatua Interpretatio*: The Background and Purpose of John of Forde's Condemnation of Jewish Exegesis," in *A Gathering of Friends*, ed. Hilary Costello and Christopher Holdsworth, CS 161 [Kalamazoo, MI: Cistercian Publications, 1996], 131–52).

78. Aelred, Oner 14.1 (CF 83:134).

79. Aelred, Oner 14.1, 3 (CF 83:134–35). [Translator's note: My ellipses, to reflect Burton's adaptation of the quotation.]

The other homily, number thirty-one, the last of the collection, relates to the second panel of Aelred's diptych, which is much better known: the formation of Christ *in Ecclesia* and *in anima*. In this homily, Aelred examines Isaiah 16:11, "my belly shall sound like a harp for Moab," opening its meanings in multiple complementary directions, all characterized by the same desire to show various faces of the harmony of contrasts and the fundamental unity existing between all things. He does so first in the context of the church (the formation of Christ *in Ecclesia*) to say that the belly in Isaiah's verse is Christ's Body, symbolizing the holy church. Just as the strings of a harp, he says, "are arranged by certain proportions and calculations in such a way that all agree in one harmony, and one beautiful tone arises from them all," so too is the church composed of various orders and ministries organized for "building up the body of Christ [Eph 4:12]."[80]

Aelred then turns to the Scriptures, which, rich in "various opinions and precepts, agreeing in the one root of faith, send forth a kind of sweet melody to both the hearts and the ears of the faithful."[81] At the same time, he evokes the church's predicatory mission, which, confronted with worldly knowledge, is to send out "the most beautiful and harmonious sound of preaching in various ways: now teaching, now admonishing, now rebuking, now coaxing, now conquering with robust reasons all the arguments of the dialectical art, namely, the support of the philosophical discipline."[82]

Finally, Aelred comes to two moral applications of the formation of Christ *in anima*. First, in the very broad context of anthropology, he underlines the integral unification of the individual. His commentary on Isaiah's passage says of the person who has succeeded in achieving this inner unity, "Happy the soul in which all things have been arranged and

---

80. Aelred, Oner 31.3, 2 (CF 83:309, 308).
81. Aelred, Oner 31.4 (CF 83:309).
82. Aelred, Oner 31.5 (CF 83:309).

ordered [*omnia composita sunt et ordinata*] like the strings of a harp, in which the virtues agree with one another [*ubi virtutibus virtutes conveniunt*] and the inner corresponds to the outer [*exterioribus interiora respondent*]."[83] Then turning from general anthropology to moral and spiritual theology, he speaks more specifically of the four cardinal virtues that edify all human action. Thus the harp strings symbolically represent each of the four virtues (temperance, justice, prudence, and fortitude), while the two pieces of wood to which they are affixed "represent the mystery of the cross," and the two images together become the symbol of the entire person's conformity with Christ, in whom all virtues, through the diversity and multitude of sounds they produce, combine "into one harmony [*in unam harmoniam componunt*]."[84]

This is to say that the sign and signal of the cross, which at the start of the *Homilies* were set "over the dark mountain"[85] of history and the world, now find themselves at the end of the collection complementarily planted in the heart of human-kind. Thereby the "Christification" of the entire universe is completed, both in the macrocosm of the history of the world, peoples, and cultures and in the microcosm of the human soul. Through this Christification, a vital continuum from one to the other is established, illuminated by the unifying light of Christ.

It could be argued that in this linking of microcosm and macrocosm we see the influence on Aelred and Cistercian au-thors in general of theological debates of the twelfth-century intellectual centers, in particular that of the Parisian School of Saint-Victor. This view is certainly plausible, since we know from a quotation in *The Mirror of Charity* (3.40.113) of Hugh of Saint-Victor's *On Meditation* that Aelred was at least somewhat familiar with this school. But regardless of this possible intel-lectual influence's meriting its own detailed examination, the

83. Aelred, Oner 31.7 (CF 83:310).
84. Aelred, Oner 31.8 (CF 83:310).
85. Aelred, Oner 3.10–11 (CF 83:41–42).

idea of a "continuum of being"[86] is so crucial to Aelred's thought that he unexpectedly expanded on the concept later in his *Dialogue on the Soul*.[87] This unfinished text, begun around 1166, consisted of three books in the form of a conversation with a disciple named John.

The *Dialogue on the Soul*: A Continuum of Life Passing Through Death

In the preceding section we showed how Aelred's interpretive method in the *Homilies* takes into account the historical and temporal complexity of the human condition and of the world—both subject to confusion—and reveals their destined unification in the person of Christ through the mystery of the cross. We showed that for Aelred a continuum of being passes through the entire depth of humanity's historic condition, whether on the individual level of the soul or the collective level of peoples, cultures, and religions. In *Dialogue on the Soul*, written almost *in articulo mortis*, no more than one year before his death, Aelred revisits the continuum of life. However, he shifts away from a teleological or macrocosmic view. He does not present it as encompassing all of human history from its creational origins, through the laborious path of history bring-

---

86. The expression is borrowed from Damien Boquet, *L'Ordre de l'affect au Moyen Âge* (Caen: CRAHM, 2005), 141.

87. A critical edition of this work, which reproduces C. H. Talbot's edition, published in London in 1952 for the Warburg Institute, can be found in Aelred of Rievaulx, *Aelredi Rievallensis Opera Omnia 1: Opera Ascetica*, ed. Anselm Hoste and C. H. Talbot (Turnhout: Brepols, 1971), CCCM 1:685–785. There exists only one contemporary French translation: Aelred of Rievaulx, *Dialogue sur l'âme*, trad. Pierre-Yves Émery (Oka, Canada: Abbaye Notre-Dame-du-Lac, 2007). Apart from Talbot's technical introduction to the 1952 edition, there are no detailed studies of the work. However, see Boquet, *Ordre de l'affect*, 119–49. Boquet situates the treatise in the broader context of Cistercian anthropological reflections on the nature of the soul, including those of, for example, William of Saint-Thierry and Isaac of Stella.

ing people and the world from dissimilarity to divine resemblance by means of the moral conversion of the individual and the societal mission of the church, to its ending in the recapitulation of all things in Christ. Instead, he narrows his perspective to the microcosmic angle of anthropology.

The reasons leading Aelred to undertake the composition of this treatise are unknown. It may have been, as the opening suggests, merely to satisfy the intellectual curiosity or quell the doubts of a disciple eager for clarification of difficult questions raised by Saint Augustine on the nature of the human soul in *Genesis according to the Letter*.[88] Nothing casts doubt on this theory, especially since Walter tells us that Aelred was in the habit of welcoming his brothers into his cell in the infirmary for spiritual and theological discussions (VA 31, 53). However, it is easy to imagine other reasons linked to the work's historical context. We know that at the end of 1165 and the beginning of 1166 a synod of bishops assembled before Henry II at Oxford to formally condemn the Cathar heresy. In the first book of *Dialogue*, Aelred alludes to this event through the voice of John.[89] In other words, even if the rarity of twelfth-century manuscripts prevents us from proving it,[90] it is tempting to imagine that in composing the *Dialogue*, Aelred took on

88. The treatise has no preface and simply begins with a question Aelred poses to his interlocutor: "What is the reason, John, for this unexpected visit of yours [*tam inopinati adventu*]?" followed by John's reply: "I have read something in the works of Saint Augustine which has somewhat disturbed me, and I should like to have your help and ask your opinion about certain questions" (Anima 1.1; Aelred, *Dialogue on the Soul*, trans. C. H. Talbot, CF 22 [Kalamazoo, MI: Cistercian Publications, 1981], 35). The book in question is Augustine's *Genesis according to the Letter*. This detail indicates the high intellectual level of certain twelfth-century Cistercian monasteries.

89. Aelred, Anima 1.60 (CF 22:66).

90. Only two late twelfth-century manuscript copies of Anima still exist: Durham, B. N. 25, and Oxford, Bod. Lib. E. Mus. 224. The manuscript never circulated on the continent, and apart from two later seventeenth-century copies of English provenance, it does not seem to have been circulated in Cistercian monasteries (Aelred, CCCM 1:684).

the responsibility of performing one of the tasks he otherwise assigns to the church: combating all forms of worldly knowledge and heretical doctrines that deny and reject Christ's truth, through its mission to teach and preach, and thanks to its *sensus fidei*.

The text's theological and spiritual issues were of great significance. Catharism's metaphysical dualism, irreducibly opposing flesh and spirit, body and soul, flew in the face of Aelred's fundamental anthropological optimism. Catharist dualism also collided with the Catholic doctrine that nothing created by God is bad and that the corruption of the flesh (i.e., sin or dissimilitude) is always historically second and never supplants the native and original ontological goodness of creation (i.e., similitude or resemblance).[91] There is, of course, an incontestable presence in Cistercian anthropology of what Damien Boquet rightly calls "a necessary ascetic dualism"[92] as an existential consequence and as the doctrinal expression of humankind's historic condition in the return toward the divine image through conformity with Christ. But this perspective differs from the Cathars' ideas, and Aelred had to counter Catharist metaphysical dualism by preserving and vigorously reaffirming the indissoluble unity and absolute ontological goodness and dignity of the human being, inseparably both body and soul.

Aelred bases his argument on the previously noted metaphysical principle of the "continuum of being" connecting the microcosm of the human being to the macrocosm of the universe and history, and he expands these notions anthropologically and

---

91. This doctrine echoes the biblical anthropology of humankind's creation "in God's image," which was embraced by the Cistercian fathers as it had been by the church fathers. It will be recalled that, in the final seven homilies of his commentary *On the Song of Songs* (SS 80–86), Saint Bernard engages all his intelligence and spiritual sensitivity to show the anthropological, spiritual, and theological richness of this doctrine.

92. Boquet, *Ordre de l'affect*, 145.

spiritually. He thus has to demonstrate the importance of placing "the question of the body-soul union at the center of man's knowledge as he makes his way toward God"[93] since, as Boquet explains "it is *within the human being* that *matter and spirit are joined*, and therefore that *all of creation is welded together and finds its ultimate coherence.*"[94] In a way, Aelred has to show that "what holds for animate creatures holds for all creation,"[95] and vice versa—that is to say that "the universe, in its extreme diversity, is permeated by the [same] dynamic returning it to the One."[96]

Structuring the Treatise: General Problematics (Books 1–2) and Specific Questions (Book 3)

In the *Dialogue on the Soul*, Aelred executes this demonstration in three complementary manners, each corresponding to the treatise's three books. In the first book, Pierre-Yves Émery explains, Aelred attempts "to surmount the excessive dualism inherited from Plato and suggest a path between soul and body conforming to the Scriptures . . . in such a way as to safeguard the unity of the human being, while at the same time preserving the substantive difference between body and soul."[97] In concrete terms it is a question of showing that just as God is the life of the soul, so the soul is the life of the body: a sort of "subtle force [*vis subtilior*],"[98] not located in any specific part of the body but one that nevertheless invests the entire body with life[99] and "directly precedes man's imaginative, rational, and intellectual forces."[100]

93. Boquet, *Ordre de l'affect*, 145.

94. Boquet, *Ordre de l'affect*, 145 (emphasis Burton's).

95. Boquet, *Ordre de l'affect*, 126.

96. Boquet, *Ordre de l'affect*, 126.

97. Pierre-Yves Émery, "Introduction," in Aelred of Rievaulx, *Dialogue sur l'âme*, 8.

98. Aelred, Anima 3.2 (CF 22:112).

99. Aelred, Anima 1.62 (CF 22:68).

100. Boquet, *Ordre de l'affect*, 139.

In the second book, Aelred changes perspective and instead of demonstrating the tie connecting the soul to the body, shows the fundamental unity of the human soul, a unity existing despite the diversity of its three principal faculties or operations. The first of these faculties is memory, the space of recall and the imagination, and also precursor to conceptual abstraction. The second is reason, or the space of moral discernment and wisdom. The third of these is the will, whose function, closely associated with humankind's self-determination, "consists of agreeing and consenting to that which reason determines based on elements furnished by memory."[101]

Finally, in the third book, Aelred shows his originality, stepping beyond his Cistercian contemporaries and predecessors by raising two questions relating to the state of the soul once it has separated from the body. One is the general issue of what happens to the soul upon the body's death; the other is the justification of intercessory prayers and the spiritual communion of the dead with the living. Apart from the more or less convincing arguments that Aelred borrows from Augustine on these questions, the argument he proposes in the final paragraphs of his treatise is probably the last thing he wrote before dying a few weeks or months later. In fact, his proposition is less a speculative argument than the final focus of his faithful gaze upon the face of Christ. To look upon him and aspire, with Saint Paul, "to depart this life and be with Christ" (Phil 1:23), is to contemplate, like Saint Benedict, the whole world "enclosed, as it were, in one sunbeam,"[102] brought into the light of inner contemplation.

Much like Gregory the Great, who reports the event from Benedict's life,[103] Aelred specifies that this statement does not

---

101. Émery, Introduction, 15. Aelred reprises much of the anthropological doctrine he had already developed in the first book of *Mirror*. A fundamentally Augustinian doctrine overall, it borrows much from Bernard's treatise *On Grace and Free Choice*.

102. Aelred, Anima 50 (CF 22:148).

103. Grégoire le Grand, "Vie de saint Benoît," in *Dialogues* II.36.6, trans. Paul Antin (Paris: Les Éditions du Cerf, 1979), 241.

mean that heaven and earth are in any way contracted. Rather, he says, "the mind of the one who saw it, being rapt in God, was enlarged and could see everything that is beneath God." And, he continues, it is precisely because "souls . . . enjoy in their vision of God that immensity of divine light [*illa immensitate divini luminis in Dei visione fruentes*]"[104] allowing them to contemplate the entire universe that they are able to intercede in favor of the living. Thereafter, in God the deceased see all things, and "it is in that light that they see us, for in it we live and move and have our being [Acts 17:28]. In that light they hear us [*nos audire*], they take note of what we desire, [and] look at what we need."[105]

Cosmic and Mystical Vision Align in the Eyes of Charity

The importance of justifying prayers of intercession is clarified by two other passages in Aelred's writings composed just before *On the Soul*. The vision experienced by the deceased as Aelred describes it here is related to the "intellectual vision [*visio intellectualis*]," of which he wrote in the second homily on the *Burdens of Isaiah* regarding the nature of prophetic visions. There as well, he explained it as "the very light of Truth [*in ipsa luce Veritatis*]. Here all things past, present, and future are true and truly are. Future things are no different from past, nor the present from past or future, but all things are always and in the same way together. Whatever Truth reveals is contemplated [*contemplare*] by an inner gaze [*interiori intuitu*]."[106]

The continuity between the two passages is evident. The third book of *On the Soul* simply offers a new and final aspect to the gaze focused on the world, encompassing not only the cosmic vision of human history through the three modalities of time, but also the eschatological vision of human destiny,

---

104. Aelred, Anima 3.50 (CF 22:148). [Translator's note: My ellipsis, to fit the English quotation to Burton's phrasing.]
105. Aelred, Anima 3.51 (CF 22:148).
106. Aelred, Oner 2.14 (CF 83:34).

gathering the living and the dead together in a single embrace beyond the limits of time in the communion of saints and the blessed expectation of its full realization and definitive consummation in God: "Therefore, we should honor, praise, and glorify the saints with all possible devotion. We should contemplate their bliss, as far as lies within our power, imitate their behaviour and desire their company. For surely they have a care for us and they pray for us all the more devoutly in proportion as they realize that their own supreme happiness is unattainable without us."[107]

That is, the communion of saints is brought about by the reciprocal prayers of the living for the dead and of the dead for the living, in the sharp awareness that living and dead have mutual need of one another. The final beatitude of the deceased depends upon the morality of the life led on earth by the living. Thus it is with a view to universal charity nourished by mutual prayers that Aelred, on the verge of death, can finally connect his two visions: his cosmic vision of history, and his mystical vision of a fraternal brotherhood among all things. This is what he had hinted at some years earlier in 1160–1162, when he had recommended that his sister the recluse not distract herself with works of charity, which were ill adapted to her way of life, but rather to accomplish the charitable act *par excellence* of intercessional prayer for the benefit of the world:

> What is more useful than prayer? Let this be your largesse. What is more humane than pity? Let this be your alms. So embrace the whole world with the arms of your love and in that act at once consider and congratulate the good, contemplate and mourn over the wicked. In that act look upon the afflicted and the oppressed and feel compassion for them. In that act call to mind the wretchedness of the poor, the groans of orphans, the abandonment of widows, the gloom of the sorrowful, the needs of travellers, the prayers of virgins, the perils of those at

---

107. Aelred, Anima 3.51 (CF 22:149).

sea, the temptations of monks, the responsibilities of prelates, the labors of those waging war. In your love take
them all to your heart, weep over them, offer your prayers
for them.[108]

Intercessory prayer is therefore a prayer of loving-kindness
embracing all men and women without distinction, the same
embrace of divine love that permits them to conform "to the
likeness [*ad eius se similitudinem conformare*] of him who makes
his sun shine on both the good and the wicked and his rain fall
on the just and the unjust."[109] Or, to put it in the terms used in
the third book of *Mirror*, intercessory prayer is "the summit of
fraternal charity. In it a person is made a son of God; in it the
likeness of divine goodness is more fully restored."[110] Finally,
we see this idea in the dual symbolism of places and times used
by Aelred throughout *Mirror*.[111] It is seen particularly in "sanctuary," the place one finally enters after a fierce struggle against
greed and after the efforts expended in the construction of
bonds of fraternity within a community. Having entered sanctuary, one may at last aspire all the more ardently to the joys of
a more assured divine embrace, and savor perfect repose:

the soul . . . inflamed with utmost desire, . . . goes beyond the veil of the flesh and, entering into that sanctuary
where Christ Jesus is spirit before its face, it is thoroughly
absorbed by that ineffable light and unaccustomed sweetness. All that is bodily, all that is sensible, and all that is

108. Aelred, Inst incl 28 (CF 2:77–78).
109. Matt 5:45. Aelred, Spec car 1.87 (CF 17:140).
110. Aelred, Spec car 3.10 (CF 17:228).
111. Aelred articulates the structure of *Mirror* around three fundamental
forms of charity: love of self, love of neighbor, and love of God. Onto this
structure he grafts multiple symbolisms, including that of numbers (especially
one, three, and seven), of places (secret room, inn, and sanctuary), of Babylon
(confusion and greed), of Jerusalem (inner unity and vision of peace), and of
time of repose (the three sabbaths—of days [love of self], of weeks [Pentecost
and love of one's neighbor], and years [Jubilee or the love of God]). Here it
is a question of the third form of love.

mutable are reduced to silence. The soul fixes its clear-sighted gaze on what is and is so always and is in itself: on the One. Being at leisure it sees that the Lord himself is God, and in the tender embrace of charity itself it keeps a sabbath, doubtlessly the Sabbath of sabbaths.[112]

Nothing more remains to be said except that, in a way, Aelred ends his earthly life where he began his monastic life. The sole difference is that while he began with a desire for inner unification, his life ends on a note of accomplishment, in the embrace of charity. In charity, conforming to the image of Christ, he seeks through the richness and extent of his pastoral ministry as abbot and counselor to princes to "become all things to all" (1 Cor 9:22), so that in truth "God may be all in all" (1 Cor 15:28).

Walter was no doubt a privileged witness and the nearly daily chronicler of Aelred's progressive transformation to resemblance with the person of Christ. In his capacity as Aelred's secretary and nurse, Walter was in close proximity to Aelred in the closing years of Aelred's life, in particular during his final illness. Through the last thirteen chapters of his hagiographic narrative, Walter shows his readers on an almost day-by-day basis the slow and inexorable progression of Aelred's condition. Walter also shows that Aelred never ceased to renew his inner self (see 2 Cor 4:16) until he became a transparent being through whom divine light shone. It is to these final chapters of *The Life of Aelred* that we now turn our attention.

Aelred's Final Years according to Walter Daniel

In the thirty-first *Homily on the Prophetic Burdens of Isaiah,* Aelred gives multiple interpretations to the Isaian verse, "my belly shall sound like a harp for Moab." Among other mean-

---

112. Aelred, Spec car 3.6.17 (CF 17:232). [Translator's note: My ellipses, to match the English quotation to Burton's French.]

ings, Aelred gives the verse a moral sense that is itself broken into two layers of meaning. The first is in terms of a general coherence of life. The second is more specifically articulated around the mystery of the cross by way of the four cardinal virtues, nourishing human actions as the source of ethical coherence in all individual behavior: "Happy the soul in which all things have been arranged and ordered [*omnia composita sunt et ordinata*] like the strings of a harp, in which the virtues agree with one another [*ubi virtutibus virtutes conveniunt*] and the inner corresponds to the outer [*exterioribus interiora respondent*]. Virtues are like spiritual strings, which, stretched between two pieces of wood, the upper and the lower, represent the mystery of the cross [*crucis mysterium praefigurant*]."[113]

Even though Walter did not express it this way, it is reasonable to think that he had one true aim in composing the life of his abbot: to make manifest to his readers' eyes that which constituted the "coherence of Aelred's life." He did so by showing specifically that life as wholly founded on a close participation in the mystery of the cross. We now turn our attention to this point, in two stages, beginning with certain hermeneutical keys allowing us to approach Walter's narrative with an appropriate blend of indulgence and critical distance. Following this we show in passages from the *Life* how Walter succeeded in his authorial project.

From Life to Narrative: *The Life of Aelred* as Icon or "Mirror of Holiness"

Among Walter's surviving works are three texts directly dealing with Aelred, his life, and his death. Chronologically first is the *Lament for Aelred*, composed immediately after Aelred's death on January 12, 1167. The second is *The Life of Aelred*, undated but obviously composed after January 12, 1167.

---

113. Aelred, Oner 31.7–8 (CF 83:309–10).

Finally there is the *Letter to Maurice*, originally conceived as a reply to critics who had in various ways cast doubt on Walter's credibility and the historical reliability of his narrative.[114] Only one known copy of these three manuscripts exists. All three were transcribed, one after the other but in a different order, in the fourteenth-century Durham manuscript in Cambridge, Jesus College MS QB 7. Here we will examine only *The Life of Aelred* and *The Letter to Maurice*.

The particular value of this manuscript is obvious, as without it we would never have known of the unabridged *Life's* existence, since until its discovery in 1922 by Maurice Powicke, the *Life* was known only through abridged versions dating from the sixteenth and seventeenth centuries. However, beyond the manuscript's obvious value, we must consider the crafting of the manuscript itself. In keeping with a desire expressly formulated by Walter at the end of *The Letter to Maurice*, this manuscript disrupted the chronological order of the two texts, first presenting *The Letter to Maurice*, then the *Life*. This inverted order is not without significance. First, it reveals Walter's awareness of his authorial responsibility. Additionally, it shows the text to be the expression and the fruit of a mature, well-conceived editorial plan. Because of its liminary position, *The Letter to Maurice* cannot be read simply as an circumstantial refutation of criticisms aimed at *The Life*. Rather, it must be viewed as a reader's guide, providing not only a simple "list of contents"[115] but also an interpretive framework giving access to the meaning of Aelred's life as he lived it and as Walter wrote it.

114. For more detail on this question, see Pierre-André Burton, "Walter Daniel, un biographe injustement critiqué? À propos de la réception de la *Vita Aelredi*. Entre vérité historique et vérité mythique," Cîteaux 53 (2002): 223–67. For similar material in condensed form, see Pierre-André Burton, Introduction, in Walter Daniel, *La Vie d'Aelred*, trans. Pierre-André Burton (Oka, Canada: Abbaye Notre-Dame-du-Lac, 2004), 13–34. This section presents essential details drawn from those two sources.

115. Walter Daniel, *The Letter to Maurice*, in *The Life of Aelred of Rievaulx*, trans. F. M. Powicke, CF 57 (Kalamazoo, MI: Cistercian Publications, 1994), 158.

Three Hermeneutical Keys Provided by The Letter to Maurice

Each of the three sections of *The Letter to Maurice*, responding to criticisms of the *Life*, constitutes a hermeneutical key for the *Life's* readers.

The first objection leveled at Walter relates to the historical foundation of the miracle narratives the *Life* presents. According to detractors, these narratives fail to offer the reader sufficient means to verify their authenticity. In response to this criticism, Walter presents an exhaustive list of eye witnesses, on whose testimony he says he relied to compose his accounts.[116] But as if he viewed such an appeal to witnesses as insufficient to show that Aelred's thaumaturgical power was real, Walter adds four new miracle stories,[117] each destined to reveal the full extent of that power. These accounts show that Aelred possessed this thaumaturgical capacity throughout his life, from his earliest childhood (*infantia*), through his later childhood (*pueritia*) and adolescence (*adulescentula*), all the way to old age (*senectus*). Furthermore, he exercised it on all the elements of created matter—earth, air, water, and fire. Thus Walter's account cannot be attacked on the basis that it does not fully conform to the historical truth of facts and events. There is nothing recounted in the *Life* that is not firmly based on the testimony of witnesses, Walter says, each more trustworthy than the last. Those who would call into doubt the narrative's credibility, he says, do so only out of jealousy toward Aelred and a patent lack of faith. In truth, he says, men of the church who show such incredulity should be ashamed of themselves, for it is their duty to be models of faith.[118]

This said, Walter was also sharply criticized for having deceptively sugar-coated Aelred's life, in particular on two points. The first is Walter's assertion that Aelred had "lived

116. Walter, Letter 10–20 (CF 57:148–49).
117. Walter, Letter 30–52 (CF 57:151–54).
118. Walter, Letter 1–29 (CF 57:150–51).

like a monk in the court of the king of Scotland,"[119] even though Aelred himself had always refrained from any such pretension and, at the same time, was notorious for having "occasionally deflowered his chastity."[120] Moreover, his detractors argued, Walter wrote without "sufficient caution" when describing "the body of the dead Aelred as glowing like a carbuncle and smelling like incense."[121]

Walter's response to criticisms of his narrative's reliability is enlightening, providing the second hermeneutical key he offers his readers. Walter shifts the critics' intended emphasis from the truth of events in the narrative and its historical reliability to the alternative realm of its literary formulation. Some critics, in fact, reproached him for following "the rules of rhetoric"[122] in his use of two tropes—hyperbole and synecdoche—to emphasize certain aspects of Aelred's life. However, anyone who rebuked him for this, he says, is like a "a peasant or an ignorant man [*rusticis et idiotis*]," unschooled in the art of eloquence.[123] Furthermore, there is nothing extraordinary in his rhetoric, as many of the best ancient writers, for example Sulpicius Severus in his *Life of Saint Martin*, had used the same devices. Therefore the beauty of the *Life's* narrative does not detract from the truth of Aelred's life as he lived it; rather, the text's literary quality reinforces that truth.

Walter therefore implies that for a reader to understand his narrative, the criterion of objective truth is insufficient on its own. It must be joined to the criterion of rhetorical technique, taking into account the work's literary amplifications, derived from its oratorical formulations. Furthermore, one has to understand that in its treatment of Aelred, the *Life* aims not to present just any type of truth. Rather, through its miracle nar-

---

119. Walter, Letter (CF 57:154), re. VA 2 (CF 57:91).
120. Walter, Letter (CF 57:154).
121. Walter, Letter (CF 57:155), re. VA 58 (CF 57:138).
122. Walter, Letter (CF 57:154).
123. Walter, Letter (CF 57:155).

ratives and oratorical techniques, the work aims to remove the veil of external appearances from the reader's eyes. The historical events it recounts are merely the external signs of the invisible reality that is Aelred's spiritual physiognomy, as Walter explains in the third part of his *Letter to Maurice*.[124]

In composing the *Life of Aelred*, Walter was driven by two concerns: to recount Aelred's life truthfully, with an emphasis on historical truth and narrative credibility, and to recount Aelred's life well, with an emphasis on the truth of expression and the use of oratorical techniques to reveal the deeper truth hidden within the historical events themselves. The last portion of Walter's *Letter*, addressed to Maurice, is devoted to the transition from the visible truth of historical events to their invisible spiritual signification.

Expanding on the epistemological reflections at the beginning of the *Letter*, Walter invites his correspondent to broaden the debate surrounding Aelred's miracles. Like Saint Paul, he bids him not to focus on the "material" aspect of the miracles, but to situate them in the proper spiritual context (1 Cor 13:4-5 and 1 Tim 1:5). Beyond their historical contingency as events, he says, it is necessary above all to see them as examples of charity. Indeed, it is less important to admire the miracles themselves, however extraordinary they may be, than to admire the charity informing them. If Aelred's powerful works are to be measured by the yardstick of charity, one must consider his entire life as a veritable "martyrdom" to charity.

The *Letter* is not the first place where Walter expresses this idea. He had already stated it in chapter 8 of the *Life*. But here he reprises the idea as a criterion for interpreting Aelred's entire life, both as history and as text, a life filled with examples of charity made manifest, examples so numerous they defy counting.[125] Thus a single example suffices to close the letter: the famous narrative of the "epicurean" brother who tried to

124. Walter, *Letter* (CF 57:156–58).
125. Walter, *Letter* (CF 57:158).

throw the moribund Aelred into the fire by which he warmed himself.

The last part of the *Letter* reveals a third hermeneutical key. If Walter himself, witness and interpreter of Aelred's life, offered an accurate relation of that life that was both factually and rhetorically true, he also sought to offer the reader a guide to reading the *Life* as a text: a "legend" in the proper and most noble sense of the term. In other words, he presents the *Life* as an invitation to the reader to move as through a mirror, beyond the appearance of historical truth to the spiritual and ethical truth of Aelred as martyr of charity. The reader is invited to pass from the description of events to the icon, and from the visible aspect of history to the invisible aspect of Aelred's reflection of divine splendor as a mirror of holiness.

Thus armed with three hermeneutical keys—the true, the beautiful, and the good—we can now assess the unity of Aelred's life as Walter presented it.

Aelred as Icon of Christ and Reflection of Divine Splendor

Between January and December 1166, Aelred conversed with one of his brothers on questions about the nature of the soul and its relationship to the human corporal condition. The result of these discussions was *Dialogue on the Soul*, a work consisting of three books. The third of these was never finished, and the extant text closes with a quotation from the "Life of Saint Benedict" taken from the second *Dialogue* of Gregory I. To establish the legitimacy of intercessory prayer by the living for the dead and to account for the spiritual communion of the dead with the living, Aelred reports Gregory's statements regarding the vision Benedict had just before his death. This testimony states that in a ray of the Creator's light and in the light of his inner contemplation, the space of Benedict's soul had effectively expanded to the point where, raised beyond the world in the light of the spirit, he was able to see, gathered in a single ray of sunlight, the totality of the world.

Walter himself, possibly inspired by this page from Aelred's work—as well as by the second homily *On the Prophetic Burdens of Isaiah* linked to it—similarly evoked his abbot's meditative vision of "the reformation of the whole world by the Grace of Christ, when 'he shall deliver up the Kingdom to God, even the Father,' and God shall be 'all in all.'"[126] It is probably on the basis of such passages that Walter came to insist on the contemplative aspect of Aelred's life and to show that at the end of his earthly sojourn, fully assimilated to the Light from which Aelred had never turned his gaze, he himself became the pure radiance of divine light, one in whose light could be contemplated the light of God itself.[127] All of this is certainly plausible given the numerous pages of the *Life* that bear the mark of Aelred's own writings.

In any case, one thing at least is certain. Walter harbored no doubt that his abbot was truly shining with divine light and that he drew this light from a life of intensive prayer and a profound union with Christ, in whose "sweet memory"[128] he rooted himself ever more firmly and intimately. These two aspects of Aelred's life—contemplative prayer and configurative union with Christ—are complementary, as certain chapters of *The Life* demonstrate. Thus the spiritual portrait that Walter paints of his abbot parallels all that we have shown of Aelred's theological and mystical doctrine, centered on the mystery of the cross and on Christ's ministry of universal reconciliation, occurring first in his own body (Christ the Head) and then over the course of human history in the church (Christ's mystical Body).

126. Walter, VA 10, citing 1 Cor 15:24, 28 (CF 57:103–4).
127. Walter, VA 58, citing Ps 36:10 (CF 57:139).
128. This is an allusion to the hymn *Dulcis Iesu memoria*. The hymn's author is not known for certain, but it was quite possibly written by Aelred. For more on this attribution, see Charles Dumont and Michel Coune, "L'hymne *Dulcis Iesu memoria*: Le *Jubilus* serait-il d'Aelred de Rievaulx?" Coll 55 (1993): 233–43.

"In His Light We See Your Light," or Aelred's Contemplative Prayer

Walter never doubted for a moment that Aelred's life truly shone with divine light. This fact is so true that when in chapter 58 of the *Life*, a chapter sharply criticized by his detractors, Walter describes the luminous beauty of Aelred's earthly remains, he boldly borrows the image "in your light we see light" from Ps 36:10, alters the wording, and applies the result to Aelred in a statement addressed to God: "in his light we see your light."[129]

The fact that Walter reformulates this affirmation in the first of the four new miracles related in *The Letter to Maurice* makes the assertion all the more significant. In this brief narrative, he places his reader before Aelred's cradle to contemplate the shining light emanating from the infant's face even at that early age:

> The infant Aelred was lying in his cradle; a visitor, a man of remarkable grace, William son of Thole, an archdeacon, comes to his father's house. He was a kinsman of Aelred and very fond of the child's father and mother. Entering the house, as I have said, where Aelred was lying in his cradle, he sees his *face turned to the likeness of the sun, shining in dancing rays of splendour*. It had gathered into itself so much light that when he put out his hand, it cast a shadow on the outer side while the outstretched palm, turned towards the infant's face, *shone with the radiance of solar light*, so that, as he looked at it, the serene countenance of the baby could be discerned gazing upon its own image perfectly reflected as in a mirror. The man marvels at the *new sun* which had risen in the house and tells the parents about the incomparable glory which he had seen in their child's face. They listen with joy and are happy in the thought that the shoots of felicity had sprouted in the soil of Aelred's infancy. They declare that one on

---

129. Walter, Vita A 58 (CF 57:139).

whose earliest days such outstanding grace had smiled
would later in life be a man of virtue.[130]

The value of this narrative is twofold. First, in parallel with
chapter 58 of the *Life*, the passage allows Walter to frame
Aelred's existence from the cradle to the grave in the radiance
of two similar events. Walter thus suggests that Aelred's entire life from start to finish reflected divine light, a trait he
anticipated in chapter 47, recounting that approximately a
year before Aelred's death, one of the brothers of Rievaulx
dreamed of seeing Aelred's soul haloed in light and rising to
heaven.[131]

Walter also specifies the source of this light. He underlines
the fact that witnesses to the scene saw in it the dazzling sign
of how "one on whose earliest days such outstanding grace
had smiled would later in life be a man of virtue." Indeed the
Life's entire second chapter is a showcase of the moral and
spiritual virtues with which Aelred was graced from an early
age, and which his sojourn at the Scottish court with King
David consolidated.[132]

However, Walter limits himself to this simple affirmation.
If Aelred indeed shone with divine light, it was not merely
because of his personal and moral qualities. Walter shows that
it was because of an ardent life of prayer that only intensified
in Aelred's final four years. This comes out in chapter 43 of the
Life, where Walter reports that during Aelred's later years,
Aelred habitually withdrew to his chamber—a *cubiculum*,[133]
or nuptial chamber, according to the Song of Songs—specially
arranged to accommodate his precarious state of health. There,
bathed in shining divine light, he conversed face-to-face like

130. Walter, Letter [1] (CF 57:151); Burton's emphasis.
131. Walter, VA 47 (CF 57:130–31).
132. Walter, VA 2 (CF 57:90–92).
133. Walter employs the term, which has mystical importance as a place
of intimate meeting with God (Walter, VA 22 [CF 57:113]).

a new Moses with "heavenly spirits," so that when he returned, "he revealed by the color of his countenance and a change in his face that he had been in the presence of spiritual agencies of the divine light and had contemplated heavenly visions."[134]

Several passages of the *Life* offer insight into what Aelred contemplated in these intimate moments with God, to be examined in the next section, also revealing the second element of Aelred's spiritual life: his union with Christ and his gradual conformation to the paschal mystery of the cross.

Aelred, Icon of Christ, Fully Conformed to the Paschal Mystery of the Cross

Between 1160 and 1166—a more precise date cannot be established[135]—Gilbert of Sempringham consulted Aelred on the subject of an extraordinary phenomenon that had occurred at Watton, a convent that Gilbert had founded near York around 1150. Confronted with the miraculous liberation of a young woman, delivered simultaneously from a sinful and unwanted pregnancy and the cruel confinement in chains inflicted upon her as punishment for it, Gilbert wondered what was to be done. He either had to enforce once more the punishment imposed by her fellow nuns or allow the young woman her freedom on the evidence of divine intervention. Aelred's reply was unequivocal: one must not bind her whom God has unbound.

We revisit this event because it furnishes proof that Aelred was considered by his contemporaries, in this case Gilbert of Sempringham, as a discerning spiritual authority on uncommon religious and mystical phenomena. Additional proof is seen in Aelred's second sermon from the *Homilies on the Prophetic Burdens of Isaiah*, which, written in more or less the same time frame, between April 1163 and April 1164, brought Aelred into contact with this Gilbertine community.

134. Walter, VA 43 (CF 57:129).
135. See the earlier discussion of *Miracle* in chap. 9.

In the narrative of *Miracle,* Aelred praised this community, reputed not only for the quality of its religious life but also for the mystical graces bestowed upon some of its members: "There the handmaids of Christ, along with their daily manual labor and customary psalmody, were consecrated to spiritual duties [*spiritualibus officiis*] and heavenly contemplation [*theoriis coelestibus*], so that many [*pleraeque*], as if leaving the world and all that is in it, were often transported into indescribable ecstasies [*saepe in quosdam indicibiles rapiantur excessus*], seeming to join in angelic choirs [*angelicis videantur interesse choris*]."[136]

The second homily from *Burdens* sheds a good deal of light on what Scannerini has somewhat humorously called "a kind of 'mystical epidemic.'"[137] To explain "intellectual vision [*visio intellectualis*]," a type of vision that characterizes truly prophetic sight, Aelred recounts what occurred in a Gilbertine community: "I know of a monastery of virgins serving under the venerable and deeply respected holy Father Gilbert where they daily send the rich fruit of their modesty to heaven. There was a certain virgin—perhaps she is still there—who, when she shut out from her breast all love of the world, carnal affection, care for the body, and exterior concern, began with burning mind to feel distaste for earthly things and a desire for the heavenly."[138]

Her desire was so great, Aelred continues, that she was graced on multiple occasions with mystical ecstasies, and in those times "she began to know Christ himself not according to the flesh [see 2 Cor 5:16], as she had before, because the spirit before her face, Christ Jesus, led her into the truth itself."[139]

136. Mira 1; Aelred of Rievaulx, "A Certain Wonderful Miracle," in Aelred of Rievaulx, *The Lives of the Northern Saints,* trans. Jane Patricia Freeland, CF 71 (Kalamazoo, MI: Cistercian Publications, 2006), 110.

137. Guglielmo Scannerini, "Mistica o Misticismo," 134.

138. Aelred, Oner 2.17 (CF 83:35).

139. Aelred, Oner 2.18–19 (CF 83:35–36), citing 2 Cor 5:16. This excerpt echoes a passage from *Mirror* 3.6.17 (CF 17:232). There is a striking parallel between these two texts, one written in 1142–1143, the other in 1163–1164.

Once she explained "this form [*modus*] of ecstasy" to her sisters, "many began to imitate the excellence of this vision," so that in turn several of them were graced with the same gift.[140] Among them was one, Aelred says, who, mistrusting and prudently skeptical, knowing that she must "not trust *every spirit* [1 John 4:1]," had at first "thought that all of this should be attributed to sickness [*morbo*] or phantasmal illusions [*phantasticis illusionibus*]."[141] But on the Good Friday when she herself was graced with such a vision, she felt herself raised to such heights in such an ineffable way that "her weak eye was unable to bear that *inaccessible light* [1 Tim 6:16]," and finally, "She asked to be called back, if possible, to the vision of the Lord's passion." Aelred then concludes the narrative in these terms: "Having suddenly seen [*quasi raptim*], as it were, being itself, she descended from the higher to the lower. She is brought to that spiritual vision, and sees in the spirit Jesus hanging on the cross, attached by nails, pierced by the lance, with blood flowing from the five wounds, kindly gazing at her [*ipsamque mitissimo oculu respicientem*]."[142]

This narrative allows us to glimpse a phenomenon that appears to have been widespread in medieval women's monasteries.[143] Additionally, the story is rich with spiritual doctrine. Aelred here reiterates the essence of mystical life in the contemplation of Christ crucified, the source of all tenderness and all mercy. Aelred also provides a discreet preview of what some centuries later with Margaret Mary Alacoque became devotion to the Sacred Heart of Jesus. However, the principal concern

140. Aelred, Oner 2.20 (CF 83:36).
141. Aelred, Oner 2.21 (CF 83:36).
142. Aelred, Oner 2.23 (CF 83:37).
143. In the Cistercian tradition, two German convents come to mind: Bingen in the twelfth century with Hildegarde, and Helfta in the thirteenth century with Gertrude the Great (d. 1291) and Mechtilde of Hackeborn (d. 1299). Certain twelfth- and thirteenth-century Flemish mystics also come to mind: Saint Lutgardis of Aywières, the three Idas of Nivelles, Léau, and Louvain, as well as Alice of Schaerbeek and Beatrice of Nazareth.

here is the story's focus on Walter's testimony about Aelred's spiritual life. According to Walter, Aelred's existence consisted of an ever-intensifying union with Christ until he arrived at a state of perfect conformity with him. In the *Life*, Walter testifies to this process through a focus on Aelred's mystical experience in his increasingly constant contemplation of the cross, as well as by the form of his narrative, which models Aelred's agony on that of Christ's passion.

Aelred's Intentio Cordis: *Union with Christ Through Contemplation of the Cross*

Walter puts Aelred's devotion to Christ's cross on a firm foundation. Its first mention in the *Life* appears in chapter 10, "Aelred in Meditation." Here Walter points out that while Aelred was in meditation, "the whole strength of his mind was poured out like a flood upon God and his Son; it was as though he had fastened to the crucified Christ a very long thread whose end he had taken back as far as the seat of God the Father. By this thread I mean the strain and concentrated vigor of his mental being."[144] According to Walter, Aelred's entire life, and especially his four final years, consisted of an intense and loving contemplation of Christ's cross, a point Walter confirms by mentioning Aelred's gaze in different chapters of the *Life*. Chapter 54, relating events around January 7, 1167, offers Aelred's loving sigh given up for Christ: " 'For the love of Christ, hasten.' When I said to him, 'What, lord?' he stretched out his hands, as to heaven, and, fixing his eyes like lamps of fire upon the cross which was held there before his face, said, 'Release me, let me go free to him, whom I see before me, the King of Glory. Why do you linger? What are you doing? What are you waiting for? Hasten, for the love of Christ, hasten.' "[145]

144. Walter, VA 10 (CF 57:103).
145. Walter, VA 54 (CF 57:136).

Similarly, in chapter 56, about the eve of Aelred's death on January 11, Walter tells of Aelred's being unable to utter a word. When the narrative of Christ's passion was read, Walter says, his whole being shook at every detail, as if he were himself an actor in it. Finally, in chapter 57, around the night of January 12, the date of Aelred's death, Walter, serving as Aelred's nurse, prompts him thus: "Lord, gaze on the cross; let your eye be where your heart is." Aelred finds sufficient strength to raise his eyelids and turn his pupils full of light (*pupillas luminum*) "to the figure of truth depicted on the wood"[146] and to articulate the final statement of his life, one that shows his resemblance to Christ, whom he never ceased to contemplate and whose words pronounced on the cross he appropriates: "You are my God and my Lord. You are my refuge and my Saviour. You are my glory and my hope forever more. Into your hands I commend my spirit."[147]

146. Walter, Vita A 57 (CF 57:138). Walter may have been inspired by a passage from *The Formation of Recluses* (Inst incl 26) in which Aelred recommends that his sister keep on her oratory altar nothing other than "a representation of our Savior hanging on the Cross; that will bring before your mind his Passion for you to imitate, his outspread arms will invite you to embrace [*amplexus*] him, his naked breasts will feed you with the milk of sweetness to console you" (Inst incl 26 [CF 2:73]). *Formation* not only resembles the second of the *Homilies* but also bears the imprint of Saint Bernard. In particular the themes of lactation (Christ nourishing the soul with the milk of his tender and compassionate humanity) and the embrace of Christ crucified are both frequent occurrences in the medieval iconography of Bernard. On the subject of lactation, see Cécile Dupeux, "Saint Bernard dans l'iconographie médiévale: l'exemple de la lactation," in *Vies et légendes de saint Bernard de Clairvaux. Actes des rencontres de Dijon, 7–8 juin 1991*, ed. Patrick Arabeyre, Jacques Berlioz, and Philippe Poirier (Cîteaux: Saint-Nicolas-lès-Cîteaux, 1993), 167–72. On the subject of the embrace or *amplexus*, see Franz Posset, "*Amplexus Bernardi*: The Dissemination of a Cistercian Motif in the Later Middle Ages," Cîteaux 54 (2003): 251–400. Finally, on the subject of the spiritual and doctrinal issues involved, see André Louf, "Bernard fut-il un iconoclaste?" *Bulletin de littérature ecclésiastique* 113 (1992): 49–64, esp. 58–61, 60. On those pages Louf presents the topic of the *imago crucis*.

147. Walter, VA 57 (CF 57:138).

Thus throughout the *Life* Walter suggests Aelred's full and final conformation to his Lord Jesus crucified, in various details of the narrative's formulation. We enumerate four examples here.

Aelred's Life as a Path Toward Full Conformity with Christ

The first trait by which Walter assimilates Aelred into the image of Christ has already been seen in our examination of Aelred's pastoral mission, noting that chapters 15, 22, and 28 of the *Life* are devoted to the unstable monk and Aelred's efforts to ensure that he give up his plan to leave monastic life. In the second of these three chapters, Walter frames his narrative in a way suggesting a living example of the parable of the prodigal son (Luke 15:11-32). Furthermore, Walter shows in this narrative that Aelred, as a "merciful man [*vir misericordiae et miseratus*]," plays the role of the compassionate and forgiving father set on the stage by the evangelist Luke (*pater misericordia motus*).[148] In other words, he assimilates Aelred into the image of Christ the good shepherd.

A second such trait is seen in Walter's *Lament* for Aelred. Here he compares Aelred to a wise physician, "good at dispelling harm and all sorts of weaknesses from every brave soul" (Lament 26).[149] He also affirms this point in the *Life*, stating that Aelred was "a friend of the sick [and their] physician."[150] In monastic literature, this image is a traditional representation of the abbot's role—indeed it is encountered in the Rule of Saint Benedict. Here it assimilates Aelred into the image of Christ through his desire to heal hearts as well as souls, a desire frequently seen in the synoptic gospels.

---

148. Walter, VA 15 (CF 57:107).

149. Walter Daniel, *Lament for Aelred*, trans. Jane Patricia Freeland, in *The Life of Aelred of Rievaulx*, trans. F. M. Powicke, CF 57 (Kalamazoo, MI: Cistercian Publications, 1994), 142.

150. Walter, VA 27 (CF 57:116).

Finally, a third such trait is seen in the parallel between Aelred's suffering and agony and Christ's. This parallel appears primarily toward the end of the *Life*, in Walter's day-by-day account of the inexorable progression of Aelred's illness. Three passages stand out. In chapter 49, relating events from 1166, one year before Aelred's death, Walter describes a particularly painful moment of suffering, demonstrating that Aelred's spirit became stronger as his physical health declined. Walter frames the scene by showing Christ's agony of the Mount of Olives transcribed on Aelred's face, "sweating [blood] in anguish."[151] More discreetly, but still in keeping with the theme, in chapter 55 one of the brothers, perhaps Walter himself,[152] falls asleep "from weariness"[153] while keeping watch over the moribund Aelred two days before his death, an echo of the scene on the Mount of Olives where Jesus found three of his disciples "sleeping from grief." Finally, chapter 57 shows January 12, 1167, the day of Aelred's death, the day of his contemplation of the cross and conformity to the paschal mystery of Christ. Walter begins by evoking these things separately and sequentially. First comes Aelred's last look, with "eyes like lamps of fire upon the cross,"[154] and then Aelred's last words, those that Jesus himself spoke as he died upon the cross: "Into your hands I commend my spirit."[155]

Aelred's final gaze and last words are followed in Walter's narrative by a long wait in the silence of the night until "close

151. Walter, VA 49 (CF 57:133). [Translator's note: My bracketed addition, as the word "blood" appears in Burton's French but not in the English translation.]

152. The same incident is seen in *The Letter to Maurice* (CF 57:75), clearly referring to Walter himself.

153. Walter, VA 55 (CF 57:137). [Translator's note: The French translation used by Burton gives "accablé de tristesse" or "overcome [wearied] by grief." The term *grief*, absent from the English translation, reinforces the connection between the French version of the *Life* and the subsequently quoted verse (Luke 22:45).]

154. Walter, VA 57 (CF 57:136).

155. Walter, VA 57 (CF 57:138).

on the fourth watch" of January 12. But Walter then focuses sharply on Aelred's death itself: "Then, when we were aware that death was near, he was placed, as the monastic custom is, on a hair-cloth strewn with ashes, and, as the brethren with the four abbots who were there gathered about him, he surrendered his spotless spirit into the hands of the Father and was at rest in Christ."[156]

This final instant is highly significant. The "monastic custom [*more monachorum*]"[157] to which Walter alludes is known from the *Ecclesiastica Officia*.[158] According to the *Book of Liturgical Practices* used in all twelfth-century Cistercian monasteries, when the nurse noticed that a brother was near death, the dying man was to be placed on the floor upon a large woolen cloth, which itself was laid upon a bed of ash in the form of a cross (*in modum crucis*).[159]

Obviously this standard rite was applied to all brothers without distinction between classes (choir brothers or lay brothers) or ranks (priests or non-priests, *officiales*, *obedientales*, or *claustrales*). But Walter's allusion to it may not be insignificant. Of course he may have simply wanted to indicate that in keeping with the prescribed ritual, the Rievaulx community fulfilled the funerary duties to which Aelred was entitled. However, it is also possible to interpret the scene symbolically as Walter's attempt to show, by alluding to this rite, that at the moment of his death Aelred had arrived at a state of full conformity with Christ crucified and that now "his spotless spirit"[160] could find in Christ the repose to which he had aspired from the day of his conversion in 1134, and to which he

156. Walter, VA 57 (CF 57:138).

157. Walter, VA 57 (CF 57:138).

158. *Les* Ecclesiastica officia *cisterciens du XIIe siècle,* ed. Danièle Choiselet and Placide Vernet (Reiningue: Abbaye d'Oelenberg, 1989).

159. On this practice, see "Comment se comporter auprès d'un défunt," Ecclésiastica Officia 94; 268–69, 453 n. 189.

160. Walter, VA 57 (CF 57:138).

had marked out a path in stages for his brothers so that they too might attain it.

In any case, shortly afterward—perhaps January 13 or 14 as Walter is not clear on the date—Aelred's body was bathed (VA 58). It was then anointed all over despite the miniscule quantity of oil on hand, a quantity small enough to be contained in a vial little larger than an almond (VA 59). Finally, Aelred's earthly remains were transported to the abbey church, where a funeral Mass was celebrated. His body was then "taken for burial in the chapter-house next to his predecessor, the venerable, saintly and first Abbot of Rievaulx, William."[161]

On his death, Aelred left to his immediate successors, Dom Roger (1167–1170) and Dom Sylvanus (1170–1188), a flourishing community of no fewer than "one hundred and forty monks and five hundred *conversi* and laymen."[162] By contrast, some four centuries later when by the order of Henry VIII Rievaulx's thirty-eighth and final abbot, Dom Rowland Blyton, signed the formal documents dissolving the monastery[163] in the presence of the king's representatives,[164] on December 3, 1538, there remained only twenty-three monks and about one hundred servants and attendants.[165] But that is a different story, whose telling we shall leave to other historians. What remains for us now is our general conclusions.

---

161. Walter, VA 60 (CF 57:140).

162. Walter, VA 30 (CF 57:119).

163. The abbot also signed accords guaranteeing the future of the brothers of Rievaulx.

164. The royal representatives were George Lawson, Richard Bellasis, William Blythman, and John Rokeby.

165. Although most monastic lands were dismembered and sold off piece by piece, Rievaulx's land fell intact into the hands of Thomas Manners, Count of Rutland. For more detail on Rievaulx's fate after its dissolution, see Peter Fergusson and Stuart Harrison, *Rievaulx Abbey: Community, Architecture, and Memory* (New Haven: Yale University Press, 1999), 175–86, 226–37 (the latter page range contains an appendix showing the material and financial state of Rievaulx at the time of its dissolution).

Chapter Eleven

General Conclusions.
From Divided Man to
Unified Being in Christ

Configuring the Self and the World
in Christ; Aelred's Universal
Mystical Theology of History

In a 1960 article devoted to the study of "Historical Factors in the Formation of Aelred of Rievaulx," Aelred Squire rightly points out that, "If Walter Daniel's *Life*, and still more Aelred's own writings produce an impression of wholesome consistency and integrity, this may be because it gradually becomes clear that his own past, from which Aelred seemed to turn on entering the monastery, was never blindly repudiated. Everything significant about it eventually fell into place."[1] Immediately thereafter, documentary evidence in hand, Squire adds "that this impression is no mere fancy!"[2]

---

1. Aelred Squire, "Historical Factors in the Formation of Aelred of Rievaulx," Coll 22 (1960): 265.
2. Squire, "Historical Factors," 265.

At the end of our narrative, we fully concur with Squire's affirmation. But now we are in a position to support it much more firmly. To do this, it suffices to reiterate in broad brushstrokes our principal lines of inquiry, or rather to reiterate, one by one, the threads used to weave the weft of our narrative, which progressively permitted us, we hope, to trace Aelred's portrait fairly faithfully.

The Validity of Walter Daniel's *Life of Aelred* as a Reliable Historical Source

Despite certain undeniable flaws such as its inflated and affected style, its tendency toward the fantastic, and various other traits that may rub the contemporary reader the wrong way, *The Life of Aelred*, written by Walter shortly after his abbot's death, has revealed itself to be a worthy and highly reliable historical source. Of course, this statement refers neither primarily to the historical precision of the facts related therein nor to the breadth of the approach. In each of these aspects, the *Life* has flagrant lacunae. The most important are an almost non-existent concern for rigorous and precise chronology, a surprising disproportion between the different parts of the narrative (with more than one third of the *Life* devoted exclusively to Aelred's final years), and the near-total obliteration of Aelred's "public face." We have tried to mitigate these weaknesses as best we could. If the *Life* appears to be a valuable source of information, it is therefore in another sense entirely. It "tells the truth" about Aelred's existence, in the sense that its primary aim is not to describe that existence in an exhaustive, objective, or historically reliable manner.

That aspect of the question is certainly pertinent to Walter, but it is secondary to his main focus. Contrary to what the contemporary historian would like, Walter's principal aim is to reveal not Aelred's exterior public face, but rather his "invisible" or "hidden" face. Walter's intention was to provide not a simple portrait of Aelred, but an icon. In short, while basing his narrative on the facts of historical truth, Walter meant to help his reader move beyond the external appearances of a purely event-based description of history in order to permit access to Aelred's ethical and spiritual truth. In this sense it cannot be said that he falls short. We admire the manner in which he makes us feel, from within, the richness of Aelred's spiritual physiognomy, largely because many pages of the *Life* are largely inspired by certain pages of Aelred's own writings.

The Three "Threads" of Historical Weft: From "Divided Man" to "Rightly Ordered Desire" to "Unified Being"

How do we account for Squire's "impression of perfect consistency and total integrity" regarding Aelred's life? To answer this question, we have only to reprise the words of Franco-German philosopher Éric Weil from this study's epigraph. Here we find the key to interpreting any life lived by a man of conscience, a man who desires to shape himself into a person of righteous "bearing," a man whose life "has bearing" in the sense of relevance and meaning, and whose life has "a bearing" in the sense of a course or direction: "man, by his moral action, realizes and recovers wholeness only by unifying the world in a way that unifies himself."[3]

Along the Timeline

This pursuit of interior unity, realized only through moral action and unifying the world only insofar as one unifies himself by it, was the sole quest of Aelred's earthly existence. We see it in Aelred's life at every stage: first as a man (1110–1134, before he entered Rievaulx), then as a monk (1134–1142, from entering Rievaulx until becoming novice master), and finally as abbot and pastor of the two communities entrusted to him

---

3. Éric Weil, *Philosophie morale* (Paris: Vrin, 1981), 33.

(1143–1147 at Revesby and 1147–1167 at Rievaulx, founding the former, becoming the illustrious third abbot of the latter in the footsteps of William "of blessed memory" and Maurice, "the second Bede"). Aelred pursued this very quest as abbot of Rievaulx, in particular from 1153–1154 onward, when, in addition to his pastoral charge, he "entered politics," so to speak, and began to play an increasingly public role as counselor of kings and princes.

That year represented a major turning point both in Aelred's life and in English history. It saw the end of the long civil war (1134–1153), which for nearly twenty years had pitted the partisans of King Stephen of Blois against those faithful to the Empress Matilda and her son, the future Henry II, and had bled England nearly to death. But this was also the moment when Aelred chose to publish his first two historical works: the relatively short *Battle of the Standard* and, of greater scope, the combined *Lament for David, King of the Scots,* and *Genealogy of the Kings of the English.* These publications were later followed by many others, but these two in particular mark at an early stage Aelred's undeniable desire to intervene on the public stage and to have his voice heard by the world's major figures. He aspired to this goal in the hope that his counsel would have if not a lasting impact on the world's history at large, at least an active role in moving toward some form of national reconciliation in his own country.

Numerous factors justified this hope. First was the immense network of relations Aelred had established over time through his various charges, which crossed political boundaries (England and Scotland), cultural boundaries (Celtic and Anglo-Saxon, Latin and Franco-Norman), and ecclesiastical boundaries ("old" monasticism and "new" forms of religious life). Second was what Squire calls "the characteristically conciliatory temper of his mind."[4] Apart from making Aelred particularly sensitive

4. Squire, "Historical Factors," 265.

to any form of divisiveness, this temper led others to request his service as mediator early in his life. King David made such requests while Aelred was still at the Scottish court (seen in the famous mission to York, in 1134), as did Dom William, Aelred's abbot, shortly after Aelred entered Rievaulx (as in the 1142 journey to Rome to resolve the question of who would succeed Thurstan as archbishop of York). Finally, Aelred could pretend to intervene on the political stage alongside the secular princes of his time, perhaps primarily because before taking on any form of engagement external to monastic life, and before presuming to address a larger public in a voice that might be taken as "authoritative," he had first had to deal with the personal challenge of unifying his own inner being.

The determining role of this challenge in Aelred's choice to embrace Cistercian monastic life in 1134 appears in scattered autobiographical evidence in different passages of his works, especially *The Mirror of Charity*, the Prologue to *Spiritual Friendship*, certain paragraphs from *Formation of Recluses*, and various liturgical sermons.

An Existential Thread

Thus the four-period chronological thread just presented is spun together with a second existential thread. Indeed it is no longer a question of following the simple chronology of Aelred's life. Rather, it is a question of teasing out that life's human and personal issues. In 1134 when Aelred decided to enter Rievaulx, these issues were significant—literally a question of life and death. In the boiling enthusiasm of his youth and adolescence, Aelred had discovered profound joy in friendships made at the Scottish court. At the same time, this discovery left a bitter emptiness in his heart that led him to the edges of despair.

If life at the Scottish court allowed him to discover the infinite potential of his emotions and the unsuspected riches of a heart avid to love and be loved, Aelred simultaneously perceived with pitiless lucidity that affection alone threatened to shatter his very being. "What use is it," he must have wondered, "to give oneself up to the delights of love, if it only leads to this?" In short, he became so disgusted with himself that he contemplated suicide. It was then that he was touched by divine grace and envisioned the possibility of another solution, perhaps suggested by his friend Waldef, who had recently become an Augustinian canon, to "make himself"[5] a monk. But because the major obstacle to this possibility was Aelred's struggle to master his emotions and his "carnal desires [*cupiditas*]," Aelred would not, like his friend, choose one of the older religious orders such as the Benedictines or the canons regular, for these were insufficiently demanding in his eyes. Rather, he chose to enter a form of monastic life reputed in its time for its high austerity in the wake of recent reform. He selected the new Cistercian monastery near York, at Rievaulx. He opted to go here and nowhere else, for he hoped that at Rievaulx he could finally bring an end to his torment. In this he would indeed succeed, but by means different from those he had initially envisioned.

Aelred had believed that to recover the inner unity his scattered affective relationships had cost him, he had to ruthlessly stifle his heart's slightest natural urges and, through merciless asceticism, repress his body's rebellion against the Spirit of God. At the moment of his conversion, this implacable asceticism was the only means he saw to pass from his splintered affectivity to the inner unity he so desired. It is as if there was in his mind at that time a radical incompatibility between his aspiration to inner unity and the natural flowering of his affective life. Indeed, he believed it was impossible to have the one without completely renouncing the other. But under the

5. [Translator's note: Burton uses the French term "se faire" in quotations, playing with the idea of becoming a monk, but also of "constructing" himself or "shaping" himself into something by becoming a monk.]

guidance of Abbot William (a monk instructed in the school of Saint Bernard), novice master Simon (an open-minded man), and a certain "most reverend" Prior Hugh (a mentor and close friend named in the Prologue to *Mirror*), Aelred soon discovered that he was on a false path and that there was no need to oppose his quest for inner unity and his natural inclination toward friendship, as he had originally thought. Thanks to these three instructors, Aelred learned that the inner unity he sought did not require him to sacrifice affectivity on the altar of rigorous, intransigent, dehumanizing asceticism—far from it. The heart's natural urges, which, through a process of splintering, lead to all of a person's desires, could be dealt with instead by correctly aligning his natural tendency to love.

In short, the Cistercian school of charity taught Aelred that the shortest path from a rich and overflowing affectivity to the unity of the human person passed not through the castrating eradication of emotions, but through proper ordering. Such ordering through charity certainly did require recourse to an appropriate asceticism: in Aelred's case, the observances of monastic life were sufficient. These observances, however, were not to be experienced as an end in themselves. Rather, they needed to be perceived as a means of learning to love in the manner God had revealed to humankind through the prototype or exemplar of his son, the Word made flesh and Wisdom incarnate in time. In other words, Aelred came to realize that the two elements he had placed in oppositional tension— affective life and inner unity—had to be placed instead in a cooperative relationship.

To do so, Aelred had to renounce the third element that he had up until then, heroically but vainly, employed to reduce that tension. Understanding that he had to relinquish the path of rigorous and intransigent asceticism, he had to substitute a new third element for it. He had to create a new path, just as demanding as the one he was abandoning, but far more liberating and fulfilling. This was the path of a Christocentric mysticism, allowing him to justify all of the components of his humanity: heart and body, body and spirit, intelligence, memory, and will. He set aside the tension between affectivity and unity that he had sought to suppress through harsh, uncompromising asceticism. Instead, he fused them in a conjoined relationship by means of a simple monastic asceticism conceived as the union with and conformation to the person of Christ, the standard of measurement for all love.

To put it in more existential and anthropological terms, Aelred marked out the path of his personal inner unification not in two but in three stages. Now it became for him a question of passing from the "divided man" of unbridled affectivity focused on the self to the man of Christian monastic life gradually conforming to Christ through the baptismal path, and finally to the "unified being" cohering in God, through charity. This is what we have identified as "the path of the formation of Christ *in anima*," which, in chronological terms, coincides roughly with Aelred's pre-monastic period and the time of his initial monastic instruction. This period was the time of the divided man. It was a time of slow and gradual assimilation of monastic values and observances that would serve as the path of inner unification through conformity with Christ.

We insist at length on this first existential and spiritual passage of Aelred's life because in many ways it had a determining impact on the rest of his life. Indeed, beginning in 1142–1143, Aelred was firmly encouraged, one might say authoritatively invited, by Bernard himself to publish the fruits of his experience in a sort of "manual of instruction for Cistercian monastic life." He had initially begun by creating small thematic dossiers, whose trace is still found in the final copy, probably for his personal use. He gathered these together to give them the quantity and substance of a larger treatise that fully examined the question and permitted him, on a solid scriptural basis, to establish the value of Cistercian monastic asceticism theologically as an instrument of personal unification. This text was *The Mirror of Charity*, whose title Bernard seems to have imposed upon his promising young disciple, in whose experience he no doubt saw a reflection of his own.

In any case, Aelred's masterful synthesis in *Mirror* became the starting point for all future developments in his monastic and theological doctrine. What he had discovered over the course of his initial monastic instruction and through the responsibilities gradually entrusted to him, he later transposed to every domain of human existence. Becoming novice master and then abbot, Aelred discovered that he must never limit the question of the formation of Christ solely to a personal level. The question also applied to the monastic community, made up of individuals called upon to weave fraternal relations of exchange, reciprocity, and sharing, each of whom was also invited to become a member of the body of Christ.

The personal quest for inner unity, constituting the principal and major challenge of Aelred's life at the start of his monastic experience, now unfolded on a far greater scale. From the unification of the individual it was necessary to pass to the unification of the community of individuals, which again found its place in Christ's person, the cornerstone of both the individual and the community. This we have termed "the formation of Christ *in Ecclesia,*" denoting simultaneously the "community of individuals" and "communal individualism." Chronologically this concern, supplementing rather than replacing the preceding one, coincides with both the period during which Aelred served as novice master (1142–1143) and roughly his first ten years as abbot at Revesby (1143–1147) and Rievaulx (1147–1153).

This first change of scope and perspective was soon followed by a second. The particular historical circumstances in which Aelred lived gave rise to it. From 1134 to 1153, in the silence of the cloister, Aelred had been the saddened and powerless witness to the dynastic and interethnic quarrels ravaging England in a devastating civil war that cost the country its national unity and cohesion. He was all the more afflicted by the presence of persons dear to him on both sides. Two names serve to illustrate this fact. On the English and Franco-Norman side, supporting King Stephen, there was Walter Espec, founder of Rievaulx. On the Scottish side, supporting the Empress Matilda, was King David of Scotland, who had been a second father to Aelred and to whom Aelred owed a great deal. On Christmas Day 1153, the Treaty of Wallingford was signed, establishing an agreement between King Stephen and the future Henry II and bringing an end to the long civil war. It was at this moment that Aelred chose to step onto the public stage and publish his first treatises on the history of England.

We considered earlier the reasons for this entry onto the public spotlight. Let us consider now the resulting substance. Aelred's historical treatises constitute a manifesto of political theology expressing Aelred's desire for the establishment of peace and justice. But the essential condition for arriving at that end, he knew, was that the English nation had to unite around the person of King Henry II. Aelred's desire for that unity was so strong that he invested Henry with messianic signs. If in the image of Christ we see the cornerstone who "might create in himself one new person in the place of two, thus establishing peace" (Eph 2:15), so Aelred called upon Henry too to make possible the unification of peoples and cultures that had hitherto struggled violently with each other within his country.

Aelred initially set the challenge of unity within the individual, constituting the ethical element of Christ's formation. He then extended it to monastic communities, constituting unity's ecclesiological element. Here he expanded the concept of unity once more to civic, social, and political dimensions. This is what we have termed the "formation of Christ *in historia*," that is, in the history of peoples, cultures, and religions. This third concern absorbed a substantial part of Aelred's energy during the last fifteen years of his life, from 1153 to 1167. This we have identified as the fourth and final period of Aelred's existence and the second period of his long abbacy at Rievaulx.

Nearing the end of his life, between 1162 and 1164, Aelred gave the third element of Christ's formation its fullest expression. In 1162–1163, it took hagiographic form in *The Life of Edward, King and Confessor*, written in the wake of *Genealogy*. But it appeared most vividly the following year in 1163–1164, in

Aelred's extensive thirty-one-homily commentary on certain chapters of the book of Isaiah, emphasizing three of the eleven burdens prophesied to fall upon the nations. This work's compositional and interpretive complexity reflects his two explicit intentions. First, it offers the mirror of the true historical condition of all humanity plunged into the most profound confusion at all levels, from individuals to communities, peoples, nations, cultures, and religions. Second, it shows that, marching toward its ultimate end, humanity will finally find its unity, cohesion, and harmony, its peace and repose, in the sole person of Christ, the beginning and the end of history, him in whom, by the mystery of the saving cross, all history is recapitulated.

In the *Dialogue on the Soul*, his final, unfinished work, begun in 1166, Aelred addresses the fourth and final component of his cosmic vision. According to his teleological and macrocosmic vision of human history, the unity of all things must at the end of history realize itself in the person of Christ. This unity of all things in Christ, according to his microcosmic vision of the vital continuum, effects the intimate joining of matter and spirit and the secret union of the soul and the body. Furthermore, this unity also transcends the boundaries of time to bring about the communion of saints, joining together the living and the dead in a communion of destiny and reciprocal prayers.

Friendship and Unity in Christ: Three Complementary Aspects of a Single Process

The entire body of Aelred's writings, like the entire course of his life, is sewn together by three threads wound together into a single history. As a man (until 1134), monk (1134–1143), abbot (1143–1167), and counselor of kings (from 1153 on), Aelred was haunted by a single thought: faced with the confusion that threatens all existence and that reigns at every level of human experience, we must find a way to attain unity within the individual, the monastic community, and the larger communities of peoples, cultures, and religions.

Every time he confronted this problem, Aelred arrived at the same solution, drawn from his inaugural monastic experience and progressively broadened to include all aspects of human existence whether personal or ecclesiastical, social or political. For Aelred, the only unification possible on any level is in the person of Christ. It is this principle that provides the three facets of Aelred's theological theme of the formation of Christ. Aelred inherits his notion of the formation of Christ from Bernard and Bernard's disciple Guerric d'Igny. The formation of Christ must be realized not only *in anima* and *in Ecclesia*, the two facets privileged by Aelred's predecessors, but also *in historia*. This third facet, or at the very least the value attached to it, represents Aelred's original contribution to such considerations.

What truly shows the originality of Aelred's theological and spiritual doctrine, though, is that in the formation of Christ *in anima*, *in Ecclesia*, and *in historia*, Aelred proposes a single path to achieving unity. This path is based in Aelred's pre-monastic experience of friendship and enriched with his later readings and a biblical and philosophical vision of the world and history. The vision is biblical in that it is founded on the book of Wisdom, to which Saint Bernard himself so often had recourse, and according to which divine wisdom "spans the world from end to end mightily and governs all things well" (Wis 8:1). The vision is philosophical in that it borrows from Stoicism, according to which the organization of the cosmos, or Creation, is founded entirely on a universal harmony by virtue of which all created things maintain with one another a relationship of complementarity, reciprocity, and mutual exchange.

Aelred had experienced this principle in his early personal friendships. As a monk, then as abbot, and finally as counselor to kings, he continued to show, as his instructors certainly encouraged him to, that the principle of a friendship firmly established in Christ could serve as a legitimate foundation on which to construct the unity of the individual, of communities, and of all human history from its origin in God to its recapitulation in Christ. Aelred thus removes friendship from the sphere of mere emotional life, where it had existed in his pre-monastic experience, to build it into a major philosophical and theological concept. In Aelred's eyes, friendship becomes a paradigm for all aspects of human existence, the possibility of whose historical concretization lay in the model of fraternal life offered by the apostolic community as described in the Acts of the Apostles.

In practical terms, Aelred extends this paradigm outward in wider and wider concentric circles to include the ethical and ecclesiastical elements of the individual and the community, the social and political elements of peoples and nations, and finally the cosmic and transhistorical elements of creation and the communion of saints. Whatever his own level of responsibility, Aelred assigned himself the task of extending the reign of friendship everywhere, to ensure that between all things and in all interpersonal, intra-communal, intercultural, and international human relationships, an increasingly denser and broader network of solidarity and reciprocity would be woven. This network would allow all, from individuals to ecclesiastical and social institutions, fully to appropriate the Augustinian adage that "What belongs to one belongs to all, and what belongs to all belongs to each" (*singula omnium, omnia singulorum*).

By building all forms of social life on the foundation of each individual's gifts shared for the benefit of all, Aelred underscored the social principle of humanity's historic condition. On this basis, he hoped to return the world to the original form in which God had created it for all eternity, thus reflecting the cosmic or protological principle of history. Additionally, he intended to make of every ecclesiastical and civil community that lived or wanted to live in this way—in particular monastic communities and Christian societies—the partially realized sign and expression of what we have joined Christian de Chergé in calling an "eschatology of hope." This sign is, in the course of time and for present history, both the sacrament and the anticipation of the eternal kingdom. It is the "already-there" of the *signum* and the plenitude "yet-to-come" of the *res*, in the eschatological principle of history advancing toward its final ending.

To put it yet another way, whether viewed in the personal terms of individual ethics, the collective terms of social life, ecclesiastical praxis, and sociopolitical ethics, or the universal terms of the cosmos and ecological ethics, Aelred always saw the drama of history unfold in three successive acts. The matrix of this drama, seen in *The Mirror of Charity,* is both theological and trinitary. The drama begins from creation, the protological beginning in God, the Father and Creator, in whom all things originate. It then passes along the laborious path of sanctification of world, humankind, and time, broken in the wake of the irruption of sin. This path exists in human historical time as the interim, or the "ethical space," of a slow process conforming the world to the plan of creation, in the power of the Spirit and charity. Christ, by his incarnation, is the center and the standard of this process. The drama finally arrives at redemption and glorification in the eschatological completion and ending of history in God the Son.

Aelred presented this three-act play of history in various ways, but always with a remarkable coherence and unity of thought throughout his life and his writings. Four examples will suffice to demonstrate this.

The first example, present throughout this biography, is anthropological and reflects the course of Aelred's own life as a man, unfolding in the following sequence. Aelred begins as a divided man. He then becomes a monk who progressively conforms himself to the image of Christ through the mystery of the cross—that is, through baptismal life and monastic observances. Finally he reaches a state of unified being.

Next, if we join this sequence with the various modes of love Aelred identifies in *The Mirror of Charity,* the sequence unfolds as follows. One begins with "*cupiditas* [greed]," then proceeds to an ordering of the power or faculty of loving (*amor*)—a structuring of one's emotional life through monastic asceticism, coupled with spiritual friendship (*amicitia*) conceived as the conformity of human feelings to those of Christ and conceived as a step (*gradus*) toward a larger fraternal charity. Then one finally arrives at the very state of charity (*caritas*) itself.

The first of the above lines of progression is anthropological and individual. The second is affective and communal. If we attach to them a third, more political and cosmic line of progression, relating to the history of peoples and all humanity, the sequence unfolds in the following way. The world begins in chaos. Then political and church authorities collaborate, each respecting the other's particular competences according to Aelred's moderate conception of the two swords. This collaboration establishes relationships founded on justice and peace both within society and between societies. In their own right these relationships affect the equilibrium of the world and the natural forces governing it, thus contributing to the universal prosperity of all—what might be considered a precursor to ecological responsibility. Finally the world reaches a definitive state of harmony.

This three-act drama of salvation, whether read on a personal, communal, or universal level, manifests itself through expressions and images that both Scripture and the patristic tradition placed at Aelred's disposal. With respect to biblical imagery, the picture of a holy people traveling toward the Promised Land holds a particular place of privilege. The image can be used to express the aforementioned progression in terms of biblical geography. First there is a departure from Babylon, the city of confusion. Then there is a long journey through the desert, an exodus, whose numerous stages Aelred enumerates in various manners, all modeled on biblical history. Finally the travelers arrive in Jerusalem, the vision of peace. With respect to the patristic tradition, Aelred superimposes teachings from works such as Augustine's *City of God* and *Genesis according to the Letter*, and Bernard's *On Grace and Free Choice*. To show this pattern fully would require a detailed study in and of itself. However, in this context, the human-divine drama of salvation takes the form of a return to the "perfect resemblance [*ad patriam / regio similitudi-nis*]," which, by the "path [*in via*]" of conforming oneself to Christ ("I am the way and the truth and the life," John 14:6), takes one away from the "country of dissemblance [*regio dissimilitudinis*]," as Aelred expresses it succinctly and frequently with the phrase "through Christ to Christ" (e.g., S 7.5).[6]

In short, we see once more a single thread divided into three parts: order / disorder / reordering, formation / deformation / conformity, and creation (resemblance to the image) / sin (de-creation or dissemblance) / re-creation (restoration of re-semblance). These parts form a single drama, consisting of the completion of all history in the person of Christ, reduplicated in three increasingly larger, successive circles integrating the individual through the formation of Christ *in anima*, the com-munity through the formation of Christ *in Ecclesia*, and the universe through the formation of Christ *in historia*. Among these circles, Christ upon the cross is the universal, connecting element: "The Mediator [*Mediator*] of God and men hangs midway between heaven and earth [*inter caelum et terram me-dius pendens*], unites the heights with the depths [*ima superis unit*], and joins the things of earth to the things of heaven [*coelestibus terrena coniungit*]. Heaven is aghast, earth marvels [*Stupet Caelum, terra miratur*]."[7]

To express it through another image, there are three fibers bound into a single "thread of intent," as Aelred's entire life, doctrine, and representation of human history are bound into Christ. This single thread is stitched through and binds to-gether the three-ply cloth of Aelred's worldview, consisting of the mystery of personal history or the unification of the indi-vidual; the political and mystical theology of human history,

---

6. Aelred of Rievaulx, *The Liturgical Sermons: The First Clairvaux Collection*, trans. Theodore Berkeley and M. Basil Pennington, CF 58 (Kalamazoo, MI: Cistercian Publications, 2001), 143.

7. Inst incl 31; Aelred of Rievaulx, "A Rule of Life for a Recluse," trans. Mary Paul Macpherson, in *Aelred of Rievaulx: Treatises. Pastoral Prayer*, CF 2 (Kalamazoo, MI: Cistercian Publications, 1971), 89.

or the solidarity of nations, peoples, and cultures; and the cosmic vision of universal history, or the *harmonia mundi*. All of these are summarized in Christ, who creates the unity of all things in God through the paschal mystery of the cross.

Indeed Saint Paul himself sings of this understanding in a hymn in praise of Christ's primacy as sovereign of the universe, telling men and women to give

> thanks to God the Father, who hath made us worthy to be partakers of the lot of the saints in light:
> Who hath delivered us from the power of darkness and hath translated us into the kingdom of the Son of his love,
> In whom we have redemption through his blood, the remission of sins:
> Who is the image of the invisible God, the firstborn of every creature:
> For in him were all things created in heaven and on earth, visible and invisible, whether thrones, or dominations, or principalities, or powers. All things were created by him and in him.
> And he is before all: and by him all things consist.
> And he is the head of the body, the church: who is the beginning, the firstborn from the dead, that in all things he may hold the primacy:
> Because in him, it hath well pleased the Father that all fullness should dwell:
> And through him to reconcile all things unto himself, making peace through the blood of his cross, both as to the things that are on earth and the things that are in heaven. (Col 1:12-20)

Aelred's entire doctrine, presented through the course of this biography, can be defined as a vast and admirable unfurling of this Pauline vision of salvation history, in which the entire world is in conformity with Christ. For in Christ those whom God

> foreknew, he also predestinated to be made conformable to the image of his Son: that he might be the Firstborn amongst many brethren. And whom he predestined,

them he also called. And whom he called, them he also justified. And whom he justified, them he also glorified.

What shall we then say to these things? If God be for us, who is against us?

He that spared not even his own Son, but delivered him up for us all, how hath he not also, with him, given us all things?

Who shall accuse against the elect of God? God is he that justifieth:

Who is he that shall condemn? Christ Jesus that died: yea that is risen also again, who is at the right hand of God, who also maketh intercession for us. Who then shall separate us from the love of Christ? Shall tribulation? Or distress? Or famine? Or nakedness? Or danger? Or persecution? Or the sword?

(As it is written: For thy sake, we are put to death all the day long. We are accounted as sheep for the slaughter.)

But in all these things we overcome, because of him that hath loved us.

For I am sure that neither death, nor life, nor angels, nor principalities, nor powers, nor things present, nor things to come, nor might,

Nor height, nor depth, nor any other creature, shall be able to separate us from the love of God which is in Christ Jesus our Lord. (Rom 8:29-39)

May this grandiose vision of hope shed a light on the path in humanity's tentative march through the shadows of history.

Désert, December 31, 2009

Colophon

Having come to the end of this biography, we acknowledge its numerous imperfections as well as the immense debt we owe to our predecessors: Powicke, Talbot, Squire, Hoste, Raciti, Dumont, Dutton, Freeman, and so many others cited in these pages.

The merit for all that is good in this biography falls to them. The blame for any errors or imprecisions in this work lies with us alone.

And you, dear reader, having reached the final page of this book, remember kindly our great effort to offer it to you and, in so doing, deign to pray for us, as we too will remember the trouble you took to read it.

Let us both, for each other's benefit, offer this prayer for December 31, the seventh day of the Roman Missal's Octave of Christmas, and let us thus together close this biography:

> Almighty ever-living God,
> who in the Nativity of your Son
> established the beginning and fulfillment of all religion,
> grant, we pray, that we may be numbered
> among those who belong to him,
> in whom is the fullness of human salvation.
> Who lives and reigns with you in the unity of the Holy Spirit,
> one God, for ever and ever.[8]

---

8. *The Liturgy Archive: Christmas Time*, accessed June 2016, http://www
.liturgies.net/Liturgies/Catholic/roman_missal/christmasmass.htm#dec31.

Appendices

Appendix I

Chronological Chart

Date	Age	Events
1066		January 5: Death of King Edward the Confessor
		October 14: Defeat and death of Edward's successor Harold at the Battle of Hastings
		December 25: Coronation of William the Conqueror of Normandy as king of England
1075		Gregory VII's *Dictatus papae*, a decree of twenty-seven propositions giving back to the church its autonomy in the naming of bishops
1110–1124	0–14	Aelred's birth, followed by primary and secondary education
1114	4	Application of ecclesiastical norms to Aelred's father's tenure at Hexham
1122		September 23: Concordat of Worms, ending the Investiture Controversy opposing Emperor Henry V and Pope Callixtus II
1124	14	Aelred arrives at the court of David I, king of Scotland
1131 or 1132	21	Named *economus* or *dispensator* of King David I
		Founding of Rievaulx by Clairvaux Abbey
		Affair of Saint Mary's Abbey, York

1134	24	Aelred's mission to the archbishop of York
		Aelred's conversion and entry at Rievaulx
1135		Death of Henry I and start of the English Civil War
		Usurpation of the English throne by Stephen of Blois
1138		Battle of the Standard
1138	28	Death of Aelred's father, Eilaf
1139–1140		Death of Archbishop Thurstan of York, and issue of succession
1142	32	Aelred sent to Rome to protest naming of William Fitzherbert as archbishop of York
1142	32	Aelred named novice master at Rievaulx
1143	33	Aelred named abbot of Revesby
1145		Death of William, first abbot of Rievaulx
		Election of Maurice of Durham as second abbot of Rievaulx
1147	37	Resignation of Maurice from abbacy of Fountains Abbey
		Aelred's election as third abbot of Rievaulx
1152		June 12: Death of Prince Henry of Scotland
1153		Death of Walter Espec, founder and patron of Rievaulx
		May 24: Death of King David of Scotland
		July 8: Death of Pope Eugene III
		August 20: Death of Saint Bernard of Clairvaux
		December 25: Treaty of Wallingford, signed by King Stephen and Henry Plantagenet, ending the English Civil War

1154		October 25: Death of King Stephen
		December 19: Henry II crowned king of England
1160		Schism begins between Pope Alexander III and Antipope Victor IV
1161		Edward the Confessor canonized by Pope Alexander III
1162		June 3: Thomas Becket named archbishop of Canterbury
1163		Death of Maurice of Durham, second abbot of Rievaulx
		October 11: Political conflict begins between King Henry II and Thomas Becket, archbishop of Canterbury
		October 13: Edward the Confessor's relics transferred to Westminster; Aelred preaches at the translation
1164		April: Death of Antipope Victor IV
		November 2: Thomas Becket in exile in France
1167	57	January 12: Aelred's death
1170		December 29: Assassination of Thomas Becket, archbishop of Canterbury

Appendix II

Aelred of Rievaulx's Works Categorized by Seven Spiritual Paths

Path	Title	Date
Path of Relationships	*The Mirror of Charity*	1142–1143
	On Spiritual Friendship (book I)	1143–1144(?)
	On Spiritual Friendship (books II–III)	After 1159
	Correspondence (lost)	
Path of Contemplation	*On Jesus at the Age of Twelve*	1154–1155
	The Formation of Recluses	1160–1162
Path of Conversion	*Homilies on the Prophetic Burdens of Isaiah*	1163–1164

Path of Imitation	of Christ:	*The Liturgical Sermons*	
	of the Saints:	*The Life of Ninian*	1154–1160
		Lament for David, King of the Scots	1153–1154
		The Saints of the Church of Hexham	1155
		The Life of Edward, King and Confessor	1162–1163
Path of History	*The Genealogy of the Kings of the English*		1153–1154
	The Battle of the Standard		1153–1154
	A Certain Wonderful Miracle		1163–1165
Path of Anthropology	*Dialogue on the Soul*		1166
Path of the Pastor	*The Pastoral Prayer*		1163–1166
Path of the Liturgy	The hymn *Dulcis Iesu Memoria*		*(dubia)*

Appendix III

Foundations in the Filiation of Rievaulx

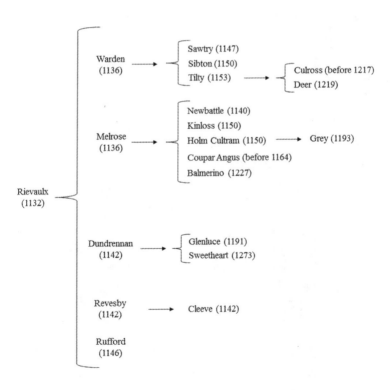

Appendix IV

Genealogical Relations Between the Anglo-Saxon, Franco-Norman, and Scottish Royal Families

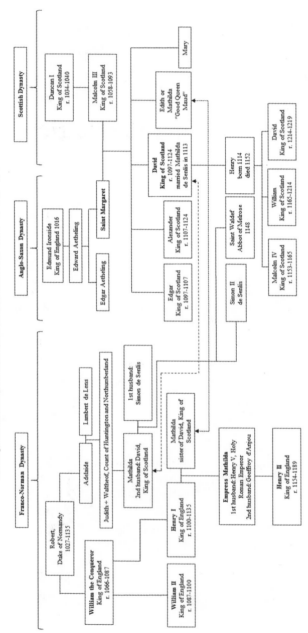

Selected Bibliography[1]

Aelredian Bibliographies

Burton, Pierre-André. *Bibliotheca Aelrediana Secunda. Une bibliographie cumulative (1962–1996).* Louvain-la-Neuve: Fédération internationale des Instituts d'études médiévales, 1997.

———. "Bibliotheca aelrediana secunda: Supplementa." In *A Companion to Aelred of Rievaulx (1110–1167),* edited by Marsha L. Dutton. Brill Companions to the Christian Tradition 76. Leiden/Boston: Brill, 2017. 295–324.

De Place, François. "Aelred de Rievaulx." In *Bibliographie pratique de la spiritualité cistercienne médiévale.* Bégrolles-en-Mauge: Abbaye de Bellefontaine, 1987. 27–36, chap. 2.

Dutton, Marsha L. "Aelred of Rievaulx." In *Oxford Bibliographies in Medieval Studies,* edited by Paul E. Szarmach. www.oxfordbiblographies.com. New York: Oxford University Press, 2018.

Hoste, Anselme. *Bibliotheca Aelrediana: A Survey of Manuscripts, Old Catalogues, Editions and Studies Concerning St. Aelred of Rievaulx.* Steenbrugge: Nijhoff, 1962.

———. "A Supplement to the Bibliotheca Aelrediana." Cîteaux 18 (1967): 402–7.

---

1. Translator's note: With some exceptions, Burton's bibliography lists works and articles in French, citing works in other languages only in footnotes. I have added sources from footnotes as well as Aelredian editions, translations, and studies that have appeared in or since 2010.

Primary Sources

Editions of Works by Aelred and Walter Daniel

Aelred of Rievaulx. "Aelred of Rievaulx's *Oratio pastoralis*." Ed. Marsha L. Dutton. CSQ 38 (2003): 297–308.

———. *Beati Aelredi Rievallis Abbatis*. Ed. J.-P. Migne. PL 195:209–796. Paris, 1855.

    De bello Standardii. 701–12.

    De genealogia regum Anglorum. 711–38.

    De sancto rege Scotorum David. 713–16.

    De sanctimoniali de Watton. 789–96.

    De spirituali amicitia. 659–702.

    Sermones de oneribus. 361–500.

    Sermones de tempore et de sanctis. 209–360.

    Speculum charitatis. 501–629.

    Vita S. Eduardi regis confessoris. 737–90.

———. *De Sanctis Ecclesiae Haugustaldensis*. In *Acta Sanctorum ordinis sancti Benedicti*, edited by Jean Mabillon. Paris: Billaine, 1672. Saec. III, Pars Ia: 228–32.

———. *De Sanctis Ecclesiae Haugustaldensis*. In *The Priory of Hexham: Its Chroniclers, Endowments, and Annals*, edited by James Raine. Surtees Society 44. Durham: Andrews and Co., 1884. 1.173–203.

———. *Epistola Aelredi Abbatis Rievallis ad Gilbertvm Venerabilem Episcopvm Lvndoniensem*. In Aelred of Rievaulx, *Opera Omnia*, vol. 5. 2005. CCCM 2D:3–5.

———. "Eulogium Davidis Regis Scotorum." In *Pinkerton's Lives of the Scottish Saints*, revised by W. M. Metcalfe. 2 vols. Paisley, Scotland: Alexander Gardner, 1889. 2:267–85.

———. *For Your Own People: Aelred of Rievaulx's Pastoral Prayer*. Ed. Marsha L. Dutton, trans. Mark DelCogliano. CF 73. Kalamazoo, MI: Cistercian Publications, 2008.

———. *Gesù dodicenne. Preghiera pastorale*. Trans. and intro. Domenico Pezzini. Milan: Paoline, 2001.

———. *Instrumenta lexicologica latina* (CM1). Microform (fasc. 53, CM1). Turnhout: Brepols, 1989.

    Contents:

    De anima. Ed. C. H. Talbot. 685–754. Reproduction of C. H. Talbot, ed. *De Anima*. London: Warburg Institute, 1952.

De Iesu puero duodenni. Ed. Anselm Hoste. 249–78. Repr. of *Quand Jésus eut douze ans,* ed. Anselm Hoste, trans. Joseph Dubois. Paris: Cerf, 1987.

De Institutione inclusarum. Ed. C. H. Talbot. 637–82. Reproduction of C. H. Talbot, ed. *The* "De Institutis Inclusarum." *Analecta Sacri ordinis cisterciensis* 7 (1951): 167–217.

De Spirituali amicitia. Ed. C. H. Talbot. 287–350.

Oratio Pastoralis. Ed. André Wilmart. 757–63. Repr. of André Wilmart, ed. "L'oraison pastoral de l'abbé Aelred." RBen 37 (1925): 263–72, with brief correction in RBen 41 (1929): 74.

Speculum caritatis. Ed. C. H. Talbot. 3–161.

———. *Instrumenta lexicologica latina* (CM2). Microform (fasc. 54). Turnhout: Brepols, 1989.

———. "In translacione sancti Edwardi confessoris." In Peter Jackson, " 'In translacione sancti Edwardi confessoris': The Lost Sermon by Aelred of Rievaulx Found?" CSQ 40, no. 1 (2005): 66–82.

———. *Opera omnia 1. Opera ascetica et mystica.* Ed. Anselm Hoste and C. H. Talbot. CCCM 1. Turnhout: Brepols, 1971.

Contents:

De anima. Ed. C. H. Talbot. 683–754.

De Iesu puero duodenni. Ed. Anselm Hoste. 245–78.

De institutione inclusarum. Ed. C. H. Talbot. 635–82.

De spiritali amicitia. Ed. Anselm Hoste. 279–350.

Liber de speculo caritatis. Ed. C. H. Talbot. 1–161.

Oratio pastoralis. Ed. Andre Wilmart. 755–63.

———. *Opera omnia 2–4. Sermones I–CLXXXII.* Ed. Gaetano Raciti. CCCM 2A, B, C. Turnhout: Brepols, 1989.

———. *Opera omnia 5. Sermones in Oneribus Propheticis Isaiae.* Ed. Gaetano Raciti. CCCM 2D. Turnhout: Brepols, 2005.

———. *Opera omnia 6. Opera Historica et Hagiographica.* Ed. Domenico Pezzini. CCCM 3. Turnhout: Brepols, 2017.

Contents:

De quodam miraculo mirabili. 253*–69*, 135–46.

De sanctis ecclesie Haugustaldensis et eorum miraculis. 179*– 217*, 75–110.

Genealogia Regum Anglorium. 69*–149*, 1–56.

Liber de Vita Religiosi David Regis Scotie. 78*–91*, 5–21.

Relatio de Standardo. 150*–178*, 57–73.

Vita Niniani. 218*–52*, 111–34.

———. *Opera omnia 7. Opera historica et Hagiographica (Vita sancti Ædwardi regis et confessoris).* Ed. Francesco Marzella. CCCM 3A. Turnhout: Brepols, 2017.

———. *Regola delle recluse.* Trans. and intro. Domenico Pezzini. Milan: Paoline, 2003.

———. "Relatio Venerabilis Aelredi, Abbatis Rievallensis, de Standardo." In *Chronicles of the Reigns of Stephen, Henry II, and Richard I,* edited by Richard Howlett. 4 vols. Rolls series no. 82. London, 1884–1886. 3:lviii–lx, 179–199.

———. "Une allocution familière de S. Aelred conservée dans les mélanges de Matthieu de Rievaulx." Ed. Gaetano Raciti. Coll 47 (1985): 267–80.

———. "Vita Niniani." In *Historians of Scotland,* edited by A. P. Forbes. Edinburgh: Edmonston and Douglas, 1874. 5:135–57.

———. "Vita Niniani." In *Pinkerton's Lives of the Scottish Saints,* edited by W. M. Metcalfe. Paisley, Scotland: Gardner, 1889. 1:9–39.

———. "Vita Niniani." In *Vitae antiquae Sanctorum Scotiae,* edited by Johannes Pinkerton. London: Nichols, 1789. 1–23.

Walter Daniel. "Epistola ad Mauricium." In *The Life of Ailred of Rievaulx,* edited and translated by F. M. Powicke. Oxford: Clarendon, 1950, 1978. 66–81.

———. "La lamentation de Walter Daniel sur le mort de la bienheureux Aelred de Rievaulx." Ed. C. H. Talbot. Coll 5 (1938): 9–20.

———. *The Life of Ailred of Rievaulx.* Ed. and trans. F. M. Powicke. Oxford: Clarendon, 1950, 1978.

Translations of Aelred's and Walter Daniel's Works

Aelred of Rievaulx. "Abbot Aelred of Rievaulx's Letter to Gilbert, Venerable Bishop of London." Trans. R. Jacob McDonie. CSQ 45, no. 2 (2010): 119–24. Repr. in Jean Truax, *Aelred the Peacemaker.* CS 251. Collegeville, MN: Cistercian Publications, 2017. 242–49.

———. "The Battle of the Standard." In Aelred, *The Historical Works,* 2005. CF 56:245–69.

———. "A Certain Wonderful Miracle." In Aelred, *The Lives of the Northern Saints,* 2006. CF 71:109–22.

————. *Dialogue on the Soul.* Trans. and intro. C. H. Talbot. CF 22. Kalamazoo, MI: Cistercian Publications, 1981.

————. *Dialogue sur l'âme.* Trans. and intro. Pierre-Yves Émery. Oka, Canada: Abbaye Notre-Dame-du-Lac, 2007.

————. *For Your Own People: Aelred of Rievaulx's* Pastoral Prayer. Trans. Mark DelCogliano, ed. and intro. Marsha L. Dutton. CF 73. Kalamazoo, MI: Cistercian Publications, 2008.

————. "The Genealogy of the Kings of the English." In Aelred, *The Historical Works,* 2005. CF 56:71–122.

————. *The Historical Works.* Trans. Jane Patricia Freeland; ed. and intro. Marsha L. Dutton. CF 56. Kalamazoo, MI: Cistercian Publications, 2005.

————. *Homélies sur les fardeaux selon le prophète Isaïe.* Trans Pierre-Yves Émery. Oka, Canada: Abbaye Notre-Dame-du-Lac, 2006.

————. *Homilies on the Prophetic Burdens of Isaiah.* Trans. Lewis White; intro. Marsha L. Dutton. CF 83. Collegeville, MN: Cistercian Publications, 2018.

————. "In translacione sancti Edwardi confessoris." Translated by Tom Licence. In Peter Jackson, "'*In translacione sancti Edwardi confessoris*': The Lost Sermon by Aelred of Rievaulx Found?" CSQ 40, no. 1 (2005): 66–82.

————. "Jesus at the Age of Twelve." Trans. Theodore Berkeley. In Aelred of Rievaulx, *Treatises. Pastoral Prayer,* 1971. CF 2:1–39.

————. "Lament for David, King of the Scots." In Aelred, *The Historical Works,* 2005. CF 56:45–70.

————. *L'amitié spirituelle.* Trans. and intro. Gaetane de Briey. Bégrolles-en-Mauge: Abbaye de Bellefontaine, 1994.

————. *La prière pastorale.* In Aelred of Rievaulx, *La vie de recluse, La prière pastorale,* translated and intro. by Charles Dumont. Paris: Cerf, 1961. 171–203.

————. *La vie de recluse.* In Aelred of Rievaulx, *La vie de recluse, La prière pastorale,* translated by Charles Dumont. Paris: Cerf, 1961. 7–169.

————. *Le miroir de la charité.* Trans. Charles Dumont and Gaetane de Briey. Bégrolles-en-Mauge: Abbaye de Bellefontaine, 1972.

————. "Le récit *La Bataille de l'Étendard.*" Trans. Pierre-André Burton. Cîteaux 58 (2007): 23–41.

————. "The Life of Ninian." Trans. Winifred MacQueen. In John MacQueen, *St. Nynia with a Translation of the Miracula Nynie*

Episcopi and the Vita Niniani. Edinburgh: Polygon Books, 1990. 102–33.

————. "The Life of Ninian, Apostle of the Southern Picts." In Aelred, *The Lives of the Northern Saints*, 2006. CF 71:35–63.

————. "The Life of Saint Edward, King and Confessor." In Aelred, *The Historical Works*, 2005. CF 56:123–243.

————. *The Liturgical Sermons: The First Clairvaux Collection, Advent-All Saints. Sermons One – Twenty-Eight.* Trans. and intro., Theodore Berkeley and M. Basil Pennington. CF 58. Kalamazoo, MI: Cistercian Publications, 2001.

————. *The Liturgical Sermons: The Second Clairvaux Collection, Christmas-All Saints. Sermons 29–46.* Trans. and Intro. Marie Anne Mayeski. CF 71. Collegeville, MN: Cistercian Publications, 2016.

————. *The Liturgical Sermons: The Durham and Lincoln Collections. Sermons 47–83.* Vol. 3. Trans. Kathryn Krug, Lewis White, and *Catena Scholarium*. Introduction by Ann Astell. CF 80. Collegeville, MN: Cistercian Publications, 2017.

————. *The Lives of the Northern Saints.* Trans. Jane Patricia Freeland. Ed. and intro. Marsha L. Dutton. CF 71. Kalamazoo, MI: Cistercian Publications, 2006.

————. *Mirror of Charity.* Trans. Elizabeth Connor; intro. Charles Dumont. CF 17. Kalamazoo, MI: Cistercian Publications, 1990.

————. "*Oratio Pastoralis*: A New Edition." Ed. Marsha L. Dutton. CSQ 38 (2003): 297–308.

————. "The Pastoral Prayer." Trans. R. Penelope Lawson. In Aelred, *Treatises. Pastoral Prayer*, 1971. CF 2:103–18.

————. "Prière d'un pasteur." In Aelred of Rievaulx, *Sermons pour l'année V*, translated by Gaetane de Briey. Oka, Canada: Abbaye Notre-Dame-du-Lac, 2005. 261–70.

————. *Quand Jésus eut douze ans.* Ed. Anselm Hoste, trans. Joseph Dubois, intro. Anselm Hoste. Paris: Cerf, 1987.

————. "A Rule of Life for a Recluse." Trans. Mary Paul Macpherson. In Aelred of Rievaulx, *Treatises. Pastoral Prayer*, 1971. CF 2:41–102.

————. "The Saints of the Church of Hexham and Their Miracles." In Aelred, *The Lives of the Northern Saints*, 2006. CF 71:65–107.

————. "Sermon for the Translation of the Relics of Edward the Confessor." Trans. Tom License. In Jean Truax, *Aelred the Peacemaker*, 2017. CS 251:260–73.

————. *Sermons pour l'année I, II, III, IV, V.* Trans. Gaetane de Briey. Oka, Canada: Abbaye Notre-Dame-du-Lac, 1997, 2002, 2005.

————. *Spiritual Friendship.* Trans. Lawrence Braceland. Ed. and intro. Marsha L. Dutton. CF 5. Collegeville, MN: Cistercian Publications, 2010.

————. *Treatises, Pastoral Prayer.* Ed. M. Basil Pennington. CF 2. Kalamazoo, MI: Cistercian Publications, 1971.

Walter Daniel. "Epistola ad Mauricium." In *The Life of Ailred of Rievaulx,* ed. and trans. F. M. Powicke. Oxford: Clarendon, 1950, 1978. 66–81.

————. "La lamentation pour la mort d'Aelred." In *La Vie d'Aelred,* trans. and intro. by Pierre-André Burton, 2003. 155–68.

————. *La Lettre à Maurice.* In *La Vie d'Aelred,* translated and introduced by Pierre-André Burton, 2003. 169–93.

————. "Lament for Aelred." Trans. Jane Patricia Freeland. In *The Life of Aelred of Rievaulx,* 1994. CF 57:140–47.

————. *The Life of Aelred of Rievaulx and The Letter to Maurice.* Trans. and intro. F. M. Powicke. New intro. by Marsha L. Dutton. CF 57. Kalamazoo, MI: Cistercian Publications, 1994.

————. *The Life of Ailred of Rievaulx.* Trans. with notes and Introduction F. M. Powicke. Oxford: Clarendon, 1950, 1978.

————. *La Vie d'Aelred, abbé de Rievaulx.* In *La Vie d'Aelred, abbé de Rievaulx, La Lamentation pour la mort d'Aelred, La Lettre à Maurice,* translated by Pierre-André Burton. Oka, Canada: Abbaye Notre-Dame-du-Lac, 2003. 43–153.

————. "Walter Daniel's Letter to Maurice." In *The Life of Aelred of Rievaulx,* translated and introduced by F. M. Powicke, 1994. CF 57:147–58.

————. "Walter Daniel's Letter to Maurice." In *The Life of Ailred of Rievaulx,* trans. and intro. F. M. Powicke, 1978. 66–81.

Aelredian Dubia

"Dulcis Jesu memoria." Trans. Michel Coune. Coll 55 (1993): 239–43.

"Maurice of Rievaulx." Trans. F. M. Powicke. *The English Historical Review* 36 (1921): 26–29.

Editions and Translations of Other Authors

Bernard of Clairvaux. "A Letter of Bernard Abbot of Clairvaux, to Abbot Aelred." In Aelred of Rievaulx, *The Mirror of Charity.* 1990. CF 17:69–75.

————. *The Letters of Saint Bernard of Clairvaux*. Trans. and ed. Bruno Scott James. London: Burns Oates, 1953.

————. "Monastic Obligations and Abbatial Authority: St Bernard's *Book on Precept and Dispensation*." Trans. Conrad Greenia. In Bernard of Clairvaux, *Treatises I*. The Works of Bernard of Clairvaux. CF 1. Spencer, MA: Cistercian Publications, 1970. 71–150.

————. *On the Song of Songs II*. Trans. Kilian Walsh. CF 7. Kalamazoo, MI: Cistercian Publications, 1976.

————. "St Bernard's Apologia to Abbot William." Trans. Michael Casey. In Bernard of Clairvaux, *Treatises I*. The Works of Bernard of Clairvaux, 1. CF 1. Spencer, MA: Cistercian Publications, 1970. 1–69.

Cicero. *De Amicitia*. In Cicero, *De Senectute, De Amicitia, De Divinatione*, translated by William Armistead Falconer. Cambridge, MA: Harvard Uuniversity Press, 2001. 103–211.

Dugdale, William. *Monasticon Anglicanum*. London: Bohn, 1846.

"Exordium Parvum." In *Narrative and Legislative Texts from Early Cîteaux*, edited by Chrysogonus Waddell. Cîteaux: *Commentarii Cistercienses*, 1999. 199–259.

Gilbert of Hoyland. *Sermons on the Song of Songs, III*. Trans. Lawrence C. Braceland. The Works of Gilbert of Hoyland. CF 26. Kalamazoo, MI: Cistercian Publications, 1979.

Guerric of Igny. *Liturgical Sermons*. Trans. Monks of Mount Saint Bernard Abbey. 2 vols. CF 8, 32. Spencer, MA: Cistercian Publications, 1971, 1999.

Jocelin of Furness. "The Life of Waldef, Abbot of Melrose." In "An Edition and Translation of The Life of Waldef, Abbot of Melrose," translated by George Joseph McFadden, dissertation, Columbia University, 1952. (Ann Arbor: University Microfilms International, 1952.)

"La vie de St. Édouard le confesseur par Osbert de Clare." Ed. Marc Bloch. *Analecta Bollandiana* 41 (1923): 5–131.

Les Ecclesiastica officia *cisterciens du XII* siècle. Ed. Danièle Choiselet and Placide Vernet. Reiningue: Abbaye d'Oelenberg, 1989.

The Life of King Edward Who Rests at Westminster. Ed. and trans. Frank Barlow. 2d ed. 1962; Oxford: Clarendon Press, 1992.

Orderic Vitalis. *Histoire de Normandie*. 4 vols. Paris: Guizot, 1826.

Raine, James, ed. *The Priory of Hexham: Its Chroniclers, Endowments, and Annals*. 2 vols. Surtees Society 44. Durham: Andrews and Co., 1864.

RB 1980: The Rule of St. Benedict. Ed. and trans. Timothy Fry. Collegeville, MN: Liturgical Press, 1981.

Richard of Hexham. *De statu et episcopo Hagulstadensis ecclesiae.* In James Raine, ed., *The Priory of Hexham,* 1864. 2:1–62.

Sallust. *The War with Catiline, The War with Jugurtha.* Trans. J. C. Rolfe; rev. John T. Ramsey. Cambridge, MA: Harvard Uuniversity Press, 2013.

Waddell, Chrysogonus, ed. and trans. *Narrative and Legislative Texts from Early Cîteaux: Latin Text in Dual Edition with English Translation and Notes.* Cîteaux: Commentarii Cistercienses, 1999.

William of Saint-Thierry, Arnold of Bonneval, and Geoffrey of Auxerre. *The First Life of Bernard of Clairvaux.* Trans. Hilary Costello. CF 76. Collegeville, MN: Cistercian Publications, 2015.

Studies

Astell, Ann W. "To Build the Church: Saint Aelred of Rievaulx's Hexaemeral Miracles in the *Life of Ninian.*" CSQ 49, no. 4 (2014): 455–81.

Aubé, Pierre. *Saint Bernard de Clairvaux.* Paris: Fayard, 2003.

———. *Thomas Becket.* Paris: Fayard, 1988.

Basset, Lytta. *Le Pardon originel.* Geneva: Labor et Fides, 1995.

Bell, David N. "*Agrestis et infatua Interpretatio*: The Background and Purpose of John of Forde's Condemnation of Jewish Exegesis." In *A Gathering of Friends,* edited by Hilary Costello and Christopher Holdsworth. CS 161. Kalamazoo, MI: Cistercian Publications, 1996. 131–52.

———. "Ailred [Aelred, Æthelred] of Rievaulx (1110–1167)." In *Oxford Dictionary of National Biography,* edited by H. C. G. Matthew and Brian Harrison. Oxford: Oxford University Press, 2004. 1:491–93.

———. "From Molesme to Cîteaux: the Earliest 'Cistercian' 'Spirituality.'" CSQ 34 (1999): 469–82.

Bequette, John P. "Aelred of Rievaulx's *Life of Saint Edward, King and Confessor*: A Saintly King and the Salvation of the English People." CSQ 43, no. 1 (2008): 17–40.

Biffi, Inos. "Aspetti dell'imitazione di Cristo nella letteratura monastica del secolo XII." *La Scuola Cattolica* 96 (1968): 150, n. 2, 451–90.

———. "Bibbia et liturgia nei sermoni liturgici di Aelredo di Rievaulx." In *Bibbia et spiritualità: Biblioteca di cultura religiosa,* edited by Cipriano Vagaggini and Gregorio Penco. Rome: Paoline, 1967. 517–98.

Boquet, Damien. "Affectivity in the Spiritual Writings of Aelred of Rievaulx." In Dutton, ed., *A Companion to Aelred of Rievaulx,* 2017. 167–96.

———. *L'ordre de l'affect au Moyen Âge. Autour de l'anthropologie affective d'Aelred de Rievaulx.* Caen: CRAHM, 2005.

Boswell, John. *Christianity, Social Tolerance, and Homosexuality.* Chicago: The University of Chicago Press, 1980.

Bouyer, Louis. *La Spiritualité de Cîteaux.* Paris: Flammarion, 1955.

Bredero, Adriaan M. *Cluny et Cîteaux au XIIᵉ siècle: L'histoire d'une controverse monastique.* Amsterdam: Holland University Press, 1985.

Briey, Gaetane de. "Observance cistercienne et charité chrétienne selon le *Miroir*." Coll 55 (1993): 169–85.

Brooke, Christopher. "St. Bernard, the Patrons and Monastic Painting." In *Cistercian Art and Architecture in the British Isles,* edited by Christopher Norton and David Park. Cambridge, UK: Cambridge University Press, 1986. 11–23.

Burton, Janet. "The Estates and Economy of Rievaulx Abbey in Yorkshire." Cîteaux 49 (1998): 29–94.

———. "The Foundation of the British Cistercian Houses." In *Cistercian Art and Architecture in the British Isles,* edited by Christopher Norton and David Park. Cambridge, UK: Cambridge University Press, 1986. 24–39.

———. *The Monastic Order in Yorkshire, 1069–1215.* Cambridge, UK: Cambridge University Press, 1999.

———. "Rievaulx Abbey: The Early Years." In *Perspectives for an Architecture of Solitude,* edited by Terryl N. Kinder (Turnhout: Brepols, 2004), 47–53.

Burton, Pierre-André. "Aelred face à l'histoire et à ses historiens. Autour de l'actualité aelrédienne." Coll 58 (1996): 161–93.

———."Aelred prédicateur. De la visé à la vision, ou l'art d'apprendre à toujours regarder avec les yeux dans la tête." Introduction to Aelred of Rievaulx, *Sermons pour l'année III: Sermons 29–46,* translated by Gaetane de Briey. Oka, Canada: Abbaye Notre-Dame-du-Lac, 2002.

———. "Aelred, tel un second Noé: l'abbé de Rievaulx, un bâtisseur à la recherche de la coudée unique." Cîteaux 52 (2001): 231–318.

———. "À propos de l'amitié dans la doctrine spirituelle d'Aelred. Dans un 'entre-temps' qui prépare—dans le Christ—à une charité d'amitié universelle." Coll 58 (1996): 243–61.

———. "Aux origines de l'expansion anglaise de Cîteaux. La fondation de Rievaulx et la conversion d'Aelred, 1132–1134 (I–II)." Coll 61 (1999): 186–214, 248–90.

———. "The Beginnings of Cistercian Expansion in England: The Socio-Historical Context of the Formation of Rievaulx." CSQ 42, no. 2 (2009): 395–411.

———. "Contemplation et imitation de la Croix: un chemin de perfection chrétienne et monastique d'après le *Miroir*." Coll 55 (1993): 140–68.

———. "An Illiterate, or a True Master of Spiritual Teaching?" In Dutton, ed., *A Companion to Aelred of Rievaulx*, 2017. 197–220.

———. "Le *Miroir de la charité* ou les trois premiers cercles de l'amour." Coll 64 (2002): 80–104.

———. "Le récit de la *Bataille de l'Étendard* par Aelred de Rievaulx. Présentation: les enjeux implicites d'un récit apparemment anecdotique." Cîteaux 58 (2007): 1–22.

———. "Le *Traité sur l'amitié spirituelle* ou les trois derniers cercles de l'amour." Coll 64 (2002): 197–218.

———. "Une lecture 'aux éclats' du Cantique des cantiques. Les enjeux de l'herméneutique biblique selon saint Bernard. Un commentaire du *Sermon 23 sur le Cantique*." Cîteaux 57 (2006): 165–241.

———. "Walter Daniel, un biographe injustement critiqué? À propos de la réception de la *Vita Aelredi*. Entre vérité historique et vérité mythique." Cîteaux 53 (2002): 223–67.

Bynum, Caroline. *Jesus as Mother: Studies in the Spirituality of the High Middle Ages*. Berkeley: University of California Press, 1982.

Callerot, Françoise. Introduction to Bernard de Clairvaux, *Sur le précept et la dispense*. Paris: Les Éditions du Cerf, 2000. 21–140.

Casey, Michael. "An Introduction to Aelred's Chapter Discourses." CSQ 45, no. 3 (2010): 279–314.

Chenu, Marie-Dominique. "Theology and the New Awareness of History." In *Nature, Man and Society in the Twelfth Century*, translated by Jerome Taylor and Lester K. Little. Chicago: University of Chicago Press, 1968. 162–201.

Chergé, Christian de. *L'Invincible Espérance*. Paris: Bayard, 1997.

Choiselet, Danièle, and Placide Vernet, eds. *Les Ecclesiastica officia cisterciens du XIIe siècle*. Reiningue: Abbaye d'Oelenberg, 1989.

Clark, Robert L. A. "Spiritual Exercise: The Making of Interior Faith." In *The Oxford Handbook of Medieval Christianity*, edited by John H. Arnold. Oxford: Oxford University Press, 2014. 271–86.

Courcelle, Pierre. "Ailred de Rievaulx à l'école des *Confessions*." *Revue des études augustiniennes* 3 (1957): 163–74.

———. "Confession et contemplation au temps d'Ailred de Rievaulx." In *Les Confessions de saint Augustin dans la tradition littéraire. Antécédents et postérité*. Paris: Études augustiniennes, 1963. 265–305.

De Connick, Léon. "Adaptation ou retour aux origines? Les Exercices spirituels de saint Ignace." *Nouvelle revue théologique* 70 (1948): 918–45.

Delhaye, Philippe. "Deux adaptations du *De amicitia* de Cicéron au XIIᵉ siècle." *Recherches de théologie ancienne et médiévale* 15 (1948): 304–31.

Dietz, Elias. "Aelred on the Capital Vices: a Unique Voice among the Cistercians." CSQ 43, no. 3 (2008): 271–93.

———. "Aelred on the Humanity of Christ: A Theology in Images." CSQ 45, no. 3 (2010): 269–78.

———. "Ambivalence Well Considered: An Interpretive Key to the Whole of Aelred's Works." CSQ 47, no. 1 (2012): 71–85.

Dumont, Charles. "Aelred de Rievaulx." In Georgius Marie, *Théologie de la vie monastique*. Paris: Aubier, 1961. 527–40.

———. "Aelred de Rievaulx. Introduction à sa vie et à ses écrits." In Dumont, *Une éducation du cœur*. 191–236. (Trans. of Dumont, "Introduction." In Aelred of Rievaulx, *The Mirror of Charity*. CF 17:11–67.)

———. "Autour des sermons *De Oneribus* d'Aelred de Rievaulx. Les éditions et la tradition manuscrite. Influence de Gilbert Foliot." Coll 19 (1957): 114–21.

———. "Chercher Dieu dans la communauté selon Aelred de Rievaulx." Coll 34 (1977): 78–88. Repr. in Dumont, *Une éducation du cœur*, 1996. 273–308.

———. "La méditation selon Aelred de Rievaulx." In *Une éducation du cœur*. 375–96.

———. "L'amitié spirituelle dans l'école de la charité." In *Une éducation du cœur*. 359–74.

———. "L'amour fraternel dans la doctrine monastique d'Aelred de Rievaulx." Coll 51 (1989): 78–88. Repr. in *Une éducation du cœur*, 1996. 335–48.

————. "Le personnalisme communautaire d'Aelred de Rievaulx." Coll 39 (1977): 129–48. Repr. in *Une éducation du cœur*. 309–34.

————. "L'équilibre humain de la vie cistercienne d'après le bienheureux Aelred de Rievaulx." Coll 18 (1956): 177–89.

————. "L'hymne *Dulcis Iesu memoria*: Le *Jubilus* serait-il d'Aelred de Rievaulx?" Hymn translated by Michel Coune. In *S. Aelred de Rievaulx: Le Miroir de la Charité. Journées d'Études, Abbaye de Scourmont, Belgium, 5–9 October 1992*. Coll 55 (1993): 233–43.

————. "Pourquoi le *Miroir* a-t-il été publié? L'identité cistercienne hier comme aujourd'hui." Coll 55 (1993): 14–27.

————. *Sagesse ardente. À l'école cistercienne de l'amour dans la tradition bénédictine*. Oka, Canada: Abbaye Notre-Dame-du-Lac, 1995.

————. *Une éducation du cœur. La spiritualité affective de saint Bernard de Clairvaux et de saint Aelred de Rievaulx*. Oka, Canada: Abbaye Notre-Dame-du-Lac, 1996.

————. "Walthéof." *Dictionnaire de spiritualité*. Paris: Beauchêne, 1995. 16:1311–12.

Dupeux, Cécile. "Saint Bernard dans l'iconographie médiévale: l'exemple de la lactation." In *Vies et légendes de saint Bernard de Clairvaux. Actes des rencontres de Dijon, 7–8 juin 1991*, edited by Patrick Arabeyre, Jacques Berlioz, and Philippe Poirier. Cîteaux: Saint-Nicolas-lès-Cîteaux, 1993. 167–72.

Dutton, Marsha L. "Ælred comme historien et acteur dans l'histoire. La philosophie politique de ses quatre traités historiques." *Intentio Cordis: Temps, histoire, mémoire chez Aelred de Rievaulx*. Coll 73, no. 1 (2011): 38–55.

————. "Aelred, Historian: Two Portraits in Plantagenet Myth." CSQ 28, no. 2 (1993): 112–43.

————. "Aelred historien: deux nouveaux portraits dans un manuscrit de Dublin (Trinity College Dublin ms. 172)." Coll 55 (1993): 209–30.

————. "Aelred of Rievaulx: Abbot, Teacher, and Author." In Dutton, ed., *A Companion to Aelred of Rievaulx*, 2017. 17–47.

————. "Aelred of Rievaulx and the Charge of Sexual Obsession: An Invented History." ABR 47 (1996): 414–32.

————. "Aelred of Rievaulx on Friendship, Chastity, and Sex: The Sources," CSQ 29 (1994): 121–96.

————. "Antiphonal Learning: Listening and Speaking in the Works of Aelred of Rievaulx." CSQ 54, no. 3 (2019): 267–85.

————. "Christ Our Mother: Aelred's Iconography for Contemplative Union." In *Goad and Nail: Studies in Medieval Cistercian History, X,* edited by E. Rozanne Elder. CS 84. Kalamazoo, MI: Cistercian Publications, 1985. 21–45.

————. "The Cistercian Source: Aelred, Bonaventure, Ignatius." In *Goad and Nail: Studies in Medieval Cistercian History, X,* edited by E. Rozanne Elder. CS 98. Kalamazoo, MI: Cistercian Publications, 1985. 151–78.

————. "The Conversion and Vocation of Aelred of Rievaulx: A Historical Hypothesis." In *England in the Twelfth Century,* edited by Daniel Williams. London: Boydell, 1990. 31–49.

————. " 'Galwegians and Gauls': Aelred of Rievaulx's Dramatisation of Xenophobia in *Relatio de Standardo.*" In *Monastic Life in the Medieval British Isles: Essays in Honour of Janet Burton,* edited by Karen Stöber, Julie Kerr, and Emilia Jamroziak. Cardiff: University of Wales Press, 2018. 115–86.

————. "Getting Things the Wrong Way Round: Composition and Transposition in Aelred of Rievaulx's *De Institutione Inclusarum.*" In *Heaven on Earth: Studies on Medieval History, IX,* edited by E. Rozanne Elder. CS 68. Kalamazoo, MI: Cistercian Publications, 1983. 90–101.

————. "A Historian's Historian: The Place of Bede in Aelred's Contributions to the New History of his Age." In *Truth as Gift: Studies in Cistercian History in Honor of John R. Sommerfeldt,* edited by Marsha L. Dutton, Daniel M. La Corte, and Paul Lockey. CF 204. Kalamazoo, MI: Cistercian Publications, 2004. 407–48.

————. "Intimacy and Imitation: The Humanity of Christ in Cistercian Spirituality." In *Erudition at God's Service: Studies in Medieval Cistercian History, XI,* edited by John R. Sommerfeldt. CS 98. Kalamazoo, MI: Cistercian Publications, 1987. CS 98. 33–70.

————. Introduction to "Aelred of Rievaulx: *The Pastoral Prayer.*" CSQ 37, no. 4 (2002): 453–59.

————. "A Model for Friendship: Ambrose's Contribution to Aelred of Rievaulx's *Spiritual Friendship.*" ABR 64, no. 1 (2013): 39–66.

————. "The Sacramentality of Community in Aelred." In Dutton, ed., *A Companion to Aelred of Rievaulx,* 2017. 246–67.

————. "Saints Refusing to Leave: Aelred of Rievaulx's *The Saints of Hexham* as an Inverted *Translatio.*" In *The Medieval Translator,* vol. 15, *In Principio Fuit Interpres,* edited by Alessandra Petrina. Turnhout: Brepols, 2013. 187–200.

———. "*Sancto Dunstano Cooperante*: Collaboration between King and Ecclesiastical Advisor in Aelred of Rievaulx's *Genealogy of the Kings of the English*." In *Religious and Laity in Northern Europe 1000–1400: Interaction, Negotiation, and Power*, edited by Emilia Jamroziak and Janet Burton. Turnhout: Brepols, 2007. 183–95.

———. "That Peace Should Guide and Society Unite: Aelred of Rievaulx's Political Philosophy." CSQ 47, no. 3 (2012): 279–95.

———. "This Ministry of Letters: Aelred of Rievaulx's Attempt to Anglicize England's King Henry II." In *Monasticism Between Culture and Cultures: Acts of the Third International Symposium, Rome, June 8–11, 2011*, edited by Philippe Nouzille and Michaela Pfeifer. *Analecta Monastica* 14. Turnhout: Brepols, 2013. 169–93.

———. "Were Aelred of Rievaulx and Gilbert of Sempringham Friends? Speculating from a Close Reading of *A Certain Wonderful Miracle*." ABR 68, no. 3 (2017): 274–300.

Dutton, Marsha L., ed. *A Companion to Aelred of Rievaulx (1110–1167)*. Brill Companions to the Christian Tradition 76. Leiden/Boston: Brill, 2017.

Fein, Suzanna Greer. "Maternity in Aelred of Rievaulx's Letter to his Sister." In *Medieval Mothering*, edited by John Carmi Parsons and Bonnie Wheeler. New York: Routledge, 1996. 139–56.

Fergusson, Peter. "Aelred's Abbatial Residence at Rievaulx Abbey." in *Studies in Cistercian Art and Architecture*, vol. 5, edited by Meredith P. Lillich. CS 167. Kalamazoo, MI: Cistercian Publications, 1998. 41–56.

Fergusson, Peter, and Stuart Harrison. *Rievaulx Abbey: Community, Architecture, and Memory*. New Haven: Yale University Press, 1999.

Freeman, Elizabeth A. "Aelred as a Historian among Historians." In Dutton, ed., *A Companion to Aelred of Rievaulx*, 2017. 113–46.

———. "Aelred of Rievaulx's *De Bello Standardii*: Cistercian Hagiography and the Creation of Community Memories." Cîteaux 49 (1998): 5–28.

———. "The Many Functions of Cistercian Histories Using Aelred of Rievaulx's *Relatio de Standardo* as a Case Study." In *The Medieval Chronicle: Proceedings of the First International Conference on the Medieval Chronicle*, edited by Erik Kooper. Amsterdam/Atlanta: Rodopi, 1999. 124–32.

———. *Narratives of a New Order: Cistercian Historical Writing in England, 1150–1220*. Turnhout: Brepols, 2002.

Ghislain, Gabriel. "À la recherche de la réponse juste: un novice interroge son père maître (*Miroir*, Livre II, ch. 17–21)." Coll 55 (1993): 78–109.

Gobry, Ivan. *Les moines d'Occident, vol. V: Cîteaux.* Paris: Guibert, 1997.

Golding, Brian. *Gilbert of Sempringham and the Gilbertine Order.* Oxford: Oxford University Press, 1995.

Gourevitch, Aron. *La Naissance de l'individu au Moyen Âge.* Paris: Seuil, 1997.

Groń, Ryszard. *"Spór o Aelreda": W poszukiwaniu prawdziwego oblicza Aelreda z Rievaulx (The Debate about Aelred: Looking for the True Face of Aelred of Rievaulx).* Introduction, Marsha L. Dutton. Kety, Poland: Antyk, 2005.

Hallier, Amédée. *The Monastic Theology of Aelred of Rievaulx.* Trans. Columban Heaney. CS 2. Kalamazoo, MI: Cistercian Publications, 1969.

Heurre, Denis. "L'initiation monastique aujourd'hui." *Liturgie* 98 (1996): 165–90.

———. "Vie commune et transcendance." Coll 71 (2009): 124–43.

Hoste, Anselm. "Aelred de Rievaulx et la dévotion médiévale au Crucifié." Coll 29 (1967): 37–43.

———. "A Survey of the Unedited Work of Laurence of Durham and an Edition of his Letter to Aelred of Rievaulx." *Sacris Erudiri* 11 (1960): 249–65.

Huille, I. "Grâces ordinaires et grâces spéciales dans le livre II du *Miroir*." Coll 55 (1993): 78–109.

Iglesia, Roberto de la. "La comunidad monástica, realización completa de la Iglesia según Elredo de Rievaulx." *Cistercium* 244 (2006): 389–437.

———. "La ecclesiologia monástica de san Elredo de Rievaulx." *Cistercium* 250 (2008): 81–101.

Ingledew, Francis. "The Book of Troy and the Genealogical Construction of History: The Case of Geoffrey of Monmouth's *Historia regum Britanniae*," *Speculum* 69, no. 3 (1994): 665–704.

Jackson, Peter. "*In translacione sancti Edwardi Confessoris*: The Lost Sermon by Aelred of Rievaulx Found?" Trans. Tom License. CSQ 40, no. 1 (2005): 45–83.

Jamroziak, Emilia. "Rievaulx Abbey and its Patrons: Between Cooperation and Conflict." *Cîteaux* 49 (1998): 59–71.

Jarrett, Bede. "Saint Aelred of Rievaulx." In *The English Way*, edited by Maisie Ward. London: Sheed and Ward, 1933.

Javalet, Robert. *Image et ressemblance au XIIᵉ siècle: De saint Anselme à Alain de Lille*. 2 vols. Paris: Letouzey et Ané, 1967.

Kinder, Terryl, ed. *Perspectives for an Architecture of Solitude: Essays on Cistercians, Art and Architecture in Honour of Peter Fergusson*. Turnhout: Brepols, 2004.

King, Edmund. *The Anarchy of Stephen's Reign*. Oxford: Oxford University Press, 1994.

Knowles, David. *The Monastic Order in England: A History of its Development from the Times of St. Dunstan to the Fourth Lateran Council (940–1216)*. Cambridge, UK: Cambridge University Press, 1976.

La Corte, Daniel M. "Aelred on Abbatial Responsibilties." In Dutton, ed., *A Companion to Aelred of Rievaulx*, 2017. 48–69.

Lange, Marjory E. "A Reading of Aelred of Rievaulx's *De Anima*: Through Ciceronian Dialogue to Personal Testament." CSQ 45, no. 4 (2010): 401–20.

Lazzari, Francisco. "Il *contemptus mundi* in Aelredo di Rievaulx." Coll 29 (1967): 61–62.

Leclercq, Jean. *Bernard de Clairvaux*. Paris: Desclée de Brouwer, 1989.

——. *L'Amour des lettres et le désir de Dieu. Initiation aux auteurs monastiques du Moyen Âge*. Paris: Cerf, 1990.

——. "Les deux rédactions de la lettre de saint Bernard à Aelred de Rievaulx." In *Jean Misrahi Memorial Volume: Studies in Medieval Literature*, edited by H. R. Runte, H. Niedzielski, and W. L. Hendrickson. Columbia: French Literature Publications Co., 1977. 210–28. Republished in Jean Leclercq, *Recueil d'études sur saint Bernard et ses écrits* 4. Rome: Edizioni di Storia e letteratura, 1987.

——. *Nouveau visage de Bernard de Clairvaux. Approches psychohistoriques*. Paris: Cerf, 1976.

Le Goff, Jacques. *La civilisation de l'Occident médiéval*. Paris: Arthaud, 1991.

——. *L'imaginaire médiéval: Essais*. Paris: Gallimard, 1985.

——. *Saint Louis*. Paris: Gallimard, 1995.

Lemoine, Matthias. "Le moine et le saint roi: La qualité de confesseur dans la *Vita Edwardi* d'Aelred de Rievaulx (I–II)." Coll 68 (2006): 34–47, 218–27.

——. "Saint Édouard, roi et confesseur dans la *Vita* d'Aelred de Rievaulx." M.A. thesis, Université de Provence, 2005.

Louf, André. "Bernard fut-il un iconoclaste?" *Bulletin de littérature ecclésiastique* 113 (1992): 49–64.

Lubac, Henri de. *The Four Senses of Scripture.* 4 vols. Grand Rapids: Eerdmans, 1998.

MacQueen, John. *St. Nynia, with a Translation of the* Miracula Nynie Episcopi *and the* Vita Niniani. Edinburgh: Polygon, 1990.

Maiorino, Anna. "La christologie affective d'Aelred de Rievaulx," Coll 29 (1967): 44–60.

Mayeski, Anne Marie. "'At the Feet of His Dearest Mother'": Aelred's Teaching on Mary in the Sermons of the First Clairvaux Collection." In Dutton, ed., *A Companion to Aelred of Rievaulx,* 2017. 149–66.

———. "Clothing Maketh the Saint: Aelred's Narrative Intent in the *Life of Saint Ninian*." CSQ 44, no. 2 (2009): 181–90.

———. "'The Right Occasion for the Words': Situating Aelred's Homily on Saint Katherine." CSQ 33, no. 1 (1998): 45–60.

———. "*Secundum naturam*: The Inheritance of Virtue in Aelred's *Genealogy of the English Kings*." CSQ 37 (2002): 221–28.

McGuire, Brian Patrick. *Brother and Lover: Aelred of Rievaulx.* New York: Crossroad, 1994.

———. *Friendship and Community: The Monastic Experience (350–1250).* CS 95. Kalamazoo, MI: Cistercian Publications, 1988. 296–338.

———. "Monastic Friendship and Toleration in Twelfth-Century Cistercian Life." In *Monks, Hermits and the Ascetic Tradition,* edited by W. J. Sheils. Oxford: Blackwell, 1985. 147–60.

———. "Sexual Awareness and Identity in Aelred of Rievaulx (1110–1167)." ABR 45 (1995): 184–226.

Miquel, Pierre. "Spécificité et caractères de l'expérience spirituelle chez Aelred." Coll 29 (1967): 3–11. Repr. Pierre Miquel, in *Le Vocabulaire latin de l'expérience spirituelle dans la tradition monastique et canoniale de 1050 à 1250.* Paris: Beauchesne, 1989. 123–32.

Miterre, Paul. *Saint Bernard de Clairvaux: Un moine arbitre de l'Europe au XIIᵉ siècle.* Genval, Belgium: Lannoy, 1929.

Molac, Philippe. "Théologie de l'histoire chez Aelred d'après les sermons *De oneribus*." In Intentio Cordis: *Temps, histoire, mémoire chez Aelred de Rievaulx.* Coll 73 (2011): 86–98.

Morris, Colin. *The Discovery of the Individual: 1050–1200.* Toronto: University of Toronto Press, 1987.

Noblesse-Rocher, Annie. *L'Expérience de Dieu dans les sermons de Guerric, abbé d'Igny (XIIᵉ siècle).* Paris: Cerf, 2005.

Norton, Christopher. "Richard of Fountains and the Letter of Thurstan: History and Historiography of a Monastic Controversy, St. Mary's Abbey, York, 1132." In *Perspectives for an Architecture of Solitude: Essays on Cistercians, Art and Architecture in Honour of Peter Fergusson*, edited by Terryl Kinder. Turnhout: Brepols, 2004. 9–34.

Nouzille, Philippe. *Expérience de Dieu et théologie monastique au XIIe siècle: Étude sur les sermons d'Aelred de Rievaulx*. Paris: Cerf, 1999.

Ouaknin, Marc-Alain. *Bibliothérapie: lire, c'est guérir*. Paris: Seuil, 1994.

Pezzini, Gaetano. "Aelred's Doctrine of Charity and Friendship." In Dutton, ed., *A Companion to Aelred of Rievaulx*, 2017. 73–97.

———. "Aelred of Rievaulx's *Vita sancti Eduardi regis et confessoris*: Its Genesis and Radiation." Cîteaux 60 (2009): 27–76.

———. "The Genealogy and Posterity of Aelred of Rievaulx's *Vita sancti Eduardi regis et confessoris*." In *The Translation of Religious Texts in the Middle Ages: Tracts and Rules, Hymns and Saints' Lives*. Berne: Peter Lang, 2008. 333–72.

———. "La théologie politique chez Aelred de Rievaulx d'après ses oeuvres historiques." In Intentio Cordis: *Temps, histoire, mémoire chez Aelred de Rievaulx: Proceedings of an International Monastic Colloquium, Toulouse, France, March 2010*. Coll 73, no. 1 (2011): 56–85.

———. "The Sermons of Aelred of Rievaulx." In Dutton, ed., *A Companion to Aelred of Rievaulx*, 2017. 73–97.

Pfeiffer, Michaela. "Trois styles de la mystique cistercienne: Bernard, Guillaume, Aelred." Coll 65 (2003): 89–110.

Polek, Wincenty. "Teologia dell'amicizia negli scritti di Aelredo di Rievaulx (1110–1167)." *Cistercium Mater Nostra* 2 (2008): 79–104.

Posset, Franz. "*Amplexus Bernardi*: The Dissemination of a Cistercian Motif in the Later Middle Ages." Cîteaux 54 (2003): 251–400.

Powicke, F. M. *Ailred of Rievaulx and His Biographer Walter Daniel*. Manchester: University Press-Longmans Green, 1922.

Raciti, Gaetano. "Deux collections de sermons de saint Aelred (une centaine d'inédits) découvertes dans les fonds de Cluny et de Clairvaux." Coll 45 (1983): 165–84.

———. "L'apport original d'Aelred de Rievaulx à la réflexion occidentale sur l'amitié." Coll 29 (1967): 77–99.

———. "L'option préférentielle pour les pauvres dans le modèle communautaire aelrédien." Coll 55 (1993): 186–206.

———. "Une allocution familière de saint Aelred conservée dans les mélanges de Matthieu de Rievaulx." Coll 47 (1985): 267–80.

Radcliffe, Timothy. *Pourquoi donc être chrétien?* Paris: Cerf, 2005.

RB 1980: The Rule of St. Benedict. Ed. and trans. Timothy Fry. Collegeville, MN: Liturgical Press, 1981.

Regnard, Joël. "Le traité *Du précepte et de la dispense* et les origines cisterciennes." Coll 60 (1998): 31–58.

Renna, Thomas. "Aelred of Rievaulx and Isaiah." In *The Joy of Learning and the Love of God: Studies in Honor of Jean Leclercq*, edited by E. Rozanne Elder. CS 160. Kalamazoo, MI: Cistercian Publications, 1995. 253–68.

Rudolph, Conrad. *"The Things of Greater Importance": Bernard of Clairvaux's "Apologia" and the Medieval Attitude Toward Art.* Philadelphia: University of Pennsylvania Press, 1990.

Russell, J. Stephen. "Aelred and Augustine: *Affectus* and Imagination." CSQ 47, no. 4 (2016): 417–28.

———. "The Dialogic of Aelred's *Spiritual Friendship*." CSQ 47, no. 1 (2012): 47–69.

———. "Vision and Skepticism in Aelred's *De Oneribus*." CSQ 49, no. 4 (2014): 483–97.

S. Aelred de Rievaulx: Le Miroir de la Charité: Journées d'Études—Abbaye de Scourmont (5–9 octobre 1992). En Hommage au Père Charles Dumont. (1993) Coll 55, nos. 1–2.

Salenson, Christian. *Christian de Chergé: Une théologie de l'espérance.* Paris: Bayard, 2008.

Scannerini, Guglielmo. "Mistica o Misticismo? Un approcio patristico ad Aelredo di Rievaulx, *De Oneribus S. 2 (3)*." Analecta Cisterciensia 54, no. 1–2 (2002): 134–85.

Sommerfeldt, John R. *Aelred of Rievaulx: On Love and Order in the World and in the Church.* New York: Newman, 2006.

———. *Aelred of Rievaulx: Pursuing Perfect Happiness.* New York: Newman, 2005.

———. "Anthropology and Cosmology: The Foundational Principles of Aelred's Spirituality." In Dutton, ed., *A Companion to Aelred of Rievaulx*, 2017. 98–112.

———. "The Roots of Aelred's Spirituality: Cosmology and Anthropology." CSQ 38 (2003): 19–26.

Squire, Aelred. "Aelred and the Northern Saints." Coll 23 (1961): 59–69.

———. *Aelred of Rievaulx: A Study.* 1969. CS 50. Kalamazoo, MI: Cistercian Publications, 1981.

———. "Aelred par lui-même." Coll 29 (1967): 259–77.

———. "Historical Factors in the Formation of Aelred of Rievaulx." Coll 22 (1960): 261–82.

Stacpoole, Alberic. "The Public Face of Aelred," *The Downside Review* 85 (1967): 183–99, 318–25.

Stiegman, Emero. "*Woods and Stones* and *The Shade of Trees* in the Mysticism of Saint Bernard." In *Truth as Gift: Studies in Medieval Cistercian History in Honor of John R. Sommerfeldt*, edited by Marsha L. Dutton, Daniel M. La Corte, and Paul Lockey. CS 204. Kalamazoo, MI: Cistercian Publications, 2004. 321–54.

Talbot, C. H. "Aelred's Sermons: Some First Drafts." *Sacris Erudiri* 13 (1962): 153–92.

Tepas, K. M. "Aelred's Guidelines for Physical Attractions." Cîteaux 46 (1995): 339–51.

———. "Sexual Attraction and the Motivations for Love and Friendship in Aelred of Rievaulx." ABR 46 (1995): 283–307.

Thévenot, Xavier. *Compter sur Dieu: Études de théologie morale*. Paris: Cerf, 1992.

———. "Conversion chrétienne et changement psychique." In *Compter sur Dieu: Études de théologie morale*. Paris: Cerf, 1992. 273–94.

Torrell, Jean-Pierre, and Denise Bouthillier. *Pierre le Vénérable, abbé de Cluny: Le courage dans la mesure*. Chambray: CLD, 1988.

Truax, Jean. *Aelred the Peacemaker*. CS 251. Collegeville, MN: Cistercian Publications, 2017.

Ullman, Walter. *The Individual and Society in the Middle Ages*. Baltimore: Johns Hopkins University Press, 1967.

Vallery-Radot, Robert. *Bernard de Fontaines, abbé de Clairvaux: Le Prophète de l'Occident, 1130–1153*. Tournai: Desclée, 1968.

Vaujour, Sophie, and Pierre-André Burton, eds. Intentio Cordis. *Temps, histoire, mémoire chez Aelred de Rievaulx: Proceedings of an International Monastic Colloquium, Toulouse, France, March 2010*. Coll 73, no. 1 (2011); Forges, Belgium: Cisterciensia, 2011.

Waddell, Chrysogonus. "The Hidden Years of Aelred of Rievaulx: The Formation of a Spiritual Master." CSQ 41 (2006): 51–63.

Warren, W. L. *Henry II*. Berkeley: University of California Press, 1973.

Weber, Edouard-Henri. *La personne humaine au XIIIe siècle*. Paris: Vrin, 2002.

Weil, Éric. *Philosophie morale*. Paris: Vrin, 1981.

White, Lewis. *"Bifarie itaque potest legi*: Ambivalent Exegesis in Aelred of Rievaulx's *De Oneribus*." CSQ 42, no. 3 (2007): 299–327; repr. CSQ 52, no. 4 (2017): 395–423.

Williams, David H. "The English Cistercians in the Times of St. Aelred, Abbot of Revesby (1143–1147) and of Rievaulx (1147–1167)." *Cistercium Mater Nostra* 2 (2008): 13–30.

Wilmart, André. "L'instigateur du *Speculum Caritatis*." RAM 14 (1933): 369–94, 429.

———. "L'oraison pastorale de l'abbé Aelred." RBen 37 (1925): 263–72.

Woytyla, Karol. *The Acting Person*. Trans. Andrzej Potocki. Boston: D. Reidel, 2005.

Yohe, Katherine M. "Aelred's Recrafting of the Life of Edward the Confessor." CSQ 38 (2003): 177–89.

Zuanazzi, Giovanni. "Introduction." In Aelredo di Rievaulx, *L'amicizia spirituale*, translated by Giovanni Zuanazzi. Rome: Città Nouva, 1997.

Indices

Index of Scriptural References

Scriptural references are cited by page number.

Index of Names

Names are cited by page number.

Index of References to the Works of Aelred and of Walter Daniel

References are grouped by author and cited by page number.

Walter Daniel's Works